T0323676

# Strategies for Managing Uncertainty

All organizations must cope with future uncertainties. These uncertainties affect the strategic choices they make. They must commit scarce organizational resources to future outcomes which they have little assurance will come into being. Marcus explores how decision makers in the energy industry made choices in the face of such uncertainties, specifically examining two major uncertainties they confronted in the 2012–2018 period – price volatility and climate change. Marcus tells the story of how different companies in the integrated oil and natural gas sector and in the motor vehicle sector responded to these uncertainties. In the face of these challenges, companies in the energy industry hedged their bets by staking out paradoxical or contrasting positions. On the one hand, they focused on capturing as much gain as they could from the world's current dependence on fossil fuels and on the other hand they made preparations for a future in which fossil fuels might not be the world's dominant energy source.

ALFRED A. MARCUS is Professor and Edson Spencer Endowed Chair in Strategy and Technological Leadership at the Carlson School of Management, University of Minnesota. He is the author, co-author, or editor of seventeen books, including *Innovations in Sustainability: Fuel and Food* (Cambridge University Press, 2015), which won the Academy of Management ONE 2016 Outstanding Book Award.

# Organizations and the Natural Environment

*Series Editors*

Jorge Rivera, *George Washington University*
J. Alberto Aragon-Correa, *University of Surrey*

*Editorial Board*

Nicole Darnall, *Arizona State University*
Magali Delmas, *University of California, Los Angeles*
Ans Kolk, *University of Amsterdam*
Thomas P. Lyon, *University of Michigan*
Alfred A. Marcus, *University of Minnesota*
Michael Toffel, *Harvard Business School*
Christopher Weible, *University of Colorado*

The increasing attention given to environmental protection issues has resulted in a growing demand for high-quality, actionable research on sustainability and business environmental management. This new series, published in conjunction with the Group for Research on Organizations and the Natural Environment (GRONEN), presents students, academics, managers, and policy makers with the latest thinking on key topics influencing business practice today.

*Published Titles*

Marcus, *Innovations in Sustainability*
Bowen, *After Greenwashing*

*Forthcoming Titles*

Gouldson and Sullivan, *Governance and the Changing Climate for Business*
Sharma and Sharma, *Patient Capital*

# Strategies for Managing Uncertainty

## Booms and Busts in the Energy Industry

ALFRED A. MARCUS
*University of Minnesota*

# CAMBRIDGE
UNIVERSITY PRESS

University Printing House, Cambridge CB2 8BS, United Kingdom

One Liberty Plaza, 20th Floor, New York, NY 10006, USA

477 Williamstown Road, Port Melbourne, VIC 3207, Australia

314–321, 3rd Floor, Plot 3, Splendor Forum, Jasola District Centre, New Delhi – 110025, India

79 Anson Road, #06–04/06, Singapore 079906

Cambridge University Press is part of the University of Cambridge.

It furthers the University's mission by disseminating knowledge in the pursuit of education, learning, and research at the highest international levels of excellence.

www.cambridge.org
Information on this title: www.cambridge.org/9781107191150
DOI: 10.1017/9781108120586

First published 2019

Printed and bound in Great Britain by Clays Ltd, Elcograf S.p.A.

A catalogue record for this publication is available from the British Library.

ISBN 978-1-107-19115-0 Hardback
ISBN 978-1-316-64168-2 Paperback

*This book is dedicated to Ariel, David, and Laura, the next generation, and to my maternal grandfather Ignaz Fried, who influenced me in many ways but from whose life I learned that calculated wagers and hedging are important.*

# Contents

# Figures

# Tables

# Acknowledgments

My wife Judy showed patience during the long hours I put into writing this book and inspired me with her everyday wisdom on the topics with which the book deals. I want to thank Valerie Appleby and Tobias Ginsberg of Cambridge University Press and Stephen Acerra, and Paula Parish formerly of Cambridge University Press. They shepherded this book through the review process and gave me encouragement during the long process of writing. I want to thank the students in the online Washington, DC-based version of the course on the energy industry I first delivered in the Carlson School of Management Industry MBA for sharpening my ideas: Joseph Arlt, Amelia Breinig, Jason Buck, Rory Heslington, Trevor Miller, Meris Petek, Marietta Shapiro, Joseph Stanoch, Patrick McCarthy, Jeffrey Beck, John Flaherty, John Jones, Christopher Mulvanny, Parker Haymans, Edward Wytkind, and Emily Trapani. Maryna Zubtsova was the teaching assistant for the course and her help in course delivery was invaluable. Hyoju Jeong worked with me as PhD student research assistant. She had many original and important insights about the energy industry. Melissa MarKay served as an undergraduate honor student research assistant for the book and Merav Levkowitz edited earlier drafts. I was inspired by my colleagues at the University of Minnesota Technological Leadership Institute where I also teach, in particular by Massoud Amin, Steve Kelly, and Tariq Samad. Phil Miller of the Carlson School of Management provided me with encouragement throughout my writing of this book, which I truly appreciated. Some of the people with whom I shared early drafts of the book are Alex Wilson and Moshe Barak of the Strategic Management and Entrepreneurship Department at the Carlson School. I am heavily indebted to all department members, but especially to the department chair, Shaker Zahra, for his support. The research ideas of Mary Benner, Gurneeta

Vasudeva Singh, Paul Vaaler, Ian Maitland, Aseem Kaul, and Jiao Luo of the department have crept into this manuscript, probably unbeknownst to them. Other people with whom I shared early drafts of some chapters include Daniel Yergin, Dan Sperber, and Jason Bordorf.

# Introduction
## Calculated Wagers and Hedging

All organizations must cope with future uncertainties. These uncertainties affect the strategic choices they make. They must commit scarce organizational resources to future outcomes which they have little assurance will come into being. This book explores how decision makers in the energy industry made choices in the face of such uncertainties. Specifically, it deals with two major uncertainties they confronted in the 2012–2018 period – that is price volatility and climate change. This period was one in which the price of oil slipped from a high of about $100 a barrel to a low below $30 a barrel, in the process of wiping out about 30 percent of the revenue of the large integrated oil and natural gas companies and providing opportunities for automotive firms to sell more SUVs, pickups, crossovers, and light duty trucks. This period was also one of mounting pressure on energy companies to respond to climate change, which culminated in the Paris climate change agreement of 2015 in which nearly all countries in the world committed to lower their carbon footprint by introducing tight new fuel efficiency and air quality standards.

In the face of these challenges, companies in the energy industry hedged their bets by staking out paradoxical positions.[1] On the one hand, they focused on capturing as much gain as they could from the world's current dependence on fossil fuels, and on the other hand, they made preparations for a future in which fossil fuels might not be the world's dominant energy source. This book tells the story of how different sectors in the energy industry and different companies – ExxonMobil, BP, Shell, and TOTAL in the integrated oil and natural gas sector and GM, Ford, VW, and Toyota in the motor vehicle sector – responded to these uncertainties. They had to make long-term strategic investments without knowing what future conditions would be and if these investments would pay off. Their investments in fuels and in vehicles not only had major effects on the companies, but also on society at large as they would play an important role in determining the degree to which humans would be able to cope with climate change, one of the most pressing issues of the twenty-first century. If the energy industry companies discussed in this book miscalculated and made imperfect choices, the effects could be devastating for them and for the planet. On the other hand, their choices could also have the beneficial effect of bringing about needed adjustments in the global economy and company business models.

## The Motivation for the Book

In other words, the stakes involved were high, and how companies in this industry made their decisions was of the utmost importance. Thus, my reasons for writing this book were very compelling. The immediate motivation came when I was asked to design a new course for a special industry-based MBA the Carlson School of Management offered to Washington, DC Congressional staffers. I have subsequently offered and am offering this course as an elective to other Carlson School MBAs. I feel capable of writing on this topic, as I have a long history in researching energy policy. In 1992, I wrote a book called *Controversial Issues in Energy Policy* (Sage Publications) in which I tried to explain the sudden decline in energy prices in the 1980s, and in 2015 I wrote *Innovations in Sustainability* (Cambridge University Press) in which I tried, among other things, to explain the rise of alternatives to fossil fuels and the movement toward cleaner energy among startups and venture capitalists.[2] In between, I have written many academic articles about the energy decision making of governments and companies.[3] This topic has been a nearly life-long obsession which began in the mid-1970s when I wrote my dissertation at Harvard on the US Environmental Protection Agency's origins and its early attempts to implement major new clean air and clean water legislation.[4] I subsequently worked for five years as a research consultant in the late Carter and early Reagan presidencies analyzing a host of issues relating to energy and business from the commercialization of then new technologies to the costs and benefits of forest practices to the dangers of accidents at nuclear power plants and how to mitigate these dangers through better management practices. In the 1990s, along with co-authors, I participated in an attempt by the Clinton administration to reform environmental regulation by relying on companies going beyond what was required by law in exchange for regulatory leniencies.

The book we wrote, *Reinventing Environmental Regulation*, documented the difficulties of business–government cooperation to achieve environmental goals they both considered important.[5]

In addition, I have been intrigued by the problem of uncertainty in strategic management as I have taught the strategic management course for almost thirty years starting at MIT where I did my sabbatical in 1991–1992 and also at the University of Minnesota Technological Leadership Institute as well as the Carlson School, and the Technion, where I have also served as an adjunct professor. I have written a strategic management textbook, many strategic management cases, and a trade book in strategy, *Big Winners and Big Losers*.[6] In my work in strategy, the question that I keep coming back to is how businesses make long-term and expensive strategic investments, when their understanding of the conditions that will prevail in the future, when the decisions have to pay off, are uncertain. This question is a classic one in business literature, one that University of Chicago economist Frank Knight raised in his early twentieth-century book, *Risk, Uncertainty, and Profit*.[7] It is quite clear that grappling with future uncertainty is a major challenge that managers of almost all organizations confront. If they miscalculate and make the wrong choices, their organizations can go out of existence, a not uncommon event in the history of companies. On the other hand, if they somehow intuit correctly what is to come next, their companies can thrive. The key strategic choices involve making the correct bets on the future. However, as Knight argued so persuasively, the data to understand the future well and correctly does not typically exist and the future is unknown so that decision makers' guesses often go awry. They make wrong choices and their companies suffer, often with broader negative social impacts of dislocated workers and other malaises.

Thus, my motivation for writing this book has also been to better understand how decision makers in the energy industry confront long-term choices when the future is uncertain. The energy industry is a particularly apt one for such an analysis as the decisions are long term in nature and socially impactful. Thus, this book analyzes the uncertainties that managers in the energy industry faced in the turbulent period from 2012 to 2018 when the rules governing their behavior were changing. Energy prices were flip-flopping in ways they almost had never before done in history. Global regulation of companies in the energy industry was stiffening, but in different ways in different parts of the world, with respect to fuel efficiency and air emissions. As businesses, energy industry companies were experiencing poor results, overcapacity, stiff competition, and somewhat declining demand, with the exception of China and eastern Asia. How should managers of energy companies respond to this situation and make long-term, expensive capital intensive, often irreversible, investment decisions in energy assets when they operated in a situation of great upheaval and uncertainty? This book tries to answer the question, given the extent of uncertainty that existed, how did they cope? What strategies did they employ? How did these strategies affect their organizations financially, and, as importantly, the broader societies of which we are a part?

## The Key Features

Here are some of the key features of this book. It proposes a new strategic management approach to managing uncertainty, a theory of hedging, and illustrates the theory with examples from the energy industry, in particular from these sectors within this industry, the integrated oil and natural gas and motor vehicle sectors. It explores in depth major uncertainties that companies in these sectors faced, that is energy price volatility – booms and busts in prices and the threat of climate change. It explores these uncertainties while at the same time depicting the difficult business conditions that prevailed in these sectors – weakening demand, increasing competition, and adverse events like major accidents, recalls, and scandals. The book shows how major companies in the integrated oil and natural gas and motor vehicles sectors – ExxonMobil, BP, Shell, TOTAL, GM, Ford, VW, and Toyota – developed ways to cope with these issues, that is, how they reacted to the uncertainties they confronted, and made wagers on the future. Thus, the book is an important contribution to the literature on the strategic management of uncertainty, which is probably the most important issue in strategy, as well as the literature on sustainability due to its focus on climate change. The book provides an up-to-date analysis of the three major sectors in the energy industry – electrical generation, as well as oil and natural gas, and automotive – and offers case studies on the following major oil and natural gas and motor vehicle companies in the period before and after oil prices plummeted – ExxonMobil, BP, Shell, and TOTAL in the oil and natural gas sector and GM, Ford, VW, and Toyota in the automotive sector. The analysis is up to date in that it includes an assessment of the divergent strategic paths of these eight firms in 2017–2018 and reveals the differences in their strategic responses to the challenges of price volatility and climate change. It contributes to the institutional literature on strategy, in that difference in responses, or heterogeneity, has become a major theme in this literature.[8]

## Calculated Wagers

Part I of this book lays out the main theme of risk and uncertainty brought on by growing price volatility – the booms and busts of 2012–2016 – and climate change. It points to major miscalculations energy companies made in the past and to the unsettled issues they confront in the future. In managing risk and uncertainty, energy industry managers cannot anticipate with assurance what is to come next. They have to make calculated wagers. These gambles are not unbiased but are subject to the individual and organizational short-comings that affect nearly every decision that an individual or organization makes as laid out in behavioral psychology and behavioral theories of the firm. Specifically, they cannot be certain of where the world is heading, what the impact of these changes will be on their industries and on their sector, and how to respond to what is taking place now and what might take place next. Under these conditions, because they do not know the chances of payoffs and losses or their magnitude, they cannot simply rely on rational/analytical decision making, but must bring to bear their hunches and intuition or what Keynes referred to as their "animal spirits."[9] Despite good efforts, they are subject to minor and serious miscalculations and can make major mistakes. They tend to recognize the limitations, and the less they feel they are able to avoid error, the more cautious they become – that is, the more they try to protect their organizations from harm by hedging their bets. In these circumstances, they may become defensive and try to delay or avoid departures from the status quo unless there are strong factors that mitigate such caution. Unless they feel they have no choice and they have been backed into a corner, or they have relative assurance that they can exploit the situation they perceive is emerging for gain, hedging their bets prevents them from making bold new moves.

Yet, this book shows that by 2018, almost all the major energy companies that it scrutinizes – ExxonMobil, BP, Shell, and TOTAL in the oil and natural gas sector and GM, Ford, VW, and Toyota in the automotive sector – made or were on the verge of making such moves.

- ExxonMobil adjusted its stance, however slightly, on climate change and widely publicized an effort on its part to develop petro-algae.
- BP disgorged large amounts of its fossil fuel assets to save itself from bankruptcy after the Deepwater Horizon oil spill.
- Shell also restructured, letting go of large amounts of its oil assets and acquiring natural gas assets instead, which led to a major commitment to build liquefied natural gas (LNG) infrastructure.
- TOTAL moved in a different direction than other integrated oil and natural gas companies, as it owned advanced battery and solar panel companies and started to secure European electric utilities for itself.
- GM upgraded its product safety and quality policies after a major ignition-sticking recall, introduced an electric plug-in and the all-electric Bolt, and made the unprecedented move of leaving Europe entirely, selling its European division to Peugeot, and in the process of abandoning hope of ever regaining the position of being the world's largest auto maker.
- Ford, wavered in the face of weak financial results unsure how much it should commit to its global bestselling F-150 series light truck versus moving to hybrids and to the opportunities of new transportation models, but it did make a number of important decisions, both in making the F-150 series lighter with an aluminum body replacing some of the metal body and in effect departing completely from the North American sedan market.
- VW, with its back against the wall because of a blatant disregard for law and ethics and its cheating on diesel emission standards, reversed its commitment to proclaiming that diesel was the world's greenest solution, and promised that it would make almost all its models available in some type of electric option no later than 2030.
- Toyota facing challenges to the quality and safety of its vehicles for virtually the first time and confronting weakness in the US market because it did not have a large selection of small trucks, tried to position itself as a leader in crossover vehicles, and in the future promised the most far-reaching transformation of any automaker with regard to offering for sale hybrid and fully electric vehicles.

## Hedging

This book explores the broad context in which these companies in the energy industry found themselves, the specific conditions they faced with respect to energy prices and societal pressures around climate change, and their use of hedges as a way to strategically deal with these uncertainties. Firms in the energy industry faced at least two major uncertainties with which this book grapples. The first of these uncertainties had to do with volatile prices, the boom and bust conditions that prevailed from 2012 to 2016, when oil prices plunged from a height of about $100 a barrel and fell to a low of about $30 a barrel, in the process of wiping out about a third of major integrated oil and natural gas company revenue and providing motor vehicle companies with the opportunity to sell more highly profitable light duty trucks, pickups, SUVs, and crossovers. The second of the major uncertainties was the ongoing threat of climate change brought about by the incessant burning of fossil fuels that the integrated oil and natural gas and motor vehicle companies facilitate. Climate change introduces physical uncertainty in that meteorological conditions in the world which allow the global economy to function will no longer be operable, and legal uncertainty in that almost every government in the world tightened its standards on fuel efficiency and air emissions and stretched the technological capabilities of integrated oil and natural gas and motor vehicle companies to their limits in trying to arrive at ways to comply with the laws the world's governments have enacted. All of the firms in the integrated oil and natural gas and motor vehicle sectors were preparing for a future in which fossil fuels will be less dominant, but their preparations for this future differed in significant ways that this book helps to clarify. Some acted more than others on the assumption that reduced reliance on fossil fuels was imminent, and this assumption led them to make different strategic investments and bets than those of their peers. How companies reacted to the dual uncertainties of price volatility and climate change are this book's major theme.

Given the uncertain future conditions they faced, the companies examined in this book had assumptions about the future that led each to adopt a strategy of hedging their bets in somewhat different ways to ensure that their organizations would survive, if not prosper, regardless of what happened. This book introduces and develops the concept of hedging as a method companies used to manage the risks and uncertainties they confronted. Hence, hedging strategies are a major topic of the book.

It is worth pointing out from where I started to derive my thinking about hedging as a means to grapple with company uncertainties. For the book *CSR and Climate Change Implications for Multinational Enterprises* (edited by McIntyre, Ivanaj, Ivanaj, and Kar), I wrote a chapter with Joel Malen called "Techniques for Navigating the Risks of Investing in Cleaner Energy Technologies."[10] In that chapter, we tried to encapsulate conclusions from my earlier book about hedging, *Innovations in Sustainability*.[11] In *Innovations in Sustainability*, I started to develop a theory of hedging.[12] My aim in writing *Strategies for Managing Uncertainty: Booms and Busts in the Energy Industry* was to understand how key players in the oil and natural gas and automotive sectors hedged their bets in making long-term decisions, when the results of those decisions were unknown in advance. Hedging is a theory of decision making that is different from the efforts corporations make to optimize returns. It also differs from bounded rationality, which claims organizations cannot optimize, though they may attempt to do so, because they lack knowledge, their time is limited, and they suffer from other decision-making shortcomings.[13] Hedging is more akin to the risk-averse biases that prospect theory has proposed, but it applies the notion of risk aversion to organizations as a whole and attempts to define the mechanisms organizations use to protect themselves from losses and ensure their survival when the future is unknown and they cannot predict with certainty whether the strategic bets they have made will pay off, or instead turn out to be grave miscalculations, which can end their existence.[14]

The term "hedging" is borrowed from finance, where it means moving in more than one direction at once to offset the chance of adverse movements in markets. Technically, to hedge means to make investments that have a negative correlation. That is, it means, to use the literature of strategic management, to take the ambivalence felt about the future direction of the state of the world and to make simultaneously contradictory bets about what is to come next. Hedging is a way to manage paradox. When the future is unknown an organization cannot responsibly or prudently place all its eggs in one basket; it must bet on *more than one world* coming into being at the same time, in the hope that its positive bets will more than offset the negative ones, or that its bets will alternately sustain it in moments when different future conditions prevail. Uncertainty about the future leads to ambivalence about which strategic moves to make and this ambivalence leads to contradictory choices and hedging. The purpose of this book has been to uncover the hedging mechanisms of integrated oil and natural gas and motor vehicle companies in the energy industry. How have they tried to shield themselves from disastrous consequences in the event that the vast strategic bets they make go awry? This book suggests that their goal is not necessarily to maximize returns to shareholders, but to survive whatever contingency takes place and with some luck to prosper if the best of conditions they assume might take place actually arise. The track record of energy industry company decision making in the past has been anything but perfect, and serious miscalculations have put nearly every firm in jeopardy and on the brink of demise at some point in time. However, there has not been any major demise of an energy industry company, even in the face of bankruptcy (GM). In this sense, the hedges of the companies in this industry have succeeded in protecting them.

## How the Book Is Organized

This book contributes to the literature on strategic management and sustainability by investigating how companies made decisions, against a background of uncertainties with which they had to grapple, by relying on hedges.

- Part I of the book sketches out the problem of risk and uncertainty in the energy industry, the management of this risk and uncertainty in general, hedging, and the industry's recent history of booms and busts.
- Part II examines the challenges to three major sectors in the industry – oil and natural gas companies, motor vehicle companies, and electric utilities.
- Part III depicts the strategies of four of the world's largest integrated oil and natural gas companies – ExxonMobil, BP, Shell, and TOTAL – before and after the 2014–2015 price collapse. How did they hedge their bets in this period of intense uncertainty?
- Part IV depicts the strategies of four of the world's largest motor vehicle companies – GM, Ford, VW, and Toyota in the same period. How did they hedge their bets in this period? While the precipitous fall in energy prices was a major threat to the oil and natural gas

companies, it was an opportunity for the motor vehicle companies to sell more profitable SUVs, pickups, crossovers, and light duty trucks, particularly in the US market.

- Part V updates the strategies of the oil and gas companies and the motor vehicle companies in 2017–2018 and indicates how each of them pivoted from prior strategies and adjusted to new realities. In light of the institutional literature's concern with this issue, the heterogeneity of their responses is a matter of great interest.[15] These companies did not respond similarly to conditions they confronted. Their strategies diverged more than they converged. This divergence had implications both for the companies and society at large.

The importance of the companies' divergent strategies is an important theme of the book.

The book ends with a discussion of how ambivalence about what to do, given the uncertainties the companies confronted, influenced their strategies. As indicated throughout this introduction, these companies set out on paradoxical paths simultaneously. These paths, one may say, had one foot in the past and one foot in the future. The companies wanted to protect their assets and current position while preparing their organizations for a time when their current operating assumptions and business models would no longer be relevant. In the future, demand for petroleum might peak, electric vehicles might become very common, autonomous driving might be the norm, and ride-sharing could largely replace private vehicle ownership. This world might be very different from the world that the oil and natural gas companies and motor vehicle companies previously occupied. How they coped with this situation by hedging their bets is this book's main theme.

## Notes

1. Farjoun, Moshe. "Beyond Dualism: Stability and Change as a Duality." *Academy of Management Review* 35.2 (2010): 202–225.
2. Marcus, Alfred A. *Controversial Issues in Energy Policy.* Los Angeles: Sage, 1992; Marcus, Alfred A. *Innovations in Sustainability.* Cambridge, UK: Cambridge University Press, 2015.
3. For example, see Ginsberg, Ari, and Alfred Marcus. "Venture Capital's Role in Creating a More Sustainable Society: The Role of Exits in Clean Energy's Investment Growth." In *Sustainability, Stakeholder*

*Governance, and Corporate Social Responsibility* (eds.) Sinziana Dorobantu, Ruth V. Aguilera, Jiao Luo, and Frances J. Milliken. Bingley, West Yorkshire, England: Emerald Publishing Limited, 2018. 145–168.

4. The dissertation was published as Marcus, Alfred Allen. *Promise and Performance: Choosing and Implementing an Environmental Policy.* Santa Barbara, CA: Praeger, 1980.

5. Marcus, Alfred Allen, Donald A. Geffen, and Ken Sexton. *Reinventing Environmental Regulation: Lessons from Project XL.* Washington, DC: Resources for the Future, 2002.

6. Marcus, Alfred A. *Management Strategy: Achieving Sustained Competitive Advantage.* Homewood, IL: McGraw-Hill, 2011; Marcus, Alfred A. *The Future of Technology Management and the Business Environment: Lessons on Innovation, Disruption, and Strategy Execution.* Upper Saddle, NJ: Pearson Education, 2016; Marcus, Alfred A. *Big Winners and Big Losers.* Upper Saddle River, NJ: Wharton School Publishing-Pearson Education, 2006.

7. Knight, F. H. *Risk, Uncertainty and Profit.* Mineola, NY: Dover Publications, 2012.

8. Greenwood, R., Raynard, M., Kodeih, F., Micelotta, E. R., and Lounsbury, M. "Institutional Complexity and Organizational Responses." *Academy of Management Annals* 5(1) (2011): 317–371.

9. "Keynes. *The General Theory.*" www.economicshelp.org/blog/613/economics/quotes-by-john-maynard-keynes/; also see, Koppl, Roger. "Retrospectives: Animal Spirits." *Journal of Economic Perspectives* 5.3 (1991): 203–210.

10. McIntyre, John R., et al., eds. *CSR and Climate Change Implications for Multinational Enterprises.* Cheltenham, UK: Edward Elgar Publishing, 2016.

11. *Innovations in Sustainability.*

12. Hedging allowed venture capitalists and startups, which were the major subject of the earlier book that invested in cleaner energy technologies, to mitigate their decision-making risk. For investors in cleaner energy, the hedging mechanisms highlighted were late and calculated entry, diversification, and side benefits. For the startups, the hedging mechanisms were patient financial backing, flexible business models, and staged, but achievable, goals.

13. Simon, Herbert Alexander. *Models of Bounded Rationality: Empirically Grounded Economic Reason.* Cambridge, MA: MIT Press, 1997 (3rd edition).

14. Kahneman, Daniel, and Patrick Egan. *Thinking, Fast and Slow.* New York: Farrar, Straus and Giroux, 2011.
15. Greenwood, Royston, Oliver, C., Lawrence, T. B., and Meyer, R. E. eds. *The Sage Handbook of Organizational Institutionalism.* Thousand Oaks, CA: Sage, 2017.

# PART I

# The Problem

The Problem

# 1 | Risk and Uncertainty in the Energy Industry

This book is about strategy making under risk and uncertainty. The terms risk and uncertainty are interchangeable in ordinary speech. Nonetheless, Frank Knight, one of the major figures in early twentieth-century economics, distinguished between them.[1] Risk is the condition in which past information is sufficient to compute the odds of what is likely to happen next, while uncertainty is the condition in which past information is not sufficient to compute the odds of what is likely to occur next. The capacity to predict what is likely to take place next, according to Knight, is based on empirical observations, knowledge derived from these observations, deductions from assumed principles, and judgments, which individuals and groups make.

Knight maintained that risk and uncertainty have important implications for competitive rivalries among business firms. He argued that the ability to make good bets about the future is the key to achieving competitive advantage. Under risk, all firms have access to similar information. If they use this information well, no firm sustains competitive advantage for a long period. On the other hand, under uncertainty, some firms may have the exceptional foresight to discern the future (or they may be just lucky); and if they can extend the gap between what they and their competitors know about the future, they achieve long-term competitive advantage. When uncertainty prevails, the stakes are high – the larger the uncertainty, the greater the possible gain; however, this condition increases the possibility of failure.

This book takes up the question of how major firms in the energy industry, defined here as the oil and natural gas and motor vehicle sectors, formulated their understanding of the future in light of the risks and uncertainties that they confronted. It examines the strategies of major energy industry companies in 2014–2015, when oil prices plummeted. How did their formulations about the future affect the actions they took, the strategies they carried out, and moves they made? How have these actions in turn affected their performance? Given the uncertainty these firms faced about future oil prices, to what extent did they shift their long-term investment priorities? The strategies and methods these companies employed to cope with the situation they faced has important implications for society. This book contributes to the strategic management literature by investigating how companies in the energy industry decided what to do in these circumstances.

## A Hedge against Failure

The book explores how companies in the energy industry tried to mitigate the risk and uncertainty they confronted. When risk and uncertainty exist about the future, companies in industries as volatile as oil and natural gas and motor vehicles could not easily place their bets on a single outcome or solution. Their lack of certain knowledge about the future compelled them to invest in a variety of options that corresponded to different visions about what might take place next. The diversity of the bets that they made were mainly a hedge against failure. Yet this hedge was not foolproof. It could not completely insulate them from impending events they could neither foretell nor control.

This book shows that while the hedges, which companies in the energy industry took to protect themselves against the unknown, over-all were similar, the particular hedges of the companies varied in slight, but important and subtle ways. Moreover, the diversity of the bets they made and the strategic initiatives they took gradually shifted over time. Locked in by existing commitments, they responded to rivals' moves and reacted to feedback from their stakeholders. Their financial health and performance also affected what they did. Their insights about the future swayed them, but not completely, because the future was so difficult to fathom with a high degree of certainty.

The package of strategic investments they made to hedge against the unfolding of alternative futures was not static. It progressed in a dynamic way in which companies carved out separate competitive spaces, positioning themselves in dissimilar niches for different eventualities. The unfolding of variances in the strategies of these firms is a major theme of the book. All the integrated oil and natural gas companies suffered drastic losses in revenue and profitability from lower energy prices, while all the motor vehicle companies enjoyed growing demand for light trucks and SUVs because of low gasoline prices. However, after the perturbation of 2014–2015, the competition among firms in both the oil and natural gas and the automotive sectors started to shift. The companies this book examines distanced themselves from each other in new ways. The book traces the path by which ExxonMobil tried to become a major player in shale, while BP rapidly shed assets to pay off its continuing Deep Water Horizon obligations. Shell, on the other hand, essentially dropped the shale option entirely and moved in the direction of natural gas, while TOTAL invested in renewable energy and storage and started to acquire electric utilities.

The major motor vehicle manufacturers the book examines also moved in different directions. GM sold its European subsidiary, Ford announced it would no longer sell sedans in the United States, and both companies in their own way doubled down on autonomous vehicles and electrification. Reeling from the emissions scandal, VW maneuvered out of diesel and tried to top all motor vehicle companies in the number of electric models it would offer, while Toyota played to its strength in hybrids and promised to deliver even more electric vehicles than VW.

This book portrays the long-term investment decisions and strategies of major energy companies as they hedged their bets in dissimilar ways against an uncertain future. When information is available to all, competitive interactions converge and no firm is likely to benefit more than any other does. However, when information about the future is hard to come by and firms have diverse understandings of the future, their competitive interactions diverge, which is the story about these firms that this book tells.

The remainder of this chapter further discusses the distinction between risk and uncertainty. It then applies these concepts to escalating energy price volatility in the energy industry, reveals past miscalculations energy companies made in the face of inconstant prices, and concludes with a list of unsettled issues decision makers in this industry continue to face with particular emphasis on climate change.

## Risk and Uncertainty

Knight maintained that under risk, the likely distribution of outcomes is known, while under uncertainty, the distribution of outcomes is largely unknown because of the uniqueness of the situation.[2] John Maynard Keynes, the great English economist, made a similar distinction.[3] Risk, he argued, was like roulette. The outcomes were subject to probability. On the other hand, there was no scientific basis on which to form a calculable probability with respect to uncertainty and likely outcomes were unknown. In the category of outcomes that were unknown, Keynes placed the prospect of a European war, the price of copper, the rate of interest twenty years into the future, and the obsolescence of an invention. These were uncertain events, without odds of prediction, and not risky ones.

Nassim Nicholas Taleb, the contemporary analyst, focuses on the problem of randomness, and has brought attention to risk's limits in the form of outliers he calls "Black Swans" wherein it is nearly impossible to form a calculable probability.[4] Ex-US Defense Secretary Donald Rumsfeld has pointed to instances of absolute uncertainty, with the distinction he has made between "known" unknowns and "unknown" unknowns.[5] Statisticians too speak about the distinction between risk and uncertainty, arguing that variations that come about because of common causes constitute risk, while those that come about because of special causes constitute uncertainty. The former yield quantifiable, regularly observed patterns, while the latter produce nonquantifiable and irregular patterns, whose frequency and severity human beings cannot predict with confidence.

When companies in the energy industry make long-term, expensive, capital-intensive, and often irreversible investment decisions, they face known and unknown unknowns as well as black swan-like outliers. They cannot be definite about where they are along this continuum. Outliers and unknown unknowns challenge them in many ways. They must consider the state of technology, politics, and society in which their firms find themselves and where the economy is headed. They must make sense of infrequently occurring events, such as technological breakthroughs, embargos, revolutions, wars, invasions, economic expansions, and contractions, and interpret their meaning and long-term impact, which is particularly difficult, since knowledge of past events does not necessarily provide good insights about what to expect next.[6] Events in different spheres such as the economy and technology are related, which makes the capacity for prediction more onerous.

Unsettled issues weigh heavily on decision makers because of the uncertainty, and serious miscalculations are possible. Under these circumstances, rational calculation may not be a fully reliable guide, and, according to Keynes, it must be supplemented by "animal spirits." He wrote that "as living and moving beings, we are forced to act ... [even when] existing knowledge does not provide a sufficient basis for a calculated mathematical expectation."[7] He then quipped that to act at all in these circumstances, it is necessary to put aside the thought of rational calculation "as a healthy man puts aside the expectation of death."[8]

Patterns may become obvious after the fact, but before the fact, when it really counts, the ability to recognize and control the future is limited. The effectiveness of decision makers is curtailed. How can energy decision makers cope, given the large role that special causes and uncertainty play in the context in which they operate? The argument in this book is that decision makers in the energy industry must make bets on the future without certainty of the outcomes. They frame problems and try to give meaning to their choices without full knowledge of the long-term impacts. They manage by making assumptions about the future that sometimes are based on very spurious assumptions. Without sufficient past evidence upon which to draw, they cannot construct sound causal inferences about what is to come next.[9]

## Escalating Price Volatility

Decision makers in the energy industry have confronted considerable uncertainty about energy prices. Since 1973, the history of energy prices has been one of booms and busts; they have risen and fallen for unique and hard-to-predict reasons. Their rise and fall have been a consequence of events, such as the 1973 Arab oil embargo, the Iranian Revolution, and the Iran–Iraq War, the growth of Southeast Asian economies, the global financial crisis, and the rise of hydraulic fracking as a substitute for conventional oil and natural gas. From 1880 to 1970, price stability was greater; the conditions decision makers confronted more stable with some exceptions, such as the 1890s, when growing European production increased supply, and the 1920s, when the automobile's adoption increased demand. However, after 2000, decision makers confronted continued oil price booms and busts (see Figure 1.1). Natural gas prices, also unstable, in turn affected electricity prices.

Everything else being equal, when prices were lower they should have lifted economic growth. Greater economic growth then should have stimulated demand for more energy. However, the relationship between energy prices and economic growth is complicated. Lower energy prices do not necessarily spur additional economic activity;

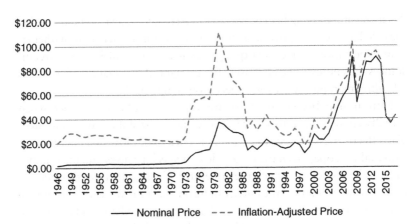

**Figure 1.1** Annual average domestic crude oil prices
(Inflation adjusted July 1946–July 2017 in $/barrel)
Derived from US Energy Information Administration data

rather, they may be a sign of economic weakness and signify less energy demand. A reason they may indicate less demand has been shifts in the advanced economies of the world from material goods to information and services. If the Chinese economy were to swing strongly to services or, conversely, slow because of bad loans, or even a meltdown, energy demand also would weaken and prices would fall.

Declines in energy prices have also come about because of greater supply. The growth of hydraulic fracking was of vital importance because it opened up previously untapped supplies of oil and natural gas. Its arrival on the scene led to questions about whether oil supplies would ever peak. Indeed, major oil companies took note of peak demand rather than peak supply in their calculations. Shell predicted it could occur as early as 2025 and BP forecast that it could take place by 2035. On the other hand, ExxonMobil denied it would ever happen. These different assessments of the future had implications for the strategies the companies adopted, as later chapters will show.

Another implication of the decline in fossil fuel prices was their impact on renewable energy. Though renewables amounted to just a fraction of the energy used, their gain had been remarkable. However, with lower fossil fuel prices, their further progress could be curtailed.

Greater supply of fossil fuels first led Saudi Arabia to increase production in order to drive the frackers out of business and restore its dominant market share. However, this strategy lowered prices to the point that the kingdom's revenues fell. The Organization of the Petroleum Exporting Countries (OPEC), under its leadership, then chose to restrict oil supplies, but whether this decision would stick, and for how long, was unknown. Would OPEC have enough discipline to maintain supply restrictions? Petro-dominated states such as Russia, Iran, Venezuela, Nigeria, and Iraq might choose not to keep oil from the market to protect their fragile economies and societies. Security in the world could grow because low oil and gas prices held petro-dominated states like Russia, Iran, and Venezuela in check. On the other hand, it could deteriorate as these nations became more desperate under the stress of low oil prices.

## Miscalculations

The focus of this book is on decision makers in fossil fuel and motor vehicle companies. The former explored for oil, natural gas, and, to a very small extent, coal, and transported, produced, refined, and sold these resources. The motor vehicle firms relied on fossil fuels to provide people with the mobility they were seeking. Electric utilities generated power, much of it from fossil fuels, but also from alternatives like renewables, and they transmitted and distributed electricity to end users. The choices of the fossil fuel, motor vehicle, and electric utility companies interacted with each other yielding unintended consequences and compounding the uncertainties they confronted. While low fossil fuel prices negatively affected the oil and natural gas companies, they were a boon to the motor vehicle firms because they allowed them to sell more larger and profitable light trucks and SUVs. The energy industry is not coordinated, which contributes to company misunderstanding about the meaning of prices. The following examples illustrate some of the miscalculations energy decision makers made because of their confusion about future price signals.

### Fossil Fuels

A miscalculation brought on by a mistaken anticipation of high oil prices occurred in Kazakhstan.[10] This country was home to the world's largest single oil discovery since 1968, a vast oil field in Kashagan about fifty miles offshore the northeast Caspian Sea. Shell and other oil companies with which it collaborated, including ExxonMobil, Eni,

TOTAL, and ConocoPhillips, expected huge rewards from this field, which, after the end of the Cold War, was the world's biggest oil development. Kazakhstan's president Nursultan Nazarbayev gave the oil companies nearly unrestricted access in hopes that, in turn, this former Soviet republic would be able to modernize its economy. The oil companies invested immense sums. By 2005, they expected that more than 1.5 million barrels of oil would reach markets daily, an amount roughly equal to the needs of a country the size of the United Kingdom. Instead, nine years later, the project was $30 billion over budget, and the project had produced no oil. With losses incurred by the parties of more than $50 billion, the oil companies put the Kashagan project on indefinite hold. They made numerous blunders. At the prices then prevailing, producing oil from Kashagan was not worth it and it was unclear if prices ever would be high enough to justify a resumption of the project. The project also suffered from many management disputes, as it turned out to be hard to coordinate the efforts of so many companies with diverse interests. The parties involved completely underestimated the obstacles of producing in this field.

## Motor Vehicles

Another miscalculation of note was GM's 1990s plunge into electric cars.[11] After the company demonstrated a concept electric vehicle (EV) at the 1990 Los Angeles Auto Show, the California Air Resources Board (CARB) put in place a zero-emission vehicle mandate that called for 2 percent of auto company fleets sold in the state to be emission free by 1998, 5 percent by 2001, and 10 percent by 2003. GM's response was to introduce a first-generation EV powered by lead–acid batteries with a range of between 70 and 100 miles. It followed up in 1999 with a second-generation EV that had nickel–metal hydride batteries and slightly better range. By 2002, GM had sold more than 1,100 EVs. Customers could also acquire the cars via a leasing program. Though driver reaction was generally favorable, GM viewed the initiative as a failure. Battery technology had not advanced, vehicle range continued to be low, and gasoline prices did not justify widespread acceptance. The company made far more money selling sports utility vehicles and light trucks than EVs. At the insistence of GM and the other automakers, CARB agreed to rescind its clean car mandate. GM then canceled the EV program and declared that it had lost over a billion dollars. Against the protest of drivers, the company destroyed all the electric cars it produced. To much fanfare and relative success Toyota, on the other hand, introduced the hybrid electric Prius, just before gasoline prices started to rise again.

## Renewable Power

US venture capitalists (VCs) miscalculated with the renewable power investments they made in the first decade of the twenty-first century.[12] These investments looked good before the fact, yet took a turn for the worse as a series of unexpected events unfolded. The acceleration of the investments occurred before the VCs knew that the US Congress would not pass climate change legislation, the 2007–2008 financial crisis would take place, Europe's recovery would be slow, and European incentives to renewable power would weaken. In addition, Chinese companies rushed existing low-cost wind and solar technologies into the market, which made the advanced technological choices that VCs favored look foolish. Even more important was the role of hydraulic fracking in lowering fossil fuel prices, a surprise that few expected. It was a feasible and cost-effective technology that revitalized US natural gas and oil production. Clean energy investors did not foresee this development, and many of their investments failed.

## Nuclear Energy

Another miscalculation had to do with nuclear power.[13] Hope for a revival led to Toshiba's 2006 $5.4 billion purchase of Westinghouse's nuclear power production capabilities. Analysts warned that the company was paying too much. Japan's Fukushima disaster made the decision seem mistaken, yet Toshiba, despite delays and the downsizing of many projects, reaffirmed its commitment to nuclear power. Its involvement in a project for the first nuclear power plant reactors built in the United States in decades was years behind schedule and billions of dollars over budget. The company had to lay off 78,000 workers, and its CEO had to resign. In 2016, Toshiba was close to bankruptcy.

## Unsettled Issues

Long-term and expensive investments in projects in the energy industry can go awry. To launch these large-scale projects decision makers must have optimistic biases, but the problems their companies encounter often snowball, and the companies must withdraw as their losses mount. Unsettled issues, including the following, continue to weigh heavily on decision makers in the energy industry:

- *Many nations are in turmoil politically.* Governments play a central role in incentivizing actors in the energy industry to take up certain activities, and, conversely, they play a disproportionate role in discouraging them from taking up other activities. The impact of government policies on the energy industry is uneven, inconsistent, hard to predict, and subject to sudden shifts. The types of regimes that will be in power and the choices they will make to subsidize, encourage, suppress, and regulate companies are unclear. How will companies operate when there are non-liberal, autocratic democracies in place in many countries? The global security picture is also in doubt because of failed states in the Middle East and ongoing warfare.
- *Technologies have been shifting rapidly.* The shale oil revolution could spread to Europe, China, Africa, and much of the rest of the world. Renewable energy has also made substantial progress and has become a feasible alternative to fossil fuels in some situations. A number of different technological revolutions are merging. The forging together of information technology with transportation, industry, housing, and commercial building may bring about shifts in business models. New systems of driving, producing goods and services, and heating and cooling buildings are possible and can lead to substantially greater efficiency in the use of energy. Communities of scientists and engineers continue to forge ahead with technologies that can disrupt calculations about what is economically feasible and prudent. How far can they go? Will rapid advances in petro-algae technology, for example, take place? Will a breakthrough in battery technology occur? What effect would these developments have on energy industry decision making?
- *The global economic future is unclear.* There are threats of trade wars, vast amounts of bad debt in China, and the lingering stasis of European Union (EU) countries. How much growth there will be and where it will take place are in doubt. Also uncertain is to what extent this growth will translate into increased demand for energy.

## Climate Change

At the forefront of issues the industry faces, and one of the most uncertain factors it confronts, is climate change. This threat could tip the balance of human survival and compel nations to take new steps to combat this problem. While it remains somewhat hard to trace the direct causal consequences to the accumulation of human-created greenhouse gas emissions (GHGs) in the atmosphere, they already were having an impact on the occurrence of extreme weather and the price of agricultural commodities. Almost certainly, with the melting of glaciers and ice sheets, there would be a rise in sea levels, the full impacts of which were unknown.

The evolution of policies to offset climate change has had an uneven history. In the 1992 Earth Summit, the United States agreed, along with many other countries, to work to stabilize GHGs at levels that prevent dangerous interference with the climate system. Under the plan then in effect, nations had "common, but differentiated responsibilities," which meant that industrialized countries, mainly responsible for historical emissions, had to act first, and sustainable development became the highest priority for developing countries.

The next step was the Kyoto Protocol. Signed in 1997, but only ratified in 2005. Under the accord, industrialized countries committed to reducing average annual emissions in 2008–2012 to 5 percent below 1990 levels. The EU's commitment was for an 8 percent reduction, while the United States was supposed to reduce its emissions by 7 percent, but the US Congress (in the Byrd–Hagel resolution of 1997) unanimously rejected the Kyoto agreement, ostensibly because of a lack of commitment from developing nations to reducing their own emissions. The Kyoto accord allowed industrialized nations to buy emission allowances and reductions from developing countries or each other, rather than reducing their own emissions.

A breakthrough took place in 2016 with the Paris summit. Both developed and developing nations agreed to limit their emissions and submit to regular reviews. Developing nations promised to help finance poorer nations' emission reductions and bring them aid to cope with climate change's negative consequences. Country commitments under the Paris Accord were voluntary, however; and even if carried out, there was likely to be a planetary warming of almost 3 degrees above pre-industrial levels, which would mean that droughts, floods, heat waves and sea level rises still were likely to arise.

Under the Trump administration, the United States declared that it would abandon its Paris commitments. The fate of the Paris Climate Accord, therefore, was in doubt. After the administration declared it would leave the Accord, would other governments also threaten to do the same? Without the United States, could the Accord survive? Its implementation was far from certain, which created another unknown for energy-industry decision makers.

Climate change and relevant policies related to it had major effects on the companies that produced and consumed energy. They raised the price of doing large-scale energy projects. ExxonMobil, for example, since exploiting the carbon-rich tar sands of Canada no longer seemed economical, had had to follow its peers and take a $2 billion write-down on its oil reserve in this region.[14]

## Conclusion

This chapter has presented the problem of this book: strategic choice under risk and uncertainty among companies in the energy industry. It has argued that it is a unique challenge whose scope and problematic nature is not easy to reduce. A key element in the challenge is price volatility, which rests on a host of political, economic, and technological considerations and unsettled issues. Another key challenge is climate change. Funders of energy developments regularly have to reassess where to put their money. Companies make short- and long-term bets on different energy sources. Where they are likely to invest next is challenging because of the lack of precedents given the risks and uncertainties they face.

## Notes

1. Knight, Frank. *Risk, Uncertainty and Profit*. Mineola, NY: Dover Publications, 2012.
2. Ibid.
3. Keynes, John Maynard. *The General Theory of Employment, Interest, and Money*. New York: Springer, 2018.
4. Taleb, Nassim Nicholas. *The Black Swan: The Impact of the Highly Improbable*. New York: Random House, 2007.

5. Rumsfeld, Donald. *Known and Unknown: A Memoir.* New York: Penguin, 2011.
6. March, James G., Lee S. Sproull, and Michal Tamuz. "Learning from Samples of One or Fewer." *Organization Science* 2.1 (1991): 1–13.
7. "Keynes. *The General Theory.*" www.economicshelp.org/blog/613/eco nomics/quotes-by-john-maynard-keynes/
8. Ibid.
9. Pearl, Judea. *Causality: Models, Reasoning, and Inference.* New York: Cambridge University Press, 2009.
10. *"Kashagan Oil Bubble: Project Failures and Consequences."* http://crude accountability.org/kashagan-oil-bubble-project-failures-consequences/
11. Marcus, Alfred. *Innovations in Sustainability: Fuel and Food.* Cambridge, UK: Cambridge University Press, 2015.
12. Ibid.
13. *"Toshiba's Chairman Resigns as Its Nuclear Power Losses Mount."* www.nytimes.com/2017/02/14/business/toshiba-chairman-nuclear-loss .html
14. *"Exxon's Big Oil Sands Write-Off Could Help It Dodge SEC Troubles."* http://fortune.com/2017/02/23/exxon-mobil-oil-sands-sec/

# 2 | The Management of Risk and Uncertainty

Decision makers in the energy industry have no easy way to reduce the risk and uncertainty about what is likely to take place next, how it affects them, and how they should respond. Therefore, the return companies make on a project, if it materializes, may be short-lived as economic and political conditions shift; technologies change; and competitors, substitute products, and new entrants cut off the possibility of gain. In general, decision makers in businesses try to gain control of such uncertainties, coping in various ways. They try to anticipate the future and attempt to take calculated bets. This chapter summarizes previous academic literature about the management of risk and uncertainty. Specifically, it analyzes the decision-making limitations that research has found to exist when decision makers contend with important strategic issues.

## Anticipating the Future

The prior literature suggests that there are at least four ways to anticipate the future, each of which has limitations.[1]

1. **Trends.** Though trends in one area often lead to developments in another, the trends must be analyzed with caution. Just because a trend is moving in a particular way does not mean it will continue. It can flatten out, become more pronounced, or reverse direction. Inflections take place. Tipping points occur. Simple extrapolation can be deceiving if it does not take into account different future conditions, the impact of trends on each other, and how human responses change their direction. Trend analysis leaves insufficient room for surprises and unexpected developments. For example, in *The Rise and Fall of American Growth* economist Robert Gordon argues that it is not certain that the remarkable improvements in

people's lives that took place in the century that started in 1870 will continue.[2] He points out that since 1970 US productivity growth has stalled, technological progress has slowed, and the benefits of this growth have not been widely shared. The information technology revolution, he comments, is no match for indoor plumbing, autos, electricity, air travel, antibiotics, and air conditioning.

2. **Experts.** Relying on expert opinion is not much better than relying on trends. Even the most trusted experts are fallible. An expert panel asserted that the analytical engine that Charles Babbage, later the inventor of the computer, created had no practical value. A committee of experts found no potential in Thomas Edison's incandescent light bulb. Experts declared that intercontinental ballistic missiles could not accurately deliver their payload thousands of miles away. In *Superforecasting: The Art and Science of Prediction,* Philip Tetlock and Dan Gardner report that experts are right less than 50 percent of the time.[3] Groups of laypeople typically make better predictions. Seers project the future, but their predictions do not necessarily foretell what is to come next. In the book *Megamistakes,* author Steven Schnarrs lists many errors that experts have made in forecasting the future.[4] He includes the supersonic air transport (SST) that at speeds of 2,000 miles per hour forecasters suggested would be followed rapidly by hyper-supersonic transport at even greater speeds of 4,000 miles per hour.

3. **Analogical reasoning.** Decision makers may compare known aspects of current conditions with corresponding characteristics of past phenomena. If the match is good, they assume that prior cases can provide a good understanding of contemporary events. The closer the match, the stronger the indication that the analogy they are using is good. Teasing lessons from the past, however, is not easy. In using analogical reasoning, the analyst must be careful to highlight the relevant similarities and differences between previous and present events. The analyst cannot ignore unlikely Black Swan events, though people tend to disregard them as they did in the Great Financial Crisis of 2007–2008. Like Robert Gordon, *Wall Street Journal* writer Greg Ip argues that the past performance of the global economy is no indicator of its future performance.[5] He suggests that the future might be very different from the past because the world has harvested the gains in science, medicine, and technology that are the easiest to achieve. Additional advances

are costly and complex, and they could be prone to failure. Barriers for transforming ideas into commercially successful products have grown. Yet, Ip admits that countertrends do exist. For example, future innovations that affect the energy industry might come from many sources including artificial intelligence, gene therapy, robotics, and software. Ip asks whether a jump as large as that, which occurred, from oil and kerosene lamps to electric lighting is possible. He maintains that no amount of analogical reasoning can answer the question of whether a golden age is on the horizon because of technological breakthroughs.

4. **Baysean judgment.** As the situation changes, analysts can update estimates based on new information. With the new information, learning is possible. The Baysean perspective thus offers room for constant adjustment, but it is not foolproof. For example, we know the probabilities of rolling dice. Even if not known, we could roll the dice and record the results. Thus, empirically, after enough tosses of the dice, we could arrive at a fairly good estimate of the odds, and with each observation, we could update and improve our estimate. Eventually, we would come very close to knowing the actual odds based on what we have observed. However, the dice exist as a fixed system. They do not exhibit any dynamism. There is no change in the twelve possible outcomes. However, if the system shifts, then it is hard to learn from a series of observations in which we record the results, since the odds of what the outcomes will be are not stable. When a system exhibits fundamental shifts, it is very hard to learn from its past behavior. For example, what if, unbeknownst to the observer, someone slightly altered the weight of the dice after each roll. No matter how faithfully we observed the rolls of the dice and recorded the results, we would not have a good sense of the odds. It would not be possible to arrive at accurate probabilities based on observation and our Baysean updating. Thus, economist Hyman Minsky has argued that because every economic era is different it is nearly impossible to extract reproducible lessons from any of them.[6]

## Taking Calculated Risks

For these reasons, and others like them, decision makers cannot fully anticipate the future. Nonetheless, they must take calculated risks based on their expectations of future returns. How certain can they be that they will achieve such payoffs? As argued in the last chapter, animal spirits play a role. Decision makers rely on their guts as much as on their reason –that does not mean that they leave reason entirely behind, yet however good they are at reasoning it only gets them so far, since fundamentally the future is unknown. Thus, to get proposals off the ground and projects funded, they have to exhibit optimism. They have to display confidence that they know what they are doing. They need to lay out the risks and uncertainties and indicate what their assumptions are. Then, they can indulge in the use of various caveats and qualifiers to maintain their credibility, inserting vague phrases like reasonable, likely, possible, or hoped-for into assertions they make, and, when pressed, they might have to attach hard numbers to the guesses.

For instance, Shlomo Maital provides the following example of taking a calculated risk.[7] Let us say that decision makers agree that a big energy project provides a 10 percent chance of $10 billion returns, but there is a 30 percent chance it might lose $0.1 billion, and a 60 percent chance the same project might result in a $1 billion loss. The decision makers have based their estimates of the odds of the likely returns on reasonable guesses. They have examined the experience of their organization and others with similar projects. They have updated their understanding with advances in technology and economic forecasts. They operate in a reasonable way. They rely on their judgment and good sense as far as it will take them. Yet, they have made a series of estimates to arrive at these odds, which together can compound the error, so the ground on which they are operating is only as good as the assumptions they have made.

Let us take for granted for a moment that their assessments of the odds are reasonably sound. Then, in the example that Maital gives, the expected gain before subtracting the expected losses is $10 billion times 0.1, or $1 billion. The expected losses are $1 billion times 0.6, plus $0.1 billion times 0.3, or $0.63 billion. Putting it together, the likely payback from this project goes down, but it remains positive, as $1 billion minus $0.63 billion is $0.37 billion. Pending opportunity costs and expected interest rates, Maital asks, should decision makers approve a project of this nature? Recall that the possibility of the $10 billion return that generates the $0.37 payback is just *10 percent* while the possibility that the loss could be as low as $0.1 billion or as high $1 billion is *90 percent*. Maital suggests that since people tend to be loss averse, as the psychologists Adam Tversky and Daniel Kahneman demonstrate, the decision makers in the example are not likely to pursue this initiative.[8] They will forego the expected gain of $0.37 billion, which is the most likely payback, because of fear of a loss, although, as a compromise, they might try to find an alternative where the loss is lower, but the expected gain is less.

This example suggests that even when decision makers quantify the risk, however imprecisely, the problem of what to do does not go away. To what extent are important organizational decisions actually made in this fashion? Do organizations always make their most important choices after similar quantifications? In most instances, they do not get to a point where they have enumerated the benefits and costs with such precision. Therefore, people in organizations depend on argument and counter-argument. Factions take up different sides. Only if they had perfect knowledge would they be fully rational. Lacking full knowledge, they make compromises. They hedge what they do, fearing to go out on a limb and get themselves and their organizations into excessive trouble.

Their hedging is the phenomenon this book later examines, that is how decision makers in major energy companies show caution and hedge their bets when they lack full knowledge of the future. Organizations have to hedge because they carry out few important strategic undertakings with full knowledge and hence total certainty. Their operational and technical decisions may be rooted in sound engineering knowledge that yields stable and reliable outcomes, but not their strategic choices. The essence of strategy is that in making strategy decision makers face an unknown future. Limitations of time, money, and analytical power mean that residual uncertainty nearly always plays a role. Under conditions of perfect ignorance, the strategic choices decision makers would make would be entirely random. They would be unable to link outcomes to alternatives. If results conformed to expectations, it would be a matter of luck. Under residual uncertainty, the choices they make are generally better than mere luck; they are not entirely random, but they are not perfect. Understanding that they are not perfect, organizations protect themselves, and thus decision makers hedge the choices they make. Given the randomness, hunches play an important role. Maital reports that when Sony decided to license the rights to the transistor in the early 1950s, the value of the technology was entirely unclear.[9] Company co-founder Masaru Ibuka made the decision based on a sleepless night's hunch during a visit to New Jersey's Bell Lab. The history of the company on its website states "an idea flashed through his mind." With hindsight, this hunch paid off, but many others do not.

## Individual and Organizational Shortcomings

Not all strategic decisions are pure hunches yet all contain some guesswork. The psychological and sociological literature has portrayed how decision making takes place when guesswork plays a role. It has portrayed the shortcomings that exist at individual and collective levels. What follows is a thumbnail sketch of some of the essential points this literature makes.

### *Individual Biases*

Psychologists Kahneman and Tversky showed that people have unreasonable expectations of early results and their replicability.[10] No matter what the implications of further evidence are, natural starting points or anchors act as aids in judgment. Humans display such perceptual biases as:

- Anchoring – putting too much stock in initial information.
- Recency – placing too much emphasis on information recently acquired.
- Salience – placing too much emphasis on information that stands out.
- Availability – placing too much emphasis on easily acquired information.
- Clustering – seeing patterns in this information when there are none.
- Overconfidence – being too certain that the patterns give accurate findings.
- Confirmation – placing too much emphasis on information that supports the findings.
- Conservatism – placing too high a burden of proof on disconfirming evidence.

Another common perceptual error is that people tend to be blind to events on their periphery. When psychologists carry out experiments in which they show a film of teams passing a ball and ask how many times the teams have passed the ball, most subjects provide the right answer.[11] Nonetheless, more than 90 percent fail to notice if a gorilla walks through the scene and taunts the players. Among those who notice the gorilla, less than half get the count right. Subjects who repeat the experiment usually get the count right and spot the gorilla, but fail to notice changes like a person leaving the game or a change in the color of the background curtain. Thus, most people can see beyond the known knowns (the ball passing hands) and spot the unknown knowns (the taunting gorilla), but it is hard for them to recognize the unknown unknowns (players leaving the game and the change in curtain color).

## Group Limitations

Collective errors compound individual judgmental impediments.[12] Groups working on decision-making problems may suppress doubts and develop illusions of invulnerability. Group consensus and group-think reinforce such attitudes. They mean insulation from external criticism and promotion of a dominant views to the exclusion of others.

Moving from the group to the organization, organizations also are limited in the choices they make. When considering the same conditions, they reach different conclusions. Objectives, capacities, and interests lead the people in organizations to present facts in a biased way. They cope with indeterminateness by simplifying tasks and narrowing the range of information they take into account, limiting the information they analyze, and confining themselves to a few responses. They recall and emphasize congenial information and ignore or suppress critical information. They select a course of action before they consider all the plausible outcomes because they are constrained by time pressures. They also use information for its manipulative or propagandistic value in promoting acceptance of their points of view.

Even when they discover error, they do not promptly correct it. They may be reluctant to admit error because of fear of blame. They may recognize the error slowly because their training leads them to stick to a prevailing course of action even when they start to sense it is defective. Thus, they will fail to distinguish true signals from the noise and not make sound use of knowledge they possess. The correction of error arising from the inadequacy of previous assessments depends not only on its recognition. People in organizations must have the power to act based on updated information they obtain.

## State, Effect, and Response

Francis Milliken argued that three types of uncertainty – state, effect, and response – affect the decisions organizations make.[13] State uncertainty has to do with the conditions in the world, effect uncertainty concerns the impact of those conditions on a particular organization, and response uncertainty relates to what the organization should do next. In each instance, there are no clear answers, which compounds the problem. Below is a summary of some of the literature on how state, effect, and response uncertainty affect organizational decision making.

### State Uncertainty

State uncertainty becomes a central problem for organizations because of complexity in their external environments. Complexity arises because of the number of factors decision makers in organizations must consider. They confront multiple external environments – technical, economic, political, and social – that change at different rates, conflict with each other, and impose inconsistent demands. Separate interacting technical, economic, political, and social logics create myriad possible futures. Technological change, for instance, takes place in a discontinuous pattern. A dominant technological design comes under threat, which disrupts the dominant design. Another dominant design, though, may come under threat, but maintain itself and withstand the disruption. In the societal sphere, some societies are disproportionately young, while others are disproportionately old. They confront different types of economic stresses – on the one hand, nurturing the young and, on the other hand, caring for the elderly. Change in the social realm also regularly arises from fluctuations in fashion, tastes, attitudes, and values. Tipping points can occur in any realm, whether it be technical, economic, political, or social, and suddenly change the rules of the game and realign the relationships among realms. Related technical, economic, political, and social changes are not in harmony. Each moves at its own pace. Governments influence the course of events. Their actions affect the economy, society, and technology. Some governments are stable, but clearly not all are. Some are in the midst of regime change. Other governments have collapsed entirely. They exist in a failed condition. For all these reasons, decision makers must contend with the question of whether the laws and public policies in place today will be the same in the future.

## *Effect Uncertainty*

Changes in the technical, social, and political environments are dynamic and complex, patterns change, and decision makers in organizations may not have enough time to adjust. Even with the time, it is unclear what the effects will be on their organizations. What are the threats and what are opportunities for them? Can they make sense of the impacts of what it is taking place on them? Can they draw the relevant connections? Though they try to hedge their bets, there is no simple firewall they can erect to protect their organizations from the technical, economic, political, and social volatility. With disparate events converging, surprises can multiply. Even if more information were available, it would not be clear how to assess it. There may be too much information as well as too little of it. Thus, decision makers organize what they know based on what stands out and is noticeable, trying to impose meaning and order on events, perhaps framing what they observe relying on various shortcuts, mental models, heuristics, lenses, and protocols for the purposes of interpretation.

## *Response Uncertainty*

Before decision makers fully know what is happening they must act – this is why hunches and professional judgment play such an important role, but uncertainty makes them hesitate, unsure of what to do next. The uncertainty may instill in them anxiety, fear, dread, perhaps even panic. It activates emotions that function at odds with rationality. Ensuing doubt and unease can lead to procrastination and delay, paralysis, drift, or retreat. As is well known, within an organization, individuals with different objectives provide different and competing interpretations about what is taking place and what the organization should do. People with different interests engage in struggles for power and influence. They may build a consensus, but if the internal organizational conflicts escalate, the consensus may break down. Lack of a consensus may result in a myopic focus on the present with blind spots regarding the future. The instinctive responses of the decision makers may then lead them down well-trodden paths, with organizational imprinting, path dependence, and sunk costs adding to inertia.

Thus, decision makers may escalate commitment to the current course of action. They find justifications for their actions based on how their organizations have been doing in comparison to various reference points. As a reference point, they might compare how well their organizations did in the past to how well they are doing now. If current performance is not out of line with past performance, they will stick with what has worked in the past. They may also benchmark performance relative to their peers. If the performance of their organizations is not out of line with that of their peers, they will continue to match what the peers are doing. Only if performance is very out of line with the past and/or peers might decision makers initiate a search for new solutions. They also may then find that it is difficult to buffer their organizations from change – it is difficult to muddle through; no longer is it possible to resist, or stall. Being defensive and fighting change is not possible.

## Being a Leader

Rather than fighting change, decision makers may choose to adapt by taking a leadership position, but doing so is hazardous. Being a first mover can yield unanticipated consequences. Decision makers may conclude that it is far better for other organizations to test the waters. Thus, they might resist being a leader. The primary concern is to protect an organization's existing assets – to hedge – and the reasoning used is that there is no reason to go out on a limb if it means putting these assets in danger. Because of these factors, before entirely reconfiguring a prior business model, decision makers may aim for some type of compromise. They will mostly stick with what they have done thus far, but not entirely. They exploit the current business model, but undertake some exploring for new approaches just in case. On the margins, they open up and try to be flexible.

If they conclude they face some type of non-linear change, they try experiments. To cope, they may enter new markets; develop novel products or services; try out alliances, mergers, and acquisitions; globalize; and innovate with alternative business models. They take these steps and then evaluate and reassess them before going further. If they have exaggerated the threat and/or misperceived the opportunity, they may abandon the fresh approaches. Along with flexibility, they need the capacity to revert to their prior condition if they have made a mistake. Hesitating to move forward too vigorously in new directions, they flip-flop between new and old positions and approaches. Different organizations go through this process in different ways. These variations are a key element in the case studies found later in the book.

## Profiting from Risk and Uncertainty

In his book *Profiting from Uncertainty*, Paul Schoemaker promises strategies for firm success no matter what the future brings.[14] He argues an organization can profit from risk and uncertainty if it follows these recommended steps:

- embrace uncertainty;
- prepare the mind;
- experience multiple futures;
- build a robust strategic vision;
- create flexible options;
- engage in dynamic monitoring and adjustment;
- implement, accepting the uncertainty;
- then successfully navigate the future.

Though there is much merit in this type of advice, actual decision making in the face of risk and uncertainty is not likely to be either this orderly or successful.

Rather it is likely to be hedged. Incumbent companies in industries poised for change are likely to adapt to risk and uncertainty by exploring and pursuing a variety of different options at the same time, but their commitment to these options is likely to be provisional. Taking out options that decision makers can reverse is a fine balancing act. It is a stretch for organizations to keep re-orienting themselves in opposing directions simultaneously, to be ambidextrous, and to engage in the art of paradox and dialectics. Sequential investment, in which they raise and lower stakes based on changing perceptions of the gains and losses, is not easy. To assemble and reassemble capabilities, to structure and restructure organizations, and to configure and reconfigure business models is a daunting activity. For example, how far can organizations go in re-pivoting themselves from being comfortable specialists in a chosen field to amateur generalists in many domains? With too many lightweight experiments they take on, the chance of spreading themselves too thin grows. Beyond a certain level, variety does not increase their odds of survival. It decreases it. The consequences of a wrong decision can be profound. There are no guarantees. Outright failure can take place. Many examples exist of once-indomitable firms such as Xerox, Kodak, Lucent, Nokia, Motorola, and Blackberry that did not adequately adjust to the mobile revolution. Just 12.2 percent of the *Fortune* 500 companies in 1955 continued to be on the list 59 years later. The rest were bankrupt, merged, or had fallen so much in revenue that they no longer were major companies. Many companies on the 1955 list are long forgotten.[15]

## How Companies Adapt

This chapter has covered the decision-making limitations that exist when organizations confront the type of risk and uncertainty with which decision makers in the energy industry must contend. Incumbent companies in industries like the energy industry that seem poised and ready for change are likely to adapt to the risk and uncertainty by hedging. The following behaviors are likely to accompany their hedging:

• Decision makers in more risky and uncertain environments (hard to predict the future) are likely to rely less on rational/analytical decision making because they do not know chances of payoffs/losses and their magnitude. They are more likely to rely on hunches and intuition or what Keynes calls animal spirits.
• The less they rely on rational/analytical decision making, the more other factors such as organizational politics, imitation (what their rivals do), and what analysts say will affect the choices they make.
• The less they rely on rational/analytical decision making the more cognitive and collective errors they are likely to make, despite their best efforts.
• The less they feel they are able to avoid these errors, the more cautious they may become – the more they will try to protect their organizations from harm by hedging their bets. Under these circumstances, they become defensive and try to delay and avoid departures from the status quo.

Such factors, as the following, however, might mitigate their caution about departing from the status quo:

- the degree to which they perceive external change as competence enhancing or detracting;
- the extent to which they have sunk costs (stranded assets) wrapped up in the status quo;
- the degree to which their organizations have been and are well diversified;
- the extent to which their organizations are performing well in comparison with peers and other reference points;
- the extent to which their organizations have the slack resources to experiment and make changes.

Under these conditions, their hedging might move from protecting their organizations from harm to exploiting the situation that they reckon is emerging for gain. The case studies that come later in this book examine the slight, but significant, departures from the status quo incumbents in the energy industry made in response to the uncertain changes taking place in their external environment.

## Notes

1. Marcus, Alfred. *Strategic Foresight: A New Look at Scenarios.* New York: Palgrave MacMillan, 2009.
2. Gordon, Robert. *The Rise and Fall of American Growth: The US Standard of Living since the Civil War.* Princeton, NJ: Princeton University Press, 2017.
3. Tetlock, Philip E., and Dan Gardner. *Superforecasting: The Art and Science of Prediction.* New York: Random House, 2016.
4. Schnaars, Steven. *Megamistakes: Forecasting and the Myth of Rapid Technological Change.* New York: Free Press, 1989.
5. Ip, Greg. "The Innovation Paradox: The Global Economy's Hidden Problem – Innovation is Slowing, Hampering Improvements in Living Standards." *Wall Street Journal,* December 7, 2016: A1.
6. Minsky, Hyman. *Stabilizing an Unstable Economy.* New York: McGraw Hill Education, 2008.
7. Maital, Shlomo. *Executive Economics: Ten Essential Tools for Managers.* New York: Free Press, 2011.

8. Tversky, Amos, and Daniel Kahneman. "Loss Aversion in Riskless Choice: A Reference-dependent Model." *The Quarterly Journal of Economics* 106 (1991): 1039–1061.
9. Maital, *Executive Economics*.
10. Kahneman, Daniel. *Thinking, Fast and Slow*. New York: Farrar, Straus, and Giroux, 2013.
11. Chabris, Christopher, and Daniel Simons. *The Invisible Gorilla*. New York: MJF Books, 2010.
12. Marcus, Alfred. "Risk, Uncertainty, and Scientific Judgement." *Minerva* (1988): 138–152.
13. Milliken, Frances J. "Three Types of Perceived Uncertainty about the Environment: State, Effect, and Response Uncertainty." *Academy of Management Review* 12 (1987): 133–144.
14. Schoemaker, Paul. *Profiting from Uncertainty: Strategies for Succeeding no Matter What the Future Brings*. New York: Simon and Schuster, 2012.
15. *"Fortune 500 Firms in 1955 vs. 2014; 88% Are Gone, and We're All Better Off Because of That Dynamic 'Creative Destruction'."* www.aei .org/publication/fortune-500-firms-in-1955-vs-2014–89-are-gone-and-were-all-better-off-because-of-that-dynamic-creative-destruction/

# 3 | *Hedging in the Energy Industry*

The firms within the energy industry with which the book deals are among the largest in the world as calculated by indexes like the *Fortune* Global 500. Almost all of these companies have suffered major setbacks in recent years, whether financial and driven by the sudden 2014–2016 drop in energy prices or a result of a serious safety incident, or both. Each company tried to make a comeback and faced vital long-term investment choices that involved key issues. Strategically, how did these companies make their bets on the future given the conditions of risk and uncertainty they confronted? This question is central to the case studies that appear later in the book. The premise of the cases is the idea that decision makers in the energy industry are unable to predict with confidence where the market will be in the future. Despite this limitation, they choose strategies to guard against the negative consequences of volatility.[1]

Affecting their decisions are perceptions of their companies' strengths and weaknesses. Also, affecting their decisions are perceptions of macro-environmental and industry risks. The macro-environmental risks they consider include those relating to economics, international security, domestic politics, law, technology, and climate change. The industry risks they evaluate include those that relate to their suppliers, customers, competitors, substitutes, and new entrants. On the bases of these judgments, they formulate assumptions about what the future may bring. The assumptions are to some degree guesswork. They justify the moves they feel constrained to make because of the assets and capabilities that they have that are tied to the status quo. If the assumptions deviate far from what they took for granted in the past, they might have to entirely abandon paths they have previously taken, a course of action that would be too cognitively and emotionally difficult for decision makers in incumbent energy organizations to make. Thus, in the moves they make they hedge their bets.

As the last chapter argued, decision makers have ways to try to anticipate what will occur next. For instance, they can draw on the past for analogies, which unfortunately are far from perfect. Still, these factors may be less important than their views of their companies' strengths and weaknesses and their dedication to continue cultivating these strengths and weaknesses by perpetuating them as best they can in the face of external threats and their perceptions of the risks.

## A Balancing Act

Thus a balancing act takes place with accommodation on the margins to the threat of a future that may be far different from the present and a strong desire to continue to exploit their existing strengths for gain. This type of balancing influences the sets of options they take seriously. They must exclude some options because they would be too threatening to the dominant logic and organizing principles of their organizations. As the last chapter argued, psychological and organizational dynamics influence how decision makers in these organizations perceive their options and which moves that they can make are worth pursuing. It would be psychologically uncomfortable and organizationally unsafe to stray too far from the status quo. Decision makers are moved by the emotion of defensiveness because they have much to defend.

What makes their task especially daunting is that they may have to consider and simultaneously plan for many futures, some of which would be easier to handle, such that these get more play. A continuation of business as usual is easier to handle; but a substantial deterioration in current conditions may take place. Even a substantial improvement in these conditions might be challenging. It is within these boundaries that decision makers in the energy industry try to operate. They tinker on the edges. Later chapters of this book examine how they tinker and adjust their strategies. Though the future is unknown, decision makers in the energy industry do not wish to stray far from their comfort levels. Straying from their comfort levels is difficult to accommodate since the so many of their assets are dedicated to the status quo. Any of the following are possible. There could be a near-total collapse, a surprise, or an unknown unknown. There could be a high-level breakdown in the system, a tipping point, or a radical inflection, or the world could continue operating largely as it has in the past.

The understanding of decision makers of future states changes as time passes and they obtain more information and what they perceive to be a better sense of what is actually taking place. They can and should update what they know but they may be reluctant to go too far in pushing the refresh button. The challenge they face is to continually reimagine what is happening and to engage with a volatile and uncertain field to provide stability and buffer their organizations regardless of what takes place. That is the purpose of hedging – to protect their organizations. Hedging itself is not static. It, too, evolves, as there is recognition of emerging realities that decision makers cannot avoid. Regardless of when and how organizations practice it, hedging becomes an imperative when organizations face risk and uncertainty. Their decision making is far from optimal and not simply boundedly rational, but in the face of risk and uncertainties, the moves that they take are hedged.

## A Definition and Some Examples

Hedging involves having sufficient backups in place to deal with the different contingencies that are possible. It also relates to the timing of when, how, if, and under what circumstances, if at all, to implement the backups, and to what degree they should be implemented. It is the phasing in of a series of moves over time, and, for most organizations, not making all decisions at once, but rather gradually modulating the intensity of commitment to different courses of actions as perceptions of the risks and uncertainties shift and basic assumptions about the likely path of the future change. Hedging their moves is how decision makers try to mitigate risks and uncertainties and make progress despite the lingering irresolution of what is to transpire next.

Legally, as public corporations, decision makers are accountable and must take cognizance of risks and uncertainties, lay bare their assumptions, and then reveal how they have hedged their bets so that their organizations can survive and with some luck thrive. This type of structured decision making is found in the annual reports of publicly traded corporations and is the foundation for the analyses of the incumbent-organization decision making in the energy industry that comes later in this book. In this sense, the hedging in which these organizations take part is not a financial instrument like a forward contract; nonetheless the intention is similar in that it can minimize downside losses and can increase the chance of gain regardless of what occurs.

In the face of multiple possibilities, decision makers in companies in the energy industry engage in hedging and contingency planning to increase the chances that their companies stay afloat, if not thrive, regardless of what ensues. By hedging the moves they take, they try to limit the downside losses, stabilize the gains, and reduce the volatility their organizations face. Each sector in the energy industry has a preferred and time-honored hedging strategy, which this book analyzes later. Oil and natural gas companies carry out different hedging strategies from those adopted by automobile companies. In each instance the hedging strategies of an industry sector must be analyzed.

The energy industry is well suited to an investigation of how decision makers hedge, as its future is beset by so much risk and uncertainty. Before rolling out a set of options that decision makers in the industry pursue, they must settle on a set of assumptions to back up their choices. Yet, the movement from risks and uncertainties to assumptions is rarely logically tight. It is subject to judgment. The movement from risks and uncertainties to assumptions sets the stage for making strategic choices about how to allocate assets and make bets on the future.

## Trying to Reduce Risks and Uncertainties

Decision makers try to reduce risks and uncertainties to manageable proportions before they proceed. They are able to accept small deviations from business as usual, but not large ones because this type of deviation would overwhelm the capacity of their organizations to cope. Their organizations are too locked in financially. The mindset of their employees and standard operating procedures is a barrier to moving far from the status quo. Still, the companies must adjust somewhat. Within limits, they have to make marginal adjustments to ensure their firms have not overcommitted to a mistaken course and will be unable to recover should the external environment move in a way they do not want. The difficulty is to build some element of flexibility into their choices so that they are able to adapt to circumstance regardless of how conditions evolve. Thus, there is a need to search for and find a mix of long- and short-term commitments that do not wind up leaving their organizations too much at risk.

There are different paths they can take to build this balance. By external collaborations and partnerships, internal belt tightening, and appropriate levels of R&D, they may be able to bolster the capacities of their companies to respond. Steven Coll in *Private Empire: ExxonMobil and American Power* offers ExxonMobil as an example of the hedging of a prominent firm in this industry, a firm that will be the subject of additional treatment later in the book.[2] The company's hedging strategies have helped it minimize the degree to which it has faced the danger of extinction. For instance, it coped with the nationalization of its global oil reserves by acquiring Mobil. Through emphasis on the recovery of offshore oil, it tried to cope with the threat of peak supply. It dealt with the Valdez spill by tightening its internal operations, implementing a very insular, technical, and rule-bound system, the strictly enforced operating integrity management system it carries out so well. It also fought a vigorous political and public relations campaign against claims of climate change, which resulted in its becoming entangled in ongoing controversy.

How well did these hedges work? As a preview to what comes later, it is worth noting that the deterioration of ExxonMobil's profits was so great in the first quarter of 2016 that rating agencies lowered its bond rankings. Has belt tightening been a sufficient strategy for this already highly efficient operator to pursue?

Another oil and natural gas firm BP, to which this book compares to ExxonMobil, also hedged to protect itself. It was acclaimed for its "beyond petroleum" campaign, which it has since abandoned. In 2010, it had the unfortunate Deepwater Horizon oil spill, the worst disaster in the history of the oil and gas industry, and then came record losses in 2016 after oil prices plummeted, which affected it like ExxonMobil. BP still was reeling from the Deepwater Horizon oil spill when prices plunged. Its financial payout exceeded $60 billion and the payout may go even higher.

Given its limited resources, how well has BP hedged its bets about the future? What types of strategic long-term investments did it make? In its 2016 annual report, the company wrote that the purpose of its strategy was to ensure that it would be "good for all seasons." In other words, in an uncertain environment, it wanted to create options that would permit it to operate under many different contingencies. These options would permit the company to do well in a world of many different circumstances, "a world of volatile oil and gas prices, changing customer preferences and, of course, the transition to a lower carbon future."

This book examines how decision makers in the energy industry made sense of the risk and uncertainty they confronted, what types of assumptions they formed, and how these assumptions affected the decisions they made. To what degree did they put in place the right mix of hedges to allow their organizations to survive, if not prosper, and protect them from contingencies? How did they take on this challenge and communicate their actions to shareholders and relevant stakeholders in public proclamations such as their annual reports? What were the assumptions energy decision makers formulated to justify how they responded to the risks and uncertainties that by law they had to acknowledge in their statements to investors? To what extent were the tactics they used to persuade investors that they were on top of the situation persuasive? The form their rhetoric took is subject to further analysis in this book. To what extent did they appeal to their audiences' emotion, logic, and values? Their movement from risks and uncertainties to assumptions and decision making was not just for themselves. They meant to convince stakeholders that they were in command and they had some control over the situation.

## Choosing What to Do

Once decision makers in the industry acknowledged the risks and uncertainties and formulated a set of assumptions, they then faced a set of choices upon which to hedge their companies' bets for the future. In the oil and natural gas sector, for example, they had to choose where in the value chain to focus, upstream or downstream. They also had to consider whether the emphasis should be on oil or more on natural gas. Choices also had to be made about where to pursue exploration and development – on-shore or offshore, in fields with tar sands or in fields with underground shale potential.

In the auto sector, decision makers had to make long- and short-term choices about vehicle models (large or small) for different global markets and engine types (diesel, gas, electric, or fuel cell) to propel these vehicles. They were held accountable to confront the risks and uncertainties, establish reasonable assumptions about the future, and then make fundamental choices about the directions in which to take their companies, with the understanding that they too had to hedge their bets against the possibility of undesirable future conditions. It is worth further sketching briefly the background conditions for hedging in the two sectors that are the subject of further investigation in this book.

## The Conditions for Hedging in Fossil Fuels

Upcoming chapters of this book are devoted to cases in which managers in the oil and natural gas sector hedged their bets. The chapters highlight ExxonMobil and BP, the two largest US oil and natural gas companies, and Shell and TOTAL.

### Demand and Supply

These companies shared the assumptions of forecasters such as the Organization of the Petroleum Exporting Countries (OPEC), who, among others, predicted that almost all continued growth in demand for oil would come from Asian, Middle Eastern, and Latin American markets. Oil demand among the advanced industrial nations in the OECD had peaked in 2005 and was likely to decline (for further discussion of these forecasts see the next chapter). World supply of conventional oil was likely to remain nearly flat until the year 2030. The forecasts predicted that almost all the growth in supply was supposed to come from so-called unconventional sources, deep-water offshore oil extraction, Canadian tar sands, and fracking. Deepwater drilling was expensive and had obvious safety risks; its safeguards had been tragically shattered in BP's Gulf of Mexico oil spill. The world's largest oil reserve was bitumen embedded in clay in the Orinoco belt of Venezuela. However, it largely remained undeveloped because of technical and financial challenges. If bitumen was included, Saudi Arabia's total reserves were second to those of Venezuela. Saudi Arabia's daily production had soared to more than 12 million barrels per day in 2016, which moved it ahead of Russia, but then it cut back as part of OPEC's efforts to limit supply. Moreover, there were some questions about how limitless Saudi oil actually was. Its large Ghawar field, which contained more than half of its oil, was more than half gone, and speculation was that the Saudis would have to rely more and more on secondary and tertiary recovery to extract the oil from this field. While Department of Energy projections suggested that the Saudis could extract as much 22 million barrels per day, their own projections did not exceed 15 million barrels per day. Among the highest producers in the world was Russia (over 10 million barrels per day), but Russia had only the eighth-largest known oil reserves in the world, which was less than a third of the amount estimated to exist in Venezuela.

In a surprise nearly no one anticipated, US production soared to a peak of about 9 billion barrels a day prior to 2016 because of fracking, though estimated US reserves were not in the top ten. Frackers knew how to remove oil and natural gas from US fields located in many parts of the country by means of horizontal drilling and the infusion of high-pressure water and chemicals. However, these same methods had not proved effective in removing the oil and natural gas from the shale rock deposits found in many other parts of the world because, among other reasons, the soils were different. Too much clay existed for the methods that worked in the United States to work in countries like Poland or China. In addition, fracking had risks of water-supply contamination and earthquakes, and while a number of US states had welcomed fracking as a job creation boom, others had banned it or nearly banned it because of these potential drawbacks.

When the Saudis increased their production to almost 12.5 million barrels a day and prices started to free fall, fracking no longer made as much economic sense, and many smaller companies engaged in this practice in less attractive fields went bankrupt. Even at $40 a barrel for fracking, it had been barely profitable in most locations in the United States, but the frackers were making progress and starting to improve their efficiency, and in some parts of the United States their breakeven point had fallen to as low as $30 a barrel. High-interest loans that bankers had made to these companies could no longer be paid back and this put stress on the financial system. Due to these circumstances, the financial condition of large oil and natural gas companies deteriorated and their managers had to make difficult choices about what type of strategic investments to make.

## The Choices for Companies

With the nationalization of most oil-producing countries' supplies, the big oil and natural gas companies no longer had large direct oil hold-ings. However, they still regularly applied their technical expertise to high-risk developments in rugged parts of the world where weather and other factors stood in the way. Should this be their way forward; or should their emphasis be downstream in oil and/or natural gas refining and distribution? To what extent should they switch to the liquefaction of natural gas resources and its transport to countries around the world? To what extent could they switch from a primary focus on oil to natural gas to the building and maintenance of pipelines? Refining had been an important hedge, but its usefulness was beginning to wane as a result of overcapacity and commodification.[3] To what extent should the downstream activities of refining based on technical innovation, in which the oil and natural gas companies would have to invest in both the processing of oil and the creation of valuable oil byproducts with new uses, become the primary priority of oil and natural gas companies?

## The Conditions for Hedging in Motor Vehicles

Upcoming chapters of this book also are devoted to cases in which managers in the motor vehicle sector hedged their bets. The companies highlighted are GM and Ford, the two largest US automakers, and VW and Toyota, the global companies with the largest international market share.

### Future Gasoline Prices

Projections of future gasoline prices were an important consideration for managers in the motor vehicles sector. The more volatile gasoline markets were, the harder it was for automotive industry managers to choose the technologies in which to invest. The extremely unstable conditions that prevailed in the twenty-first century, starting with a large but gradual increase in real prices to levels not experienced since the 1979 Iran–Iraq War, the sudden price collapse after the financial crisis of 2008, prices soaring again from 2010 to 2012 only to precipitously collapse starting in 2014, were unsettling. With such volatility, it was difficult for automotive industry executives to make firm long-term commitments. Projected returns on investment were likely to shift.

Another factor that managers in the motor vehicle sector confronted was differing gasoline prices and tax schemes in different countries of the world, which affected the demand for their product. For instance, the US Corporate Average Fuel Efficiency (CAFE) standards increased substantially for the first time since 2003 in 2016 and a single goal of

54.5 miles per gallon prevailed for US cars and light trucks, but the Trump administration was trying to reverse this change.

## The Choices for Companies

A major issue for automakers was that this sector was mature, the growth of global markets very slow in the United States and Europe, and the industry extremely competitive. A major opportunity was the Chinese market, which surpassed the United States as the market with most autos sold on an annual basis. Within the Chinese market, however, domestic producers, with whom the major global firms collaborated, could become global competitors. The rise of Hyundai as a strong global player in the industry served as a warning that new entrants could emerge and challenge the position of the major players. Energy price volatility as well as technological developments like the greater use of software, lighter materials, and the prospect of autonomous driving affected the prospects of new entrants and the long-term strategic investments of the firms in the sector. Historically, low gasoline prices meant that US manufacturers GM and Ford did better than companies like VW and Toyota, as both their sales of profitable SUVs and light trucks and their profits picked up.

An important strategic question that decision makers in the motor vehicle's sector continued to face was the extent to which they are going to commit to different engines and different models of vehicles and sizes of vehicles in various time horizons. Any decisions they make today about this question would only come to fruition many years later. For instance, putting in place a new manufacturing plant for a vehicle that had a different engine platform, like an electric vehicle, was, at minimum, a five-year undertaking. R&D choices made today will have repercussions ten and twenty years from now.

Upcoming chapters explore areas in which managers in the motor vehicle sector have had to hedge their bets. The chapters highlight the two largest US automakers, GM and Ford and the two largest global automakers, VW and Toyota. What mix of technologies have they committed to in order to maintain their place in this highly competitive industry? GM had introduced the hybrid plug in Volt. It was going head-to-head with Tesla with a moderately priced, all-electric Bolt. Volkswagen was committed to diesels, but the scandal concerning its cheating on the $NO_x$ emissions standard test arose largely out of this commitment and changed its priorities. To what extent would Volkswagen be able to turn around its business after such a horrendous public beating?

Globally, hybrid vehicle sales could take off and this would benefit Toyota. Until now, Toyota has been the leader in hybrids. However, hybrids constituted no more than 3.5 percent of world auto sales. Toyota had placed more emphasis on fuel cells than other automakers. Was this choice wise? Ford also increased the number of its hybrid offerings, but relied to some extent on licensing Toyota technology. It undertook active efforts in the area of autonomous vehicles, as has GM, Toyota, and VW.[4] Ford sacked its CEO of many years, Mark Fields, however, for not delivering adequate returns to shareholders. Where it would go next was still in doubt.

## Sufficient Backups for Multiple Contingencies

This chapter points to hedging as a common approach on which decision makers in the energy industry relied when faced with the kinds of risks and uncertainties they faced. Hedging involved having sufficient backups in place to deal with different contingencies. In the face of multiple possibilities, decision makers in the energy industry had to engage in contingency planning to increase the chances that their companies would survive and thrive regardless of what later ensued. By hedging their bets, they might be able to limit downside losses, increase gains, and reduce volatility. Each of the firms studied in upcoming chapters hedged slightly differently.

This book provides related cases that deal with the ongoing challenges that companies in the energy industry confront. The cases are open-ended because the challenges that companies in the energy industry confront are not over. The companies discussed in the book remain in the midst of deciding what to do next. The reader is invited to take part in this process. Which strategic choices should these firms adopt next to fulfill their obligations to their shareholders and their stakeholders, and which are of utmost importance to society?

The book describes the hedging strategies that major companies in the energy industry have pursued, why they pursued these strategies, and the results they have been trying to achieve. Before analyzing the firms' hedging strategies, however, it is necessary to take a closer look at booms and busts in the industry, which have been a partial cause of the unsettled conditions these firms have faced.

# Notes

1. See Mathews, J. A. "Ricardian Rents or Knightian Profits? More on Austrian Insights on Strategic Organization." *Strategic Organization* (2006): 97–108.
2. Coll, Steven. *ExxonMobil and Private Power.* New York: Penguin, 2012.
3. "Oil Price Upheaval Finally Hits Refiners." *Wall Street Journal* May 3, 2016. www.wsj.com/articles/oil-price-upheaval-finally-hits-refiners-1462316442.
4. "GM, Lyft to Test Self-Driving Electric Taxis." May 5, 2016. www.wsj.com/articles/gm-lyft-to-test-self-driving-electric-taxis-1462460094.

# 4 | Booms and Busts in the Energy Industry

Booms and busts characterize uncertainty in the energy industry. Energy demand and supply are main reasons for the booms and busts. A key factor affecting energy demand is economic growth. Higher levels of growth, all else being equal, mean more demand for energy. A key factor influencing supply is technology. Technological advances, all else being equal, should expand supply. However, all else is not equal. For instance, conflict between and within states can threaten supply. Predicting the progression from booms to busts and estimating the duration of these stages therefore is difficult. Conditions oscillate from state to state; they are unstable, yet they form the background against which decision makers operate and bound the future in terms of what can happen. The purpose of this chapter is to consider what these conditions reveal about the risks and uncertainties decision makers confront and understand why it is hard for them to make long-term strategic investments. Over a quarter century or more, it is hard to know for sure if payoffs will materialize from their long-term energy investments. Under these circumstances, decision makers hesitate, not sure if they should alter their assumptions and reverse their commitments.

As it is not possible to eliminate the risks and uncertainties, decision makers hedge their bets by putting in place options that will provide protections for their organizations under a variety of circumstances. They aim to shield their organizations from the worst results while positioning the organizations to benefit from the best outcomes. This chapter discusses the booms and busts requiring hedges, while subsequent chapters discuss the hedges of specific companies. The focus is on the nature of the risks and uncertainties energy companies face due to fluctuations in demand and supply. Influential forecasts by three organizations are examined – the US Department of Energy (DOE), the International Energy Agency (IEA), and the Organization of the Petroleum Exporting Countries (OPEC).[1] Each organization became a prominent player after the 1973 oil crisis. President Jimmy Carter

54

created DOE in 1977 to consolidate US energy policy making. OPEC, founded in 1960 in response to price cuts by major oil companies, consisted of these original members: Iran, Iraq, Kuwait, Saudi Arabia, and Venezuela. Ineffectual until 1973, the year it took cartel-like action, it restricted the flow of oil to the world in the wake of the Arab–Israeli war. It thereby quadrupled world oil prices, introducing a major shock into the world economy. OPEC has since added other oil-producing nations (Algeria, Angola, Ecuador, Gabon, Libya, Nigeria, Qatar, and the UAE) to its founding members. Countries in the Organization for Economic Co-operation and Development (OECD), mostly high-income, high-petroleum consumption nations most affected by the crisis, created the IEA in 1974. In its origins, this organization was supposed to be a counterbalance to OPEC. The United States is a member of the IEA along with other nations in Europe and Asia.

## Economic Growth

These three organizations provide reference case models of global energy demand that hinge on assumptions about economic growth. They assume that global growth will be in the range of 3.4 percent per year up to the year 2040. Their assumptions vary a little, as shown next. Yet they fail to consider fully the possibility that world economic growth will greatly exceed or fall far short of this range. They also do not fully take into account volatility, the ups and downs in economic growth that result from the business cycle.

### The Business Cycle

The business cycle does not produce even growth from year to year. Though the US business cycle achieved increased stability from 1981 to 2006, the 2007–2008 crisis was an example of extreme volatility. It was the worst decline since the Great Depression. Since 2010, greater stability returned, yet global GDP annual growth rates were only in the range of around 2 percent per year. Even if average growth rates amounted to around 3.5 percent up to the year 2040, alternating rounds of booms and busts introduced complications for energy industry decision makers who might prefer steadiness to high growth levels.

As of 2017, another surprise took place; US policies broke from the past and the impact of a new US administration on the global economy was unclear. The positive effects of large infrastructure and military spending, tax cuts, and regulatory relief could mean that economic growth would exceed 2 percent annually. That was the administration's goal for the United States. On the other hand, the economic growth rate could fall because of trade wars, principally with China, and due to immigration restriction, abandonment of multinational institutions, modifications in US foreign policy, and Federal Reserve tightening of interest rates. Global political shifts in countries like Venezuela and Iran and in the world's policies toward these countries were likely to affect both the world's annual rate of economic growth and its steadiness. Euromonitor, a forecasting organization, imagined five tracks for the future of the US economy, with the range in economic growth in these tracks being significant – from over 3 percent, as forecast by DOE, the IEA, and OPEC, at the high end, to negative growth at the low end.[2]

## Secular Stagnation

After the Great Recession of 2007–2008, economists pointed to the phenomenon of secular stagnation, in which actual GDP growth in developed countries like the United States, the Euro area, Japan, and the United Kingdom was not matching past performance. It was not living up to past trends. The deviation from past trends after the crisis was low growth even though there had been years of near-zero interest rates. Economists who posited a theory of secular stagnation described at least four structural headwinds that stood in the way of better performance: (i) lack of population growth in the United States, the Euro area, Japan, and the United Kingdom; (ii) stagnant education levels; (iii) growing inequality; and (iv) expanding public debt. These economists did not see the factors abating quickly. The consensus among them was that secular stagnation in developed economies would persist, and growth in developed economies would be affected.

There was no reason to count on continued rapid expansion. Some forecasts took the warnings about lower growth into account. The consulting firm PwC maintained that the world economic growth rate heading to the year 2050 would be under 3 percent annually, a projection 0.4 percent lower than the estimates of DOE, IEA, and OPEC.[3] PwC anticipated a substantial slowing in the growth rates of

India and China in the upcoming decade. India's projected growth rates for those decades would be higher than other countries, but not significantly higher. China, in particular, would exhibit growth rates no higher than the United States or the United Kingdom. The United States, the United Kingdom, and the EU could not pick up the slack for weaker growth in such countries as India, China, Brazil, and Russia.

Unlike the DOE, IEA, and OPEC, PwC did not have a single forecast. It created four scenarios for annual world economic growth to the year 2050. In none did annual world economic growth surpass 3 percent per year. In two of the scenarios, annual world economic growth was less than 2.5 percent annually. PwC signified that the major constraints on growth in developing economies were political instability and weak investment as a result of this instability.

## Undue Optimism?

In comparison to PWC, the DOE, IEA, and OPEC forecasts for world economic growth, which were the basis for their projections for growth in energy demand, were optimistic. In *The Art of the Long View*, Peter Schwartz noted that in the 1990s major oil companies' scenarios for energy demand were on the high side, while actual energy demand turned out to be substantially lower and these mistaken scenarios led to mistaken decisions.[4] To the extent that energy companies relied on the DOE, IEA, and OPEC forecasts, the companies could repeat these mistakes. The DOE, IEA, and OPEC forecasts admitted to uncertainties, but did not fully acknowledge the range of contingencies that could diminish or amplify global economic growth in coming years. Let us examine these forecasts in more detail.

## DOE's 2016 Outlook

The DOE let it be known that its projections were not statements of what will happen, but what *might* occur given the assumptions and methods upon which it relied.[5] It characterized these assumptions as being no more than simplified representations. It anticipated linear advances in energy demand, not foreseeing random and unexpected events, yet declared with assurance that significant growth in worldwide energy demand would occur. The specific number it attached to this growth was an increase of 48 percent in the years 2012–2040 based on known technologies and policies in place. Yet, the policies were already changing. Under the US Clean Power Plan (CPP) the Obama administration aimed to increase renewable energy use by 37 percent and reduce coal use by 24 percent. The DOE was transparent and it admitted that it had not considered this policy in its projections, with the question later becoming one of the degree to which the policy would stick under the Trump administration.

## Economic Growth
The DOE projected weak economic growth for the thirty-five developed OECD nations, but non-OECD country growth would take up the slack for weak growth in OECD countries. Rising living standards, the need for better housing, transportation, and appliances, and growing industrialization would sustain high growth rates in these countries. The economic growth rates of non-OECD countries had been 4.9 percent per year from 1990 to 2010, while OECD-country economic growth rates had been less than half. The DOE imagined that these trends would continue. Going forward, it expected non-OECD-country GDP growth rates to be 4.2 percent per year. It accepted that there would be some slowdown as these countries moved away from heavy industry to service-based economies (Table 4.1). On the other

Table 4.1 *DOE projections of GDP annual growth by region 2012–2040*

|                | Reference point growth % |
|----------------|--------------------------|
| Non-OECD       | 4.2                      |
| Europe/Eurasia | 2.8                      |
| Asia           | 4.7                      |
| Middle East    | 3.7                      |
| Africa         | 4.8                      |
| Americas       | 2.6                      |
| OECD           | 2                        |
| Americas       | 2.5                      |
| Europe         | 1.7                      |
| Asia           | 1.3                      |
| **Total World**| **3.3**                  |

Derived from US DOE World Energy Outlook to 2040

hand, OECD-country growth would remain steady at about 2 percent per year. Thus, overall, global GDP growth would be 3.3 percent in the period from 2012 to 2040.

To its credit, the DOE recognized the limitations of its model. Thus, it introduced a slightly altered version, with a range of 0.7 percentage points above and below the 3.3 percent reference case. In the high economic growth case, OECD GDP would expand at a 0.3 percentage point rate and non-OECD GDP would expand at a 0.4 percentage points more than the reference case. In the low economic growth case, OECD GDP would fall 0.4 percentage points and non-OECD GDP growth would fall 0.3 percentage points less than the reference case. In sum, regardless of what occurred, average world economic growth would be at least 3 percent per year, according to the DOE.

## Oil Prices

The DOE projection of the price of a barrel of oil, unadjusted for inflation, would be $141 by 2040. The DOE also analyzed the possibility that oil prices could be lower or higher than the $144 a barrel. If GDP growth in non-OECD countries fell to 3.9 percent per year, the price of a barrel of oil, unadjusted for inflation, would plummet to $76 a barrel, while if the growth rate rose to 4.5 percent per year, the price of a barrel of oil, unadjusted for inflation, would rise to $253 a barrel. Thus, changes in GDP growth had large impacts in DOE projections on energy prices. In the reference case, world spending on oil would increase at a rate of 1.6 percent per year, which was not as fast as the 3.3 percent per year projected rise in GDP, meaning that the DOE expected that the world economy would shift to less intensive uses of energy and be more energy efficient.

## IEA's 2016 Outlook

Unlike the DOE, the IEA took into account policy change and incorporated the climate pledges that countries made as part of the Paris Accord into its projection of energy demand.[6] It viewed the pledges countries negotiated at the meeting as relevant. The participants, the Conference of the Parties (COP) of the United Nations Framework Convention on Climate Change (UNFCCC), converted their pledges into Nationally Determined Contributions (NDCs). However, the IEA anticipated that the parties to the agreement would implement their pledges in a sluggish manner. To facilitate NDC achievement in developing countries, developed countries had to agree to assistance payments of $100 billion per year. The IEA also acknowledged that technological change was relevant.

For these reasons, it had three separate scenarios of world energy demand. One scenario did not incorporate the pledges countries made under the UNFCCC. Two went beyond these pledges. The reason to go beyond the pledges was that the UNFCC had not found a pathway to limit long-term global warming to 2 degrees Celsius above preindustrial levels. Scientists warned of serious consequences if the countries around the world did not achieve this limit. Thus, the IEA had a scenario in which the world found a pathway to limit long-term global warming to 2 degrees Celsius above preindustrial levels, and another scenario in which the world found a pathway to limit it to 1.5 degrees Celsius above preindustrial levels.

## Economic Growth
According to the IEA, the rate at which the world economy was likely to grow was the main driver of energy demand. It assumed an annual world GDP growth of 3.4 percent to the year 2040, 0.1 percentage points higher than DOE's reference case. It conceded that this scenario was not a forecast, but rather a "point" that energy decision makers should consider. How did the IEA arrive at this number? Its projection of non-OECD growth was 0.2 percentage points higher than the DOE's, and its projection of OECD growth was 0.2 percentage points higher. The primary driver of increased economic growth was growth in the world's population from 7.3 billion people in 2015 to an estimated 9.2 billion in 2040. In the early 2020s, India would surpass China as the world's most populous country. Thus, the IEA estimated Indian economic growth was likely to be a full percentage point higher than the DOE projection. Under these circumstances, the IEA emphasized the importance of providing everyone on earth – including people in such countries as India – with safe, reliable energy.

## Oil Prices
Continued low oil prices were not conducive to meeting this goal of providing everyone on earth with safe, reliable energy. To meet the goal, the IEA expected oil prices to start rising in 2020 because

production would not keep pace with demand. As the world depleted existing reserves, producers would increasingly obtain oil from challenging and complex reserves that would be expensive to develop like US shale, Canadian tar sands, and offshore fields. The IEA, therefore, admitted that it was difficult to predict energy prices with precision. Markets were likely to remain volatile. If the economy grew less than expected, prices would fall. In addition, OPEC again could choose to flood the market with cheap oil to prevent key non-OPEC producers, such as the United States and Russia, from gaining market share.

Like the DOE, the IEA was also unwilling to assume that there was a one-to-one relationship between economic growth and energy demand. It asked whether the world had broken the link between rising economic activity, energy demand, and energy-related $CO_2$ emissions. Structural change in the composition of GDP was the driver of this trend. Services accounted for the largest share of global GDP. From 2000 to 2014, GDP growth was associated with less energy use in OECD countries. At 62 percent, services' share was rising and could reach 64 percent or even more by 2040. China was on a less energy-intensive path than in the past. The IEA expected that industry's share in China's GDP would decline from 42 percent in 2016 to 34 percent in 2040.

With additional investment in efficient and low-carbon technologies under COP policy agreements, the IEA maintained that the relationship between rising economic growth and energy demand, already declining, would go down even more. An expansion in services, as opposed to industry such as iron and steel, cement, and petrochemicals, would mean less growth in energy demand per unit of GDP growth. For every percentage point rise in non-OECD economic growth, energy demand grew by 0.7 percent from 2000 to 2014. These changes had important implications. They meant that demand for energy, and hence energy prices, could go down, even as the world economy expanded at a higher rate.

## OPEC's 2016 Outlook

OPEC's main theme in its outlook for world energy prices was uncertainty.[7] The price of a barrel of oil had fallen from over $100 to close to $20 from 2014 to 2016. This 80 percent decline was the largest in 30 years. The cause was low demand given that supply was ample. The question OPEC posed in its report was whether demand would pick up. The obstacle to higher demand was global economic weakness since the financial crisis. OPEC also had concerns about Brexit. To what extent would the global economy experience a really strong comeback? OPEC also was anxious about the Paris Climate Agreement and alternative fuel vehicles.

### Economic Growth

The OPEC report, like those of the DOE and IEA, did a detailed analysis of the prospects for economic growth in different regions of the world. OPEC's projections for world annual economic growth per year up to 2040 were 3.5 percent per year. These projections were higher than the DOE's, which were 3.3 percent, and the IEA's, which were 3.4 percent. The source of high demand would not come from already developed countries. OPEC's reference case suggested developed-country (OECD nations) demand would grow by just 0.1 percent per year, while growth in developing country demand from 2014 to 2040 would be 2.1 percent per year. Like the IEA, according to OPEC, the reason for this difference was higher population and economic growth in developing countries. Like the DOE and IEA, OPEC highlighted India and China as being the leaders in world economic growth. Because of aging populations, the developed countries would lag significantly behind.

### Oil Prices

Unlike the IEA, which anticipated that $80 a barrel for oil was possible by 2020, OPEC projected oil prices starting in 2021 to be just $60 a barrel. Not until 2040 did it anticipate that prices might reach $92 a barrel in 2015 inflation-adjusted terms, which was equivalent to $155 a barrel in nominal terms. OPEC's 2040 forecast was higher than the DOE's as it anticipated that oil prices would be $11 more than the DOE's reference case by that year. However, OPEC cautioned that this rise in oil prices would take place only if the demand for oil grew, but without a healthy and vibrant world economy, the demand for oil would not grow. Even with a really robust recovery, OPEC was anxious about a movement away from fossil fuels that was underway and had gathered momentum. This movement from fossil fuels had many sources – initiatives to reduce greenhouse gases after the Paris summit were but one of the actors. Other factors that OPEC deemed important were technological changes, such as battery advances, which could stimulate rapid introduction of electrical vehicles (EVs) that were likely to reduce fossil fuel demand.

**The Paris Agreement**
Unlike the DOE, OPEC pointed to energy demand weakening because of the COP21 Paris Agreement. The main impact of COP21 on energy demand was likely to be new technology developments, such as alternative fuel vehicles, which would reduce demand. Yet, according to OPEC, even with the Agreement, oil and gas would continue to meet more than 50 percent of the world's energy needs in 2040. COP21 would affect the electricity-generating sector more heavily because of a shift away from coal toward renewables, but renewables still were not likely to account for more than 5 percent of total energy supply by 2040.

The problem with COP, according to OPEC, was that it introduced new uncertainties into the system, as it was hard to predict in what ways and to what extent individual countries would meet their commitments. Regardless of how they met these commitments, the result, according to OPEC, was likely to be an increased focus on energy efficiency and alternative-fuel vehicles. Therefore, there would be less energy demand. The OPEC report estimated the reduction in energy demand under different scenarios, and for OECD countries the reduction in demand could be as much as 10 percent under one of its scenarios.

**Alternative Fuel Vehicles**
The report estimated that by 2040 the total number of motor vehicles in the world was likely to more than double, with most of this increase being concentrated in developing countries, especially China and India. The composition of the fleet also was expected to change, with hybrid electric vehicles (HEVs), plug-in hybrid electric vehicles (PHEVs), battery electric vehicles (BEVs), compressed natural gas (CNG), liquefied petroleum gas (LPG), and fuel-cell vehicles (FCVs) playing a growing role. OPEC estimated that non-conventional powertrain passenger vehicles would constitute 22 percent of the passenger car fleet by 2040, an increase from 3 percent in 2014. Most of the growth would come from BEVs. Fuel-efficiency improvements, the penetration of alternative fuel vehicles, and fewer miles travelled would outbalance the greater number of vehicles on the road.

Less demand for fossil fuels would mean less income for oil-producing states. It lowered the incentives for making long-term investments in fossil fuel exploration and refining development. From 2014 to 2016, OPEC noted that the relevant parties had deferred making $300 billion in investments. By 2040, it calculated that they would have to invest $10 trillion. Without these investments in new fossil fuel capacity and infrastructure, the industry would be unable to meet global demand. The global economy would suffer, ushering in a vicious cycle of decline.

Despite these challenges, OPEC was convinced there was no need for pessimism. The energy industry's history of resilience and its innovative nature would help to weather the storm and deliver the required energy.

## How Realistic?

How realistic were the DEO, IAE, and OPEC projections? Each projection depended on the world economy expanding at a rate greater than 3 percent per year until 2040. How likely was this outcome?

### Higher Economic Growth

On the one hand, the projections for future economic growth might be too low. Economic growth could take off and be greater than the DOE, IEA, and OPEC expected. The slowdown in growth in OECD nations, for example, could end. This improvement would hinge on technological progress and improved productivity. The digital revolution would move to a new stage, with artificial intelligence and machine learning stimulating hard-to-imagine gains in economic vitality. Population aging, which figures prominently in IEA and OPEC analyses, would no longer be a barrier to growth. Medical advances would elevate life expectancy and quality of life. The elderly would make significant economic contributions later in life than currently. Their accumulated experience would become an asset rather than the disabilities of aging being a liability. Societies with younger populations that had to take care of a surfeit of dependent children would not be able to match older societies in their economic accomplishments.

Younger societies as well might do even better. Policy reform would aid in this process of achieving higher global economic growth.

Political parties could come together and reach consensus about a cohesive set of policies that would diffuse social unrest and stimulate the growth of developing as well as developed nations. These policies would raise educational levels and make people more job ready. They would promote innovation with greater incentives for business R&D. With the greater R&D incentives, there would be more business start-ups. Global economic growth in the next decades could be far greater than 3.4 percent per year.

## Lower Energy Demand

However, would an era of rapid economic growth necessarily lead to greater energy demand? As the IEA discussed, the relationship between economic growth and energy demand was weakening. The decline in manufacturing and the move to services was one of the reasons. Another was the diffusion of energy-saving technology. Concerns about climate change, and global policies to diminish climate change's effects played a role. Changes in the pattern of car ownership in developed countries also could take place as the OPEC report discussed. China and India might not reach the car ownership and driving levels of developed nations. Ride sharing could become common and car ownership fall off. An autonomous transportation system, which reduced energy demand, might take hold even as growth in GDP soared. No longer would households in many countries have two cars per family.

Peak car ownership might mean less consumption of energy. It could take place without a diminution in mobility and it might require greater economic activity as it would mean the need to build new infrastructure to substitute for the old. Similarly, in the building sector, demand for energy efficiency could stimulate economic growth as it necessitated lighting, heating, and air conditioning improvements and the introduction of building energy controls and sensors that made buildings smarter. The economic case for retrofits and new construction lines not only were lower long run costs but the increased comfort. A construction boom of this nature would grow GDP. It would yield plenty of good jobs, while at the same time lowering energy consumption. Efficiency gains would be possible not just in the building sector, but also in manufacturing. Industry could progress in using less energy per unit of output. Without adding to energy use, the world was also likely to witness economic progress because of advances in automation, nano-technology, 3D printing, robotics, sensors, and computer controls. Even if global GDP growth did take off, it would not necessarily mean energy consumption would grow proportionately. Transportation, buildings, and industry could become more efficient and less energy intensive. People could enjoy more of the goods and services they needed and wanted while at the same time the demand for energy could stay stable or even go down. The close relationship between consumption and a growing demand for energy did not neces-sarily have to prevail in the future in the same way as it had in the past.

## Less Economic Growth

Yet the future could be far different and darker and the reason for a decline in energy consumption might reflect a situation in which optimistic scenarios for global economic growth were not realized. The close-to-business-as-usual projections of the DOE, IEA, and OPEC that the global economy would grow at a rate of about or above 3.4 percent per year in coming decades might be unrealistic. The times ahead could be very difficult. The DOE, IEA, and OPEC projections looked back to the 1990–2016 performance of the world economy. They projected similar trend lines and outcomes coming next. Developing countries were making significant advances, while rich nations were just getting by. The DOE, IEA, and OPEC looked to the emerging economies, such as China, India, Brazil, and Russia, as the engines of growth. Even if there was some softening in the Chinese economy, the DOE, IEA, and OPEC did not see abatement in the vitality of other emerging economies. If the Chinese economy was a weak link, India would more than make up for it. It could become the world's next economic miracle. Brazil's setbacks were important, yet it too had great potential. The DOE, IEA, and OPEC analyses hardly mentioned Africa, despite its burgeoning population. They barely considered the Middle East and did not adequately factor Latin America into their analyses. What if these regions turned it around and flourished? On the other hand, what if the situation in these regions deteriorated further, chaos grew, and their economies stagnated? What would be the impact on the demand for energy? What if disorder intensified and brought down the rest of the global econ-omy? The DOE, IEA, and OPEC did not envision expansion in the rich countries, however, they equally did not take into account the possibility that these economies could decline. According to the projections of the DOE, IEA, and OPEC, the rich economies of the world would not overcome their inertia, nor would they grow by much, but they would get by. Thriving emerging economies would drive economic growth. Without the blossoming of these economies, the global economy could not grow at a rate of about or above 3.4 percent per year in coming decades. The projections did not account for anything similar to Trump tariffs and their dampening effects on global growth. The prosperity of emerging economies and the stability of developing countries were not inevitable. With little effort, one could make different projections than those of the DOE, IEA, and OPEC, which would preclude the world from achieving economic growth of 3.4 percent per year.

## A Chinese Meltdown?

China, the world's largest economy, was navigating a complex transition. Bumps along the way could have substantial negative effects not only on China but also on other emerging markets and developing countries.[8] Just as the Japanese economic bubble burst, so, too, could the Chinese economy crash, but with greater impact as a Chinese collapse could spread and trigger weak economic growth throughout the world. Worth pondering was the degree to which the Chinese economy was built on unstable foundations. Here were some of the weaknesses:

- Its population, as result of the one-child-per-family policy, was aging faster than many developed nations, including the United States.
- Pollution in its cities was debilitating. The country could have a major public health crisis brought on by dirty air and water.
- Its food production could decline because of water scarcity.
- China's bloated housing market bore a very close resemblance to the swollen Japanese housing market of the early 1990s.
- Employment in China's state-supported coal mining, mineral, chemical, and metal industries was out of proportion with global demand.
- Political repression had increased and civil disorder could erupt.

An important issue was whether China's government would be able to maintain control and mobilize its people to tackle the immense challenges it faced.

The authoritarian nature of the ruling elite's dominance had been effective in stifling dissent, but if the Chinese government did not adequately deal with the many problems it faced, the chances of disorder would increase. The many bad loans in the system alone could spark a breakdown. Estimates made at the end of 2016 were that 22 percent of the Chinese financial system's loans and assets were nonperforming and that these bad loans could lead to greater than $4.4 trillion in actual losses, about half the country's annual economic output.

If a meltdown took place in China, it would reveal lingering contradictions in other developing countries' institutions. Cronyism and corruption existed everywhere. They are a main reason for the fact that Brazil has fallen on hard times, they are a defining feature of the Russian kleptocracy, and they negatively affect India as well. With the institutional weaknesses of these nations exposed, their leadership role in global economic growth would be undermined. Investment in these and other emerging economies would ease and their economic progress would slow. As a result, these countries would build fewer roads, buy fewer cars, construct less infrastructure, grow at a slower level, if at all, and consume less energy.

The developed world would suffer along with developing countries. Cronyism and corruption were not absent in developed countries. A Chinese-led debt fiasco, for instance, would affect the EU, which also was struggling with a multitrillion-dollar debt problem that had sapped the economies of countries such as Greece and Italy. Perhaps aging would bring down the welfare systems of a host of developed countries as global dependency rose and productivity declined. Many problems would ensue and they would hurt the United States as well. For instance, debt pressure would result in a decline in federal R&D spending in the United States. The result would less basic research, fewer good investment opportunities for venture capital, less business formation, decreased job creation and mobility, greater inequality and resentment, and more political unrest, which would feed a cycle of despair. The effects on the distribution of income would be even greater inequality. Already, the politics of most nations had turned sour, economic nationalism was on the rise, and the necessary global cooperation to deal with emerging problems was weakening. Politicians were blaming their countries' woes on foreigners and immigrants and setting off trade wars that were further diminishing the prospects for steady growth. This state of affairs could get worse.

## How the World Would Cope

Contemplating tragedies that could ensue might reveal pathways for coping with them. Grim scenarios were not at all inevitable. Unattractive conjectures were guesswork but so too were the business-as-usual projections of the DOE, IEA, and OPEC. There were additional developments that might shake the contours of energy markets, technologies that could create energy abundance, on the one hand, and worldwide tensions and insecurity that could threaten energy supply, on the other. As much as future energy demand was highly uncertain, so, too, was energy supply. The second decade of the twenty-first century saw extraordinary technical advances in fossil fuel extraction, and in lowering renewable resource costs; these held out the promise of energy abundance. On the other hand, because of the breakdown of the nation-state and global conflict, supply disruptions remained possible. It is to these possibilities that this chapter now turns.

## Abundant Supplies

After 1973, the United States – resigning itself to a long and slow decline of fossil fuel production – began to import more oil than it exported. However, some 35 years later this situation profoundly moved in a different direction, and the United States started to experience a boom in natural gas and oil production, achieving near self-sufficiency in both fuels. Moreover, it appeared that the United States would have abundant supplies for many years to come. Plentiful supplies of fossil fuels were a consequence of technological revolutions in shale gas and oil. Yet, at the same time, investment in renewable energy had been growing to all-time highs, surpassing fossil fuel in providing additions to new electrical generation capacity. Fossil fuel executives had dismissed renewables as being expensive, unreliable, and not cost-competitive without substantial public subsidies. Yet, R&D on renewable energy, initiated after 1973, had started to pay off. Renewables' contribution to electrical generation had grown by a large amount since 1973, though their overall contribution remained small. Both developments – the vast increase in US natural gas and oil supplies and in renewables – had been prompted by high and growing energy prices in the period leading up to the financial collapse of 2007–2008.

## The Fracking Revolution

The fracking revolution played a large role in US energy abundance.[9] US daily use of natural gas grew to more than 70 billion cubic feet and from 1990 to 2005. Supply was tight and prices rose from $2 to $14 per thousand cubic feet. However, by 2011 prices fell to below $3 per thousand cubic feet, as shale gas output increased as a result of the fracking revolution. The combined technologies of horizontal drilling and hydraulic fracking made for much more productive wells. Companies started to drill down vertically into shale formations, then curve horizontally through a longer expanse of rock layer to expose more of a formation. They drilled down and then sideways a mile or more. After drilling, they commenced with hydraulic fracking in which they then shot water and chemicals deep underground to tear up the rock and get natural gas as well as oil to flow. They relied on both techniques – horizontal drilling and fracking – to make the breakthrough. Because of these technologies, from 2007 to 2010, natural gas supplies grew by 14 percent.

The story of how these technologies came together to produce a breakthrough is fascinating. Could other breakthroughs of this nature take place in the future? People in the oil and natural gas industry always understood that horizontal drilling was possible. They knew of this potential as far back as the late 1920s. However, the French company Elf Aquitaine only demonstrated the commercial viability of horizontal drilling in the 1980s. People in the oil and natural gas industry also recognized that hydraulic fracking was an alternative way to extract fossil fuels. They understood the potential of fracking as far back as the mid-1860s, when Edward Roberts received a patent for an explosive torpedo lowered into oil wells filled with water that improved flow by as much as 1,200 percent. However, the nitroglycerin explosive he and others had used to make the underground explosion was not safe. Companies made advances in the post-World War II period by finding substitutes for nitroglycerin led by Stanolind, which patented a process in which the producers inserted gelled gasoline and sand into gas-producing limestone and followed it up by an injection of a gel breaker. This method did not produce significant production increases until Halliburton obtained the exclusive license to the method and made a number of improvements. Assisted by US Department of Energy research, production increases of up to

75 percent then became common, and the pace of hydraulic fracking (but not hydraulic fracking combined with horizontal drilling) had picked up. By the 1970s, the extraction process was in regular use in various basins in the United States.

## Mitchell Energy's Role

The company most responsible for combining hydraulic fracking and horizontal drilling was Mitchell Energy, a feat it did not achieve successfully until the late 1990s. Its accomplishment came after more than a decade of persistent attempts by the company that the major global oil companies and the US Department of Energy dismissed as both futile and unproductive. They simply did not think it would work. Instead, the big oil companies chased offshore discoveries and invested in tar sands in projects in Canada in this period to make up for what they viewed as inevitable decline in energy supply.

Mitchell Energy was an independent company founded by petroleum engineer and geologist George Mitchell. The path Mitchell's company took to successful commercialization of horizontal drilling and fracking was not an easy one. During the 1980s and early 1990s, it drilled many wells, whose sites Mitchell often determined. For 15 years, the company struggled to show that its methods could produce reliable and economical natural gas. Chasing after a good way to make the technologies of horizontal drilling and fracking work, the company fell heavily into debt. The board of directors removed Mitchell from a position of decision-making authority because he stubbornly insisted that efforts to combine horizontal drilling and fracking could succeed despite the costs. The Board installed a new CEO, Bill Stevens from ExxonMobil, whom it charged with the goal of winding down these efforts. The Board would not tolerate the company's bankruptcy because it was chasing the futile dream of its founder. Nonetheless, company engineers, urged on by Mitchell, persisted. They continued to experiment with different means by which they could more effectively deliver a powerful underground force to stimulate the release of the natural gas trapped within shale formations. They used diverse formulations, mixing chemicals, sand, and water to break up the rock where fossil fuels existed.

In a last gasp effort, they decided to use fewer chemicals and more water. Why did they make this decision? They were under intense pressure from the board and from the CEO the board had installed, Stevens, to lower costs, and water was less expensive than the chemicals on which they had been relying. In 1997, at one of the shale gas wells on which they experimented, Mitchell's team of Dan Steward Nick Steinsberger, Kent Bowker, Mark Whitley, and Lee Utley had a breakthrough that showed that fracking could be financially viable. The decision to use fewer foams and gels proved to be a winning formula. An injection of additional water and sand was less expensive than the use of foams and gels. Mitchell's team also discovered that it was necessary to adjust this method on a well-by-well basis. They did not arrive at a cookie cutter formula for fracking that suited all cases.

Fracking was as much an art as a science, one that depended on the experience and capabilities of the frackers. This type of experience did not belong to the large integrated oil and natural gas companies. Early frackers poured mixes of about 750 gallons of water, gelled crude oil, or gelled kerosene into the ground to extract embedded fuel. Modern frackers might use up to 8 million gallons of water and 75,000–320,000 pounds of sand. The fluids in this mixture continued to have some foams and gels, but the modern frackers needed less of these expensive chemicals than prior experts originally thought were necessary. The slick water mix modern frackers concocted might also consist of some benzene, hydrochloric acid, friction reducers, guar gum, biocides, and diesel fuel. In addition to requiring less expensive chemicals, in comparison to early fracking, the hydraulic horsepower this mixture generated upon entering the ground was twenty times more powerful for average projects and more than 100 times more powerful for large and difficult projects. These innovative techniques were revolutionary.

Despite more than 15 years of failure, Mitchell and his team of dedicated engineers persisted. On the other hand, the US DOE and the large oil companies had resigned themselves to the inevitable decline of conventional natural gas and oil. Supply would necessarily shrink and prices would go up, a trend that they were seeing in the first decade of the twenty-first century and one they thought was unstoppable. The discovery of fracking was not one that experts elsewhere in the industry had anticipated. Chevron had spent part of its $30 million annual exploration budget trying to figure out how to extract natural gas from shale rock, but gave up. ExxonMobil was not even willing to give this method much of a try. Mitchell engineer Kent Bowker had been involved in Chevron's efforts and came over from Chevron to work for Mitchell Energy. His 3D seismic analyses showed estimates of recoverable natural gas three times the size of prior estimates. Chevron had been skeptical of such claims. Despite these doubts, the team at Mitchell Energy persevered in its belief that they could release the colossal reserves trapped in the rocks.

Mitchell had the company engineers focus on the Barnett basin around Fort Worth, Texas, where natural gas pipelines existed. The market for the gas they extracted was Chicago. In the year the team showed how to break through the shale rock in a cost-effective way, George Mitchell was 87 years old. In 2002, Devon Energy purchased his company for $3.1 billion, but it took time for the fracking momentum to take off and for other companies to follow. The high prices of energy in the early part of the twenty-first century helped. By 2012, more than a third of all US natural gas production relied on such techniques. The US Department of Energy projected that by 2035 more than half of US natural gas production would use these techniques. It estimated that the price of natural gas was unlikely to exceed $6 per thousand cubic feet in current dollars, supplies would be ample, and that recoverable US reserves were capable of lasting more than 100 years.

## Fracking Outside the United States

Following the Great Financial Crisis of 2007–2008, the boom in US natural gas production helped ease the US economy back to recovery.[10] By 2010, it had created 190,000 jobs. By 2020, the US Department of Energy projected that it would create 370,000 new jobs. Low-cost natural gas supported up to half a million other jobs in the allied chemical, steel, and aluminum industries. It added $150 billion to the US economy. High potential shale fields existed throughout the United States. By 2012, technically possible recoverable US shale gas exceeded the proven natural gas reserves of all other countries in the world combined. By 2015, 67 percent of marketed natural gas in the United States came from hydraulically fracked wells.

In contrast to the United States, which had an abundance of natural gas because of fracking, Europe was heavily dependent on obtaining natural gas from Russia via pipelines that passed through the Ukraine. The main alternative to Russian gas was liquid natural gas, which came by ship from Qatar. With added US supply in global markets, European electric utilities, like E.ON, were able to negotiate better terms for the delivery of Russian natural gas. Nonetheless, natural gas, which sold for the equivalent of $20 a barrel of oil in United States, cost twice as much in Europe. In Asia, it could cost six times as much.

Significant shale resources were found in many places in the world, including China, Argentina, Mexico, South Africa, and many European nations, though conditions were not yet ripe for their development.[11] Soil conditions were different, the water needed for fracking might not be plentiful, and infrastructure was not in place to bring in and apply the chemicals needed to extract natural gas and oil from fracked wells. In Western Europe, citizen opposition prevented the resource's development. Legally, the incentive did not exist for fracking in Europe because neither individuals nor companies could exert the right of their ownership of underground resources.

Nonetheless, combining the technologies of horizontal drilling and hydraulic fracking had great promise not only in the United States, but globally. The use of these technologies in tandem could not only free the world from dependence on politically fraught Russian natural gas, but also unshackle it from reliance on Iran, a major supplier of natural gas to Asia.

## Shale Oil as Well as Gas

Using the same techniques of horizontal drilling and hydraulic fracking, oil production in the United States grew rapidly.[12] Drillers also obtained light crude oil locked in rock formation by combining hydraulic fracturing with horizontal drilling. In 2007, North Dakota's oil production grew from 150,000 barrels a day to 400,000. By 2011, in North Dakota and the Permian Niobrara, Eagle Ford, Haynesville, Marcellus, and Utica basins more than 900,000 barrels a day of shale oil were being produced in the United States. This increase enabled a rapid reduction of US imports. The United States was assured of an adequate oil supply as long as the price of a barrel of oil was $60 a day, because that was considered the breakeven point for shale oil. Even at prices lower than $60 a barrel, shale oil was competitive in some fields. If prices were significantly higher, the United States might be able to tap additional shale oil deposits in the West, where it once considered mining, crushing, and heating the shale to extract oil. Estimates were that the United States could extract at least two million more barrels of oil per day if prices rose substantially.

The process of obtaining oil from hydraulic drilling and fracking was quick and relatively simple. After a drilling rig was in place, it took about a month to drill the well. Once producers completed drilling, it took another two months or so to complete the well and the infrastructure needed to extract the oil. Though the wells might operate for five years or more, the producers extracted most of the oil within the first six months of operation. The first 180 days of production were the critical ones. Nonetheless, wide variations existed among companies in terms of how much oil they could extract from their wells.

## An Unstable Oil Market

Shale destabilized the global oil market. A reason the Saudis had flooded the oil market at the start of the 1980s was to keep prices out of the reach of US producers, who had new oil to extract in Alaska. The Saudis supplied enough oil to keep prices on an even keel until 1985. They wanted to maintain market share and market leadership. They also released enough oil to keep prices steady after a temporary price spike shook the world when Iraq invaded Kuwait.

Starting in 2000, prices rose because of global GDP growth and rapid expansion of automobile ownership in China and other countries. Oil prices plunged during the Great Financial Recession, and quickly rebounded in 2010 and remained high until 2015. High prices stimulated the development of alternatives to conventional oil such as tar sands and deep offshore oil as well as shale. Canadian tar sands were a mix of clay, sand, and oil. Once considered too costly to develop, in the high price environment after 2010 that changed, and companies in Canada produced 1.5 million barrels a day from tar sands. Total reserves were enormous, as much as 1.7 trillion barrels, according to some estimates.[13] The DOE forecasted a production potential of 6 million barrels a day by 2030 and the United States promised pipeline construction to transport the oil to markets. High oil prices also made deep water drilling more attractive. Though more expensive and dangerous than drilling in shallow water, there was a reason for developing deep offshore oil throughout the world if oil prices were high. Bio-based fuels also existed. In Brazil, ethanol came from sugarcane and in the United States from corn. Sugar-based ethanol was the fuel that nearly half the motor vehicles on Brazilian roads used. The US Congress mandated the production of one million barrels of oil-equivalent ethanol a day by 2020, a goal that was proving hard to achieve. Research on second- and third-generation biofuels, however, was underway. Made from plant materials and algae that did not compete with food consumption, the second-generation material promised additional supply.

OPEC-affiliated nations had long understood that the production of conventional oil was likely to flatten out and that future supply growth would emanate from unconventional sources like tar sands, deep off-shore wells, and biofuels. The existence of the unconventional sources repudiated the argument that the world someday would run out of the resource. There would be no peak to oil production. As long as the price of oil was elevated, the substitutes for conventional oil had great potential. However, when the shale revolution occurred, OPEC-affiliated nations, with their large reserves of conventional oil, became anxious about lost market share.

Understanding the threat that shale and other unconventional sources posed, the Saudis, with some assistance from other OPEC members and Russia, flooded the market with conventional oil with the aim to drive down prices to the point that the alternatives were not viable. They pursued this goal although it reduced their revenues. Once they pushed unconventional alternatives from the market, they could limit supplies and return prices to levels they deemed acceptable. Indeed in 2015, excess oil in the market led to a sudden and unexpected price crash, which made unconventional, but high priced, alternatives unattractive to produce.

A problem was that though the Saudis could withhold oil from the market, they could not keep the other producers in OPEC and the Russians entirely in check. Countries like Iran and Russia relied on oil revenues to keep their economies afloat and their governments in power. They had strong reasons not to completely abide by agreements to withhold oil from the market. They were likely to cheat to some extent and to try to bring more oil to market than they promised. The Saudis therefore had to take unilateral action for the supply restrictions to stick. The question was how far they were willing to go. Their move to lower prices took away incentives to develop deep offshore oil and tar sands and they bankrupted many shale oil producers, but Saudi revenues also decreased, which in the long run was not in its interest.

## Ongoing Price Uncertainty

For all these reasons, the exact price of oil going forward was uncertain. Because of so many supply options – deep offshore oil, tar sands, ethanol, and shale – the price of oil essentially had a cap, but it was unclear what this cap was. US shale oil production, depending on price, could move from 2,000 to 11,000 barrels per day.[14] Rig count, a simple measure of drilling activity, might fall for about a year or so if prices were low. A decrease in drilling activity also would result in shale oil production declining. However, the shale producers were resilient and resourceful and they were able to make improvements in productivity. In 2014, their average breakeven price was about $60 a barrel; by 2016, in some basins, it approached $45 a barrel. The producers discovered ways to be more efficient with techniques covering a wide spectrum of practices, including different water chemical combinations, more pressure to break up rock, more wells drilled in the same place, and using drones and sensors to discover the best locations. They rapidly recovered because they could get loans at low rates. So long as interest rates remained low, they could pay off their debts. Shale oil producer bankruptcy filings peaked in 2016. They then went down.

Four key regions accounted for most US shale production, they were Bakken, Permian, Niobrara, and Eagle Ford. The cost of oil from shale was falling in all these regions. Opening new oil shale production fields in these regions happened quickly, as did their shutting down. They did not require the same type of capital-intensive investment as tar sands, deep offshore drilling, and ethanol projects. A limitation was pipelines and other means of getting the oil to markets. The added market supply, however, had drawbacks. With so much oil entering the market, prices could fall again. The DOE, IEA, and OPEC forecasts did not adequately consider the new boom and bust cycles in energy markets.

## Renewables' Rise

At the same time as fossil fuel markets were changing, breakthroughs took place in renewable energy.[15] The motivation again partially came from higher oil prices. Renewable energy was starting to make a dent in fossil fuel dominance, in this case in electrical generation, its attractiveness enhanced by its potential to reduce greenhouse gas emissions, which had government support not only in the United States, but also globally, especially in the EU. Coupled with Chinese incentives, renewable electricity came close to being competitive with fossil fuel energy, in some instances even being less expensive. A push toward electric vehicles could further stimulate the demand for renewable.

With benefits arising from increased deployment, greater economies of scale, more competition, and falling costs, renewable energy had made substantial progress. Of particular note were improvements in onshore wind, which brought it within the same cost range as new fossil fuel capacity. Onshore wind average investment costs dropped by about two-thirds from 1983 and 2015. When wind costs reached the range of five to ten cents per kilowatt hour (¢/kWh), wind installations grew substantially. In the United States, wind generation grew about threefold from 2008 to 2015. By 2015, the United States had more than 980 utility-scale wind farms and over 50,000 wind turbines in operation. Offshore wind power, still in its infancy, might have the potential for significant cost reductions and growth.

Solar photovoltaics (PV) costs also dropped from 2008 to 2015. The drop of more than 60 percent made possible a significant increase in supply. The cost of installing utility-scale photovoltaics fell from $5.70 per watt to $2.08 per watt, becoming competitive with conventional generation in parts of the United States. The best utility-scale solar PV projects in 2015 in parts of the United States provided electricity at eight cents per kWh without subsidies compared to 4.5–14 cents per kWh for the addition of new fossil fuel power plants. A 75-percent drop in module costs was the main factor in the reduced costs. China-made modules flooded the market in response to European subsidies. In country after country, governments sued the Chinese for dumping below-cost-of-production modules on the market.

Distributed solar relying on PV modules generated power on the roofs of homes and commercial buildings. It saw its prices fall by half from 2008 to 2015. Though it remained slightly more expensive to install than utility-scale PV, it grew in popularity, with more than a million distributed PV systems running in the United States. Customers who could not afford the upfront costs found third parties, including utilities and companies like Google, to finance and help install the panels. The third parties played an increasing role in US installations. From 2008 to 2015, US solar PV capacity in all applications (residential, commercial, and utility) grew thirty fold.

Battery costs also fell from $1,000 per kWh in 2010 to $227 per kWh in 2016, with prices projected to be $190 per kWh by 2020 and $100 per kWh in 2030. In 2016, electric vehicles continued to be more costly than comparable conventional models because of battery costs. However, if the predicted cost reductions came about, then electric vehicles might become cheaper.

LED lighting saves as much as 85 percent of the energy used by incandescent bulbs. As LED bulbs became cheaper to install and use, they gained increased adoption. In 2008, less than a half million LED bulbs had been installed, but by 2016 that number had grown to more than 200 million, stimulated by price decreases of more than 90 percent. By 2035, 85 percent of all new lighting was likely to be LED. In addition to reducing greenhouse gas emissions, LEDs had the potential to save billions of dollars in energy costs.

From 2008 to 2015, cost reductions of between 41 and 94 percent had been achieved in wind, PVs, batteries, and LEDs. In each instance, lower costs meant greater supply. Each of these technologies was on a trajectory in which continued progress was likely regardless of public policies. In contrast, there were fewer changes in more mature renewable technologies such as biomass, geothermal, and hydropower, as their prices remained relatively stable and they did not see the same jump in supply as for wind, PVs, LEDs, and batteries.

Global renewable electricity generation, hydro included, accounted for around 23 percent of all electric generation in 2015. China was the largest market, accounting for more than 20 percent of global renewable electricity generation that year, followed by the European Union at 17 percent, and the United States at 11 percent. In 2015, China installed more than half of global onshore wind additions. The EU came in second, and the United States was third, followed by Brazil and India. China and Japan accounted for more than half of the growth in solar PV capacity in 2015. Over forty countries highlighted renewable electricity as part of their greenhouse gas (GHG) reduction strategy. India pledged to more than double its wind capacity and to increase its solar capacity by twenty five times.

## Supply Threats

Fossil fuel *and* renewable energy advances were making supply abundant. A threat to this abundance was geopolitical developments, primarily in the Middle East, where conflicts risked damaging production capacity and transport in the region that accounted for 30 percent of global oil.[16] Wars and conflicts had affected oil supply and prices in the Middle East and North Africa in the past. They included the Suez Crisis (1956), the Arab–Israeli wars (1967–1973), the Iran–Iraq war (1980–1988), the Iraqi invasion of Kuwait (1990), and the US invasion of Iraq (2003). From 1972 to 1974, Arab states lowered production by 5 million barrels per day, causing the price of oil to increase fourfold, from $3 to over $12 a barrel. The 1978–1979 Islamic Revolution in Iran resulted in the loss of two to 2.5 million barrels of oil per day, leading to another jump in oil prices. The subsequent 1979–1980 war with Iran led to the loss of 6.5 million barrels per day, resulting in oil prices more than doubling from $14 in 1978 to $35 per barrel by 1981. Wars resulted in long-term supply losses and declines in countries' productive capacities. After the US invasion, Iraq's production did not return to pre-invasion levels. Petro-states were unstable and violent, with conflict involving not just state conflict, but also subnational participants like ISIS, Al-Qaeda, and militias seeking to control of oil production and refining installations.

## Vulnerable Countries

Vulnerable countries included Iraq, Venezuela, Libya, and Yemen. Iraq could be a crucial source of supply to meet future demand growth. The IEA expected it to account for 60 percent of growth in OPEC capacity to the year 2020. While Iraqi production potential was large, the risks were also great. The ISIS campaign to form an Islamic caliphate in northern Iraq and eastern Syria had involved intensive efforts to gain control of oil-producing fields. ISIS had capitalized on existing oil-smuggling operations and its control of fields to help fund its operating costs. It obtained between one and three million dollars daily from draining pipelines, storage tanks, and pumping stations. However, it lacked technical knowhow and its fighters had to stave off attacks to recapture key fields. In 2014, the organization captured six oil fields in northern Iraq, which had pre-war production capacity of about 0.06 million barrels per day. Though it quickly lost these fields to Iraqi forces, production from these fields did not rebound after the Iraqi army retook them. The Baiji refinery in Anbar province was the scene of intense battles. ISIS also controlled the Ajeel field, located near

Tikrit. The Kurdistan Regional Government regained control over oil hub Kirkuk after confrontations with ISIS. However, most Iraqi oil came from the south and ISIS did not have control over this predominantly Shia area of Iraq where oil production and exports were concentrated. Isolated attacks on key infrastructure, though, had affected the market and increased prices. Over the long term, capacity expansions to meet production targets would be difficult for Iraq's fragmented government to achieve.

Venezuela had the largest oil reserves of any nation in North or South America. Among oil producers in the North American continent, however, it was the most politically unstable. It relied on high oil prices to prop up a corrupt and incompetent government. Within OPEC, to which it belonged, it pushed the other members to restrict production even as it produced as much oil as possible because of a desperate need for revenue. Mismanagement of its oil sector resulted in production stagnation that was well below potential, while mismanagement of the economy yielded domestic unrest, which posed a threat to world oil markets.

With the start of protests against Gadhafi in 2011, Libyan oil production, which had stood at 1.6 million barrels per day, stopped. This loss amounted to about 1.8 percent of global production. Global prices increased almost 24 percent when the protests started. During the civil war that followed, the country's production fluctuated. Output fell due to ISIS attacks on energy facilities, including some fields jointly owned with Western companies. Yemen was a small energy producer, but its infrastructure also was a frequent target of militants.

Russia's role in global energy markets also introduced instability. Oil and natural gas comprised about 70 percent of Russia's export revenue and about half of the central government's budget. About a third of Europe's natural gas supply came from Russia, passing through Ukrainian pipelines. Ukraine, in turn, obtained about half its natural gas supply from Russia. Russia had threatened removing the favorable natural gas prices it gave to Ukraine if Yanukovych, the country's former president, did not halt his country's plans to forge closer ties with the EU. The Russians then initiated an ongoing crisis by taking military action and occupying Crimea. Russia turned to the Middle East, specifically the Syrian Civil War, with the goal of exploiting Shia–Sunni tensions to gain influence. The fields most affected by the Syrian crisis had been formerly operated by Shell and TOTAL and had contributed around one million barrels per day to world oil supply. That contribution fell to 0.015–0.035 million barrels per day. Sanctions that the world imposed on Russia coupled with low oil prices weakened the country.

## Transport Insecurity

In the Middle East, the United States had the Fifth Fleet at sea near the Strait of Hormuz, stationed there to protect the navigation of oil through this narrow strait.[17] Approximately 17 million barrels per day of oil flowed through the strait, about a fifth of the total volume of oil traded in world markets. The strait could become a major chokepoint, whose closure would prevent much of the world's oil from moving to these markets. Both China and the United States had an interest in the free flow of oil through the strait since most of that oil was destined for points east. A sustained disruption of oil through the strait would immediately lower oil supply and cause prices to skyrocket. Iran had threatened to close the strait in response to global sanctions,

Vulnerabilities other than the Strait of Hormuz existed. Bab el-Mandab was at the southern entrance to the Red Sea. The Suez Canal and SUMED pipeline linked the Red Sea and Mediterranean, and the Bosporus connected the Black Sea and Mediterranean. Other important lines of transit included: the Caucasus, from Azerbaijan through Georgia to Turkey and the Mediterranean; northern Iraq, including the autonomous Kurdish region, through Turkey to the Mediterranean; and various routes from Iran to Pakistan and India and other points in Central Asia. The Strait of Hormuz, which carried more oil than any chokepoint, was also an LNG route. There were few alternatives to using it. At its narrowest point, it was just thirty miles wide, with only two shipping lanes, each about two miles wide. These vulnerabilities were real and could seriously affect energy supply.

## At Least Four Worlds

The purpose of this chapter has been to review the risks and uncertainties of future energy demand, supply, and price. Managers making long-term investment choices faced at least four possible worlds (Table 4.2): plentiful supply and demand, abundant supply but weak demand, limited supply but ample demand, and both feeble supply and

Table 4.2 *Booms and busts in energy markets*

| Energy demand | High | Low |
|---|---|---|
| **Energy Supply** | | |
| High | BOOMS | GLUTS (prices decline) |
| Low | SHORTAGES (prices increase) | BUSTS |

demand. In each instance, energy prices would be different and the returns from investments would vary.

Growth in demand was anything but assured. Standard projections, with their incremental adjustments going forward, did not do justice to the possibility of far less *or* far more demand than anticipated. They assumed that the future would continue trends that started in the past and did not account for surprises in which demand might accelerate or fall off in unexpected ways. At the same time, projections of future supply did not fully incorporate the vast possibilities opened up by technological innovation in oil production and in renewable energy generation and energy efficiency. Energy supply could be far more ample than expected. The many avenues for making this supply available had not been tapped fully. On the other hand, instability in oil-producing states had to be considered. Serious instability, not at all unlikely, could lead to a partial or complete shutdown in world oil and natural gas trading, with supply being withheld from the market and shortfalls. To deal with the risks and uncertainties, managers had to hedge their bets. How they hedged is explored in coming chapters.

## Notes

1. IEA. *World Energy Outlook to 2040*. Washington, DC: US Department of Energy, 2016; IEA. *World Energy Outlook 2016*. Paris: International Energy Association, 201; OPEC. *2016 World Oil Outlook*. Vienna: Organization of Petroleum Exporting Countries, 2016.
2. Euromonitor. *Global Economies and Consumers in 2017*. Paris: Euromonitor, 2017.
3. PWC. *The World in 2050: Will the Shift in Global Economic Power Continue?* PWC: London, 2015.
4. Schwartz, Peter. *The Art of the Long View: Planning for the Future in an Uncertain World*. New York: Doubleday, 1996.

5. EIA 2016.
6. IEA 2016.
7. OPEC 2016.
8. IMF. *World Economic Outlook*. Washington, DC: International Monetary Fund 2016.
9. Zuckerman, Gregory. *The Frackers: The Outrageous Inside Story of the New Billionaire Wildcatters*. New York: Portfolio, 2013.
10. Ibid.
11. Flowers, Simon, and Wood MacKenzie. "Exporting Fracking: 8 Countries Ripe for Tight Oil Drilling Outside the US," *Forbes* 19 December 2017. www.forbes.com/sites/woodmackenzie/2017/12/1 9/where-are-the-tight-oil-plays-outside-the-us/#2d07ee061a99.
12. Lasky, Mark. *The Outlook for US Production of Shale*. Washington, DC: Congressional Budget Office, 2016.
13. *Natural Resources Canada*. n.d. 3 August 2018. www.nrcan.gc.ca/ene rgy/oil-sands/18085.
14. Lasky.
15. *Renewables 2016*. Paris: Renewable Policy Network for the 21st Century, 2016.
16. Kalicki, Jan (ed.). *2015 Global Energy Forum: Revolutionary Changes and Security Pathways*. Washington, DC: Wilson Center, 2015.
17. Mills, Robin. *Risky Routes: Energy Transit in the Middle East*. Doha: Brookings, 2016.

# PART II

# Challenges in Major Sectors

# 5 | The Oil and Natural Gas Sector

This part of the book covers the context for energy decision making in three sectors starting with oil and natural gas and progressing to motor vehicles and electrical generation. Chapter 5 discusses key challenges major oil and natural gas companies have faced. It defines the sector and examines its key weaknesses, including low and erratic prices, diminished global demand growth, mounting competition, substitutes, and the threat of new entrants. It poses the question – what should companies in this sector do next?

## The Sector Defined and Characterized

Oil and natural gas sector companies engaged in upstream and downstream activities. Upstream was exploring for, developing, and producing oil and natural gas, while downstream was conveying the oil and natural gas, primarily by tanker and pipelines, and storing, refining, and selling these resources and their byproducts. The transportation and storage of oil and natural gas were often referred to as midstream activities. Large integrated oil and gas companies like ExxonMobil, BP, Shell, and TOTAL were involved in all these activities. However, there were companies – other than the large integrated firms like ExxonMobil, BP, Shell, and TOTAL – not active in all of these activities. Some specialized in a single activity or just a few, which made the sector's structure complicated. The sector had many kinds of firms with different specialties. The companies heavily involved in fracking that the book discussed in the last chapter restricted themselves to the upstream activity of exploring for and producing oil and natural gas. Other firms just focused on the downstream activity of refining. Firms that focused on a particular activity were smaller than the large integrated firms.

*Customers*

Throughout the economy, the sector had many types of customers. The motor vehicle sector, the topic of the next chapter in this book, was a major customer. Every person who regularly drove a car, truck, or other vehicle, or relied on public transportation to get from place to place used oil. Indeed, even the asphalt in the roads on which they drove was composed of an oil byproduct. Another important customer was aviation – pilots of military, as well as commercial, aircraft, depended on gasoline. The military needed a stable and adequate supply of fuels to move troops and supplies and power tanks and the instruments of war. Still another important customer was the marine industry, which had a military component, but also consisted of ocean-going vessels, which made international trade possible. Then, there were the cruise ships, yachts, and recreational boats, which also required the generation of power to sail. Fishing boats too depended on these fuels. The modern fishing industry could not exist without them. Aluminum, steel, and chemical production depended on oil and natural gas. Oil and natural gas byproducts were in plastics, detergents, and pharmaceuticals. Modern agriculture could not function without oil and natural gas which contributed to feeding the world. Roofing material came from oil byproducts.

Electric utilities were also customers. This sector is the subject of the chapter after next. Stoves, ovens, microwaves, refrigerators, washers and driers, and other appliances such as electric shavers and tooth-brushes, toasters, and blenders functioned because of electricity, a high percentage of which came from natural gas. Residential and commercial buildings relied on natural gas for the provision of heating and cooling, cooking, and lighting. Owners and renters could not heat air condition buildings, prepare food, or do laundry without oil and natural gas. Perhaps of greatest importance, computers could not operate and create the flow of information and other vital transactions on which modern societies depended.

*Revenue*

In 2016, crude oil accounted for slightly more than two-thirds (68.1 percent) of upstream revenue, while natural gas accounted for the remaining third (31.9 percent) of revenue.[1] Since 2012, the proportion of oil had declined, while that of natural gas had increased. The remarkable progress in hydraulic fracturing and directional drilling, discussed in the previous chapter, made natural gas, a cleaner and less environmentally harmful source of energy than oil, more plentiful in the United States. Natural gas overtook coal as the fuel most used for US electric power generation in 2016. This shift to natural gas reflected its greater availability and lower price. Companies made ongoing investments in LNG pipelines and infrastructure so they could export US-produced natural gas to other countries.

The oil sold in world markets varied from light and sweet to heavy and sour crude. The quality of the former was greater than that of the latter. Over time, the quality of the oil on the world market had declined. More of it was low quality. The amount of low-quality oil was likely to grow because, as older wells neared their end, the remaining oil tended to be lower quality. Low-quality crude contained more sulfur than high-quality crude, and was costlier to refine and bring to market.

Revenue to companies in the sector also came from the offshoots of oil and natural gas. They obtained revenue from byproducts like chemicals, pharmaceuticals, solvents, fertilizers, pesticides, plastics, adhesives, detergents, and sealants. Revenue sources for these firms were the derivatives of oil and natural gas found in such products as resins, fibers, lubricants, gels, rubber, rayon, nylon, polyester to tubing, piping, dyes, printing, packaging, PVC bottles, and engine coolants.

Most companies in the sector did not mine coal. Like oil and natural gas, coal was a fossil fuel formed in the geological past from the remains of living organisms. All fossil fuels, even coal, which was more plentiful than oil and natural gas, had limits and were finite resources. It was unclear how much remained. However, fracking pushed their limits into the future. As time passed and technologies got better, they might push the limits even further. As nonconventional methods of extracting oil and natural gas became common, they reduced concern about supply constraints. When the revenues of companies in the sector went up, they were freer to invest in unconventional extraction methods. Obtaining resources from tar sands and deep offshore assets, for example, became more attractive.

In contrast to fossil fuels, renewable energy from the sun, wind, and plants, in theory, at least was infinite. At some point, the supply of fossil fuels would end. Global societies would have little choice but to move toward renewables. They would have little choice not only because of inadequate supply but because of the impacts on climate change. The time horizon for this transition, however, was unknown. That a transition of this nature was likely, though the time horizon was not known, weighed heavily on decision makers in this sector.

## Government

Because of the sector's centrality to the global economy, governments the world over heavily subsidized and regulated it. They provided tax breaks. They tried to control the upstream and downstream stages, starting with drilling equipment and oil field leases and ending in refining and product marketing. Government's involvement had a substantial impact on the revenues companies in the sector could earn.

Governments also regulated and provided incentives for using energy more efficiently. Their engagement extended to the development and use of renewable energy, for which they put rules in place and provided subsidies. These subsidies had an effect. Renewables such as wind, solar, and biomass made up a very small proportion of the world's energy consumption, but their costs declined as they were subsidized and their use grew (see Chapter 4). Their consumption was on the rise, while that of coal was falling, a trend that the policies of most governments in the world supported. As coal was more polluting than oil and natural gas and its contribution to climate change was greater, government mandates often dictated indirectly, if not directly, that natural gas and renewables should replace coal. In the United States, coal had been in decline for quite some time. Yet globally, if not in the United States, coal remained the most commonly used fuel for the production of electricity.

Globally, the dominance that fossil fuels had over renewables was beginning to erode, but slowly. The extent to which governments throughout the world were beginning to favor energy efficiency and renewables and subsidizing those more than fossil fuels was unclear. If governments were beginning to favor energy efficiency and renewable energy, it would be a reversal of their historic policies – they had always favored fossil fuels. It was not clear whether tax breaks for energy efficiency and renewable energy were surpassing those for oil and natural gas in the United States and other countries. What was clear was that the policy environment was dynamic and evolving. It changed regularly, as did the relative emphasis governments gave to renewable energy and fossil fuels. Many European nations had pulled back on their support for renewable energy. The Trump administration did the same. Its policies favored coal over renewables.

Economists called for an even playing field and the elimination of all subsidies; the market, and not government, should decide on the sources of energy that people used.[2] However, undoing the many and complex types of government intervention was unlikely. Governments considered their reasons for intervening in energy markets to be legitimate. The sector was critical to national security. It had an important influence on job creation and economic prosperity. It affected such important indicators as economic growth and inflation.

Energy production and consumption also produced externalities, a host of harmful side effects that were outside the price system. Thus, governments were obliged to exert control over energy production and eliminate negative side effects. Energy companies tried to shape the influence of government. They lobbied vigorously and used the vast resources at their disposal to sway the political process. Non-government organizations (NGOs) contested their actions. Energy sector politics were highly adversarial, though in some instances opposing sides reached accommodations and cooperated. An important point is that government policies regularly changed in response to this jockeying for power, while energy companies preferred stability. It would be far easier for them to make long-term decisions in a stable environment.[3] They were constrained from committing because they were uncertain what policies might be in place in the future.

## International Trade and Pricing

Nearly half the oil produced was traded internationally, while only about 30 percent of natural gas traded was similarly traded.[4] Most global trade in oil was via oceangoing tankers that had to traverse long distances through strategically sensitive areas like the Strait of Hormuz (see Chapter 4). In contrast, most global trade in natural gas was via pipeline. Yet, the pipelines also had to traverse strategically sensitive areas like the Ukraine. The pipelines limited how far natural gas could be transported. If liquefied, it could be transported longer distances. As facilities to convert natural gas to liquid multiplied, seaborne trade in LNG grew. However, transporting LNG in this way added to the expense. The LNG, moreover, could not be stored in large quantities. To be traded globally required special storage facilities.

Common international standards, in use since the 1990s, applied to oil prices. They tended to converge at similar levels. The four standards were West Texas Intermediate (the United States), Brent (Europe, Africa, and Asia), Dubai and Oman (the Middle East), and Dated Brent (Asia-Pacific). Unlike oil prices, natural gas prices were set at a local level. In the United States, the federal government and state regulatory commissions regulated prices. Global trade in natural gas was based on the prices the parties to particular agreements established. Prices tended to be far lower in the United States than other parts of the world. High natural gas prices deterred other countries from switching from coal to natural gas. Their electrical production still was largely coal-based.

## Natural Gas Producing Nations

The main natural gas producing nations in the world were the United States, Russia, and Iran.[5] Europe, the world's biggest natural gas importer, obtained most of its natural gas from Russia. For Iran to sell natural gas directly to Europe, Iran would have to build a pipeline. Doing so would require the cooperation of many countries that lay between Europe and Iran. Otherwise, the only way to get Iranian natural gas to Europe was in the form of LNG. Similarly, the only way to move US natural gas outside North America was in the form of LNG.

Natural gas markets were diverse. Electricity generators were the major market, absorbing about 35 percent of global production in 2017.[6] The industrial sector consumed another 30 percent, primarily for petrochemicals, pulp and paper, and pharmaceutical manufacturing. Residential and commercial consumption made up the remaining 20 and 15 percent, respectively. It was mostly for heating and cooking. The direct market for oil was somewhat less diverse than the market for natural gas. The main downstream users were refineries. In addition to producing gasoline, these refineries made many byproducts from oil including lubricants and plastics.

## Petroleum Producing Nations

The world's main petroleum producing nations were Saudi Arabia, the United States, and Russia. Most major producers in the Middle East and North Africa belonged to the Organization of the Petroleum Exporting Countries (OPEC). Even without Russia, which was not a member of OPEC, but often cooperated with it, OPEC countries typically produced about 40 percent of the world's oil.[7] Their exports represented about 60 percent of the oil traded internationally. OPEC claimed that its members also had about 80 percent of the world's oil reserves.

The organization came into existence in 1960 following a decision by multinational oil companies to reduce oil prices (see Chapter 4). From 1945 to 1973, three-fourths of the world's oil discoveries had taken place in OPEC countries. In 1973, OPEC supplied over 80 percent of non-Communist country exports. When OPEC imposed an oil embargo on the world in 1973–1974, it had a tighter hold on world production and reserves than it had in the twenty-first century's second decade.

OPEC's goal was to coordinate and unify petroleum policies among its member countries. Prior to its rise, the large multinational oil companies, the predecessors of companies like ExxonMobil, BP, Shell, and TOTAL, possessed the necessary technology and skills for exploration and production and they ruled the oil sector without OPEC interference. OPEC was born with the intention of reducing the influence of these multinationals; it succeeded in this effort and, over time, it learned to cooperate with them when necessary. OPEC and the large oil companies, although not always without tension between them, were partners in many deals and endeavors.

Venezuela, a founding member of OPEC, had been the largest oil exporter in North America (see Chapter 4). Oil was central to its economy, constituting about half of the government's revenue and a third of the country's GDP. It had the largest reserves in the world, more than Saudi Arabia (Figure 5.1), but some of the reserves were very poor quality and not easily exploitable. Brazil was also a producer of oil and, to a lesser extent, natural gas, but because of high domestic needs, it had to import both fuels. Overall, South America only produced about 8 percent of the world's total oil.[8]

Southeast Asia accounted for about 6.5 percent of the world's oil and natural gas production.[9] It had a large amount of oil in Kazakhstan and Azerbaijan and large natural gas producers existed in Turkmenistan and Uzbekistan. Indonesia and Malaysia also were producers. China accounted for about 4 percent of global oil and natural gas output, and

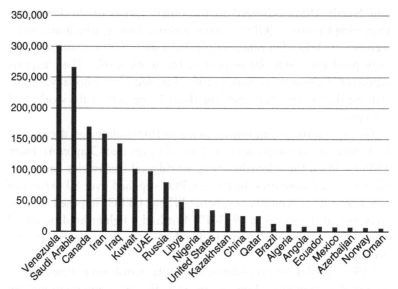

**Figure 5.1** Proven oil reserves 2017 (millions of barrels)
*Source*: US EIA

Australia accounted for about 1 percent.[10] Because of all these countries being involved in world oil markets, after 1973, the world's suppliers of oil and natural gas were more diverse than they had been before it, and OPEC's hold on the world oil market declined.

## Lack of Pricing Power

Not only did the number of nations, which had their own oil and natural gas resources, grow, but overall supply of oil and natural gas also increased. With the supply increase, came reduced pricing power for sector participants. Pricing power weakness was one of the factors that played a role in gasoline prices in the United States plummeting from $3.50 a gallon in 2011 to $2.00 a gallon in 2014. Oil and natural gas price history is worth reviewing.

### Oil and Natural Gas Price History

From 1981 onward, oil and natural gas prices had a number of peaks and valleys.[11] Demand fell in 1981 because of a deep worldwide recession. Growing energy efficiency, after the prior decade of high prices, played a role in declining demand. Many users, especially in the electric utility sector, when able, also switched from oil to natural gas and oil supplies grew. New non-OPEC oil came on the market, mainly from Russia, Mexico, and the countries bordering the North Seas.

The OPEC states, divided, were in no position to impose pricing discipline on producers. In 1980, they chose not to meet at all because of differences with respect to the Iran–Iraq War. The organization's radical camp – consisting of Iran, Algeria, and Libya – favored restricting supply and raising prices to maximize their short-term revenues. The moderate faction, led by Saudi Arabia, sought less restrictive policies, which would allow for lower prices and lead to long-run revenue growth. The Saudis organized their allies within OPEC as the Gulf Cooperation Council (GCC) and the GCC won the battle with the radicals. In 1983, therefore, OPEC decided for the first time to act to reduce prices. Discipline among its members was hard to maintain, however, and oil-producing nations made separate deals with oil-consuming nations. By 1986, the cartel could no longer enforce an acceptable market-sharing scheme. With its unraveling, the price of oil remained steady and relatively low in the 1980s and 1990s.

Southeast Asian economic growth drove oil demand up in the first decade of the twenty-first century. However, with the Great Financial Crisis of 2007–2008, the rise in demand came to a halt. Then, during the Arab uprisings of 2011, supply concerns came to the fore. These concerns, however, proved to be temporary, as fracking gained traction and the global supply of natural gas and oil increased (see Chapter 4). By 2016, fracked oil constituted more than half of US output, an exceptional feat given that fracking had accounted for less than 2 percent of US production in 2000.[12] Only 23,000 fracking wells produced about 100,000 barrels of oil a day in 2000. By 2016, there were 300,000 wells, yielding 4.3 million barrels per day.

Not to be outdone by the new US producers, Saudi Arabia opted to flood the market with oil in 2014.[13] The unstated aim was to try to drive frackers from the market. Saudi Arabia boosted its output from 9.5 million barrels to 10.6 million barrels a day, adding significantly to the world's supplies, a maneuver that had its intended effect, for with oil under $40 a barrel, it became very hard for some of the US frackers to survive. Some did go under, but others waited, were patient, and tried to lower their costs and achieve greater efficiencies so that they could compete even if prices remained low. When OPEC, led by Saudi Arabia, decided to reverse its policy, restrict supply from the market, and tried to raise prices and gain additional revenue, these frackers benefitted and made a comeback.

Unlike oil after the 2007–2008 Great Financial Crisis, natural gas prices in the United States did not recover. Less affected by global events, natural gas was shielded from the disturbances that affected oil. Prices stayed relatively low in the United States, largely because of the increased supply that frackers brought to the market. Consumers benefitted from natural gas producers lacking pricing power as this translated into declining US electricity rates in 2013 and 2014, and the low natural gas and oil prices of that period helped to facilitate the US economic recovery, but other countries in the world continued to be burdened by high natural gas prices.

## Diminished Performance

Low prices were a significant blow to oil and natural gas companies. With the exception of China's Sinopec, every major company underperformed the S&P 500 Index from 2011 to 2016. ExxonMobil managed to eke out a small gain of about 5 percent, though it did not match the S&P's performance, and Shell, BP, and TOTAL lost about 30 percent, 26 percent, and 16.5 percent of their value, respectively. Firms in the sector's supply chain were losers as well. They specialized in refining, marketing, field services, transportation, and storage. The market capitalization of the sector as a whole went down by about a quarter, from approximately $6 trillion to $4.5 trillion.[14]

The weakness meant that the sector experienced huge job losses, totaling about 350,000 workers worldwide. Upstream workers who had been involved in exploration, production, and drilling were hit especially hard. In this segment, employment fell by about 43 percent, and global layoffs exceeded 135,000 employees.

Companies covered in upcoming chapters – ExxonMobil, BP, Shell, and Total – suffered revenue losses of about a third each as they shrank considerably in size. With some variations their profits also declined considerably (Figure 5.2). The main reason for the decline in the market value of these companies was the decline in oil prices. Prior to 2014, the performance of these companies was roughly consistent

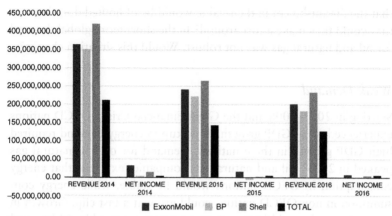

**Figure 5.2** Decline in ExxonMobil, BP, Shell, and TOTAL revenue and profits: 2014–2016

with the S&P 500, if slightly lower, but when oil prices dropped, the gap between their performance and the S&P index widened appreciably. TOTAL withstood the onslaught somewhat better than the other companies in Figure 5.2 and its revenue drop, though substantial, was slightly less.

## Making Investments in a Low-Price Environment

Making investments in a low-price environment was difficult for these integrated oil and natural companies. They had less cash and the payoffs from the investments they made were less certain. Producing oil in deep water was complicated and dangerous. Companies therefore curtailed some of the investments they had made in offshore oil production. None of them had been important players in the fracking revolution, which had opened the potential for previously unreachable reserves. It was unclear to them whether they could reverse this situation. Smaller companies had the capability and were far ahead of them (see Chapter 4). They considered investments in LNG production facilities and in the ships used for the transport of LNG, but US laws restricted exports of this commodity.

The dilemma the companies faced was how they should react to being considerably smaller and weaker than they had been just a few years earlier. Was their decline a historical watershed? Was there hope that the diminishment in their value would be of limited duration and they could they make a turnaround? In the short term, global demand for oil and natural gas was not robust. Would this situation change?

## Weak Demand

Starting in 2007–2008 and the Great Financial Crisis, OECD nations experienced weak GDP growth. A pickup in energy demand required high GDP growth in these nations. Demand for oil and natural gas peaked in 2005. Oil and natural gas companies expected that energy consumption in OECD nations would be stable, while energy consumption in non-OECD nations could grow at a fast clip. Growth in future demand would have to come from countries, like China; and India would have to replace China, if China faltered as the main driver for rising demand. In both OECD and non-OECD nations, energy intensity, that is, the amount of energy needed to produce a unit of GDP, was falling, as services replaced manufacturing.

## Strong Upstream Rivalry

National oil companies (NOCs), not private firms like ExxonMobil, BP, Shell, and TOTAL, owned most of the oil. The largest of these NOCs, Aramco, the Saudi Arabian Oil Company, had control of about 8.6 percent of the market in 2016.[15] Other NOCs, none of which had more than a 3 percent market share, controlled the rest. In 2017, the next companies after Aramco were Gazprom (Russia), NIOC (Iran), Petro-China, and ExxonMobil. Together, they controlled about 7.4 percent of the market in this year. They were geographically dispersed and the rivalry among them was intense. None, not even Aramco, was large enough to manage the sector's output effectively.

Aramco was founded in 1933 when US-based Standard Oil of California started to explore for oil in Saudi Arabia. Since 1944, it had gone by the name Arabian American Oil Company (Aramco). The Saudi Arabian government was full owner, though Saudi Arabia was thinking of taking the company public. Aramco was the world's largest oil and natural gas company. In recent years, it had produced from 9 to 11 million barrels of oil per day. Aramco was also the world's largest exporter of oil. Most of Saudi Arabia's oil and gas reserves were found in the eastern part of Saudi Arabia, where the

Table 5.1 *Estimated decline in Aramco revenue 2012–2016*

| Year | Revenue $million | Percentage change in revenue | Production volume million barrels per day | Percentage change in the production of oil |
|------|------|------|------|------|
| 2012 | 365,329 | 6.1 | 9.5 | 4.4 |
| 2013 | 357,272 | –2.2 | 9.4 | –1.1 |
| 2014 | 333,746 | –6.6 | 9.4 | 0.0 |
| 2015 | 273,672 | –18.0 | 12.5 | 33.0 |
| 2016 | 232,621 | –15.0 | 13.0 | 4.0 |

*Source*: Annual Reports

population was largely Shia and hostile to the ruling Sunnis. Saudi Arabia was not just one of the world's largest producers; it also had about 25 percent of the world's oil reserves. Questions were raised, however, about the accuracy of these estimates.[16] The Saudi fields were old, and although vast, up to half their oil was gone. To remove the rest, Aramco might have to rely increasingly on more expensive secondary and tertiary recovery.

Aramco, like ExxonMobil, BP, Shell, and Total, suffered from the oil price decline, losing more than $200 billion in revenue from 2012 to 2016 (Table 5.1). Three-quarters of the losses were in oil revenue, and another quarter were in natural gas revenue. Of note was that though revenue consistently had fallen in this period, production volume actually *had gone up*, highlighting that Aramco sold the oil at a low price. A 33 percent increase in volume in 2015 took place at the same time that revenue dropped by 18 percent.

Aramco's revenue always correlated closely with oil prices. Its revenue contracted, during the global recession, when prices fell, recovered when prices then rose, and dropped again when prices again declined. Aramco had the lowest production breakeven costs in the world, which allowed it to increase production in 2015. Its actions further depressed prices and did not grow its revenue, but the strategy did help maintain its market share. In a reversal, Aramco then worked with OPEC and with non-OPEC countries like Russia to try to limit supply and thereby raise prices, an effort that partially succeeded.

The Russian firm Gazprom was the world's second largest oil and natural gas company, estimated to have about a 3 percent share of the world's market share in 2017.[17] Most of its reserves were located in Russia, but it had operations in countries such as Venezuela and Bolivia. Russia's daily oil output, about 9–10 million barrels of oil equivalent per day, was very close to that of Aramco's. However, its breakeven prices and its profits were lower. When oil prices fell, they hurt Gazprom more than Aramco. While Aramco was the world's largest oil producer, Gazprom was the largest natural gas producer.

The third largest oil and natural gas company in the world was the National Iranian Oil Company (NIOC).[18] Its estimated market share was 2.9 percent in 2017. Like Aramco, it was government-owned and had ambitions to be a large exporter, but these ambitions were held in check by global sanctions imposed on the Iranian government because of its nuclear program. In the 1970s, the country's output reached 5.5 million barrels per day, but since 2011, output had fallen to less than half that figure. The country's oil reserves were vast. NIOC owned 10 percent of world oil reserves and controlled 13 percent of OPEC's reserves. Like Aramco, its production costs were low. They were in the range of $10–$15 a barrel. After the world lifted sanctions against Iran in 2016, companies like Shell and the Russian firm Lukoil showed interest in investing in Iranian oil and natural gas. Companies from France, Italy, Malaysia, and the United Kingdom got around the sanctions. NIOC also did some investing outside Iran, owning a 50 percent stake in Britain's largest untapped gas field in the North Sea. It did not publicly reveal information about itself. Therefore, it was difficult to estimate the exact amount of losses it suffered because of the fall in oil price, but the United States Department of Energy suggested its losses from 2012 to 2017 were about $70 billion, which was on par with other oil companies.[19]

Petro China, with an estimated market share of 2.8 percent in 2017, was the next-largest national oil and natural gas company in the world.[20] Much of its business was downstream. It was heavily involved in the production and sale of oil- and natural gas-related products. Nonetheless, it explored for and produced about 4.4 million barrels of oil a day as well as transporting, refining, and selling many petroleum-derived products. Petro-China had attempted to expand overseas by acquiring stakes in refineries, oil fields, and tar sands in countries such as the United Kingdom, Iraq, Canada, and Australia. With the price of oil declining, its revenue also fell. Like other NOCs, its revenue dropped by some $70 billion from 2012 to 2017.

ExxonMobil's estimated market share was just 1 percent in 2017.[21] The NOCs were the dominant players in this sector; they owned most of the reserves and carried out a significant amount of the production. Of note were the significant reserve production imbalances. Companies like ExxonMobil, PetroChina, BP, Shell, and Chevron had low reserves but high levels of production, while companies in Qatar, Iraq, Venezuela, Nigeria, and Libya NOCs had high reserves and low production levels. Unlike Venezuela, the United States and Russia had low reserves and high production. The companies and countries producing high amounts of oil that had low reserves would eventually run out of oil if they did not find ways to replenish their reserves. Thus major oil companies like ExxonMobil, BP, Shell, and TOTAL were investing heavily in finding new reserves as later chapters in this book will show.

## Strong Downstream Rivalry

Strong rivalry was not confined to upstream activities. The intense rivalry extended to the downstream part of the oil and natural gas business. Indeed, the downstream part of the business experienced even more intense rivalry than the upstream part of the business. Many specialized companies were involved, not just the large integrated oil and natural gas companies.[22] There was overcapacity and the segment suffered from weak demand. From 2014 to 2015 revenue fell off by almost 40 percent, and it was lower than it was during the Great Financial Crisis. Environmental restrictions and the push for efficiency meant that fewer refineries had been built, though capacity remained steady (Figure 5.3). Major players like ExxonMobil and Shell rapidly lost ground to the specialty companies. Shell's US refining revenue declined by more than 35 percent in 2015, and its profits fell by over 33 percent after declines of more than 30 percent in 2014 and 14 percent in 2013. ExxonMobil's US refining revenue plummeted by more than 38 percent in 2015, and its profits were down by over 6 percent after declines of more than 27 percent in 2014 and 38 percent in 2013. It was unclear what, if anything, could change these trends. The major integrated oil and natural gas companies regularly shut

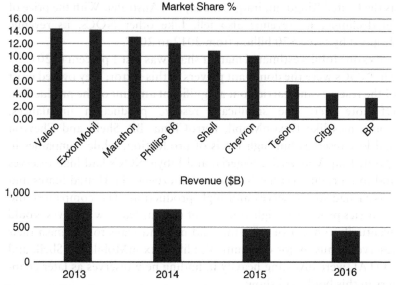

**Figure 5.3** US refiners' market share in 2016 and sector revenue 2013–2016 Derived from IBIS *Fueled Up* 2016

down refineries and initiated campaigns to cut costs and make existing refineries more efficient.

## *Advances in Unconventional Energy*

Unconventional fracked oil and shale yielded very rapid US production growth as noted in the previous chapter. US energy progress could be measured by the actual amount of energy the country produced versus forecasts that had been made. As Chapter 4 showed, the forecasts missed the possibility that unconventional fracked oil and shale would have a major impact.[23] They vastly underestimated how much fracked oil and natural gas could be produced. Unconventional fracked oil and shale yielded a very rapid import decline and brought the United States to the point where it was close to the long-sought-after goal of energy independence.

Offshore oil and tar sands also were thought to have had great production promise, but they were not competitive with abundant unconventional fracked oil and natural gas, especially at prices as low as they were in 2015. Tar sands, mostly of Canadian origin, had an almost unlimited potential for exploitation, but the costs were high and the environmental damage great. The United States had large untapped offshore potential, but 87 percent of federal offshore acreage was off-limits to development. Deep-sea oil and gas exploration and extraction expanded, but it was both expensive and dangerous, as the Deepwater Horizon oil spill showed.

Shale oil and natural gas were not only found in the United States. There was global promise for the exploitation of this resource, but it had rarely been pursued (see Chapter 4). Among the most important barriers to the development of fracking outside the United States were access to sufficient amounts of water, the ability to make legal purchases of property for this purpose, adequate and intimate knowledge of soil conditions, and the capacity to move the fracked gas and oil by truck or pipeline to markets.

Some of the risks associated with fracking might yet prove to be worse than they had seemed. These included the risks of earthquakes, spills, and water or chemical contamination. The financing of the fracking producers was a considerable risk. They were heavily leveraged. Another issue was that only in some US locations was oil shale exploitable at prices below $60 a barrel. The Middle East producers, on average, had breakeven prices of less than $30 a barrel. However, the frackers were not holding still. They were improving the efficiency of their operations, so that they could compete with lower priced Middle Eastern oil.

## Advances in Renewable Energy

A high percentage of future energy growth was expected to come from renewable sources like solar, wind, and biomass. They could easily increase from about 8 to about 14 percent of total energy consumed by 2040.[24] While solar and wind had exceeded expectations, ethanol, on the other hand, fallen short of expectations.

Other developments that could shift the landscape were that fuel consumption by new cars and trucks could decrease more than expected and alternatives to gas-powered engines like electric vehicles could gain traction. New forms of mobility like shared driving and autonomous vehicles might result in substantially less consumption of oil.

However, if the price of fossil fuels kept falling, these developments were less likely to occur. On the other hand, if the effects of global climate change were more severe than anticipated then governments might have to take rapid and dramatic action.

## What Comes Next

The risks and uncertainties that the managers of major oil and natural gas companies faced were great. Consider the following: with low prices for oil and natural gas, where was the incentive for exploration? Would petroleum and natural gas exploration and production decline because prices were low? Would the feedback then be insufficient supply, and sudden and unexpected price hikes? Already, because of low prices, drilling had fallen off, returning to levels like those witnessed prior to the boom that began in 2010.[25]

Another factor influencing investments in new oil and natural gas arose from the political risks in countries with known large fossil fuel deposits. Production in countries with known reserve levels like Saudi Arabia, Kuwait, Mexico, Iraq, Nigeria, and Iran posed these risks. Another issue was the excessive corruption in these countries.

Decision makers in this sector had to ask themselves to what extent the low oil prices with which companies in the oil and gas sector had confronted represented a watershed. Revenues of the companies in this sector declined from 2012 to 2016 (Table 5.2). The dramatic fall-off was almost entirely due to erosion in the

Table 5.2 *Decline in revenue in the oil and natural gas sector*

|      | Revenue ($m) | Annual % change | Crude oil output (billions of barrels) | Annual % change |
|------|--------------|-----------------|----------------------------------------|-----------------|
| 2012 | 3,536,484.60 | 6.8             | 90                                     | 2.3             |
| 2013 | 3,698,828.30 | 4.6             | 91                                     | 0.6             |
| 2014 | 3,888,774.60 | 5.1             | 93                                     | 2.4             |
| 2015 | 2,287,546.90 | −41.2           | 95                                     | 2.5             |
| 2016 | 1,966,629.10 | −14             | 96                                     | 0.7             |

*Source*: Derived from IBIS World, Industry Report Global Oil & Gas Exploration & Production, 2016

price of oil and natural gas. Crude oil output remained steady or even increased, while revenue dropped. Thus, major companies in the oil and gas sector earned far less for each barrel of oil that they sold.

An important question was whether the decline in revenue could be reversed. Companies had to engage in extensive belt-tightening, though many already had highly efficient operations.

What these companies should do was not at all clear. To what extent should they pursue merger and takeover activity, with a focus on boosting their oil and gas reserves? Some companies had already acquired other companies or formed joint ventures. Concentration could go up with volatile energy prices spurring additional activity of this nature.

There was doubt as to where the sector was heading. Other key strategic choices companies could make related to where in the value chain they should focus: upstream or downstream. Also, they had to ask themselves, should their emphasis be on oil or natural gas? Still another concern was where to pursue exploration and development activities. In what countries and how? Should it be onshore or offshore, tar sands, and/or hydraulic fracking? Should the emphasis be on building and maintaining natural gas pipelines, liquefying natural gas for transport, or investing in innovative processing methods? What kinds of commitments, if any, should companies in this sector make to renewable energy and energy efficiency? Even if future oil prices were not as volatile as they were from 2014 to 2016, the major integrated oil and natural gas companies faced the question of what they should do next.

## Notes

1. "Global Oil & Gas Exploration & Production." IBIS World Industry Report, 2016; also see Inkpen, Andrew, *The Global Oil and Gas Industry*. Phoenix: Thunderbird, 2016.
2. Climate Action, 2017. August 5, 2018. www.climateactionprogramme. org/news/leading-economists-and-major-corporations-call-for-the-end-of-fossil-fuel-i.
3. Marcus, Alfred, J. Alberto Aragon-Correa, and Jonatan Pinkse. "Firms, Regulatory Uncertainty, and the Natural Environment." *California Management Review* 54 (2011): 5–16.
4. "Global Oil & Gas Exploration & Production."

5. Ibid.
6. Ibid.
7. Ibid.
8. Ibid.
9. Ibid.
10. Ibid.
11. Marcus, Alfred. *Controversial Issues in Energy Policy.* Newbury Park, CA: Sage, 1992.
12. Sieminski, Adam. *International Energy Outlook 2016.* Washington, DC: Center for Strategic and International Studies, 2016.
13. Mourdoukoutas, Panos. Forbes. May 29, 2016. www.forbes.com/sites/panosmourdoukoutas/2016/05/29/saudi-arabias-second-big-gamble-w ill-take-the-oil-market-for-a-rough-ride/.
14. Huddleston, Tom. Fortune. January 9, 2015. http://fortune.com/2015/01/09/energy-companies-market-value/.
15. "Global Oil & Gas Exploration & Production."
16. Kemp, John. Reuters. July 5, 2016. www.reuters.com/article/us-saudi-oil-kemp-idUSKCN0ZL1X6.
17. Ramaswamy, A. K. *Gazprom: The Evolution of a Giant in the Oil and Gas Industry.* Phoenix: Thunderbird, 2009.
18. "Global Oil & Gas Exploration & Production."
19. Ibid.
20. Ibid.
21. Ibid.
22. Witter, David. "Fueled Up: Improving Global Economic Conditions Will Sustain Demand for Petroleum Products." IBIS World Industry Report, 2016.
23. Sieminski.
24. Ibid.
25. Ibid.

# 6 | The Motor Vehicle Sector

Drivers consumed most of the gasoline produced by oil and natural gas companies. Motor vehicle companies such as Toyota, VW, GM, and Ford fought for the loyalty of these drivers, seeking to increase their share of a barely growing global motor vehicle market. However, demand for motor vehicles in developed economies was leveling off, as it had for oil, while in emerging economies, it was climbing. China had become the world's largest consumer and producer of passenger cars, while in North America light trucks had largely replaced passenger cars as the vehicle of choice. These factors affected suppliers to the motor vehicle sector; forced to simultaneously cut costs and improve quality, they too experienced heightened competition for a dwindling market. On the horizon were even more significant shifts, such as electric and autonomous vehicles. They could make all companies in this sector, with their specialization on the internal combustion engine (ICE), less relevant. Companies tried to adapt to this situation without a clear roadmap of what would come next. This chapter explores the changes transforming the motor vehicle sector, its slow growth, the heightened competition among producers, the rise of China, the ascendance of light duty trucks in the North American market, the struggles of the suppliers, and the prospects for alternative technologies.

## The Sector Defined and Characterized

Major companies in the motor vehicle sector – firms like Toyota, VW, GM, and Ford– were OEMs (Original Equipment Manufacturers). They were at the apex of a vast supply chain and their performance depended critically on their capacity to manage their relations with the companies in this supply chain. They designed, marketed, and assembled vehicles and relied on companies in a supply chain to make the parts they needed including brakes, powertrains, transmissions, tires, wheels, exhaust systems, radiators, and filters. Their payments to their suppliers constituted more than 75 percent of their costs, while they spent just 7.5 percent on workers' wages and 2 percent on marketing.[1] Their profit margins, at 5.2 percent in 2016, were low compared to such sectors as healthcare, technology, and finance.

## Slow Growth Except for Asia

Growth in demand for new vehicles had been slow since 2013. Sales approached a saturation point of about 75 million units or so sold annually.[2] The automakers adjusted by reducing the number of cars and commercial vehicles they manufactured. Despite the 2014–2015 collapse in gasoline prices, which should have made car ownership more affordable and brought it within the reach of more people, production slowed down.

The location of markets also shifted. No longer were North America and Europe dominant. Rather, Asia had become the world's main market for the sale of new automobiles. It had the highest volume of new car sales in 2016 – more than 40 percent of the cars sold worldwide.[3] US sales volume in that year was only about 14 percent of cars sold worldwide and Europe's about 25 percent. Stagnant North American and European demand was likely to continue. The tipping point was 2009. Until that year, US auto sales were greater than China's, but after it. China surpassed the United States in auto sales. China's lead had grown every year since. China's rise was an unintended consequence of the Great Financial Crisis, from which China recovered at a faster pace than other countries. From 2004 and 2014, Chinese car and truck sales grew at a compound annual rate of 11.4 percent, while in the rest of the world they grew at a compound annual rate of 2.7 percent.[4] In Europe, the compound annual growth in car and truck sales in this period was 1.4 percent and in North America, it was 0.9 percent. In Japan, sales declined at a compound annual rate of 0.5 percent.

While the market for new motor vehicles declined in developed economies, there could be as much as a doubling in motor vehicle sales in emerging economies by 2030 in comparison to 2015. US sales were not likely to grow at a fast pace for a number of reasons. Sales slowed because drivers kept their cars on the roads longer. The cars were better made. Consumers were often cash-strapped and unable to afford a new vehicle. When they shopped, they looked for used vehicles that were more affordable. Consumers were also less fashion conscious and had less interest in buying the next model. In 2000, the average age of a vehicle on the road in the United States was about nine years.[5] By 2015, it was close to twelve years. In addition, car sharing had become a trend especially among the young living in large cities. In dense urban areas like the New York metropolitan area, where car ownership made little sense, this trend was projected to grow. If this trend continued, the result would be a reduced demand for individual car ownership.

## Intense Global Competition

While growth in demand slowed, competition heated up. At the top among automakers in market share were Toyota and VW; these companies fought it out to become the world's largest automaker. In 2016, Toyota slightly edged VW. With 10.8 million units sold in that year, it had a market share of 11.8 percent.[6] VW, in comparison, sold 9.53 million units and had a market share of 11.5 percent. In third place was GM, followed by Renault-Nissan, Hyundai, and Ford. Of note was that no automaker had a share greater than 12 percent and that Hyundai, a relative newcomer to this sector, was ahead of Ford, one of the sector's oldest participants. As indicated, though the sector was highly competitive, there was still room for new companies to gain a foothold.

The 2014 "Dieselgate" scandal affected the competition between VW and Toyota. To meet US nitrogen oxide standards, VW intentionally programmed its diesel engines to activate emissions controls only while in lab testing (see Chapter 14). The engines emitted up to forty times more nitrogen oxides in real-world driving. Prior to the scandal, VW, not Toyota, had been the world's largest producer. It achieved this status largely because of its dominance over Toyota in China. From 2010 to 2015, the performance of both VW and Toyota slipped. In 2015, the year Dieselgate became widely known, VW's performance fell far more than Toyota's. In that year, VW revenue fell by almost 11 percent, and its operating profit was down by more than 60 percent.

Overall, before the event, VW had been growing much faster than Toyota. In 2010, its revenue was about $150 billion, while Toyota's was close to $200 billion. Starting in 2012 and continuing in 2013 and 2014 Volkswagen surpassed Toyota in both revenue and operating profit. With the scandal, VW's rise ended, but it recovered rapidly and did surprisingly well in subsequent years. The decline in both Toyota's and Volkswagen's revenue should have given other automakers the chance to advance, but that did not happen.

Toyota's problem in China, the world's fastest growing market, was that Japanese products were shunned because of the country's conduct in the Second World War. Were it not for China, Toyota's market share lead over VW would have been higher. VW prevailed in China. It was the top-selling automaker in the country with a market share of about 15 percent in 2016.[7] Toyota was far behind, in sixth place. Its Chinese market share was just 4.6 percent. General Motors trailed VW and was in second place in China, with a 14.5 percent market share and Hyundai was in third place with a 7.6 percent market share. These were the big three in the Chinese market. Renault-Nissan's market share was 4.8 percent, and the Chinese producer Changan had a market share of 4.6 percent. Ford was behind Toyota; it had a market share of only 4.4 percent. Ford strived hard to overcome this problem (see Chapter 12). The Chinese manufacturers BAIC and Dongfeng had 3.9 percent and 3.7 percent market share, respectively. Honda had a market share of 3.6 percent market share; it suffered like Toyota from its Japanese origins.

## China's Ascendancy

The top twenty-three foreign brands in China sold slightly over 12 million cars in that country in 2014. They prevailed over domestic Chinese brands, which sold about 7.5 million cars.[8] The top eight domestic brands were Wuling, Changan, Dongfend, Chery BYD, Haval, Geely, BAIC, and JAC. Outside of China, the names of the domestic Chinese brands were virtually unknown. In the future they might become very well known as these companies pursue foreign markets, especially in emerging countries to which their vehicles are well suited.

Foreign firms were not allowed to operate in China without a Chinese joint venture partner. Each foreign firm active in the country had at least one such partner, if not more. The largest of the joint venture partners active in China was the state-owned automotive manufacturing company, FAW. It had partnerships with VW, Audi, and Toyota. Together with its partners, FAW sold more than four million cars in China in 2014. Another state-owned company Dongfeng was the partner of Infiniti, Peugeot, Citroen, Kia, and Nissan. With its partners, it sold more than two million cars in China in 2014. Shanghai Motors, otherwise known as SAIC, was still another state-owned company, and it partnered with Chevrolet, Buick, Cadillac, and VW. It too sold more than two million cars in China in 2014 with its joint venture partners. Changan, another state-owned Chinese auto company, partnered with Ford, Suzuki, Citroen, Mazda, and Volvo. It also sold more than a million cars in China in 2014 with its partners. Finally, there was Beijing Motors (BAIC), the last of the main state-owned companies, which partnered with Hyundai and Mercedes-Benz, and with its partners also sold more than a million cars in China in 2014.

Chinese consumers not only bought more new cars than any country in the world, but its workers also produced more of these cars than any country, far outdistancing its nearest rival, Japan, in 2015.[9] Chinese workers assembled more than 22 million passenger cars in 2015. In comparison, Japanese workers assembled just almost eight million cars in that year, German workers about six million, and both US and South Korean workers about four million cars, respectively. Other countries, whose workers produced a million cars, or more in that year, were India, Spain, Brazil, Mexico, the United Kingdom, France, the Czech Republic, Russia, and Slovakia.

China, however, was the center of world auto production. It exported about a third of the cars it made in 2015 to the rest of the world, a number that was growing.[10] In 2009, its exports had been about 13 million, while in 2020, they were projected to be about 35 million. If this projection came about, almost half of the autos produced in the world in that year would be Chinese made.

## Light Duty Trucks in the US

Passenger cars were not the only market in which the major motor vehicle firms competed. More than 55 percent of the US market in 2015 consisted of light duty trucks.[11] These came in a number of varieties. In the US market as a whole, crossovers were in the lead at 29.1 percent, followed by pickups, sport utility vehicles, and vans. About 45 percent of the global market in 2015 also consisted of light duty trucks, with crossovers again being in the lead at 21.6 percent, followed by the other types of such trucks. Pickups, sport utility vehicles (SUVs), crossover utility vehicles (CUVs), and minivans represented a $200 billion global market.[12]

The collapse of gasoline prices provided motivation for consumers to switch from passenger cars to the various types of light duty trucks. In the United States as prices went down, consumers bought more of these vehicles. The gasoline price plunge was a boon for US auto companies. They were a challenge for foreign automakers like VW and Toyota, which had fewer light duty truck models. Oil and natural gas companies suffered, while the automakers had new opportunities. A high percentage of Americans, if given the chance, preferred to drive a large, multi-purpose vehicle as opposed to a small one, which saved gas. So long as gas prices were not markedly high, they preferred these vehicles because they gave them a feeling of greater freedom and safety. Consumers valued the versatility, the enhanced space, and the hauling capacity.

In the midst of the major plunge in gasoline prices in 2015, Ford's F-Series pickup trucks became the US brand with the highest market share, followed closely by the Chevrolet Silverado, and Chrysler's Ram Charger. Together, they commanded 11.6 percent of the US market.[13] Other light duty trucks that sold well in 2015 were Toyota's RAV4, Honda's CR-V, the Ford Escape, GMC's Sierra, Nissan's Rogue, and the Jeep Cherokee. In contrast, the largest selling passenger cars were the Toyota Camry, the Honda Accord, the Honda Civic, and the Toyota Corolla. Together, they controlled 8.4 percent of the US market; and when gas prices went down, their market share fell. In 2016, passenger car sales fell by 9 percent, while light duty truck sales increased by 8.4 percent.[14] The top-selling light duty truck brand, the Ford F-Series had growing sales, while the top-selling passenger car brand, the Toyota Camry, had declining sales. There were some exceptions. Sales of the Chevrolet Equinox and Silverado, which were small trucks, declined, while sales of the Honda Civic and Nissan Sentra passenger cars grew.

With plummeting gasoline prices, GM, Ford, and FC (Fiat Chrysler) did well because of their focus on light duty trucks. Foreign manufacturers like Toyota, Honda, and VW fought hard to catch up. They introduced new light duty truck models and heavily promoted those they already sold. The operating profits of the light truck divisions of

GM, Ford, and FC rose steadily when oil prices plunged, while the financial performance of the major oil and natural gas companies examined in the last chapter fell. Their interests were not in alignment. Declining fortunes for one side were a boon for the other.

## Suppliers

Global motor vehicle companies heavily depended on their suppliers; hundreds existed operating in many categories – brakes, electronics, metal stamping, seating and interiors, steering and suspension, transmission and powertrains, tires and wheels, exhaust, HVAC (heating, ventilation, and air conditioning), filters, and radiators. Many of the suppliers to the motor vehicle manufacturers had moved to Asia, where the action was. The highest percentage of suppliers had Asia locations (37.3 percent), followed by Europe (32 percent), and North America (29.3 percent).[15]

Although most of the suppliers' sales (60.9 percent) were to motor vehicle manufacturers in their own countries, a considerable export (23.8 percent) and aftermarket (15.3 percent) business existed. Supplier sales growth had fallen from nearly 6 percent in 2012 and 2013 to about 2 percent in 2014. The suppliers saw a pickup in their business when oil prices collapsed and they grew at a rate of almost 6 percent in 2015, yet their growth again fell to under 2 percent in 2016. Projections for their future growth were no better than this number.

### Strong Competitive Pressures

Competition was high in the markets in which the suppliers competed. The OEMs had choices. The two largest suppliers in the world were the German company Bosch and the Japanese company Denso.[16] Between them, they had about 5 percent of the world market share. The remaining 95 percent of market share belonged to many suppliers. Bosch did better in 2013, prior to the plunge in gasoline prices, than after the 2014 plunge. Its performance improved somewhat in 2015, but it did not sustain these gains in 2016. Denso, on the other hand, did well in 2014 and poorly in 2015, but its performance picked up again in 2016.

The following list breaks down the different categories of US suppliers, with their 2016 revenues in parenthesis.[17]

- metal stamping and forging ($34 billion);
- transmission ($41 billion);
- steering and suspension ($15 billion);
- interiors ($29.1 billion);
- brakes ($12.3 billion);
- batteries ($11.3 billion);
- electronics ($25.6 billion);
- tires ($18.3 billion);
- iron and steel ($78.8 billion).

About 750,000 Americans worked either directly or indirectly for these suppliers.[18] Most of these jobs were located in Michigan, Ohio, Indiana, and Kentucky, where they made up just under half of all employment. Another 1.5 million or so Americans worked in jobs indirectly tied to the suppliers. Automation, pressure from the auto manufacturers to keep costs under control, and weak US motor vehicle sales growth were expected to lower the level of employment. Many, but not all, of the suppliers' products were tied to the internal combustion engine and their fortunes would decline to the extent that electric vehicles gained ascendancy. The sector's difficulties are worth examining in more detail.

## Metal Stamping and Forging

Companies in this segment worked for aerospace, the military, and agricultural equipment companies as well as for the automakers. Their work for the motor vehicle sector made up about a third of their revenues.[19] By any measure – revenue, number of establishments and enterprises, employment, and wages – US metal stamping and forging companies were in decline (Figure 6.1). The uptick in demand for light duty trucks in the US made little difference. Broader economic trends worked against metal stampers and forgers.

No company absolutely dominated this category. The two companies with the largest market share were Allegheny Technologies Incorporated (ATI), with a 4.3 percent market share in 2016, and Alcoa, with a 3.7 percent estimated market share in that year.[20] Both firms did better in 2014 after oil prices dropped and there was a pickup

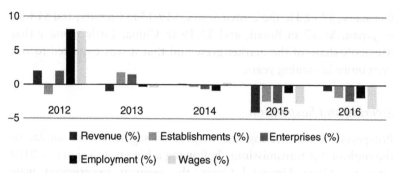

**Figure 6.1** The percentage decline of the US metal stamping and forging segment 2012–2016
*Source*: Derived from IBIS World, *Metal Forging and Stamping in US*, 2016

in small truck demand, but they were not able to sustain these gains in 2015 and 2016.

*Transmissions*

This segment produced other products, such as axles, transaxles, differentials, drivetrain components, torque converters, clutches, and transmission gears, but automatic and manual transmissions for light duty trucks, passenger cars, heavy-duty vehicles, and buses made up 51.8 percent of the segment's sales in 2016.[21] Coming out of the Great Financial Crisis of 2007–2008, the segment's revenues grew rapidly, but they had been stagnant ever since and the segment had experienced no real growth since 2010. Only one company had significant market share – Dana at 5.7 percent – and though it had experienced a small rebound in 2016, Dana had negative growth in revenue and operating income in most of the years after 2012.[22] It benefited little from the decline in oil prices. The main reason was an increase in imports. About 41 percent of the $41 billion of US auto firm spending on transmissions in 2016 went to imports; 37 percent of total imports came from Mexico, 22.3 percent from Japan, and 11.4 percent from Canada.[23] Low wages, not surprisingly, drove the shift to low-cost foreign suppliers. The wage divide between Mexico and other countries was quite large. Mexico paid workers in the automotive sector $3.29 an hour in 2015.[24] The average hourly wage rates for workers in other countries in 2015 were $26.25 in

Germany, $23.88 in the United States, $19.13 in Canada, and $14.88 in Japan, $6.17 in Brazil, and $5.19 in China. Little wonder that Mexico's share of the market grew and that it was expected to rise even more in coming years.

## Steering and Suspension

Prospects for the steering and suspension segment were similar to the outlook for transmissions. Following a big growth spurt in 2010 after the Great Financial Crisis, the segment experienced little growth and was not expected to grow much in the future. A high percentage of segment sales was devoted to manufacturing SUVs and light trucks. In 2015, this percentage was 41.7 percent, while 31 percent of segment sales went to the manufacture of passenger cars.[25] The remainder was devoted to exports (11.3 percent), heavy trucks and buses (8.6 percent), and the aftermarket (7.4 percent). TRW, with 9.1 percent, and Tenneco, with 5.2 percent, were the 2015 market share leaders.[26] TRW's performance fell dramatically in 2014 and picked up some in 2015 and 2016. Tenneco did not have a dramatic fall, but did not show substantial improvement. Again, there was a high percentage of imports, which accounted for 54 percent of sales in 2016. Mexican imports captured 37.6 percent of this business.[27]

## Interiors

This segment showed similar signs of stress. There was no ongoing recovery after the Great Financial Crisis. The Mexican factor again played a large role. The main product was seats, 38.7 percent of the business, followed by trimmings 30.7 percent, seat belts 15.4 percent, and seat frames, covers, and car interior trims 15.2 percent.[28] Since 2012, the segment had close to no growth and the expectation for the future was for little improvement. At 14.8 percent, Johnson Controls had the largest market share, followed by Lear at 7.9 percent.[29] Johnson Control's business declined between 2014 and 2016 in comparison to 2013, while Lear's improved. Imports constituted 26.6 percent of sales, with Mexican imports making up 63.3 percent of this total.[30] An advantage the segment had over companies that made transmission and steering and suspension was that in the event of the rapid introduction of electric vehicles (EVs), the need for the segment's products would continue while the need for transmission, steering, and suspension capabilities would decline.

## Brakes

This segment also was weak. After recovering from the Great Financial Crisis, it showed little growth. Most of the revenue came from sales to the OEMs, 57.2 percent in 2016, with some coming from exports, 21.7 percent, and the automotive aftermarket, 16.4 percent.[31] The companies with the highest market share were Tokyo-based Akebono Brake, at 12.3 percent, and TRW, at 10 percent.[32] Akebono's profits picked up in 2014, when oil prices started to collapse, but the company's performance thereafter declined. TRW's performance went down in 2014. Imports constituted 41.4 percent of US brake sales, with Chinese imports making up 30.4 percent of the total and Mexican imports 26.7 percent of the total.[33]

## Batteries

This segment did fine after the Great Financial Crisis, but by 2013 fell to a near no-growth condition, which was expected to continue even if EVs gained momentum. Battery company expertise was in lead acid batteries and not in lithium ion batteries on which EVs relied. The 2016 market was divided among motor vehicle companies, at 36.6 percent, exports, at 33.6 percent, and the aftermarket, at 29.8 percent.[34] Through consolidation, Johnson Controls became the dominant US player, with a 23.9 percent market share.[35] Its brands included Advance Auto Parts, AutoZone, Costco, NAPA, O'Reilly, Sears, and Walmart. The oil price shock of 2014–2015 did not yield significant improvement in Johnson Control's business. Imports were a significant factor, with more than 40 percent of the market. The Chinese were the leading importer and had 33.2 percent of this market.[36]

## Electronics

An upward spurt after the Great Financial Crisis and then a subsequent leveling-off also took place in the electronics segment.

However, there was a difference. These firms were the source of many of the innovations in the motor vehicle sector in this period. They were at the center of the process in which motor vehicles introduced more and more electronics into the new models of the vehicles they sold. Segment sales were divided as follows: 20.4 percent was for control systems, 17 percent was for information and entertainment systems, 13.7 percent was for starters and spark plugs, and 8.5 percent was for alternators, generators, and regulators.[37] The segment was expected to make further gains because of greater use of devices such as the GPS in new cars. Japanese-based Denso, with 24.1 percent, had the highest market share, and Delphi was in second place with 14.6 percent.[38] Imports from Mexico, China, and other low-wage nations were not a significant factor.

## Tires

After this segment recovered from the Great Financial Crisis, demand for US-made tires was flat, with no improvement expected in the immediate future. Most companies in 2016 were producing for the replacement market (81.7 percent); 14.9 percent of the tires made were sold to OEMs.[39] Japan-based Bridgestone commanded the largest market share, with 21.3 percent; France-based Michelin was second, with 21.2 percent.[40] Neither company did well in 2014 and 2015 when oil prices declined, but both performed slightly better in 2016 (Figure 6.2).

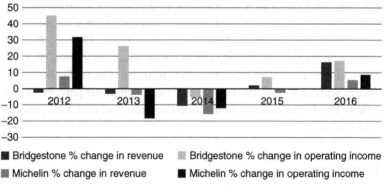

**Figure 6.2** The performance of Bridgestone and Michelin tires 2012–2016 Derived from IBIS World, *Tire Manufacturing in US*, 2016

## Iron and Steel

Iron and steel firms served many more markets than just the motor vehicle market. Only 8.2 percent of sales were to motor vehicle companies.[41] Following the Great Financial Crisis, the decline in these companies' revenue was far steeper than that of other suppliers, and their rebound, although strong, did not match that of other suppliers. The company that had the greatest US market share in 2016 was Nucor, at 18.4 percent; it faced competition from India-based ArcelorMittal, which had 16.1 percent market share.[42] When oil prices plummeted, both companies did well, especially Nucor, but the performance improvement did not persist. ArcelorMittal's profits remained slightly better than Nucor. The segment faced major global competition, with imports entering the United States from Canada, South Korea, Brazil, and Japan. Imports amounted 33 percent of the iron and steel consumed in the United States in 2016.[43]

## Vehicle Electrification

Because of imports, the companies that supplied the motor vehicle sector had not benefitted much from the decline in oil prices and the increased demand for larger, heavier vehicles that took place. Most of them confronted the threat of vehicle electrification. Progress in electrifying the automotive fleet, however, was slow. In 2005, just three hybrid models – the Honda Civic, the Honda Insight, and the Toyota Prius – were sold in the United States. Though EPA rated these cars capable of getting up to fifty miles per gallon (MPG), their market share was very low. In 2013, US hybrid penetration peaked at about 3 percent of vehicles sold.[44] The 2014–2015 drop in oil prices saw hybrid market share in the United States decline to less than 2.5 percent. More hybrid cars were sold in China (336,000 cars) and Europe (215,000 cars) in 2016 than in the United States (160,000 cars). Norway had the highest electrical vehicle penetration of any country in the world in that year with 30 percent. No other country other than the Netherlands exceeded a penetration rate of more than 5 percent.

Honda reduced its involvement in the US hybrid race, leaving Toyota, with various models of the Prius, Lexus, and Avalon, in control. To compete with the popular Prius and the all-electric Nissan Leaf, Chevrolet launched a plug-in hybrid, the Volt, in 2010. As an extended range vehicle, the Volt ran on its battery until the charge dropped; then the internal combustion engine kicked in to extend the car's range. As with other hybrids, regenerative braking contributed to the car's fuel efficiency. As rated by the US EPA, the Volt was the most fuel-efficient car with a gasoline engine in the United States. With different styling, GM sold plug-in hybrids such as the Vauxhall Ampera in the United Kingdom and the Opel Ampera in the rest of Europe. GM's vice chair Robert Lutz had been the main developer of the Volt. He initially proposed that Chevy make not a plug-in hybrid, but an all-electric vehicle. However, the VP for global vehicle development, Jon Lauckner, advised against doing so because of battery cost and insufficient charging stations. Lauckner suggested a car with a smaller battery and a small internal combustion engine. GM's plug-in hybrids had sales of about 70,000 units worldwide at the end of 2013.[45]

## The History of Electric Vehicles (EVs)

EVs had a long history.[46] Pre-twentieth-century EVs, propelled by non-rechargeable batteries, traveled at speeds under 20 miles per hour and went less than 50 miles before having to be recharged. Women tended to like them, but male drivers wanted powerful ICE vehicles. Ironically, the 1910 introduction of an electric charger eliminated the need to crank-start ICEs and led to the ICE's dominance. Henry Ford mass-produced ICE vehicles, selling them for $850. By 1915, more than a million ICE vehicles were on the roads, and their number grew rapidly.

By 1935, US automakers produced practically no EVs. EVs made a short comeback in the late 1990s. GM introduced zero-emission lead acid and nickel metal hydride (NiMH) battery vehicles to meet California's strict anti-pollution laws. In addition to less pollution, these EVs had certain advantages over ICEs. EV motors were nearly twice as efficient as ICE engines. The waste heat loss was less than 60 percent, compared to nearly 80 percent in ICE vehicles. EVs were also quiet. Unlike the complex ICE, whose powertrain had many moving parts, they required little maintenance. EVs also weighed more and therefore tended to do better than ICE vehicles in a collision.

The EVs that GM built in the late 1990s, however, had distinct drawbacks. Their range was less than 140 miles. The cars were small two-seat compacts because the batteries took up so much space. Public charging spots were not available in large numbers, and the charging of the batteries was slow, up to 12 hours. GM's EV cost $35,000 and the company claimed that the market for it was not sufficiently large for the company to make much money. Its plan was to sell just 300 cars per year. California weakened its anti-pollution laws under pressure from automobile companies, and by the end of the 1990s, GM recalled all 1,138 EVs it sold and destroyed them.

## Tesla's Path Forward

Instability in oil-producing countries and petroleum prices following the 9/11 attack revived interest in EVs.[47] Almost every government in the world created incentive packages for promoting alternative transportation. Elon Musk was an early investor in the all-electric auto company Tesla. He maintained that his motivation was that the world was running out of fossil fuels. The company's purpose was to expedite the move from a "mine-and-burn hydrocarbon economy" to a sustainable solution, a solar electric economy.[48] Musk became CEO in 2008 when Tesla failed to meet its deadlines for its first product, the Roadster sports car. He invested another $40 million of his own money in the company. The business model was to enter the high end of the automotive market first, since in this segment customers were likely to be prepared to pay a premium, and then to move down the market to greater volume and lower prices with each successive model.

Building an all-electric car, however, was not an easy task. EV companies had settled on lithium ion as the battery of choice. The same battery as in laptop computers, its capacity per weight was relatively high in contrast to the lead acid and nickel metal hydride batteries in GM's original all-electric vehicle. For use in autos, a manufacturer had to combine many lithium ion modules in a pack. The batteries were expensive, but the hope was that that these costs would decline with greater volume and experience. Tesla chose Panasonic as its battery supplier. Tesla innovated by putting the battery pack underneath the vehicle, not in the trunk as GM had done. This placement provided a lower center of gravity, which meant better handling – an important selling point. Tesla's first car, the high-end Roadster sports car, had a range of 245 miles. In comparison, the Leaf, a midsize all-electric vehicle Nissan sold, had a range of about seventy miles. The Roadster battery had 7,100 cells as opposed to the 192 cells in the Leaf. Chevrolet's Volt plug-in hybrid had 288 cells. The drawback of so many cells was not just the weight; the heat the cells generated was a problem. Tesla innovated to solve this problem and did what no other EV maker had done previously. It installed all-embracing thermal sensors and wiring needed to keep the batteries cool. Otherwise EVs could ignite if not cooled properly.

To sell the Roadster, Tesla focused not on the car's environmental benefits, but its speed, styling, comfort, and handling. The vehicles were eligible for a $7,500 federal tax credit, and California offered another $2,500 tax credit. Other benefits that some states offered were reduced home electric bills, free parking, and the use of high occupancy vehicle and carpool lanes. Tesla took until 2009 to sell more than 1,000 Roadsters. Between 2007 and 2011, the global electric vehicle market took off, admittedly from a very low base. It grew at a compound annual rate of 135 percent, compared to an ICE compound annual growth rate of 2 percent in the same period. EV sales were projected to continue to grow at a rate of 26 percent per year from 2012 to 2020. Even then, the total penetration of EVs in the automotive market would amount to less than 1 percent. Musk remained upbeat despite the difficulties which were often overwhelming and declared with bravado that EVs would be the only type of vehicle available for sale in the United States by 2030. By mid-century, he claimed, it would not be possible to find ICEs of any kind on global highways.

Tesla's immediate challenge was to get beyond a sports car and move toward a more affordable vehicle. The company's second car, the Model S, cost somewhat less than the Roadster, but was still priced in the luxury premium category. *Consumer Reports* gave it the highest rating it ever gave to a car, and it won the magazine's 2014 car of the year award. The magazine lauded the Model S for its styling, handling, fuel efficiency, and safety. The car competed in the same category as the Audi A6 and the BMW 5 series, but accelerated from zero to 60 miles per hour 10 percent faster than those cars. From 2009 to 2012, reservations for the Model S grew at a 64 percent compound annual rate. It achieved its biggest success in Norway, where it was the overall top-selling vehicle. In 2013, Model S US sales were greater than the Mercedes S Class, the BMW 7 series, the Lexus LS, and the Audi A7. By the spring of 2014, Tesla had sold more than 31,000 vehicles.

The world awaited Tesla's introduction of its third EV model, one that would sell for about $35,000 and have mass appeal. Tesla revealed that a half-million people had put down money to reserve one of these cars. Yet, the company continually missed its production deadlines and it was running out of money. Musk, himself, appeared to be breaking under the pressure. Thus, it was unclear whether Tesla would reach its goals and even survive.

## Overcoming Existing Obstacles

Tesla also faced considerable competition. It was no longer the only EV player. Before Tesla came out with its third EV, GM already had introduced the all-electric Bolt model at the same price point as the Model 3 and it had very similar features. The Bolt obtained a five-star rating from *Car & Driver* magazine and like the Model S, *Motor Trend* declared it its 2017 car of the year.

The competition showed the vitality and staying power of EVs. Nonetheless, they continued to face many challenges. They included development lead times for less expensive models. In failing to meet its goals, Tesla had shown how difficult the challenges were. They included the high capital investment, the availability of critical components, and sufficient capacity utilization to achieve the learning and economies of scale for low-cost production. In addition, many consumers continued to perceive the costs of EVs to be too high. They persisted in having concerns about fuel storage, limited range, and insufficient refueling infrastructure.

Despite the challenges, nearly every major motor vehicle company had serious EV programs underway. They planned to introduce EVs in greater numbers in the coming decades. A factor pushing them forward was that many countries had future bans in place for ICEs, and others were considering the bans.[49] The United Kingdom banned sales of new gasoline and diesel cars starting in 2040. By 2050, all cars on its roads would have to be zero emission. France's intention also was to end sales of gas- and diesel-powered vehicles by 2040. After that date, automakers only would be able to sell cars that ran on electricity or other cleaner sources of power, including hybrids. India mandated that that every vehicle sold in the country would have to be electric by 2030. Norway's transportation plan outlined a target that all new passenger cars and vans sold in 2025 should be zero-emission vehicles. German Chancellor Angela Merkel wanted to set a deadline for her country to end sales of cars fitted with gasoline or diesel engines. Other countries that had set official targets for a ban on gasoline and diesel cars and the introduction of EVs were Austria, Denmark, Ireland, Japan, the Netherlands, Portugal, Korea, and Spain. At least eight US states had such goals.

China too had made far-reaching commitments to the Paris climate accord that called upon it to:

- top off its carbon dioxide emissions around 2030 and make its best efforts to peak earlier;
- lower its carbon dioxide intensity (carbon dioxide emissions per unit of GDP) by 60–65 percent from the 2005 level; and
- increase the share of non-fossil fuels in its primary energy consumption to around 20 percent.

These commitments signified that China might be very close to being ready to announce that it was establishing a ban on ICEs like that of other countries.

## Ambitious Goals

Motor vehicle companies had ambitious EV goals, even if there was no assurance they could meet them.[50] In 2016, Volkswagen declared that it would attempt to bring thirty or more EV models to market by 2025, with a target of two to three million sold, equaling roughly 25 percent of its total sales. In 2017, the company increased these numbers and vowed to create electric versions of all 300 of its models. In 2017, Daimler (owner of Mercedes-Benz) announced it would have ten new EV models on the market by 2022. That same year, Volvo declared that all the models it would introduce in 2019 and thereafter would be hybrid or electric. Jaguar Land Rover made the same promise.

Nonetheless, in 2016, at 0.2 percent, EVs were a tiny proportion of the automotive market. None of the International Energy Agency (IEA), the US Department of Energy (DOE), the Organization of the Petroleum Exporting Countries (OPEC), or the major oil and natural gas companies, for that matter, foresaw major EV inroads in line with the plans of the above-mentioned countries (see Chapter 4). ExxonMobil expected that alternatives to the ICE would constitute a very small proportion of total 2040 vehicle sales (see Chapter 16). However, Bloomberg New Energy Finance's updated outlook for 2017 projected 54 percent of new car sales in 2040 would be EVs, up from the 35 percent it had projected the previous year, meaning that about one-third of the global passenger fleet would be electric by 2040.[51]

A move to EVs could be accelerated if the steady, incremental improvement in batteries analysts forecast moved forward more rapidly. R&D in batteries was growing and faster progress was not out of the question, though batteries had been researched for years and few real breakthroughs had taken place. Another possibility was that climate change became so severe that governments the world over *had to* impose more stringent restrictions on ICEs and introduce larger incentives for alternative vehicles. Still another factor that could lead to a tipping point was that consumer demand could pick up considerably. It could pick up for a number of reasons. High gasoline prices were certainly one of them. Then again, demand could increase on its own if consumers became comfortable with EVs, they started to enjoy the benefits, and found them more attractive than conventional vehicles.

For demand for EVs to grow, policy makers would have to help by better funding infrastructure and alleviating anxiety about insufficient charging stations. Furthermore, the capacity to produce EVs inexpensively had to rise. Their price had to come down if they were going to gain wide acceptance. On the other hand, contingencies could arise that could slow down gains, such as:

- continued consumer resistance;
- automakers reneging on their promises or not meeting their deadlines;
- governments not carrying through on their climate change commitments;
- insufficient critical metals for battery mass production;
- a high-profile accident or technical malfunction; and
- an inability to standardize charging infrastructure.

Questions remained as to whether, when, and to what extent EVs would start to replace conventional vehicles as the main means people used to get from place to place.

## Low Priced Gasoline in the United States

Substantially lower US gas prices than in other countries continued to be a roadblock to EV adoption. The average equivalent US electricity costs of a gallon of gasoline were in the range of $1.15–$1.25 in 2015. If US gasoline prices at the pump were higher because of taxes, as they were in most other countries, the gain to an EV owner would be greater and the incentive to drive an EV higher. In 2015, the federal government tax on gasoline was $0.18 per-gallon and the state and local governments' average gas tax per gallon was about $0.35 per gallon, for a combined tax rate of about $0.53 per gallon.[52] This rate was about a fifth that of the world's thirty-four other advanced economies, where the average tax rate on a gallon of gasoline was $2.62. Mexico was one of the few countries that had a lower tax rate than the United States.

The US rate was less than half of that of Canada, where driving long distances was also common and necessary. In addition, almost all the world's advanced countries also placed a value added tax (VAT) on gasoline, so that their effective tax rate was even greater. In nearly every country in the world other than in the United States, drivers would save substantial sums of money by switching to electric.

Instead of stiff gasoline taxes, the US government had imposed corporate average fuel efficiency (CAFE) standards on automakers to lower the amount of fuel consumed per mile. If these standards originally had been set at a high level and then successively raised, the automakers would have had much greater motivation to go electric. However, the US government did not increase CAFE standards from 1975 until 2007, when President Bush signed the Energy Independence and Security Act (EISA), which increased them by 40 percent and set a goal for a 35-miles-per-gallon (mpg) national standard for all vehicles by 2020. Previously, there had been separate CAFE standards for passenger cars (about twenty-eight miles per gallon), and for light trucks (about twenty miles per gallon). However, by the first decade of the twenty-first century, the US market share for light trucks was over 50 percent, whereas it had been under 10 percent when the law first took effect. The 2007 requirement, in contrast, applied to all vehicles – passenger automobiles and light trucks alike – but unfortunately its implementation was delayed. The Obama administration proposed new combined standards of 54.5 mpg by 2025, which under pressure from the auto industry, the Trump administration had decided to try to overturn.

## What Comes Next

For companies in the motor vehicle sector, it still was unclear how real the challenge of electrification was to their standard way of doing business. Their problem was what types of innovative technology investments they should make. They had many vehicle paths from which to choose. They also had many fuel use possibilities, fuel pricing possibilities, vehicle-pricing possibilities, and market adoption possibilities to consider. Fuel-cell vehicles, another alternative, whose fate waxed and waned, might make a comeback. With fuel cells added to the mix, automakers had to choose from three main vehicle types: ICE-based vehicles, battery-based vehicles, and fuel-cell-based vehicles. Battery-based vehicles offered a number of possibilities – HEV, plug-in hybrid vehicles, and pure electric vehicles. Fuel-cell-based vehicles could be hybrids or standalone. Each of these might advance together or separately. ICEs would not stand still. Over time, they would also make advances in fuel efficiency. The electric vehicle options needed more powerful and cheaper batteries to overcome the ICE's lead.

### Lighter Materials

All of the options benefitted from lighter materials. No matter which option motor vehicle companies chose to emphasize, that option would do better if there were material science advances, such as the replacement of heavy iron and steel with lighter aluminum and plastic, a trend that was already underway in vehicle design and production. Any option chosen also would benefit from a better understanding of the aerodynamics of motion and resistance. In 1994, the clean energy visionary Amory Lovins developed a concept for a vehicle that was ultra-light and safe.[53] It had an aerodynamic body and used advanced composite materials like carbon fiber to keep its weight down. It had fewer parts and was easier to assemble. It had low-drag design, and a hybrid drive and was meant to achieve a threefold to fivefold improvement in fuel economy, equal or better performance and affordability, and have the same amenities as conventional automobiles, or even better. These concepts, still relevant, would revolutionize the motor vehicle sector, if realized, even if it did not make a full turn toward electric.

If realized, the concepts would also have a negative effect on suppliers, who were already suffering. Without a major transformation of the suppliers, this concept and others would not come into being. The entire motor vehicle ecosystem, including suppliers and infrastructure, had to be ready and *eager* for change.

## Connected Vehicles

Additional advances were taking place in connected vehicles. New vehicles were being equipped with communication technologies that connected them to each other and to infrastructure so they could precisely locate other cars and road barriers. Mobility preferences were also shifting, with more pay-per-use and pay-per-trip mobility options, which made it less necessary to own a car and deal with it in dense urban centers where the cost of ownership was very high, the traffic impossible, and public transportation a reasonable alternative.

## Autonomous Driving

Furthermore, the emergence of an autonomous driving system was somewhere on the horizon, with major investments by tech companies in the sensors and knowhow required to make this vision a reality. With autonomous driving already in the proof-of-concept stage and various companies experimenting with it in major US cities, the question was not whether but when and how it would be more widely used. Autonomous driving involved far-reaching transformations in the way people lived and it had many unknown side effects.

Was the self-guided electric the inevitable car of the future, and would it be the centerpiece of an autonomous driving system? Such a car would have sensors, lasers, radar, and cameras to detect objects in all directions. The design would be for a rounded shape to maximize the sensors' field view and increase its efficiency. The design of the interior would be for riding and not driving. Travelers would not have to concentrate on the road, but would have the freedom to read, scan their smartphones, daydream, or just sleep. A computer program would direct steering, and braking. It would have to have redundant backup systems in case of failure. Who would own such a vehicle? Would it be the individual driver or would the traveler only order such a ride from a third-party provider or ride sharing services when needed?

## Hedging

With no certain path forward, motor vehicle companies had hedged their bets by investing in a portfolio of complementary power options. They had committed themselves not just to the ICE, but also to electric powertrains and to a lesser extent, fuel cells, to lighter materials, to connected vehicles, and to autonomous driving. They made these commitments because of the future risks and uncertainties. They understood that no powertrain necessarily satisfied all the necessary criteria for economics, performance, public policy, and the environment.

The current disruption they faced was far from simple. It had been underway for quite some time and it related to many factors. With even more dramatic disruption possible, would hedging by adopting a portfolio approach where they dabbled in all the options stand up?

## Evolution or Revolution

If the next stage was evolutionary, the changes affecting companies in the sector might be gradual and incremental. The mobility system would retain most of its current features. The key players, their assets, and the structure would not change that much and the changes which would take place would be orderly, linear, and mostly predictable. The companies in the sector could rest assured that their place in the new system would be central. They were safe. The hedging they had done to protect themselves had paid off. They would be able to retain their assets and capabilities.

The task the major companies in the sector had set for themselves was to experiment and try out the possibilities to discover what worked and what did not. Their hedging via commitment to a portfolio approach of dabbling in the many options that existed made perfect sense, because the future was uncertain. On the other hand, if the next stage was revolutionary, the changes affecting companies in the sector would not be gradual and incremental. They would confront a more fundamental challenge. They might have to take more radical and focused action; otherwise, they might lose out in a big way.

Should they concentrate their efforts? This decision hinged on whether there would be a tipping point and if they could recognize the tipping point beforehand, which probably was impossible. Therefore, the likelihood was that they would continue their hedging tactics of investing in a diversified portfolio of options as a means to ensuring that they would remain viable if not the dominant force in the transportation system of the future. Yet it was not completely clear how the major companies in the sector should cope. What they should do was an open question.

## Notes

1. IBIS World Industry Report. "Global Automobile Engine and Parts Manufacturing." 2016.
2. IBIS World Industry Report. "New Car Sales." 2016.
3. Ibid.
4. Ibid.
5. IBIS World Industry Report. "Average Age of Vehicle Fleet." 2016.
6. Statista. *Global Car Market Share of the World's Largest Automobile OEMs in 2016.* 2016 www.statista.com/statistics/316786/global-mar ket-share-of-the-leading-automakers/.
7. IBIS World Industry Report. "Global Car and Automobile Sales." 2016.
8. Ibid.
9. "Global Automobile Engine and Parts Manufacturing."
10. Ibid.
11. IBIS World Industry Report. "SUV and Light Truck Manufacturing in the US." 2016.
12. Ibid.
13. Ibid.
14. Ibid.
15. "Global Automobile Engine and Parts Manufacturing."
16. Ibid.
17. IBIS World Industry Report. "Car and Automobile Manufacturing in the US." 2016.
18. Ibid.
19. IBIS World Industry Report. "Metal Stamping and Forging in the US." 2016.
20. Ibid.
21. IBIS World Industry Report. "Automobile Transmission Manufacturing in the US." 2016.
22. Ibid.
23. Ibid.
24. *Average Hourly Rate for Auto Workers in Select Countries.* 2016. http:// topforeignstocks.com/2016/10/26/average-houry-rate-for-auto-workers- in-select-countries/.

25. IBIS World Industry Report. "Automobile Steering and Suspension in the US." 2016.
26. Ibid.
27. Ibid.
28. IBIS World Industry Report. "Automobile Interior Manufacturing in the US." 2016.
29. Ibid.
30. Ibid.
31. IBIS World Industry Report, "Automobile Brakes in US." 2016.
32. Ibid.
33. Ibid.
34. IBIS World Industry Report, "Battery Manufacturing in US." 2016.
35. Ibid.
36. Ibid.
37. IBIS World Industry Report, "Automobile Electronic Manufacturing in US." 2016.
38. Ibid.
39. IBIS World, "Tire Manufacturing in US." 2016.
40. Ibid.
41. IBIS World, "Iron and Steel Manufacturing in US." 2016.
42. Ibid.
43. Ibid.
44. *Hybrid Electric Vehicles in the United States.* 2018. https://en
    .wikipedia.org/wiki/Hybrid_electric_vehicles_in_the_United_States.
45. Ibid.
46. Marcus, Alfred. *Innovations in Sustainability: Fuel and Food.*
    Cambridge, UK: Cambridge University Press, 2015.
47. Ibid.
48. Ibid.
49. *Countries Are Announcing Plans to Phase Out Petrol and Diesel Cars.*
    2017. www.weforum.org/agenda/2017/09/countries-are-announcing-p
    lans-to-phase-out-petrol-and-diesel-cars-is-yours-on-the-list/
50. *Here's How Every Major Automaker Plans to Go Electric.* 2017. http
    s://mashable.com/2017/10/03/electric-car-development-plans-ford-gm/
    #rW_qEOF6Eiqw
51. *Electric Vehicle Outlook 2017.* https://data.bloomberglp.com/bnef/sites/
    14/2017/07/BNEF_EVO_2017_ExecutiveSummary.pdf
52. *How High Are Other Nations' Gas Taxes.* 2017. https://taxfoundation
    .org/how-high-are-other-nations-gas-taxes/
53. *The Hypercar Lives.* 2014. https://medium.com/solutions-journal-sum
    mer-2014/the-hypercar-lives-meet-vws-xl1-97603e97612f

# 7 | The Electric Utility Sector

The speed and extent of any electric vehicle transition that would take place depended on developments in the electric utility sector. This chapter reviews key challenges that this sector has faced, including weak demand, a shift in the US away from coal, restructuring, deregulation, and the movement to renewables. The chapter closes with some speculations about the paths that this sector could take in the future.

## The Sector Defined and Characterized

In the United States, people mainly consumed electricity for residential and commercial purposes. In 2016, almost three-quarters of US consumption was for these ends. The remaining consumption mostly was for industrial purposes, with the top consuming industries being wood pulp, inorganic chemicals, and aluminum. Since 1978, the US Congress had pursued legislation to encourage the efficient use of electricity. Congress promoted energy conservation and encouraged utilities to introduce demand-side management (DSM) systems. Agencies of the federal government mandated or incentivized companies and individuals to upgrade and improve lighting, HVAC, washers, driers, dishwashers, dehumidifiers, motors, refrigerators, freezers, and electronics. US states created local appliance standards, building codes, and other measures, such as price breaks for interrupted service, advanced metering, and time of use peak and off-peak pricing. Smart grid technologies were under development. The point of these programs was to do away with as much waste as possible in energy consumption, since conserving energy was often less costly than constructing new power plants. Demand for power in the United States stayed low despite higher than normal temperatures in some regions and mounting air conditioning use. It stayed low despite prices for electricity not being especially high. Indeed, US electricity's share of the average household budget was relatively low.[1]

Tiered pricing in the United States meant that residential and commercial electricity users paid almost twice as much as industrial users, but this pricing scheme did not stimulate increased industrial demand for electricity, as the United States, overall, was deindustrializing. In contrast, China continued on its path of intensive industrialization and its electricity consumption overall was growing and was mostly for industrial and agricultural ends. About three-quarters of Chinese consumption was for these purposes in 2016.[2] The top four consuming industries in China were ferrous metal, non-ferrous metal, building materials, and chemicals. Yet even in China electricity demand was starting to slow. In 2015, it grew by just 0.5 percent.

Globally, growth in demand for electricity from 2012 to 2016 – except for the Asia Pacific region – was nearly flat.[3] Global growth in demand was just 2.2 percent in 2016 and 1.6 percent in 2015; it trailed the 2.8 percent ten-year average growth rate. Demand for electricity in emerging economies had risen since 2010. In 2016 it grew by 4.0 percent compared to 2.6 percent in 2015. In fact, increasing global demand for electricity was primarily a phenomenon in the world's largest emerging economies. Japan, on the other hand, was a drag on demand growth. In 2016, demand for electricity fell in Japan by 3.2 percent.

## Gradually Moving Away from Fossil Fuels

The types of fuels the world used to meet the demand for power was shifting gradually from a reliance on fossil to non-fossil fuels.[4]

- In 1973, about 75 percent of the world's generation of electricity came from coal, oil, and natural gas, but in 2016, this number had fallen to 66 percent.
- Oil was the fossil fuel with the largest decline, from 24.8 percent of electricity generated in 1973 to but 4.1 percent in 2015.
- Natural gas, on the other hand, went from 12.1 percent of the electricity generated in 1973 to 22.9 percent in 2015.
- Nuclear energy went from 3.3 percent of electricity generated in 1973 to 10.6 percent in 2015.
- Renewables went from 0.6 percent of electricity generated in 1973 to 7.1 percent in 2015, an increase of nearly 92 percent.
- Hydropower, however, fell from 20.9 percent of electricity generated in 1973 to 16.0 percent in 2015.

Coal remained the world's largest source for electricity generation. In 1973, it totaled 38.3 percent of the electricity generated globally and in 2015, the figure stood at 39.3 percent, a slight increase.

In the United States, about 80 percent of mined coal was used for the production of electricity, about 14 percent exported, and about 6 percent used by industry.[5] Coal's main industrial uses were for the production of steel and cement. The largest US coal company was Peabody Energy.[6] In 2016, it had a market share of about 10 percent. The next largest US coal company was Arch Coal with a market share of about 8 percent in 2016.[7] Both companies were in decline. Peabody Energy's revenue fell by 12.3 percent in 2015 and by 15.2 percent in 2016. It lost $185.5 million in 2013, $80 million in 2014, $922 million in 2015, and $404 million in 2016. Arch Coal's losses were even steeper. Its revenue dropped in each of the years from 2012 to 2016 from 2.6 to 20.0 percent and it lost from $474 million to $2,865 billion.

In China, in contrast to the United States, the dominant state-owned coal-mining companies had a combined market share of slightly more than 40 percent in 2015.[8] Coal was critical to China's industrialization, yet the revenue of the large state-owned coal mining companies in China had also dropped. From 2012 to 2015, the revenue decline of Chinese coal companies was greater than 30 percent, though in 2016, these companies regained some of their lost ground.

## The Decline of Coal in the United States

The use of coal in the United States fell off for a number of reasons. Extensive pollution control standards put in place because of coal's negative health effects curtailed growth. The 1970 and 1977 Clean Air Acts mandated emission reductions that forced new plants to install expensive systems to curtail pollution and older plants to end operations unless the utilities that owned these plants comprehensively remodeled them. EPA's 2011 mercury and air toxics standards continued to compel utilities to make expensive changes. Another concern that led to reduced growth in the use of coal arose from the greenhouse gases that coal-fired power plants emitted. Their emissions of carbon dioxide per unit of electricity generated were far greater than electricity plants that relied on natural gas. Under the 2015 Paris Accord, the US goal was to reach a 26–28 percent reduction in greenhouse gas

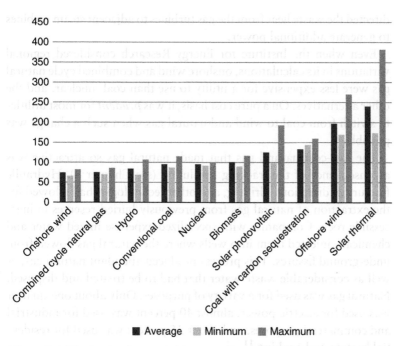

■ Average  ▓ Minimum  ■ Maximum

**Figure 7.1** The levelized cost of electricity ($/megawatthour)
Derived from Institute for Energy, The Levelized Cost of Electricity from
Existing Generation Sources, 2016

emissions by 2025.[9] Thus, state-by-state mandates called for less use of
coal; if the mandates were carried out, many coal-fired plants would
have to be shut down.

In any case, it was more expensive to generate electricity from coal
than wind or natural gas. Based on Department of Energy figures, the
Institute for Energy Research calculated the levelized cost of new generation of different methods in 2016 (Figure 7.1).[10] Its calculation took
into account capital, fixed costs, and fuel, transmission, variable operations, and maintenance costs based on a 30-year cost recovery period,
using a 6.1 percent real after tax weighted average cost of capital.
The lowest cost technology, onshore wind, was an intermittent source
of power; for a utility's baseload it was not reliable. The lowest cost
non-intermittent generation method was combined cycle natural gas.
Combined-cycle relied on gas and steam turbines to produce as much as
50 percent more electricity than one-cycle plants. The technology

directed the waste heat from the gas turbines to adjacent steam turbines to generate additional power.

Even when the Institute for Energy Research considered regional variations in its calculations, onshore wind and combined cycle natural gas were less expensive for a utility to use than coal, nuclear, and the other alternatives. On a pure cost basis, it was *prudent* for most utilities to switch from coal to wind and natural gas when such a change was possible.

The low-cost natural gas that made natural gas so attractive was a consequence of the fracking revolution (see Chapter 4). Hydraulic fracturing, directional drilling, and other technologies had allowed for the extraction of natural gas from previously buried reserves in inaccessible rock. Companies with specialized expertise mixed water and chemicals, injected them into wells where the natural gas flowed from underground fissures. This process produced abundant natural gas, as well as considerable waste water that had to be treated and disposed. Natural gas was used for a variety of purposes. Only about one-quarter was used for electric power, almost 40 percent was used for industrial and commercial purposes, and about 35 percent was used for residential heating and cooking.[11]

Most top fracking companies in the United States were not large, integrated oil and natural gas firms. The exception was ExxonMobil which had acquired XTO. Other large fracking companies included Chesapeake Energy, Andarko, Devon Energy (the successor to Mitchell Energy), Encana, ConocoPhillips, Southwest Energy, Chevron, Williams Energy, and BP. Because of fracking, natural gas prices had declined or smoothed out in most parts of the United States. The price of natural gas had been as high as $8 per 1,000 cubic feet in 2008. Eight years later it was as low as $2.50 per 1,000 cubic feet.[12] If winters in the United States were particularly cold, demand for natural gas could surge and prices increase.

For all these reasons, natural gas overtook coal as the top US source for electric power generation in 2016.[13] Many coal-burning power plants were retired from production between 2011 and 2016. Coal production in the Appalachian region was down by a half. However, converting coal-fired power plants to natural gas was mostly a US phenomenon, mainly because fracking had not come to China or Europe where natural gas was significantly more expensive, as much as twice to three times its cost in the United States.

## The Restructuring of the US Electric Utility Sector

The US electric utility sector had evolved over time as a result of a series of reorganizations. To understand the sector, the history of these reorganizations is worth reviewing.[14]

Shareholder-owned utilities produced a high percentage of the power in the United States. Monopoly franchises had exclusive service territories and a government-mandated obligation to serve. Their status as monopolies had been justified by the need for greater efficiencies and economies of scale. As redundancies in overhead power lines were a waste, electric utilities were viewed as natural monopolies. Public utility commissions (PUCs) regulated the rates they charged, allowing them to recover infrastructure, operations, maintenance, and other costs plus earn an acceptable rate of return. In determining the rate of return, the PUCs had to balance the interests of the utilities' consumers, who wanted low electricity prices, and investors, who wanted maximum profits.

In addition to shareholder-owned utilities, some government-owned utilities existed. A prominent example was the Tennessee Valley Authority (TVA). In some regions, publicly owned utilities, such as the TVA, generated most of their power from hydroelectric dams the government had been instrumental in building.

The 1935 Public Utility Holding Company Act limited the size of US shareholder-owned utilities. Their expansion, however, continued from the 1940 to 1970s, as demand for electricity increased, consumption grew, and large central power plants were needed. In constructing these plants the aim was to provide reliable power and to keep the costs of electricity as low as possible. The utilities were fully integrated entities. The power plants they owned generated electricity. The transformers they managed converted the electricity from low to high voltage for efficient transport. At substations they converted the electricity back to low voltage for distribution to homes, offices, and factories.

Managing this system presented many challenges, however. The electricity could not be stored and demand was not constant. Yet the system had to be built to supply power when demand was at its apex. Thus, the system had to be built with overcapacity so it could meet the highest levels of demand.

*Consolidation*

Starting in the 1990s, US investor-owned utilities began a process of consolidation; they merged, acquired other utilities, and moved from their home bases in one state across state lines. The result of this activity was that Duke, Southern, and Nextera became the largest US investor-owned utilities.[15] Each was headquartered in the South, Duke in Charlotte, North Carolina, Southern in Atlanta, Georgia and Nextera in Juno Beach, Florida. Other large US investor-owned utilities were Exelon of Chicago, Illinois and Dominion Resources of Richmond, Virginia.

Each of these utilities had somewhat different specializations.[16]

**Coal and Natural Gas Generation:** Duke and Southern were the largest coal and natural gas generators in the United States. Duke, which merged with Progress (formerly Carolina Power & Light) in 2012, increased its revenue from coal and natural gas power via the merger by more than 50 percent. Over 60 percent of its 2016 revenue of about $23 billion came from coal and natural gas power production. The company owned and operated more than 58,000 megawatts of generation capacity and had 7.2 million customers in a service territory that extended 104,000 square miles. It maintained 250,200 miles of distribution and also owned and operated more than 4,300 megawatts of generation capacity in Latin America and Saudi Arabia, and it had natural gas holdings as well as being an electricity producer. Duke's operating income increased by double digits every year from 2012 to 2015, but in 2016 declined by 1.4 percent.

Like Duke, Southern was a very large utility. It owned and operated more than 42,000 MW of generation capacity and had 4.3 million customers in four states – Alabama, Georgia, Florida, and Mississippi. It served 120,000 square-mile territory and had 27,000 miles of distribution lines. About 40 percent of its revenue of about $20 billion came from coal and natural gas production. Yet, it was gradually retiring some of its coal-generating capacity. The company's operating income varied from an 18.8 percent increase in 2015 to a 26.2 percent decrease in 2013.

NextEra also was very big, but in some ways it was very different than Duke or Southern. This was because it not only had a combined capacity of 42,500 megawatts of natural gas, nuclear, and oil capacity, but it was also the largest owner and operator of wind and solar in North America. It owned eighty-five wind farms in seventeen US states and three Canadian provinces and was the co-owner and operator of Solar Energy Generating Systems (SEGS), which was the world's largest solar power generating facility.

**Nuclear Generation:** Exelon and Dominion were the largest nuclear utilities. Exelon achieved this status when it merged with Pepco, which served the states of Delaware, Maryland, and New Jersey. About a third of its $33 billion in revenue came from nuclear power. It owned and operated 35,000 megawatts of electricity and produced, traded, and distributed power in forty-seven states, Canada, and Columbia, South America. Dominion Resources owned and operated about 24,000 megawatts of electricity and maintained 64,000 miles of electric transmission lines.

**Transmission, Distribution, and Wholesale:** Exelon also specialized in transmission, distribution, and wholesale. In 2012, it merged with Constellation which allowed it to expand its wholesale sales and its involvement in natural gas. Exelon's operating income therefore varied from going up 96.3 percent in 2015 to going down 75 percent in 2012. Other large transmission, distribution, and wholesale utilities were PG&E and Southern Cal Edison in California.

As a point of comparison, the largest Chinese electric utilities, unlike US electric utilities, were state-owned monopolies supported by the government.[17] The major players were State Grid which had a market share of about 80 percent and China Southern Power which had a market share of around 17 percent. State Grid had assets worth close to $500 billion by 2015 and its revenue was more than $330 billion. It was ten times the size of Exelon. It had seen double-digit growth revenue for nearly a decade until 2015 when revenue fell by 2.9 percent. China Southern had a similar profile. Though it was only a fifth the size of State Grid, by US standards it still was very large. It had about $75 billion in revenue in 2015. Its revenue growth fluctuated from 23.1 percent in 2008 until 2015 when it fell by 2.9 percent. China wanted to cut down the size of these large state-owned behemoths. It was in the midst of transmission and distribution deregulation which it started in 2014.

*Deregulation*

US electric utilities had undergone a process of gradual, partial, and ultimately flawed deregulation.[18] Until the late 1970s, their status as monopolies rarely had been challenged. The oil shocks of the era, however, led to a search for lower energy costs. In addition, environmental awareness had grown. A movement toward deregulation therefore arose. It rested on a number of important legal changes. The most important of them was the 1978 Public Utility Regulatory Policies Act (PURPA), which allowed avoided cost pricing for energy that utilities purchased from qualified third parties. In this way, the government opened one part of the utilities' business, generation, to competition. A number of states granted independent power producers (IPPs) the right to produce and sell power to the utilities.

At the same time, the utilities became reluctant to build additional capacity because of high costs, long lead times, and uncertainty about whether the capacity would be needed. Thus, with some reluctance, they welcomed this change. By the early 1990s, many utilities also sought the right sell their excess generation as their load growth often did not meet their expected demand levels.

Many state governments moved toward this type of deregulation in this period. The Federal Energy Regulatory Commission, in its 1996 Order 888, opened up transmission to all suppliers, incorporated the IPPs more fully into the system. The first state to take the plunge completely toward deregulation was California. It created an entire system to access and to transmit the generation of the wholesale power IPPs sold to the utilities. Other states followed. Large commercial users hoped that deregulation would bring lower prices, but these experiments did not always work. The design of the Californian system was flawed in that it relied too heavily on spot markets for the utilities' purchase of electricity. Reliance on spot markets led to excessively high costs when California experienced unusually high temperatures in 2000–2001 and the demand for power skyrocketed. The California Electric Utility Restructuring Law took effect in 1996 with the intent of increasing competition and lowering electricity prices. However, the 2000–2001 drought and heat wave significantly raised electricity prices because of the plan's heavy spot market dependence. The insufficient supply of electricity led to blackouts. The then Governor Gray Davis declared a state of emergency. Though the state was in dire need, Enron traders withheld electricity from the California market and subsequently faced charges of price manipulation. The main utility serving Northern California, PG&E filed for bankruptcy and the main utility serving Southern California, Southern California Edison, was in dire straits. The California deregulation initiative backfired and led to the recall of Governor Davis and his replacement by Arnold Schwarzenegger.

The Federal Regulatory Commission's antidote was to introduce long-term contracts, but this cure for a defective design came too late and after the fact. As a consequence, the national movement for deregulation stalled. California suspended its deregulation initiative, but twenty states still maintained some form of competition. To contain and lower prices, some states required that their utilities entirely divest their generation holdings. Others permitted the utilities to hold generation assets but only as affiliated companies. Still others required a functional separation between generation and other tasks the utilities carried out like transmission and distribution. In the Midwest and Southeast, twenty-six states entirely rejected deregulation. After what happened in California, other states repealed or suspended the restructuring in which they were involved, delayed starting it, or limited their programs, for example, by restricting them to only large customers who could purchase their power directly from the IPPs.

Even so, partial deregulation did reshape the industry in that it allowed new IPPs to emerge. They managed unregulated generation assets they accumulated, generated power using these assets, and sold it to utilities and other parties needing electricity. The largest of the new IPPs were NRG, Calpine, and Dynegy.[19] Regulated utilities such as Exelon, NextEra, and PSEG also participated in this market, selling excess power on the open market. In the second decade of the twenty-first century, the IPPs were earning about 14 percent of the revenue from electricity generation in the United States. The investor-owned utilities still earned about 60 percent of this revenue. Generating power with unregulated assets was inherently riskier than generating power as a regulated entity. It was riskier since the entity selling the power was not protected from price fluctuations. The IPPs benefitted when prices went up, but their economic fortunes declined when prices went down.

## Regional Coordinating Organizations

Starting in 1999, the Federal Energy Regulatory Commission (FERC) attempted to create more order in the system by *suggesting* to the utilities that they establish regional transmission organizations (RTOs) to coordinate their activities.[20] Within the RTOs, IPPS and new transmission developers could compete with established utilities.

As the establishment of the RTOs was voluntary, not all regions complied with the FERC order. The Pennsylvania, Jersey, Maryland Power Pool (PJM) was an RTO that coordinated the movement of wholesale electricity in all or parts of these states as well Delaware, Illinois, Indiana, Kentucky, Michigan, North Carolina, Ohio, Tennessee, Virginia, West Virginia, and the District of Columbia. The Midcontinent Independent System Operator (MISO) did the same for all or parts of fifteen states in the upper Midwest and the Canadian Province of Alberta. New England's independent system operator administered wholesale power markets and trading in electricity and transmission in six states in the region. The Southwest Power Pool coordinated power delivery in parts or all of fourteen states: Arkansas, Iowa, Kansas, Louisiana, Missouri, Montana, Nebraska, New Mexico, North Dakota, Oklahoma, South Dakota, Texas, and Wyoming.

Some states, however, opted out of these arrangements. They did not want to be burdened by costs if the benefits crossed state lines and they could not fully capture them. For the most part, the state of Texas remained separate and independent and it had its own Electric Reliability Council. California was also mostly independent and had its own system administrator. Large parts of other states in the West and the Southeast resisted forming regional transmission organizations and therefore lacked the means to coordinate wholesale electricity sales and reliably transmit power. They did not form RTOs because the 1999 FERC order was voluntary. Nonetheless, the order did mandate regional planning and cost allocation for transmission construction so the states had to find ways to work together.

As a result of a system of inconsistent coordination, the building of new transmission fell behind. Another reason it lagged was that regulated utilities had to give access to unregulated entities, the IPPs, that wanted to use the transmission to sell and move the power they produced. This requirement took away some of the incentive that the regulated utilities had to build transmission. Thus, investment in this important part of the system often stalled.[21] Station equipment, poles and fixtures, overhead lines and devices, underground lines and devices, towers, and other fixtures did not keep up with demand. During the 2003 Northeast blackout, awareness of this problem was acute, which gave impetus to efforts to redress it.

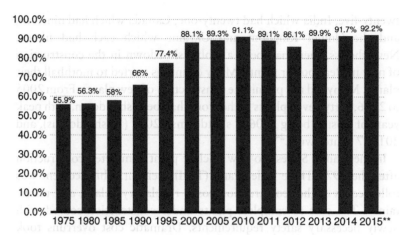

**Figure 7.2** Capacity factors of US nuclear power plants: 1975–2015
Derived from Nuclear Regulatory Commission Statistics

## Nuclear Spinoffs

Another development was that many regulated utilities spun off their nuclear generation capabilities. Many utilities in the United States had either abandoned having nuclear power plants of their own, or they had divested the running of these plants. By 2016, nearly half of nuclear power generation were in this category.[22]

Nonetheless, the United States still had the most nuclear power plants in the world, and it was operating them efficiently, running them with few unexpected interruptions and high capacity factors (Figure 7.2).[23] Although the United States had more nuclear power plants than any other country, its nuclear utilities were generally smaller than nuclear utilities in countries such as France, Russia, and South Korea. For example EDF, the French nuclear utility, ran all of that country's plants, while Exelon, the largest of the US nuclear utilities, had control over only a relatively small proportion of US plants.

There were about 100 nuclear power plants in the United States, France had fifty-eight, which supplied around 80 percent of that country's electricity, and Japan had forty-three, but was shutting down a large part of its nuclear power plants because of Fukushima. Other countries with large commitments to nuclear were Russia, which had thirty-five plants, China which had thirty-two, South Korea which had twenty-five, India which had twenty-one, Canada which had nineteen, and the United Kingdom and Ukraine which each had fifteen. Nevertheless, there had been a global slowdown in the construction of new nuclear power plants. Many countries started to mothball their plants. Many did not permit the construction of new plants. From 2005 to 2016, forty-seven plants in the world had been shut down, with peak years of closure being 2006 (8 shutdowns), 2011 (13 shutdowns), and 2015 (7 shutdowns).[24]

In the United States, no new nuclear plant completed construction after the 1979 Three Mile Island (TMI) accident. This accident was followed by higher construction costs, regulatory delays, and uncertainty. The cost to complete plants under construction soared with newly necessary safety requirements. Dramatic cost overruns took place at many plants under construction, and many were cancelled before their completion. The demand for electricity did not justify the construction of new nuclear facilities in any case, as it did not increase as much as anticipated in the United States in the 1980s. Thus, the need for large new nuclear plants did not exist. Then came the major incidents at Chernobyl in 1986 and Fukushima in 2011 that exacerbated fears and accelerated plant closures in the United States and abroad.

Nonetheless, outside the United States and countries like Germany, the construction of new nuclear power plants continued. China, Russia, and India were not deterred by these problems. In 2012, the United Arab Emirates started to build its first nuclear power plants. In the same year, Georgia Power obtained permission to construct two new nuclear reactors in the United States as did South Carolina Electric and Gas. The original costs had been $14 billion, but they ballooned to $23 billion. This overrun resulted in the bankruptcy of Toshiba's nuclear division (see Chapter 1), which it had purchased with much fanfare from Westinghouse Electric. It nearly led to the company's complete demise. Georgia Power continued in its attempt to complete the nuclear plants it started, but South Carolina Electric and Gas dropped out.

## Renewable Inroads

Renewable energy, meanwhile, made inroads as a means of generating electricity. One reason for this was concern about climate change. For the electric utility industry the quandary was that at 30 percent, it was responsible for the highest percentage of US greenhouse gas emissions.[25] Though other sectors contributed – transportation produced about 25 percent of the emissions, other industries about 20 percent, the residential and commercial sector about 12 percent, and agriculture about 10 percent – electric utilities were the largest emitters.

## Greenhouse Effects

The concern was not just with carbon dioxide. Other greenhouse gases were methane, nitrous oxides, and a variety of others. Carbon dioxide was the source of about 55 percent of greenhouse gases, methane was the source of about 30 percent, nitrous oxides about 10 percent, and other gases the remainder. These gases blocked solar radiation from escaping into the atmosphere. The greenhouse effect took place when solar radiation passed through the atmosphere. Some of it was absorbed and warmed the earth and some reflected outward and was lost in space. However, not all of it escaped into the atmosphere. Greenhouse gases prevented solar radiation from leaving the atmosphere. Some trapping of solar radiation was perfectly normal; it made the earth's climate tolerable in comparison to that of other planets. However, the higher the concentration of greenhouse gases, the greater the blockage that took place; and the greater the blockage that took place the warmer the atmosphere became. The concentration of greenhouse gases could increase to a point where the climate could heat up in an extremely dangerous way.

The following were among the most troubling negative impacts that an increasing concentration of greenhouse gases could cause:

- more extreme weather such as droughts and hurricanes;
- the melting of glaciers and ice sheets;
- sea levels rising and flooding;
- small island states disappearing;
- wildfires growing in number and severity;
- oceans becoming substantially warmer;
- the destruction of coral reefs;
- the alteration of animal migration patterns;
- unpredictable and increased levels of rain and snow;
- severe changes in plant life cycles, with negative impacts on agriculture and food production.

The impact on agriculture was ambiguous. On the one hand, increased concentration of greenhouse gases could yield longer growing seasons, while on the other less arable land would be available and the soil would be drier, which would mean reduced food production. Particularly vulnerable to the negative impacts of climate change were developing nations, if their food supplies were threatened.

## Global Agreements

Globally, the world had taken a number of steps to curb greenhouse gas emissions. The 1992 Rio Treaty, signed by George H. Bush and ratified by the US Congress, established a goal of "stabilization" of greenhouse gases at a level to "prevent dangerous interference with ... (the) climate system." Each nation in the world, under this treaty, would have a "common" but "differentiated" responsibility for addressing the problem, meaning that the industrialized nations, who were most responsible for the problem, had to act first. They owed a substantial amount of their affluence to the greenhouse gases they had emitted. For developing countries the highest priority was sustainable development, in effect meaning that that their economic growth came before their requirement to address greenhouse gas emissions.

The next step the world took after Rio was that in 1997 almost all nations signed the Kyoto Protocol. The world did not fully ratify the protocol until 2005 when Russia came on board. According to this protocol, industrialized countries had to reduce their average annual emissions by 5 percent in the years 2008–2012 in comparison to 1990. Some participants went further. The EU agreed to reduce its 2008–2012 average annual emissions to 8 percent below 1990 levels and the US seemed to have accepted a plan to reduce its 2008–2012 average annual emissions to 7 percent below 1990 levels. To achieve these goals, the industrialized nations could choose to buy emissions allowances and reductions from developing countries, or to buy them from each other, and could make these purchases instead of reducing their own emissions.

This plan did have great promise, but the US Congress refused to ratify US participation in it. The Clinton administration had agreed to Kyoto, but the Senate opposed it. The vote in the Senate was nearly unanimously against Kyoto. Even progressive Senators such as Minnesota's Paul Wellstone of Minnesota voted against it. The coal lobby claimed the

job losses that would accompany implementation would be unacceptable. The other argument Senators made against the protocol was that the
sole burden was on developed countries. Under Kyoto, developing
countries had no commitment to reduce their emissions. The Byrd-
Hagel resolution the Senate passed declared the issue would have to be
tabled until developing nations took on some of the burden.

*US Policies outside Kyoto*

In the absence of the United States signing the Kyoto Protocol, the
country did take steps to reduce its emissions. After 2009, the US EPA
assumed the obligation to regulate greenhouse gas emissions and barred
new coal power plants from construction without carbon capture and
sequestration (CCS) technology. As the expense of CSS technology was
so great, EPA's action, in effect, prohibited the construction of new
US coal-fired plants. Outraged, Congressional Republicans threatened
to strip the EPA of its authority, but in a historic decision, the Supreme
Court affirmed the EPA's right to regulate greenhouse gases.

In addition to the EPA's actions, California's Air Resources Board
attempted to obtain greenhouse gas reductions via a cap-and-trade
system. Starting in 2009, the states of Connecticut, Delaware, Maine,
Maryland, Massachusetts, New Hampshire, New York, Rhode Island,
and Vermont followed the lead of California and created their own
greenhouse gas cap-and-trade program modeled after California. After
the Great Financial Crisis, the federal government took additional
steps. The 2009 Recovery and Reinvestment Act put aside $57 billion
for energy infrastructure and efficiency, smart grids, renewables, and
transmission. Congress also maintained the wind-production tax credit
of 2.3 cents per kilowatt of electricity generated for any facility built
before 2020. However, the amount of the credit was set to decline
each year from 2017 to 2019. Congress also extended a solar investment and tax credit of 30 percent for residences and commercial
establishments through 2016 that helped the solar industry's revenue
grow, but concern also existed whether this incentive would continue.

*VC Funding*

Government policies were not the only driving force. Venture capitalists
(VCs) also played a role in helping to bring about growth in renewable

energy.[26] From 2004 to 2008, US VCs increased the amount of money they invested in various forms of renewable energy. The most active US private equity VCs were Khosla Ventures and KPCB and the most active corporate VCs were Intel Capital and Google Ventures. Initial returns had been high, but over time, the overall results were mixed. The degree of difficulty associated with introducing cleaner energy technologies was not low and the entrenchment of less-clean fossil fuel technologies was a formidable challenge. Questions existed about the potential size of the market for renewable energy technologies, whether customers would accept them, whether these technologies would work, and whether they could be produced at sufficient scale and at low enough prices. There were also questions about whether government policies to promote these technologies would be strong, predictable, and sufficiently effective to result in commercialization.

The extent to which VCs were a suitable vehicle for investing in cleaner energy was also questionable. A main reason was that the period for the full maturation of cleaner energy technologies was decades, while that for returning a significant payoff to VC investors was under ten years. Even so, many VCs did provide financing to renewable energy companies and in the first decade of the twenty-first century, in particular, they funded promising startups.

## Renewable Energy Progress

From 2005 to 2014, countries throughout the world added large amounts of wind and solar capacity. Texas became the US wind energy leader. It achieved this status because it faced fewer of the legal constraints that prevented other states from building the transmission needed to transport wind energy to major population centers.[27] Other states with significant wind resources like Minnesota could not keep up with Texas because they were much more deliberate in building transmission. By 2016, Texas' wind energy capacity was nearly 18,000 Megawatts (MW). The state had nearly three times the wind capacity of any state. Behind Texas were Iowa and California with about 6,000 MW of wind energy capacity apiece. Minnesota, which had wind potential equal to, if not greater than, Texas had just around 3,000 MW of capacity in that year.

The global leader in wind energy installations, though, was China. Projections were that in the future, renewable energy would maintain a rapid growth rate. However, the mix among renewable energy additions was forecast to change. By 2020, solar was expected to overtake wind.[28] Wind additions would increase slightly, while solar, as prices continued to come down, could take off. The world's leading solar adopter had been Germany. Other countries making rapid progress in solar were Spain, Japan, and Italy. However, all these countries cut their subsidies, a main reason being budgetary constraints. Their actions reduced the chances that solar would meet ambitious targets that forecasters predicted.

The most common PV type was crystalline silicon.[29] It could reach efficiencies of about 16 percent in converting sunlight to energy. Crystalline silicon efficiencies were higher than thin film. Thin film could do no better than convert sunlight to energy at 13 percent efficiencies. The main disadvantage of crystalline silicon was that it weighed more, but because it was more efficient it required less space than thin film. Due to high silicon prices, crystalline silicon had been more expensive than thin film in 2009–2010. However, when silicon prices dropped in 2011 crystalline silicon sales grew rapidly and took the lead. Crystalline silicon had the majority of the global market in 2016. On the horizon was multi-junction crystalline silicon; it set efficiency records of 46 percent, but was far more expensive to produce and it had a very small market share in 2016.[30]

The remaining solar option consisted of concentrated solar. The advantage over PVs was greater potential for energy storage. However, the costs were far higher. Concentrated solar projects needed extensive Department of Energy loan guarantees to succeed. California was the leading state in utility scale solar power installations followed by Texas and Florida. Many US states had no installations of this nature.

At the same time that the world was increasingly adopting renewable energy technologies, energy efficiency was growing. The carbon intensity of major economies in the world was falling. Total $CO_2$ emissions from energy consumption per dollar of GDP were expected to continue to go down as the economies in the world deindustrialized and used less energy.[31] Carbon intensity in the United States and Europe had been falling since the 1990s, but China's carbon intensity had grown at the same time as manufacturing that once had taken place in developed countries shifted to that country. China's economy carbon intensity went up, but it was expected to peak and to start to decline as the country met its commitment under the Paris accord and invested in clean energy.

### Companies with the Capabilities of Benefitting

The rise in renewables benefitted companies that had capabilities in these fields. GE became the main US producer of wind power systems.[32] It had more than 35 percent of the US market for wind energy in 2016. The German company Siemens and the Danish company Vestas were also significant players in the United States and each controlled about 15 percent of the US market in that year. These companies' revenues and profits from selling wind power systems varied greatly from year to year, however.[33] GE's revenue from wind power peaked at more than $7 billion in 2012 and its profits in that year were almost $1 billion, but in 2013, the company's wind revenues declined by 83 percent and its profits fell by about 86 percent. In 2016, the company's wind revenue recovered to around $5 billion, but its profits were just $0.35 billion. Erratic government policies were to blame. In 2013, uncertainty existed about whether Congress would renew US wind energy subsidies. The experience of Siemens and Vestas in the United States was similar to GE's experience. Like GE, Siemens and Vestas suffered in 2013. Siemens and Vestas lost just about all their US revenue. However, by 2016, the situation improved, both companies recovered, and they both had about $2 billion of US wind energy revenue.

With about 20 percent of the US market, First Solar was the main US producer of PVs in 2016.[34] SolarWorld was in second place with about 17 percent of the US market that year. First Solar was the world leader in thin film (cadmium telluride) cells. However, it did more than make cells. It manufactured, designed, installed, constructed, financed, operated, and maintained solar systems. It had manufacturing plants in Malaysia, Vietnam and Germany as well as the United States. However, because of slack demand for thin film solar, the Vietnam and German plants were up for sale. First Solar had total revenue of about $3 billion in 2016. Except for 2015, its US business revenues fell every year from 2011 to 2016. It posted net losses in 2011 and 2012 and from 2013 to 2016 it had operating income of just between $25 and $43 million annually in the United States.

The second major US solar producer was SolarWorld.[35] It was a German based company with US manufacturing in Hillsboro,

Oregon. Like First Solar, it was fully integrated and did more than manufacture solar cells, and, like First Solar, it also had financial difficulties. Its US revenues fell sharply every year from 2012 to 2015. In 2016, it made a recovery and its US revenues grew by about 28.5 percent; however, the only year from 2011 to 2016 that SolarWorld had profitable US operations was 2014. Its losses in this period ranged from $0.8 million to around $0.26 billion.

Major Chinese producers dominated the global solar PV market.[36] They included the CHINT Group, JA Solar Holdings, Jinniu Energy, Suntech Power, Yingli, China Sunergy, and Hanwha SolarOne. Almost 40 percent of the revenues of the Chinese companies came from exports. Their focus was on crystalline silicon cells, though they did make some thin film cells. Their costs had fallen with the fall in silicon prices. Their output grew at the rate of about 20 percent annually from 2010 to 2016. They provided inexpensive cells and panels to US and European installers and took advantage of European subsidies; however, the European market was weakening. Many countries pulled back on their solar commitments. The number of new solar projects in Europe declined. Therefore, the Chinese manufacturers faced a slowdown in 2016. Increasingly their sales would have to come from Asia, where demand had been growing at double-digit levels. They benefitted from a feed-in-tariff which the Chinese government had introduced in 2011.

NextEra, NRG, and SunEdison were the main owners of large-scale US solar power installations.[37] Yet NextEra only had a US market share of about 4.8 percent, NRG about 4.7 percent, and SunEdison about 4.2 percent. NextEra had installations in New Jersey, New Mexico, Nevada, and Canada. NRG had sixteen installations. David Crane, its CEO in 2016, was a well-known spokesperson for renewable energy. He was eventually fired for his failure to deliver consistently positive financial results from his company's renewable investments. SunEdison had sixteen projects in the states of Texas, Nevada, Arizona, California, Delaware, and North Carolina. In 2016, it went bankrupt because of its aggressive expansion plans. All these companies were also involved in wind energy. NRG, for instance, had thirty-six wind farms and SunEdison had acquired First Wind in 2014.

The installation of solar panels in the United States had become a more profitable business than the manufacture of solar panels.[38] Total estimated revenue in 2016 was $10.3 billion. About 35 percent of the revenue came from roof-mounted panel installation, 25 percent from solar tracking panel installation, 20 percent from ground mounted panel installation, 15 percent from fixed rack panel installation, and 5 percent from monitoring. The largest US installers in 2016 were SunPower and SolarCity, each controlling about 3.5 percent of the market. These companies benefitted from low-cost Chinese imports. They were harmed by tariffs. When the US Coalition for American Solar Manufacturing (CASM) got the Department of Commerce to impose a tariff of from 2.9 to 4.7 percent on Chinese manufacturers, it raised the costs of the US installers and slowed solar's US diffusion.[39] The Trump administration continued with these policies of imposing tariffs of solar panel imports, which went against the interest of the installers and led to declines in their business.

## The Paris Agreement

The breakthrough part of the Paris Climate Agreement was that both developed *and* developing countries had agreed to limit their greenhouse emissions. This compromise was reached when developed countries promised to aide poor nations to help them meet their commitments. If climate disasters took place that disproportionately affected poorer nations, developed countries would come to their assistance. The parties also agreed that if the science supported an increase they would increase their commitments. Though the agreement was historic, it did not go far enough inasmuch as the caps, which the parties accepted, were still likely to lead to a warming of 2.7–3.0 degrees centigrade above pre-industrial levels.[40] Many scientists warned that breaching the 2.0 degree centigrade threshold would result in irreversible droughts, floods, heat waves, and sea level rise.

The Obama Clean Power Plan – designed to cut utility carbon emissions 32 percent from 2005 levels by 2033 – came after the signing of Paris Accord. Under this plan, each state had the right to choose how to accomplish this goal. It could use some combination of natural gas, efficiency, nuclear power, and renewables to reduce emissions.

The Obama plan came on top of renewable portfolio standards and goals that thirty-seven states and the District of Columbia had adopted. States like California and Colorado aimed to generate 33 percent of their electricity using renewables by 2020. Illinois, Minnesota, and Oregon promised to generate 25 percent of their electricity using renewables by that year. These states had met, or were very close to meeting, these targets. For the states in the Northeast, however, achieving the goals they had set for themselves in their renewable portfolio standards would be difficult, as they lacked inexpensive onshore wind.

Almost no Southeastern region state adopted a renewable portfolio standard. Politics played a role, as did the influence of the large utilities that relied on coal-fired power like Duke and Southern, but another important factor was the lack of renewable potential in states that had little inexpensive wind and only moderate potential for inexpensive solar energy. These states had high biomass potential but the development costs for biomass were still very high. Few anticipated that Trump would win the presidency and then his administration would try to end US participation in the Paris Accord.

## What Comes Next?

By 2040, the electric utility companies faced many possibilities. Below is a list of what might happen by 2040 – a list that is by no means comprehensive, as the risks and uncertainties with respect to what might happen next are very great.[41]

- Many governments might scale down their ecological targets because of a series of economic crises: climate protection would be of secondary importance, with growth and employment issues being the first priority.
- Energy consumption might grow significantly as private households stepped up their use of mobility, increased automation of homes, heating, and other conveniences.
- Carbon capture and storage systems might be able to reconcile the goals of climate protection with the use of fossil energy sources.
- The Internet of Things might coordinate power generation and consumption; all electrical appliances would autonomously report their energy demand online and respond to supply and price movements, with lower overall power consumption.
- Only a few technical functions, such as operation of networks, might remain within the sphere of responsibility of electric power companies, while electricity would be generated by many small producers and network management would become the domain of international IT companies.

- Major internet companies and the data and IT industry might become the largest energy players given their capability to process large data volumes and their ability to manage supply and demand on an automated basis.
- The growing middle classes in emerging economies such as China and India might force their countries' governments to adopt even more stringent sustainable energy policies.
- Policy makers' top priority would be to fight environmental pollution and a rising share of growing energy demand would be renewable.
- The largest CO2-emitting countries might take decisive action to change course as a result of a series of ecological disasters; sustainable energy systems would have to be promoted, and economic and energy policies would have to be aimed at fighting climate change.
- A global climate regime with binding and ambitious targets for the reduction of carbon emissions might be in place.
- An effective regional system for the pricing of carbon emissions (e.g. emissions trading or a carbon tax) could be in operation.
- Changing values in society might turn a sharing economy into a reality; the new paradigms would be ecological efficiency, consumer restraint (sufficiency), and the dematerialization of production.
- Consumers might expect businesses, products, and services to be sustainable on a comprehensive scale. Sustainable products would be mainstream. Non-sustainable forms of production would be considered unethical.
- China might extend its lead as the world's largest developer of sustainable energy technologies and the dominant innovator in this field.
- An all-electric society might become a reality.
- Electricity, especially power generated from renewable sources, would also provide mobility and heating, and displace petroleum and natural gas in many industrial processes.
- A consequence of the expansion of intermittent renewable energy generation would be that uninterrupted availability of electricity would no longer be a standard service offered by energy companies, but would become an extra service to be purchased separately by the customer.

For energy industry businesses, unclear as to which of these and many other possible developments were most likely and why, what might take place next was not apparent. The impacts on other sectors in the energy industry – oil and natural gas and motor vehicles – were also unclear. Yet long-range strategic investments had to be made with their payoffs being extremely uncertain.

## Notes

1. *"Lower Residential Energy Use Reduces Home Energy Expenditures as Share of Household Income."* www.eia.gov/todayinenergy/detail.php? id=10891
2. IBIS World Industry Report, "Electricity Transmission and Distribution in China." 2015.
3. *"IEA World Energy Outlook 2016."* www.iea.org/media/publications/weo/WEO2016Chapter1.pdf
4. Ibid.
5. IBIS World Industry Report, "Coal Mining in the US." 2016.
6. Ibid.
7. Ibid.
8. IBIS World Industry Report, "Coal Mining in China." 2015.
9. *"What Is US Commitment in Paris."* https://blogs.ei.columbia.edu/2015/12/11/what-is-the-u-s-commitment-in-paris/
10. *"The Levelized Cost of Electricity from Existing Generation Sources."* www.instituteforenergyresearch.org/wp-content/uploads/2016/07/IER_LCOE_2016-2.pdf
11. IBIS World Industry Report, "Natural Gas Distribution in the US." 2016.
12. IBIS World Industry Report, "World Price of Natural Gas." 2016.
13. *"Natural Gas Overtakes Coal as Top US Power Source ... "* www.stltoday.com/business/local/natural-gas-overtakes-coal-as-top-u-s-power-source/article_4077bac1-bc70-5659-a834-57c6cb23488a.html
14. Navigant, "Evolution of the Electric Utility Industry Structure in the US and Resulting Issues." 2013.
15. IBIS World Industry Report, "Coal and Natural Gas Power in the US." 2016.
16. Ibid.
17. IBIS World Industry Report, "Electric Transmission and Distribution in China." 2015.

18. "Evolution of the Electric Utility Industry Structure in the US and Resulting Issues," Prepared for Electric Markets Research Foundation by Navigant Consulting, Inc., Washington, DC, October 8, 2013.

19. IBIS World Industry Report, "Electric Power Transmission in the US." 2016.

20. Fremeth, Adam, and Alfred A. Marcus. "The Role of Governance Systems and Rules in Wind Energy Development: Evidence from Minnesota and Texas." *Business and Politics* 18 (2016): 337–365.

21. Ibid.

22. IBIS World Industry Report, "Nuclear Power in the US." 2016.

23. *"Number of Operable Nuclear Reactors"* www.statista.com/statistics/ 267158/number-of-nuclear-reactors-in-operation-by-country/

24. Ibid.

25. *"Global Greenhouse Emissions Data."* www.epa.gov/ghgemissions/ global-greenhouse-gas-emissions-data

26. Marcus, Alfred. *Innovations in Sustainability: Fuel and Food.* Cambridge, UK: Cambridge University Press, 2015.

27. Fremeth and Marcus.

28. *"IEA World Energy Outlook 2016."*

29. *Innovations in Sustainability.*

30. IBIS World Industry Report, "Solar Power in the US." 2016.

31. *"IEA World Energy Outlook 2016."*

32. IBIS World Industry Report, "Wind Turbine Manufacturers in the US." 2016.

33. Ibid.

34. IBIS World Industry Report, "Solar Power Manufacturing in the US." 2016.

35. Ibid.

36. IBIS World Industry Report, "Solar Panel Manufacturers in China." 2016.

37. IBIS World Industry Report, "Solar Farm Development in the US." 2016.

38. IBIS World Industry Report, "Solar Panel Installation in the US." 2016.

39. *Innovations in Sustainability.*

40. *"The Paris Climate Accord Didn't Go Nearly Far Enough ... "* www .thenation.com/article/the-paris-climate-accord-didnt-go-nearly-far-enough-can-bonn-do-better/

41. *"Delphi Energy Future 2040."* www.pwc.com/gx/en/energy-utilities-mining/pdf/delphi-energy-future.pdf

# PART III

# Oil and Natural Gas Company Strategies

# 8 | Strategies to Try to Offset Plummeting Prices: ExxonMobil

This part of the book moves to the responses of individual companies to the conditions sketched out in prior chapters. The purpose of this chapter is trace the responses of ExxonMobil to changing conditions in the years 2012–2016, when there were particularly volatile oil prices, and to consider where it might go next with its strategies. The chapter starts with an introduction to the company and then goes on to cover the condition of the company between 2012 and 2014, before the dramatic fall in oil prices that took place, and between 2014 and 2016, after the fall. From 2011 to 2014, the average price of a barrel of oil was above $93. In 2015 it fell below $50 a barrel, a drop of close to 50 percent, and it continued for the next three years to be priced at approximately this level. How did ExxonMobil view the situation? What were the risks and uncertainties it supposed it confronted, its assumptions about the future, and the hedges it put in place to protect itself against the losses it experienced? To what extent did the price shock affect its performance? To what extent did it change the strategies it pursued because of plummeting prices?

## ExxonMobil in 2012

In 2012, Brent crude oil averaged $111.67 per barrel, slightly above the 2011 average of $111.26. With the price of oil this high, ExxonMobil was the subject of an *Economist* article entitled "Oozing Success."[1] Not only was it the largest of the integrated oil and natural gas companies at the time, it also was the most profitable. If it were a country, its revenues would have made it the twenty-first among world countries in GDP.[2] However, as the *Economist* pointed out, many criticisms had been directed at the company, including that its product was one of the most polluting in the world, that its search for oil and gas had entangled it in messy situations throughout the globe, and that its fierce support for climate-change skepticism had aroused the ire of environmental groups.

159

To achieve the position as the world's top oil company in 2012, ExxonMobil had surmounted many obstacles. In the 1950s, when the firm still went under the name of Standard Oil of New Jersey, US oil supplies had started to diminish. No longer was the company as welcome in countries in which supplies were ample. To compensate, it embarked upon a worldwide search to replenish its dwindling oil stocks, which led it into politically fraught situations throughout the globe.[3] Then came the 1989 Exxon Valdez oil spill, which forced it to tighten up its operations.

The next serious challenge it confronted was climate change. With Lee Raymond as CEO from 1999 to 2005, the company conducted a disinformation campaign against the science of climate change.[4] Rex Tillerson followed Raymond as CEO and gradually moved ExxonMobil from a position of extreme climate change rejection. Under Tillerson, the company, like other oil companies, called for a carbon tax. However, it remained firmly committed to the oil and natural gas industry and not to the alternatives. Its concessions to alternative energy were minor, unlike BP, which at a similar point in time branded itself as being "beyond petroleum."

## The Drop in Oil Prices

Among private oil companies, as shown in Chapter 5, ExxonMobil had the world's largest oil and gas reserves, but it was far behind national oil companies like Aramco, NIOC, and Gazprom. ExxonMobil also stood out for its refining and chemical businesses, which, in 2012, contributed more to its revenues than upstream oil and gas exploration, though they were less profitable. The drop in oil prices, which took place in 2015, changed this situation (Figure 8.1). By 2016, ExxonMobil had no upstream profits whatsoever. Downstream revenue drastically declined, almost by half, but at least the downstream part of the business continued to be profitable.

Having upstream and downstream assets was a hedge the integrated oil and natural gas companies erected against the contingency that prices might fall. If prices fell, then downstream raw material costs would drop as well and they would more than make up for poor upstream performance. The year 2015 was a turning point, however, in showing how imperfect this hedge was. The profits ExxonMobil earned from the downstream part of its business were no match for the

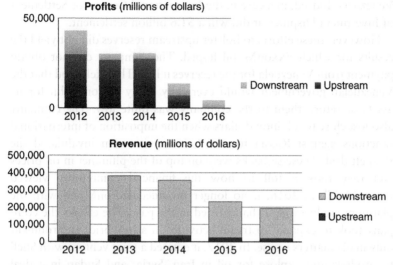

**Figure 8.1** ExxonMobil profits and revenue 2012–2016
Derived from Company Annual Reports

profits it lost when the upstream part of the business turned sour. In facing this challenge, ExxonMobil was not alone, as all major global integrated oil and natural gas companies had made this hedge. Now all of them had to deal with the issue.

In the period of high oil prices, most of ExxonMobil's capital spending, and as well as that of other major integrated oil and natural gas companies, was bound up in upstream investments, since this was where they could earn large profits. The companies supported upstream spending at the expense of downstream, because downstream profits, though steady, were not as spectacular. For instance, in 2008, ExxonMobil had phased out of the retail market in the United States and sold or franchised most of its service stations, because they did not meet its profitability standards. On the other hand, the company expanded its upstream activities, when it acquired XTO in 2010. Among other reasons, this was in order to gain a foothold in oil shale and natural gas production. In 2011, it entered into a strategic cooperation deal with the Russian national oil company Rosneft to gain access to Russian reserves. In the next year, it made a deal to produce and explore for oil and natural gas in the Kurdistan region of Iraq, and in the following year, it tried to recover production assets it lost in

Venezuela. Indeed, in a case in the International Centre for Settlement of Investment Disputes, it did win a $1.6 billion settlement.

However, these efforts to bolster upstream reserves did not yield the results for which ExxonMobil hoped. The company did not obtain payment from Venezuela for the reserves it lost. The likelihood that the Venezuelan government would ever fully repay ExxonMobil for its assets or return them to the company was quite low. The company also lost close to a billion dollars when the imposition of international sanctions against Russia for the Crimean invasion invalidated the Rosneft deal. These setbacks were on top of the plummet in oil prices and they took a toll in how the financial community viewed ExxonMobil; in 2016, it no longer provided ExxonMobil with the platinum credit rating it had earned in the past. The efforts the company took to expand upstream activities in a low-price environment only made matters worse. In 2017, it entered a joint venture with Shell to produce and explore for oil in Iran, Syria, and Sudan in a deal running counter to US sanctions against these countries. The company's argument that it was working with a European-based firm, which was not under US jurisdiction, did not stand up to scrutiny. The attempt ExxonMobil made to expand and protect its upstream holdings in such places as the shale basins of the United States, and in Venezuela, Russia, Iraq, Iran, Syria, and the Sudan did not succeed.

## Climate Change Pressures

At the same time, the company became vulnerable to attacks that it had allegedly concealed prior knowledge of climate change. Pressure, for instance, came from the Rockefeller Family Fund (RFF). Family members of the company's founder, who controlled this fund, accused ExxonMobil of failing to disclose the findings of its past research on climate change and of distorting the evidence.[5] When they chose to divest their holdings from the company, they admitted to be turning against the firm that had created most of their wealth.

ExxonMobil denied the charges the family members made, but the denial did not stop the New York attorney general in 2015 seeking documents to determine whether the company had lied to investors and consumers and kept information about climate change effects secret.[6] The pressure intensified when the Center for International Environmental Law released decades-old documents that appeared to show that the firm had investigated and understood fossil fuel climate change impacts for a number of years.[7] Attorneys general from various states then demanded the release of information about the company's research and its funding of climate change denial advocacy. ExxonMobil vigorously fought these actions, calling the accusations against it inaccurate and misleading.

At its 2016 annual meeting, the company was inundated with climate-related demands.[8] This meeting was raucous. It required that the company warn those present about rules of conduct, which prohibited inappropriate comments, and other types of interference with the meeting, such as the distribution of literature. Of eight shareholder proposals concerning climate change made at the meeting, one did pass and with a 62 percent majority. Support for the proposal came from the company's largest shareholders, such major financial backers as BlackRock, Vanguard, State Street, and CALPERs. This proposal gave shareholders (with 3 percent or more of the company's shares for more than three years) the right to nominate a quarter of the board. Activists believed the proposal would lead to the appointment of a climate advocate to the board. The company faced another hostile proposal at its 2017 annual meeting. In a non-binding resolution, over 62 percent of shareholders voted that the company should conduct a detailed assessment of the impacts of climate change on the firm.

The Securities and Exchange Commission (SEC) also had concerns about the value of ExxonMobil's upstream assets. In a significant move in 2016, it compelled the company to write down the value of its oil reserves by about a fifth.[9] Other oil companies had taken these actions voluntarily, but ExxonMobil had refused and the SEC had to force the company to do a write-down. The research group Carbon Tracker concluded that oil companies were wasting trillions of dollars in investments in oil development.[10] Their investments would generate 380 billion tons of carbon dioxide by 2035. Within a decade, demand for oil would decline, and ExxonMobil, with the most stranded assets of any oil company, had the most to lose.

Darren Woods, who replaced Rex Tillerson as CEO, accepted that ExxonMobil should take the climate change issue more seriously and make changes in its approach. Along with other companies, ExxonMobil was part of the Climate Leadership Council, which advocated for a gradually rising and revenue-neutral carbon tax with carbon dividend payments to American families. It also continued to participate in the activities of the US National Research Council and the Intergovernmental Panel on Climate Change (IPPC), the United Nations body that was responsible for the assessment of climate change.

## Prior to and After the 2014–2015 Price Collapse

A more detailed examination of ExxonMobil's strategies before and after 2014–2015 follows. This assessment has been carried out based on a careful reading of the company's annual reports and other communications to shareholders.[11] In these documents, the company gave an account of its perceptions of the risks and uncertainties it confronted and its assumptions about the future. Based on these perceptions and assumptions, it offered justifications for the strategic choices it made. Like other integrated oil and natural gas companies, it hedged its bets about what it would do next. Its hedging strategy featured a focus on operations, especially safety; the upstream investments it needed to make to replenish its reserves; its downstream refining activities, which it had to streamline and modernize; and the R&D investments it made, which could lead to breakthroughs and provide it with future competitive advantage.

The company's moves in these four areas, the essence of a business model it adopted to protect it from current and future uncertainties, had significant implications for the company's performance. The company's performance then fed back and influenced the ways it adjusted its subsequent strategies.

### *Before the 2014–2015 Price Collapse*

#### Perceptions of the Risks and Uncertainties

Prior to the 2014–2015 price collapse, the risks and uncertainties that ExxonMobil acknowledged in its annual reports and other communications with shareholders were those of price volatility, government actions of various kinds, climate change, and timely completion of its ongoing projects.

#### *Price Volatility*

Just about the biggest risk the company confronted was price volatility. It admitted that energy price changes were very hard to control. They depended on demand and supply factors over which the company had little influence. Demand, for instance, was swayed by economic growth rates, which in turn were affected by population growth and decline, inflation and exchange rates, government spending, debt, and fiscal and monetary policies, not to mention civil unrest and the weather. Refining and petrochemical manufacturing capacity and technological change had an effect. So, too, did OPEC countries' production quotas, hostile actions, wars, natural disasters, and distribution and transportation channel openness and availability.

### Government Actions
A second important risk and uncertainty came from governments. Their influence was felt in many ways, including expropriation threats, taxes and royalty rates, price controls, transparency requirements, and environmental regulation. The company relied on the legal system to protect its property rights. However, even in countries with well-developed systems, it confronted uncertainty and litigation risks. As a US firm, it was subject to laws restricting it from doing business in many parts of the world and it needed the government's help to protect it from security concerns, acts of sabotage and terrorism, and cybercrime.

### Climate Change
ExxonMobil considered climate change and greenhouse gas restrictions a threat. It noted that countries were adopting or considering regulation to reduce greenhouse gas emissions such as cap-and-trade regimes and carbon taxes. They had introduced restrictions on permitting, which extended the firm's project implementation times. Countries might require carbon emission sequestration. They were tightening efficiency standards and providing renewable energy incentives and mandates, thereby shifting demand away from oil to natural gas. The subsidies they offered and mandates they established for alternative energy were altering consumer preferences, pushing consumers from gas-powered vehicles toward alternative-fueled ones.

### Timely Project Completion
For it to meet its financial goals, ExxonMobil had to bring oil and natural gas resources into production on schedule and within budget. This task was complicated by the negotiations it had to conduct with governments, suppliers, customers, joint venture partners, and contractors. The company also had to manage shifting operating costs, including managing the costs of vendor equipment and services such as

drilling rigs and shipping. Furthermore, it had to prevent and respond to unanticipated technical difficulties that could delay the completion of projects, while minimizing human error that could jeopardize safety or lead to spills. This process depended on models to optimize performance to complete complex, long-term, capital-intensive projects, but much could go wrong.

## Assumptions about the Future

Despite the growing importance of natural gas, renewables, and nuclear power, ExxonMobil was convinced that oil would remain the largest energy source in 2040. It predicted that oil would constitute 30 percent of global consumption and natural gas 25 percent. The energy source that would decline the most, according to its assumptions, would be coal, which would fall to 20 percent. Despite oil's continued dominance, its production would shift from conventional to non-conventional methods. The company also assumed international accords and national and regional regulations with respect to greenhouse gases were evolving with uncertain timing and outcome. The impacts would be movement toward natural gas to generate electricity and some improvement in renewables and nuclear power prospects.

### Oil's Dominance
The reasons for oil's continued dominance were that world population would grow from 7 billion in 2010 to between 8.8 and 9 billion in 2040. In addition, average GDP would increase 3 percent per year, and energy demand would rise by 35 percent. Under these conditions, 40 percent of energy demand growth would be for transportation fuels, 65 percent of it in developing countries, as their economies expanded and their need for these fuels increased, while demand in developed countries evened out with advances in efficiency. On the other hand, demand for energy would be flat in OECD nations even as their output increased, because of such factors as high-efficiency natural-gas power plants and such technologies as hybrid auto engines.

### Conventional Oil in Decline
Conventional oil production would decline. Thus, supply increasingly would have to come from deep-water fields and other less conventional sources, such as tight oil, oil sands, shale gas, and to an extent biofuels.

The cost of developing these resources in a responsible way would be significant. ExxonMobil predicted that the investment required to meet oil and gas energy needs worldwide from 2012 to 2035 would be about $19 trillion measured in 2011 dollars, or approximately $800 billion per year on average.

Greenhouse Regulation
The world would adopt policies to reduce greenhouse gas emissions, as well as to improve local air quality, but the timing and types of polices were uncertain. Regardless, the upshot of the policies was that worldwide demand for natural gas would grow and the prospects for renewable energy and nuclear power would improve.

- ExxonMobil projected that worldwide demand for natural gas would rise by as much as 65 percent from 2010 to 2040. A main reason would be growing demand for electricity. Demand would grow by 85 to 90 percent by 2040, with natural gas becoming the main source for generating this electricity, which would require new sources of supply. Thus, the natural gas found in shale and other rock formations would constitute roughly a third of global natural gas supplies, an increase from less than 15 percent in 2010. The worldwide LNG market would grow correspondingly and approach about 15 percent of global demand for natural gas by 2040.
- The prospects for energy supplied from wind, solar, and biofuels would improve. ExxonMobil anticipated that total energy supplied from wind, solar, and biofuels would grow about 450 percent from 2010 to 2040, though its combined share of world energy consumption would constitute just 3–4 percent. If biomass, hydro, and geothermal were included along with wind and solar in the count of renewables, renewables would reach about 15 percent of total energy consumed in 2040. Nuclear power would lag at about 11 percent because of the negative repercussions of the Fukushima nuclear power plant disaster.

*After the 2014–2015 Price Collapse*

Perceptions of the Risks and Uncertainties
The company's main concerns after the price collapse were weak margins and environmental laws and regulations. It also acknowledged ongoing turmoil in Europe.

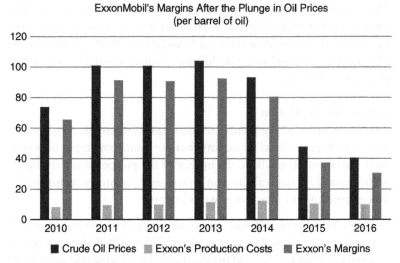

**Figure 8.2** ExxonMobil's declining margins
Derived from Company Annual Reports

## Margin Slippage

Declines in the price of oil threatened the company's margins. ExxonMobil was concerned that technologies to enhance recovery would lower prices and growth in demand would not offset greater supply. By unlocking abundant North American unconventional supplies, technological innovation was hurting the firm's margins. The margins the company earned were equal to prevailing oil and natural gas prices minus the costs of removing oil and natural gas from the ground. In 2014, its costs for removing a barrel of oil from the ground were about $13 a barrel. They did not vary that much from year to year. Thus, the key factor affecting profits was oil prices. As prices plummeted in 2014–2015, margins fell (Figure 8.2), the gap led to a lower breakeven point, and the company would have to write down reserves.

## Aggressive Environmental Laws and Regulation

ExxonMobil remained concerned about environmental laws and regulations that could prevent the company from engaging in offshore drilling, extracting oil from tar sands, and fracking. The costs of these projects were increasing at a time when the company could earn less because of falling prices. The company was involved in environmental lawsuits, claims, and legal proceedings, in which it had to pay significant damages, fines, and penalties for remediation of contamination.

## European Turmoil

ExxonMobil also showed concern about government austerity programs, sovereign debt downgrades, defaults, and the inability to access debt markets due to credit and legal constraints. It highlighted the role that a liquidity crisis could play; the breakup and the restructuring of fiscal, monetary, and political systems, such as the EU; and other events or conditions that could damage the global market.

## Assumptions about the Future

ExxonMobil lowered its expectation of energy demand growth in 2040 to 25 rather than 30 percent. It projected global GDP doubling by that year. It expected that improvements in energy efficiency and changes in the energy mix would slow the growth of $CO_2$ emissions, which would peak in 2030. By 2040, the global economy's $CO_2$ intensity level would be cut in half.

## Continued Demand Growth

ExxonMobil continued to anticipate that rising world population and burgeoning middle class, along with economic progress, would drive growth in energy demand from 2014 to 2040. New sources of energy would therefore be needed. Growth in energy demand would come mainly from non-OECD nations, whose middle classes would grow to three billion people. More energy also would be needed to reduce global poverty and advance the world's living standards. Oil would remain the largest global energy source. In 2040, its share would stay at close to one-third of consumption. Additional supplies would come from unconventional sources – deep-water oil, tight oil, and oil sands – and from increasing extraction from existing sources. Technology would underpin the gains. The costs would be significant. Investments to meet total oil and gas energy needs over the period from 2014 to 2040 were likely to be $28 trillion (measured in 2013 dollars), or more than one trillion dollars per year on average. Though the current market was long on supply and low on demand, in the future, there would be increased demand for oil driven by transportation and chemicals.

## CO2 Emission Restrictions

ExxonMobil remained concerned that international accords and underlying regional and national regulations covering greenhouse gas emissions continued to evolve with uncertain timing and outcomes, making it difficult to predict their business impact. Even with increasingly stringent policies relating to greenhouse gas emissions, the company anticipated a new era of energy abundance and diversity. This new era would emerge despite continued price volatility. Demand for natural gas would grow as a result of greater power consumption and increased need on the part of industry. Natural gas would meet 40 percent of the growth in energy demand, more than any type of energy. Most natural gas supply growth would come from fracking. Demand for LNG would also take off. It would triple by 2040, and demand for electricity would increase by nearly 85 percent, led by developing countries. While starting from a relatively low base, nuclear and renewables would have the highest growth rates among all types of energy. ExxonMobil would be faithful to meeting the dual challenge of mitigating climate risk and providing affordable and reliable energy. Its assumptions were in accord with commitments that countries had made in the Paris climate agreement.

## Hedging

Like other large integrated oil and natural gas companies, the approach ExxonMobil took to managing the risks and uncertainties, based on its assumptions, involved four layers of hedging: (1) maintaining operational excellence; (2) continuing to make upstream investments; (3) relying on downstream integration; and (4) carrying out high-impact R&D. Described next is how the company applied these hedges before and after the 2014–2015 price crash.

## (1) Operational Excellence

### Before the 2014–2015 Price Collapse

ExxonMobil prided itself on having rigorous operating systems, proven processes, and best practices and routines, to which it meticulously adhered. The goal of its Operations Integrity Management System (OIMS), created in the wake of the Valdez oil spill, was to ensure safety, reliability, and efficiency.[12] A sign that it worked was the company's industry-leading results in lost-time injuries and illnesses. ExxonMobil tried to scrupulously follow world-class project management methods in the efficient completion of large-scale, complex projects in challenging environments.

### After the 2014–2015 Price Collapse
A relentless focus on fundamentals was the key to reducing risk and maximizing reliability. Goals for operational integrity and excellence yielded high levels of personnel and process safety as well as an efficient cost structure and disciplined project execution. The company would not slip or skimp on safety and would retain its safety leadership. After the price collapse, it had a renewed interest in environmental impact and was systematically identifying, assessing, managing, and monitoring risks to reduce emissions and releases. It was focusing on reducing flaring, venting, and fugitive emissions in its refineries and on energy efficiency. It made use of cogeneration technology, when feasible. It owned a third of the world's carbon capture and sequestration capacity. It tried to engage in constructive dialogue with environmentalists. It had avoided 8.8 million tons of greenhouse gas and other emissions and made significant progress on spills.

## (2) Upstream Investment

### Before the 2014–2015 Price Collapse
Before the collapse, a number of themes dominated upstream investment including developing new oil and natural gas resources, with a greater emphasis on natural gas, and increased monitoring of the company's progress.

**Developing New Resources.** ExxonMobil had a disciplined approach to choosing attractive upstream projects. It set objectives in an annual planning process based on its long-term economic assumptions. It annually updated field production profiles and expected product prices. It tested the objectives it had against a number of scenarios to ensure their robustness and it reappraised and readjusted its decisions if needed. In this way, it evaluated opportunities across a range of market conditions and time horizons covering decades. It tested the viability of projects to ensure that it had identified and appraised relevant financial, commercial, environmental, and technical risks and that it could manage them effectively.

The company only approved projects with the potential to achieve superior returns and provide long-term shareholder value. To ensure profitable future growth it had a balanced portfolio of projects in forty countries. In 2012, its capital and exploration budget was $36 billion, and for the next five years, it was ready to spend another $190 billion, with the aim of initiating twenty-eight new project startups. Prominent examples of the projects it funded were oil sands and offshore oil projects in Canada, offshore oil projects in Angola, LNG projects in Papua New Guinea and Australia, and deep-water oil projects off the coasts of the United States. The company also had a strategic agreement with Rosneft, mentioned previously, to jointly assess and develop oil and natural gas resources in Siberia and North America. Natural gas represented a growing percentage of the company's project startups.

ExxonMobil was engaged in projects that required the use of specialized and sophisticated technologies like Arctic and deep-water drilling, heavy oil sands recovery, the construction of liquid natural gas facilities, and fracking. It aimed to grow North American oil and natural gas output from 32 percent to 35 percent in total volume by 2017 and increase its capacity for converting natural gas into LNG. The company had a diversified portfolio of projects, yet concentrated on extracting unconventional resources like heavy and sour oil from deep water and oil sands and from hard-to-access regions like the Arctic. Despite being dedicated to LNG, ExxonMobil viewed it as having an uncertain future, so long as pipeline-delivered natural gas was readily available. ExxonMobil closely monitored progress in achieving its goals. It reappraised its projects and adjusted them to improve performance and divested or abandoned projects when they no longer were viable.

### After the 2014–2015 Price Collapse

After the price collapse, ExxonMobil tried to become even more disciplined in the investments it made; it practiced greater selectivity in choosing projects, but did not desist from initiating new projects.

### A More Disciplined Approach to Developing New Resources

ExxonMobil did not back away from making investments in energy projects after the price collapse. It reemphasized the disciplined approach it used that focused on capital efficiency and creating value for shareholders. Nonetheless, it did require that the investments be smaller and tried to restrict them to very high-quality projects. In 2012, its plans were to invest between $35 and $40 billion per year over the next five years, but the 2014–2015 plunge in oil prices brought dramatic losses in the income the company earned from its upstream activities. The net income of the upstream division fell from over $27 billion in 2014 to about $7 billion in 2015, and in 2016, it again dropped to just $0.2 billion. In response, the company cut capital expenditures to about $30 billion in 2015, cut them again to about $25 billion in 2016, and had no plans for future growth. Its budget for exploration was 25 percent lower in 2016 than it had been in 2013.

To maintain a diverse portfolio of exploration and development opportunities under these conditions, the company had to be very selective in choosing which projects to approve. It tried, nonetheless, to maintain a diversified portfolio of conventional, unconventional, heavy oil, and LNG projects and to continue to pursue diverse, high-quality opportunities throughout the world. In 2016, it produced 2.3 million barrels of liquid fuels and 10.5 billion cubic feet of natural gas daily, and it had a fossil fuel stockpile consisting of 25 billion oil-equivalent barrels (BOEB) in twenty-four countries. It had 100 projects under investigation that had a potential to yield 91 BOEB. In 2015, it initiated six major projects, including ones involving offshore African oil and Canadian oil sands, and it added nearly 300,000 barrels per day to its production capacity. The projects started ahead of schedule and stayed within budget.

ExxonMobil planned to initiate ten more projects in 2016–17, including offshore Canadian and UAE oil projects. It was evaluating the potential of offshore Guyana resources, which could add 1.5 BOEB to its fossil fuel stockpile. It had ten shale projects underway and tried to make progress in developing US shale resources. Shale could potentially unlock more than 15 BOEB to the company's industry-leading fossil fuel stockpile. The company also tried to capitalize on growing global LNG demand, but it had to keep the costs as low as possible. The Asia Pacific region was showing promise as a place for additional resources development. ExxonMobil had significant assets in Papua New Guinea and elsewhere in the region. It was looking to develop assets in Australia and in East Africa.

Despite less money available for investment, ExxonMobil was committed to these projects, convinced that the size and diversity of its project inventory, along with its financial strength, gave it the flexibility to invest despite its financial difficulties. Assisting it was a decline in project costs, with upstream costs falling by as much as 30 percent compared to 2014. The company did not consider peak energy demand to be a real threat. Despite warnings that as much as half the money it spent was at risk if the world vigorously moved in the direction of meeting its climate change targets, ExxonMobil dedicated more than 80 percent of its 2016 capital and exploration expenditures to upstream projects.

## (3) Downstream Investment

### Before the 2014–2015 Price Collapse
Before the price collapse, ExxonMobil tried to maintain downstream revenues at a profitable level by heeding the downstream challenges it faced.

**Heeding Challenges.** The company cultivated its downstream assets, which were the source of most of its revenue, if not its profits, as a hedge against upstream problems. In 2012, the downstream assets consisted of thirty-two refineries closely tied to the upstream assets. In addition to gasoline, they produced a mix of commodity (e.g. plastics) and specialty (e.g. high-end polymers and lubricant additives) chemicals. The company relied on geographic and product diversity to maintain stability. It expanded in Singapore to increase its ability to sell lucrative premium products in economically growing Asia.

Downstream assets provided stable earnings through the business cycle. As oil and natural gas were the main input, they benefitted when oil and natural gas prices fell. However, ExxonMobil understood that the downstream industry environment was challenging because of demand weakness and refining overcapacity that put pressure on margins. Volume might grow but profits would not increase. The company, thus, aimed to reset its downstream portfolio to take advantage of the fact that some regions had stronger margins than others did. It divested less profitable facilities in Latin America, Malaysia, Switzerland, and Japan, while constructing new ones, such as a joint Saudi Aramco venture that produced low-sulfur fuels.

### After the 2014–2015 Price Collapse

After the price collapse, downstream did not quite live up to the counter-cyclical balancing role it was supposed to play. Despite ExxonMobil's initiatives, operating downstream remained challenging.

**Not Living Up to Its Countercyclical Role.** Downstream was supposed to play a balancing role in generating cash that would allow the company to meet its financial obligations and maintain returns if upstream revenue and profits weakened. If prices plummeted, the company had access to low-cost feedstock. Lower oil prices translated into less expensive raw materials, thus providing the company with a resilient business model. Downstream margins did grow after the price collapse, but not as much as anticipated. Overcapacity, competition, and weak and declining demand limited downstream financial performance. Downstream prices fell as well as upstream prices. The low prices negatively affected both parts of the business. Downstream therefore was not a perfect hedge. Its performance correlated too much with upstream performance. ExxonMobil did not compensate for upstream weakness with downstream strength.

After the price collapse, the company still had to address downstream weakness. It had thirty refineries in seventeen countries. There were somewhat fewer refineries than prior to the oil price collapse. The refineries continued to turn crude oil into gasoline, jet fuel, and a variety of products. To increase the refineries' revenue and profits, the company expanded production in some, and it introduced new high-value products. Nonetheless, the long-term outlook was that refining margins would remain low as new capacity outpaced growth in demand. To counter these trends, ExxonMobil tried to enhance the efficiency of its refineries and improve their logistics. It developed a proprietary hydrocracking process to improve how it made lubricants and how it manufactured low-sulfur diesel fuel. It became involved with Saudi Arabia in a joint venture to make rubber. These actions, though, could not prevent downstream's ongoing decline. Sales continued to fall; in 2016, they were 30 percent lower than they had been at their peak in 2003.

### *(4) High Impact R&D*

#### Before the 2014–2015 Price Collapse

Another hedge was carrying out high-impact R&D. The company had a variety of upstream, downstream, and environmentally related projects. It divided its one billion dollar R&D budget in the following ways.

**Upstream.** The bulk of the investments benefitted the upstream business, such as early reservoir modeling using seismic technology and high-performance computing, drilling record-length wells, and producing oil and natural gas in harsh environments such as ultra-deep water and the Arctic.

**Downstream.** Projects of benefit to downstream included improvement in motor oil fuel economy and in flexible packaging.

**The Environment.** The goal of other projects was to reduce the company's environmental footprint. Since 2009, ExxonMobil had invested $0.6 billion into an algae-based biofuels project. It was also carrying out research into alternative energy and carbon sequestration. In addition, the company was a main sponsor of a global climate and energy project at Stanford University.

### After the 2014–2015 Price Collapse

Despite its weakened financial position, ExxonMobil tried to keep R&D spending at a level of more than a billion dollars per year, making slight cuts in 2014, but restoring spending to this level by 2016. The company justified R&D spending by claiming that its success depended on technological leadership. Its commitments were to fundamental science and scalable applications, enhanced long-term value, and profitability through innovation, discovery, and technological leadership.

**Upstream.** The goal of upstream R&D was to improve profitability by means of high-performance computing, extended-reach drilling, and hydraulic fracturing.

**Downstream.** The downstream goal, also to improve profitability, was to work on advanced motor oils and performance plastics.

**The Environment.** The purpose of these initiatives was to reduce emissions and carbon intensity. The company had interests in carbon capture and storage, second-generation algae, and biofuels. It pursued innovations in the reduction of methane emissions, internal combustion engine efficiency, power-generation technologies, automotive light weighting, reduced packaging, and industrial process efficiency.

The company had ongoing interests in climate science, economics, policy, and renewable energy systems. It was not just seeking to reduce its own emissions, but also to help consumers reduce their emissions. In supply options and efficiency savings, it secured partnerships with universities and private sector companies, such as Georgia Tech, Purdue, Berkeley, TDA Research, ECN, Fuelcellenergy, Michigan State, the Colorado School of Mines, Synthetic Genomics, and REG.

## Performance

### *Before the 2014–2015 Price Collapse*

In 2012, ExxonMobil's results had been stellar. It had earnings of $45 billion. It had peer-group leadership on return on capital employed (ROCE) of 25 percent. It made 2.9 billion oil-equivalent barrels (BOEB) of discoveries in a host of countries – Australia, Canada, Nigeria, Papua New Guinea, Romania, Tanzania, and the United States – and achieved 115 percent replacement of its proved reserves, the nineteenth consecutive year it did so. The following year's results showed slippage on every front: earnings fell to $32.6 billion, return on capital invested declined to about 18 percent, and reserve replacement barely reached the 100 percent level. The bulk of the earnings decline was in the company's downstream operations.

### *After the 2014–2015 Price Collapse*

Despite the strategies ExxonMobil used, it could not stem the tide of continued performance decline. Its 2016 revenue was more than $200 billion lower and less than half what it had been at its peak in 2011; and its 2015 earnings were more than $20 billion lower and less than half what they had been at their peak in 2012. Its return on average capital (ROACE) employed fell by more than half its average in the previous five years, and the company reported reserve replacement rates of less than 100 percent. Proven reserves declined 20 percent from 2011. The US Security and Exchange Commission forced it to write down the value of its reserve estimates. Total debt grew from $11.581 billion in 2012 to $38.687 billion in 2015. In 2015, net debt to capital rose to 16.5 percent from 1.2 percent in 2012. The company, therefore, had to dedicate a substantial portion of its cash flow to debt payments.

## Trying to Stay the Course – The Correct Response?

ExxonMobil, like other companies in the oil and natural gas sector, confronted a largely unexpected and massive fall in the oil prices in 2014. Prices peaked at roughly $110 a barrel in June of that year and by the end of the year declined by nearly 50 percent. This chapter has examined how ExxonMobil responded to plummeting prices. To what extent did it change its assessments of the risks and uncertainties? To what extent did its alter its assumptions and adjust a strategy that it used to hedge itself against such possibilities? How effective was it in hedging its bets in an environment of low oil prices?

The company analyzed the risks and uncertainties and made assumptions based on the analysis. It made adjustments, but behaved largely as it had in the past. It tried to stay the course in response to plummeting oil prices. Accommodating to some extent the external pressures – it could not avoid them entirely – it exhibited some flexibility and made incremental changes. It altered its tone and policies with regard to climate change. It remained committed to operational excellence. It expected petroleum to have continued dominance, but had to impose additional discipline on its upstream investment choices. Nonetheless, it persisted, albeit at a lower level, in making big bets on the discovery and development of new oil and natural gas fields throughout the world and tried to accumulate additional reserves to replace the oil and natural gas consumed. The company also recognized that the downstream parts of its business had become less competitive. The downstream part of the business needed modernizing and restructuring. It was not as good a hedge against the weakness in the upstream part of its business. At the same time, the company maintained a high level of R&D investments to bolster its capacity to develop and sell oil and natural gas, and reduce environmental impacts in the future. Still, its performance suffered, though it made these adjustments

The effect of the collapse in prices on ExxonMobil's performance was clearly negative. Could the company have done better had it followed a different path? Of greater significance is to ponder what it should do next

# Notes

1. *"Oozing Success."* www.economist.com/books-and-arts/2012/08/11/ oozing-success
2. Ibid.
3. Coll, Steven. *ExxonMobil and Private Power.* New York: Penguin, 2012.
4. *"Inside an Investigation into Exxon Mobil's Climate Change Misinformation."* www.theverge.com/2017/8/23/16194366/exxon-mobil-knew-climate-change-misinformation-harvard-study
5. *"The Rockefellers vs. the Company That Made Them Rockefellers."* http://nymag.com/daily/intelligencer/2018/01/the-rockefellers-vs-exx on.html
6. *"Exxon Mobil Investigated for Possible Climate Change Lies by New York Attorney General."* www.nytimes.com/2015/11/06/science/ exxon-mobil-under-investigation-in-new-york-over-climate-statements .html
7. *"Oil industry knew of 'serious' climate concerns more than 45 years ago."* www.theguardian.com/business/2016/apr/13/climate-change-oi l-industry-environment-warning-1968
8. *"Exxon Mobil's Shareholders Meeting Was Totally Overrun by Climate Demands."* https://grist.org/climate-energy/exxon-mobils-sharehold ers-meeting-was-totally-overrun-by-climate-demands/
9. *"Exxon Has Wiped a Whopping 19.3% of Its Oil Reserves off Its Books."* https://qz.com/917178/exxon-wiped-19-3-of-its-oil-reserves-off-its-books-in-2016/
10. *"Oil and gas companies 'risk losing $2tn.'"* www.bbc.co.uk/news/busi ness-34921867www.bbc.co.uk/news/business-34921867
11. *"ExxonMobil Summary Annual Report 2012."* https://cdn.exxonmobil .com/~/media/global/files/summary-annual-report/news_pub_sar-2012 .pdf; "2012 US Security and Exchange Commission Form 10K Exxon Mobil Corporation." www.sec.gov/Archives/edgar/data/34088/0000034 08813000011/xom10k2012.htm
    *"ExxonMobil Summary Annual Report 2013."* https://cdn.exxonmobil .com/~/media/global/files/summary-annual-report/2013_exxonmobil_ summary_annual_report.pdf; *"2013 US Security and Exchange Commission Form 10K Exxon Mobil Corporation."* www.sec.gov/ Archives/edgar/data/34088/000003408814000012/xom10k2013.htm
    *"ExxonMobil Summary Annual Report 2014."* https://cdn.exxonmobil .com/~/media/global/files/summary-annual-report/2014_summary_ annual_report.pdf; "2014 US Security and Exchange Commission Form

10K Exxon Mobil Corporation." www.sec.gov/Archives/edgar/data/340 88/000003408816000065/xom10k2015.htm
*"ExxonMobil Summary Annual Report 2015."* https://cdn.exxonmobil .com/~/media/global/files/summary-annual-report/2015_sar_new.pdf
"2015 US Security and Exchange Commission Form 10K Exxon Mobil Corporation." www.sec.gov/Archives/edgar/data/34088/00000340881 6000065/xom10k2015.htm
*"ExxonMobil Summary Annual Report 2016."* https://cdn.exxonmobil .com/~/media/global/files/summary-annual-report/2016_summary_ annual_report.pdf
*"2016 US Security and Exchange Commission Form 10K Exxon Mobil Corporation."* www.sec.gov/Archives/edgar/data/34088/0000034088 17000017/xom10k2016.htm

12. *"Operational Integrity Management System."* https://cdn.exxonmobil .com/~/media/global/files/energy-and-environment/oims_framework_ brochure.pdf

# 9 | Strategies to Try to Offset Plummeting Prices: BP

The purpose of this chapter is trace the responses of BP to changing conditions in the years 2012 to 2016, when there were particularly volatile oil prices, and to consider where it might go next with its strategies. The chapter starts with an introduction to the company, emphasizing the Deepwater Horizon disaster, whose legacy BP found hard to shake. It then goes on to cover the state of the company between 2012 and 2014, before the dramatic fall in oil prices that took place, and between 2014 and 2016, after the fall. It asks the same questions about BP that the last chapter asked about ExxonMobil. How did BP view the situation? What were the risks and uncertainties it confronted, its assumptions about the future, and the hedges it put in place to protect itself against the losses it experienced? To what extent did the price shock affect its performance, and to what extent did it change the strategies it pursued because of the drop in prices?

## The Legacy of Deepwater Horizon

Unlike ExxonMobil, which was in a very strong position prior to 2012, BP was in distress because of the lingering impacts of the 2010 Deepwater Horizon oil spill, the largest in history, which resulted in unprecedented damage. The spill was an economic, legal, public relations, and human disaster. Guilty of eleven counts of felony manslaughter, two misdemeanors, and a felony count for lying to Congress, BP had to make the largest criminal payment in US history, more than $4.5 billion. It also came to terms with five states to clean up the damages, which cost it $18.5 billion. Overall, the company lost upwards of $60 billion because of the incident.[1] Even for a large, integrated oil and natural gas company like BP, that amount was substantial.

The company was not new to controversy. BP had a reputation for taking risks and had committed many safety breaches.[2] Even in the 1960s it had the worst safety record in the sector. In 1967, it was responsible for the Torrey Canyon oil spill off the British coast. In 1995, John Browne became CEO and moved the company in the direction of aggressive expansion.[3] In 1998, it merged with AMOCO, at the time one of largest US integrated oil and natural gas companies. In 2000, it acquired another large US oil and gas firm, Arco. With these acquisitions, BP became second in size to ExxonMobil among US oil and natural gas companies. It remained headquartered in London. From there it was active in more than seventy-two countries.

Browne tried to repair the company's poor safety record. However, after the acquisitions BP was strapped for cash. Neither Browne nor his successor Tony Hayward had sufficient funds to upgrade worn-out facilities. Thus, BP continued to have safety incidents.[4] In 2005, fifteen workers died and more than 170 workers sustained injuries in a Texas City Refinery explosion. In 2006, a production platform in the Gulf of Mexico, known as Thunder Horse, almost sank in a hurricane because workers had installed a valve backwards. In the same year, corrosion on a pipeline in the Prudhoe Bay oil field on Alaska's North Slope resulted in a major oil spill. From 2007 to 2010, BP refineries in Ohio and Texas accounted for 97 percent of the "egregious" and willful" violations identified by the US Occupational Safety and Health Administration (OSHA).

Viewed in the context of these issues, the 2010 Deepwater Horizon accident was not a surprise. The only way BP could pay for the damages it caused was to sell about $38 billion of assets, after the spill. The largest sale was to the Russian oil firm Rosneft in 2012. BP obtained $12.3 billion in cash and a 19.5 percent stake in Rosneft, when the two parties ended a prior joint venture.[5]

Nonetheless, the oil spill hurt the company profoundly and led to a sharp decline in its share price. Under Bob Dudley, who succeeded Hayward as CEO in 2010, BP tried to turn the situation around, but it was not able to do so fully. While the S&P shot up by nearly 60 percent from 2007 to 2017, BP shareholders lost nearly 50 percent. From 2012 to 2014, the company's downstream refining business, though like ExxonMobil's constituting a much larger percentage of BP's revenues than upstream, was less profitable than upstream (Figure 9.1). In 2014, downstream had losses and upstream remained profitable, though upstream profits also went down. As was the case with ExxonMobil,

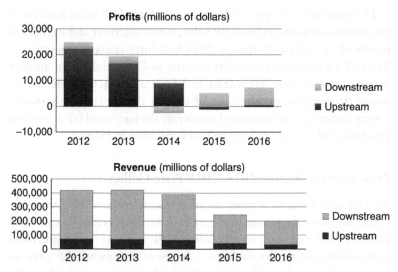

**Figure 9.1** BP profits and revenue 2012–2016
Derived from Company Annual Reports

however, this situation changed. In 2015, upstream lost money and all BP's profits were in the downstream part of its business.

## Climate Change

Among large integrated oil and natural gas company CEOs, BP's John Browne was the first to acknowledge publicly the threat of global climate change. In a 1997 speech at Stanford University, he stated, "we must now focus on what can and what should be done, not because we can be certain climate change is happening, but because the possibility can't be ignored."[6] He affirmed, "It falls to us to begin to take precautionary action now."[7] And he maintained that it was necessary "to go beyond analysis to seek solutions and to take action."[8] BP then adopted a green sunburst logo and rebranded itself as the company that was beyond petroleum. BP made many initiatives in the field of alternative energy. Between 2005 and 2011, it spent $8.3 billion on renewable energy projects that employed, at their height, over 5,000 people, yet activists criticized the company for greenwashing.[9]

The costs of the Deepwater Horizon spill forced BP to cut back on its green commitments. It closed BP Solar, a manufacturer and installer of photovoltaic solar cells that in 2011 had forty years of operation.[10] Tony Heyward, who succeeded Browne as CEO, claimed in another Stanford speech that renewables had been a distraction. He recommitted the company to safety, but BP did not abandon all its alternative energy initiatives and continued to operate thirteen wind farms in seven US states and to have an interest in a wind farm in Hawaii.

## Prior to and After the 2014–2015 Price Collapse

This chapter turns to a more detailed examination of BP's strategies before and after the plunge in oil prices. Like the previous ExxonMobil chapter, it is based on a careful reading of BP's annual reports and other communications to shareholders.[11] In these documents, BP gave an account of the risks and uncertainties and its assumptions about the future. Based on these perceptions and assumptions, it offered a justification for its strategic choices. Like ExxonMobil and other large integrated oil and natural gas companies, it hedged its bets focusing on: operations, especially safety; upstream investments; downstream refining; and R&D. These moves were the essence of a business model meant to protect and insulate it from uncertainty. They had implications for the company's performance, and the company's performance in turn influenced how the company adjusted its strategy.

## BP Before the 2014–2015 Price Collapse

### Perceptions of the Risks and Uncertainties
Though BP understandably emphasized operational safety more than ExxonMobil did, it recognized similar risks and uncertainties. The main risks it foresaw were price volatility, climate change, and the problem of completing projects on time.

### Operational Safety
Many factors could lead to safety incidents – natural disasters, extreme weather, human error, and technical failure. The company conducted activities in hazardous, remote, and environmentally sensitive locations. Significant incidents like Deepwater Horizon, as disastrous as they were, were hard to prevent. Most projects the company undertook relied on

contractors and sub-contractors, whose responsibility for damages was insufficient and whose safety standards could be lax. Cybersecurity was another concern, as breaches or attacks could disrupt operations and cause losses and liabilities. The company had to shore up prevention and response and be able to restore operations quickly.

*Price Volatility*
Like ExxonMobil, BP emphasized that its financial performance was subject to fluctuating oil and natural gas prices. Erratic shifts in supply and demand and volatile prices could destabilize margins, affect company investments, and invalidate the choices it had made. Prolonged low oil prices were a disincentive for making long-term investments. It impaired the value of the oil and natural gas properties the company owned. Inflation, on the other hand, made access to the resources needed to develop additional oil and natural gas supplies costly and uncertain. The company preferred stable prices, neither too high nor too low nor changing too often.

*Politics and Climate Change*
The diverse nature of its global operations exposed BP to political developments that could alter its operating environment. The company's concerns extended to OPEC actions, conflict situations, and other political developments. The regulatory climate and laws, with which it had to contend, had pitfalls. Like ExxonMobil, BP was worried about climate change. Carbon pricing policies could mean higher costs that could reduce future revenue and hinder further growth.

*Completing Projects*
Like ExxonMobil, completing projects on time and on budget also was a central concern. The company had to make good on the investment choices it had made. It was concerned that joint ventures and other contractual arrangements, as in the Deepwater Horizon spill, risked disrupting successful project execution. They would make it difficult to recover quickly and effectively from disruptions or incidents that occurred.

*Assumptions about the Future*

Like ExxonMobil, BP assumed that rising populations and increasing industrialization in previously poor nations would create strong demand for energy and continued dependence on fossil fuels.

According to BP, the world's population would grow by 1.3 billion from 2011 to 2030. Real income would double in this period, and energy demand and consumption would increase accordingly.

### Continued Demand

BP projected that energy demand and consumption would have to grow to meet the needs of an increasing population. About 93 percent of the growth would take place in non-OECD countries. It forecasted average increases in energy demand of 1.5 percent annually to 2035. The company imagined a future much like the past in which recoverable oil reserves grew over time. In 1981, the world's oil reserves had been about 700 billion barrels, while in 2011 they grew to 1,650 billion barrels, even though the world consumed 800 billion barrel of oil in the intervening decades. A reason to be optimistic about natural gas was fracking. BP predicted that from 2012 to 2035, shale gas would contribute 47 percent to the growth in global natural gas supplies.

### Climate Change

BP estimated that even under an ambitious climate-policy scenario, oil and natural gas would still represent 50 percent of world energy demand in 2030. Like ExxonMobil, BP assumed that meeting global energy demand required a diverse set of fuels and technologies, including unconventional ones such as oil sands, shale gas, deep water oil, natural gas, biofuels, and renewables. The company viewed renewable energy, growing at a 7.6 percent rate, as the fastest-growing energy source, but like ExxonMobil concluded that renewables, including biofuels, but excluding hydro, would meet a small fraction of global energy demand, under 6 percent by 2030. The company declared that without subsidies alternative energy was not competitive with fossil fuels. It noted that using natural gas instead of coal for electrical power could reduce $CO_2$ emissions by half.

## BP After the 2014–2015 Price Collapse

### Perceptions of the Risks and Uncertainties

After the price collapse, the company's assessment of the risks and uncertainties covered the problems of low prices and having an adequate pipeline of future projects. Climate change and other government policies continued to be perceived as risky and uncertain.

*Low Oil Prices*
The company's financial performance had been subject to fluctuating prices of oil, gas, and refined products. Factors that were hard to control shaped supply and demand and influenced prices, including fracking, technological change, OPEC, and changes in the global economy. Regardless of whether prices fell or climbed, so long as they were volatile, their impacts were hard to absorb. If prices went down, the company's revenue, margins, and profitability declined. A prolonged period of low prices would compel BP to question the viability of its current and future projects and write down a portion of its assets. On the other hand, a significant rise in prices, if accompanied by inflation, would make it harder to access and develop resources for.

*Bolstering the Project Pipeline*
BP depended on having a strong pipeline of future projects. Renewing the company's upstream resources and replacing its reserves was essential to its future performance. Obstacles to achieving this goal were technical and geographical challenges and heightened political risks. The political risks included expropriation and nationalization of property as well as sanctions, civil strife, strikes, insurrections, terrorism, and war. Given BP's large stake in the Russian oil company Rosneft, the company was especially concerned about Russia, in particular further trade restrictions that would adversely impact its Russian investments.

*Climate Change and Government*
Climate policies came on top of a host of other government requirements that made BP take stock of environmental, health and safety and controls in the drilling for oil and in the decommissioning of oil and natural gas fields. It already had to be wary of such policies as nationalization, expropriation, royalty and tax changes, and the cancellation or non-renewal of contract rights. Because of the threat of $CO_2$ and other greenhouse gases, BP was fearful that government policies would increase oil and natural gas costs, reduce future revenue, and limit its growth. It shared with ExxonMobil the view that carbon pricing via a well-constructed carbon tax or cap-and-trade system was the best way to limit greenhouse gas emission. Carbon pricing would affect the value of the company's assets, its costs, its ability to generate revenue, the demand for oil and natural gas, and its ability to grow. It would make energy efficiency more attractive and lower-

carbon energy sources, such as natural gas and renewables, more cost competitive.

## Assumptions about the Future

BP assumed a world of change in which all forms of energy – fossil fuels and renewables – would become more abundant and less costly. Its role was to provide the world the energy it needed for heat, light, and mobility, and create a lower-carbon world. It also had to get the remaining liability for the Gulf spill behind it. The changing landscape BP foresaw had short- and long-term components. In both, petroleum would remain the dominant transportation fuel.

### Short-Term Price Pressures

The energy landscape was changing, with demand moving from developed countries to emerging markets that needed energy to accelerate economic growth. Oil prices had been low since 2014, mainly because of oversupply. It would take time for an adjustment to take place. High inventories would continue. The company expected demand for oil to fall in the short term, with oil prices remaining under pressure.

### Long-term Possibilities

In the long term, the world was moving toward a lower carbon future, with the energy mix changing, driven by technological improvements and environmental concerns. BP had a main scenario and a number of alternatives. In the main scenario, it anticipated that the world economy would double in size in twenty years and that demand for energy would increase by around 30 percent. These estimates of world economic growth and demand for energy were about the same of those of ExxonMobil and the forecasts of DOE, the IEA, and OPEC (see Chapter 4). The emerging economies would be the leaders in future growth. In the future, there would be improvements in energy efficiency, a shift toward less energy-intensive activities, policies that incentivized low-carbon activity, and compliance with pledges made as part of the 2015 Paris climate accord. Nonetheless, BP assumed that renewables, other than hydro, would account for no more than 10 percent of consumption by 2035, and oil would still have around a 29 percent share. Throughout the world, natural gas would start to overtake coal in generating electricity. As a cleaner alternative to coal, the use of natural gas would grow. Natural gas would be up slightly to 25 percent of global energy consumption, placing it ahead of coal and not far behind oil.

This scenario was BP's main one, but it proposed alternatives in which oil and natural gas still would constitute about 50 percent of the 2030 energy mix and about 44 percent of the 2040 energy mix. Under the alternatives, the leading global economies price carbon at $100 a ton and the world takes effective action and limits the rise in global temperatures to 2 degrees Celsius. Renewables, other than hydro, then provide between 16 and 23 percent of the world's energy. The proportion provided by hydro and nuclear goes up from 12 to 15 to 17 percent, while coal declines from 23 to between 13 and 18 percent. The share of natural gas also declines, but only slightly. Emerging technologies, such as improved batteries, solar conversion, electricity storage, and autonomous vehicles, would advance. If 6 percent of all vehicles on the road became electric, then demand for oil would decrease by about a million barrels a day. There also would be significant growth in ride pooling and autonomous vehicles.

### Oil's Dominance

Regardless of how the world evolved, BP assumed that oil would remain the world's dominant fuel because it has advantages other fuels cannot match. The advantages are that oil is a liquid that is easy to transport and has high-energy density. Vehicles using oil can go further with less weight to bear than with alternative fuels. For transportation, oil is ideal and indispensable and therefore would continue to account for about 90 percent of transportation fuels in use. The upshot was that BP and the other oil companies had to develop new sources of hydrocarbons, even if they were difficult to reach, extract, and process. This conclusion was the same one that ExxonMobil had reached.

### Hedging

Like other large integrated oil and natural gas companies, the approach BP took to managing the risks and uncertainties, based on its assumptions, involved four layers of hedging: (1) maintaining operational excellence; (2) continuing to make upstream investments; (3) relying on downstream integration; and (4) carrying out high-impact R&D.

Described next is how the company applied these hedges before and after the 2014–2015 price crash. After the crash in oil prices, BP, like ExxonMobil, did not deviate much from these strategies, though how it carried them out shifted somewhat.

## (1) Operational Excellence

**Before the 2014–2015 Price Collapse**
To earn back trust and improve relations with governments, NGOs, and local communities, BP worked very hard to enhance safety after Deepwater Horizon. The core of BP's 2012 and 2013 strategy – its main priority – was to address the litigation from the oil spill. It fought for its interests in the courts, even as it still had very large Gulf commitments to meet, yearly payments into a $20 billion trust fund. BP needed to become a safety leader, and it did make some improvements. Recordable injury frequency for employees and contractors was better than in 2010, the year of the accident, but not significantly better than prior to the accident, and BP had not caught up to ExxonMobil, which had about one-third fewer injuries in 2013.

**After the 2014–2015 Price Collapse**
A relentless focus on safe and reliable operations remained BP's top priority, but despite striving to be one, it was still not a world-class operator. It gradually made improvements in a number of important indicators, like reported recordable injury frequency, process safety events, and loss of primary containment. It also made progress in lowering its greenhouse emissions, from 59.8 million tons of CO2 equivalent in 2012, to 50.3 million in 2013, to 48.7 million in 2014, to 49 million in 2015, but then went back up to 50.1 million in 2016.

## (2) Upstream Investment

**Before the 2014–2015 Price Collapse**
Certain themes were prominent in BP's upstream investments prior to the price collapse, which differed from ExxonMobil's: including asset sales to pay for Deepwater damages and declining investments even before prices plummeted. Ironically, the company proclaimed in its official documents that it still had exceptional deep-water skills, and

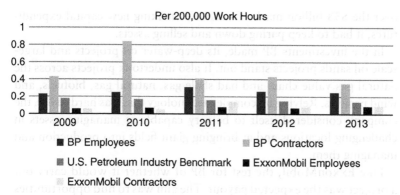

Figure 9.2 BP and ExxonMobil safety incidents: 2009–2013
Derived from Company Annual Reports

it continued to invest in select long-life, high-return projects in many parts of the world.

**Discipline.** While ExxonMobil grew its investments before the 2014–2015 price collapse, BP's expenditures fell from $29 billion in 2011 to about $25 billion. Its priority was not to expand its assets; it had to have a disciplined investment approach, and it could not support just any project. Once it finished divesting assets, it could expand exploration, reload the upstream pipeline, and play to its strength in doing high-value projects.

Under these conditions, with operating cash flows declining from 2011 to 2013, it had to rely on dividend payments and buybacks to maintain shareholder loyalty. They grew from around $2.5 billion in 2011 to over $9 billion in 2013.

To meet its Deepwater Horizon commitments, BP sold many assets, disposing of them and using the money to help pay for its oil spill obligations. Each year from 2011 to 2013, BP disposed of additional assets. It had also dissolved the partnership with Rosneft in which it sold 50 percent of the shares in this venture to Rosneft for $12.3 billion and a 19.75 percent interest in that company. With Rosneft still a partner BP had the largest oil and natural gas reserves among publicly traded companies in the world. BP also sold half of its upstream installations and pipelines and a third of its oil and natural gas wells in order to raise $38 billion to help it pay for Gulf damages. It intended to raise another $10 billion by means of asset sales in order to put it over the $38 billion mark. To continue making new capital expenditures, it had to keep paring down and selling assets.

In the investments BP made, its deep-water oil projects and large-scale oil sands projects stand out. It also undertook projects across the natural gas value chain and had shale gas, natural gas, biofuels, and wind projects. Relying on complex technology that was hard to use, the company considered itself to be very capable at managing assets in challenging locations and at bringing giant fields into production and managing them.

Like ExxonMobil, the test for BP of whether it would carry out a project was the expected payout. The aim was to find opportunities to strengthen the company's portfolio of long-life, high-return assets. The margins had to be high. Decision making started with an annual capital expenditure budget; then, the company screened potential projects for those with the best likely payoff. Delivering the projects efficiently on time and on budget was important. When working with suitable partners made sense, BP did so, but a takeaway from the oil spill was that it had to carefully monitor its partners for safety and ensure their compliance with its production standards.

**Many Parts of the World.** Like ExxonMobil, BP tried to reduce its risks by carrying out projects in many different parts of the world. In 2012, BP suspended Alaska development, but gained access to six new areas, adding acreage in Brazil, Canada, Egypt, Namibia, Uruguay, and the Gulf of Mexico. It had projects in the North Sea and Norway as well as an LNG project in Angola. It added shale acreage in the United States, with its US shale play growing to 25 percent of its US production. Even after the Deepwater spill, BP held onto to leading offshore positions in the Gulf of Mexico, Libya, Egypt, India, and Uruguay. It also retained significant offshore stakes in Nova Scotia, the Arctic, Angola, Brazil, South China, and Australia. In 2012, it did exploratory drilling in nine wells against a target of twelve and had five major project startups against a target of six.

In 2013, BP spent nearly $25 billion on upstream investments, growing its position in exploration by participating in projects in Angola, Brazil, Egypt, India, and the Gulf of Mexico. The company drilled seventeen exploration wells in 2013, more than the two previous years combined. Though the EPA temporarily barred BP from new US government contracts in the Gulf of Mexico, it still had seven rigs operating there. It had three major project startups, one in the Gulf of Mexico, one in Angola, and one in Australia. It invested heavily in Azerbaijan natural gas and oil, made a natural gas discovery in India, and tried to increase oil delivery from the Mad Dog deep-water project in the Gulf of Mexico. By 2015, it aimed to drill fifteen new test sites throughout the world.

### After the 2014–2015 Price Collapse

After the price collapse, the company's priorities had to change. It lowered its capital expenditures, applied more discipline in choosing where to invest, continued to divest properties, and increasingly shifted its focus to natural gas. BP also started to use carbon pricing in its evaluation of new projects. Though it cut costs, it continued to invest in new projects. Among BP's investments were a small number in renewable energy.

**Cutting Costs.** Like ExxonMobil after the 2014–2015 price collapse, BP experienced a dramatic drop in its upstream revenue; by 2016, upstream revenue was about 50 percent lower than it had been in 2014. Like ExxonMobil, BP also had to decrease capital expenditure; by 2015, it was about 20 percent lower than it had been in 2014. The plan was for capital expenditure to stay at about this level until further notice. If it stayed at this level, it would be about a quarter lower than ExxonMobil's capital expenditure. BP continued to divest about $3 billion of assets per year, moves based on its conclusion that oil prices would be "lower for longer." It also had to reduce the workforce. By 2016, it cut about 6,000 jobs in every part of the business, a reduction of about 17 percent compared to its 2014 workforce. By releasing these workers, it considered itself to be in a better position to make a fresh start after the oil spill. It would be better able to compete effectively in a world of volatile oil and gas prices, which was transitioning to a lower-carbon future.

**Even More Financial Discipline.** In a period of lower oil and natural gas prices, the company not only had to cut back unnecessary activities, but also have a simpler and more focused set of investments that emphasized its distinctive strengths, capabilities, and technologies in project execution and management. The purpose of the investments BP made was to reshape the company and strengthen it so that it would be more resilient and better able to withstand short-term price volatility. As a result, it applied a rigorous cost discipline to how it managed its portfolio of projects, continuing to concentrate on the areas it considered its strengths, specifically deep water, giant fields, unconventional natural gas and oil, and select parts of the natural gas value chain. The company wanted to obtain margins in the new projects in which it invested that were 35 percent higher than it accepted in the projects in which it had previously invested. The projects had to be low cost and in existing basins, where the company could maximize recovery, extend the basin's life, or manage the basin's decline.

Before BP funded a project, it painstakingly vetted it to make sure it met its return threshold. Like ExxonMobil, it screened each project it was considering against a range of prices in an attempt to ensure that the project would be profitable in the short and long term. It faced the same fortunate situation as ExxonMobil in that the breakeven prices of the projects it supported were declining since suppliers slashed their prices in response to reduced demand. Thus, BP renegotiated contracts with suppliers and took advantage of the suppliers' lower prices. By the end of 2016, it had renegotiated 40 percent of the contracts it had with suppliers. In addition, it simplified its organization to achieve greater efficiency, while attempting not to jeopardize safety, a balancing act that was difficult to carry out.

**Adding Carbon Pricing.** BP anticipated that greenhouse gas regulations might someday be in place. Thus, in evaluating potential projects, it factored in a carbon price based on the then-current price of $40 per ton of carbon dioxide equivalent in industrial countries and stress tested the proposed investments it could make at a carbon price of $80 per ton.

**Emphasizing Natural Gas.** Though it imposed new investment criteria, BP still aimed for a diverse and balanced portfolio across resource types, geographies, and operating conditions. Unlike ExxonMobil, it chose to tilt more from oil to natural gas and to seek new opportunities in natural gas. Its aim was that about three-quarters of the projects that it planned to start up by the year 2021 would be natural gas projects. The company acquired interests in offshore natural gas exploration blocks in Mauritania and Senegal and gained approval for LNG expansions. It highlighted its natural gas focus, yet also signed an agreement for the future development of Azerbaijan oil and renewed its Abu

Dhabi onshore oil concession, where it had operated for more than seventy-five years. It obtained an extension to 2050 in exchange for a 2 percent stake in the Abu Dhabi National Oil Company.

**Using Production Sharing Agreements.** BP wanted a significant part of its portfolio to be in the form production-sharing agreements. The revenues it earned in these agreements were typically less sensitive to oil price fluctuations. To maintain its presence in Russia, a country with some of the world's largest oil and gas reserves, it retained its relationships with leading Russian oil and gas companies. It also worked with the China National Petroleum Corporation in an effort to help revitalize Iraqi oil production. The agreement with China National would allow it to recover its costs, irrespective of oil prices, and to obtain a fee per barrel of incremental production above a certain threshold. The company was also working with China National on shale gas exploration in that country. In Norway, it created a joint venture called Aker BP, which was the country's largest independent oil company.

**Investing in Renewables.** BP claimed its interest in renewables was greater than the other large oil and natural gas companies. BP operated a biofuels business in Brazil that used sustainable feedstock to produce low-carbon ethanol and power. It continued to have significant interests in onshore wind in the United States, which made it one of the top US producers of wind energy. The company also had a wind farm in the Netherlands and continued to invest in the development and commercialization of biobutanol for airplane fuel in conjunction with DuPont. Biobutanol was lighter than other fuels, and easier to transport, store, and manage. BP also created a venturing arm to grow renewable businesses. It collaborated with startups in an attempt to bring successful technologies to large-scale commercialization. These activities were different from ExxonMobil.

**Being Agile.** As prices, policy, technology, and customer preferences were rapidly changing, to stay competitive, BP would have to evolve and refresh its strategy in a way that would better guarantee that it did well in "all seasons." Doing better in "all seasons" meant lowering costs, tilting slightly from oil, increasing its emphasis on natural gas, paying more attention to renewables and clean energy ventures, and staying diversified. BP's aim was to be agile, flexible, and diversified in the investments that it made as a hedge against volatility. In 2016, the six major startups it initiated extended from Algeria to the Gulf of Mexico. In that year the company was in the midst of making final investment decisions on an additional five projects. Major new projects that it planned to start in 2017 in the United Kingdom, Oman, and Egypt would add significant reserves and lower per-unit costs. The company's goal was to increase production from new projects by 800,000 barrels of equivalent oil a day by 2020. In 2016, a year in which it grew its holdings to over a million barrels of equivalent oil a day, it was on track to achieve that goal.

## (3) Downstream Integration

### Before the 2014–2015 Price Collapse

**Downsizing.** Because of weak demand and capacity additions by Chinese competitors, which put pressure on margins, downstream was a less promising business than upstream. BP, like ExxonMobil, found little reason to increase investment in it. Therefore, in the same way as ExxonMobil, BP was in the process of downsizing and updating its downstream holdings. It chose to divest two major US refineries, including Texas City, selling these assets while trying to retain 90 percent of its proved reserves and production. Texas City was where it previously had a major accident. Along with the sale of the Texas City and Carson refineries, the company chose to modernize the Whiting refinery, where it had a major controversy about the facility's pollution. The company sold downstream facilities in Malaysia, as it did not expect major improvements in the demand for gasoline, diesel, aviation fuel, and LPG that these facilities produced. Demand for lubricants also remained flat and unlike ExxonMobil, BP expected that demand for petrochemicals that go into consumer products, such as paints, plastic bottles, and fibers for clothing, would decline. The company's downstream margins continued to fall. In 2013, it considered growth in non-OECD markets to be disappointing. Europe, as well, was not expanding. BP was hurt by the loss of Iranian oil caused by US and European trade embargos. Joint ventures were safer than going it alone and thus BP invested in partnerships in Asia, so long as it had as collaborators leading companies such as the Zhuhai Port Company in Guangdong, China.

## After the 2014–2015 Price Collapse

**Not Sufficiently Countercyclical.** BP's downstream profits first started to improve after 2014–2015; and the company underscored the boost in profitability that downstream provided and pointed to the geographic reach of its downstream assets and their location in growing markets. However, the improvements did not last. When oil prices crashed in 2014–2015, BP's downstream business lost about half of its revenue. As in the case of ExxonMobil, downstream did not provide an effective hedge against volatility. BP therefore had to continue to reduce the size of its downstream business to maintain strong returns. It renegotiated contracts with vendors as it had with upstream vendors. In the name of efficiency and simplification and lowering expenses, it reduced head office costs by about 40 percent. The company established a site-by-site improvement program to raise efficiency. It reorganized from nine regions to three, streamlined the lubrication business, and began to restructure petrochemicals. It also bolstered brands and tried to position products as premium in markets that were highly commoditized. In 2015, it began a marketing campaign in Spain for a range of "dirt-busting" fuels that contained proprietary additives to clean and protect car engines, remove deposits, prevent their formation, and help engines perform better.

### (4) High-Impact R&D

**Before the 2014–2015 Price Collapse**
BP's R&D investments were substantially lower than ExxonMobil's. While ExxonMobil invested about $1 billion in R&D per year, BP invested about $0.65 billion and its projects were very diverse.

**Upstream.** BP invested in upstream oil and natural gas recovery, such as advanced seismic imaging capacity with the assistance of large supercomputers, new techniques for unconventional oil and gas shale extraction, and tools to help recover high-pressure, high-temperature deep water oil, and natural gas. It also explored ways to improve its real-time decision making when working on projects such as deep water oil and natural gas that were inherently dangerous. It wanted to avoid another incident like the one it had in Gulf. Unlike ExxonMobil, BP had interests in energy efficiency and energy storage, carbon management, and renewable power.

**Downstream.** On the downstream side of the business, BP was interested in a less-polluting polyester raw material and a lubricant co-engineered with Ford to boost automotive efficiency. It also had joint ventures with DuPont to develop and market biobutanol and next-generation cellulosic biofuel technology.

### After the 2014–2015 Price Collapse

Unlike ExxonMobil, which tried to maintain its R&D spending at about the level of $1 billion per year despite plummeting oil prices, BP's R&D expenditures fell by more than a third from 2014 to 2016, to about $0.4 billion. Nonetheless, the company maintained a varied research program. The program had a broad mandate to enhance the safety and reliability of operations, create competitive advantage in energy discovery and recovery, and deploy advanced technologies, including robotics and big data analytics to improve efficiency.

**Upstream.** Upstream technology in which BP showed interest included advanced seismic imaging to help find oil and gas and enhanced recovery to extract more of it from existing fields. The Independent Simultaneous Source (ISS) technology the company developed conducted large-scale 3D seismic surveys of fields, reducing costs by using multiple surveying sources and receivers. In difficult terrain, it helped to identify early warnings of performance issues. BP also developed an automated well choke control system, which had a lower failure rate and better managed well start-up and flow during operations. In addition, it explored lower carbon energy sources. Like ExxonMobil, it had partnership arrangements with universities and global R&D centers and it was active in patenting its discoveries.

**Downstream.** Downstream R&D was carried out to improve the performance of BP's refineries and petrochemical plants and to try to create new, high-quality, energy-efficient products.

## Performance

### Before the 2014–2015 Price Collapse

BP's 2012 earnings were about $11 billion, considerably less than ExxonMobil's in that year, but the following year saw some improvement, to nearly $13.5 billion in earnings. Its reserve replacement ratio in 2012, however, was just 77 percent, the first year it had a reserve replacement ratio below 100 percent after three successive years of ratios above 100 percent. In 2013 the company made a comeback with a reserve replacement ratio of 129 percent and it did as well as it had in 2009. Nonetheless, its 2013 production continued along the downward trajectory in which it had been moving since 2010, with production coming in about 20 percent less than it had in 2009. Overall, ExxonMobil performed better than BP in this time period and ExxonMobil's performance was disappointing in comparison to what it had been previously. The main drag on BP's performance that ExxonMobil did not feel was the headwinds from BP's giant oil spill.

## After the 2014–2015 Price Collapse

BP's Gulf of Mexico obligations kept rising to over $65 billion by 2015. The plunge in oil prices thus hurt it very deeply. Ongoing oil spill compensation charges and upstream losses resulted in a loss in 2015. In 2016, the company returned to profitability, but barely. Its 2016 return on average capital employed was 70 percent less than it had been in 2014. Its reserve replacement ratio, however, improved, an indicator on which it did better than ExxonMobil in that year.

## Many Small Adjustments after the Deepwater Horizon Accident – The Correct Response?

This chapter examined how BP responded to plummeting oil prices. It showed the degree to which it changed its assessments of the risks and uncertainties, altered its assumptions, and adjusted its strategies. The effects of the collapse in prices on its performance were even more negative than the effects of the collapse in prices on ExxonMobil's performance. The same question applied to BP as applies to ExxonMobil. Could BP have done better had it followed a different path?

Both companies to some extent accommodated the external pressures they experienced. BP, probably more so than ExxonMobil, exhibited a greater degree of flexibility and made more changes to adjust to the new situation. The company loosened its assumptions about the future and considered multiple possibilities, unlike ExxonMobil. However, like ExxonMobil, it anticipated oil's continued dominance and based the decisions it made in trying to remain heavily invested in upstream exploration throughout the globe, with a continued emphasis on deep water projects, on this assumption. Both companies had to apply much more discipline to the upstream investments they made. The counter-cyclical hedge they expected downstream to provide protected neither firm. Their downstream businesses were as stressed as their upstream businesses, bringing into question the wisdom of their integrated structure as a guard against price volatility. Neither BP nor ExxonMobil, though they cut back, refrained from making big bets on the discovery and development of new oil and natural gas fields in rugged terrains throughout the world. The discovery of this new oil and natural gas required using complex technology that bore with it the chance of an accident. Though BP made safety improvements, it had not caught up with ExxonMobil. The company continued to be more accident prone than ExxonMobil.

To a greater extent than ExxonMobil, BP had to raise cash. This need to raise cash was a consequence of the Deep Water Horizon accident. Therefore, though both companies made cutbacks, streamlined operations, and divested upstream and downstream assets, BP did so more than ExxonMobil. BP also cut its R&D spending more than ExxonMobil and made different R&D investments, being more concerned about getting a handle on its short-term decision making in situations of stress and pressure. A marked difference between the companies was that although BP backed away somewhat from investing in cleaner energy, it did not back away entirely. In this regard it differed from ExxonMobil. It also showed a sensitivity to climate change as an issue in that it introduced a price for greenhouse gases in its decision making. It also shifted more than ExxonMobil from petroleum to natural gas. None of the adjustments BP made, however, could prevent it suffering a decline in revenue and profits. However much ExxonMobil's revenues and profits fell, BP's fell off much more. What this company should do next also was an open-ended question. Yet it was undeniable that its choices, like those of ExxonMobil, would have important implications for both the company and society.

## Notes

1. *"BP's Deepwater Horizon Costs Total $62B,"* www.usatoday.com/st ory/money/2016/07/14/bp-deepwater-horizon-costs/87087056/

2. *"BP's Dismal Safety Record,"* https://abcnews.go.com/WN/bps-dismal-safety-record/story?id=10763042

3. *"BP,"* www.crunchbase.com/organization/bp-3#section-overview

4. *"A history of BP's US Disasters,"* www.telegraph.co.uk/finance/news bysector/energy/oilandgas/9680589/A-history-of-BPs-US-disasters .html

5. *"Rosneft Takes Over TNK-BP in $55bn Deal,"* www.theguardian.com /business/2013/mar/21/rosneft-takes-over-tnk-bp

6. *"Climate Change Speech,"* www.documentcloud.org/documents/2623 268-bp-john-browne-stanford-1997-climate-change-speech.html

7. Ibid.

8. Ibid.

9. *"Recapping on BP's Long History of Greenwashing,"* www.greenpeace .org/usa/recapping-on-bps-long-history-of-greenwashing/

10. *"BP to Exit Solar Business After 40 Years,"* www.ft.com/content/80c d4a08-2b42-11e1-9fd0-00144feabdc0

11. *"Annual Report and Form 20-F 2012,"* www.bp.com/content/dam/bp/ pdf/investors/bp-annual-report-and-form-20f-2012.pdf; *"Summary Review 2012."* www.bp.com/content/dam/bp/pdf/investors/bp-sum mary-review-2012.pdf; *"Annual Report and Form 20-F 2013,"* www .bp.com/content/dam/bp/pdf/investors/bp-annual-report-and-form-20f -2013.pdf

*"Strategic Report 2013,"* www.bp.com/content/dam/bp/pdf/investors/ bp-strategic-report-2013.pdf

*"Annual Report and Form 20-F 2014,"* www.bp.com/content/dam/bp/ pdf/investors/bp-annual-report-and-form-20f-2014.pdf

*"Strategic Report 2014,"* www.bp.com/content/dam/bp/pdf/investors/ bp-strategic-report-2014.pdf

*"Annual Report and Form 20-F 2015,"* www.bp.com/content/dam/bp/pdf/ investors/bp-annual-report-and-form-20f-2015.pdf; *"Strategic Report 2015."* www.bp.com/content/dam/bp/pdf/investors/bp-strategic-report-2015.pdf; *"Annual Report and Form 20-F 2016."* www.bp.com/content/dam/bp/en/corporate/pdf/investors/bp-annual-re port-and-form-20f-2016.pdf

*"Sustainability Report 2016,"* www.bp.com/content/dam/bp/en/corporate/ pdf/sustainability-report/group-reports/bp-sustainability-report-2016.pdf

# 10 | *Strategies to Try to Offset Plummeting Prices: Shell*

The purpose of this chapter is trace the responses of yet another oil and natural gas company, Shell, to changing conditions in its industry in the years 2012–2016, especially to volatile oil prices, and to consider where it might go next with its strategies. The chapter starts with an introduction to Shell. Like the two previous chapters, it then covers the state of the company between 2012 and 2014, before the dramatic fall in oil prices that took place and then goes on to cover the company's condition between 2014 and 2016, after the fall. It examines the risks and uncertainties as it perceived them, its assumptions about the future, and the hedges it put in place. How did the price shock alter its performance, and to what extent did it change its strategies because of changes in its performance?

## Shell's Past

Similar to ExxonMobil and BP, the 2014–2015 fall in oil prices dug deeply into the revenue and profits of Dutch-English oil and natural gas giant Shell (Figure 10.1). Controversies dogged the company both before and after the drop in prices, including overstating its oil revenues, human rights violations, problems with Arctic drilling, and disputes over climate change. Shell's 2004 overstatement of its oil reserves resulted in loss of confidence, large government fines, payments to shareholders, and the forced exit of its then chairperson Philip Watts.[1] Nearly a decade prior, in 1995, the company stood accused of collaborating in the execution of eight leaders of the Ogoni tribe in Nigeria, including Ken Saro-Wiwa, whom the country's military rulers hanged.[2] Human rights groups brought cases against the company to hold it accountable. They accused it of crimes against humanity, torture, inhumane treatment, arbitrary arrest, and detention. Without accepting responsibility, Shell agreed to pay $15.5 million in a 2009 legal settlement. However, Amnesty International continued to report human rights problems connected to Shell's Nigerian activities.[3] Documents that the organizations released in

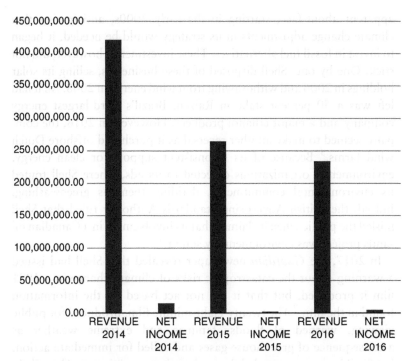

**Figure 10.1** Shell's revenue and net income 2012–2016
Derived from Company Annual Reports

2009 and 2010 showed that Shell did not end its meddling in the affairs of the Nigerian government and making regular payments to the military.

In the Arctic, the controversy evolved as follows.[4] The company started a $4.5 billion drilling program in 2006, which provoked analysts' skepticism that Shell could safely develop resources. Greenpeace and other environmental groups protested. Shell faced permit delays and lawsuits. A winter storm hit the rig Shell used in the Arctic. When the company towed the rig to the state of Washington for maintenance, the crew lost control and Shell had to ground it. Shell had invested nearly $5 billion on this initiative; whether it could ever resume drilling was doubtful.

## Climate Change

On climate change, Shell was an early member of the Global Climate Coalition, a group opposed to greenhouse regulation. But, in an apparent about-face, starting in the early 2000s, anticipating that climate change adjustments in its strategy would be needed, it began to invest in fossil fuel alternatives. These investments, however, did not stick. One by one, Shell disposed of these businesses, selling its solar holdings in 2006 and withdrawing from wind energy in 2008. All it had left was a 50 percent stake in Raizen, Brazil's third-largest energy company and a major ethanol producer. However, in 2016, the company seemed to make another reversal as it purchased offshore Dutch wind farms.[5] Because of its inconsistent support for clean energy, environmental organizations objected to its ads, where Shell touted its environmental commitments, deriding them as greenwashing. Indeed, the British Advertising Standards Authority ruled that Shell misled the public when it claimed that its involvement in a Canadian oil sands project was environmentally sound.[6]

In 2017, the *Guardian* newspaper revealed that Shell had issued a warning about the catastrophic risks of climate change in a 1991 film it produced, but that it did not act based on the information found in the film.[7] The twenty-eight-minute film, produced for public viewing, warned of floods, famines and extreme weather as a consequence of greenhouse gases and called for immediate action, but Shell had not responded. Instead, at the time, it invested heavily in fossil fuels and helped lobby against climate action. These charges brought against Shell were similar to those leveled against ExxonMobil (see Chapter 8).

## Prior to and After the 2014–2015 Price Collapse

This chapter turns to a more detailed examination of Shell's strategies before and after the plunge in oil prices. The examination, like those in prior chapters, is based on a careful reading of its annual reports and communications to shareholders.[8] In these documents, Shell gave an account of the risks and uncertainties and its assumptions about the future. Based on these perceptions and assumptions, it offered justification for its strategic choices. Like the companies depicted in previous chapters, it hedged its bets focusing on: operations, especially safety; upstream investments; downstream refining; and R&D that might lead to breakthroughs. The aim of these moves was to protect it from the uncertainties oil and natural gas companies confronted. The moves had implications for the company's performance, and the company's performance in turn influenced how the company adjusted its strategy.

## Shell Before the 2014–2015 Price Collapse

### Perceptions of the Risks and Uncertainties

Prior to the 2014–2015 price collapse Shell acknowledged risks and uncertainties which were similar in nature to ExxonMobil and BP – fluctuating prices, climate change and regulation, and completing the large projects it had started.

### Fluctuating Prices

The global economy, still underperforming after the Great Financial Crisis, had not provoked sufficiently steady demand to ensure prices would remain high. Should prices fall, Shell would have to take projects that did not generate sufficient revenue off the books as proven reserves. More than ExxonMobil or BP, Shell emphasized that should prices unexpectedly rise, the costs of carrying out projects to replenish and enhance its reserves would increase and they might become too expensive and be delayed or cancelled. High prices also reduced demand for its downstream products and raised the take of its partners in production-sharing contracts. Steady prices were desirable, yet maintaining steady prices was far from easy as many factors that were difficult to control affected supply and demand for oil and natural gas. These factors included weather, natural disasters, oil-producing country actions, political issues, and the global economy. Unexpected price movements in a downward or upward direction were not in the company's interests.

### Climate Change and Regulation

Another imponderable was climate change. To meet the world's energy needs, the company would have to increase production. More oil would come from sources such as Canadian oil sands, which emitted high levels of greenhouse gases. Flaring natural gas emissions also were likely to increase. Without solutions to these problems that were economically viable and publicly acceptable, Shell would have to delay projects and cut back on production. The growth in emissions was likely to lead to additional regulatory measures, which would come on top of the regulation already in place. In the more than seventy countries in which Shell operated, the company was subject to different levels of government control and requirements. Every country was different. Each country had a different set of nongovernmental organizations and watchdog groups. The world had subjected some countries where Shell operated to global sanctions. In each country, Shell faced different issues, including terrorism, war, and piracy.

### Completing Projects

The company's future depended on its ability to complete large and complex projects, which allowed it to replace and enhance its proven reserves. The challenges in developing these projects included geology, technology and engineering, labor, and cost overruns. Large capital projects exposed the company to a wide range of health, safety, security, and environmental threats. The state of the global economy and politics put many projects in jeopardy. In developing countries, such as Iraq and Kazakhstan, where Shell was active, these problems were common. Shell faced the same issues in the Arctic. The company acknowledged a deteriorating situation in Nigeria involving the safety of people, sabotage theft, limited infrastructure, higher taxes, and an inability to enforce contractual rights. National oil companies intervened and curtailed Shell's influence. Shell could not afford further violations of anti-bribery and corruption laws, which had resulted in fines and exposed the company and its employees to criminal sanctions and civil suits in the past. Major projects were usually joint ventures, in which the company did not fully control its partners. Disruption of critical IT services and breaches of information security were possible. For all these reasons, Shell might be in a position where it would have to delay or cancel major projects.

## Assumptions about the Future

Like ExxonMobil and BP, Shell assumed that energy demand would continue to grow strongly in the decades ahead and that it would have to carry out major projects, however risky and uncertain. Demand for natural gas would also grow in the future. Should there be volatile prices and unstable revenue, the company assumed that it was strong enough to withstand them.

### Rising Demand

By 2050, Shell assumed that global energy demand was likely to increase as living standards grew and the world's population increased from 7 to over 9 billion. Though economic growth was contracting in Europe and moving forward at a very slow pace in the United States, high growth rates prevailed in China and other developing countries; these were key assumptions Shell shared with ExxonMobil and BP. Global energy demand was set to grow as world population expanded and large numbers of people in emerging economies benefitted from higher incomes. With consumer expectations mounting and the demand for energy expanding, average annual global growth in energy consumption would continue. The price of oil would not fall below $80 a barrel and thus the company had to maintain a long-term, strategic view about investing in energy.

### Greater Use of Natural Gas

Shell assumed that fossil fuels would remain dominant. They would satisfy about two-thirds of the world's energy demand, but demand for natural gas, especially in the form of LNG, would go up. As more governments around the world recognized the environmental advantages of natural gas-fired power, global demand would increase. Replacing coal with natural gas in Asia's rapidly expanding cities would reduce nitrogen oxides and particulate pollution as well as greenhouse gases. Although renewable energy could also help meet the challenge of satisfying rising energy demand while significantly reducing $CO_2$ emissions, it would take many years, perhaps up to 2050, before renewables could provide 30 percent of the world's energy.

## Shell After the 2014–2015 Price Collapse

### Perceptions of the Risks and Uncertainties

After the price collapse, the company's assessment of the risks and uncertainties remained focused on fluctuating prices, climate change, and the completion of large, complex projects.

### Fluctuating Prices

Shell continued to be concerned about fluctuating prices and factors that influenced supply and demand that it had difficulty controlling, including natural disasters, weather, political instability and conflicts, economic conditions, the actions of major oil- and gas-producing countries, and operational issues. It viewed the short-term outlook for energy markets to be problematic. Low oil prices were a major challenge. Asset impairment was possible and could result in the debooking of reserves. Yet, the company continued to emphasize that an environment of unexpectedly high prices also was not desirable.

### Climate Change

As Shell had anticipated, rising climate-change concerns were leading to additional legal and regulatory measures that had the potential to produce project delays and cancellations. Even more regulation was likely and the results would be the same – the company would face higher costs and less demand.

### Completing Projects

In a low-price environment, Shell generated less revenue from upstream production. The upshot was that long-term projects were not as profitable or incurred losses. If oil and natural gas prices remained at low levels, the company would not be able to maintain its long-term capital investments at the same level and might have to cancel projects. In the more than seventy countries with different degrees of political, legal, and fiscal stability in which it operated it faced social instability, civil unrest, terrorism, piracy, and acts of war. The challenges were particularly large in countries like Nigeria, Iraq, and Kazakhstan and in regions like North Africa and the Middle East.

## Assumptions about the Future

In the short term, Shell assumed that the world economy was going through a period of oversupply and slow economic growth. Weak economic growth in Russia and Europe coupled with robust production had driven down prices. Technological advances had unlocked vast shale reserves, and renewable sources were gaining ground. They would be vital to limiting carbon emissions, but only in the long term. In the long term, the outlook for energy demand continued to be strong because of population growth and improvements in living standards.

### Investing to Meet Demand

Shell expected demand for energy to continue to rise as populations and prosperity increased. To meet the energy needs of a growing population, oil and natural gas would play vital roles in supplying the world's energy in the second half of the twenty-first century. Billions of people relied on oil and natural gas to improve their living conditions. Global energy demand would grow from 2012 to 2040. In this period, roughly $25 trillion of investment would be needed to bolster oil and natural gas supplies. The long-term investment case for oil and natural gas, therefore, was strong, despite a temporary fall in oil prices. The problem was that low prices might spur insufficient motivation to invest in the projects needed to ensure an adequate long-term supply. Without sufficient investment, demand growth would outstrip supply availability and prices would go up.

### The Centrality of Fossil Fuels
Shell's main scenario, which took into account existing government commitments and plans with regard to carbon emissions, pointed to a 14 percent rise in oil consumption and a 55 percent rise in natural gas consumption by 2040. Even with effective policies to tackle climate change, the world's energy needs would expand. Though important, the Paris Accord would not undermine the centrality of fossil fuels. Natural gas, though, would play a much larger role, and renewable energy would also start to meet an increasing share of global energy needs.

### Carbon Pricing
Like ExxonMobil and BP, Shell argued for a carbon-pricing system to drive the movement from coal to natural gas-fired power generation. It also supported greater energy efficiency and wanted more incentives for the development of carbon capture and storage (CCS). To encourage the type of change needed to meet the challenge, all sectors of society would have to be involved.

### Hedging
Like ExxonMobil and BP, the approach Shell took to managing the risks and uncertainties, based on its assumptions, relied on four layers of hedging. They were: (1) maintaining operational excellence; (2) continuing to make upstream investments to replace lost oil and natural gas; (3) relying on downstream integration for steady profit and revenue growth; and (4) carrying out high-impact R&D for future competitive advantage. After the crash in oil prices, Shell like the other companies discussed in previous chapters deviated little from this

model. Discussed next is how it applied these hedging strategies before and after the 2014–2015 price crash.

## (1) Operational Excellence

### Before the 2014–2015 Price Collapse

Like the other oil companies, Shell sought to improve operational safety. Its overall safety performance had been getting better, yet the company was disappointed that off-coast drilling in Alaska still had problems. It safely completed preliminary drilling, but there were problems in deployment, a damaged containment dome, and difficulties in moving the oil rig from place to place. Because of these difficulties, it had to put in place capping and containment equipment, make use of oil spill response vessels, instigate other safeguards, and work closely with regulators, the local community, and environmentalists to deal with their concerns, but the company continued to face regular protests and a court order forced it to retreat, pause, and then suspend these operations.

### After the 2014–2015 Price Collapse

Shell wanted to lower operating expenses, but it could not lose focus on safety. Despite the many steps it took to improve safety, it still had incidents such as an explosion that took place in a chemical plant in the Netherlands and a fire in its Singapore refinery. Nearly every year, it reported the deaths of employees. Four people lost their lives in 2014, seven in 2015, and three in 2016, and many others were injured. The company was trying to learn from these incidents. The number of its unplanned releases did go down from fifty-one in 2015 to thirty-nine in 2016. However, in 2016, Shell had more recordable injuries per million working hours than it had had in 2015.

Shell's goal was to avoid harm and to achieve zero leaks. Thus, the company bolstered its standards and control systems. It established processes to avert spills, leaks, technical failures, and breakdowns. It carried out regular emergency response drills. It tried to enhance safety initiatives among employees and contractors. If the work they were doing appeared unsafe, Shell encouraged them to stop it. In the case of a spill or leak, the company upgraded its recovery measures to contain the damage. It also upgraded the system of physical barriers, requiring that all offshore wells have at least two independent barriers to stop uncontrolled releases. To ensure that the barriers were effective, the company regularly inspected, tested, and maintained them.

## (2) Upstream Investment

### Before the 2014–2015 Price Collapse

The key themes prior to the collapse were relying on a disciplined process to keep up the pace of investments, a process that would take care of price volatility because of careful adding and culling of assets. In adopting this disciplined system, Shell was like ExxonMobil and BP. Shell chose to cut assets in the United States and elsewhere, emphasize natural gas and deep-water projects, and acknowledge climate change.

**A Disciplined Process.** The market plus local operating and regulatory conditions drove the pace of Shell's capital allocation decision making. The company expected future oil and gas prices to be volatile and considered a range of possible future prices. It tested the economic performance of projects against price ranges of $70 to $110 per barrel for oil and three to $5 per MMBtu for natural gas, and these price ranges were subject to review and change. The company carried out sensitivity analyses to examine the impact of high-price drivers, such as strong economic growth and low investment in new production, and low-price drivers, such as economic weakness and high investment in new production. It evaluated these drivers in the short, medium, and long term. It designed the portfolio of projects it funded to benefit from high prices and to deal with weakness when prices fell. It scrutinized supply and demand and took into account geopolitics, and OPEC actions and assessed the degree of political disruption. Relying on historical analysis, it paid attention to short-term events, such as relatively warm winters or cool summers. It examined the role statistical volatility played in the trends it examined. Whether a project fit into the portfolio of its other projects was a consideration. The emphasis was on medium-term financial returns and growth.

**Cutting US Shale and Other Assets.** In 2013, Shell decided to divest its positions in tight-natural gas and liquids-rich petroleum shale in the United States. Its capital expenditures in the United States had been higher than in any other country in which the company invested

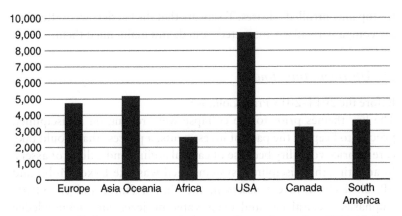

**Figure 10.2** Shell's upstream capital expenditures by region 2013 (dollars million)
Derived from Company Annual Reports

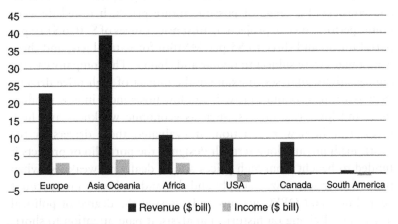

**Figure 10.3** Shell's revenue versus income by Region 2013
Derived from Company Annual Reports

(Figure 10.2), though it lost money in the United States, mainly because of high exploration costs and depreciation expenses (Figure 10.3). Tight-gas and liquids-rich shale in the United States was not the type of opportunity that Shell was able to exploit well. Its proven 2013 oil and natural gas reserves were concentrated in Asia, not the United States. In North America, the company chose to expand its conventional oil and natural gas businesses and further develop its oil sands operations in Canada.

The company also cut back its assets elsewhere. Through additional sales and impairments, it exited, when it could, from mature, cash-generating properties that it viewed as not having sufficient growth potential. It generated $16 billion from sales of assets from 2011 to 2013. Shell cut overall capital spending in 2014 to around $37 billion, which was about $9 billion less than the previous year. In that year, it also embarked on a new program of asset sales designed to generate an additional $15 billion in divestment proceeds. With the sale and disposal of these assets, the company's balance sheet would be stronger and more robust and it would be able to make additional investments in the future growth. At the same time as ExxonMobil was growing its assets, Shell as well as BP were selling.

**Investing in Natural Gas and Deep Water Drilling.** Shell decided that natural gas outside the United States, in particular LNG, was a primary growth opportunity. Natural gas already made up about 50 percent of its production. Though it sold a stake in an Australian LNG facility in 2014, it wanted to make bigger Australian investments. It relied on advanced technology to tap Australian natural gas fields and to process, store, and transfer the LNG. The company worked in South Korea to build a floating LNG facility, the largest in the world. In Qatar, it also was committed to LNG. It had natural gas opportunities in established resources basins of the Gulf of Mexico and offshore Europe, and held that the Arctic, Iraq, Kazakhstan, and Nigeria provided future natural gas opportunities for the company.

Deepwater wells also had investment potential. Shell touted a production-sharing contract for the giant Libra oilfield off the coast of Brazil as an opportunity to showcase its deep-water expertise in one of the biggest deep-water fields in the world. The company also expanded its portfolio of deep-water projects in the Gulf of Mexico and Malaysia.

**CO2 Reductions.** The company saw business potential in finding cost-effective ways to manage CO2 emissions. Natural gas, carbon capture and storage technologies, and energy efficiency had potential. The company had a joint venture with Raizen in Brazil, which produced low-carbon biofuel from sugar cane.

**After the 2014–2015 Price Collapse**
After the collapse in prices, Shell continued to engage in disciplined growth. It reinforced its commitment to natural gas by acquiring the natural gas powerhouse BG (British Gas), incurring a large debt in making this acquisition. It did more to lower greenhouse gas emissions, and to afford the BG acquisition it sold assets.

**Disciplined Growth.** Shell did not want to miss growth opportunities, though they seemed less affordable under low price conditions. The company was cautious and curbed spending, though it did not view the volatility as novel in light of industry history, from which it learned to keep a lid on spending, while not ignoring growth. The company eliminated 7,500 jobs in 2015, but expected energy demand would rise. Curtailing capital investment and divesting assets were necessary, but new sources to meet rising long-term energy demand still had to be developed. In a manner similar to the other companies discussed in previous chapters, the company tried to make disciplined choices. It cut back its capital investments and exploration expenses from a 2013 peak of more than $40 billion in 2013 to $26 billion in 2015. It tried to rein in the costs of projects and make tough decisions about which projects were not competitive. In 2015, it stopped construction of an in-situ oil project and a sour gas project in the UAE, and in 2016, it postponed investing a project off the Nigerian coast.

**Committing to Natural Gas and Deepwater Drilling.** In 2016, Shell decided to purchase the giant British natural gas firm, BG, for $53 billion. The move came when low oil prices hurt profits throughout the oil and natural gas sector. To afford the acquisition, Shell had to shed yet another 2,800 jobs. Yet the move strengthened the company's already strong position in the fast-growing LNG market and made it into the largest foreign oil company in Brazil, with offshore oil assets second only to Brazil's scandal plagued national oil company, Petrobras. The company's goals were to focus on natural gas and deep water oil drilling and to become even more competitive and innovative in these domains. Shell was evolving. It was becoming more of a natural gas producer than an oil producer. The BG acquisition more than offset the expiration of an oil production license in Abu Dhabi oil production. As an example of technological advances the company was making, it pointed to the large floating LNG production facility, called Prelude, that it built in Western Australia, which allowed it to access natural gas resources and convert them to LNG in remote waters.

**Lowering Greenhouse Gas Emissions.** Since natural gas emits less carbon gas than petroleum, Shell was trying to find new uses for the fuel. For instance, it was exploring greater use of natural gas in transport. The Brazilian joint venture Raízen also made it one of the world's largest biofuel producers from sugar cane. It continued to examine technologies like carbon capture and storage. It had a project called Quest in which it was trying to capture and safely store CO2 from a Canadian oil sands facility. It was planning to create another carbon capture project for use in a natural gas-fired power plant in the United Kingdom. In addition, it set up a New Energies business division in 2016 to search for opportunities in alternative fuels. This division was supposed to be an incubator for game-changing technologies. Among the division's interests were identifying how technologies like natural gas and renewable could work together more effectively and better ways to connect energy producers and consumers using digital technology.

**Selling Assets.** After the BG acquisition, Shell was constrained from making additional investments, not only by the low price of oil, but also by its debt. The company had to sell assets to reduce the debt. Its $20 billion in asset sales in 2014–2015 more than exceeded its goal of $15 billion. In 2016–2018, it intended to increase its asset sales to $30 billion, planning to exit from between five and ten countries. The company insisted that it was selling assets only if it obtained value in return and its overall portfolio improved. In 2016, it completed $4.7 billion in divestments, and started negotiations for further asset sales. If the market allowed, it was ready to disgorge even more assets, though it did not want to miss opportunities for growth if these arose. The net effects of the changes it made were that the company's oil and natural gas production declined by 4 percent compared to 2013.

## (3) Downstream Integration

**Before the 2014–2015 Price Collapse**

**Downsizing and Upgrading.** Since there was excess refining capacity globally, Shell embarked on a review of its downstream holdings, with the intention of streamlining them as well by means of asset sales, closures, and impairments. In reshuffling its downstream portfolio, it tried to increase the value of its global network of refineries and chemical plants. In 2013, it sold its stake in a Czech refining business and most of its stake in the refineries it owned in Italy and Australia. In 2014, it sold its stake in a German refinery. Instead, it took steps to meet growing refinery demand in Asia. Convinced that downstream refining margins in Asia would be strong, it created additional production capacity in China and expanded its Jurong Island petrochemicals plant in Singapore.

### After the 2014–2015 Price Collapse
**Continued Streamlining.** Shell continued streamlining, for example, by selling most of its Italian and Australian holdings. It decided not to proceed with a proposed project with its Qatar partner because of the cost. At the same time, it made investments to make its downstream portfolio more competitive. For example, it expanded capacity at a Netherlands refinery and a US chemical plant. Like other energy companies, it endeavored to bring high-performance lubricants to the market. It tried to develop biofuels that would reduce motor vehicles' environmental impact and worked with auto manufacturers. It also collaborated with the government of Iraq and Mitsubishi to capture flared natural gas from non-Shell southern Iraq oil fields and supply the natural gas to local power plants.

### *(4) High-Impact R&D*

### Before the 2014–2015 Price Collapse
**More Spending on R&D than Other Companies.** The company publicized that it spent more on R&D than any other integrated oil and natural gas company – more than $1 billion annually after 2007. In 2013, its R&D expenses grew to $1.32 billion, from $1.31 billion in 2012 and $1.12 billion in 2011. Shell pinned its future performance on the successful development of new technologies. Innovation was a way in which it could stand out from its competitors, obtain better performance from its existing businesses, and be on the cutting edge of future developments.

**Upstream, Downstream, and Environmental Impact.** Upstream spending was devoted to seismic processing and visualization, drilling equipment, and oil recovery. Downstream investments were in crude oil and LNG refining processes as well as new fuel and lubricant formulations. The company's focus also was on technologies to reduce its environmental footprint, especially in the area of water recycling and reuse.

**Global Partnerships.** Increasing its presence in China and India, the company expanded its global network of technology centers. The partnership it formed with the China National Petroleum Corporation was to develop techniques to drill multiple wells for tight shale.

### After the 2014–2015 Price Collapse

**Cutbacks.** By 2015, Shell had to cut its R&D spending by 23 percent in comparison to 2013, yet it managed to keep spending above $1 billion. It maintained major technology centers in India, the Netherlands, and the United States while also carrying out research in Canada, China, Germany, Norway, Oman, and Qatar. Its newest global research center was in India.

**Improving Operational Efficiency.** Shell invested in projects to improve the efficiency of existing operations, processes, and products. Its R&D provided technical services to keep upstream and downstream assets operating safely and efficiently. R&D helped to design, engineer, and construct projects; provided leadership in global contracting and procurement; and carried out troubleshooting at facilities at which performance fell below expectations.

**Emphasizing Safety and the Environment.** R&D's goal was to maintain the competitiveness of existing businesses, and to support company safety and environmental initiatives. Thus, Shell had a carbon storage research center in Qatar. It invested in research to help develop and commercialize advanced biofuels. It aimed to develop nascent technologies into value-generating products and technologies that would aid in the transition to a low-carbon economy.

**Supporting Innovation.** Shell also had programs through which external parties could share the rewards and risks of innovation. Among oil companies examined so far, these programs were unique.

One provided financial and technical support to prove the commercial viability of new ideas. Since 1996, more than 1,700 innovators had approached Shell and the company had helped more than 100 of them bring their ideas to fruition. An initiative that came from these efforts was Prelude, the facility that produced LNG at sea. The company's venture arm connected it with early-stage startups, business incubators, and seed-capital accelerators. Shell both invested in and collaborated with companies, not only in oil and gas and new energy, but also in information technology. For example, it invested in a California company that created software to design, connect, and operate energy storage systems and microgrids. Another investment was in a Massachusetts company that developed a device to monitor home appliances with mobile devices. Still another investment was in a UK company to support the technical and commercial development of high-altitude wind power. The winner of a Shell-organized competition developed an electrochemical technology that recycled carbon dioxide into chemicals and fuels. Another Shell program was meant to accelerate the adoption of proven technologies from other industries. It concentrated on computational science and data analysis, including the modeling of the flow of oil through underground rock layers. This program also explored chemical reactions in internal combustion engines, refinery engineering, chemical processing, gas-liquefaction, and catalysts. The company collaborated with private firms to develop a method for robot submarines to detect hydrocarbons that seep naturally from the seabed and to prove the seabed was an attractive spot for exploration.

## Performance

Despite these moves, Shell's profit margins hit rock bottom in 2015 and hardly improved the following year. Its performance was moving in a downward direction prior to the plunge in oil prices in 2014–2015 and it got worse after oil prices dropped. Net capital investment, which went up in 2013, shifted downward in 2014. Return on capital invested fell by about half from the levels achieved in 2012. Net capital investment continued to go down in 2015 and 2016. Return on capital invested reached a nadir in 2015. It started to improve somewhat in 2016.

## The Shift to Natural Gas and Deepwater Drilling – The Correct Response?

Shell struggled with some of the same issues as ExxonMobil and BP. Like both of these companies, it viewed the risks and uncertainties that it faced in similar terms and had similar assumptions about the long-term outlook for energy. Specifically, the risks and uncertainties centered on volatile prices, climate change and regulation, and getting projects done on time and on budget. Like ExxonMobil and BP, Shell envisioned rising demand for energy in the future, sparked mainly by the growing economies of Asia, the continued centrality of fossil fuels, and greater reliance on natural gas. All these companies continued to emphasize the imperative of growth in a volatile world that was facing many difficult challenges.

Like ExxonMobil and BP, Shell rested its hedging strategy on the pillars of sound operations, upstream growth, downstream integration, and high-impact R&D. Shell did not match ExxonMobil in operational excellence. Though it did not confront a safety lapse as large as BP's Gulf spill, it had difficulties in offshore drilling in the Arctic, in an explosion that took place in a chemical plant in the Netherlands, and in a fire in its Singapore refinery.

ExxonMobil, BP, and Shell had to show new discipline and sell assets that they considered less central to their missions. Shell significantly cut back on its global assets, such as choosing to pass on the shale revolution in the United States because it was losing money. It shed assets and looked for new opportunities but then settled on natural gas, particularly on LNG, and offshore drilling, and took a big plunge with its purchase of BG. Unlike ExxonMobil, which tried to stay the course, and BP, which made many small adjustments in the face of plummeting oil prices, it made a big shift, buying BG, which made it into an LNG and deep-water drilling power. Though both ExxonMobil and BP also recognized the growing importance of natural gas and tilted to some extent in this direction, Shell went further than either company did in emphasizing natural gas.

Though Shell chose to focus more than ExxonMobil and BP on natural gas, it still held a diverse portfolio of assets. All of these companies continued to be convinced that such diversity would provide them with the hedge they needed to withstand economic headwinds, no matter what they might be. They needed diversity to thrive in the future since the future was so uncertain. Like the other companies, Shell also worked diligently to streamline its downstream operations. On the other hand, it went further than either ExxonMobil or BP in emphasizing R&D and having programs in place to stimulate innovation.

The question to consider with Shell, as with ExxonMobil and BP, is whether it could have managed its affairs differently. What assumptions should guide their decision making going forward and how should they continue to adjust their strategies to what might come next?

## Notes

1. "Shell Says Overstated Reserves Led to Exaggerated Profits," www .nytimes.com/2004/07/03/business/shell-says-overstated-reserves-led-to-exaggerated-profits.html
2. "Shell Pays Out $15.5m Over Saro-Wiwa Killing," www.theguardian.com/ world/2009/jun/08/nigeria-usa
3. "*Nigeria: A Criminal Enterprise? Shell's Involvement in Human Rights Violations in Nigeria In The 1990s*," www.amnesty.org/en/documents/ AFR44/7393/2017/en/
4. "*3 Reasons Why Shell Halted Drilling in the Arctic*," https://news.natio nalgeographic.com/energy/2015/09/150928–3-reasons-shell-halted-dril ling-in-the-arctic/
5. "*Shell Takes Cautious Approach to Green Energy Transition*," www .ft.com/content/85a32136-a1f9-11e7-9e4f-7f5e6a7c98a2
6. "*Shell Rapped By ASA for 'Greenwash' Advert*," www.theguardian.com/ environment/2008/aug/13/corporatesocialresponsibility.fossilfuels
7. "*Shell Knew Fossil Fuels Created Climate Change Risks Back in 1980s, Internal Documents Show*," https://insideclimatenews.org/news/05042 018/shell-knew-scientists-climate-change-risks-fossil-fuels-global-warm ing-company-documents-netherlands-lawsuits; "'*Shell Knew': Oil Giant's 1991 Film Warned Of Climate Change Danger*," www .theguardian.com/environment/2017/feb/28/shell-knew-oil-giants-1991-film-warned-climate-change-danger
8. "*Annual Report and Form 20-F 2012*," http://reports.shell.com/annual-report/2012/servicepages/about_disclaimer.php; "*Sustainability Report 2012*," http://reports.shell.com/sustainability-report/2012/servicepages/ welcome.html; "*Annual Report and Form 20-F 2013*," http://925.nl/cm s_img/shell_annualreport_2013_en2.pdf
   "*Sustainability Report 2013*," http://reports.shell.com/sustainability-report/ 2013/servicepages/welcome.htmlf

"*Annual Report and Form 20-F 2014*," http://solutions.vwdservices.com/
documents/CorporateCommunicationDocuments/B_10127_JV_EN_2014
.pdf?c=AIkkuHOSYeJ8MSaQgnf7BOXmckGQDdmuyohMqU7BoFKeD
lTYfuvKdc9pjSKPN7gb
"*Sustainability Report 2014*," http://reports.shell.com/sustainability-report/
2016/
"*Annual Report and Form 20-F 2015*," https://solutions.vwdservices.com/
products/documents/8d5ce06a-6d6e-4f51-a646aa9667b92ed5/?c=jcXBL
JDNGC4zvVK2BiVK9qwLNlqtdCoWs1PZNNMksJMwFAVPOU6UN
VF7wSUbGAhN
"*Sustainability Report 2015*," http://reports.shell.com/sustainability-report/
2015/f; "*Annual Report and Form 20-F 2016*," https://reports.shell.com/
annual-report/2016/servicepages/disclaimer.phpf; "*Sustainability Report
2016*," http://reports.shell.com/sustainability-report/2016/

# 11 | Strategies to Try to Offset Plummeting Prices: TOTAL

The purpose of this chapter, like the previous ones on ExxonMobil, BP, and Shell, is to trace the responses of TOTAL to changing conditions in its industry in the years 2012–2016, especially to volatile oil prices, and to consider where it might go next with its strategies. The chapter starts with an introduction to TOTAL. Like earlier chapters, it then covers the state of the company between 2012 and 2014, before the dramatic fall in oil prices that took place and then goes on to cover the situation of the company between 2014 and 2016, after the fall. It examines the risks and uncertainties as the company perceived them, its assumptions about the future, and the hedges it put in place. How did the price shock alter its performance, and to what extent did it change its strategies because of changes in its performance? How did its strategies to offset plummeting prices compare with those of ExxonMobil, BP, and Shell, and what do they suggest about what TOTAL should do next?

## TOTAL's History

Founded after World War I, when the French Prime Minister Raymond Poincaré rejected forming a partnership with Shell, TOTAL started out as the French Petroleum Company. Like other companies in the sector, it had many foreign entanglements.[1] For example, after 1990, it was significantly involved in Iran.[2] In 2006, it collaborated with Aramco on a refinery and petrochemical complex in Saudi Arabia.[3] In 2009, it partnered with the Chinese National Petroleum Company (CNPC) and the Malaysian National Oil Company, Petronas, to develop oil in southern Iraq.[4] In 2013, it joined other companies in developing Kashagan's oil and natural gas.[5]

As a company with foreign entanglements, TOTAL got caught in a number of corruption scandals. The company's managing director and ten other executives in Italy were arrested for bribery in 2008.[6]

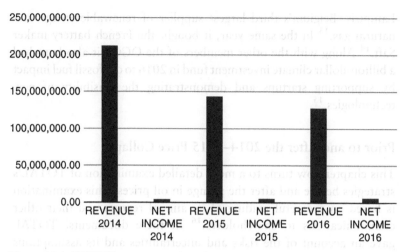

Figure 11.1 TOTAL's revenue and net income 2012–2016
Derived from Annual Reports

The US government fined TOTAL $398 million for paying an Iranian official $60 million as a consulting charge to gain access to natural gas fields.[7] Under the UN Oil-for-Food Program in Iraq, the company was accused of paying off Iraqi officials to secure contracts.[8] In Malta, TOTAL's main energy supplier barred it and its agents from operating because of the company's corrupt past.[9] Similar to ExxonMobil, BP, and Shell, the 2014–2015 drop in oil prices dug deeply into the company's revenue (Figure 11.1).

## Climate Change

Unlike other oil and natural gas companies, TOTAL was less resistant to the reality of climate change and made stronger commitments to renewable energy. It was an early member of the Oil and Gas Climate Initiative (OGCI), a CEO-led effort to show positive climate change leadership.[10] In 2011, it bought a 60 percent stake in US photovoltaics company, SunPower.[11] In 2016, it published its first Climate Report in which it revealed the actions it would take to meet growing energy demand while limiting climate impact.[12] It promised to achieve a 20 percent low-carbon energy mix by 2030 by emphasizing energy efficiency and developing renewable sources. In 2016, TOTAL bought

Lampiris, Belgium's third largest supplier of renewable energy and natural gas.[13] In the same year, it bought the French battery maker Saft.[14] Along with the other members of the OGCI, it also launched a billion-dollar climate investment fund in 2016 to cut fossil fuel impact by supporting startups and demonstrating the feasibility of new technologies.[15]

## Prior to and After the 2014–2015 Price Collapse

This chapter now turns to a more detailed examination of TOTAL's strategies before and after the plunge in oil prices. This examination is based on a careful reading of its annual reports and their other communications to shareholders.[16] In these documents, TOTAL gave an account of the risks and uncertainties and its assumptions about the future. Based on these perceptions and assumptions, it offered justification for its strategic choices. Like ExxonMobil, BP, and Shell it hedged its bets focusing on: operations, especially safety; upstream investments; downstream refining; and R&D that might lead to breakthroughs and give it competitive advantage. The goal of these moves was to protect it from price perturbations and other uncertainties that had implications for its performance. The company's performance in turn influenced how the company adjusted its strategy.

### TOTAL Before the 2014–2015 Price Collapse

#### Perceptions of the Risks and Uncertainties
Prior to the 2014–2015 price collapse, TOTAL acknowledged risks and uncertainties which were somewhat similar in nature to ExxonMobil, BP, and Shell. TOTAL like the other integrated oil and natural gas companies, was concerned with fluctuating prices, regulation, and preventing depletion of its reserves. To this end, it had to be able to start and finish projects on time. To this list of risks and uncertainties, it added regional vulnerabilities.

#### Price Fluctuations
Like ExxonMobil, BP, and Shell, TOTAL acknowledged that prices fluctuated due to many factors over which it had little control, including:

- economic and political developments in resource-producing regions, such as the Middle East, Africa, and South America;
- the influence of the Organization of the Petroleum Exporting Countries (OPEC) and other producing nations on production levels and prices;
- the supply of unconventional energy sources, like fracked oil and natural gas and oil sands;
- the existence of new technologies;
- politics, civil wars, violent conflicts, terrorism, and social unrest;
- demographic changes;
- economic instability;
- consumer preferences; and
- IT disruptions.

Like Shell, TOTAL wanted stable prices. If prices were exceptionally high for a considerable period, the negative effects were less demand for the firm's refined products and a decline in downstream earnings. In an environment of high prices, costs went up for the investments TOTAL made. On the other hand, substantial or extended falls in oil and natural gas prices also had adverse effects on the company's performance. They reduced the economic viability of the projects TOTAL planned, or had in development, and negatively affected the value of assets the company had and might wish to divest. They made it more difficult to finance capital expenditures for new projects and might cause the company to cancel or postpone them. A prolonged period of low prices would lead to review of the company's properties and could result in a reduction in reported reserves and impairment charges.

### Environmental Regulations
Like the other large integrated oil and natural gas companies, TOTAL was subject to stringent environmental, health, and safety laws that imposed significant costs. Growing public concern in a number of countries over greenhouse gas emissions and climate change, as well as stricter regulations in this area, could adversely affect sales, increase operating costs, and reduce profitability. More of its future production was expected to come from unconventional sources so it could help meet the world's growing demand for energy, and the carbon gas intensity of oil and gas production from unconventional sources was higher than production from conventional sources, and thus was likely to induce governments to create even more stringent requirements.

## Reserve Depletion

To be a profitable oil and natural gas firm in the long run, the company had to replace the reserves it depleted. Its long-term viability depended on the cost-effective discovery, acquisition, and development of new reserves. However, the development of oil and natural gas fields, including the construction of facilities and drilling, were capital intensive activities and required costly technology. Furthermore, due to a number of different challenges, cost projections were difficult to make because of many factors, including:

- the geological nature of oil and natural gas fields;
- the risk of dry holes;
- equipment shortages, failures, fires, blow-outs, and accidents;
- adverse weather;
- competition from NOCs;
- an inability to develop or deploy new technologies;
- government regulations, taxes, royalties, retroactive claims, and legal title issues;
- lack of control over the partners with whom the company carried out projects.

These factors could lead to cost overruns and impair the ability of the company to make profitable discoveries and acquisitions or complete development projects.

## Regional Vulnerabilities

TOTAL was especially vulnerable because of the regions of the world in which it operated. They included:

- Africa, which represented about a third of its 2012 liquids and gas production. It had its highest hydrocarbon production in Nigeria and Libya.
- The Middle East, which represented about a fifth of TOTAL's 2012 liquids and gas production. This region was undergoing significant violent conflict and social unrest, especially in Syria. EU economic sanctions against producing oil and gas were in place in Syria and in Yemen.
- South America, which represented 8 percent of the company's 2012 liquids and gas production. Here too some countries also suffered from conflict and social unrest, such as Venezuela and Argentina.

Nonetheless, the company had not stopped from exploring for and developing new reserves in regions of the world that were politically, socially, and economic instable, such as the Caspian Sea where it had large projects underway.

## Assumptions about the Future

Like ExxonMobil, BP, and Shell, TOTAL assumed that energy demand would continue to grow strongly in the decades ahead. Therefore, the company was justified making substantial long-term investments in new energy supplies. Demand for natural gas and renewable energy would also grow in the future. Where TOTAL parted ways from ExxonMobil, BP, and Shell was in a greater emphasis on renewable energy.

### Demand Growth

Projecting to the year 2030, TOTAL, like the other oil companies, anticipated growing demand led by developing countries. It also envisioned a diversified energy mix, but with oil remaining the primary energy source. An economic slowdown that dampened oil demand from OECD countries would be more than offset by the increasing dynamism of emerging countries, particularly in Asia. The dynamism of these economies would sustain overall growth in demand. TOTAL was in agreement with ExxonMobil, BP, and Shell in that it viewed the challenge as being the need to satisfy the world's growing global demand for oil. New incremental production would not come from traditional sources. Rather, all the oil companies would have to rely increasingly on unconventional sources like deep offshore oil, extra heavy oil, and tight oil (i.e. fracking).

### Natural Gas

Like ExxonMobil, BP, and Shell, TOTAL was bullish about natural gas, which it expected to replace coal as the second most important energy source. Demand for LNG would go up because of strong growth in Asian economies. The prices for natural gas in Asia would be high. On the other hand, US prices would be low due to abundant shale gas supply.

### Renewable Energy

Unlike ExxonMobil, BP, and Shell, TOTAL emphasized that growth in renewable energy was likely to be rapid; however, in agreement with its peers, it did not envision that this growth would take place in the near term. Cuts in subsidy programs had taken place and many renewable energy companies were in bankruptcy because of excess production. Photovoltaics, temporarily in decline, nonetheless, had the potential to grow as the EU moved to meet its Kyoto climate commitments. In moving toward a lower-carbon economy, TOTAL agreed with ExxonMobil and Shell that carbon capture and storage was likely to play an important role.

## TOTAL After the 2014–2015 Price Collapse

After the price collapse, the company's assessment of risks and uncertainties remained focused on fluctuating prices, climate change, and completion of large, complex projects.

### Perceptions of the Risks and Uncertainties

*Fluctuating Prices*

The sharp decline in oil and natural gas prices and return to volatility were not welcome. TOTAL calculated that $10-per-barrel decreases in oil prices lowered its profits by about $2.5 billion. It had little control over the factors that determined prices, such as general economic and political conditions, dollar exchange rates, OPEC, technological developments, demography, consumer preferences, global security, and adverse weather. The company could not influence whether the world targeted countries for sanctions or other restrictions, and the sanctions had curtailed its ability to do business in Iran, Syria, and Russia.

*Climate Change*

Like other oil and natural gas companies, TOTAL was also concerned about climate change regulations that could adversely affect its business. In addition, it was apprehensive about the physical effects of climate change unleashing negative weather patterns, such as wildfires in Canada that could harm its operations.

*Project Completion*

The company was subject to a wide variety of operational concerns that affected its ability to complete projects, including accidents, fires, explosions, equipment failures, toxic leakages, discharges, ecosystem damage, terrorism, death and injury to employees and people in the communities where it located its facilities, inadequate performance of contractors, as well as malicious acts against pipelines and computer systems. The security situations in Nigeria and Yemen were troubling. TOTAL had to build precautions into every activity it undertook and have crisis management systems in place to handle the threats that could develop, but they still did not provide complete protection.

## Assumptions about the Future

The company expected the sharp oil price decline, driven by excess supply due to increased US production and lower demand, would continue because, even with OPEC- and non-OPEC-announced production cuts, inventories were likely to stay high. The anticipation of low prices extending into the future led TOTAL to assume that it would have to delay and cancel projects. At the same time, companies in the sector would increasingly have to incorporate the threat of climate change.

### Delay and Cancelation

The likelihood of an oil price rebound was not high due to:

- the robustness of the US shale business;
- weak growth in global GDP;
- improved energy efficiency, as a result of innovation; and
- OPEC and other geopolitical factors.

Oil-producing states needed and benefitted from low prices. The major industry players would have to delay and cancel projects, reduce their capital and operating expenses, and rely on downstream to hedge their bets.

### Long-Term Growth

TOTAL projected that in the long-term demand for oil would grow at a 0.6 percent compound annual rate. That meant that 50 million barrels a day of new production would be necessary by 2030. To bring on the supply, there had to be significant investment in high tech and innovation in exploration and production. For the investment to take place, prices would have to rise. The world would be short of about a fifth of the oil it needed, if oil prices continued to be less than $90 a barrel.

## Climate Change

The company would have to incorporate the challenge of climate change into its business plans. It believed the goal of limiting the rise in global temperatures to two-degrees Celsius was realistic. It would have to provide solutions to the climate change problem, while, at the same time, satisfying the needs of a growing world population for affordable energy.

## Hedging

Like ExxonMobil, BP, and Shell, the approach TOTAL took to managing the risks and uncertainties, based on its assumptions, relied on four layers of hedging: (1) maintaining operational excellence; (2) continuing to make upstream investments to replace lost oil and natural gas; (3) relying on downstream integration for steady profit and revenue growth; and (4) carrying out high-impact R&D for future competitive advantage. After the crash in oil prices, TOTAL like the other large oil and natural gas firms deviated little from this model. Discussed next is how TOTAL applied these hedging strategies before and after the 2014–2015 price crash.

## (1) Operational Excellence

### Before the 2014–2015 Price Collapse

As with the other major oil and natural gas companies, safety was a core value. TOTAL touted the improvements it made. It had total recordable injury and total lost time injury rates that were 57 percent and 56 percent less than 2008. These gains were made though the number of million hours worked had increased. TOTAL, nonetheless, had to deal with accidents in the North Sea and Nigeria in 2012, as well as safety issues in its facilities in Yemen. The company was also close to achieving its target of reducing natural gas flaring by 50 percent and water discharges by 40 percent and making annual energy efficiency improvements of 1.5 percent. The goal was to reduce internally generated greenhouse gas emissions by 15 percent from 2008 to 2015.

The company had a "Health Safety Environment Quality Charter," in which it set out its principles for safety and the environment, which were supported by its management systems. In these areas, TOTAL relied on ISO 14001 and ISO 9001 assessments and certification, complied with laws and regulations, and carried out systematic risk assessments at many points – prior to approving new projects, investments, acquisitions, and disposals as well as periodically during operations. Before releasing new chemicals, it conducted toxicological studies and life cycle analyses. TOTAL monitored its progress in achieving safety and environmental objectives by means of a program of inspections, audits, training, and raising awareness. It set out the rules for occupational safety in a document called the 12 Golden Rules. It provided strong incentives to report anomalies and near misses. Its internal statistics showed that employees generally followed the rules.

Though the emphasis was on prevention, TOTAL also took steps to prepare for crises that it identified. After BP's large spill in the Gulf, it created task forces to carry out risk analyses and issue recommendations. The company implemented more stringent controls and audits of its drilling operations. Yet it admitted that no matter what it did, it was impossible to guarantee completely that such contingencies would not arise. Thus, it had carefully drawn up emergency plans and procedures to respond in the case of spills or leaks.

### After the 2014–2015 Price Collapse

Safety and the environment remained central, as it was for all the major oil companies. A senior-level "Executive for Health, Safety, and the Environment" officer, located in the Division of People and Social Responsibility Division, implemented a unified safety and environmental plan. Management systems continued to be in place to meet the requirements of ISO 14001, ISO 9001, and OHSAS 18001. The company meant to meet the requirement of the future ISO 45001. Unlike other companies discussed in previous chapters, TOTAL placed great emphasis on these certifications. It did not stop from carrying out regular assessments of the risks and impacts of activities in the areas of process safety, the environment, and protection of workers and local residents prior to approving new investments, acquisitions, releasing new products, and disposing of assets. It also maintained the inspections and audits it carried out, as well as engaging in training and making efforts to raise the awareness of employees and contractors. The company had steps to prepare for incidents based on various scenarios. It had objectives, and action plans in place. On most indicators, it showed improvement. The target of achieving less than 1.15

recorded injuries per million hours worked was achieved in 2016. The number of accidental deaths per million hours worked was among the best in the industry in that year.

## (2) Upstream Investment

### Before the 2014–2015 Price Collapse

Before the collapse, TOTAL had many long-term global contracts and joint ventures to produce oil and natural gas. It aimed to optimize its portfolio through asset sales as well engaging in new projects to ensure that its investments would pay off. It also had commitments to renewable energy and biomass.

**Global Investment.** In 2009, TOTAL set up a joint venture with the US shale company Chesapeake to produce natural gas in the Barnett Shale Basin in Texas. It owned 25 percent of this venture. In 2011, it signed another joint venture agreement with Chesapeake, in which it acquired a 25 percent share in liquid-rich Utica shale fields in Ohio. TOTAL also produced and exported coal for over thirty years from South Africa, mainly to Europe and Asia. A subsidiary of the company owned and operated five mines. TOTAL often had a percentage interest in oil and natural gas fields, with the balance held by joint venture partners. The joint venture partners were frequently state-owned oil companies and government entities as well as other oil and natural gas companies. In many instances, but not always, in its joint venture partnerships, TOTAL was the party responsible for the technical operations. By having joint venture partnerships, it hedged its bets.

In 2012, about half of TOTAL's proved reserves were oil and about half were natural gas. It had both productive oil and natural gas wells and developed and undeveloped oil and natural gas acreage all over the world. The highest percentage of its oil production was in the UAE and the highest percentage of its natural gas production was in Russia (Figure 11.2). Its reserves were located in Europe (mainly in Norway and the United Kingdom), in the Middle East (mainly in Qatar, the UAE, and Yemen), in Asia (mainly in Australia, Kazakhstan, and Russia), in Africa (mainly in Angola, Gabon, Libya, Nigeria, and the Republic of the Congo), and in the Americas (mainly in Canada, Argentina, and Venezuela). The company was a pioneer in LNG and a leading player with stakes in liquefaction plants in Qatar, the UAE,

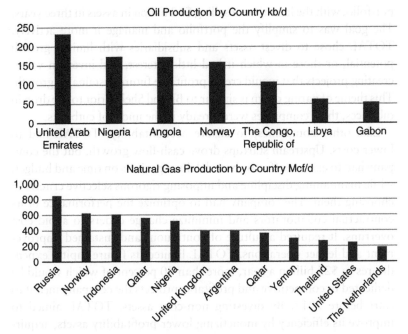

**Figure 11.2** The locations of TOTAL's oil and natural gas production
Derived from Company Annual Reports

Oman, Nigeria, Norway, and Yemen, as well as a supply agreement in Indonesia.

With the exception of North America and part of the United Kingdom, Norway, and Argentina, TOTAL sold the majority of its natural gas production under long-term contracts, not on the spot market. It based the long-term price contracts on oil prices and inflation. Yet, sometimes, it was required to deliver natural gas on an as-needed basis. Delivery commitments varied in duration and in scope from contract to contract.

**Optimizing the Portfolio.** Like the other oil companies discussed in previous chapters, TOTAL evaluated exploration opportunities based on a variety of geological, technical, political, and economic factors (including taxes and license terms) and projected oil and gas prices. In 2013, it started to transition. Like the other companies, it moved from an intensive investment phase toward optimizing capital expenditures based on stricter investment criteria. It chose to pare down its portfolio, with the intention of selling $10 billion in assets in three years. The goal was to simplify the portfolio and manage it more actively. TOTAL chose to divest assets and subsidiaries with limited growth potential, or those in which it had little interest, and invest in value-creating projects that would create profitable future sustainable growth. This theme of paring down is similar to BP and Shell. Prior to the drop in oil prices, these companies were already in the midst of cutbacks.

Like other companies, to ensure accountability, TOTAL had to lower costs. Upstream startups drove cash-flow growth, but the company had to execute effectively and deliver projects on time and budget, while maintaining discipline and imposing rigorous selective criteria in choosing them. The company had to optimize the performance of its contractual collaborators and minimize change orders to avoid cost overruns. It required a culture of continuous and sustained improvement and leaner operations. TOTAL limited its future capital expenditures to $25 billion a year, more than 80 percent of which would be dedicated to competitive and profitable projects the company meant to start before 2017. By divesting non-core assets, TOTAL aimed to improve its efficiency by monetizing lower-profitability assets, acquiring new core resources, and better balancing its country exposure. It planned that one-third of its new projects would be deep offshore, with LNG being another key emphasis. In 2013, it established an LNG facility in Angola and continued with ongoing LNG projects it had started in Australia, Russia, and Nigeria.

**Investing in Renewables.** To complement its investments in hydrocarbons (oil, natural gas, and coal), TOTAL also invested in renewable energy in a different way from the companies discussed in previous chapters. Its focuses were on solar energy (primarily, but not exclusively, crystalline silicon photovoltaics) and biomass. It kept an active watch on other technologies. Following a friendly takeover of SunPower of San Jose, California of which it owned 66 percent in 2011, and a capital infusion it gave to SunPower in 2012, it integrated Tenesol, its own solar subsidiary, with SunPower. SunPower designed, manufactured, and supplied high-efficiency solar panels. It was active throughout the solar power value chain, from cells to the design and construction of power plants. It manufactured cells in the Philippines and Malaysia and assembled them into modules and solar panels in Asia, North America, Europe, and South Africa. Tenesol mainly operated in Europe and Africa. TOTAL also held a 50 percent interest in Photovoltech, a Belgian company that specialized in manufacturing multicrystalline photovoltaic cells. Photovoltech won a 2010 contract to construct a concentrated solar power plant in Abu Dhabi, in which it would sell electricity to the country's leading water and Electricity Company. In other renewable energies, TOTAL owned a 12-megawatt wind farm in Mardyck (near Dunkirk, France). In marine energy, it held a 26.6 percent share in Scotrenewables Tidal Power, located in the Orkney Islands in Scotland.

TOTAL was exploring a number of avenues for developing biomass. The methods were likely to vary depending on the resource used, markets targeted (e.g. fuels, lubricants, petrochemicals, specialty chemicals), and the nature of the conversion processes. Since 2010, TOTAL strategically partnered with Amyris, a US company specializing in biomass. TOTAL held an 18.5 percent stake in this company, which owned a cutting-edge industrial synthetic biological platform designed to create and optimize microorganisms that could convert sugars into molecules of interest through fermentation. Amyris' research laboratory and pilot units were in California as well as in Brazil and it opened up a production facility in Paraiso, Brazil at the beginning of 2013.

TOTAL also was assessing the potential of phototrophic processes and the bioengineering of microalgae. It had entered into a partnership with Cellectis S.A. to conduct exploratory work in this field.

**After the 2014–2015 Price Collapse**
After the collapse, the company's focus was on restoring its cash flow. It continued to reorganize, cut back on spending, and reduce the size of its portfolio. In taking these steps, it was similar to the companies discussed in previous chapters. It also remained committed to deep offshore projects, yet, unlike the other companies, TOTAL retained more assets that would provide it with a hedge against a low-carbon future than they did.

**Restructuring the Portfolio.** TOTAL searched for a robust response to the price collapse and a clear path forward. It needed to increase its cash flow to maintain access to financial markets under favorable conditions. To do so, it made significant reductions in operating expenditures ($1.2 billion), freezing upstream recruitment and reducing downstream headcount. By 2017, it aimed to cut corporate staff by 15 percent.

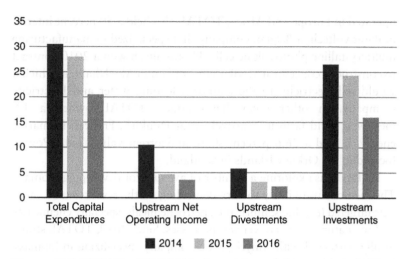

**Figure 11.3** TOTAL's 2014–2016 downsizing of its upstream business (billions of dollars)
Derived from Company Annual Reports

Together, the cash-flow impact of having fewer employees would be $8 billion. This step of letting go employees was like other companies. TOTAL, like other companies, also continued to sell upstream assets (Figure 11.3) and reduced green-field and brown-field spending. It disposed of its coal mines. The changes it made from 2012 to 2014 – the sale of these non-core and downstream assets and simplification of and exiting from businesses – raised $28 billion. The 2017 goal was to divest assets worth slightly more than $3 billion per year, for a total of $10 billion in asset sold over three years.

The company lowered capital expenditures by about 33 percent, from around $30 billion in 2014 to around $20 billion in 2016. With more than $15 billion in cash and more than $10 billion in credit lines, TOTAL had liquidity and the financial flexibility to continue to invest. Like other companies, it imposed discipline on its investing. It strictly screened new project opportunities, subjecting them to ongoing strategic review to prioritize the most promising ones. The criteria TOTAL applied was that 50 percent of new projects had to be in basins with proven hydrocarbons, 25 percent had to be in and around producing assets, and just 25 percent could be in new-frontier basins. The company wanted to reduce the uncertainty. Like its peers, it kept costs down by being more selective. It largely allocated its 2017 exploration and production budget to major development projects already under construction. These were in the Republic of the Congo, Angola, and Nigeria. It also had LNG projects in Russia and Australia and was Sub-Saharan Africa's largest producer. Its 2016, exploration expenditure, $1.4 billion, was mainly in the United States, Norway, Papua New Guinea, Brazil, Iraq, Bulgaria, Myanmar, and the United Kingdom. This amount compared to $1.9 billion in exploration expenditures in 2015 and $2.6 billion in 2014.

TOTAL thus was cutting its exploration expenditures by about a half. It projected that its 2017 exploration budget would be just $1.25 billion. With regard to the eight project startups TOTAL had in 2015, about 50 percent were production-sharing agreements, where it could share the risk and hedge again unforeseen contingencies; 60 percent were TOTAL-operated; and 60 percent were deep offshore projects. In these deep offshore projects, TOTAL was building on a core capability. Like BP, it considered itself a leader in deep offshore developments. They constituted more than 10 percent of its production in 2014.

The company also renewed a contract it had with Abu Dhabi's national oil company. However, its equity interest in Abu Dhabi's national oil company was just 10 percent, though in this agreement it did obtain higher margins than in the one it had in the past. The new agreement would last forty years and the production plateau was 1.8 million barrels per day.

The company wanted a stronger, but smaller, portfolio, mainly focused on a few key assets. Yet, it continued to look for ways to enter Qatar, acquire US shale assets, and make deals in countries such as Brazil, Uganda, and Iran to increase production. After the fall in oil prices, it emphasized, like the other oil companies, strong cash-flow growth from the new projects it funded. Like the other companies, it expanded its cost-reduction initiatives. It wanted to keep lowering its breakeven point. The goal was to reach a breakeven point to $40 per barrel of oil, and create an energy mix with progressively decreasing carbon intensity.

**Investing in Renewables.** TOTAL created a new business division for natural gas and renewable energy. It also created a new division dedicated to social responsibility and people. These divisions were additions to its existing divisions, which were devoted to exploration, production, refining, chemicals, marketing, and services. Biofuel was not part of the new natural gas and renewable energy division.

It continued to be a part of refining and chemicals. The company developed activities in low-carbon and renewable energy with the aim of achieving an energy mix with less carbon intensity that would hedge its bets against the possibility that the world was going to limit global temperatures increases to no more than two degrees Celsius.

As part of the effort to diversify, TOTAL maintained its majority share in SunPower. This company also built solar farms in Latin America and South Africa. However, in light of the strong 2016 deterioration in global solar market and overcapacity of PV cells production, it had to reduce its operational costs and it closed its Philippines plant. Besides SunPower, TOTAL had other interests in solar farms and solar R&D. For instance, it held a 20 percent interest in an Abu Dhabi solar power plant. TOTAL also invested in storage. It bought the remaining portions of Saft, the French battery company that it did not own in a 2016 voluntary takeover bid. Saft maintained its specialization in high-tech batteries for industry. With just under $1 billion in sales, it was a leader in nickel and primary lithium batteries for industrial infrastructure. It also made lithium ion batteries for space and defense purposes and was witnessing steady growth in emerging economies and in Asia, Latin America, and Russia.

TOTAL continued to hold a 23.5 percent interest in Amyris, which now tried to produce biojet fuel. Amyris had successful demonstration flights with Air France, KLM, and Cathay Pacific. This company was studying microalgae bioengineering and had acquired R&D platforms in California that were dedicated to fermenting and processing molecules for biofuels with the goal of developing new bio-components.

## (3) Downstream Integration

### Before the 2014–2015 Price Collapse

**Restructuring to Improve Profitability.** Like other large oil and natural gas companies, TOTAL leveraged its downstream businesses to support its upstream growth. For this strategy to be effective, the company had to restructure its downstream businesses to improve their profitability. Like other companies discussed in previous chapters, TOTAL's goal was to increase the competitive performance of the downstream business and boost their profitability. It wanted to increase their profitability from six percent in 2010 to 13 percent in 2015.

Refining and chemicals was a large group encompassing many businesses and selling a range of different products. TOTAL was a leader in the specialty chemicals market for lubricants, LPG, jet fuel, special fluids, bitumen, heavy fuels, and marine fuels. Its businesses also included the processing of adhesives and plastics with elastic properties. In addition, it did electroplating for the automotive, construction, electronics, aerospace, and convenience goods markets. Through a French subsidiary, it manufactured and marketed nitrogen fertilizers from natural gas.

Through active portfolio management, TOTAL tried to reduce its European exposure. It aimed to lower its European breakeven points by means of increased synergies and greater efficiencies. It concentrated its investments in the best European platforms, modernized these sites, and further integrated their production of refinery products and chemicals. From 2011 to 2014, TOTAL cut back the capital it employed in Europe by 30 percent, and it was in the process of reducing European capacity by another 20 percent by 2017. TOTAL moved the capital it employed from slower growing European markets to faster growing markets elsewhere in the world. It had major refining and chemical platforms in France and Belgium as well as the United States, Saudi Arabia, Qatar, and South Korea, and while the company cut back on its operations in France and Belgium, it expanded its manufacturing platforms in Saudi Arabia, Qatar, and South Korea.

**Clean Energy.** TOTAL participated in the Clean Energy Partnership in Germany that focused on hydrogen distribution. An "H₂ Mobility" study examined the deployment and implementation of a hydrogen fuel distribution network in Germany. In addition, it played a role in developing fast-change electric vehicle fueling stations in various European countries. It had pilot programs in place that offered services that discouraged energy consumption, along with others to create hybrid fuel and photovoltaic technical solutions and facilitate access to energy in rural Africa.

### After the 2014–2015 Price Collapse

**Further Increasing Productivity.** TOTAL reduced downstream investments by about 40 percent, from around \$26.5 billion in 2014 to around \$16 billion in 2016. The company persisted in divesting its non-core assets and systematically tackling underperforming ones. Between 2011 and 2017, it aimed to reduce its

European capacity by another 20 percent. On the other hand, in Africa it was the market leader and was building on its presence on that continent. It was also expanding a high-return lubricant business, building a major hub in Singapore, and creating new partnerships with Korean and Chinese companies. TOTAL lowered its European refining and chemicals breakeven point by about 50 percent from 2011 to 2014. By 2016, the company had reduced production costs for a barrel of oil to $5.90 compared to $9.90 in 2014. It aimed to continue to cut costs, with the goal of bringing them down to $5.50 a barrel in 2017. Among major oil and natural gas companies, TOTAL had the highest downstream return on capital invested. The company had fewer downstream assets than in the past but their profitability had grown (Figure 11.4).

## (4) High-Impact R&D

### Before the 2014–2015 Price Collapse

TOTAL's R&D expenditure in 2012, about $1.3 billion, was very high in comparison to its peer companies. Yet it had lowered the number of people engaged in this role from 4,087 in 2010 to 3,946 in 2011, while increasing the number to 4,110 people in 2012. It had twenty-one R&D sites worldwide and about 600 partnerships with other companies, universities, and academic institutes. It also had a permanent network of scientific advisors to monitor and advise it on its R&D activities, and was actively engaged in protecting its innovations through the patent system.

**Upstream.** The company's upstream R&D priorities were relevant to:

- deep offshore projects, natural gas resources, and very cold regions;
- computing, exploration, seismic acquisition, and processing tools for the appraisal of hydrocarbon reservoirs and simulation of field evolution, especially for tight, very deep reservoirs;
- shale gas and oil, with a strong focus on water management during fracking;
- enhanced oil recovery from mature reservoirs;
- recovery of heavy oil and bitumen with reduced environmental impacts;
- $CO_2$ capture and storage; and
- water management.

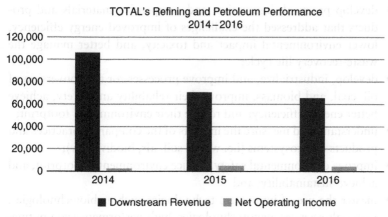

Figure 11.4 TOTAL's downstream revenue and profits 2014–2016
Derived from Company Annual Reports

**Downstream.** The company's downstream R&D priorities were relevant to energy efficiency, safety, and the environment and included:

- new LNG solutions;
- synergy between industrial units;
- improved safety, performance, and energy efficiency of processes;
- differentiated fuel and polymer products;
- meeting environmental obligations;
- non-conventional oil and second-generation biomass;
- higher performance and energy-saving fuels and oil;
- material sciences skills and innovations for an energy-efficient car;
- sustainable binder assembly and electroplating solutions for reduced energy and less environmental impact;
- detection and reduction of air pollution emissions;
- prevention of soil contamination and site rehabilitation; and
- environmentally friendly conversion processes for coal and biomass to polymers and biomass to fuels.

**New Energy Systems.** The focus of TOTAL's R&D efforts was not just on advancing knowledge, tools, and technological mastery of discovering and profitably operating complex oil and gas resources, but also on new energy systems. Specifically TOTAL aimed to:

- develop and industrialize solar, biomass, and carbon capture and storage technologies;

- develop practical, innovative, and competitive materials and products that addressed the challenges of improved energy efficiency, lower environmental impact and toxicity, and better manage the waste-recovery life cycle;
- develop, industrialize, and improve processes for the conversion of oil, coal, and biomass, improve their reliability and safety, achieve better energy efficiency; and reduce their environmental footprint;
- understand and measure the impacts of the company's practices and products on ecosystems (i.e. water, soil, air, biodiversity);
- improve environmental safety, reduce environmental footprint, and achieve sustainability; and
- master the use of innovative technologies such as biotechnologies, materials sciences, nanotechnologies, high-performance computing, information and communications technologies, and new analytic techniques.

TOTAL pursued R&D in crystalline silicon and concentrated solar power. It had partnerships to optimize the photovoltaic solar chain (silicon, wafers, cells, modules, and systems) by cutting production costs and multiplying applications, while increasing electric-efficiency conversion.

**After the 2014–2015 Price Collapse**
TOTAL's R&D expenditures fell slightly below $1 billion per year in 2015, but the cut was only temporary and the company increased spending to above $1 billion a year again in 2016 (Figure 11.5). It had fewer global R&D sites – eighteen, but more partner agreements – 1,000, and it maintained an active intellectual property protection effort in filing for patents. More than half of its R&D expenditures, or $689 million in 2016, were devoted to oil and natural gas, but it continued to make investments relevant to new energy systems, upstream oil and natural gas production, and downstream refining and chemicals. In making diversified R&D investments, TOTAL, like the other oil companies, hedged its bets against different possible future worlds.
**Upstream.** Among the upstream topics receiving emphasis were the following:

- improving exploration, geological structures, seismic acquisition, and imaging technologies;

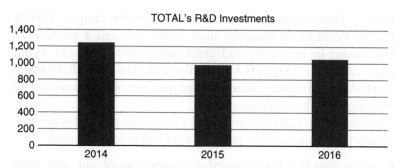

**Figure 11.5** TOTAL's R&D spending 2014–2016 (millions of dollars)
Derived from Company Annual Reports

- characterizing hydrocarbon reservoirs and simulating field evolution during production;
- enhancing oil recovery (particularly important given the company's Mideast partnerships);
- deep offshore especially as it supports major technological innovation, such as in Brazil;
- well operation and safety;
- robotics, nanotechnology, and supercomputers for decision support.

Like BP, TOTAL was interested in decision support systems.

**Downstream.** Among the downstream topics receiving emphasis were the following:

- refining of differentiated chemicals products especially bio-sourced products and liquid fuels from natural gas;
- catalysts;
- new additives for cold-weather performance;
- limited-sulfur-content fuels;
- sugars for biofuels conversion.

TOTAL was unique among oil companies in having interests in sugars for biofuels conversion.

**New Energy Systems.** TOTAL continued to have an active portfolio of projects around topics such as $CO_2$ capture, use, and storage; health, safety, and environment; renewable energy, and energy efficiency. The company maintained future-generation photovoltaic cell research in partnership with leading scientists and engineers like those at

France's Photovoltaic Institute on the Paris-Saclay campus. TOTAL Energy Ventures, in existence since 2009, managed a portfolio of investments in innovative and clean energy technology. In having a special venture unit, TOTAL was like Shell. The R&D division was also tasked with creating a consolidated roadmap of studies around the two-degrees-Celsius scenario.

In addition to carbon capture and storage and soil and water contamination management, topics that were highlighted included:

- weight reduction for improved diagnostic control and safer, more comfortable, more responsible mobility;
- ways to improve how SunPower produced cells and modules;
- ways that Saft could produce low-cost lithium ion storage batteries that reduced environmental impacts;
- software tools and algorithms for intelligent electric power management.

The detail and breadth of TOTAL's R&D efforts were impressive, both before and after the oil price drop.

## Performance

For 2012–2016, TOTAL's revenue, net income, and profit margins slipped less than Shell's, though both companies were smaller than they had been in 2012. Shell's profit margins hit rock bottom in 2015 and hardly improved the following year, while TOTAL's profit margins did not fall as far as Shell's did, and they started to make a small recovery the next year. Like Shell, TOTAL increased capital spending in 2013 and grew it more in 2014. Despite all the moves it made, however, its return on invested capital fell from year to year. It was not meeting its goal of a 15 percent return, but it bested Shell's in this category in 2012 and it increased its lead over Shell in 2014. From 2014 to 2016, TOTAL's capital spending continued to fall and so did its return on invested capital, but it once again did better than Shell in both 2015 and 2016.

## Gradual Movement to a Low Carbon Future – The Correct Response?

TOTAL's strategies differed from its peers both in its understanding of the risks and uncertainties and its assumptions about the future. These differences were not extremely large, but they were important in how TOTAL responded. Like the other companies, TOTAL had a robust hedging strategy in place that rested on the pillars of sound operations, a balanced set of upstream growth opportunities, downstream integration, and high-impact R&D. Its safety and environmental programs, more than the other companies, depended on external certification and assessment. It had rigorous goals in these domains and made some progress. Similar to the other oil companies reviewed in previous chapters, it actively engaged in a process of paring down its portfolio in response to reduced revenues and profits after prices plummeted. Like the other companies, it streamlined its downstream operations in order to maintain its profitability. More than any of these companies, it made big bets in renewable energy. While Shell, too, had investments in this area, TOTAL's outright ownership of renewable energy companies, and the degree to which it highlighted renewable energy in its R&D was different. These bets make it stand out from Shell, or for that matter, from ExxonMobil and BP. TOTAL apparently was more concerned about protecting itself against the contingency of less carbon intensive world than the other companies were, which is not to say that Shell also was not concerned, but it expressed this concern by making a turn to natural gas, while TOTAL expressed its concern by outright ownership of renewable energy assets and an R&D program that was broadly inclusive in the realm of alternative energy and environmental protection.

The question to ponder was whether TOTAL could have managed its affairs differently during the period of the price collapse. None of the oil companies examined entirely effectively fought the headwind of declining oil prices. What future risks and uncertainties would TOTAL face? What assumptions should guide its decision making? What should it do in the future and how should it further adjust its strategies? Its responses had important implications for the firm and for society.

## Notes

1. *"Compagnie Française des Pétroles and Its Contribution to the Re-establishment of France's Position among the Oil Countries after the Second World War,"* https://web.archive.org/web/20130512121843/http://thebhc.org/publications/BEHonline/2006/sassi.pdf

2. "*Total Signs Deal with Iran, Exposing It to Big Risks and Rewards,*" www.nytimes.com/2017/07/03/business/energy-environment/iran-tota l-france-gas-energy.html

3. "*Total CEO Confirms Plan to Enlarge Joint Venture with Saudi Aramco,*" www.oilandgaspeople.com/news/16440/total-ceo-confirms-plan-to-enlarge-joint-venture-with-saudi-aramco/

4. "*TOTAL in Iraq,*" www.total.com/sites/default/files/atoms/files/total_in_ iraq_en_ara.pdf

5. "*TOTAL in Kazakhstan,*" www.total.com/en/kazakhstan

6. "*Head of Total Italy Arrested in Graft Probe,*" www.ft.com/content/6 ef1109a-cb9f-11dd-ba02-000077b07658

7. "*Total Settles US Bribe Probe For $398 Million; CEO May Be Tried,*" www.reuters.com/article/us-total-iran-idUSBRE94S11020130529

8. "*Total Fined by French Court in Iraq Oil-For-Food Case,*" www .reuters.com/article/us-france-total-iraq-idUSKCN0VZ1AM

9. "*Malta Bans Trafigura, Total Unit from Oil Supply Tenders,*" www .reuters.com/article/malta-oil-enemalta/update-1-malta-bans-trafigura-total-unit-from-oil-supply-tenders-idUSL6N0BLDRU20130221

10. "*Catalyst for Change,*" http://oilandgasclimateinitiative.com/

11. "*Total and SunPower Partner to Create a New Global Leader in the Solar Industry,*" www.total.com/en/media/news/press-releases/tota l-et-sunpower-creent-un-nouveau-leader-mondial-de-lindustrie-solaire

12. "*Integrating Climate into Our Strategy.*" www.total.com/sites/default/files/atoms/files/rapport_climat_2016_en.pdf

13. "*Total Acquires Lampiris to Expand Its Gas and Power Distribution Activities,*" www.businesswire.com/news/home/20160614005759/en/ Total-Acquires-Lampiris-Expand-Gas-Power-Distribution

14. "*Oil Giant Total to Acquire Battery Maker Saft for $1.1 Billion,*" www .greentechmedia.com/articles/read/oil-giant-total-to-acquire-battery-m aker-saft-for-1-1-billion#gs.TFemFQM

15. "*Catalyst for Change.*" http://oilandgasclimateinitiative.com/

16. "*Annual Report and Form 20-F 2012,*" www.total.com/sites/default/fi les/atoms/files/total-form-20-f-2012.pdf; "*Factbook 2012.*" www .total.com/sites/default/files/atoms/files/factbook_2012.pdf; "*Annual Report and Form 20-F 2013,*" www.total.com/sites/default/files/atom s/files/form_20-f_2013.pdf

"*Factbook 2013,*" www.total.com/sites/default/files/atoms/files/total-factbook-2013_0.pdf

"*Annual Report and Form 20-F 2014,*" www.total.com/sites/default/ files/atoms/files/form_20-f_0.pdf

"*Factbook 2014,*" www.total.com/sites/default/files/atoms/files/fact
book_2014_v2_0.pdf ;"*Annual Report and Form 20-F 2015,*" www
.total.com/sites/default/files/atoms/files/form_20-f_2015_web_version
.pdfN
"*Factbook 2015.*" www.total.com/sites/default/files/atoms/files/factbook-
2015-bd.pdf; "*Annual Report and Form 20-F 2016,*" www.total.com/sit
es/default/files/atoms/files/2016_form_20-f_web_0.pdf; "*Factbook
2016,*" www.total.com/sites/default/files/atoms/files/factbook_2016_web
.pdf

# Motor Vehicle Company Strategies

# 12 | *Strategies to Take Advantage of Plummeting Prices: GM*

Now that the book has covered the major integrated oil and natural gas companies, it moves to the major motor vehicle firms, GM, Ford, VW, and Toyota. Much of the gasoline that the major oil and natural gas companies make ends up in the gas tanks of motor vehicles (see Chapter 5). The major automotive companies also reacted to the plunge in oil prices. What was a threat to the oil and natural gas companies was an opportunity for the automotive companies as driving became less expensive and they could sell large, profitable vehicles in greater numbers. To what extent were the automotive companies able to take advantage of this opportunity? Each firm in the sector reacted somewhat differently and had a different capacity to deal with this change.

This chapter's purpose is to trace the responses of GM to changing conditions in the automotive sector from 2012 to 2016, especially due to volatile oil prices, and to consider where the company might go next with its strategies. It starts with an introduction to the company. Then, it covers the company's strategies from 2012 to 2014, before the fall in oil prices, and 2014 to 2016, after prices dropped. What were the risks and uncertainties that GM perceived in this period, its assumptions about the future, and the hedges it had in place to protect its business during the period of high gasoline prices? The chapter seeks to understand the extent to which the oil price shock altered GM's strategies and affected its performance. To what extent were strategies adequate, and what do they suggest about what the company should do next?

## The New GM

GM had been the world's largest automaker from 1931 to 2007. However, in 2009, because of the Great Financial crisis, its US sales fell 60 percent from over five million vehicles in 2008 to about two million in 2009.[1] This decline in sales resulted in very heavy indebtedness and the company's bankruptcy. To bail it out, the US Treasury provided the company with $49.5 billion under the Troubled Asset Relief Program.[2] To survive, the company had to eliminate such brands as Saturn, Pontiac, Oldsmobile, and the Hummer, and sell the Saab brand. In 2010, the new GM was born in what was, at the time, one of the world's largest initial public offerings (IPOs). Purchasing a majority of the old firm's assets, including the General Motors name, it was the new GM that now took on the task of designing, assembling, marketing, and distributing vehicles, and selling parts and financial services, but it was no longer the world's largest motor vehicle company, as Toyota and VW held that position. The US government estimated that the bailout of the company saved more than 1 million jobs. Had it not bailed out GM, the government would have lost $35 billion in tax revenues. In 2010, the new GM company was profitable. The government was a part owner, only selling its shares in 2013.

## Defective Ignition Switches

The new GM appointed Mary Barra CEO in 2013, ending a period of turmoil in which the company had three different chief executives between 2009 and 2011. Barra was fifty-one years old at the time of her appointment. She was previously GM's executive vice president for Global Product Development, Purchasing and Supply Chain and had a lifelong career at the company, where she rose through the ranks. Immediately after her appointment, she faced a serious test: a safety defect in ignition switches that the old General Motors had installed in millions of vehicles.[3] The defect had caused 124 deaths, for which GM now had to compensate the survivors. The company faced seventy-nine lawsuits seeking upwards of $10 billion in damages. The National Highway Traffic Safety Administration (NHTSA) fined it $35 million in 2014 for failing to recall the brands that were responsible, the Cobalts, Pontiacs, Saturns, and Chevrolets the new GM no longer made, claiming that General Motors had known for a decade or more about the faulty switches and had not acted to correct the problem. NHTSA imposed the maximum fine it could, as evidence showed that the violation of safety rules had been egregious. In total, GM had to recall 2.6 million vehicles, with direct costs to the firm of several billion dollars. The company's profits declined, it lost sales, its stock market value fell, and its reputation for safety and quality, not high to begin with, was diminished.

## Trying to Turn the Company Around

Barra tried to turn GM around, abandoning unprofitable operations and investing in profitable ones.[4] Her goal was to make GM slimmer and have it focus on North and South America and Asia, where it was strong, as opposed to Europe, where it was weak. In Europe, GM had been struggling for quite some time; by 2016, it had had sixteen straight years of losing money there. These losses added up to more than $15 billion from 2000 to 2016. In 2016, GM lost about a quarter of a million dollars in Europe. Though the European division generated 11.8 percent of the company's vehicle sales in 2016, after years of trying to achieve a turnaround, Barra made the decision in 2017 to sell the European brands, Vauxhall and Opel, to Groupe PSA (Peugeot).[5]

In 2017, GM had four remaining divisions: North America, International, South America, and Financial. The company sold five brands: Chevrolet, Cadillac, Buick, GMC, and Holden (Table 12.1). The largest and most profitable division was North America. The international division, which included China, was the fastest growing. Since 2010, GM had sold more vehicles in China than it did in the United States. The South American division continued to be troubled because of ongoing turbulence in GM's principal South American markets, Venezuela and Brazil.

Each of GM's brands played a different role in its strategy. The oldest, GMC, stood for powerful heavy-duty trucks and for sports utility vehicles (SUVs). Buick had become a bestseller in China. Cadillac continued to be a luxury brand, though its premier status had waned, and GM had to act to restore its luster. Chevrolet, the company's mainstay, which made the largest contribution to its sales, embodied solid performance and reliability. GM sold Holden vehicles only in Australia and New Zealand.

Table 12.1 *GM brands and major global markets*

| Brand | Year joined GM | Main markets (Chinese joint venture partners in parenthesis) |
|---|---|---|
| GMC | 1901 | North America, The Middle East |
| Buick | 1908 | North America, China (Shanghai GM) |
| Holden | 1908 | Australia, New Zealand |
| Cadillac | 1909 | North America, Europe, The Middle East, China (Shanghai GM), Japan, South Korea |
| Chevrolet | 1917 | Global (Shanghai GM in China), except Australia and New Zealand |
| Wuling | 2002 | China (SAIC) low-cost vehicles |
| Baojun | 2010 | China (SAIC) low-cost vehicles |
| Jiefang | 2011 | China (FAW) heavy and light duty trucks |

Derived from Company Annual Reports

In China, GM had to work with joint venture partners.[6] All of GM's partners were state owned. They were Shanghai GM, SAIC-GM-Wuling, and FAW-GM. Shanghai GM made Chinese-built Buicks, Cadillacs, and Chevrolets. It owned 34 percent of SAIC-GM-Wuling and it made low-cost Baojuns. They competed with other Chinese low-cost domestic brands such as Chery, Geely, and BYD. Microvans – no larger than a compact – were pillbox-size trucks used for commercial deliveries. With starting prices of around $10,000, GM sold about five million of the low-cost vehicles annually in China. This market, larger than the French and UK markets combined, consisted mostly of first-time Chinese buyers. FAW-GM, on the other hand, produced Jiefang, a heavy and light-duty truck well known in China because it reproduced a Russian-made army truck that had been a mainstay of the People's Liberation Army.

Outside China, GM had joint venture partners in Russia, Pakistan, Uzbekistan, India, Egypt, and South Africa. In India, the company produced 1.6 million cars annually. It halted its sale of vehicles in India in 2017, though it continued to manufacture for export. GM maintained a majority stake in GM Korea, but in 2012 discontinued the Daewoo brand replacing it with Chevrolet. In Australia, the company persisted in selling vehicles under the Holden name, though it stopped manufacturing the car in Australia. GM exited South Africa in 2017 and though active in more than 140 countries, its primary focus was North America and China.

## Alternative Fuel Technologies

Another side to its business was its involvement in alternative fuel technologies. The 1966 Electrovan was the first hydrogen fuel-cell car.[7] General Motors started spending about $100 million a year on FCVs in 2002. It expected full-scale commercialization by 2020, but it would have trouble reaching this goal. On the other hand, the company had a leadership position in ethanol-burning flexible-fuel vehicles. By 2012, it offered twenty flex-fuel models in the United States, more than any automaker.[8]

In conjunction with AeroVironment, General Motors built the Sunraycer in 1987, which won the inaugural World Solar Challenge.[9] Much of the technology in the Sunraycer found its way into the company's Impact electric vehicle (EV), which General Motors introduced in the 1990s to meet California pollution laws.[10] On sale in 1996, the Impact was the first all-electric car any automaker put on the market, but it was available at only a few dealerships and ultimately was leased rather than sold outright. After losing billions of dollars on the Impact, GM ceased production and destroyed all vehicles it had made. Tesla later incorporated features General Motors developed into its electric vehicles (EVs).

GM carried out most of its research on alternative fuel technologies at its Michigan Technical Center and Proving Grounds. The company had six laboratories, six science offices, and many collaborative relationships with universities, governments, and suppliers in more than twelve countries. When oil prices shot up in the first decade of the twenty-first century, the company's interest in fuel economy rose and it sold the first full-sized hybrid pickup, the half-ton Silverado/Sierra, in 2004. However, the Silverado/Sierra did not fully incorporate hybrid technology. GM supported the US government's 2006 Corporate Average Fuel Economy (CAFE) standard increase from 27 to 35 mpg, and that year, it offered full hybrid systems in the Chevrolet Tahoe, GMC Yukon, and Cadillac Escalade, as well as its half-ton pickups.

The landmark year for alternative vehicles at GM was 2010, when the company introduced the plug-in electric Volt. It also set up a Shanghai auto research center to develop hybrids and electric vehicles and other alternative fuel engines and technologies. But GM did not sell many hybrids or plug-ins and its commitment to them, always somewhat doubtful, started to lag. Critics continued to lambast the company for its weak fuel-economy efforts.[11] It countered that it offered economy models and had R&D programs in small cars, but the demand for efficient cars was not large enough to justify additional investment. It claimed that most consumers, if given the choice, preferred light trucks and SUVs to small cars. They only moved to efficient modes of transportation when gas prices really soared and their move was slow and grudging and they quickly swung back to large vehicles and trucks when gas prices went down. Nonetheless, GM pushed ahead in its efforts to innovate, setting up an automotive battery laboratory in Michigan in 2011 and producing the all-electric Spark.[12] The company collaborated with the Korean firm LG to make the battery pack and many of the drivetrain components and it assembled the vehicle itself and sold the car in Korea in 2013. The availability of the Spark, however, was limited to Korea, the United States, and few other global markets. While GM pursued electric vehicles, it did not abandon fuel cells. In 2013, it formed a partnership with Honda to develop an FCV. Along with Honda, it had more automotive fuel cell patents than any company.

In addition, the company increasingly moved forward with advanced technology for safety, security, and information, which it incorporated into alternative fuel technology vehicles. Its OnStar subsidiary offered many of these services. At the Intelligent Transport Systems World Congress in 2014, the company disclosed that it would introduce autopilot features in some 2017 models. In 2016, it revealed it would begin testing self-driving vehicles on public roads in Michigan. Recognizing that driving was going in a progressively more connected, seamless, and autonomous direction, GM invested $1 billion in Lyft in 2016. Later that year, it bought Cruise Automation, a San Francisco self-driving vehicle startup, an investment meant to bolster Lyft and keep it competitive with Uber. Finally, GM offered the Chevrolet Bolt electric vehicle for sale ahead of Tesla in 2016. Though the Bolt did not match all of Tesla's features, on a mile-for-mile basis in the range it went without having to be recharged it did as well as Tesla.[13]

## Prior to and After the 2014–2015 Price Collapse

This chapter now turns to a more detailed examination of how GM's strategies changed before and after the 2014–2015 collapse in gas and oil prices. Based on its annual reports and other communications to

shareholders, the analysis that follows examines the company's perceptions of the risks and uncertainties and its assumptions about the
future.[14] It shows how GM hedged its bets by focusing on safety and
the quality of its operations and by choosing the countries in which it
would be involved, the brands and models it would bring to market,
and the R&D it would do. GM's performance affected the moves it
made, and these moves in turn had an impact on its performance.

## GM Before the 2014–2015 Price Collapse

### Perceptions of the Risks and Uncertainties

Prior to the 2014–2015 fall in prices, GM's lists of risks and uncertainties included: global economic conditions, competition and alliances,
sales, production, quality, and costs, government policies, oil prices,
fuel economy, and climate change. Its lists were long and comprehensive and can be summarized with the following bullet points.

*Global Economic Conditions.* The company was concerned about:

- unstable global exchange and interest rates;
- high unemployment and/or inflation levels;
- volatile commodity and housing prices;
- economic weakness;
- an inability to fulfill the company's pension obligations.

*Competition and Alliances.* Principal concerns were:

- excess capacity;
- inability to price improved models to cover costs;
- industry mergers, acquisitions, and alliances;
- low-cost Chinese and Indian penetration into markets.

*Sales.* GM's central concerns were to induce its customers to:

- buy sufficient vehicles to keep production volume high and costs
  low;
- buy sufficient high-margin full-size pickup trucks, SUVs, and luxury
  cars to maintain and increase profitability.

*Production.* GM's central concerns were:

- assuring suppliers' ability to deliver parts, systems, and components;
- avoiding disruptions from causes such as natural calamities, war,
  and terrorism;

- maintaining availability of low cost, critical raw materials (e.g. steel, aluminum, copper, platinum, and palladium);
- preventing security breaches and IT network disruptions;
- overcoming joint venture partner unreliability and unaccountability.

*Quality.* The company's central concerns in this domain were:

- ongoing expenses from the ignition switch recall – the continued investigations, fines, penalties, and lawsuits it faced;
- a need to avoiding future recalls that could lead to a negative reputation and higher costs.

*Costs.* The company's central concerns were overcoming:

- high-fixed costs of closing facilities;
- difficulties in making labor-force adjustments.

*Government Policies.* GM was concerned they would unsettle markets by:

- changing safety and recall policies;
- conducting aggressive recall campaigns, litigation, and investigations into auto industry practices;
- engaging in trade wars and imposing tariffs.

*Oil Prices.* The company's unease centered on:

- oil shortages and price volatility, as a result of political instability in the Middle East, Africa, and elsewhere;
- sustained oil price increases, resulting in higher gasoline prices and lower demand for high-margin full-size pickup trucks and SUVs.

*Fuel Economy and Climate Change.* The company's concerns were about:

- new regulation, treaties, and/or taxes that added to costs, forced modifications in the product portfolio, and lowered demand;
- lack of technological alternatives and insufficient liquidity to finance, fund, and commercialize new vehicle models.

## Assumptions about the Future

Given this large list of risks and uncertainties, achieving future returns would not be easy. Unlike the integrated oil and natural gas companies, which published thirty- or forty-year outlooks, neither GM nor the other automakers issued statements about the long-term future. Rather, their statements were about their expectations for earnings, about how well they would do in comparison to competitors, about the health of their suppliers, about the prospects for government regulation, and about transformations in personal mobility.

### Earnings Expectation

The company assumed that it would have to raise margins to 9–10 percent to meet its earnings goals. Global industry vehicle sales had to grow at around 3 percent per year for it to accomplish these goals. Under these conditions, the company had to sell more full-size SUVs and pickup trucks. It could not be deterred by unfavorable foreign currency movements. The company expected solid North American demand for midsize pickups and full-size vans and good sales for the new Chevrolet Colorado and GMC Canyon pickups. It was hopeful that its Chinese sales would also grow. A similar expectation applied to South America, though problems due to unsettled conditions in Venezuela, Brazil, and Argentina were not likely to abate. In 2014–2015 GM still wanted to improve its earnings in Europe based on new product launches and lower manufacturing costs. Overall, the company aimed to increase sales from new or remodeled products by 40 percent by 2020.

### Competitors and Suppliers

However, the competition the company faced was intense. Capacity in the sector exceeded demand, yet closing production facilities was difficult. Moreover, competitors enhanced their sales by cutting prices, subsidizing financing and leasing, and offering costly incentives. Chinese and Indian manufacturers were starting to enter some markets. Their inexpensive vehicles were very attractive to first-time buyers in emerging markets and blocked avenues for GM's expansion. During and after the bankruptcy, competitors had been successful in persuading customers to abandon its vehicles. To win back these customers, GM had to design, build, and sell safe, high-quality vehicles. Achieving this goal required extensive capital investment. It was a tough challenge to enhance quality and safety through better design, engineering, and manufacturing. The supply chain concern was that just-in-time manufacturing hinged on having bare inventories and the emphasis on lean operations made the company vulnerable to supply chain disruptions. As if these issues were not enough, the company also needed to recruit fresh talent.

## Government Regulation
The company could not violate safety or emissions standards. It had to avoid recalls and the associated fines and penalties. Government regulations throughout the world were tightening. Compliance with federal Corporate Average Fuel Economy (CAFE) and California Air Resources Board (CARB) greenhouse gas requirements meant that it would have to sell more hybrids and other fuel-efficient vehicles. China, too, was moving toward aggressive new fleet fuel-consumption standards and it was likely to increase its subsidies for fuel-efficient vehicles, plug-in hybrids, and battery electric and FCVs. Europe was also in the process of tightening its emission standards for diesel and conventional engines. Global noise standards and lending regulation could stiffen. The United States and Canada were taking green chemistry initiatives, mandating life-cycle analysis and product stewardship standards that could mean the banning or restriction of materials GM used and China and the EU could implement the same requirements.

## Transformations in Personal Mobility
Meanwhile, social and technological trends were rapidly transforming personal mobility. GM estimated that the number of people using shared mobility was likely to increase from 15 million in 2015 to 50 million in 2020. The automotive sector was experiencing more change than it had in fifty years and had no choice but to commit to new technologies. Thus, there was a need for continued investments in OnStar connectivity and alternative propulsion vehicles like the Volt and Bolt. There was a need to become more involved in car sharing (Maven and Lyft) and autonomous driving (the acquisition of Cruise Automation). If competitors advanced faster than GM, GM would be shut out of these markets. Its path in moving toward a new automotive future had to be smoother than paths it had taken in the past. Technologies it wanted to deploy, such as hydrogen fuel cells and advanced batteries, had experienced unexpected setbacks. The long-term agreement with Honda to co-create a next-generation fuel cell and hydrogen-storage system had stalled and the two companies were not meeting their deadline.

## GM: *After the 2014–2015 Price Collapse*

**Perceptions of the Risks and Uncertainties**
After the 2014–2015 fall in oil prices, the list of risks and uncertainties remained about the same, though the emphasis shifted somewhat from globalization, competition, and cost control to technology disruption.

### Technological Disruption
The introduction of new technologies, products, services, and business models like autonomous vehicles, car and ride sharing, and transportation-as-a service threatened to disrupt previous ways of doing business. GM's ability to respond had limits. Improvements in design, engineering, and manufacturing required massive investment. Consumer confidence, unemployment, inflation, political unrest, interest rates, and other factors could get in the way. The company's profits largely derived from the sale of full-size pickup trucks and SUVs. Increases in oil prices or shortages could shift consumer preferences to smaller, more fuel-efficient vehicles. Climate change, emissions controls, and safety regulation made the future even more uncertain. If GM ran afoul of government mandates, it risked being subject to punitive damages, fines, lawsuits, criminal penalties, sanctions, and recalls that could result in modifications to its business practices, interruptions in production, and reputational damage. The Takata airbag recall had harmed all auto companies, exposing them to penalties and reduced consumer confidence. If fuel prices, styling, economic conditions, and regulation significantly shifted, the innovations that GM aimed to make would not pay off.

### Globalization, Competition, and Cost Control
Meanwhile, dealing with the international scale and footprint of its operations put GM at risk. Large competitors such as Toyota, Volkswagen, and Ford fought for market share with GM in an industry that had excess capacity. Each company's fixed costs were high, and they could not easily close facilities. To maintain sales volume, all the companies lowered prices and offered costly incentives. GM, moreover, did not benefit from same economies of scale as its competitors. Toyota and VW were larger than GM. They might ally or perhaps merge at GM's expense. The company's Chinese joint venture partners were moving on their own into low-cost segments in emerging markets. While foreign governments protected their domestic manufacturers, GM was not receiving as much support from the US government.

The company found it hard to carry out necessary restructuring, as its pension liabilities limited its ability to act. The cost of protecting against security breaches and IT problems were also growing. Finally, global supply chains were becoming less secure as governments threatened to make changes in international trade and investment, introduce higher tariffs, erect entry barriers, stiffen anti-corruption laws, and impose labor restrictions.

## Assumptions about the Future

After the 2015–2016 oil price collapse, GM continued to assume it could achieve margins of 9–10 percent on earnings. Its goal was to be at, or near, the top among its industry peers on this indicator (Figure 12.1). It assumed that it could meet this goal by offering a better customer experience and industry-leading products. Its top brands, Chevrolet and Cadillac, had to grow in the United States, China, and elsewhere. It had to be a leader in innovation, which meant investing in OnStar 4G LTE, the connected car, alternative means of propulsion, urban mobility via Maven and Lyft, active safety features, and autonomous features. The resources needed for these investments were high. To raise resources, the company had to cut costs. As of 2016, it had realized around $4 billion in annual savings compared to 2014. GM assumed that additional cost savings could help offset the investments it had to make. Its North American breakeven point had fallen and would have to go down further.

## Global Sales

Sales in China in 2016 had increased by 12.9 percent compared to a year earlier, but the company's market share fell to 13.8 percent, which was 1.1 percentage points lower than the preceding year. Strong increases in Cadillac, Buick, and Baojun sales were offset by lower Chevrolet and Wuling sales. GM expected only moderate industry growth in China in 2017 and a continuation of pricing pressures. A weak economy had reduced automotive industry demand in the rest of Asia Pacific, Africa, and the Middle East, and had led to a decline of 3.2 percent in sales in 2016 compared to 2015. GM assumed that these operating environments would remain challenging and it would have to keep restructuring and rationalizing its

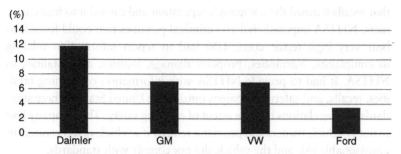

**Figure 12.1** Earnings before interest and taxes of major auto producers in 2015
Derived from annual reports

operations. It hoped that conditions in the South American automotive industry would ultimately get better. Sales in 2016, however, were 12.3 percent less than they had been in 2015. The company's Brazilian market share, at 16.9 percent, had not improved much because of a refreshed product portfolio. To further increase sales, the company would have to launch new models, change the vehicle mix, and make even more cost reductions.

## Hedging

The approach GM took to managing risks and uncertainties involved layers of hedging designed to protect the company against various contingencies. The hedges in which the company engaged were to try to: (1) ensure the quality and safety of its vehicles; (2) invest globally in diverse markets; (3) adjust its brand and model mix; and (4) devote itself to technological innovation that might bring with it future competitive advantage. GM did not deviate from these strategies even when oil prices fell, though there was some shift in how it executed them. How it applied these strategies before and after the 2014–2015 price crash is described next.

## GM Before the 2014–2015 Price Collapse

### (1) Assuring Quality and Safety

GM had no doubt that safety was every bit as important to customers as design, price, quality, options, reliability, and fuel economy. It understood that recalls harmed the company's reputation and caused it to lose customers. NHTSA imposed civil and criminal penalties that could force it to bear very high repair costs. GM had to report information relating to complaints, warranties, property damage, injuries, and fatalities to NHTSA. It had to provide NHTSA with information concerning fatalities, recalls, and safety campaigns outside the United States, where standards and regulations had the intent of ensuring safety. The company had to notify vehicle owners and provide a remedy if a vehicle defect created an unreasonable risk and the vehicle did not comply with standards.

**The Ignition Switch Recall.** From 2014 to 2015, GM had to repair about 2.6 million ignition switches in which loss of electrical power prevented the airbag from deploying in the event of a crash. The problem also involved ignition lock cylinders in which the key could come loose when the engine was running. In response to these recalls, GM initiated a comprehensive review, which showed that it would have to recall another 36 million vehicles:

- 12.1 million vehicles to rework or replace ignition keys because the ignition switch could move out of the run position, impact power steering and braking, and result in airbags not deploying;
- 2.7 million vehicles to modify the brake lamp wiring harness, which could corrode due to micro-vibration;
- 1.9 million vehicles to replace either the power steering motor, the steering column, the power steering motor control unit, or a combination of the above;
- 1.5 million vehicles to replace front safety lap belt cables, which could fatigue and separate over time;
- 1.4 million vehicles to replace a shift cable that wore out resulting in mismatches of the gear position;
- 1.3 million vehicles to replace parts essential for the deployment of side impact restraints that were not serviced when the airbag warning light became illuminated;
- 1.1 million vehicles to repair loose battery cables that affected warning systems;
- 0.7 million vehicles to repair ignition keys that came out when the vehicle was in the run position;
- 0.6 million vehicles to replace wave plates in transmissions, which could crack; and
- 10.1 million vehicles which had other safety issues.

The total recall costs would amount to more than $4 billion. The impact on sales and revenue was difficult to determine. Of the approximately 36 million vehicles subject to recall, about 10 million were subject to multiple recalls. In addition, approximately 63 percent were vehicles the new GM no longer produced or sold. They were models the old General Motors made such as the Chevrolet Cobalt, Pontiac G5, and Saturn ION.

**GM's Response.** In response to these problems, GM conducted an in-depth review of its safety policies. It hired a former US attorney to carry out an investigation and provide recommendations. It disciplined employees. It created a new Global Vice President of Safety responsible for safety performance and it created a new Global Product Integrity Organization within the Global Product Development Department. The company made enhancements to its investigation process and consumer-facing processes. It implemented new standards to facilitate information sharing and aid decision making, and added an estimated 100 additional technical resources globally to support new processes. It also launched its Speak Up For Safety Program to encourage employees to report on issues and tried to ensure that issues would be brought to the highest levels in the company.

### (2) Investing in Global Markets

In order to hedge its bets, GM sold vehicles throughout the world, but its market share was highest in the United States at 17.4 percent in 2014. South America came in second place, where GM's market share was 16.6 percent. However, in terms of the number of vehicles sold, China was dominant; GM's market share in that country was 14.8 percent in 2015 and it sold 3.54 million vehicles there (Table 12.2). From 2012 to 2014, GM's sales grew by 24.8 percent in China and 13.1 percent in the United States while Europe continued to be the weak link. Total retail vehicle sales in Europe in 2015 were 1.26 million and the company's market share fell to 6.7 percent compared to 2012, when its market share had been 7.9 percent. In South America, GM also experienced fewer vehicle sales as well as a loss of market share. Sales were down from 1.05 million in 2012 to 0.88 million in 2014 – a decline of 16.2 percent, and the company's market share fell from 18 percent to 16.6 percent.

**Consolidation.** To bolster the company's international operations, GM consolidated global development. It created a single organization

**Table 12.2  GM product sales and global market share 2012–2014**

| | 2014 product sold (in thousands) | As a % of industry | 2013 product sold (in thousands) | As a % of industry | 2012 product sold (in thousands) | As a % of industry |
|---|---|---|---|---|---|---|
| United States | 2,935 | 17.4 | 2,786 | 17.5 | 2,596 | 17.5 |
| North America | 3,413 | 16.9 | 3,234 | 16.9 | 3,019 | 16.9 |
| Germany | 237 | 7.1 | 242 | 7.4 | 254 | 7.5 |
| United Kingdom | 305 | 10.7 | 301 | 11.6 | 272 | 11.7 |
| Russia | 189 | 7.4 | 258 | 9.1 | 288 | 9.6 |
| Europe | 1,256 | 6.7 | 1,393 | 7.6 | 1,469 | 7.9 |
| China | 3,540 | 14.8 | 3,160 | 14.2 | 2,836 | 14.6 |
| Asia/Pacific, The Middle East and Africa | 4,378 | 10.2 | 4,058 | 9.8 | 3,755 | 9.7 |
| Brazil | 579 | 16.6 | 650 | 17.3 | 643 | 16.9 |
| South America | 878 | 16.6 | 1,037 | 17.5 | 1,051 | 18 |
| Total Worldwide | 9,925 | 11.4 | 9,722 | 11.5 | 9,294 | 11.5 |

Derived from Company Annual Reports

for automotive architecture, which supported a common set of components, subsystems, and interfaces. This new organization collaborated closely with development teams in various parts of the world. While the development teams worked on vehicle exterior and interior design and tuning, the new organization had responsibility for such systems as steering, suspension, brakes, and heating. It set common performance ranges, characteristics, and product dimensions, which the development teams applied to brands in different countries.

**Cost Cutting and Product Launches.** GM also tried to improve its global position via cost cutting and new product launches. In North America, where it had the industry's largest market share, such product launches as the following were meant to drive growth – the Corvette Stingray, Chevrolet Impala, Cadillac CTS, and new Chevrolet Silverado and GMC Sierra full-size trucks. These products received recognition for their excellence and many won quality awards. In Europe, GM achieved Opel and Vauxhall market share growth for the first time in fourteen years. Nonetheless, the European division continued to operate at a loss and GM shut down facilities, such as the vehicle and transmission production unit in Bochum, Germany, but only after agreement from the German labor union. New vehicle launches enabled the company to retain the number-two market share in Asia Pacific, the Middle East, and Africa. In South Korea, it was engaged in protracted litigation with employees over wages. In South America, where it derived more than 60 percent of its vehicle sales from Brazil, the company continued to have the number-one market share. However, in Brazil it was only number three. GM was attempting to improve its position in South America via new product launches, restructuring, and creating better deals with labor. Venezuela was an ongoing trouble spot.

### (3) Adjusting the Brand and Model Mix
GM hedged its bets by having a full line of vehicles that would appeal to a customer throughout the life cycle, from a sturdy car for college, to a crossover or SUV for family life, to luxury models for well-healed older customers.

**Cadillac.** At the apex of this process was Cadillac. Sold and made in the United States and China, Cadillac's image had to improve and its sales had to grow. GM aimed to bring it back globally and return it to the forefront of performance, design, and driving. It set up a second assembly plant for Cadillac in China. It launched a new top-of-the-line model, the CT6, which weighed less, incorporated advanced performance features, and included technologies that enhanced safety, efficiency, and connectivity. Its goal was to launch eight new Cadillac models to restore the brand to a position of global luxury leadership. The company set up a separate business unit for Cadillac in 2014. Sales of the brand grew by 5 percent that year, led by a 47 percent increase in China driven by the popularity of the new Escalade. Globally, the expectation was that the luxury segment would expand by 35 percent by 2020. To take advantage of this trend, GM invested heavily in vehicle-to-vehicle connectivity and Super Cruise control, which it aimed to introduce by 2017.

**Chevrolet.** Chevrolet was well established and had more than 70 million customers around the world. The challenge was to leverage its growth in the United States and expand its sales in China, Brazil, and other developing markets. As an example of its potential, GM launched a new small crossover, the Trax. Other launches were new midsize pickups, the Chevy Colorado, and GMC Canyon. Though industry experts dismissed the midsize pickup segment, GM persisted in product introductions and received good reviews and awards, including *Motor Trend's* truck of the year and *Autoweek's* best truck. GM had a full pipeline of additional product launches that it planned, including new versions of the Malibu, Equinox, Camaro, Spark, and Volt.

**Buick and GMC.** As a style leader, Buick was a core element in GM's growth strategy in China. Consumer rating organizations, such as J.D. Power and Associates and *Consumer Reports*, consistently ranked the brand at a top level for reliability and dealer service. In China, GM relied on a multi-brand growth strategy that included Chevrolet, Cadillac, Baojun, Jiefang, and Wuling as well as Buick. To succeed, this strategy required that the company maintain good relations with its joint venture partners. GM also enhanced the marketing of GMC, a brand it sold mainly in the United States.

**The European Brands.** To rebuild the Opel/Vauxhall brand in Europe, GM introduced new products, such as Mokka and ADAM; they helped Opel/Vauxhall gain market share. It also launched a fifth generation of the Corsa, a new small car, called Karl, and the Astra and expected that these vehicles would represent about half of Opel/Vauxhall's volume.

The company invested €245 million to prepare Opel's assembly plant in Rüsselsheim, Germany, to produce a new flagship SUV. It invested more than half a billion euros in engine and transmission plants in Rüsselsheim and Kaiserslautern, Germany, as well as Tychy, Poland, so that Opel/ Vauxhall would have the fuel-efficient engines European customers wanted.

### (4) Technological Innovation

From 2012 to 2014, GM's R&D expenses remained steady at slightly more than $7 billion annually. GM's spending on R&D far exceeded that of the oil and natural gas companies discussed in previous chapters. In its R&D, the company hedged its bets by seeking improvements in conventional powertrains, automatic transmissions, and lighter, front-wheel drive architecture. It also emphasized vehicle emissions controls, safety, and fuel economy and had other priorities such as alternative fuels, electrification, fuel cells, and connectivity, as elaborated below.

**Alternative Fuels.** To reduce gasoline consumption, GM took a number of steps to learn from the experience and capability it had accumulated in flex-fuel vehicles. These vehicles ran on gasoline-ethanol blends fuels, CNG, and LPG. The company offered thirteen flex-fuel models in the United States in 2015 for ordinary drivers plus an additional four models for fleet and commercial drivers. The Chevrolet Express, GMC Savana full-size vans, Chevrolet Silverado, and GMC Sierra 2500 HD pickup truck were able to switch between gasoline, diesel, and CNG. The company also sold a CNG bi-fuel Chevrolet Impala full-size sedan. In Brazil, a substantial majority of the vehicles the company sold were flex-fuel. It also marketed these vehicles in Australia, Thailand, and other global markets. The company produced CNG bi-fuel-capable vehicles in Europe, such as the Opel Zafira. GM offered LPG capable vehicles in select global markets depending on infrastructure, regulatory focus, and natural resource availability. Along with the development of biodiesel blend fuels as alternative diesel fuels produced from renewable sources, it continued to study the future role flex-fuel vehicles could play in the United States and elsewhere in light of regulatory and other developments.

**Electrification.** GM invested in multiple technologies offering increasing levels of vehicle electrification, including eAssist, plug-in hybrids, and extended range and BEVs. In the United States, it had seven models featuring some form of electrification. In 2014, it introduced the Cadillac ELR extended-range luxury coupe. It continued to develop other extended-range vehicles, such as the Opel Ampera. The Volt was its plug-in hybrid electric vehicle and GM sold an EV, the Chevrolet Spark. The Volt averaged about 100 miles per gallon and customer satisfaction ratings were high, but sales were disappointing.

**Fuel Cells.** As part of GM's long-term strategy, the company continued to develop hydrogen fuel-cell technology. The Chevrolet Equinox fuel-cell electric vehicle demonstration program had accumulated nearly three million miles of real-world driving experience. It allowed the company to identify consumer and infrastructure needs to determine if it could make the business case for this technology. GM and Honda had a long-term agreement to co-develop a next-generation fuel-cell system and hydrogen-storage technologies, aiming for a 2020 time frame. They based the collaboration on a sharing of expertise, economies of scale, and common sourcing strategies.

**Connectivity.** Across all of its brands, GM offered 4G LTE and OnStar globally. OnStar, LLC (OnStar) was a wholly owned subsidiary of the company serving more than 6.8 million subscribers in the United States, Canada, Mexico, and, through a joint venture, China. GM expected to expand OnStar to Europe. OnStar provided connected safety, security, and mobility solutions and gave its subscribers up-to-date vehicle information on oil level, tire pressure, and fuel level. GM made advanced information technology available in the majority of its 2015 vehicles. Key services included automatic crash response, stolen vehicle assistance, remote door unlock, vehicle diagnostics, hands-free calling, and wireless connectivity. The system alerted first responders when a crash took place.

## GM After the 2014–2015 Price Collapse

### (1) Assuring Quality and Safety
GM still had to make payments for the ignition switch recall of more than a billion dollars a year. Almost 300 actions for alleged death and injury and more than 100 legal actions for diminution in vehicle value remained standing in US and Canadian courts. Five trials in 2016

yielded results favorable to GM, while the parties came to a voluntary settlement in another three.

**A Fundamental Commitment.** Hoping that focus on product quality was a key enabler of safety, the company continued to add resources and implement a revamped approach to safety in which it encouraged employees, suppliers, and dealers to voice their concerns.

**Top Safety Picks.** GM aimed to have its new models designated as top safety picks by rating agencies. Models that achieved this status in 2016 and 2017 were the Chevrolet Sonic, Chevrolet Malibu Limited, Chevrolet Equinox, Buick Encore, GMC Terrain, Chevrolet Volt, Chevrolet Malibu, Buick Envision, and Cadillac.

**Initiatives for Young Drivers, the Internet, and Seatbelts.** GM had specific initiatives designed to address the main causes of severe accidents – young drivers, Internet use, and the lack of seatbelt use:

- The 2016 Chevy Malibu had a teen driver system to inculcate safe driving habits. GM hoped to install this system in more than 60 percent of Chevy vehicles sold in 2017 and make it available in Cadillacs, Buicks, and GMCs.
- To facilitate hands-free calling, texting, and app use, the company placed controls in steering wheels and it had voice-controlled OnStar commands.
- It had an assurance system that prevented vehicles from starting until everyone buckled up that it was testing in a limited number of vehicles. It provided nearly $70 million to help educate parents about passenger safety, it donated car seats to families in need, and it provided child safety seat inspections.

**(2) Investing in Global Markets**
With low gasoline prices, GM's North America revenue and profit margins were the highest ever. Sales in emerging markets, however, lagged because of low household incomes and new regulations that aligned with those in more developed countries. These new regulations raised costs, and thus made affordability an issue.

**China.** GM continued to sell more vehicles in China than it did in the United States (Figure 12.2). Along with its joint venture partners, it

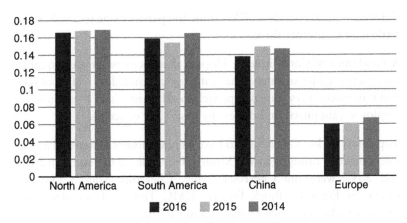

**Figure 12.2** GM's global market share by region 2014–2016
Derived from Company Annual Reports

launched thirteen new or refreshed models in 2016 and sold a record 3.87 million vehicles in China. The growth rate in vehicles sold in that country continued to be high, but the company's market share fell. Everywhere in the world, the company lost market share (Figure 12.2). It continued to face challenging conditions in South America. It chose to exit Russia and cease manufacturing there and sold fewer Chevrolets in Europe.

### (3) Adjusting the Brand and Model Mix
GM's specialty in trucks and crossovers not passenger cars paid off with the drop in gasoline prices, but it hurt EV sales.

**An Emphasis on Trucks.** GM planned twenty-six new product launches in 2017 and more than 50 percent of these launches would be profitable trucks, crossovers, and SUVs. In China, it planned to launch eighteen more models and to emphasize higher margin SUVs, crossovers, and luxury vehicles. Between 2017 and 2020, GM expected that approximately 38 percent of its volume would come from recently introduced models, up from 26 percent the preceding six years.

**The Challenge of Selling Electrified Vehicles.** With gasoline prices low and consumers' desire for more fuel-efficient vehicles falling, GM had trouble selling EVs. It tried to maintain momentum by introducing the Bolt, adding it to a lineup that included a new Volt and Malibu hybrid.

The Bolt was the world's first electric vehicle to combine long range with affordable pricing. It got an EPA-estimated 238 miles per charge at a price below $30,000 after government incentives. It won many awards including *Car and Driver's* "10 Best Cars for 2017," *Green Car Journal's* "2017 Green Car of the Year," and the "2017 *Motor Trend* Car of the Year."

The company also ramped up production of the second-generation Chevrolet Volt, which offered a pure EV range of fifty-three miles and a gasoline equivalent of 106 mpg. The Chevrolet Malibu Hybrid got an EPA-estimated city-highway fuel economy of forty-seven miles per gallon. GM also introduced a Cadillac CT6 plug-in hybrid, which achieved an EPA-estimated city-highway fuel economy equivalent of 62 mpg.

GM was trying to bring electric mobility to countries outside the United States where gasoline prices were not so low. In Norway, it introduced the Ampera-e car. This sold out almost immediately. GM aimed to launch the vehicle in other European countries soon after. It tried to bring electrification to Korea. It debuted energy-efficient models in China in 2016 – the Buick LaCrosse hybrid, Chevrolet Malibu XL hybrid, and Cadillac CT6 plug-in. It was in the process of rolling out more than ten new energy-efficient vehicles in China through the year 2020. Yet the company acknowledged that with low gasoline prices, fuel efficiency was not a top priority and that customers still were not convinced that the future of mobility was electric.

**(4) Technological Innovation**
GM kept increasing its R&D spending; in 2014, it was $7.4 billion, in 2015, $7.5 billion, and in 2016, $8.1 billion. It hedged its bets in its research spending, however by funding improvements in existing products and new product development plus initiatives in emissions control, fuel economy, safety, mobility, and autonomy. The company also continued to have programs in flex-fuel vehicles, fuel cells and electrification, and connectivity.

**Flex-fuel Vehicles.** GM offered eleven flex-fuel vehicles in the United States to retail customers and seven additional models to fleet and commercial customers. It had a program to offer a wide selection of truck and van options operating on CNG or LPG, suitable for fleet and commercial applications and retail customers. In Brazil, a substantial majority of the vehicles it sold were flex-fuel vehicles capable of running on 100-percent ethanol blends. The company also marketed flex-fuel vehicles in Europe. It produced CNG bi-fuel-capable vehicles in Europe, such as the Opel Zafira Tourer and the Opel Combo van. Globally, GM sold CNG- and LPG-capable vehicles in select markets depending on their infrastructure, regulatory focus, and the availability of natural resources. The company continued to support the development of bio-diesel blend fuels as alternative diesel fuels made from renewable sources. It was studying ethanol-based fuels as well as other high-octane fuel blends and the role they could play in maximizing efficiencies of future internal combustion engines.

**Fuel Cells.** As part of the company's long-term strategy to reduce petroleum consumption and greenhouse gas emissions, it remained committed to hydrogen fuel-cell technology. It explored non-traditional automotive uses for fuel cells in demonstrations with the US Army and US Navy.

**Electrification.** GM's strategy was to improve the fundamentals of traditional propulsion technology, while innovating new energy-efficient and lower-carbon technologies like EVs. It treated fuel economy and emissions not only as a highly regulated part of its business, but also as a way in which to increase customer satisfaction. It tried to work with government regulators to develop effective policies. At the 2015 North American International Auto Show, it introduced a second-generation Volt that symbolized its continued commitment to the expansion of vehicle electrification and the development of accompanying electrification technologies, including battery systems, electric motors, and advanced electronic controls. GM built on its experience with the Volt in creating the Bolt, an all-electric car that could go 200 miles on a charge and that cost under $35,000.

**Connectivity and Mobility.** GM had more 4G-equipped models than all other companies combined did. In 2016, OnStar celebrated its twentieth anniversary. In 2016, the company took steps that it hoped would redefine personal mobility. With the launch of Maven, the company had a car-sharing service. Within residential communities, approved participants had twenty-four-hour access to a variety of vehicles parked in residential community parking garages. The Maven Pro corporate car-sharing solution offered companies a solution to managing their fleets. Employees could use a smartphone app to access a pool of company-owned vehicles.

In 2016, GM expanded Maven offerings to sixteen cities across the United States. The company also purchased an ownership interest in Lyft and started a new program called Express Drive, which leveraged the Lyft relationship to expand ride-sharing offerings. The partnership with Lyft involved buying back vehicles at auction and renting them on a short-term basis to Lyft drivers, who did not want to use their own car or whose personal vehicles did not qualify for Lyft service. Under the Express Drive program, Lyft drivers in multiple cities across the United States could rent GM vehicles on a weekly basis. Like its arrangement with Lyft, GM was partnering with Uber to pilot a program under which Uber drivers could rent GM vehicles on a weekly basis.

**Autonomy.** GM planned to develop an integrated network of on-demand autonomous vehicles in the United States. Since driver error was the cause of more than 90 percent of crashes, GM saw autonomous technology leading to advances in safety as well as convenience and mobility. The company had millions of miles of real-world experience with embedded connectivity through OnStar, and OnStar's advanced safety features were the building blocks to more advanced automation features that would eventually lead to fully autonomous vehicles. An example of advanced automation was the Super Cruise, a hands-free driving customer convenience feature GM would offer in the 2017 Cadillac CT6 sedan.

## GM's 2012–2016 Performance

The collapse in gas and oil prices lifted the company's performance. It had the exact opposite effect that it had on the oil and gas companies discussed in previous chapters. In 2013 and 2014, when gasoline prices were high, GM was fighting off the effects of the ignition recall, and its profits were low. When gasoline prices fell in 2015, its profits rose and in 2016, its revenues grew (Figure 12.3). From September 2012 to September 2017, no automaker equaled the 74 percent return of the S&P 500, but GM did comparatively well as its returns to shareholders of about 70 percent exceeded those of Toyota, whose returns were about 47 percent, Ford whose returns were about 18 percent, and Volkswagen whose returns were about 10 percent.

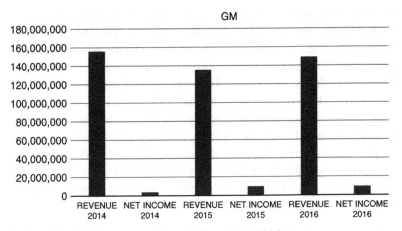

**Figure 12.3** GM's revenue and net income 2014–2016
Derived from Annual Reports

## Some Bold Moves – The Correct Response?

Under Mary Barra, GM took some bold steps. First, it fundamentally re-made its safety culture, anticipating that improvements in quality would accompany the improvements in safety it made. After the bankruptcy and recall, it had to win back customers and to do so it introduced many new models. The quality of its vehicles had to be high to maintain customer loyalty. The second bold step – one that it came to only gradually and at very end of the period under consideration – was to exit Europe. After investing billions of dollars in trying to be profitable in Europe, GM came to the realization that it was unlikely that it would ever achieve this goal. In retreating from Europe, GM gave up on the aspiration of again having the largest market share of any auto company in the world. These were bold decisions – recalling millions of vehicles, fixing its defective safety culture, improving the quality of its vehicles and their reputation, selling its weak European division, and exiting that market entirely.

For making these decisions, GM received the reward of comparatively good performance relative to its peers. Low fuel prices in 2015–2016 also helped to bolster its profits and sales. For the moment, it recognized that consumers in the United States and elsewhere in the world demanded more light duty trucks and it was in the company's interest to provide them. Yet it hoped that by committing itself to light duty and other trucks *and* alternative vehicles and electrification, whatever happened with gasoline prices, it would be safe.

The risks and uncertainties the company faced were large from changes in the global economy to oil prices, fuel economy, and climate change. It was in a highly competitive sector where the direction of government regulation was unpredictable and the pace of technological innovation was high. To compete it had to keep its costs low, yet it could not afford to compromise on quality or safety.

Its assumptions were the need for it to grow its earnings and transform itself and the sector at the same time. It assumed that sector competition would be unforgiving and it had little room for error. It had a dual turnaround task. It had to rebuild after the old GM fell into bankruptcy and it had to recover from the ignition defect recall.

Like other companies in this sector, as the chapters to come show, GM hedged by making safety a fundamental commitment, investing in different global markets, regularly upgrading a diverse set of global brands with different images and selling them at different price ranges, and maintaining a very high R&D budget. It faced the future by hedging its bets and covering all bases – safety and quality, global diversification, multi-branding, and R&D across a broad spectrum of programs. Its hedges were to achieve high levels of safety, focus mainly on the United States and China, though it still had involvement in many countries, confine itself to fewer than a dozen major brands, and play to its strength in light trucks, while at the same time innovating in alternative vehicles, connectivity, mobility, and autonomy. In its R&D, GM hedged by maintaining ongoing initiatives in alternative fuels, fuel cells, electrification, connectivity, and autonomy as well as in new product development and improving existing products.

Where GM should go next was unclear. With gasoline prices lower, it could cut back on the shifts it had made toward alternative transportation modes and put even more emphasis on its lucrative small truck, crossover, and SUV businesses. However, many countries had made promises to reduce or even end the sale of gasoline- and diesel-based vehicles (see Chapter 5). That European countries like France and the United Kingdom had made these promises did not matter much to GM any longer, but the fact that China, where forecasts suggested explosive growth in EV sales by 2040, was in the midst of moving in this direction mattered a lot. Given these developments, what GM should do next was unclear; but it was undeniable that its decisions would have important implications for the company and for society.

## Notes

1.  "*A Giant Falls,*" www.economist.com/briefing/2009/06/04/a-giant-falls.
2.  Rattner, Steven. *Overhaul: An Insider's Account of the Obama Administration's Emergency Rescue of the Auto Industry.* Boston: Houghton Mifflin Harcourt, 2010.
3.  "*GM: Steps to a Recall Nightmare,*" https://money.cnn.com/info graphic/pf/autos/gm-recall-timeline/index.html
4.  "*Mary Barra Is Remaking GM's Culture – And the Company Itself,*" www.fastcompany.com/3064064/mary-barra-is-remaking-gms-culture-and-the-company-itself
5.  "*General Motors Pulls Back from European Auto Market,*" www .washingtonpost.com/news/innovations/wp/2017/03/06/General-Moto rs-sells-car-brands-Vauxhill-Opel-in-Europe-to-PSA-Group/?utm_ term=.98053cf94bbe
6.  "*About GM China,*" www.gmchina.com/company/cn/en/gm/company/ about-gm-china.html
7.  "*1966 Electrovan,*" www.motortrend.com/news/1966-gm-electrovan-fuel-cell-prototype-turns-50/
8.  "*Fueling the Future,*" www.gmfleet.com/overview/alternative-fuel-vehicles .html
9.  Tuckey, Bill. *Sunraycer.* St. Leonards, Australia: Chevron Publishing Group, 1989.
10. Marcus, Alfred. *Innovations in Sustainability: Fuel and Food.* Cambridge, UK: Cambridge University Press, 2015.
11. "*General Motors: Corporate Rap Sheet,*" www.corp-research.org/general-motors
12. "*Chevrolet Spark EV,*" www.caranddriver.com/chevrolet/spark-ev
13. "*Chevy Bolt EV Range Is 238 Miles: Prime Time for the Electric Car?*" www.latimes.com/business/autos/la-fi-hy-bolt-ev-range-20160912-snap story.html
14. "*General Motors Annual Report 2012,*" www.annualreports.com/ HostedData/AnnualReportArchive/g/NYSE_GM_2012.pdf
    "*Connecting You to What's Important 2013 Sustainability Report;*" "*General Motors Annual Report 2013,*" www.annualreports.com/ HostedData/AnnualReportArchive/g/NYSE_GM_2013.pdf

"*A Driving Force 2014 Sustainability Report;*" "*General Motors Annual Report 2014,*" www.annualreports.com/HostedData/AnnualReport Archive/g/NYSE_GM_2014.pdf

"*Accelerating Ahead 2015 Sustainability Report;*" "*General Motors Annual Report 2015,*" www.annualreports.com/HostedData/Annua lReportArchive/g/NYSE_GM_2015.pdf

"*GM Sustainability Report 2016,*" www.gmsustainability.com/_pdf/ downloads/GM_2016_SR.pdf

"*General Motors Annual Report 2016,*" www.annualreports.com/ HostedData/AnnualReportArchive/g/NYSE_GM_2016.pdf

"*GM Sustainability Report 2017,*" www.gmsustainability.com/_pdf/ downloads/GM_2017_SR.pdf

# 13 | Strategies to Take Advantage of Plummeting Prices: Ford

The purpose of this chapter is trace the responses of Ford to changing conditions in the automotive sector from 2012 to 2016, especially due to volatile oil prices, and to consider where the company might go next with its strategies. Like the previous chapter, this chapter starts with an introduction to the company. It then covers the company's strategies from 2012 to 2014, before the fall in oil prices, and 2014 to 2016, after prices dropped. What were the risks and uncertainties that Ford perceived in this period, its assumptions about the future, and the hedges it had in place to protect its business? The chapter seeks to understand the extent to which the oil price shock altered its strategies and affected its performance. To what extent were the strategies that it adopted adequate, and what do they suggest about what the company should do next?

## Many Challenges

Ford manufactured vehicles under its own name and that of Lincoln and it once manufactured vehicles under the name of Mercury. Thus, the number of brands with which it was associated was more limited than GM. It also operated Ford Credit, and previously owned Hertz, the large automobile rental company. In addition, it formerly owned Jaguar, Volvo, Land Rover, and Aston Martin and it once had a controlling interest in Mazda.

Because of a decline in quality and a slowdown in sales, its financial stability weakened in the early part of the twenty-first century, and as oil prices rose from 2000 to 2014, its US market share slipped (Figure 13.1). Its sales fell from over $139 billion in the prior year to less than $136 billion in 2014. The upshot was that the company had to sell Jaguar, Volvo, Land Rover, and Aston Martin as well its interest in Mazda.

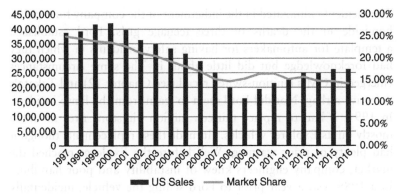

**Figure 13.1** Ford's declining US market share 1997–2016
Derived from Ford Annual Reports

## Fuel Efficiency

Where Ford stood out was that its F-Series trucks were the bestselling vehicle in the world in 2017, edging out the Toyota Corolla, VW Golf, and Wuling Hongquang; but they were also among the world's least efficient, averaging between 13 and 21 miles per gallon (mpg).[1] Ford's line-up of vehicles had other models with mpg ratings better than the F-series, however, largely because of the F-Series, SUVs, and cross-overs, the company's overall fleet average was less than 23 mpg. Though GM's fleet average was similar and Fiat-Chrysler's was even lower, Ford's was among the lowest auto company fleet averages in the United States. Fiat-Chrysler's fleet average, 25 mpg. However, Toyota's and VW's fleet averages were above 25 mpg (before Dieselgate, see Chapter 14) and Honda's was even higher at greater than 27 mpg. Because of the correlation of mpg fleet averages with greenhouse gas emissions, Ford, GM, and Fiat-Chrysler were responsible for the highest amounts of greenhouse gas emissions among US car manufacturers.

## Safety

Ford also stood out for its history of safety problems. One of its top-selling 1973 cars, the Pinto, generated a series of lawsuits, a federal investigation, a "60 Minutes" exposé, and a 1.5 million-vehicle recall.[2]

The incident culminated in the indictment of the company for reckless homicide in the deaths of three teenage girls. Ford established a template for automakers for having safety incidents in which they had foreknowledge but did little about it. The same circumstances emerged in GM's ignition-switch recall (see Chapter 12) and Takata's defective airbag. Nor did Ford seem to learn from the Pinto incident. In 1991, it had to replace thirteen million Firestone tires mounted mostly on its Explorer vehicles.[3] It made these replacements though it had plenty of prior warning. Well before the Explorer reached the market, company engineers knew of instability and poor handling. In a 1989 test, a year prior to Ford selling the vehicle, incidentally as a family-friendly one, an internal report pointed out that the vehicle was prone to excessive rollovers; yet Ford chose to ignore this problem and did not make changes to correct it. Instead, it told drivers to lower their tire pressure, even though doing so reduced the Explorer's fuel economy. The company's actions were ultimately responsible for 174 deaths and more than 700 injuries. Ford lost about $2.4 billion in damage settlements, with additional lawsuits seeking another $590 million. The company could not deny that its SUVs rolled over more frequently than other automobiles, as it built most of them with pickup-truck bodies, which ride higher and raise a vehicle's center of gravity. In 2002, it corrected this problem, as it built the next Explorer 2.5 inches lower to the ground than its predecessor.

## Financial Ups and Downs

Ford also had a history of financial ups and downs.[4] In 1908, it introduced the durable and practical Model T, for which demand was so great that it had to expand production and initiate an assembly line, the first in manufacturing history. To increase production efficiency, each worker did just one single repetitive task. This innovation remains a landmark. The founder of the company, Henry Ford, however, then went on to publish the fascist periodical, the *Dearborn Independent*, thus tarnishing his own and the company's image. In World War I, Ford produced not only large quantities of automobiles, but also trucks, airplane motors, tanks, submarine chasers, ambulances, and munitions for the military. But, the company almost went bankrupt in the 1920s, when it acquired financially troubled

Lincoln. It then fell behind General Motors when General Motors introduced the stylish and powerful Chevrolet.

To prevent unionization, Ford initially adopted very progressive labor policies; its workers toiled for just five days a week, for which the company paid them a minimum $5 per day in wages. In the late 1920s, Ford forged very close ties with the Soviet Union, viewing that country as an important ally that had great economic potential. With the Depression setting in, however, Ford barely stayed afloat and the huge losses it underwent forced it to lower wages to a $4 a day minimum. Yet, it again voluntarily raised wages to a $6 a day minimum in 1936 to prevent workers from organizing. Nonetheless, the US government cited it for numerous unfair labor practices in 1937.

Henry Ford was a vigorous opponent of US involvement in World War II almost until its commencement, but once the war began, his company actively supported the war effort. It constructed a huge government-sponsored facility, where it made the aircraft necessary to defeat US enemies. After the war, with government contracts no longer supporting Ford, it was once again on the verge of bankruptcy. To bring the company's finances under control, it hired ex-Air Force efficiency experts including Robert McNamara. McNamara, who ultimately became the CEO, copied General Motor's decentralized management practices, moved to foreign markets, and introduced strict financial controls. In the end, the financial controls proved to be the company's undoing as they were too tight and the company's staid and functional vehicles fell further behind General Motors in stylishness. Trying to catch up with General Motors, Ford then introduced the ill-fated Edsel, which turned out to be a flop and embarrassment. Ford next purchased Philco, the radio company, started to make tractors, and had great success with the Mustang, a car developed by Robert McNamara protégé, Lee Iacocca.

## The Passage of the 1970 Clean Air Act

The next stage in Ford's evolution was at the start of the 1970s, when Congress passed the Clean Air Act, which forced Ford and other US automakers to design smaller and less polluting vehicles.[5] Japanese compacts became increasingly popular and the US automakers had trouble responding. Iacocca left Ford following the Pinto incident, for which he had to take responsibility, because he was leader of the team that designed the car. By 1980, the company yet again was on the verge of bankruptcy, its US market share falling to under 17 percent. To bring about a recovery, Ford tried to copy the Japanese methods that had worked so well in lowering costs and improving quality. In 1979, it acquired a 25 percent stake in Mazda and worked closely with that company treating it as a small car division from whom it could learn Japanese methods. Ford, though, continued to face more challenges. It had to close many plants and laid off more than 100,000 workers. Its productivity only improved when it began to offshore some of its manufacturing to Mexico.

Then, Ford had a success with the launch of the Taurus in 1985, a full-size car that had taken five years and billions of dollars to develop. Sales and profits achieved record levels and in 1986, Ford surpassed General Motors in income for the first time since 1924 and its US market share grew to just under 20 percent. In 1989, the company was in a position where it could purchase Jaguar. It also became the second largest provider of financial services in the US, ranking only behind Citicorp, and its plan was to derive 30 percent of its profits from this part of the business.

However, the company bore the brunt of the economic recession that crippled the US auto industry in the early 1990s, and its sales plummeted both in the United States and globally. In 1991, it lost $2.25 billion and in 1992, $7.8 billion. These losses would have been far larger had it not been for financial services. Ford based its efforts to recover from these losses on its growing dominance in the truck and minivan market. Nonetheless, it continued to have low profit margins compared to other US automakers and thus it had to keep slashing costs. These efforts paid off in the end, to the point that by the end of the 1990s, it was the world's most profitable automaker. It was therefore able to increase its stake in Mazda to 33.4 percent in 1996 and to buy Volvo in 1999.

However, the recall of the tires on Ford's popular Explorer and other models was a serious blow.[6] In 2001, the company recalled over 300,000 vehicles and replaced over 13 million tires at a cost of $3 billion. It had the worst quality rating in the sector, according to J.D. Power & Associates, and its losses mounted to $5.45 billion. It had to deal with sluggish sales, intense price wars, and faltering employee morale. In 2002, it closed many plants, eliminated 35,000 jobs, and stopped making Mercury Cougars and Lincoln Continentals. Though it cut its losses in 2002, its market share continued to fall. In response, it launched new models the next year and anticipated forty new launches in 2004, including a new Mustang and a first SUV hybrid.

Nonetheless, in 2005, Ford, as well as General Motor, had their bonds downgraded to junk status.[7] The reasons the raters gave included an aging workforce, high US healthcare costs, soaring gasoline prices, eroding market share, and over dependence on SUV sales. As oil prices rose in the twenty-first century's first decade, profits from the sales of the large vehicles, in which both Ford and General Motors specialized, went down. To gain additional sales, the companies had to increase the incentives such as the rebates and low interest financing they offered. Ford's next moves included introducing crossover SUVs, licensing Toyota hybrid electric powertrain technologies, and exploring the future of plug-in hybrids with a utility company Southern California Edison.

## A Partial Recovery

Again these moves were not fully effective and they did not prevent the company from experiencing the largest annual loss in its history up to that point, $12.7 billion, in 2006.[8] The plan to return to profitability unveiled in 2006 called for the dropping of models that lost money, consolidating production lines, closing factories, and cutting jobs.[9] The company raised bankruptcy as an option, getting the United Auto Workers, representing approximately 46,000 hourly workers in North America, to agree to a historic contract settlement in 2007; in return, Ford got breaks in retiree healthcare coverage. This agreement established a company-funded, independently run trust, which removed retiree health care from the company's books, thereby improving Ford's balance sheet. In return for the agreement, hourly workers received guarantees of greater job security. The company still finished 2007 with a $2.7 billion loss, and in 2008, it had to sell Jaguar and Land Rover to Tata Motors.

During the Great Recession that followed Ford did not declare bankruptcy like General Motors, nor did it ask the government for a bridge loan, but requested and got a credit line of $9 billion as a backstop against its worsening condition.[10] In 2010, the company returned to profitability, earning $6.6 billion; in that year, the F-Series established itself as the best-selling US vehicle. Ford sold 528,349 F-Series trucks, a 27.7 percent increase in comparison to 2009.[11] The F-Series was about a quarter of the company's total sales of 1.9 million vehicles. Heavily dependent on the profitable sales of this one vehicle, Ford was not hedged well for a decline in the vehicle's sales, should it take place. Moreover, the company had to continue realigning its assets and sold Hertz Rent-a-Car. In 2014, it named Mark Fields as its new chief operating officer. Fields had been president of its North and South America operations and was well known as a cost-cutter whose expertise was in streamlining Ford operations.

## Prior to and After the 2014–2015 Price Collapse

This chapter now turns to a more detailed consideration of how Ford's strategies changed before and after the 2014–2015 collapse in gas and oil prices. Based on its annual reports and other communications to shareholders, the analysis examines the company's perceptions of the risks and uncertainties and its assumptions about the future.[12] It shows how the company, like GM, tried to hedge its bets by focusing on operations, especially safety and quality, and by choosing the countries in which it would be involved, the brands and models it would bring to market, and the R&D it would carry out. Ford's performance affected the moves it made, and these moves in turn had an impact on its performance.

### *Ford Before the 2014–2015 Price Collapse*

**Perceptions of the Risks and Uncertainties**
Prior to the 2014–2015 fall in prices, Ford's concerns centered on its global market share and revenue, various adverse events as well as, fuel economy and emissions controls, fuel prices, safety, and toxic substances legislation.

*Declining Market Share and Revenue*
Before the 2014–2015 price collapse, Ford's global market share and revenue continued in a downward direction in many areas of the world (Figure 13.2). From 2013 and 2014, its market share had declined in North America, South America, Europe, and the Middle East and Africa, with the only gains taking place in Asia Pacific. The company understood that these results meant that it had to expand in

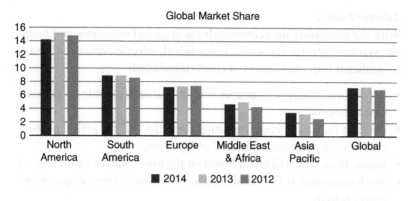

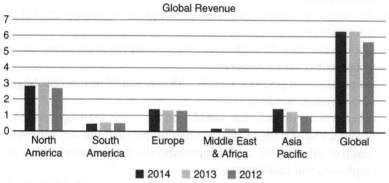

**Figure 13.2** Ford's global market share and revenue 2012–2014 (billions of dollars)
Derived from Ford Annual Reports

fast-growing newly developed and emerging markets, particularly in the Asia Pacific and the Middle East and Africa. In addition, it had to maintain and increase its sales and market share in mature markets like North America and Europe. The company had to make its products attractive across many dimensions including price, quality, styling, safety, and fuel efficiency. The price competition it faced in the sector, however, was intense, as the sector suffered from excess capacity. Because of high-fixed costs, small changes in sales and market share had a substantial effect on profitability. With so much overcapacity, Ford and the other manufacturers could not easily raise prices to offset higher costs. To grow market share and maintain sales they had to offer discounts and other incentives to buyers, moves that kept a lid on their profits.

### Adverse Events

With the increasing interconnectedness of global economic and financial systems, adverse economic, geopolitical, adverse events could have a significant impact. Matters of concern included:

- Ford's operations in countries with unstable economic or political environments;
- the debt burden of countries using the Euro and the ability of these countries to meet their financial obligations;
- higher than expected credit losses on the loans made to auto buyers;
- work stoppages at Ford and suppliers because of labor disputes and union activity;
- the company's dependence on single suppliers for some of its critical components;
- labor demands that might prevent the company from maintaining a competitive cost structure;
- the pension and postretirement health care and life insurance obligations it had to workers;
- cybersecurity threats that could lead to work interruptions and outages, loss of trade secrets, or other proprietary and competitively sensitive information and compromise the person information of employees and customers;
- exposure to hurricanes, tornadoes, other storms, flooding, and earthquakes, and the patterns of extreme weather that climate change could cause.

### Fuel Economy Plus Emission Controls

In the United States, the National Highway Traffic Safety Administration (NHTSA) had authority for vehicle fuel economy and the Environmental Protection Agency (EPA) had authority for greenhouse gas emissions. The two agencies mandated light duty vehicle corporate average fuel economy (CAFE) standards of 35.5 mpg by 2016, 45 mpg by 2021, and 54.5 mpg by 2025. Canadian and Mexican standards were similar. These standards would be very difficult for Ford and the other auto manufacturers to meet. Ford was particularly concerned about the feasibility of meeting the 54.5 mpg standard. The projected 2018 midterm evaluation of this standard, therefore, was very important to the company. Its ability to comply with the standard was unclear because of factors over which it did not have control; fuel prices had to be sufficiently high and market conditions right for consumers to buy enough electric vehicles and other fuel-efficient vehicles to meet the policy's goals. If fuel prices did not rise and market conditions remained unchanged, meeting government fuel economy and $CO_2$ standards would be extremely difficult. If a revision to the policy did not take place, the company might have to take actions that would adversely affect its sales and profits, including limiting the sales of popular models, like the F-Series trucks, and curtailing the production of high-performance cars and other full and light trucks.

It would also be difficult to comply with the more stringent EPA air emission standards, which the agency had slated to go into effect by 2017. And an even bigger challenge would be meeting California requirements to sell zero emission vehicles (ZEVs). By 2025, California mandated that around 15 percent of Ford's sales in the state should be this type of advanced vehicle. The California requirements called for substantial increases in battery electric, fuel cell, and plugin hybrid vehicles by 2025. Thirteen states, primarily in the Northeast and Northwest, had adopted the California standards. If gasoline prices did not continue to be high, sales of these vehicles were not likely to meet expectations. The market for such vehicles was uncertain and the infrastructure to support them was not in place. Full implementation of the EPA and California standards would have a substantially negative effect on Ford's sales and profits.

In Europe, stricter emission control standards also were a threat. In Europe, automakers could not take for granted the fuel economy and $CO_2$ advantages of diesel fuels. Other countries followed in the footsteps of the United States and Europe. South Korea and Taiwan had adopted US gasoline vehicle standards and European diesel standards. Canada aligned its standards with the United States. China based its emission standards on the European model. Japan had unique standards and procedures. While Brazil, Argentina, and Chile were considering what to do next, it was likely that they too would introduce more stringent controls.

Thus, Ford confronted stringent regulation in the EU, as well as the United States and other countries with additional requirements covering not only $CO_2$ and non-$CO_2$ air emissions, but also noise, recycling, safety, and more. Many member states in the EU – the United Kingdom, France, Germany, Spain, Portugal, the Netherlands, and other countries – had introduced $CO_2$ taxes to bring about the introduction of low-CO2 vehicles, but these countries had not harmonized the taxes they imposed. In addition, South Korea, China, Japan, and Latin American nations had also introduced new fuel efficiency programs and targets that increased vehicle costs. Another measure to curtail CO2 emissions in EU countries was a mandate to replace current refrigerant in auto air conditioning with one that had lower climate change potential. This mandate would also add to vehicle costs. Providing climate-change-relevant information to investors and shaping the company's business strategy with climate change in mind were important elements in maintaining the company's access to capital. Ford, therefore, had made many changes to improve fuel economy, but there were limits to how far it could go. Many additional obstacles stood in the way including the costs, the readiness of the technology, infrastructure adequacy, and consumer acceptance.

### Volatile Fuel Prices
Although the company had a balanced portfolio of small and medium as well as large cars and trucks, a shift in consumer preferences from large and more profitable vehicles – whether because of fuel prices, government actions, or other reasons – would negatively affect Ford's bottom line. Concerns about gasoline prices in the 1970s drove consumers to more fuel-efficient vehicles. However, starting in the 1980s, gasoline prices remained relatively low and sales of less fuel-efficient SUVs and light trucks gained traction. From 2006 to 2014, this trend started to shift. With the exception of the years of the Great Recession, gasoline prices increased.

Ford conceded that governments had legitimate security concerns. They wanted reductions in imports. They also had legitimate concerns about climate change. These factors provided an opportunity for automakers to deliver fuel-efficient and low-carbon products. They got them involved in research in new vehicle and battery technologies. Nonetheless, consumer segments seeking greater fuel efficiency were not yet large. Broad consumer acceptance waited for a time when fuel prices would be consistently and dependably high and demand for Ford's profitable large cars and trucks went down when prices increased.

### Safety
The year 2014 marked an unprecedented increase in the number of US safety and vehicles recalls, a main reason being NHTSA's expansion in its definition of safety defects and its shift to a significant increase in civil

penalties, actions that adversely affected the reputation of all the automakers and the acceptance of their products. Meeting or exceeding government safety standards was often costly and technologically difficult. Moreover, safety standards frequently conflicted with the weight reductions needed to comply with fuel economy standards. EU regulators had also been active in this domain. They compelled companies to adopt a number of specific safety features such as lane-departure warning systems, electronic stability controls, and automatic brake assists. Canadian regulations were similar to those in the United States. Countries in Asia and Latin American were also developing new safety and recall requirements and different national regulations added to the complexity and costs of compliance.

### Toxic Substances Legislation
In the United States, the Senate and House had proposed bills since 2010 to overhaul the 1976 Toxic Substances Control Act, but none had passed. However, California had passed a safe consumer products law, which took effect in late 2013 that required manufacturers to identify safer alternatives to a range of 1,200 chemicals known to be harmful to public health and the environment. In 2009, the United Nations called for regulations requiring a globally harmonized system (GHS) of classification and labeling of chemicals. Ford's goal was to complete US-mandated implementation of the GHS requirements by the end of 2013 and it had started with employee training. Its view was that these requirements for the handling of undesirable chemicals had created undue uncertainty because standards were different, not prioritized, and very difficult to implement.

### Assumptions about the Future

Given these uncertainties, achieving future returns would not be easy. Ford assumed new patterns of mobility would arise and that new opportunities would come from being innovative.

### New Mobility Patterns
The company assumed that as both the developed and developing worlds continued to grow, innovation and ingenuity were necessary to overcome energy and raw materials constraints. It had a long list of issues of relevance to itself and its stakeholders that included:

- product quality;
- safety;
- innovation;
- brand perception;
- customer satisfaction;
- supply chain management;
- environmental management;
- fuel economy;
- carbon impact;
- gas price volatility;
- vehicle electrification;
- ethics;
- public policy;
- community impacts;
- water.

Given that all these issues existed stabilizing atmospheric $CO_2$ emissions at 450 parts per million (ppm) would be exceptionally challenging and require unparalleled coordination.

Ford favored a comprehensive, market-based approach to reducing greenhouse emissions to lower emissions at the lowest cost per ton. This system would provide a price signal to support the billions of dollars invested in low-carbon and fuel-efficient vehicle technologies. Shared goals and regulatory harmony across national borders would ease the burden of developing new technologies to meet the goals of $CO_2$ reductions, but overcoming the patchwork of inconsistent current regulations might be too much to expect. Ford was trying to figure out what its fair share to stabilization should be by calculating the $CO_2$ emission reductions required of new light-duty vehicles (LDVs) in different parts of the world. These steps indicated that it would have to make deep cuts in nearly every part of the world.

The company assumed that the following trends would play a prominent role in its future:

- Global population would grow to 9–11 billion people by 2050.
- Much of the growth was in resource-constrained, climate-vulnerable, developing nations, while stagnant or declining fertility rates were common in developed nations.
- The world's population as a whole was aging, though at the opposite end of the spectrum there still existed vibrant young segments.

- In some parts of the world, the middle class had achieved unprecedented growth, but in other parts, the middle class was fading.
- Globalization had benefits but also disadvantages; localization was growing along with globalization.
- City populations were denser than at any time in history.
- Many in the world faced new levels of inequality.
- Big data was causing unprecedented disruption.

The trends meant that Ford would have to focus on new mobility models, conducting experiments, which would culminate in long-term leadership.

### Opportunities in Innovation

Concerns about climate change, the volatile price of fuel, and energy security created opportunities that could enable growth and expansion. Significant opportunities opened to companies because of these factors but it was unclear if Ford could take advantage of them. Ford's commitment in all its new or significantly refreshed vehicles was to offer fuel economy, and technology consistent with current thinking about climate change and the need to keep pace and stay ahead of regulatory requirements. The current period was transformative and the winners would be the innovators that were willing to break with tradition and find new solutions. Ford could not use lack of agreement on long-term climate solutions as an excuse for inaction.

The aim of the company was to create global vehicle platforms that offered superior fuel economy, safety, quality, and customer features, and to tailor each global platform to national or regional preferences and requirements. It was trying to cut the time taken to bring new vehicles to market. It would have to rely on innovation to succeed. It would have to seize the opportunities that existed. Yet, in making important decisions about the future, it lacked complete certainty about what the developments would be in technologies, markets, consumer demand, and policies. Without this certainty, it had to have the requisite flexibility to do well across a range of possible scenarios. The company had to hedge its bets.

Thus, the company was committed to a new mobility blueprint for transportation in 2025 and beyond of connected cars making driving safer, easing traffic congestion, and sustaining the environment. It assumed that because of big data and other technological advances there would be movement toward a world where vehicles could communicate and sense each other's presence and where people routinely shared vehicles and used multiple forms of transportation. It had developed the SYNC network for communications and entertainment. It would continue to equip vehicles with additional ways to link to the Internet. Vehicles better connected to each other could alert drivers about traffic and the hazards that were in front of them. The disruptions taking place in mobility redefined what was possible. The next stage in this evolution would be autonomous vehicles. They would make traveling from Point A to Point B easier than ever. These disruptions were worth embracing, if the company could play a prominent role in what might be fast approaching.

## Ford: After the 2014–2015 Price Collapse

### Perceptions of the Risks and Uncertainties

After the 2014–2015 drop in oil prices, Ford's main concerns continued to be the possibility of adverse events and clean air and fuel efficiency regulations that could increase its costs and lower its sales.

### Adverse Events

A decline in industry sales due to a number of possible events – a financial crisis, recession, geopolitical event, or other incident – could take place. Additional adverse conditions might occur because of economic and geopolitical and protectionist trade policies. They could take place because of currency fluctuations. They could occur because of labor, which might limit Ford's ability to maintain a competitive cost structure. In some instances, Ford had but a single-source of supply. Thus, there might be supplier work stoppages, limitations on production, not only because of disputes with labor, but because of natural and human disasters, tight credit markets, or other factors. Ford faced cybersecurity threats, and it continued to have to deal with high pension and post-retirement liabilities. It might confront new credit regulation that would make it harder for people to purchase new vehicles.

### Clean Air and Fuel Efficiency Regulations

Ford took note of the stringent US government clean air regulations that were coming. California's standards were already stricter than those of the federal government – about 15 percent of the vehicles Ford sold in the state in 2025 would have to be emission free. Thirteen US states had adopted California's standards. In 2015, governments around the world also took action against VW for its use of defeat devices to thwart diesel emission controls. These actions yielded billion dollar settlements as well as indictments of employees for criminal conduct. The EU was ready to expand diesel exhaust regulations. Proposed tests would mandate real-time assessments using on-board diagnostics to supplement laboratory examinations. Compliance costs were likely to be significant and might eliminate diesel's advantage in releasing fewer $CO_2$ emissions than gasoline engines.

Under NHTSA and EPA's mandates, Ford and the other auto manufacturers would have to achieve average-fleet fuel economy standards of 35.5 mpg model year by 2016. The average would go up to 45 mpg by 2021, and 51.4 mpg by 2025. Meeting fuel economy and emission standards would be difficult if fuel prices continued to be low and market signals did not compel the purchase of alternative vehicles. If gasoline prices remained low, how many fuel-efficient vehicles could Ford sell? If other states embraced California's clean air standards, Ford deemed it unlikely that the market and the infrastructure in California and elsewhere would support the sale of a large quantity of electric or other highly fuel-efficient vehicles. Other countries throughout the world were adopting versions of the US and/or EU standards, including the rapidly growing countries of the Asia Pacific region. If compliance with fuel economy and emission regulations meant a significant long-term shift from highly profitable large models, it would negatively affect the company's bottom line.

## Assumptions about the Future

Ford continued to focus on a number of trends it assumed would play a prominent role and the innovative opportunities they might create.

### Shared Mobility
An important trend was that people were moving from owning vehicles to accessing shared transportation modes. This trend was ushering in a revolution in transportation based on factors such as:

### Crowded Cities and Growing Populations:

- air pollution and congestion;
- strains on global transportation and highway systems;
- increased middle class aspirations for car ownership.

**Nature on the Edge**

- a resulting pickup in demand for energy, water and other raw materials;
- growing impacts of climate change from vehicle manufacture and use.

**Changing Priorities**

- new behaviors shaped by the digital world and sharing economy;
- an increasing appetite for ride sharing and alternative ways to own and use a car.

For Ford, these changes meant a different conception of its business. It was not just selling vehicles but providing transportation services that encompassed electrification, autonomy, and mobility.

**Opportunities for Innovation**
Because of these trends, the company had opportunities to innovate. It had reason to reduce vehicle life cycle impacts, without sacrificing vehicle power or performance. It had to ensure that switching to ultra-low/zero-emission vehicles would be to the benefit of consumers, cities, and the natural environment. The ability to take advantage of the opportunities depended on customers deciding which vehicles and fuels they would purchase. It was contingent on customers choosing how to drive and maintain their vehicles. The opportunity for Ford was to continue to invest in its core business of designing, manufacturing, marketing, financing, and servicing cars, SUVs, and trucks, while hedging its bets which meant at the same time endeavoring to help bring about a transition to new modes of mobility.

**Hedging**

Like GM, the approach Ford took to managing the risks and uncertainties involved layers of hedging to protect the company against various contingencies. The hedges in which it engaged were to try to: (1) ensure the quality and safety of its vehicles; (2) invest globally in different markets; (3) adjust its brand and model mix; and (4) devote itself to technological innovation that might bring with it future competitive advantage. Ford did not deviate much from these strategies even when oil prices fell, although it did alter the way it implemented them. The chapter next describes how Ford applied these strategies before and after the 2014–2015 price crash.

## Ford Before the 2014–2015 Price Collapse

### (1) Assuring Quality and Safety

*The Pillars of the Business*

World-class safety and quality were the pillars of Ford's business. Their foundation was in a zero-defect mindset, high aspirational goals, and a constant effort to achieve the goals. By means of a lean, flexible, and disciplined production system, Ford strove to maintain and improve product quality and safety. It applied measurable global guidelines that employees had to meet or exceed, and the scoring of the guidelines played an important role in the performance reviews of all employees including managers. The company's stringent design guidelines exceeded regulatory requirements for pre-crash, crash, and post-crash situations. The company relied on engineering, computer modeling, and testing to evaluate vehicle and component performance prior to introduction. To strengthen its vehicles, as well as keeping their weight down, it used advanced materials such ultra-high-strength steels, plastics and composites, and aluminum.

*Issues*

Nonetheless, the company still had quality and customer satisfaction issues. In 2014, it experienced forty US safety recalls (Table 13.1), which was higher than in previous years. This increase was due in part to NHTSA expanding its definition of safety defects, which led to a high number of safety recalls in the United States across all manufacturers. However, a greater use of innovative technologies had put additional demands on the company and suppliers. The company's tracking of customer satisfaction in the first three months of a vehicle being in service was steady or improving in almost every region in the world in 2014 in comparison to 2013, but Ford was behind Toyota in the number of its new cars achieving five-star safety ratings from NHTSA in 2013 and 2014. For the fourth time in Ford's history, it did not have an employee work-related fatality in 2014, but its contractors – in Kansas City, Argentina, Brazil, and China – did have four fatalities.

Table 13.1 *Indicators of Ford quality and safety 2009–2014*

US safety recalls

|  | 2009 | 2010 | 2011 | 2012 | 2013 | 2014 |
|---|---|---|---|---|---|---|
| Number | 8 | 7 | 13 | 24 | 16 | 40 |
| Millions of vehicles | 4.522 | 5.510 | 3.339 | 1.399 | 1.188 | 4,746 |

"Things gone wrong" (3 months in service per 1,000 vehicles)

|  | 2009 | 2010 | 2011 | 2012 | 2013 | 2014 |
|---|---|---|---|---|---|---|
| North America | 1,430 | 1,358 | 1,449 | 1,514 | 1,650 | 1,392 |
| South America | 2,258 | 2,126 | 1,510 | 1,416 | 1,724 | 1,472 |
| Europe | 2,224 | 1,827 | 1,747 | 1,573 | 1,302 | 1,302 |
| Asia Pacific | 2,266 | 1,979 | 1,100 | 860 | 941 | 917 |
| Middle East & Africa | 1,977 | 1,814 | 1,122 | 1,535 | 1,311 | 1,046 |

Percent of customers satisfied (3 months in service)

|  | 2009 | 2010 | 2011 | 2012 | 2013 | 2014 |
|---|---|---|---|---|---|---|
| North America | 78 | 80 | 79 | 79 | 78 | 79 |
| South America | 68 | 66 | 66 | 65 | 65 | 68 |
| Europe | 58 | 59 | 62 | 68 | 71 | 73 |
| Asia Pacific | 48 | 48 | 59 | 67 | 68 | 69 |
| Middle East & Africa | 55 | 56 | 54 | 69 | 63 | 62 |

Percent of models achieving 5-star NHTSA safety rating

|  | 2013 | 2014 |
|---|---|---|
| Ford | 32 | 41 |
| Toyota | 33 | 60 |
| GM | 43 | 40 |

Derived from Ford Annual Reports

## New Safety Features

Ford introduced many new features into its vehicles to enhance safety. Starting in 2011 the Explorer had the world's first automotive rear inflatable safety belts. The 2014 model achieved top marks in the federal government's new car safety rating program, but the fact it achieved the highest US safety rating did not mean it would get the same rating in other countries. Standards differed, which was a challenge the company faced in vehicle design. Ford offered other types of accident avoidance and driver-assist technologies on select models, such as an adjustable speed limiter, traffic sign recognition, active city stop devices, brake support, and adaptive headlights. To prevent drivers from diverting their attention from the conditions on the road, SYNC technology allowed them to use voice commands on their cell phones and MP3 players. SYNC-equipped vehicles also had a non-subscription call-for-help system. In addition, an SOS-Post Crash Alert System automatically sounded the horn and activated emergency flashers. The 2014 Mustang had a new airbag design for knee protection. Ford expanded a lane-keeping system, which was a driver assist feature, to include more vehicles. Curve control that slowed a vehicle when it sensed the driver was taking a curve too quickly became available on select vehicles. Pre-collision assist with pedestrian detection were ready for release on 2015 Ford Mondeos.

Ford also had a number of programs aimed at driver education. Driving skills for life was a free program to help new drivers. In North America and Europe, its focus was helping teenagers with distraction, speed and space management, handling, and hazard recognition. The company supported Graduated Driver Licensing (GDL) programs to reduce crashes, injuries, and fatalities involving teen drivers. MyKey was a technology it developed to help parents encourage their teenagers to drive safely. In Asia, the Middle East and Africa the focus was not just young drivers; it was drivers of all ages.

*Accountability*

A sustainability committee, part of the board, reviewed company actions with regard to safety and the environment, and held executives accountable. From 2013 to 2014, the company reduced water use by 3 percent. It achieved zero waste-to-landfill status at a manufacturing facility in Canada. It managed material use across the life cycle to eliminate troublesome and dangerous materials. All of Ford's manufacturing facilities and product development functions were ISO 14001 certified. To ensure environmental quality and safety, the company depended on more than 11,000 supplier companies. It trained 280 of these companies in 2014 in corporate social responsibility,

emphasizing human rights. The company had its own energy management system and it shared its best practices for energy as well as
greenhouse gas emissions and water use with select suppliers. It also
made outreach efforts to improve the performance of the smelters on
which it relied. It engaged in voluntary recycling, though it did not
assume that recycled materials were always the best solution. It took
into consideration whether these materials would increase vehicle
weight or raise energy demand.

## (2) Investing in Global Markets

### *Four Divisions*
Ford hedged its bets by investing in many different parts of the world.
In 2012–2014, it had divisions in Asia Pacific, Europe, South America,
and the Middle East and Africa. High fuel prices were having an impact
in all areas in which Ford operated. In North America, sales in 2014
declined 5 percent compared with 2013. At 8.4 percent, operating
margins slipped by 1.8 percentage points, and US market share was
down one percentage point, primarily due to less market share for gas
guzzling F-150 trucks. On the other hand, sales in Asia Pacific grew by
13 percent compared with 2013, and market share was at a record
3.5 percent. However, although Ford had record profits of
$589 million, operating margins in Asia Pacific were just 5.5 percent.
Even if they were 2.3 percentage points better than the previous year,
Asia Pacific operating profits were 35 percent less than they were in
North America.

### *Asia Pacific*
By 2014, Ford's presence in Asia Pacific encompassed twelve primary
markets – Australia, New Zealand, Japan, Korea, China, Taiwan,
India, Thailand, Indonesia, the Philippines, Vietnam, and Malaysia,
and the company was active in an additional thirty-one other countries.
Ford expected that 60–70 percent of its growth in the next decade
would come from Asia Pacific. Accordingly, it planned a substantial
increase in its operations there. In 2013, the company built its largest-
ever factory complex in the southwestern Chinese city of Chongqing.
It spent $4.9 billion to expand the number of cars it sold in China and
double its production capacity to 600,000 vehicles. In 2014, it
launched eight new models in the region, expanded the number of its
dealerships, and built state-of-the-art manufacturing facilities, which

would enable it to produce 2.7 million vehicles per year in the region and allow it to sell about 8 million vehicles per year there. The improvement it so far had experienced in Asia Pacific was mainly due to China. In Australia and New Zealand, the Ford Falcon had been the most popular family car, but because of high costs of making the car in these countries, manufacturing in the countries ceased.

Ford's Chinese market share grew to a record 4.5 percent in 2014. It sold more than a million vehicles in China for the first time. China's strict fuel efficiency standards, however, were a limit on how far Ford could go in the country. China's corporate average-fuel consumption target was a stringent 34 mpg in 2015. This standard was to go up to 47 mpg in 2020. The Chinese government provided incentives of about $9,700 per vehicle of Chinese made fuel-efficient vehicles like plug-in hybrids. Ford was working to increase its vehicles' fuel efficiency throughout the region. It offered EcoBoost engines in thirteen products in 2014 and planned to increase the number to twenty vehicles in 2015. It also sold three hybrid electrics in the region. Yet Ford was considerably behind GM in China. It created its first joint venture in China in 2001, six years later than GM and more than ten years after VW. The company had just 2.5 percent of the Chinese market in 2013, while VW had 14.5 percent and GM 15.6 percent of the market. In 2013, GM had more than six times the sales that Ford had in China.

Unlike GM, Ford was active in India. In 2010, it launched its first compact car in India, the Figo. It designed and priced the vehicle for the mass market. In 2011, it signed a memorandum of understanding with the State of Gujarat for the construction of an assembly and engine plant in which it planned to invest about a billion dollars.

*Europe*
In Europe, where Ford sold smaller cars than in North America, the Fiesta was the bestselling car on the continent for the third year in a row in 2014. The number of vehicles Ford sold and the revenue it earned in Europe in 2014 were higher than the previous year by 5 and 8 percent, respectively. Its 2014 market share in Europe was the highest since 2011. The company gained 0.2 percentage points in market share in that year. At eight percent, its European market share was considerably higher than its market share in Asia Pacific, though not as high as its market share in North America. Ford outperformed GM in Europe.

Like the F-150 truck in North America, the Fiesta was a hit. The car featured smart technologies and seven powertrain options. There were both diesel and gasoline models. It was fuel-efficient and on average emitted less than 100 grams of $CO_2$ per kilometer, the first non-hybrid, gasoline, family car in Europe to break this barrier. Ford also had a successful line of new line of Transit vehicles in Europe. The Mondeo models were popular and Ranger compact pickups were strong performers.

Though Ford's sales in Europe were good, its operating margins remained weak. In 2014, they were a negative 3.6 percent and the company suffered a pre-tax loss of $1.1 billion. This loss was actually less severe than it had been the previous year.

Ford's history of operations in Europe was a long one. The first cars it shipped there were in 1903 – the year of the company's founding. Ford had wholly-owned facilities in the continent and sold vehicles in fifty different European markets. Nonetheless, the dilemma Ford confronted in Europe was similar to the one it confronted in Asia Pacific. To attain profitable growth, the company would have to produce vehicles with low $CO_2$ emissions. Ford introduced Europe's first gasoline hybrid electric. It reduced the average $CO_2$ emissions of its European fleet by 18 percent from 2006 to 2014. Mondeos had three low $CO_2$ emission ECOnetic diesels and one EcoBoost petrol vehicle. Ford had a broad low-$CO_2$ vehicle portfolio in Europe, ninety-two models and variants in Europe with $CO_2$ emissions below 130 g/km of which twenty-one models or variants had $CO_2$ emissions below 100 g/km.

ECOnetic vehicles were ultra-low-$CO_2$ diesels that leveraged several advanced fuel-saving technologies. The Fiesta ECOnetic had $CO_2$ emissions of 85 g/km and fuel economy of 71 mpg, with a range of technologies helping to produce this result including gear ratios, aero-dynamics, tire-resistance, air conditioning and cooling, oil pumps, and the alternator. The engine's combustion was different and the car had start and stop features and regenerative braking. With the addition of two additional EcoBoost engines in 2014, Ford expanded the total number of these engine configurations in Europe to fifteen. In 2015, Ford was planning to introduce a Ford Mondeo with an EcoBoost engine, with fuel economy of 55.4 mpg and 119 g/km $CO_2$ emissions.

EcoBoost engines relied on turbocharging and direct injection air to the engine to deliver fuel-efficiency and $CO_2$ reductions gains. They were supposed to achieve these goals without sacrificing vehicle performance. Yet there was considerable controversy about whether they actually accomplished what Ford claimed. Ford pushed the technology, maintaining it was a less costly and more versatile way to increase fuel economy and lower $CO_2$ emissions than expanding the use of hybrid and diesel engine technologies. In 2013, *Consumer Reports*, however, challenged these claims and maintained that after testing many cars with these engines, and competitors with conventional engines, the turbocharged cars had slower acceleration and no better fuel economy. Ward's Automotive Group also tested many EcoBoost engines, and had similar findings.

Ford had three European electric vehicles – the Mondeo Hybrid, the Focus all-electric vehicle, and s C-MAX plug-in hybrid. In markets where infrastructure existed, such as Spain, Portugal, Italy, Germany and Turkey, the company sold LPGs and propane versions of the Fiesta, B-MAX, Focus, and C-MAX. It offered flex-fuel versions of the Focus in select countries. The company continuously tried to improve the efficiency and sustainability of manufacturing operations. It worked with companies in the supply chain to create alignment with them on sustainability. It had seven zero-waste-to-landfill Ford plants in Europe, and it made efforts to reduce energy and water usage.

### South America

Ford had dealt with protectionist government measures in South America throughout most of the twentieth century that forced it to build different models in different countries and kept it from rationalizing its production and achieving economies of scale in this part of the world. However, Mercosur, the regional common market, allowed it to consolidate manufacturing of the Fiesta and EcoSport in Brazil, and the Focus in Argentina, and to import the Mondeo from Europe, and the company produced a pick-up truck version of the Fiesta in Brazil. In South America, its market share grew to 14.1 percent – 1.5 percentage points higher than in 2013 and its highest market share in the region in seven years – improving its position from fourth in the industry in 2013 to second in 2014. Yet, the company suffered declines in cars sold (14 percent) and revenue (19 percent) in 2014 compared to 2013. It had a negative operating margin of 13.2 percent, and a pre-tax loss of $1.2 billion, both worse than 2013.

Ford launched new products with fuel-efficient technologies in South America, such as the new Ka and the hybrid electric Ford Fusion.

The Ka had the best compact and mid-range fuel efficiency rating among vehicles sold in Brazil. The company offered EcoBoost engines in South America. The company improved vehicle efficiency through a variety of means – less friction, greater throttle, improved gear ratios, better aerodynamics, less tire resistance, improved timing, better battery management, enhanced electric power steering, smart alternators, and dual-clutch automatic transmission.

In Brazil, the large-scale use of biofuels was a national policy. Ethanol was used as a fuel by itself or it was blended with gasoline. Many vehicles were flexible and could run on ethanol or gasoline. Diesels had to run on fuel that had a minimum of 7 percent biodiesel. Other South American countries, such as Argentina and Colombia, were becoming more like Brazil and had increased their use of biofuels.

### The Middle East and Africa
This region had a diverse range of markets with different political, cultural, and economic conditions. It had some of the wealthiest and poorest countries. It had oil exporters as well as importers. Fuel economy and CO2 had not been major priorities of governments in the region, though regulatory challenges could emerge in the future. South Africa was the exception. It already had a CO2 tax based on vehicle emission levels. In this region, the number of cars Ford sold was down 3 percent and its revenue had declined 4 percent compared to 2013. Operating margin was a negative 0.5 percent and the company had pre-tax loss of $20 million in 2014, but its performance was better than it had been the previous year. Ford expected the market in this part of the world to grow 40 percent by the end of the decade to 5.5 million vehicles and it wanted to be part of this growth. Therefore, it accelerated its activities in the Middle East and Africa. It intended to launch twenty-five vehicles in the region by 2016. It would be introducing EcoBoost engines and SYNC connectivity and safety technologies such as inflatable rear seat belts. In 2014, Ford set up a new division to cover the sixty-seven markets in North Africa, Sub-Saharan Africa, Southern Africa, and the Middle East.

### (3) Adjusting the Brand and Model Mix

### Global Integration
The company aimed for a single strategy of global integration. Ford's aim was to offer for sale a full family of vehicles – small, medium and

large; cars, and trucks – that all had high levels of quality, fuel efficiency, safety and design. To simplify operations and save money it was in the process of consolidating the number of global platforms it had from twelve to nine by 2016. The goal was to have almost all its global production come from these platforms. In 2014, Ford launched globally twenty-four all-new or significantly refreshed products, including the all-new Ford F-150, Mustang, Escort, Ka, Transit, and the Lincoln MKC, a luxury compact crossover. In 2015, it aimed to make fifteen new global product launches since new product launches were critical to its growth and profitability, and without them, its sales would be stagnant. Ford's goal was to hedge its bets with a global product mix that had many different models from very large trucks to the very small Ka/Figo all of which it would build on a few global platforms (Table 13.2).

*New Models*

The way it developed the new models it introduced was to start with its customers and determine who they were, how they lived, and what they wanted. To identify the best technologies and anticipate where the market was heading, it engaged in an annual planning process that included groups from research, product strategy, marketing, and design. The decisions it made rested on these groups making strong business cases for developing new models or extending existing ones. Once Ford accepted the business case, it set its global product development system in place to implement the idea. To ensure efficiency and quality this system relied on a set of performance measures and metrics that incorporated lessons learned from prior product introductions.

*Life-Cycle Assessment*

Ford analyzed which combinations of vehicle and fuel technologies would be most cost-effective for the long-term stabilization of atmospheric $CO_2$ concentrations. It kept track of total emissions by carrying out life cycle analyses. Most of the emissions from internal combustion engines (ICEs) were a result of driving. Most of the emissions of the electric alternatives to the ICE were a result of power generation. These emissions depended on the extent to which that power generation was low carbon. High carbon emitting coal-fired power had a worse effect than low carbon emitting solar and wind-generated electricity. With regard to total lifetime $CO_2$ emissions, Ford found that the plug-in

**Table 13.2** *Ford's product mix 2014*

| TYPE | Name | Year introduced | Product information |
|------|------|-----------------|---------------------|
| Trucks | Ranger* | 1971 | Mid-sized pickup truck |
| | F-150 | 1948 | Full-sized pickup – best seller in North America |
| | Super Duty | 1999 | Full-sized heavy duty pickup |
| SUV | Escape*/Kuga | 2000 | Compact SUV |
| | Expedition | 1996 | Full-sized SUV global platform |
| | Lincoln Navigator | 1998 | Full-sized luxury SUV |
| Crossovers | Ecosport | 2003 | Subcompact crossover |
| | Edge | 2006 | Mid-sized crossover global platform |
| | Lincoln MKX | 2007 | Mid-sized luxury crossover |
| | Explorer | 1990 | Full-sized crossover global platform (US) |
| | Flex | 2009 | Full-sized crossover global platform (Europe) |
| | Lincoln MKT | 2010 | Full-sized luxury crossover |
| Vans | Transit Connect | 2002 | Compact van developed in Europe |
| | Transit Courier | 2014 | Leisure activity van |
| | Transit Custom | 2012 | Mid-sized van |
| | Transit* | 1965 | Light commercial van developed in Europe |
| | E-Series | 1961 | Full-size van |
| Multi-purpose | B-Max | 2012 | Mini developed in Europe |
| | C-Max* | 2003 | Compact |
| | S-Max | 2006 | Mid-size |
| | Galaxy | 1996 | Large |
| Power cars | Mustang | 1964 | Muscle car |
| | GT | 2004 | Super car |
| Passenger cars | Ka/Figo | 1996 | Super mini developed in Brazil |
| | Fiesta | 1976 | Subcompact global platform |
| | Focus* | 1998 | Compact global platform |
| | Mondeo*/Fusion* | 1992 | Mid-sized global platform |
| | Lincoln MKZ | 2007 | Mid-sized luxury sedan |
| | Taurus | 1986 | Full sized global platform |

Derived from Ford annual reports; *comes in hybrid and/or all electric versions hybrid was superior to most ICE engines. A plug-in hybrid with a twenty-eight-mile driving range beat various types of internal combustion engines. It also beat a pure electric battery vehicle that had a seventy-mile driving range (Table 13.3). The results, however, varied depending on the climate in a particular region as well as its energy mix. For instance, electric alternatives to the ICE did much better in California than they did in Minnesota because batteries were not as effective in cold climates. Ford also found that ICEs with its EcoBoost technology did not significantly outperform ICEs without this technology.

Ford offered an Eco Boost alternative to reduce fuel consumption on 80 percent of the vehicles it sold, yet its analyses did not show major benefits. According to Ford's testing, an engine with EcoBoost did not run on significantly less gasoline than a conventional ICE (Table 13.4). Depending on country, region, or US state, there were variations in these findings. The regulatory standards governments introduced mattered. Different governments had miles per gallon, grams of CO2, or mega-joules per kilometer standards. How they enforced the standards, the penalties for non-compliance they put in place and the incentives for making reducing emissions, also mattered. For instance, to make up for lower gasoline taxes, some US states raised registration fees for hybrid and/or electric vehicles, while some European countries waived these fees to encourage hybrid and/or electric vehicle adoption. Ford took into account other factors. In Europe, as well as tracking CO2 emissions, it tracked air-quality impacts, recycled and renewable materials, noise, safety, the storage space and roominess of the vehicle, and the first three years' ownership costs.

To evaluate different future alternatives, the company relied on life-cycle analysis to obtain a better sense of the materials it used, the energy consumed, and the emissions generated. Included in its analyses was a broad range of impacts of automobile production and use such as mining, production of the parts, their fabrication and assembly, the operation of a vehicle, its fuel-use, maintenance, and the vehicle's disassembly and disposal. Ford concluded that because of large uncertainties about technology, costs, and regulation, it could not determine which combination of fuel and technology would be superior in the future. In the absence of future certainty, the company's goal was to make a fair contribution to global CO2 reduction goals. Each year it would try to reduce its emissions depending on factors such as energy price changes and

Table 13.3 *Ford's estimates of lifetime CO2 emissions of different engine configurations*

| Different engine configurations | Total lifetime CO2 emissions (metric tons) |
|---|---|
| Internal combustion engine (ICE) | 74 |
| ICE with auto start-stop | 72 |
| ICE with EcoBoost | 70 |
| Diesel ICE | 66 |
| Hybrid | 55 |
| Plug in Hybrid – 28-mile electric driving range | |
| US average | 53 |
| California average | 42 |
| Minnesota average | 58 |
| Battery Electric – 70-mile driving range | |
| US average | 58 |
| California average | 33 |
| Minnesota average | 67 |

Derived from Ford Reports

Table 13.4 *Ford's estimates of fuel economy of different engine configurations*

| Different engine configurations | Fuel economy (miles per gallon) |
|---|---|
| Internal combustion engine (ICE) | 26 |
| ICE with auto start-stop | 27 |
| ICE with EcoBoost | 28 |
| Diesel ICE | 35 |
| Hybrid | 37 |

Derived from Ford Reports

demand changes in the mix of vehicles consumers wanted. In 2014, its average-fleet fuel economy did not improve in the United States because consumer preferences shifted slightly from cars to trucks despite high gasoline prices, yet the total amount of CO2 it emitted did go down somewhat.

Ford's expectation was that life cycle as a methodology would improve and would become better over time in answering the question about which technology or which technologies in combination were superior. Comparing vehicles powered by ICEs and various alternatives to these engines was complex and such assessment did not yield a simple answer to the question of the relative impacts and benefits.

### The Internal Combustion Engine (ICE) and Beyond the ICE

As the question of what technology and fuel combination continued to be uncertain, in the near term, Ford chose not to substantially deviate from its current truck and car mix. It was developing a portfolio of different options to provide information about the type of cost-effective choices it would need to make to hedge its bets in the future. Life-cycle assessment did underpin the decision Ford made to increase the use of aluminum and high-strength steel in the F-50s. Life-cycle studies showed that using lightweight materials lowered overall greenhouse gas (GHG) emissions. Though the energy required to make these materials might exceed the energy to make steel, the increase was more than offset by GHG savings from reduced weight and better mpg. The use of aluminum and high-strength steel had other advantages. It made a vehicle stronger, more durable, and safer. New F-150s featured high-strength, military-grade, aluminum-alloy body and bed, which shaved 700 pounds off its weight. Ford also relied on advanced materials to cut the weight of the Fusion by 25 percent.

For now, the company's goal was to provide diversity and choice and it was taking many steps to improve the ICE's fuel economy by developing:

- nine- and ten-speed transmissions to improve fuel economy by up to 5 percent over six-speed gear boxes;
- electric power-assisted steering (EPAS) that could reduce fuel consumption and decrease $CO_2$ emissions by up to 3.5 percent in comparison with hydraulic systems;
- auto start-stop technology that turned off the engine when the vehicle stopped that could improve fuel economy by 3.5 percent, especially during city driving;
- active grille shutter technology, which could reduce aerodynamic drag by up to 6 percent, increase fuel economy, and reduce $CO_2$ emissions up to 2 percent;

- battery management systems that could increase the efficiency of a vehicle's electrical power generation system and improve fuel efficiency;
- advanced high-strength steels, aluminum, magnesium, natural fibers and nano-based materials that could reduce vehicle weight without compromising interior size, safety, performance or other features (a 10 percent reduction in weight could improve fuel economy by about 3 percent);
- smaller vehicles based on the C-car platform;
- advanced clean diesels, some of which ran on biofuels, which were 30 to 40 percent more fuel efficient than comparable gasoline vehicles.

At the same as that Ford was taking steps to improve the ICE's fuel economy, it was hedging its bets by incrementally migrating to alternative fuels and powertrains. Ford was taking a portfolio approach to reducing $CO_2$ emissions and improving fuel efficiency. It had plans to advance and expand its offerings of electrified vehicles – including HEVs, PHEVs, BEVs, hydrogen FCVs, and vehicles that ran on CNG and LPG.

### (4) Innovating

Ford's spending on engineering, research, and development increased from $5.5 billion in 2012 to $6.9 billion in 2014. The company understood that the challenge it faced was to develop a new mobility blueprint and business model.

*Blueprint for Mobility*

Ford had a multi-decade blueprint for mobility in which it imagined a future in which vehicles would communicate with each other. As vehicles sensed each other's presence, fewer accidents would take place. The sensors would warn people of traffic and infrastructure delays. People would be able to take alternative routes, saving time and reducing congestion.

In future people would routinely share vehicles and use multiple forms of transportation. The car would be part of a broader transportation network that took into account taxis, bikes, buses, and various types of public transport.

In 2014, Ford began twenty-five global mobility experiments that focused on flexible ownership and social collaboration to test such concepts and evaluate their impacts. It collaborated with universities like MIT and Stanford. Recognizing that almost every company in the industry had moved in this direction, it expressed a sense of urgency to make rapid progress. Smart mobility could be transformational.

## A New Business Model

There were likely to be profitable business models in products and services in which autonomous vehicles and big data were able to knit together the transportation system in new ways. If the company played a central role in tying people together in a broader network, where they got from point A to point B with greater ease in crowded cities and remote rural locations, it would prosper.

Like GM, Ford considered itself to be in one of the most transformative periods in automotive history. As passionate as the company was about cars and trucks, it would not be able to make and sell them as it had. Its prior business model was not sustainable in a more crowded world where more people were living in congested cities and people were less tolerant of long commutes, gridlock, and delay. Traffic jams were an immense inconvenience that stifled growth and economic progress. A new generation of millennials used smartphones to plan its trips. It did not just rely on private autos.

Ford had to be involved in the quest to transform mobility through efficient multi-modal transportation. It had to be involved in developing smart cars, roads, parking, and public transportation linked via wireless communications. The company pressed forward with these issues because of the business opportunities. It embraced disruption in order to take a leadership role in redefining what was possible

At the same time, the company's goal was to reduce its fleet-average $CO_2$ by more than 20 percent and was committed to continuing to do its share to protect the climate. For instance, its researchers were investigating how the company could assist in developing new lightweight materials that would go into vehicles of all types, no matter whether propelled by gasoline, electricity, or fuel cells. The company had active projects examining:

- automotive grade carbon fiber that could be manufactured at high volume and low cost;

- new types of steel, up to three times the strength of current steel;
- polymeric plastic foams strong enough to stabilize a vehicle's body-work in the event of an accident;
- alternative copper-based wire;
- nano-filler made up of metal and plastic composites;
- nano-clays to replace glass.

Ford hedged its bets and did research and development on gasoline and diesel technologies as well as electrical and other powertrains.

## Ford After the 2014–2015 Price Collapse

### (1) Assuring Quality and Safety

*Improvements*
Ford continued to maintain a strong commitment to design and build safe vehicles, which met or exceeded regulations and satisfied its customers' expectations. It dedicated its quality operating system to enhancing safety. It also took cognizance of the fact that product quality, customer satisfaction, and safety were improving, but not rapidly, nor in every market that it operated (Table 13.5). Safety recalls were fewer but the number of vehicles recalled, close to six million in 2016, remained high. Ford improved in the number of things going wrong in the three months after purchase everywhere it operated except Europe. Customer satisfaction in the first three months after sale was somewhat better in the United States and the Middle East and Africa, but not the rest of the world. The number of Ford's new models that achieved NHTSA's five-star safety rating increased to 71 percent in 2017, however, which was an outstanding achievement. In that year, Ford had eleven new models with five-star ranking.

In Europe, the company received seven new car assessment and six best in class awards, more than any automaker. Its vehicles provided driver assist features and semi-autonomous technologies that relied on radar, sonar, and cameras. It focused on speed limits, traffic sign recognition, cruise control, braking collision avoidance, pedestrian detection, lane management, blind spots, parking, starting on hills, and curve control. However, the features were available only on specific models in certain markets.

Table 13.5 *Indicators of Ford quality and safety 2014–2016*

**US safety recalls**

|                    | 2014  | 2015  | 2016  |
|--------------------|-------|-------|-------|
| Number             | 40    | 40    | 33    |
| Millions of vehicles | 4.746 | 4.99  | 5.97  |

**"Things gone wrong" (3 months in service per 1,000 vehicles)**

|                        | 2014  | 2015  | 2016  |
|------------------------|-------|-------|-------|
| North America          | 1,392 | 1,265 | 1,273 |
| South America          | 1,472 | 1,207 | 1,119 |
| Europe                 | 1,302 | 1,232 | 1,379 |
| Asia Pacific           | 917   | 846   | 788   |
| Middle East and Africa | 1,046 | 775   | 510   |

**Percent of customers satisfied (3 months in service)**

|                        | 2014 | 2015 | 2016 |
|------------------------|------|------|------|
| North America          | 79   | 81   | 81   |
| South America          | 68   | 70   | 68   |
| Europe                 | 73   | 75   | 73   |
| Asia Pacific           | 69   | 71   | 68   |
| Middle East and Africa | 62   | 67   | 70   |

**Percent of models achieving 5-star NHTSA safety rating**

|      | 2014 | 2015 | 2016 |
|------|------|------|------|
| Ford | 41   | 65   | 62   |

Derived from Ford Annual Reports

Employee lost work time was down in the United States, but it had increased in Europe and the Middle East and Africa. The company had two fatalities in 2016 – one in Europe and one in North America – and one contractor fatality.

The company was working to do better on safety. Its test facilities in Dearborn Michigan and Merkenich Germany had a motion-based driving simulator to research advanced driver assist features, human-machine interface, and issues like drowsy and distracted driving. It also examined the safety implications of driver assist technologies and con-nectivity, mobility and autonomous vehicles at its Palo Alto, California Research and Innovation Center.

The company had a commitment to make improvements in air emissions, CO2, energy, water, and waste. The combined average fuel efficiency of the vehicles it sold in the United States improved from 22.8 mpg in 2014 to 23.4 mpg in 2016. Ford was doing better than GM, VW, and Fiat Chrysler on this indicator and it trailed Toyota by only a small margin. However, the number of its models compliant with US government fuel-efficiency standards declined from 38 percent in 2014 to 32 percent in 2016.

## (2) Investing in Global Markets

### Good and Bad News

With gasoline prices reduced, the positive news was that Ford sold more vehicles in every region except the Middle East and Africa and South America (Figure 13.3). It sold more vehicles in the Asia Pacific region than in North America or Europe, and its market share in that area, driven by China, improved in 2016. However, its total market share slipped slightly that year in every region except for Europe, and Ford's 2016-market share was lower than it had been previously.

### Relying on Chinese Partners

Ford relied heavily on its alliance partners in China to help it improve its performance:

- Changan Ford Automobile Corporation was a 50/50 joint venture that operated five assembly plants, an engine plant, and a transmission plant. It made and distributed an expanding variety of Ford passenger vehicles.
- Changan Ford Mazda Engine Company was a joint venture among Ford (25 percent), Mazda (25 percent), and Changan (50 percent partner) that produced and marketed Ford and Mazda engines.
- JMC was a publicly traded firm with Ford a 32 percent shareholder and Jiangling a 41 percent shareholder. Jiangling was a 50/50 joint venture between Changan and Jiangling. JMC assembled the Ford Transit, Ford Everest, Ford engines, and non-Ford vehicles and engines for distribution in China and in other export markets. It had two assembly plants and one engine plant. In 2015, it opened a new plant for heavy-duty trucks and engines.

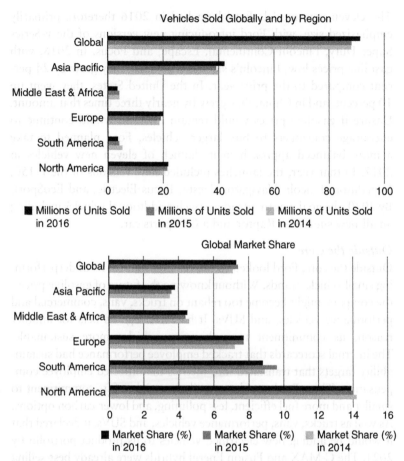

Figure 13.3  Ford's global vehicles sold and market share 2014–2016
Derived from Ford Annual Reports

## (3) Adjusting the Brand and Model Mix

### The Core Business

Ford's core business – its global leadership in trucks, vans, commercial and performance vehicles, and SUVs – was its strength, upon which it tried to enhance its position. It determined that trucks, vans, commercial and performance vehicles, and SUVs were its core business and strength based on its knowledge of customers. Through their purchase decisions, they showed the company they wanted these vehicles.

The eleven new models Ford launched in 2016 therefore primarily emphasized size, with Ford introducing new versions of the F-Series Super Duty, Lincoln Continental, Escape, and Focus. In 2016, with gasoline prices low, Lincoln's sales skyrocketed; they grew by 24 percent compared to the prior year. In the United States, they went up 10 percent, and in China, they grew by nearly three times that amount. Unsure if gasoline prices would remain low and would continue to encourage consumers to buy larger vehicles, Ford planned to take a more balanced approach in its launch of eleven new vehicles in 2017. In that year, the launches included new versions of the F-150, Expedition, Lincoln Navigator, Fiesta, Focus Electric, and EcoSport. By 2020, the goal was to introduce twelve additional vehicles including an all-new super-size Raptor and a GT sports car.

*Outside the Core*

Outside the core, Ford looked to turnaround some of its underperforming small vehicle brands. Without knowing the future of gasoline prices, the company might become too reliant on trucks, vans, commercial and performance vehicles, and SUVs. It had to hedge its bets for another reason, its commitment to making its vehicles more sustainable. The internal scorecards that tracked employee performance had sustainability targets that translated into metrics that affected employee compensation. Thus, Ford could not easily lose sight of its commitment to smaller and more fuel efficient, less polluting, and lower-carbon options. As well as trucks, vans, performance vehicles, and SUVs, it declared that it would be adding new electrified vehicles to its product portfolio by 2021. The C-MAX and Fusion Energi hybrids were already best-selling plug-in electric models. In addition, the company sold a luxury version of the Fusion plug-in, the Lincoln MKZ. By 2016, it had sold thousands of electric vehicles. Electric vehicles sales had solid sales increases in 2013, 2014 and 2016, but their sales, along with the rest of this market, had slipped in 2015, mainly due to low oil prices. Comparing 2016 to 2015, Ford's electric sales enjoyed a comeback.

By 2021, the company aimed to expand its electric offerings to eighteen models, which would mean that it would have electric versions of more than 40 percent of the models it sold. Ford invested $4.5 billion in electrification, and planned to make electric versions of the F-150, Mustang, Mondeo, Transit, Taurus, and Explorer. To justify the move toward electrification it continued to rely on life-cycle analysis. Its researchers played a leading role in an industry–government cradle-to-grave analysis of this nature, which explored the costs of reducing greenhouse gas emissions using conventional gasoline vehicles versus pursuing alternatives like electrification. The study demonstrated that a transition to electric and to other alternatives would not be cheap, but Ford seemed to be willing to pay the price. Ford pursued a dual strategy. On the one hand, it was fully committed to trucks, vans, commercial and performance vehicles, and SUVs and on the other hand, it was fully committed to electrification and other alternative technologies.

### Choice

Ford hedged by giving customers the choice of a full range of conventional and alternative vehicles. Not all the changes it expected to make involved electrification. Like GM, Ford offered flex-fuel vehicles powered by fossil and non-fossil fuels. Where demand existed, it also offered CNG vehicles. It continued to maintain interest in fuel cells, though recognizing that making further fuel-cell improvements might be very expensive. The company's intent was to provide customers a full portfolio of vehicle, fuel, and mobility choices and it would continue to explore which combinations of vehicle and fuel technologies would be most effective. With the future being uncertain, like GM, Ford did not want to limit its options prematurely.

Hedging made sense since new models of conventional gasoline-powered vehicles could incorporate innovations designed for alternatively propelled vehicles. The conventional gasoline-powered vehicles could incorporate such innovations as lighter materials and new aerodynamic designs. The company had started to introduce start and stop systems into conventional ICE models and was working on diesel aftertreatment technology. In place already were Eco Boost models changes Ford had made to the internal combustion engine.

Additional innovations it could incorporate included new engine and transmission technology, electrical system enhancements, and advanced powertrains. These innovations would make conventional ICE powertrains more fuel-efficient and less air polluting, and they would emit fewer greenhouse gases.

### (4) Innovation

Engineering, research, and development expenses grew from $6.7 billion in 2015 to $7.3 billion in 2016. They were on a par with

GM's investment in this area. The company was involved in a broad range of innovative endeavors.

*Engines*
Ford had a number of initiatives regarding engines:

- It was advancing technologies to improve gasoline engine/EcoBoost powertrain efficiency and performance. It had a new 3.5-liter EcoBoost engine, which it paired with ten-speed automatic transmission in the F-150 model.
- It was also working on innovative diesel technology, which it had introduced in Europe as an all-new EcoBlue engine. In North America, it offered advanced diesel engines in SuperDuty and Medium Duty commercial trucks, and the Transit Van. To reduce diesel air emissions, it was examining alternative oxidation catalysts, particulate filters, catalytic reduction systems, and nitrous oxide traps.
- Ford was also looking for transmission and driveline improvement and exploring the potential of an 8+ speed automatic transmission.

*Bodies*
The company also had a number of significant auto body initiatives:

- Ford continued to try enhancing vehicles aerodynamic qualities.
- It had significant ongoing programs in weight reduction. Together with Magna International, it developed a prototype carbon fiber composite sub-frame that reduced mass by 34 percent compared to the stamped steel equivalent. It developed a light but strong cargo floorboard for the new Ford EcoSport, which was made of high-strength 100 percent recycled paper and water-based glue. The company had piloted a Stratasys 3D printing system to produce lighter-weight parts.
- Ford aimed to reduce the number of materials in vehicles. The choice of materials was an important factor in sustainability and it influenced vehicle safety, fuel economy, and performance as well as the options for auto recycling and reuse. Ford prioritized materials based on their carbon footprint. It also addressed health impacts and tried to eliminate materials that might cause concern. In addition, it attempted to move toward increased use of recycled and plant-based materials. It already obtained almost 300 parts from renewable sources such as soybeans, cotton, wood, flax, jute and

natural rubber, and it was using Coke's PlantBottle plastic, in the seat fabric, trim, carpets and elsewhere in a Focus battery electric demonstration vehicle.

### Evaluating Vehicle Types

In addition to electricity, Ford was evaluating, developing, and introducing other vehicle types:

- It had initiatives on lower fossil-carbon fuels such as biofuels, CNG, LPG, and hydrogen.
- It was also working on affordable fuel-cell solutions for high-volume applications.
- Ford invested heavily in autonomous vehicles. It was road testing a fleet of such vehicles. Its intention was to have four such vehicles that fully autonomous – with no steering wheel, brake, or gas pedal – in commercial operation by 2021. To overcome the technical challenges surrounding automated driving, it collaborated with universities, government, and other automakers on vehicle-to-vehicle safety communication systems, vehicle-to-infrastructure applications, and cyber security.

### Mobility and Connectivity

Ford had initiatives in mobility and connectivity:

- It launched a subsidiary, Smart Mobility, to design, build, grow, and invest in mobility services. It acquired Chariot, an app-based, crowd-sourced shuttle service that was available in San Francisco and Austin, which it planned to expand to other cities.
- It focused on building technology platforms for connectivity. It had a city solutions team to work with municipalities and invested in an artificial intelligence company.

### Advancing Safety

Ford also had ongoing safety-related research that focused on:

- vehicle safety, occupant protection, and driver distraction;
- test devices for assessing front and side impacts;
- ensuring alternative fuel technology systems functioned as intended in the event of a crash;
- meta-analysis of crash avoidance technologies;

- the safety of lithium-ion batteries;
- the crashworthiness and fuel-efficiency benefits of lightweight materials;
- applications of nano-liquid foam technology;
- state-of-the-art computer simulation of the effects of age and other vehicle characteristics;
- human body computer models for research on the needs of the elderly and obese;
- evasive steering assist to help drivers move around stopped or slower vehicles;
- wrong way alert using windshield-mounted cameras to provide warnings not to go against the traffic;
- traffic jam assist to help drivers keep a vehicle centered in a lane and stay in pace with the vehicle in front.

Ford had more patents than any other automaker in 2016.

*Performance*
With the collapse in gas and oil prices, Ford net income and its operating margin and revenue rose. Like GM, the main effect took place from 2014 to 2015. Total shareholder return, however, lagged both the industry average return and that of the S&P 500.

## Between Past and Future – The Correct Response?

Ford's past and future seemed to be in conflict and it was unclear if it could find the right balance. The company had never had a smooth ride. It repeatedly failed in some major dimension and usually seemed to recover. Ford understood the risks and uncertainties in the period under consideration as pressures, which extended from financial burdens, involving declining market share and revenues, to fuel economy, greenhouse gases, toxics, safety, and volatile fuel prices. Many types of adverse events could take place. There was also the possibility of new models of shared mobility and other innovative opportunities.

The hopes the company had for the future blended with its anxieties. Prudence called upon it to rely on hedging mechanisms similar to those that GM used. Ford tried to: (i) stay focused of safety and quality; (ii) develop a global reach, especially in Asia; (iii) maintain different vehicle models and try to improve them; and (iv) engage in research with path-breaking potential. Ford's hedges, grounded in the present, had the potential to open up its future.

Ford did the best it could with these hedging mechanisms. It kept careful tabs on safety and quality and when it found lapses, it took action to find remedies. Its safety and quality improved due to these efforts. It worked with its alliance partners in China to try to increase sales and grow market share, but did not succeed. It had more success in Europe where it had a best-seller in the Ford Fiesta and the Focus also sold very well. In Europe and rest of the world, it had to boost the fuel mileage of its vehicles to compete. Ford had a solution it widely promoted – the eco-boost engines it offered – but whether these engines really delivered was open to question. In designing new models, Ford took seriously lowering $CO_2$ emissions and other societal considerations. It analyzed these issues carefully and methodically using life cycle analysis, made incremental adjustments and improvements to the ICE, including introducing aluminum in the F-Series trucks, and it offered hybrid vehicles for sale.

Introducing lighter aluminum in the place of steel in the F-series was a major move. It raised the vehicle's costs, enough so that customers had to have substantial loyalty to the brand or had to value the fuel saving sufficiently to continue to buy. Without continued strong F-150 sales, Ford would be in deep trouble. The F-150 was a best seller in North America and the Fiesta was a best seller in Europe.

In its ongoing reflection on its condition, Ford arrived at a philosophy of choice, wherein it hedged its bets by providing customers' options and they could choose what they wanted – whether larger muscle vehicles, smaller eco-friendlier ones, or electrified models. How to find the right balance between what Ford's customers wanted now in the present and the new products and technologies they might want in the future was not simple. The past pulled the company in one direction and the future in another. Ford moved outside its core in the present, but not too far outside it. To plunge fully into the future did not seem feasible now. Yet, Ford fully acknowledged this future and prepared for it.

That future involved new engine types, new body types, different vehicle types, and a different transportation system that ran on different rules. This new system was one for which Ford tried to prepare. Thus, it experimented with a business model that it thought might arrive some day and called it a blueprint for mobility. Rather than private ownership of individual vehicles, it involved ride sharing and perhaps autonomous driving. Ford had conflicts and was going in a number of directions at once, between different worlds, the past that it had survived and a future in which it hoped it could not only survive, but prosper. In its history, it had experienced many turbulent transitions, wars and economic downturns and worse, and bounced around before reaching a new stability, however impermanent.

How the company should approach the future remained unclear. Its choices would have important implications for the company and society. What should it do? How could it expand its business in China? Should it cut back on the shifts it had made toward alternative transportation, and put more emphasis on its lucrative trucks, vans, commercial vehicles, and SUVs? Should it give up on small passenger cars in the United States?

## Notes

1. *"Best Selling Car and Light Truck Models Worldwide in 2017."* www.statista.com/statistics/239229/most-sold-car-models-world wide/; *"Fuel Economy Data,"* www.fueleconomy.gov/feg/download .shtml
2. Birsch, D., and Fielder, J. H. *The Ford Pinto Case: A Study in Applied Ethics, Business, and Technology.* Albany, NY: Birsch, D., and Fielder, J. H., 1994.
3. *"The Firestone Tire Controversy,"* www.icmrindia.org/casestudies/cat alogue/Business%20Ethics/BECG005.htm
4. Brinkley, Douglas. *Wheels for the World: Henry Ford, His Company, and a Century of Progress.* New York: Penguin, 2003.
5. Marcus, Alfred. *Promise and Performance: Choosing and Implementing an Environmental Policy.* Santa Barbara, CA: Praeger, 1980.
6. *"Firestone Tire Recall,"* https://one.nhtsa.gov/Vehicle-Safety/Tires/Fire stone-Tire-Recall
7. *"GM, Ford Bond Ratings Cut to Junk Status,"* www.washingtonpost .com/wp-dyn/content/article/2005/05/05/AR2005050501962.html? noredirect=on
8. *"Ford Loses Record $12.7 Billion in '06,"* www.nytimes.com/2007/01/ 25/business/25cnd-ford.html

9. *"Ford: The Remake of an American Icon,"* www.forbes.com/sites/great speculations/2010/11/08/ford-the-remake-of-an-american-icon/ #22586d01108c

10. *"How Ford Stayed Strong through the Financial Crisis,"* http://archive .fortune.com/2011/01/12/autos/Bill-Ford-Alan-Mulally-carmaker.for tune/index.htm

11. *"Ford F-series US Car Sales Figures,"* http://carsalesbase.com/us-car-sales-data/ford/ford-f-series/

12. *"Ford Sustainability Report 2011–2012,"* https://corporate.ford.com/ microsites/sustainability-report-2017–18/doc/sr17-sr11.pdf; *"Ford Annual Report 2012,"* https://s22.q4cdn.com/857684434/files/doc_ financials/2012/annual/2012-annual-report.pdf

*"Ford Sustainability Report 2012–2013,"* https://corporate.ford.com/ microsites/sustainability-report-2017–18/doc/sr17-sr12.pdf; *"Ford Annual Report 2013,"* https://s22.q4cdn.com/857684434/files/doc_ financials/2013/annual/2013-annual-report.pdf

*"Ford Sustainability Report 2013–2014,"* https://corporate.ford.com/ microsites/sustainability-report-2017–18/doc/sr17-sr13.pdf; "Ford Annual Report 2014," https://s22.q4cdn.com/857684434/files/doc_ financials/2014/annual/2014-ford-annual-report.pdf

*"Ford Sustainability Report 2014–2015,"* https://corporate.ford.com/ microsites/sustainability-report-2017–18/doc/sr17-sr14.pdf; "Ford Annual Report 2015," https://s22.q4cdn.com/857684434/files/doc_ financials/2015/annual/2015-annual-report.pdf

*"Ford Sustainability Report 2015–2016,"* https://corporate.ford.com/ microsites/sustainability-report-2017–18/doc/sr17-sr15.pdf "Ford Annual Report 2016," https://s22.q4cdn.com/857684434/files/doc_ financials/2016/annual/2016-annual-report.pdf

*"Ford Sustainability Report 2016–2017,"* https://corporate.ford.com/ microsites/sustainability-report-2017–18/doc/sr17-sr16.pdf

# 14 | *Strategies to Take Advantage of Plummeting Prices: VW*

This chapter aims to trace the responses of Volkswagen (VW) to changing conditions in the automotive sector from 2012 to 2016, especially due to volatile oil prices, and to consider where the company might go next with its strategies. It starts with an introduction to the company. Covered next are the company's strategies from 2012 to 2014, before the fall in oil prices, and 2014 to 2016, after prices dropped. It examines the risks and uncertainties that VW perceived in this period, its assumptions about the future, and the hedges it had in place to protect its business. The chapter seeks to understand the extent to which the oil price shock altered its strategies and affected its performance. What were the strategies VW adopted suitable, and what do they suggest about what the company should do next?

## The Company's Rise and Fall

As a conglomerate, VW controlled a dozen different motor vehicle brands located in six European countries. In addition to its Passenger Cars and Commercial Vehicles brands in Germany, it had brands that it sold in Italy, Spain, the Czech Republic, and the United Kingdom. The brands that originated in Germany were Audi, Porsche, and Man and those that originated in Italy were Ducati, Bugatti, and Lamborghini. SEAT was the Spanish brand, ŠKODA the Czech brand, Bentley the British brand, and Scania the Swedish brand.

As the parent company for these brands, VW helped to develop, make, and sell components and to make vehicles. With the exception of VW Passenger Cars and Commercial Vehicles, each company was independent and separately managed, and each had a separate history. The emphasis in the discussion that follows will be on VW, the parent company. VW itself started production in 1937.[1] The trade union of the Nazi Party, the German Labor Front, founded the company. In the 1930s, only the richest Germans could afford a car – just one in fifty

Germans owned one – and the goal, therefore, was to make a vehicle inexpensive enough so that anyone could buy it. Ferdinand Porsche built the prototype "people's car," the Volksauto (*Volk* means "people" in German), in 1933. Porsche's prototype became the model for the Beetle, a car with a distinctive shape and a rear, air-cooled engine that was VW's trademark. Adolph Hitler endorsed the state-owned factory that began manufacturing the vehicle. When World War II broke out, VW shifted to military production, for which it relied on slave labor from the Arbeitsdorf concentration camp. With the defeat of Germany, the company had little of value that remained. When the British offered to donate its assets to Ford for free, Ford declined to accept them.

Until 1968, VW made nothing other than the Beetle, apart from a van and sports car called the Karmann Ghia. In the 1960s, sales of the Beetle took off in the United States, particularly in California, where it achieved cult-like status as a symbol of freedom from responsibility. The car also became popular in other parts of the United States, abetted by clever advertising, a reputation for reliability, and its California reputation. Indeed, over time the car became so popular that it surpassed the Model T as history's all-time bestseller. However, when the US Congress passed strict, national anti-pollution laws, the Beetle's air-cooled engine could not achieve compliance. Had VW not acquired Audi in 1964, it probably would have gone out of business. Audi gave it the expertise it needed to make a standard water-cooled front-wheel-drive vehicle to keep going.

## The Successors to the Beetle

The company then produced a number of successors to the Beetle based on Audi technology. The Passat was the first. Launched in 1973, it shared many parts with the Audi. VW then launched the Scirocco to compete with the affordable four-seater Ford Capri. The next car it launched, also in 1974, was the Golf. VW produced many generations of this vehicle, and it became the company's mainstay. VW established a manufacturing site in the United States making the car in New Stanton, Pennsylvania, outside Pittsburgh. However, due to stiff competition from Japanese vehicles with similar low-mileage features, but lower prices, US sales of the Golf dropped in the 1980s. They fell steeply from 293,595 units sold in 1980 to 177,709 in 1984. In response, VW chose to stop making cars in the United States at that time.[2]

In 1975, the company entered the supermini market in Europe with the Polo.[3] This car was a stylish and spacious three-door hatchback that competed with the Fiat 127 and Renault 5. Ford chose to enter this market and launched the Fiesta in 1991. VW then launched a third-generation Golf in 1992 and the Vento, called the Jetta in North America, in 1993. VW stood out for the fuel efficiency of its vehicles. However, stringent US government emissions regulations forced it to eliminate the diesels it sold in the United States. It had to wait until 2009 to introduce a new lineup of diesels in the United States that it maintained were compatible with US standards. At first, the company resisted introducing an SUV in the US market, as it did not regard the SUV as its specialty. It relented when it launched the Touareg, which it made in partnership with Porsche, in 2018. A heavy vehicle that did not have a third-row seat and with relatively poor fuel economy, the Touareg had modest sales.

The company set up factories in different parts of the world, manufacturing and assembling vehicles for local markets. That meant that in 2011, it once again began to produce cars in the United States; its US facility was in Chattanooga.[4] Besides Germany and the United States, VW had factories in Mexico, Slovakia, China, India, Indonesia, Russia, Malaysia, Brazil, Argentina, Portugal, Spain, Poland, the Czech Republic, Bosnia, Herzegovina, Kenya, and South Africa. An important factor was VW's ongoing relationship with Porsche, which remained very close.[5] Porsche components, including engines, gearboxes, and suspensions, found their way into many VW brands. As Porsche engineering reputation was outstanding, its relationship with VW raised VW's stature. In 2009, Porsche owned more than half of VW, though German laws did not allow it to exert effective control.

## Dieselgate

In 2015, the US EPA discovered that, starting seven years earlier, VW had illegally installed software that detected when its cars were subject to emissions testing.[6] The software enabled a pollution-control device that made it appear that the cars were in compliance. However, during normal driving conditions, this mechanism shut down in order to maintain the vehicle's fuel economy and provide the car with additional power. The cars that had the software released *forty times more* pollution than US law allowed. VW had installed the software in virtually all the diesel cars it manufactured between 2009 and 2015.

Ultimately and reluctantly, VW admitted to installing the software.[7] It had to recall about a million cars in the United States and Europe. The penalties the US government imposed amounted to more than $18 billion.[8] In 2016, the company also confronted a $15.3 billion class action lawsuit, the largest ever in the United States against an auto company. In addition, the US Federal Trade Commission brought action against VW for false advertising because the company had regularly put forward the claim that its diesel vehicles were a less polluting green alternative. The cheating occurred in eight models: the Jetta, Golf, Passat, Beetle, Touareg, Audi 7, Audi 8, and Porsche Cayenne. In Germany, VW escaped serious criticism to begin with, but ultimately the German government felt compelled to punish the company. The KBA, or Federal Vehicle Agency – an arm of the Ministry of Transport – approved a European recall. In the United States, top-level executives faced criminal charges. The costs of these scandals forced the company to plan a reduction of its workforce by some 30,000.

VW got away with the deception for many years. How was the pollution control defeating software discovered? The EU had trouble verifying that lab emissions matched on-road performance, a suspicion that led the International Council on Clean Transportation to commission research by West Virginia University's Center for Alternative Fuels. California's regulators helped by providing access to a compliance-testing laboratory.[9] The West Virginia researchers found the problem in 2014, but VW denied the results, citing weather, driving styles, and technicalities and belittling the researchers.

VW doggedly maintained its innocence for over 15 months. Only under the threat that the US EPA might withhold approval of its 2016 cars, did it admit to rigging the emissions control systems on 11 million vehicles worldwide. CEO Martin Winterkorn issued an apology and agreed to cooperate with investigators. The next day the company's stock price plummeted 20 percent and the following day it fell another 17 percent, at which point Winterkorn resigned.[10] After his departure the new CEO, Matthias Müller, continued to maintain that what had happened was a technical problem related to a misinterpretation of

US laws that he blamed on rogue engineers. Frustrated by VW denials, California regulators took additional steps to scrutinize the company's software and found the secret codes VW engineers had installed, the subroutine of parallel instructions that shut down the emissions controls when the vehicles were not operating in laboratory settings.

What caused the scandal? A 2016 *Fortune* article blamed it on the company's overweening ambition.[11] Ferdinand Piëch, grandson of Ferdinand Porsche, became CEO in 1993, at a time when VW had been performing poorly. Chief executive until 2002, and chair of VW's board from 2002 through the crisis, he infused the company with the drive to dominate the world auto industry. Under Piëch, VW succeeded in surpassing Ford in global sales in 2008. It leapfrogged GM in 2014, and then beat out Toyota in 2015. Under Piëch, employees believed it was unacceptable to admit that a task they had been given could not be accomplished. The goal of VW's CEO Winterkorn had been to triple US sales in under a decade by betting on diesels and promoting them as a clean and fuel-efficient alternative to vehicles Toyota sold in the United States. Disabling the emissions controls not only gave the cars better mileage, but also power, a feature Winterkorn thought US consumers would appreciate.

According to *Fortune*, in 2007, VW had walked away from pollution-control technology for diesels that Mercedes-Benz and Bosch had developed.[12] It chose instead to go it alone and try to create a pollution control solution by itself, but when it failed the company reverted to the practice of using defeat devices to get around pollution laws. Indeed, in 1973, the US EPA had caught VW for disabling emission control devices and had fined it $120,000. Again, in 1998, the firm's truck division reached a billion-dollar settlement with the EPA for engaging in this type of trickery. Technology that Mercedes-Benz and Bosch recommended that VW use involved mixing urea with engine exhaust to neutralize harmful diesel pollutants. This method was effective, but costly, as it required drivers to fill their tanks periodically with the urea. VW deemed it acceptable for trucks and heavier commercial vehicles, but could not imagine implementing it in the car market.

Despite the setback, VW nearly doubled its global sales from 2006 to 2016, from 5.7 million units in 2006 to 10.3 million in 2016 (Figure 14.1). Its profits fell in 2015, but they started to recover in 2016 (Figure 14.2).

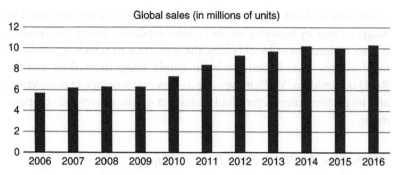

**Figure 14.1** VW sales growth 2006–2016
Derived from VW Annual Reports

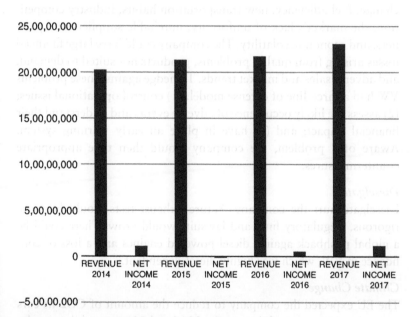

**Figure 14.2** VW dollar revenue and profits 2012–2016
Derived from VW Annual Reports

## Prior to and After the 2014–2015 Price Collapse

How did VW's strategies change before and after the 2014–2015 collapse in gas and oil prices? Based on its annual reports and other communications to shareholders, the analysis that follows examines the company's perceptions of the risks and uncertainties and its assumptions about the future.[13] It shows that the company tried to hedge its bets by focusing on operations, especially safety and quality. It also hedged them by choosing the countries in which it would be involved, the brands and models it would bring to market, and the R&D it would do. VW's moves affected its performance in these years, and its performance in turn had an impact on the moves the company made.

## VW before the 2014–2015 Price Collapse

### Perceptions of the Risks and Uncertainties

The perceived risks and uncertainties came from Dieselgate, climate change, fuel efficiency, new transportation habits, industry competition, the market's lack of uniformity, unreliable suppliers and partners, and economic volatility. The company could have large financial losses arising from quality problems, products not suited to demand, and adverse sales and market trends. To hedge against these problems VW had a three-line of defense model: (1) control operational issues; (2) assess the likely occurrence of adverse events and understand their financial impact; and (3) have in place an early warning system. Aware of a problem, the company would then take appropriate countermeasures.

### Dieselgate

Dieselgate hurt the company. Future exhaust tests would be more rigorous. Regulatory fines and lawsuits would grow. There could be a global pushback against diesel-powered engines and a loss of confidence in VW, which was highly diesel-dependent.

### Climate Change

The EU expected the company to reduce the amount of $CO2$ its cars emitted to 130 grams a kilometer by 2015 and 95 grams a kilometer by 2021. The EU's standard for light trucks was 147 grams a kilometer by 2020. By 2050, it could possibly ask for 60 percent more reduction in comparison to 1990. The EU was also considering asking for further reductions in $NO_x$ and fine particulate emissions to accompany the standards it was introducing to reduce climate change. Other governments had different emission and vehicle taxation policies, treaties, and agreements and the varying sanctions governments imposed to enforce $CO2$ regulations were a problem. In addition, extreme weather, storms, and floods – the results of climate change – could lead to the failure of information and communication technology, suppliers' incapacity to deliver, production standstills, or extended downtime of production facilities.

*Fuel Efficiency*
Many countries also developed new average, fleet fuel-efficiency standards. These countries included the world's largest markets, the United States and China. The only way to meet these standards was to launch vehicles with alternatives to conventional fossil-fuel-fired engines, such as electrical vehicles, and to make other innovations. To meet the targets that governments set depended on deployment of considerable technological and financial resources. Every auto manufacturer faced these challenges and all of them had to acquire expertise in new areas like battery technology. Even with trend analysis, customer surveys, and other assessments of customer sentiment, the needed R&D investments might not pay off.

*New Transportation Habits*
The full consequences of new transportation habits such as ridesharing and growing demand for autonomous vehicles remained unknown. Greater use would wipe out the environmental advantages that might take place.

*Competition*
Competition in the automotive sector continued to be intense. The sector was fragmented and there was no dominant player. Demand was not growing at a fast pace. Customers held onto to their vehicles longer than in the past – a trend that was accelerating because of pressure to make vehicles that were even more durable. Companies faced new competition from Tesla in the premium category and from Chinese companies selling inexpensive cars in Asia. The supply chain was such that new entrants had relatively easy access to the inputs they needed to compete with the incumbents. Further differentiation would not have much influence; each manufacturer already offered complete suites of models in nearly every category. Brand reputation and loyalty were not high. Growing digitization posed another challenge. The sector could benefit from consolidation, which would make increased economies of scale possible and drive down costs, but further consolidation was not that likely.

*Global Diversity*
Each region of the world had unique conditions, which made it hard to serve them with a single strategy, including:

• price sensitivity in growing Asian markets and a need for local production;
• the need to tailor products for the US market by producing more light trucks;
• high levels of inflation and high interest rates in Brazil;
• restrictions on operations in Russia, and the weakness of the Russian economy.

*Suppliers and Partners*
VW, like other firms, was heavily dependent on a relatively small group of suppliers. Demand that was higher than expected risked supplier bottlenecks, while overly optimistic forecasts resulted in insufficient supplier capacity utilization. Contractors and joint venture partners posed a threat because of their ability to make unauthorized use of sensitive corporate data.

*Economic Volatility*
Economic volatility was a result of many factors such as geopolitics, imbalances in global growth rates, economic power shifts, debt, social tensions, conflicts, and loss of consumer confidence. Rapid urbanization, price pressures in established markets due to market saturation, falling European demand, and potential deceleration in China's expansion were important issues. Unaccountable actions on the part of politicians and governments unhinged fiscal and social stability. The imposition of high customs barriers and local content laws could lead to global contraction.

## Assumptions about the Future

VW analyzed megatrends, tracked customer opinions, and bench-marked its competition. It conducted dialog with stakeholders and scrutinized the global media. It used the results in a ten-year planning process. Its assumptions about the future included the following:

• The world was changing rapidly because of globalization, new technologies, and the Internet.
• Customers wanted intelligent mobility.

- They expected eco-friendly products.
- Global economic conditions would likely improve, with emerging economies of Asia leading the way and the US recovery growing in strength.

VW's goal was to achieve a 4 percent sales increase from year to year, thus beating world economic growth. It had to regionalize its product portfolio, localize production and procurement, and diversify outside established business models and markets. It had to monitor world oil prices carefully, and would need to be increasingly flexible and creative.

**Digitization**
A digital transformation was underway that was affecting operational paradigms in the automotive sector. With computers, smartphones, and robots redefining how people lived, automotive digitization extended beyond the engine and chassis to communications, infotainment, and navigation. Drivers had started to benefit from automated assistance programs. Future vehicles would connect to traffic lights and infrastructure and give warnings about hazards, which would improve traffic flows. Traffic lights would establish optimal speed levels. Drivers would receive route calculations that incorporated negative weather conditions and information about road closures and free parking spaces, making the driving experience more pleasant and safer.

**Intelligent Mobility**
Dense, exhausting traffic jams in the world's big cities limited the usefulness of private auto ownership, which meant that mobility not only had to be safe and convenient but also intelligent. The sharing economy had already transformed many aspects of life. The automobile, too, had the potential to become a shared asset, but how to effectively make it a shared asset remained unclear.

**Eco-Friendliness**
Climate change, resource availability, and demography signified that autos had to be energy efficient, light, economical, and increasingly electrified. Electric mobility would be a key pillar in reaching the EU's $CO_2$ targets. However, developing new low-emission drive systems was an immense technological challenge. VW was in the midst of staging a phased and gradual transition to these technologies. It was

hedging its bets by offering a wide range of vehicles and technologies and was investing in R&D to establish new standards for drive trains and vehicle weight without knowing for sure if the R&D would pay off.

## Economic Growth

VW anticipated slightly faster world economic growth, with the emerging economies of Asia leading the way and signs of recovery elsewhere, especially in North America. India would experience some improvement. It was reasonable to expect that the double-digit growth in the number of vehicles sold in China would continue, though the country was in the midst of toughening its environmental laws and it had rising awareness of environmental issues, climate change, and air pollution. The market for trucks was on a positive trajectory in North America. The US market was favorable because of the ease with which VW could market and finance vehicles there. The country had low gasoline prices and afforded opportunities for attractive sales promotions. Germany's growth was stable and Russia's was negative, which limited growth in Eastern and Central Europe. Growth in Europe had stalled because of structural problems. The rest of the world had mixed conditions. The Canadian and Mexican markets seemed promising, Brazil might see a slight recovery, and South Africa would continue to suffer from political uncertainty and social tensions.

## *VW after the 2014–2015 Price Collapse*

### Perceptions of the Risks and Uncertainties

The risks were many: Dieselgate, problems with the macroeconomy, demand for conventional automobiles, innovations like electric drives, connected vehicles, autonomous driving, and potential procurement, quality, and production problems were among the most important. However, the system the company had in place for controlling risks would put it in good standing. Based on assessing the probability and extent of future events and developments and taking countermeasures, VW retained its three line of defense model.

### *Dieselgate*

The scandal continued with recalls, customer-related complaints, legal problems, and reputational damage. The company confronted criminal and administrative proceedings, technical-fix expenses, repurchase obligations, and financial liabilities. It was concerned that the psyche of consumers would turn against the company permanently; demand for its vehicles would decrease, prices would go down, and margins would decline. VW was unable to calculate the total amount of payments it would have to make. In 2015, it admitted the tampering affected 11 million vehicles worldwide. The German Motor Transport Authority ordered a recall of EU member state vehicles, the US Department of Justice (DOJ), on behalf of the EPA, filed a civil complaint, and the California Air Resources Board sought fines for health and safety code violations. Germany opened criminal investigations, and class actions were pending in Argentina, Australia, Belgium, Brazil, Israel, Italy, the United Kingdom, Mexico, Poland, Portugal, and Taiwan. How long it would take for VW to leave the crisis behind it was unknown. Credit rating agencies could downgrade its status, making it harder for it to secure funding. The scandal increasingly put the company on the defensive. It was under pressure to explain what happened and to demonstrate that it would not engage in such misconduct again.

### The Global Economy

Growth could shrink due to turbulence in financial markets, protectionist measures, and government deficits. Western Europe had stalled. The United Kingdom had started the process of its withdrawal from the EU. The Southern European economies were not particularly healthy. Russia was not coming through, though it had the potential to be one of the world's largest automotive markets. Its economy remained heavily reliant on oil, and it was subject to US and EU sanctions. In Europe and the United States, the company's competitors were offering excessive incentives to meet their sales targets. To grow in the US market, VW needed expand its presence. Market conditions in South America as well as Eastern Europe were not promising. High customs barriers and local content requirements in markets in South America, Eastern and Central Europe, and Asia made it difficult to increase sales. The Brazilian economy was not improving. The Indian market was not living up to its potential. China might impose additional restrictions on vehicle registrations. VW would have to introduce models especially developed for China and expand its production to defend its market position. Weak energy and commodity prices, sociopolitical tension, corruption, and inadequate governance held back emerging economies. The company lacked sufficient production facilities in the

Middle East to meet demand, where conflict escalation could cause upheavals, terrorism was a factor, and there was increased movement of people from the region because of civil wars.

### Demand Weakness
Demand could decline. Consumers were keeping their vehicles longer or holding off from buying altogether. In saturated markets such as Western Europe and the United States, where the competition was intense, consumers could purchase smaller and less-expensive vehicles. Elsewhere, governments might introduce tax increases or protectionist measures. The company had to be an innovator and remain at the forefront of those firms developing new vehicles to counter these concerns.

### Electric, Connected, and Autonomous
The company had to rely on the latest mobility technologies to meet stricter fleet fuel consumption limits. Although VW depended on diesel technology, electric drives would become increasingly common. The entry of competitors from outside the industry and the swift implementation of government edicts regarding $CO_2$ emissions were driving the pace of innovation and forcing rapid adjustments in the company's business model. EU legislation permitted some flexibility in what it could do; that is, it could obtain credits for especially innovative technology. Thus, the degree to which it could meet fuel efficiency and $CO_2$ requirements crucially depended on the technological and financial capabilities it applied.

### Procurement, Quality, and Production
To ensure continuity of production, suppliers had to deliver on time. Increasing technical complexity meant there was a need for high-grade components of impeccable quality. However, VW was not always able to identify quality problems early enough to correct them. Short product life cycles and new vehicle start-ups increased the potential for delays and added to procurement and quality problems. Overly optimistic forecasts left capacity underutilized. Overly pessimistic forecasts resulted in insufficient capacity to meet demand. The company encountered engineering mistakes. It sometimes improperly costed new vehicles, and faced issues like contract changes, weak project management, and poor supplier performance, which led to downtime, lost output, rejects, and unnecessary product reworking. Accidents, storms, and

earthquakes could disrupt supply lines. The company could encounter hazardous substances leakage problems. It could not tolerate another supplier-caused recall like the Takata airbag. Suppliers had consolidated to the extent that automotive companies needed additional competition to prevent quality deterioration and eliminate bottlenecks.

## Assumptions about the Future

Besides its own research, VW relied on estimates by third-party institutions including economic research institutes, banks, consulting firms, and other multinational organizations to formulate its assumptions. Its three main assumptions had to do with growth in demand for new vehicles, attention to ethics, and focus on sustainable mobility.

**Demand Growth**
In 2016, the pace of global economic growth had been slightly slower than the previous year, but demand for vehicles had been higher. The 2016 results could be an exception. Demand grew in the Asia Pacific region, Western Europe, North America, and Central Europe, while it fell in South America, Eastern Europe, and Africa compared to previous years. VW's assumptions about demand for new vehicles in different parts of the world in upcoming years were that:

- Western European economic growth was likely to slow because of Brexit. As the situation in Eastern Europe stabilized, demand for new vehicles would rise, unless Russia's conflict with Ukraine worsened.
- Demand in emerging economies would grow faster than developed economies, with the strongest expansion in Asia. China would grow at a high level, India at a moderate one, and Japan would be unchanged. Demand growth in China for new vehicles would be for attractively priced SUVs.
- Growth in demand for new vehicles in the United States and Canada would be higher, but in Mexico, it would be lower. As the economies of Brazil and Argentina improved, demand for new vehicles would increase in those countries.
- South African demand was not likely to grow, as its economy continued to perform poorly.

VW expected limited growth in markets for commercial vehicles. Its growth estimates would be higher if the threats of protectionism, turbulence in financial markets, government deficits, and geopolitical tension eased.

Overall, the number of passenger cars sold would grow, but at a slower pace than in the past. Nonetheless, the company's goal was to grow sales by 4 percent compared to previous years. It aimed to achieve an operating profit of between 6 and 7 percent even if net cash flow was likely to be lower than before because of Dieselgate. To continue to grow profitably, the company needed to maintain operational excellence and rely on its global presence, brand diversity, and technological innovation.

**Ethics**
The massive loss of trust that followed Dieselgate made it clear that ethics had to receive much more attention in the company. Loss of an asset as important as its reputation was not an acceptable outcome. The company could not achieve its growth goals without an impeccable reputation. It had to honor the basic principle of running the business in compliance with legal requirements. Yet, it was aware that it could never fully prevent misconduct or criminal acts on the part of individuals or control the media reaction to such activity. Nonetheless, it had to attach greater importance to its social responsibilities and deepen its commitment to behave ethically and with integrity. CEO Müller stated in 2016 that integrity would be the basis for every action the company took, His emphasis was on compliance, and the company integrated the responsibilities for compliance with risk management and internal control. The company took remedial measures when needed and it evaluated the effectiveness of these measures to ensure it eliminated corruption in all its guises. It brought in additional compliance officers to support the work of compliance in the different brands and divisions. The core values the company chose to emphasize were honesty and openness. It asked for additional input from stakeholders and outside experts on how to live up to these values. It created a board position for integrity and legal affairs to implement programs that aimed to raise integrity awareness. It launched a campaign to get employees to engage with the topic

**Sustainable Mobility**
VW also established a sustainability council with nine experts advising it on issues such as sustainable mobility and environmental protection.

The company assumed that the automotive world was undergoing rapid change, with autonomous driving, e-mobility, connected vehicle concepts, and digitization coming to the fore, affecting customer expectations, and challenging established business models. New players entered the business, innovation cycles were shorter, and the company had to spend time and money developing new competencies. These factors combined with stringent emissions standards and a highly volatile market were creating challenges for the company's continued growth. Its low-emission technology initiatives and its moves toward electrification, mobility services, and autonomous driving were bringing it into new business areas. It wanted to reduce transportation's negative environmental impacts and attain sustainable development goals like those the UN promulgated.

VW aimed to meet challenges like climate change, resource availability, and urbanization by making each new generation of vehicles more eco-friendly than its predecessor. Yet it showed some ambivalence and caution in where it was going. Electrification, for instance, presented challenges to existing production methods. It required the development of innovative battery technologies and electric and hybrid vehicles, which were not in themselves panaceas. VW had to compare these solutions with conventional vehicles in terms of the resources they consumed and the need they presented to recycle batteries.

Electrification was not the only area where the company had to address important questions. It also wished to be a leader in ride hailing and to develop or acquire attractive and profitable services such as car sharing. It had a stake in Gett and was setting up its own app-based, on-demand, connected commuting service. It also had developed a fully autonomous concept car, with an innovative control system for summoning and taking passengers to their destinations. Automated vehicles and new mobility services blurred the lines between individual and collective mobility. Depending on the data gathered, shared, and analyzed, they created issues of privacy. The ethical and legal issues associated with the moves VW was making toward sustainable mobility required stakeholder collaboration if VW was to make these moves appropriately.

## Hedging

The approach VW took to managing the risks and uncertainties involved hedging in ways similar to GM and Ford. The hedges in which the company engaged were: (1) trying to ensure the quality and safety of its vehicles; (2) investing globally in different markets; (3) adjusting its brand and model mix; and (4) devoting itself to technological innovation that might bring with it future competitive advantage. How VW applied these strategies before and after 2014–2015 is described next.

## VW before the 2014–2015 Price Collapse

### (1) Assuring Quality and Safety

VW intended to have leading positions in customer satisfaction, quality, and sustainability. The company analyzed customer satisfaction levels using standardized performance indicators for all its brands. The indicators included image, desirability, purchase-likelihood, product quality, and brand awareness. It also tracked customer loyalty and sales. The different brands could create their own measures as needed. Over the years, VW saw regular improvement in these ratings. Audi and Porsche were recognized leaders in customer satisfaction. Other VW brands did not rank as highly.

### Quality

VW had a similar global quality strategy for all its brands, but its growing number of production locations and market-specific models presented a challenge. It had 16,000 employees involved in some way in quality processes, helping to avoid and eliminate errors. To maintain consistency, a central body governed these activities, though final responsibility lay within specific markets and regions.

### Safety and the Environment

The company' goal in protecting driver safety was zero fatalities or severe injuries due to its vehicles. It provided safety benchmarks for the suppliers in its value chain. An accident research department reconstructed and evaluated accidents and the findings fed into vehicle development activities, leading to innovations, such as driver assistance, distance control, and emergency assist. Its vehicles had highly deformation-resistant passenger cells, defined front and rear crumple zones, and crash-optimized interior design. They had strong occupant retention systems, leading-edge chassis, high-performance lighting, and optimized bodywork. The company wanted to provide drivers with additional support when braking to avoid collisions. It continually tried to improve its standardized safety designs.

By 2018, VW's aim also was to be the world's most environmentally compatible automaker. To achieve this goal, it had ambitious environmental protection targets. The board was the highest decision-making authority on environmental matters. Climate protection was at the top of its agenda. The company reported regularly on its climate progress to the Carbon Disclosure Project. In 2014, this organization awarded VW ninety-nine out of a possible hundred points for transparency, and a top grade for performance. Absolute $CO_2$ emissions from in-house energy generation at production locations and from purchased energy had gone up slightly, while emissions per vehicle fell. For the German locations, which were around 45 percent of VW's production, the company had a target of a 40 percent decrease in $CO_2$ emissions in 2020 compared with 2010.

In Germany, VW brands had information on fuel consumption and $CO_2$ emissions on their websites. Beginning in 2011, all new cars had to have a weight-based energy-efficiency label similar to the labeling of household appliances. The label provided information on fuel consumption, annual fuel costs, $CO_2$ emissions, and the tax payable under Germany's $CO_2$ laws. For electric vehicles, the label provided information on electricity consumption.

VW evaluated its suppliers and business partners hoping they would live up to its standards. It subscribed to the certified environmental management systems ISO 14001 and/or EMAS, and required its suppliers to do the same. Nearly 90 percent complied. The company offered training courses and workshops to suppliers. It provided an electronic learning module on sustainability to them. At the end of 2014, 14,457 suppliers had completed this module

**(2) Investing in Global Markets**
VW's manufacturing network had 118 locations, but Europe was the heart of these activities with seventy-two locations, twenty-nine of them in Germany, where VW produced more cars than it sold. The company also had twenty-nine production locations in the Asia Pacific region, nine in South America, four in Africa, and four in North America. Europe was by far its largest market, and only 4.6 percent of its sales in 2014 were in North America, 0.2 percent less than in 2013. The US vehicle market as a whole grew in 2014 and was attractive, but because of backlash from Dieselgate, VW was falling behind in the United States. It also was having difficulty growing markets in Brazil,

Argentina, India, and Russia. These markets had great potential, despite the fact that conditions were not ideal. To strengthen VW's position in Brazil, it offered models manufactured locally specifically for that market, including the Gol and the Fox.

VW was a market leader in China, the leading foreign brand. Roughly, half of its Chinese offerings came from its two local joint ventures. The rest it imported from manufacturing it did elsewhere. The company expected that demand for motor vehicles in China, its largest market in Asia Pacific, would continue to increase, driven by the growing need for personal mobility, but growth rates in China were slowing slightly and shifting from coastal cities inland. China's guidelines to reduce $CO_2$ emissions were more exacting than the EU's. Because of traffic congestion and pollution, Chinese cities were likely to restrict the number of vehicle registrations further. Only 1 percent of the cars VW sold in China were diesel; most Chinese consumers preferred gas-consuming cars.

### China and Electrification

Sales of electric vehicles in China had surpassed both the United States and Europe. They were poised to grow at a much faster rate. To maintain its edge in China, VW would have to give strong support to the development of electric vehicles. China's goal was to be a dominant force in electric vehicles. Just as Japan and South Korea became leaders in conventional vehicles, China aspired to leadership in electric vehicles. Its declared intention was to ban *all* gas and diesel cars by 2040. VW anticipated that demand for plug-in hybrids was likely to rise before China went fully electric. The main obstacle was that there was sufficient charging infrastructure in place. To gain a foothold in the Chinese electric vehicle (EV) market, cars also would have to be low cost. The top-selling all-electric Chinese vehicle, the Zhidou, made by Geel, cost just $7,500 after subsidies. However, only cars that had Chinese-manufactured batteries qualified for these subsidies.

VW's plan, to offer consumers a choice of over twenty electric vehicles, would depend on its working with its joint venture partners. The Chinese government restricted foreign-owned electric-vehicle companies to its free-trade zones. Imported cars were subject to a 25 percent tariff. Without VW's joint venture partners, it could not effectively participate in the Chinese market. Yet these partnerships posed risks, as the partners, the FAW Group and SAIC, were state-owned enterprises, and VW had to turn over critical technology when working with them. VW tried to protect its intellectual property by keeping the manufacture of its premium brands separate from its Chinese partners. Protecting the company's intellectual property in China was a challenge, one that VW deemed to be worthwhile, as it intended to use its production in China as a springboard to expand in other markets in Asia. The company therefore decided to invest heavily with its Chinese JV partners to develop a wide range of low-cost electric vehicle models for China. Though these partnerships required 50–50 profit-sharing agreements, the size of the Chinese market was large enough that the company would be able to reap substantial benefits.

Given that the battery was a critical component of a fully electric vehicle drivetrain, meeting VW's electric vehicle production target would require purchasing large quantities of lithium batteries. Since it would have to purchase so many batteries, VW had to protect itself from supplier instability. It would do this by awarding its battery contracts to state-owned Chinese battery manufacturers. The bulk of its contracts were with CATL, one of several companies in China participating in this market. CATL also worked with the other German automakers BMW and Daimler.

### (3) Adjusting the Brand and Model Mix
In addition to relying on global diversification to hedge risks and uncertainties, VW maintained a broad product portfolio. It sold passenger cars, commercial vehicles, and many different body types from small cars to pickups, heavy trucks, and buses. Altogether VW had nine different brands, plus the vehicles it specifically made for the Chinese market with FAW and SAIC such as Lavida, New Bora, New Jetta, and New Santana. Its weakness was in the worldwide SUV market, which was the fastest-growing market segment, especially in the United States, and was the most challenging in terms of complying with $CO2$ emission regulations.

### Brand Performance
Most VW brands saw improved performance in 2014 compared to 2013. The exceptions were truck brands Scania and MAN3 (Figure 14.3). Passenger car deliveries increased 4.9 percent to about 9.5 million cars in 2014, compared to 2013. The biggest-selling models were the Golf, Jetta, Polo, Passat, Tiguan, and Lavida. Audi

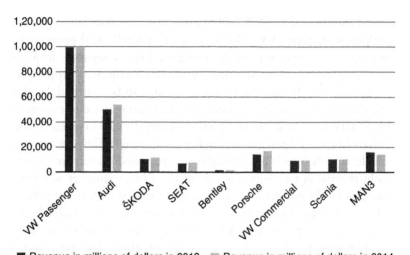

■ Revenue in millions of dollars in 2013   ▦ Revenue in millions of dollars in 2014

**Figure 14.3** VW performance by brand 2013–2014
Derived from VW Annual Reports

(10.5 percent), Škoda (12.7 percent), SEAT (10.0 percent), Porsche
(17.1 percent), and Lamborghini (19.3 percent) had made the largest
gains. VW launched the Golf Sportsvan as the successor to Golf Plus
and upgraded the Polo, Jetta, and Scirocco. Škoda introduced a new
edition of the Fabia hatchback and Porsche brought out a Macan SUV.
The Passat had a new engine and infotainment system, a lighter body,
and more driver-assist programs. VW had plans for updating more of
its models in 2015.

To reduce development costs and production times, VW consolidated the manufacture of its brands by means of a Modular Transverse
Matrix; that is it built different categories of vehicles on the same
production line, applied the same standards, and used identical parts
in different models. The system integrated conventional gasoline and
diesel engines, including hybrid and electric drives, incorporated alternative powertrains, and added the same features, such as driver-assist
programs, to each vehicle type.

In 2014, VW reported that it would spend 64 percent of its 43-billion-
euro capital budget on modernizing and extending existing brands.
The spotlight would be on expanding the product range of its SUVs
and modernizing its light commercial vehicle models. The company

claimed that sales of eco-efficient vehicles were around one-third of its total sales. About a third of the eco-efficient vehicles were VW passenger cars equipped with "Bluemotion" technology, which had the following features:

• Start-stop technology. The engine automatically stopped when the car was in neutral.
• Battery regeneration. The car took energy used when braking, stored it, and put it back into the battery that it used to start the engine.
• Low-rolling resistance tires and aerodynamic design.

Another 20 percent of eco-efficient vehicles VW sold were Audis with similar technological features.

In 2014, VW sold fewer than 15,000 hybrids and pure electric vehicles. It sold more CNG vehicles than electrified vehicles. VW tried to overcome this deficiency; in addition to the all-electric e-Golf, it launched its first high volume-production plug-in hybrid model, the Golf GTE in 2014. With the e-Golf and the plug-in GTE, VW was the first carmaker in the world to offer all relevant drive systems within one brand. It launched Audi's first plug-in hybrid and introduced the Porsche 918 Spyder as a hybrid super sports car. VW reserved its biggest electric mobility initiatives for China. If demand developed, it had the capacity to build as many as 75,000 battery electric and plug-in hybrids a year. Over the next five years, it planned to spend about €6 billion per year on environmental technology, the goal being to build emotionally appealing EVs with a range of up to 310 miles. It was looking to develop as many as thirty all-electric cars in ten years and sell two to three million per year by 2025, with its ability to achieve these goals depending on battery costs.

**(4) Innovating**
In 2014, VW invested €11.5 billion in research and development, an expenditure that it was set to increase over the next few years. Between 2015 and 2019, it was planning to invest around €85.6 billion in new models, innovative technologies, and its global presence. Around two-thirds of the investments would be dedicated to efficiency, alternative powertrains, and environmentally compatible production. The total investment of €85.6 billion did not include investment by the firm's Chinese joint ventures, which would be spending an additional

€22 billion on new factories and products between 2015 and 2019 from their own funds.

VW was hedging its bets, simultaneously moving to eco-friendly conventional diesel, gasoline and natural gas engines as well as innovative hybrid drive systems, all-electric, and FCVs. Most customers still opted for conventionally powered vehicles, therefore, electric powertrains and conventional engines would coexist for a significant period as parallel technologies. The aim was to improve drivetrain efficiency regardless of how VW powered its vehicles.

### Optimizing Conventional Engines

As conventional combustion engines would remain for the time being, they would be the main technology in use in most parts of the world, especially in growth markets like Russia, India, and Asia. VW would dedicate its R&D to further optimizing gasoline and diesel engines with Bluemotion technology. It would achieve the optimization via light weighting, engine management, direct shift gearboxes, and better aerodynamics. For instance, the 2014 Audi showed a new type of vehicle spring that offered significant scope for weight savings. Audi and an Italian supplier developed glass fiber-reinforced plastic springs that were 40 percent lighter than comparable steel springs for vehicles in the upper mid-range segment.

### Automating Driving

As part of its R&D activities, VW was drawing up feasibility studies for automated driving. These studies included safety functions that relied on sensors to scan a vehicle's environment, identify and interpret situations, and make maneuvers that benefitted the driver. Safe-parking programs plus speed, and braking controls would make vehicles less accident-prone. Vehicles would be able to take evasive actions on their own without driver involvement. The automated systems would help overcome the problem of driver distraction, a main accident cause. The reaction times of the automated system were quicker and more precise than drivers' reaction times. VW also was setting up a digital platform that would collect, process, and analyze large volumes of data. Using the same technology in each of its brands would significantly reduce deployment costs.

## *VW after the 2014–2015 Price Collapse*

### (1) Assuring Quality and Safety

VW understood that maintaining quality was critical to customer satisfaction. The diesel issue, however, had harmed its image and was a lingering problem.

### *Quality*

VW involved customers in the product development process via market research; benchmarked satisfaction, using such indicators as brand image, desirability, future purchase consideration, and quality; and asked for customer feedback prior to product launch. It updated its adherence to the ISO 9001 standard, and, as a further step, it applied multiple internal controls based on a series of cross-checks. The company established new quality specifications for components and operating fluids and tried to eliminate harmful interior odors and emissions to increase customer satisfaction. Audi and Porsche continued to be leaders in customer satisfaction in Europe, while the VW brand maintained high levels of customer loyalty and satisfaction. The emissions issue, however, lingered and hurt customers trust.

### *Safety and the Environment*

VW continued to aim for the goal of eliminating fatalities and severe injuries in vehicles it manufactured completely. Accident research played a pivotal role in how it tried to achieve this goal. It reconstructed and evaluated accidents and introduced, on the one hand, active systems, such as emergency braking and lane keeping; and on the other hand, passive systems, such as better vehicle structure and occupant retention systems. The company actively participated in the German Road Safety Council and its employees took part in safety conferences. VW brought concerns about safety to its suppliers. The European New Car Assessment Program and Insurance Institute for Highway Safety tested models it built. Tiguan received a five-star rating and the SEAT a four-star rating in 2016. Various models of Audi, Golf, Jetta, and Passat were top safety picks.

The company's environmental policies set binding, measurable targets at each stage in the value chain. Its goals were to reduce its carbon footprint, pollutant emissions, and resource consumption. Newly developed vehicles were supposed to show improvement in each of these dimensions. With suppliers, VW had agreements to integrate sustainability. They were binding contractual commitments. In Europe,

VW vehicle CO2 emissions were lower than they were in the United States and China. Thus, the vehicles in the United States and China had some catching up to do. VW's new passenger car fleet in the EU (excluding Lamborghini and Bentley) emitted an average of 120 g CO2/km. In the United States, the comparable figure was 162 g CO2/km and in China 153 g CO2/km (including cars made with SAIC and FAW).

(2) Investing in Global Markets
VW continued to produce more cars in Germany than it sold there and sell more cars outside its home country than it sold in Germany. It was seeing more growth in sales in Europe than any region. Dieselgate mostly affected its sales in North America.

(3) Adjusting the Brand and Model Mix
The range of the products it offered protected VW from the full brunt of Dieselgate. Its product portfolio comprised 336 models, covering almost all key segments and body types, including pickups, heavy trucks, and buses. It geared its product portfolio to profitable growth areas by taking into account regional customer needs and unveiling new models based on the Modular Transverse Toolkit. Because of its product range, VW was able to deal with developments in automotive markets around the world. In 2016, in a reversal of the prior two years, commercial vehicle volume and sales improved slightly more than passenger vehicle volume and sales. The only passenger vehicle to show growth in revenue, but not volume, was Porsche.

*Launching More SUVs*
Sales of eco-driven vehicles were down about 11 percent globally and 10 percent in Western Europe in 2016 compared to the prior year (Table 14.1). With gasoline prices lower and customer demand moving in that direction, VW continued to launch more SUVs in attractive, fast-growing global markets. In China, it introduced a longer version of the Tiguan. In the United States, it produced a second-generation Q5 SUV at the Audi plant in San José Chiapa, Mexico. It started to produce the Atlas SUV domestically in Chattanooga. It continued the initiative with the T-Roc, a compact crossover model. It also introduced the Teramont, a mid-class SUV that seated seven passengers. Škoda launched a Kodiaq SUV. VW would spend the bulk of its scheduled CAPEX (capitalized investments in property, plant and equipment,

Table 14.1 *VW sales of eco-friendly drive vehicles 2015–2016*

| | 2015<br>(% of total<br>vehicles sold) | 2016<br>(% of total<br>vehicles sold) | 2015–2016<br>(% change) |
|---|---|---|---|
| **GLOBAL** | | | |
| Natural-gas drives | 86,781<br>(0.90%) | 72,955<br>(0.73%) | –16 |
| Hybrid drives | 39,107<br>(0.40%) | 39,037<br>(0.39%) | –0.2 |
| All-electric drives | 17,076<br>(0.18%) | 15,729<br>(0.16%) | –0.8 |
| Total eco-friendly drives | 142,949<br>(1.48%) | 127,721<br>(1.27%) | –11 |
| **WESTERN EUROPE** | | | |
| Natural-gas drives | 34,678<br>(1.04%) | 30,807<br>(0.90%) | –11 |
| Hybrid drives | 33,759<br>(1.01%) | 33,222<br>(0.97%) | –1.6 |
| All-electric drives | 12,987<br>(0.39%) | 9,480<br>(0.28%) | –27 |
| Total eco-friendly drives | 81,424<br>(2.43%) | 73,509<br>(2.16%) | –10 |

Derived from VW Annual Reports

investment property and intangible assets) of €13 billion on new products in the SUV range.

### Conventional Powertrains
For the time being, alternatives to gasoline and diesel-powered vehicles did not constitute a high percentage of the vehicles that VW sold. With gasoline prices low, sales fell for most of the alternatives. VW aimed to boost the powertrain efficiency of each new generation of vehicle regardless of how it powered the vehicle – whether by internal combustion engine, hybrid, plug-in hybrid, all electric, or fuel cell. It hedged itself against all

the contingencies. Though its strategy ranged across all possibilities, optimizing conventional powertrains came first. Afterward, the company would gradually broaden the portfolio of its drive systems and move to the other options. In the future, conventional powertrains and electric systems would coexist. In the present, the company would try to make current internal combustion engines as clean as possible. It would reduce fuel consumption by introducing dual-clutch transmissions, lightweight construction, and better aerodynamics systems. It would fit gasoline engines with particulate filters and diesel engines with catalytic converters.

### Electrification

Nonetheless, VW did not give up on electrification. It planned to launch three new electric vehicles in China: plug-in versions of the Phideon and the Passat Estate, as well as the e-Golf. Starting in 2017, Porsche would produce a Panamera 4 E-Hybrid. VW made electric motors at its Kassel plant. Its new battery technology extended the range of the e-Golf by about 50 percent up to 300 kilometers. Ultimately, the company wanted to offer customers electric vehicles that would meet almost all their mobility needs. However, it was cognizant of the fact that most customers would want to take their vehicles on long trips, for which all-electric vehicles were not suitable. For electric vehicles to take-off, there had to be more private battery-recharging options. Charging stations had to be installed on customers' premises and supplemented by a public recharging infrastructure. As a bridge to fully electric vehicles, VW started to offer plug-in hybrids in multiple vehicle classes.

The heart of an electric vehicle was the battery, the energy content of which was the deciding factor in determining the vehicle's range. For all-electric and plug-in hybrid vehicles, VW was using lithium-ion cells assembled into battery systems at its Braunschweig factory, but the company was researching other types of batteries based on solid electrolytes, which had a higher energy density and met stricter safety standards. In 2020, it aimed to launch a new compact electric car with a battery that charged by cable or through an inductive charging interface in the front of the car. The battery would take thirty minutes to reach 80 percent capacity. VW would offer this car at a price level equivalent to a comparable Golf.

### Digitization

The company was also integrating digitalization more fully into its products. The Teramont had the latest driver-assist systems. Audi's new flagship, the successor to the Audi A8, also had numerous new driver-assist systems and new infotainment features. The revamped Golf, coming out in 2017, had a different design, a more efficient engine, and also a new infotainment system and innovative driver-assist systems.

## (4) Innovating

Early identification of pioneering developments and trends was the basis for innovation. This awareness was crucially important to the company's research and development activities. Only if the company had a reliable vision of technical possibilities could it ensure its growth. Its aim was to create overarching technologies that avoided parallel developments in different units and facilitated efficient technology transfer to reduce the costs. Its research and development activities concentrated on expanding the product portfolio and improving the functionality, quality, safety, and environmental compatibility of its products, while simultaneously reducing the number of platforms. In 2016, VW invested in new models, environmentally compatible drive technologies, and optimized production processes. It invested €11.5 billion in research and development in that year, much of it on efficiency-enhancing technologies. It had more than 45,000 R&D employees engaged in efforts to develop new models with more-efficient powertrains including electric cars powered entirely by battery, as well as plug-ins. It filed 6,465 patent applications compared with 6,244 the previous year. The year-on-year increase was primarily attributable to driver assistance systems.

### Electric Propulsion

R&D was assisting in shifting the company toward electric propulsion. However, sustainable mobility meant more than electrification. It was a holistic concept that incorporated many activities leading to greater efficiency, connectivity, flexibility safety, comfort, and environmental compatibility including the development of driver-assistance systems and autonomous piloted driving. To move in this direction, VW continued to look for partnerships and acquisitions and make venture capital investments as well as carry out R&D.

### Lightweight Bodies

Lightweight bodies remained a priority. VW used hot-formed, high-strength steels and pursued the further use of composite materials and aluminum. While these materials consumed more energy in the production process, they meant less fuel consumption from weight savings and reduced $CO_2$ emissions and energy use over a vehicle's lifetime. The body of the Audi Q7 was largely made of aluminum, as were the Porsche Panamera's roof and side panels, along with more than 30 percent of its bodywork.

### Autonomous Driving
In the field of autonomous driving, the new Passat featured an optional head-up display to improve safety. It projected trip data onto a screen that moved into the driver's field of vision. Drivers kept their eyes on the road while simultaneously taking note of on-screen information. Because alerts appeared directly in the driver's line of sight, the system reduced driver reaction times. The Audi A7 piloted-driving concept car, a research vehicle, was capable of carrying out all freeway-driving maneuvers on its own. The concept car enabled piloted driving by relying on a driver-assistance control unit that used high-performance processors to evaluate signals from sensors in real time and continuously generate a model of the surrounding environment. Long-range radar sensors, lane-keeping assistants, and laser scanners and a wide-angle 3D video camera allowed the concept car to change lanes, overtake, accelerate, and brake without human intervention.

### Big Data Analytics
VW's Data:Lab in Munich specialized in big data, advanced analytics, and machine learning, with the aim of forecasting customer wishes, predicting loyalty, and getting involved in spare-parts scheduling. Digital:Lab in Berlin conducted projects on digital mobility and systems for processing traffic-related information generated by vehicles. The Smart.Production:Lab in Wolfsburg specialized in production and logistics solutions.

### Reduced Future Spending
While fuel-efficient conventional vehicles with low $CO_2$ emissions were important R&D priorities, digitalization combined with electric mobility and autonomous driving were likely to transform VW's businesses in the long term. When this transformation was more complete, VW projected it would end up being able to reduce its R&D spending as a percentage of sales.

## Performance

Dieselgate could have led to far worse 2012–2016 performance, because of the billions of dollars in costs and negative public relations. In the United States, VW ranked dead last in reputation among the world's 100 most visible companies. As the company moved through the crisis, returns to shareholders did not keep up with Toyota, yet the company did better than Ford. Given low gasoline prices, revenues should have picked up, but they fell slightly. Profits fell and the company lost money in 2015, but by 2016, it again was profitable.

## Adjusting to the Ethical Breakdown – The Correct Response?

Saddled by risks and uncertainties, before and after 2014–2015, some relating to the scandal's lingering burden and some common to all automobile companies in this period, VW tried to make amends for its ethical breakdown. It confronted risks and uncertainties related to climate change, industry competition, global economy weakness, inconsistent standards in markets in which it operated, and technological disruption at the same time it had to deal with Dieselgate. The increasing digitization of its products and the potential for electric, connected, and autonomous vehicles were other challenges that it confronted.

Like Ford, VW was ambivalent. It had to strike a balance between moving toward new more eco-friendly propulsion systems and sticking to and strengthening its capabilities in the conventional engines, diesel and gas powered, it knew best. The high gas prices that prevailed before 2014–2015 tilted the balance in the direction of moving forward with new alternatives. The push came from China, where VW was the dominant foreign automaker. The company had to pay attention to signals from China that electric vehicles were going to play an increasingly important role.

On the other hand, in the United States, where VW was relatively weak compared to its competitors, the signals were different. Even when gas prices were high, the market slanted toward SUVs and light trucks, where VW was comparatively weak. VW wanted to grow its market share in the United States and therefore tried not only to introduce new models more compatible with that market but also to encroach on Toyota's dominant passenger car market position, with the claim that its diesel vehicles were a less polluting green alternative. Its goal was to triple US sales in under a decade by betting on diesels and promoting them as a clean, but better engineered and more powerful alternative to vehicles that Toyota sold in the United States.

The Dieselgate scandal erupted in the United States and it was in the United States where VW's image and sales suffered the most. The company would have had to pay a much higher price for the scandal had it not hedged globally and protected by its multi-brand strategy. VW could fall back on the Chinese market. The scandal hardly affected its performance in China, where it sold mostly gasoline-powered vehicles with its joint venture partners. No matter how much harm Dieselgate caused VW in Europe, it also had loyal customers there, where it was also the dominant automaker. An essential bulwark of the German economy, it had the backing of the German government and its labor unions because of the vast numbers of people it employed. Its global and multi-brand strategies again protected it from the scandal's full impact.

As VW worked its way through the scandal, it hedged its bets, like GM and Ford, between the alternatives – electrification on the one hand and light duty trucks for the United States, on the other. At the same time, VW, like GM and Ford, explored other transportation innovations that were gaining ground such as digitization and autonomy. The fall in oil prices after 2014–2015 created an unexpected opportunity, one that VW was not fully prepared to seize. The eco-friendly vehicles it had introduced and worked to bring to market declined in sales. On the other hand, the fall in oil prices opened the US market to more for SUVs and small trucks. VW, like Ford and GM, tried to fill the gap. This move did not mean it gave up on electrification, better batteries, digitization, and alternatives to conventional powertrains, just that it stretched out the time horizon for their launch. The demands of the moment were too strong to ignore.

Like Ford, VW was ambivalent about what it should do to next given the upheavals the automotive sector was experiencing. Prior to the 2015–2016 plunge in gasoline prices, the company more enthusiastically accepted electrification and cleaner mobility. After 2015–2016, it showed greater caution and some reluctance to pursue this path when immediate gain seemed more tied to expanding its global SUV and small truck fleet. The past and the future pulled the company in different directions as they pulled Ford in different directions. The situation in 2015–2016 nudged it into the past, but it did not entirely abandon the future. Thus, like Ford, VW was conflicted, and was moving in a number of directions at once, hedging its bets that it would do well no matter what took place, but unlike Ford, VW faced a fraud that would have brought down a weaker and less-hedged firm.

Given the company's history, what was the prudent and ethically correct road for it to take?

## Notes

1. Hiott, Andreas. *Thinking Small: The Long, Strange Trip of the Volkswagen Beetle.* New York: Random House, 2012; Rieger, Bernhard. *The People's Car: A Global History of the Volkswagen Beetle.* Cambridge, MA: Harvard University Press, 2013.
2. *"Volkswagen to Shut US Plant."* www.nytimes.com/1987/11/21/busi ness/Volkswagen-to-shut-us-plant.html
3. *"Volkswagen Historical Notes."* www.volkswagenag.com/vwag/vwco rp/info_center/en/publications/2008/05/chronicle.-bin.acq/qual-Binary StorageItem.Single.File/HN7e_www2.pdf
4. *"VW Picks Tenn. For Its 1st US Car Plant Since '88."* http://archive .boston.com/business/articles/2008/07/16/vw_picks_tenn_for_its_1st_us_ car_plant_since_88/
5. *"Porsche Looks at Restructuring VW Relationship."* www.nytimes.com/ 2009/04/24/business/global/24porsche.html?mtrref=www.google.com
6. *"Dieselgate" – A Timeline of Germany's Car Emissions Fraud Scandal."* www.cleanenergywire.org/factsheets/dieselgate-timeline-ger manys-car-emissions-fraud-scandal
7. *"Insight-After Year of Stonewalling, VW Stunned US Regulators with Confession."* www.reuters.com/article/usa-volkswagen-deception/insig ht-after-year-of-stonewalling-vw-stunned-us-regulators-with-confes sion-idUSL1N11U1OB20150924
8. *"How VW Paid $25 Billion for 'Dieselgate' – and Got Off Easy."* http:// fortune.com/2018/02/06/volkswagen-vw-emissions-scandal-penalties/; *"VW's Dieselgate Bill Hits $30 Bln After Another Charge."* www .reuters.com/article/legal-uk-volkswagen-emissions/vws-dieselgate-bill- hits-30-bln-after-another-charge-idUSKCN1C4271
9. *How VW's Cheating on Emissions Was Exposed.* "www.ft.com/con tent/103dbe6a-d7a6-11e6-944b-e7eb37a6aa8e"; *"Researchers Who Exposed VW Gain Little Reward from Success."* www.nytimes.com/2 016/07/25/business/vw-wvu-diesel-volkswagen-west-virginia.html

10. *"Volkswagen CEO Martin Winterkorn Resigns Amid Emissions Scandal."* www.nytimes.com/2015/09/24/business/international/volks wagen-chief-martin-winterkorn-resigns-amid-emissions-scandal.html
11. *"Hoaxwagen."* http://fortune.com/inside-volkswagen-emissions-scandal/
12. Ibid.
13. *"VW Sustainability Report 2012."* www.volkswagenag.com/ir/Y_201 2_e.pdf; *"VW Annual Report 2012."* www.volkswagenag.com/pre sence/investorrelation/publications/annual-reports/2013/volkswagen/e nglish/GB%202012_e.pdf; *"VW Sustainability Report 2013."* https:// ddd.uab.cat/pub/infsos/146241/isVOLKSWAGENa2013ieng1.pdf *"VW Annual Report 2013."* www.volkswagenag.com/presence/inves torrelation/publications/annual-reports/2014/volkswagen/english/Y_2 013_e.pdf; *"VW Sustainability Report 2014."* http://sustainabilityreport2014.volkswagenag.com/sites/default/files/pdf/ en/Volkswagen_SustainabilityReport_2014.pdf; *"VW Annual Report 2014."* www.volkswagenag.com/presence/investorrelation/publications/ annual-reports/2015/volkswagen/english/GB+2014_e.pdf; *"VW Sustain ability Report 2015."* http://annualreport2015.volkswagenag.com/gro up-management-report/sustainable-value-enhancement/csr-and-sustain ability.html; *"VW Annual Report 2015."* www.volkswagenag.com/presence/investorrelation/publications/annual-reports/2016/volkswagen/englisch/Y_2015_e.pdf *"VW Sustainability Report 2016."* www.volkswagen-newsroom.com/ en/press-releases/volkswagen-group-presents-its-sustainability-report-for-2016-1091; *"VW Annual Report 2016."* www.volkswagenag.com/pre sence/investorrelation/publications/annual-reports/2017/volkswagen/en/Y _2016_e.pdf; *"VW Sustainability Report 2017."* www.volkswagenag .com/presence/nachhaltigkeit/documents/sustainability-report/2017 /Nonfinancial_Report_2017_e.pdf

# 15 | *Strategies to Take Advantage of Plummeting Prices: Toyota*

This chapter aims to trace the responses of Toyota to changing conditions in the automotive sector from 2012 to 2016, especially due to volatile oil prices, and to consider where the company might go next with its strategies. It starts with an introduction to the company. Covered next are the company's strategies from 2012 to 2014, before the fall in oil prices, and 2014 to 2016, after prices dropped. Like the previous chapters on GM, Ford, and VW, it examines the risks and uncertainties that Toyota perceived in this period, its assumptions about the future, and the hedges it had in place to protect its business. The chapter seeks to understand the extent to which the oil price shock altered its strategies and affected its performance. To what extent were the strategies Toyota adopted adequate, and suggest what the company should do next?

## The Toyota Way

Toyota, and Toyota-produced automobiles, consistently ranked near the top in quality and reliability. Largely considered responsible was the company's management approach, referred to as the Toyota Way.[1] The company made decisions slowly and by consensus, considering the options and rapidly implementing decisions. Employees were supposed to adhere to principles, which involved teamwork, learning, continuous improvement, long-term thinking, respect for people, and problem solving. They were expected to take care of problems before they grew large and out of control. Toyota stressed quality and its approach put a heavy emphasis on lean manufacturing and just-in-time production.

Toyota's focus on quality originated in the efforts of the US government and the consultant W. Edwards Deming. In the post-World War II period, they worked to improve Japanese manufacturing capabilities. Toyota became an enthusiastic adopter of quality principles, while US auto manufacturers fell behind and were unable to put quality principles into place successfully. By the 1990s, most US consumers understood that if quality was their main concern, Japanese manufacturers offered the best option.

Japanese manufacturers overcame the image of shoddy manufacturing from which they suffered at the end of World War II.[2] The intense focus on quality helped Toyota become Japan's largest company and one of the world's most respected. In 2013, it was the first automobile manufacturer to produce more than 10 million vehicles in a year.[3] It made them under the Toyota, Hino, Lexus, Ranz, and Daihatsu names. It had a stake in Subaru and Isuzu, along with joint ventures in China, India, and the Czech Republic. The company sold sedans, coupes, vans, trucks, hybrids, and crossovers, ranging from subcompacts such as the Yaris and Scion to a compact like the Corollas, a midsize car like the Camrys, a full-size car like the Avalon, and a luxury vehicle like the Lexus. Toyota also made and sold vans, such as the Previa and Sienna; SUVs and crossovers like the Matrix, RAV4, and Highlander; and light duty trucks like the Land Cruiser.

The 1973 oil crisis first motivated many Americans to try Toyota's cars. At the time, they were most fuel-efficient cars on the market. Already in the 1960s, Toyota had fought off stiff US import tariffs. By the 1980s, to counter their effects, Toyota set up US manufacturing plants. In these years, it moved from making mostly compacts to larger and more luxurious vehicles. In the late 1990s, in response to California's zero-emissions mandate, Toyota went in another direction and produced about 1,500 all-electric RAV4s for sale in the state.

## Hybrids

An area in which Toyota stood out was as the world's hybrid leader.[4] It first introduced the hybrid Prius in 1997 and followed up with other hybrid options and models. The Prius was the world's top-selling hybrid electric vehicle (HEV). In addition to the Prius, Toyota had hybrid versions of the Camry, Lexus, Avalon, and Highlander. By 2016, Toyota's cumulative global hybrid sales had reached 10 million vehicles.[5] By combining battery-powered electric motors with conventional internal combustion engines (ICE), HEVs achieved better fuel economy than conventional cars. They emitted less greenhouse gases and caused less pollution than cars powered by gasoline engines only. However, because of the need to add batteries and an electric propulsion system, they weighed and cost more. Buyers of HEVs had to consider how many miles they would have to put on their vehicles before buying a hybrid paid off.

During the 1990s, the US government spent $240 million per year over six years funding a group of US car manufacturers to develop a new fuel-efficient vehicle. It called the initiative the Partnership for a New Generation of Vehicles (PNGV). Out of this effort came GM's Precept hybrid and Ford's Prodigy hybrid, both of which achieved PNGV's goal of 80 miles per gallon. These prototypes were American cars – that is, they were not small, but spacious mid-size sedans. This size came at a cost, however. A commercial model was likely to be significantly more expensive than petroleum-powered vehicles. Thus, GM and Ford concluded that though Americans appeared to like the idea of more fuel-efficient vehicles, most would be unwilling to pay the extra cost.

Toyota, operating with different reasoning, moved forward with its hybrid concept. Its prototype car made its first appearance at the Tokyo Motor Show in 1995. Called the Prius – the Latin word means the coming of a new era – the car used high-voltage batteries as a power source and electric motors as the propulsion system. California designers did the styling. The first commercially available model went on sale in 1997 in Japan. At its introduction, it became Japan's Car of the Year. In 2000, hybrid vehicles, marketed with an emphasis on their environmental benefits, grew in popularity. The Prius, sized between a Corolla and a Camry and priced at about $20,000, was the most popular of them. It did not hurt that hybrid owners were eligible for a $2,000 US federal tax deduction. In 2002, Americans bought more than 36,000 hybrids. Viewed as a percentage of total US vehicle sales, their sales constituted, however, just 0.24 percent of the total US market that year.

In 2003, Toyota redesigned the Prius. Redistributing the mechanical and interior space, it significantly increased rear-seat room and changed the luggage compartment. The US National Highway Traffic Safety Administration (NHTSA) gave this car a five-star driver- and four-star passenger-safety rating. The US Insurance Institute for Highway Safety scored its safety as good, even when competing with much larger vehicles. The battery pack had a 150,000-mile warranty. The EPA rated the new Prius more environmentally friendly than the previous one. Toyota's second edition of the Prius was a success. The company could not make enough of them. Consumers experienced long waits before they could get their cars. The development effort led to 530 patents, some of which Toyota later licensed to other companies. European sales started in 2000. While Japan and the United States had strong hybrid markets, Europeans preferred diesel vehicles as a way to lower energy consumption (see Chapter 14). Toyota introduced the Prius into China in 2005, but sales were disappointing because of the high price, about $15,000 higher than comparable vehicles, mainly due to tariffs that the Chinese government imposed on the vehicle.

In 2007, Toyota's US market share, at more than 16 percent, was second only to GM. In 2008, it surpassed GM and had the largest market share among world automakers.[6] Although Toyota gained the status of number one carmaker in the world, the 2008 financial crisis paved the way for the company's first annual loss in seventy years. The third-generation Prius debuted at the 2009 North American International Auto Show, and sales of this vehicle began in Japan that year. It again won the Japanese Car of the Year award. The new body design was aerodynamic, and the car received a very good safety rating. Toyota cut its price and it became the world's undisputed leader in the category. It had a commanding market share lead.

In 2009, Akio Toyoda, a direct descendant of the company's founder, became president and CEO. The following year, the company initiated a partnership with Tesla to go beyond hybrids and create all-electric vehicles. Toyota built thirty-five converted RAV4 electric vehicles for testing and evaluation with Tesla's batteries and the company's assistance. Toyota sold the all-electric RAV4 only in California, and limited its production to 2,600 units. The company later broke off relations with Tesla, and in a surprise move, indicated that it was switching its emphasis from electric vehicles to fuel cells. In 2011, it announced that it planned to launch a full set of fuel cell cars in California as early as 2015.

## Unintended Acceleration

Toyota had a significant setback in 2009–2010. In a series of global recalls, it took back more than 9 million vehicles and briefly had to halt all production and sales after reports that several of its cars and trucks experienced unintended acceleration.[7] In 2009, the US National Highway Traffic Safety Administration (NHTSA) advised the company that it had to eliminate the movement drivers experienced when the floor mats slid into the accelerator. In 2010, the agency advised Toyota to take care of this problem of crashes caused by floor mat incursions that took place without driver intent. It had to prevent its accelerators from sticking to the floor and causing vehicles to move on their own. The two recalls netted 7.5 million vehicles.[8] A third recall involved 2 million vehicles in Europe and China and the alleged number of deaths attributable to the problems was thirty-seven. The US media gave the situation a lot of coverage. However, automotive experts, Toyota officials, and even government agents contested whether the problem was as serious as the media claimed.[9] They asked if the victim reports were reliable and argued that several factors could cause sudden unintended acceleration including drivers' mistakes.

When Toyota incorrectly repaired some of the recalled vehicles, it led to additional NHTSA and Toyota investigations and multiple lawsuits.[10] In 2011, NHTSA, in collaboration with the National Aeronautics and Space Administration, carried out an investigation.[11] They failed to find electronic defects in Toyota vehicles. Rather, they determined that the problem was mechanical and that driver error could be a cause, but in 2013, a jury ruled against NHTSA, holding that the accidents were the result of electronic deficiencies.[12] It criticized NHTSA and NASA for conducting an incomplete investigation of the electronics and concluded that Toyota had not followed best software practices. Previously, the accelerators in Toyota vehicles had been entirely mechanical, but then came the advent of electronic control. The accelerator pedals in Toyota vehicles had a spring-loaded arm connected to an electronic transducer. Older mechanical pedals relied on friction to keep the pedal in a fixed position. With electronic accelerators, the friction was not sufficient, which made it difficult for drivers to maintain the accelerator in a fixed position. Drivers preferred the freer and more tactile response of the conventional system. Toyota's designers, therefore, tried to emulate the tactile accelerator response with a special friction device made of nylon or polyphenylene sulfide. The jury found that nylon or polyphenylene sulfide devices often failed, which was at the root of most sudden acceleration problems.

In the week of January 25–31, 2010, the story of unintended acceleration was the fifth most reported item on US news. Toyota dealers in the southeast of the United States pulled their advertising out of newspapers in protest against what they judged excessive reporting. Trying

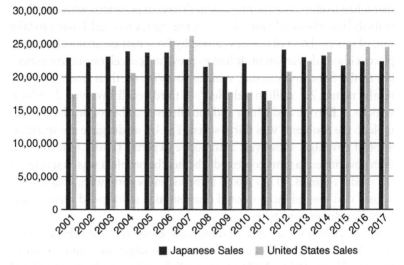

■ Japanese Sales    ▨ United States Sales

**Figure 15.1** Toyota's Japanese and US sales in dollars 2001–2016
Derived from Toyota annual reports

to emerge from the recession and already suffering from declining sales, the 2010 recall came at a difficult time for Toyota. Its US dealerships lost about $2 million a month on average in revenue. In 2008, Toyota had sold more automobiles in the United States than Japan. From 2009 to 2013, this situation changed. Toyota sold more cars in Japan than in the United States (Figure 15.1). Its US sales did not start to improve until 2012.

In 2012, Toyota spent more than a billion dollars settling a class-action lawsuit compensating owners for the lost resale value of their vehicles.[13] Toyota also agreed to pay a fine of $1.2 billion for not revealing information and misleading the public about the issue. In 2014, the company and the US Justice Department reached an agreement whereby Toyota agreed to pay a $1.2 billion criminal penalty in exchange for deferred prosecution. The agreement subjected Toyota to independent monitoring of its safety procedures and ended an investigation in which the US Justice Department concluded that Toyota had hidden information from the public and made deceptive statements to protect its image.[14] At the time, this penalty was the largest ever issued against a car company. Toyota said the agreement was difficult to bear, but necessary to put the issue behind it. Brake-override systems, then, became standard in all its vehicles, but it continued to confront wrongful death and personal injury lawsuits.

In response, Toyota set up a new global quality committee to coordinate defect analysis and future recall announcements. It also established a Swift Market Analysis Response Team in the United States to conduct on-site vehicle inspections. It expanded its Event Data Recorder system and the degree to which it relied on third-party quality consultation, and expanded its driver safety education initiatives. The recalls represented a direct challenge to the Toyota Way philosophy. The errors, it turned out, were due to design as well as quality-control problems. While these events took place, competitors like GM and others offered rebates for customers to switch from Toyota and to buy their cars. Toyota, meanwhile, promised that its global quality committee would become more responsive to consumer concerns.

## Prior to and After the 2014–2015 Price Collapse

How did Toyota's strategies change before and after the 2014–2015 collapse in gas and oil prices? The analysis that follows examines the company's perceptions of the risks and uncertainties and its assumptions about the future, based on its annual reports and other communications to shareholders.[15] It shows how the company, like GM, Ford, and VW, hedged its bets by focusing on operations, especially safety and quality and by choosing the countries in which it would be involved, the brands and models it would bring to market, and the R&D it would do. Toyota's performance affected the moves it made in these years, and these moves in turn had an impact on its performance.

### Toyota before the 2014–2015 Price Collapse

**Perceptions of the Risks and Uncertainties**
The two broad categories of risk and uncertainty on which Toyota focused were industry and business and legal and political.

*Industry and Business*
The worldwide automotive market was competitive and volatile across many factors – quality, safety, reliability, fuel economy, innovation, pricing, service, financing, and vehicle features. Competition among companies was intensifying. Sector reorganization was possible; growth

in emerging markets was slowing. The global economy had not yet fully recovered. Demand shifts were taking place because of technological disruption. Incentives, fuel costs, and government taxes and tariffs affected global demand. Demand was unstable in nearly every market in which Toyota operated. Should the world economy deteriorate, Toyota and its suppliers might not be able to raise sufficient capital to operate. Economic and political instability, fuel shortages, war, terrorism, labor strikes, and natural calamities affected Toyota. Its operations were subject to currency and interest rate fluctuations, including the effects of the yen's value against the dollar, a problem it had to deal with through local production and financial derivatives. High prices for raw materials such as steel, precious metals, aluminum, and plastic also were a concern. Toyota could not count on growing sales. To maintain its market position, the company had to respond vigorously to changing customer preferences for quality, safety, reliability, styling, and other features. With no assurance that it would succeed, it had to introduce in a timely way new vehicles at competitive prices that met rapidly changing preferences. If the company failed to reduce its development times, it would lose market share, sales, and margins.

To respond to these challenges, Toyota had to have the right technology in place. It needed a capacity for cost reduction. It had to have a supply chain sturdy enough to avoid delays. It required marketing and distribution wherewithal. It had to be able to implement safety changes rapidly to protect its image in the event or recalls. Its digital information technology networks and systems would have to stand up to malfeasance and attacks. It had little leeway for slippage.

### Legal and Political

At the same time that industry and business risks existed, there were legal and political ones. The automotive industry was subject to many governmental regulations including safety, environmental, fuel economy, and noise regulations. The threat existed of new policies or changes to existing policies. Countries had different vehicle safety and emission standards. Governments recalled vehicles that did not comply with safety standards. Aggrieved citizens sued the company. Governments also imposed tariffs and trade restrictions

**Vehicle Safety:** In 2009, the European Commission established a simplified framework, repealing more than fifty existing directives regarding vehicle safety, other than pedestrian protection, and replacing them with a single standard aimed at incorporating UNECE (United Nations Economic Commission for Europe) standards. The goal of UNECE standards, implemented in 2012, was to protect vulnerable persons from collisions and introduce new preventive safety technology such as lane-departure warning, emergency braking for pedestrian protection, and blind-spot monitors. The standards included gearshift indicators, seat-belt reminders, alcohol interlocks, speed management, and electric car requirements such as charging infrastructure and batteries. They also incorporated an emergency call system and required advanced safety systems such as electronic stability control, low-rolling resistance tires, tire-pressure monitoring, emergency braking, and lane departure warnings. While originally based on European regulations, many countries adopted the UNECE standards, including Japan, Thailand, Russia, South Africa, Morocco, Malaysia, Egypt, China, and India. Chinese vehicle safety regulations, drafted with reference to UNECE, had nearly the same coverage, with the addition of distinct Chinese features. Japan also brought its standards in line with UNECE. As a result, it updated requirements for electric vehicle recharging and introduced new approaches for lane departure warnings, emergency braking, forward field vision, child restraints, car windows, temporary parts, tire pressure monitoring, steering, braking override, interior fittings, anti-spinal injury measures, and anti-drink-driving measures.

**The National Highway Traffic Safety Administration (NHTSA):** NHTSA enforced US standards. It had the right to investigate complaints relating to vehicle safety and to order manufacturers to recall and repair vehicles found to have safety-related defects. The cost of these recalls could be substantial depending on the nature of the repair and the number of vehicles affected. The standards emphasized rollovers; tire-, lock-, roof-, and side-impact protection; seat belts; and power windows. NHTSA considered requiring rearview camera systems to prevent vehicles that were backing up from hitting children and child-restraint systems to protect children in the case of side crashes. Also of interest to the agency was the creation of standard warning sounds for electric and hybrid vehicles. In response to the unintended acceleration issue in 2010, NHTSA had examined ways to strengthen brake override systems, standardize push-start switches, and have event data recorders in vehicles.

**The EU, Emissions Control, and Fuel Economy:** As with vehicle safety, the world had adopted two different approaches to emissions control and fuel economy, one emanating from the EU and the other from the United States. The EU signed the Kyoto Protocol and agreed to reduce carbon dioxide emissions by 8 percent from 2008 to 2012 as measured by the base year of 1990. It reached a voluntary agreement with the European Automotive Manufacturers Association (ACEA) for an average emissions target of 140 grams of carbon dioxide per kilometer for new cars sold in the European Union in 2008. The Japan Automobile Manufacturers Association and the

Korean Automobile Manufacturers Association reached similar agreements. In 2008, the European Parliament lowered the standard to 130 grams of carbon dioxide per kilometer by 2012 for passenger cars, phased in gradually to 100 percent of new cars sold in 2015. In 2014, it went further and reduced the average carbon dioxide emissions targets for light commercial vehicles to 147 grams per kilometer beginning in 2020 and 95 grams per kilometer for passenger cars beginning in 2021. It also strengthened its standards to limit further emissions of diesel-powered vehicles and bring them down to a level equivalent to gasoline-powered vehicles. An increasing number of EU states also had vehicle tax laws based on carbon dioxide emission levels, a trend that was expected to continue.

The US Approach: In the United States, the California Air Resources Board (CARB) had the right to set its own standards separate from the federal government. It had adopted a zero-emission vehicles requirement for model years 2005 and beyond. Vehicles such as PHV (plug-in hybrid vehicles), hybrid cars, and alternative fuel vehicles had limited qualification as EVs (electronic vehicles) or FCVs. Toyota's battery-powered RAV4 EV compact sport utility vehicle and the Toyota FCHV qualified as a zero-emission vehicle, while the Prius plug-in hybrid and Prius and Camry hybrids qualified as a partial zero-emission vehicle. In 2012, CARB approved a new emission-control program for model years 2017–2025 called Advanced Clean Cars, for which it was developing its rules. The states of New York, Massachusetts, Connecticut, Maine, Maryland, New Jersey, New Mexico, Oregon, Pennsylvania, Rhode Island, Vermont, Washington, Delaware, and Colorado either adopted or planned to adopt regulations substantially similar to California's. To comply, Toyota would have to develop advanced alternative fuel technologies that qualified as zero-emission vehicles or partial zero-emission vehicles. In 2014, the US Environmental Protection Agency (EPA) strengthened standards for volatile organic compounds, nitrogen oxides, particulate matter, and fuel vapor emissions in phases starting in 2017 through 2025 to bring them in line with California standards. A 2007 US Supreme Court ruling gave the EPA the authority to regulate automotive greenhouse gases. In 2010, the EPA and NHTSA issued rules for 2012 through 2016 of a combined average emissions level of 250 grams of carbon dioxide per mile, equivalent to 35.5 miles per gallon. NHTSA set 2025 Corporate Average Fuel Economy (CAFE) standards at 163 grams of carbon dioxide per mile, which was equivalent to 54.5 miles per gallon. These standards were subject to reevaluation by 2018. In 2010, the EPA also approved the sale and use of fuel with a 15 percent ethanol blend (E15). The Alliance of Automobile Manufacturers (the Auto Alliance), of which Toyota was a part, appealed, and a Supreme Court decision was pending.

**Outside the EU and the United States:** Outside the EU, Japan, and the United States, other nations were also proactively introducing emission regulations. Canada's were similar to those in the United States. Compliance with Chinese emission control standards presented significant technological challenges and would require significant expenditures. The Chinese standards called for the development of advanced technologies, such as high-performance batteries and catalytic converters, as well as alternative fuel technologies. Manufacturers that were unable to develop commercially viable technologies within the time frames set by the standards had to decrease the number of types of vehicles they could sell. Other countries, such as Korea, Mexico, Brazil, Taiwan, and India, were introducing their own fuel-consumption regulations.

## Assumptions

Toyota had assumptions about the business environment, overcapacity in the automotive sector, regulation, climate change, the vision to which it adhered, and its relations to customers.

### The Business Environment

In 2013–2014, the economies of developed countries strengthened, while emerging countries' economies slowed. They did not keep pace with Japan, which expanded, and China, which accelerated, reaching double-digit growth. Nonetheless, Toyota expected future growth to come mainly from emerging countries, where automotive companies would intensively compete. Their competition would center on compact and low-price vehicles, technological change, new products, heightened global awareness of the environment, and stringent fuel economy standards.

### Overcapacity

The automotive industry might have to consolidate because of overcapacity. Auto companies had reduced costs by introducing common vehicle platforms and sharing R&D expenses for environmental and other technology. Increasingly, they were relying on alliances and joint ventures. Toyota's strategic advantages were in research and development of environmentally friendly new vehicle technologies, vehicle safety, and information technology.

### Regulation

Regulation aimed at enhancing vehicle safety, reducing harmful effects on the environment, and improving fuel economy significantly affected the industry and added to the costs of doing business. Regulation also mandated procurement of local parts and imposed tariffs and other barriers that limited operational alternatives and curbed the ability to return profits to an automaker's home country.

### Climate Change

The Intergovernmental Panel on Climate Change (IPCC) Fifth Assessment Report came out in 2013–2014. Warming of the climate system was unequivocal; the oceans were already warmer, and human activities were the main cause. The likely results would be increased frequency of adverse weather events including very heavy precipitation, high wind levels, and an increase in tropical cyclones. Climate change would also increase droughts, reduce biological diversity, and harm agricultural productivity. Japan already had felt the impact. Toyota was committed to a reduction in gases that contribute to global warming, but the whole world would have to be involved in building a low-carbon society and reduce the amount of these emissions.

### The Vision

Toyota's vision, unveiled in 2011, started with safety – the company's highest priority. Next came environmental quality, followed by exceeding customer expectations and contributing to human happiness, enriching lives, generating employment, and having good relationships with dealers and suppliers. The company was dedicated to quality, innovation, and affordable prices. It also aimed for continued awareness of the earth and environment, energy conservation, and reduction of carbon dioxide emissions. It hoped to lead the way to the future of mobility by spawning next-generation transportation in which personal mobility and information technology converged. The objective was to meet challenging goals, exceed expectations, and regularly seek to find a better way forward.

### Consumer Gratitude

Toyota owed a profound sense of gratitude to its customers; therefore, it wanted to make ever-better cars. In developing countries, it would provide customers with innovative products. For the luxury Lexus, the aim was to be an unparalleled premium brand. Its new global architecture allowed it to redo work procedures and assisted it in launching attractive products globally in a timely and efficient manner.

## Toyota after the 2014–2015 Price Collapse

### Perceptions of the Risks and Uncertainties

Toyota remained focused on the same categories of risks and uncertainties: industry and business and legal and political ones.

### Industry and Business

The timely introduction of new and redesigned vehicles was necessary to satisfy customer needs. The company's ability to satisfy changing customer preferences would have significant effects on the company's revenues and earnings. Many factors affected its profitability. The most important were sales and the mix of vehicle models and options. Also important were parts and service along with the warranties it offered. Price discounts, incentives, and marketing costs affected the amount of money it made. The company was concerned about its costs – there were R&D and raw material costs (steel, precious metals, non-ferrous alloys, aluminum, and plastic). There were the costs of the parts and components suppliers charged the company. To remain competitive, the company had to keep costs down. As it was a global company, it also had to deal with fluctuating currency values. In addition, it faced the threat of potential production interruptions because of natural calamities or other factors. Further, the extremely competitive nature of the worldwide automotive industry exerted pressure on the company.

Maintaining its global market share in these circumstances was not easy. Toyota had no guarantees that it would be able to succeed. Many of the factors that affected it were not within its control, as a host of social, political, and economic conditions influenced consumers' ability and willingness to purchase vehicles. The company faced many challenges:

- It had to respond adequately and appropriately to changing customer preferences and demand in a timely way.
- It had to stay on top of changes in quality, safety, reliability, styling, and other features.
- It had to manufacture vehicles in the most cost-efficient way possible to remain competitive.
- It required up-to-date sales techniques and distribution networks to reach customers.
- It was highly dependent on suppliers – they could not fail to deliver on time.

- The company relied on financial institutions for the credit Toyota and its customers needed – they had to stay solvent.
- The digital and information technology the company used was subject to potential disruptions and shutdowns due to hacker attacks, computer viruses, breaches, errors, and malfeasance.

The company also had to avoid adverse media attention that could negatively affect its brand and its image. While global demand for automobiles was picking up, it was not yet strong enough for Toyota to be comfortable. The US market had revived and personal consumption was growing, but the Japanese and European recoveries were moderate, and sales in these regions were not vibrant. There was some weakness in China and emerging Asian nations as well.

### Legal and Political

The company was concerned about unpredictable legal and political changes. Changes in regulations, government policies, and governmental actions could negatively affect its profitability. The laws, regulations, and policies of most concern related to vehicle safety and the environment and fuel economy.

**Vehicle Safety:** With regard to safety, recalls would be particularly damaging. Different parts of the globe had implemented different requirements. Japanese standards were largely in line with the UN regulations. Standards for filament light bulbs, gas-discharge light sources, and LEDs took effect in 2015, and those for fire prevention and side impact would take effect in 2018. Standards for vehicle exterior tire noise, friction force, and wet road rolling resistance applied in stages over four years to commence in 2018, while standards relating to illumination of rear registration plates would take effect in 2020. Unique Japanese guidelines for remote-controlled parking assistance systems and response systems for driver emergencies already were in place, while the Japanese government was considering measures for hybrid quietness, brake overrides, and stronger anti-spinal injury and anti-drink-driving standards.

**The EU:** The EU submitted a proposal clarifying recall requirements in 2016 and proposed a roadmap for the introduction of autonomous vehicles, with final authorization possible in 2017. Europe had decided to implement an emergency call system in 2018. The EU published a final report on the benefits and feasibility of a range of new safety technologies and planned to propose amendments to UN rules regarding matters the UN regulated. The goal was to have the new regulations take effect in 2020, although the target date of each regulation would vary. The possibility of regulation of information and advanced driver-assistance systems for 2020 and beyond was under consideration. Also under consideration was the regulation of advanced emergency braking, blind-spot monitors to detect pedestrians, lane departure warnings, and alcohol interlock devices.

**Other Countries:** China planned to put in place regulations related to airbags batteries, electric motors, and the charging of electric vehicles. The US NHTSA proposed amending safety standards regarding child restraint systems to improve ease of use, as well as the standard for seatbelt assembly anchors. In 2016, it proposed changes to safety standards for electrical shock protection in electric and hydrogen FCVs. In that year, NHTSA, the Insurance Institute for Highway Safety, and twenty vehicle manufacturers agreed to standardize automatic emergency brake equipment by 2022.

**Emissions and Fuel Economy:** Under the Clean Air Act, the EPA was required to review and possibly revise ambient air quality standards for six criteria pollutants, including for ozone and particulate matter every five years. It scheduled a review to start in 2015, which could also lead to additional pollution control requirements and costs. In 2015, the EPA adopted final rules to limit the use of various hydrofluorocarbons (HFCs) and HFC-containing refrigerant blends used in motor vehicle air conditioning systems for new vehicles. The final rules listed HFC-134a, the most dominant refrigerant used in vehicles worldwide, as unacceptable for use in air conditioning systems in new vehicles beginning in 2021, along with other refrigerant blends as unacceptable that were to be eliminated starting in 2017. Feasible alternatives to these refrigerants were costly and presented other problems, such as flammability and safety concerns. An EU directive on motor vehicle air conditioning units required manufacturers to replace currently used refrigerants with refrigerants having a lower global warming impact for all newly registered vehicles starting in 2017.

**Assumptions**
Toyota laid out its assumptions about the global economy, sector competition, its vision, the environment, and new types of mobility.

*The Global Economy*
The US economy would experience steady growth, while Japan's economy would lack strength, as job market improvement had not sufficiently affected income, and consumption remained low. Europe's recovery had been gradual, and monetary authorities were easing credit to create more growth. The Chinese economy had not been as strong as anticipated. Emerging market growth was slow due to weak local currencies. Nonetheless, Toyota expected growth in the automotive market to come principally from emerging markets.

*Competition*
Global competition would remain very intense. The focus would be on compact and low-price vehicles, new technologies, and new products, and heightened global awareness of the environment and fuel economy would be major factors.

*The Vision*
The basis for the company's vision was its commitment to safety, the environment, product quality, continuous innovation, customer happiness, economic vitality, and enriching lives. It cared deeply about its customers, seeking to exceed their expectations and earn their "smiles." To achieve the vision, Toyota restructured its organization in 2016, establishing product- and region-based entities in addition to the head office. At the product-based level, it streamlined operations from planning through manufacturing to enable quick, independent decision making. It aimed to increase closeness to customers by means of region-based units, while the head office worked toward realizing an overall plan and allocating resources.

*The Natural Environment*
Toyota would tackle environmental challenges via development and promotion of next-generation vehicles, including hybrid and FCVs. Efficient production put less of a burden on the environment. Vehicles and batteries had to be recycled and trees planted to promote harmony with nature and preservation of the ecosystem. Yet these activities were not sufficient given the seriousness of global warming, water shortages, resource depletion, and biodiversity degradation. In response to the situation, Toyota announced its 2050 Environmental Challenge in 2015, with the aim of reducing the environmental impact of vehicles as much as possible as well as moving

toward a net positive impact that would contribute to the realization of a sustainable society. The company promised to try to achieve a number of goals:

- zero-$CO_2$ emissions new vehicles;
- zero-$CO_2$ life-cycle emissions;
- zero-$CO_2$ manufacturing emissions;
- optimal water usage;
- establishment of recycling systems;
- moving society toward greater harmony with nature.

It would collaborate with stakeholders to gather new ideas and apply technology to tackle these problems.

### New Types of Mobility

Toyota saw a need to become involved in the development of automated driving technology. Fierce competition in this domain would intensify on a global scale. Toyota had to make progress in pioneering such new technologies, products, and businesses.

## Hedging

How did Toyota's strategies change before and after the 2014–2015 collapse in gas and oil prices? Based on its annual reports and other communications to shareholders, the analysis that follows examines how the company hedged its bets by focusing on operations, especially safety and quality and by choosing the countries in which it would be involved, the brands and models it would bring to market, and the R&D it would undertake.

### Before the 2014–2015 Price Collapse

#### (1) Assuring Quality and Safety

Toyota had a history as a quality leader, which was associated with the Toyota Way. After the unintended acceleration issue, it made efforts to upgrade its safety and its environmental programs.

### The Toyota Way

Toyota was a pioneer in the creation of the internationally recognized system of production known as the Toyota Way. Two facets of the system, designed to enhance quality and efficiency, were: (i) just in time, in which suppliers manufactured and delivered necessary parts and components in the right quantity when the company needed them; and (ii) work stoppages, in which workers could stop work immediately when production problems arose. The goal was to provide flexibility in responding to changing consumer demand without sacrificing quality or increasing costs. Employees identified issues and analyzed them at the company's production sites, being open about the process in which they engaged and taking actions to address problems they identified at source. Employees only resumed manufacturing after the company fixed the defects they identified. The system relied on a sophisticated communication system that spread awareness of the problems the employees had found and how the company had fixed them. Before Toyota produced new vehicle prototypes, it incorporated lessons in simulations that took into account the different steps in assembling a vehicle. The company had training centers in North America, Europe, and Asia, where managers and supervisors, new hires, and workers received similar training in the system. The emphasis was on continuous improvement and creating ever-better cars. Professional trainers trained trainees to become trainers.

### Safety as the Highest Priority

The unintended acceleration issue came as a rude shock. Toyota thus established a special quality committee to investigate the causes, review its processes, and implement improvements. It had a third-party evaluation carried out by the Union of Japanese Scientists and Engineers, as well assessments carried out by other external experts. It reaffirmed that safety was its highest priority; that its goal was to eliminate all casualties with safer vehicles, better infrastructure, and by means of driver education. The World Health Organization (WHO) reported that 1.24 million people died globally in traffic accidents each year, making them the eighth-leading cause of death. The number of deaths had declined in Japan, North America, and Europe, but in emerging nations, the number was growing. Traffic fatalities likely would be the fifth-leading cause of death in the world by 2030. Toyota aimed to have in place an integrated safety system that functioned before an accident, during every driving stage of driving, and after an accident, if it was unpreventable. The company analyzed accidents and incorporated what it learned into vehicle development, seeking optimal systems for every driving scenario it could identify.

Table 15.1 *Toyota's advanced automated driving technology for improved intersection safety*

| | |
|---|---|
| Vehicle-to-infrastructure | When waiting at an intersection with a traffic signal to make a turn across oncoming traffic, in-road sensors would detect and gather information concerning oncoming vehicles and pedestrians crossing the road and provide warnings to drivers. |
| Vehicle-to-vehicle | At intersections with poor visibility, the sensors would detect the presence and behavior of nearby vehicles and provide warnings. |
| Vehicle-to-pedestrian | The sensors also would gather information on the presence of bicycle riders and pedestrians from devices in their possession and notify drivers. |

Derived from Toyota annual reports

Though fatal accidents involving pedestrians and drivers were lower in Japan, among those aged sixty-five and older the decline had been slow. Approximately half of accidents in which the elderly were involved occurred at or near intersections. Toyota, therefore, was working on deploying advanced automated driving technology – vehicle-infrastructure cooperative systems that provided drivers with information about approaching vehicles and pedestrians, as a way to prevent accidents (Table 15.1).

Toyota's vehicles won many safety awards. In 2013, the Japan New Car Assessment Program (JNCAP) awarded the Crown Royal and Crown Athlete sedans five stars, its highest rank. The former model received the highest score ever for the program. These cars were equipped with a pre-collision system with enhanced brake assist and automatic braking functions, intelligent clearance sonar that reduced damage from accidents caused by pedal misapplication, and drive start control that limited sudden starts when operating the gear shift. They had advanced active safety systems including a panoramic view monitor and adaptive high beam, which provided forward visibility when driving at night.

A number of systems in the vehicles provided additional levels of safety. They included automatic driving cruise control, which relied on wireless communications with a preceding vehicle to maintain a safe distance, and lane control, which aided steering along an optimal route based on lane markings and other information. These controls reduced unnecessary acceleration and deceleration and contributed to improved fuel efficiency and lower traffic congestion. The Crown Royal had an impact-absorbing body and high-rigidity cabin and had seven airbags and seatbelt reminders as standard features. Hybrid models also featured a vehicle body structure that would reduce injury to pedestrians.

### The Natural Environment

With regard to the environment, Toyota pursued the goal of zero emissions by implementing preventive measures, supporting government policies, disclosing information, and promoting awareness. It was seeking to further expand its hybrid vehicle lineup and increase global sales of these vehicles to more than 6 million units. It reduced global $CO_2$ emissions per vehicle produced by 35 percent in comparison to 2001 and was engaged in efforts to reduce $CO_2$ emissions further. It relied on an eco-vehicle assessment system to carry out systematic analysis of a vehicle's impact on the environment over the life cycle from production to disposal. It had conducted life-cycle assessments of eight new and fully redesigned models.

### (2) Investing in Global Markets

Toyota hedged its bets by both selling and producing vehicles in many different global markets. It sold vehicles in approximately 170 countries and regions, and, along with affiliated companies, produced automobiles in more than fifty overseas facilities in twenty-seven countries. Outside of Japan, it had manufacturing plants in the United States, Canada, the United Kingdom, France, Turkey, Thailand, China, Taiwan, India, Indonesia, South Africa, Australia, Argentina, and Brazil. In addition, it made Daihatsu vehicles in Japan and in three countries outside it, including Indonesia and Malaysia, and it made Hino-brand vehicles in Japan and in ten other countries outside it, including Indonesia and Thailand. Toyota manufactured about three-quarters of the vehicles it sold overseas in overseas locations. Its primary markets were Japan, North America, Europe, and Asia. From 2012 to 2014, the company's highest unit sales were in North America (Figure 15.2). However, global sales in millions of yen were higher in Japan than North America (Figure 15.3). Compared to 2010, Toyota's North American market share fell from 16.2 percent in 2010 to 13.6 percent in 2014 (Figure 15.4).

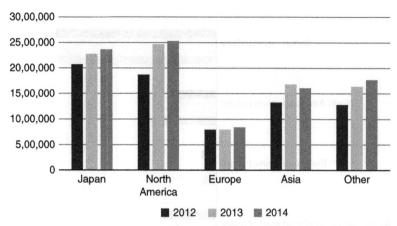

**Figure 15.2** Toyota's global unit sales 2012–2014
Derived from Toyota annual reports

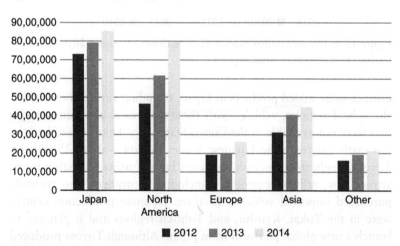

**Figure 15.3** Toyota's 2012–2014 global sales in millions of yen
Derived from Toyota annual reports

The diversity of markets in which it participated provided a hedge against weakness in any one of them. Toyota aimed to increase local production in emerging countries throughout the world.

*Japan*
The reason Toyota had greater revenue in Japan than in North America, despite selling fewer vehicles, was that it had introduced

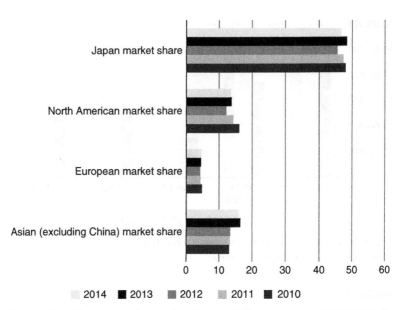

Japan market share

North American market share

European market share

Asian (excluding China) market share

0    10    20    30    40    50    60

2014   ■ 2013   ■ 2012   ■ 2011   ■ 2010

**Figure 15.4** Toyota's global market share in different regions 2010–2014
Derived from Toyota annual reports

distinct value-added products in Japan, including various Lexus models, hybrid vehicles, vehicles with three-seat rows, and mini-vehicles that were not available in the United States. The Lexus brand had the top market share in the Japanese luxury market – about 25 percent. Toyota sought to distinguish the Lexus brand further by continuing to attract new, affluent customers, including customers who typically purchased imported vehicles. Its three Japanese production centers were in the Tokai, Kyushu, and Tohoku regions and it planned to launch a new global platform from Japan. Although Toyota produced vehicles outside Japan, its Japanese operations were the source of its innovative manufacturing practices, which it tried to export to other countries. Home to five major domestic manufacturers and five specialized producers, Japan was a very competitive market, one that received a growing number of imports from the United States and Europe. The prolonged economic slump in the Japanese economy and increased environmental awareness were shifting consumer preferences toward more affordable automobiles. Although, for more than forty years, Toyota had maintained its position as the dominant producer in Japan, it could not be complacent.

## North America

After Japan, North America was Toyota's most significant market. Toyota struggled in North America after the 2008 financial crisis and the unintended acceleration issue hurt its mage. The United States was the most important part of this market, and Toyota was trying to rely more on local production; the company had North American production facilities in many states, including Indiana, Texas, Kentucky, West Virginia, and Mississippi, as well as in Mexico and Canada. It also had a separate North American Technical Center that spearheaded vehicle design, planning, and evaluation and it planned to locate its North American headquarters in Plano, Texas. The company had a wide lineup of vehicles that it offered for sale in North America. The Prius was Toyota's bestselling model in North America after the Corolla and Camry. Toyota also sold hybrids under the Lexus and Avalon brands and hoped to expand Lexus sales in North America by introducing new models.

## Europe

Toyota's principal competitors in Europe were VW, Renault, Ford, Opel, Peugeot, Hyundai, and Kia. The company produced vehicles in the United Kingdom, Turkey, Russia, and France as well as having a joint venture with PSA Peugeot Citroën, but because of slack demand in Europe, it was cutting back on European production. Although competition in this market was intense, Toyota's sales in 2013 in Europe exceeded the previous year's figures due to the introduction of new models, recovery in the Western European economy, and increased Russian sales. It aimed grow its product lineup while at the same time being attentive to the market's weakness. It planned to have an expanded lineup of hybrid models. It entered into supply agreements with BMW for diesel engines and with PSA Peugeot Citroën for light commercial ones.

## Asia

Because of high growth expectations, the Asian market was very important and Toyota planned to strengthen and solidify its business position by improving its product lineup, expanding local procurement, and increasing production capacities. It produced vehicles in Thailand, Indonesia, India, the Philippines, Malaysia, India, Taiwan, and Vietnam. Toyota made Camry hybrids and the Prius in Thailand. In India, it produced and sold the Etios compact, which it designed specifically for that market, but also exported to South Africa.

The company produced and sold Camry hybrids in Taiwan and sold US-produced Camrys in Korea. The Thailand plant produced the Hilux and Fortuner for sale outside of Asia, including in Australia and in the Middle East.

## China

Like other automobile makers, Toyota was working with joint venture partners in China. It had two major partners. With FAW, it launched the Vios, and produced and sold nine other models, including the Land Cruiser Prado, Corolla, Crown, REIZ, Coaster, RAV4, and Prius. With Guangzhou, it made the Camry, Yaris, Highlander, E'z, and CVT. Total vehicle sales in the Chinese market increased 14 percent in 2013. In the passenger vehicle market, Toyota had a market share of 6 percent. It planned to increase sales by expanding dealer numbers and product offerings for locally produced and imported vehicles, particularly in inland China. It also planned to open a plant to produce hybrid vehicle batteries.

## The Rest of the World

Toyota's vehicle sales in other regions in the world grew by 7.8 percent from 2013 to 2014. Part of the reason for the growth was strong Etios sales. The main models sold in these regions were the Corolla, Hilux, and Camry. The company had production facilities in Argentina, Brazil, and Egypt, but decided to end production in Australia by 2017. Toyota expected that South and Central America, Oceania, Africa, and the Middle East would become increasingly important and planned to develop new products for these regions' needs.

### (3) Adjusting the Brand and Model Mix

Toyota also hedged its bets with the sale of different types of vehicles. The two main types were conventional engine vehicles and hybrids. The product lineup included mini-vehicles, subcompacts, compacts, mid-size, luxury, sports, specialty, recreational, sport utility, pickups, mini-vans, trucks, and buses. The company also sold FCVs.

## Conventional Vehicles

Toyota had a broad lineup of conventional vehicles:

- **Mini-Vehicles.** Daihatsu manufactured and sold mini-vehicles with small engines as well as passenger vehicles, commercial vehicles, and auto parts under its own brand and the Toyota brand. It sold approximately 900,000 vehicles in 2014, its largest market being Japan itself, which accounted for approximately 80 percent of its 2014 sales.

• **Subcompact and Compact.** The Corolla was one of the world's bestselling models. The Yaris, marketed as the Vitz in Japan, was a subcompact designed to perform with comfort and low emissions – features particularly attractive in Europe. In Japan, Toyota had the micro-premium iQ and remodeled Passo, Ractis, Vitz, Corolla, Porte, Spade, and Auris. It introduced the Etios and Vios in India, Asia, China, and other markets. It sold the Scion as a sports model that targeted at young US drivers.

• **Mid-Size.** Toyota's mid-size models included the Camry, the bestselling passenger car in the United States for every year but one from 1997 to 2014. Along with the hybrid version, US sales were above 400,000 units. Toyota's other mid-size models were the REIZ in China, the Avensis in Europe, and the Mark X in Japan.

• **Luxury and Full-Size.** Toyota sold luxury vehicles under the Lexus brand. Lexus models included the LX, the GX, and the RX. The RX was a sport utility vehicle Toyota sold in the United States. The company's full-size cars were the Avalon, Crown, and Century.

• **Sports Utilities and Trucks.** The sport utility vehicles the company offered in North America were the Venza, Sequoia, 4Runner, RAV4, Highlander, FJ Cruiser, and Land Cruiser. The pickup trucks were the Tacoma and Tundra. The company manufactured the Sequoia, Highlander, Tacoma, and Tundra in the United States, while it manufactured the RX and RAV4 in Canada. Toyota's pickup truck, the Hilux, was Thailand's bestselling truck brand.

• **Minivans.** Toyota had many different versions. It sold the Alphard, Vellfire, Wish, and Noah/Voxy, in Europe, the Corolla Verso, the Estima, Sienta, and Isis in Japan, and the Sienna in North America.

• **Trucks and Buses.** Both Toyota and its subsidiary Hino sold trucks and buses. Hino had a significant share of the Japanese large truck market, and Toyota and Hino had significant shares of the small microbus market.

*Hybrids*

The Prius, the world's first mass-produced hybrid, ran on a combination of electric motor and gasoline engine, which allowed it to achieve better gas mileage than other vehicles of comparable size and performance. Its design resulted in 75 percent fewer emissions than Japanese regulations allowed. It was the cornerstone of Toyota's emphasis on eco-friendly transportation, but the company also had other hybrid models, such as the hybrid Crown it sold in Japan and the Lexus hybrid it sold in Japan, North America, and Europe. As of 2014, it sold thirty hybrid models in eighty countries. These included the Auris, Avalon, Camry, Corolla, Harrier, Voxy, and Noah. The number of hybrids that Toyota sold as a percentage of all vehicles it sold was growing. Worldwide sales of its hybrids topped 6 million units in 2014, and the company anticipated continued strong demand and therefore planned further ways to enhance its lineup. It calculated that as of 2014, hybrids had resulted in approximately 43 million fewer tons of $CO_2$ emissions than would have been emitted by gasoline vehicles of similar size and performance and saved about 16 million kiloliters of gasoline compared to similarly sized gasoline vehicles.

*Fuel-Cell Vehicles*
Convinced that hydrogen based-energy would someday play a central role in creating a more sustainable society, Toyota had a strong commitment to fuel cells. As supplies of oil and other fossil fuels became exhausted, demand for automobiles would grow among consumers in emerging economies, and, to satisfy this need, automakers had to diversify the energy sources on which they relied and had to hedge their bets and include fuel cells in the mix on which they counted. An advantage of hydrogen was that it was universally available; the sources were not concentrated in a few strategically important countries. An additional advantage was that it did not release carbon dioxide or other noxious emissions. Hydrogen had greater energy density than batteries, allowing for a longer cruising range, and it fueled more quickly. Thus, as far back as 2002, Toyota had started to experiment with hydrogen. It began limited sales of a fuel-cell hybrid vehicle in Japan and the United States and made breakthroughs in the technologies fuel cell engines needed for start-up and for cruising at below-freezing temperatures. In 2014, it launched a fuel cell sedan, and carried out trials of fuel cell buses, and forklifts. Yoshikazu Tanaka, who had been in charge of the Prius plug-in hybrid development, was the head its hydrogen project.

The spread of FCVs, fueled by hydrogen, however, depended on the availability of hydrogen infrastructure. The Japanese government took initial steps toward creating infrastructure for FCVs in Japan.

It promised to set up about 100 hydrogen fueling stations, mainly in Japan's four major metropolitan areas. Another issue it dealt with was the technology of the tanks and their safety. It passed legislation, which established standards for the tanks and their safe deployment.

## (4) Innovating

Toyota had fourteen major global research centers (Table 15.2) and its research expenditures were growing. They were approximately ¥910.5 billion in 2014 and had been ¥807.4 billion in 2013 and ¥779.8 billion in 2012. Yet Toyota recognized that the effectiveness of R&D was hard to measure, subject to factors outside its control, such as the advances competitors might make and the ability of its engineers and scientists to convert R&D into commercial successes. Toyota had a number of R&D themes including production efficiency; environment and energy, safety; and advanced mobility and intelligent transport.

*Production Efficiency*
Vehicles had to be able to respond flexibly to changes in consumer needs. The company needed to improve the methods for their efficient development, production, and sale. It aimed to create methods for timely, appropriate responses, including optimizing and eliminating vehicle platforms, sharing parts and components, and shortening development times. It created a system for using simulation and a system for the design and manufacture of multiple models simultaneously. The company worked closely with suppliers to increase their efficiency, pursuing aggressive cost-reduction to eliminate waste, while ensuring reliability. It focused on global sourcing distribution programs, which yielded lower costs, thereby freeing ever more money for R&D.

*Environment, Energy, and Safety*
The company promoted next-generation environmentally friendly, energy-efficient, safe vehicle technology, aiming to lower the volume of carbon dioxide emissions at all operational stages from development, production, and logistics to usage, disposal, and recycling. It did R&D on materials suitable for recycling and on designs for vehicle dismantling. It sought to maintain a leadership position in environmental technology, hedging its bets with a wide range of projects:

- With regard to conventional engines, it was interested in both gasoline-engine fuel economy and clean diesel. For gasoline engines, its

**Table 15.2** *Toyota's major research centers*

| Facility | Principal activity |
|---|---|
| **Japan** | |
| Toyota Technical Center | Product planning, style, design, and evaluation |
| Tokyo Design Research and Laboratory | Advanced styling designs |
| Higashi-Fuji Technical Center | Advanced research and development |
| Shibetsu Proving Ground | Vehicle testing and evaluation |
| Tokyo Development Center | Advanced development of electronics |
| **US** | |
| Toyota Motor Engineering and Manufacturing North America | North American production and product planning, upper body planning, evaluation |
| Calty Design Research | Design |
| Toyota Research Institute of North America | Advanced research relating to energy and environment, safety, and mobility infrastructure |
| **Europe** | |
| Toyota Motor Europe | Production, planning, and evaluation of vehicles that are produced in Australia and Asia |
| Toyota Europe Design Development | Design |
| Toyota Motorsport | Development of motor sports vehicles |
| **Asia Pacific** | |
| Toyota Motor Asia Pacific Engineering and Manufacturing | Production, planning, and evaluation of vehicles that are produced in Australia and Asia |
| Toyota Technical Center Asia Pacific Australia | Production, planning, and evaluation of vehicles that are produced in Australia and Asia |
| **China** | |
| Toyota Motor Engineering and Manufacturing | Research of new, low-energy vehicle technology, vehicle evaluation, and quality assurance in China |

Derived from Toyota annual reports

interest was in variable valve systems, and for diesel engines, its interest was in particulate and nitrous oxide reduction systems.

- It also had a focus on hybrid technologies, the mass production of electric vehicles next-generation batteries, fuel cells, and biofuel vehicles. By 2015, Toyota planned to introduce a fuel-cell sedan at a reasonable price for customers in Japan, the United States, and Europe where appropriate infrastructure was available. It was investigating biofuels that did not compete with food production and genetically modified organism (GMO) technology as a way to process sugarcane more efficiently and aimed to introduce low-ethanol-content vehicles (E10), natural gas vehicles, and high-concentration flex-fuel vehicles (FFV) that were compatible with ethanol.

*Safety*

Toyota's work focused on the development of technologies designed to prevent accidents in the first instance, as well as the development of technologies that protected passengers and reduced the damage on impact in the event of an accident. Safety technologies in development included research on protecting senior citizens, autonomous driving, pre-collision systems, and data exchange to support advanced communications.

**Pre-Collision:** Toyota was the first auto manufacturer to have a pre-collision system that relied on sensors, wave radar, and cameras to detect objects presenting hazards, employed a brake assist mechanism to minimize speed on impact, and automatically applied the brakes when a collision was inevitable. Toyota called the system Vehicle Dynamics Integrated Management. It constantly monitored the driver and vehicle and managed the engine, steering mechanisms, and brakes. It was able to stabilize a vehicle before a driver lost control.

**Distracted and Impaired Driving:** The company focused on reducing the risk of distracted and impaired driving behaviors and protecting vulnerable demographics such as young children.

- A lane-keeping assist system used a camera to detect white or yellow lane markers while driving on a highway. The system assisted in the operation of the steering wheel; it helped to keep a vehicle traveling between the lane markers by controlling the steering and warned the driver if it detected possible deviation.

- Radar cruise control allowed a vehicle to keep a constant distance between itself and the preceding vehicle, automatically slowing it down and stopping if necessary to avoid collision.
- Blind spot monitor alerted a driver to vehicles in a blind spot while changing lanes with sound and visual display.
- The Intelligent Parking Assist System enabled a vehicle to be automatically steered when backing into a parking spot or parallel parking.
- For the Crown sold in Japan, Toyota developed a driver-monitoring pre-collision system that made sure that the driver's eyes were open and tracked the direction in which the driver was facing.

### Advanced Mobility and Intelligent Transport

Advanced mobility and intelligent transport was another research theme. The company was investigating next-generation information technology that connected people, cars and infrastructure, and communities. It was examining functions that went beyond running, turning, and stopping a vehicle, including information about: (i) maintenance; (ii) congestion, traffic, accidents, and parking; (iii) theft detection; and (iv) emergency calling. It had a big data program considering what technology could do to improve traffic flows and disaster responses, looking for applications that would ease traffic congestion in emerging nation urban areas, and accelerating its initiatives in mobility sharing and route guidance.

## After the 2014–2015 Price Collapse

### (1) Assuring Quality and Safety

No matter, where in the world, Toyota's top priorities continued to be safety, quality, and the environment, as it was convinced that these would strengthen its competitiveness.

### Quality

It remained faithful to the Toyota Way. For staff working on its vehicles, it had training in its culture and way of doing business. It incorporated ergonomics into vehicle development. It continued to pursue cost-cutting and waste elimination without sacrificing safety or reliability.

## Safety

Like other automakers, Toyota installed restraint devices like seatbelts, headrests, and airbags. It tested its vehicles for frontal, side, and rear collisions and rollover accidents using dummies to estimate injury rates. It installed tire-pressure warning systems, anti-lock brakes and traction, vehicle stability, and hill-assist controls. The company also had an emergency dispatch service, which provided automatic crash notification in the event of an accident. However, it went beyond standard tests and equipment by creating a safety sense package, which relied on an in-vehicle camera and front-grille-mounted radar to detect obstacles and automatically apply a vehicle's brakes to avoid collisions. This package had such features as pedestrian detection, lane departure alert, radar cruise control to keep the vehicle at a distance from the vehicle ahead, and automatic high beams. It won the New England Motor Press Association award in 2016, and although only a few models had it as an option in 2016, Toyota promised that by 2018, all US models would have it.

## The Environment

Through the development of redesigned engines, transmissions, and other components, Toyota aimed to improve its vehicles' environmental performance. It scheduled to deploy new powertrains in conventional gasoline-powered engines between 2017 and 2021. Its cumulative global sales of hybrids from 2000 to 2016 grew to over 14 million units. About half the sales were in Japan, and the other half in other countries. The company calculated that it had eliminated approximately 77 million tons of carbon emissions because of the hybrid vehicles it sold.

## (2) Investing in Global Markets

Toyota hedged its bets by being involved in markets in many countries. It sold vehicles in 190 countries and regions, but its primary markets were the world's largest auto markets, Japan, North America, Europe, and Asia. In 2016, 23.7 percent of the company's unit sales were in Japan, 32.7 percent in North America, 9.7 percent in Europe, 15.5 percent in Asia, and 18.4 percent in other markets. Toyota manufactured around 75 percent of the vehicles it sold in overseas markets in overseas plants it or affiliated companies operated. It manufactured approximately 72 percent of its North America sales in North American plants,

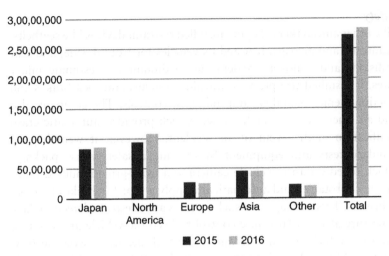

**Figure 15.5** Toyota's global unit sales 2015–2016
Derived from Toyota annual reports

and approximately 76 percent of its European sales in European plants.
From 2015 to 2016, Toyota's unit sales in North America grew more
rapidly than its sales anywhere else (Figure 15.6). Revenue in yen also
increased more in North America than elsewhere, but profits in Japan
were higher than profits in North America. Profits in North America
declined in 2016 while in Japan and Asia, they rose and revenue in Japan
continued to be greater than North American revenue (Figure 15.7).
The main reason for revenue growth in Japan was exchange rate fluctua-
tion, while low gas prices helped to create the sales increase in North
America. Like other automakers, Toyota was seeing increased interest in
sports utility vehicles in North America. European sales declined mainly
because of Russia.

*Japan*
Profits were strong in Japan because of better technology and the introduction of distinctive value-added products including new Lexus models,
hybrids, three-seat-row vehicles, and mini-vehicles. Toyota's domestic
market share grew from 46 percent in 2015 to 46.8 percent in 2016.

*North America*
Toyota reorganized production in North America in addition to
improving the product lineup. It tried to delegate additional decision
making to the North American operations. The new headquarters were

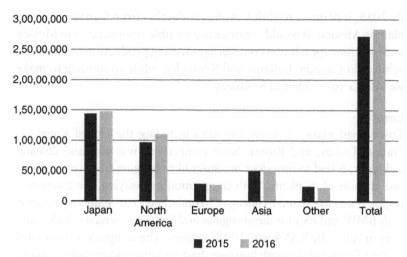

**Figure 15.6** Toyota's 2015–2016 global sales in millions of yen
Derived from Toyota annual reports

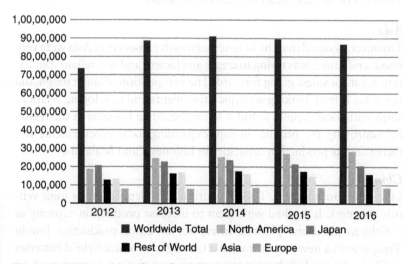

**Figure 15.7** Toyota's total number of vehicles sold 2012–2016
Derived from Toyota annual reports

located in the Dallas suburb Plano. The North American technical center spearheaded design, planning, and evaluation for the region. In 2015, Toyota entered into a long-term partnership with Mazda, which allowed it to produce light vehicles in Mazda's Mexican plant.

By 2019, it planned to shift Corolla production from Canada to a new plant in Mexico. It would continue to assemble compact cars in Mexico and in Mississippi. It was considering focusing production of mid-sized vehicles in Canada, Indiana, and Kentucky, while continuing to make various Lexus models in Kentucky.

### Europe

Toyota had plants in many countries including the United Kingdom, France, Turkey, and Russia. Since competition was stiff and demand lackluster, it had to introduce measures like changing from two shifts to one at some of its plants. With competition intensifying, the company's response was to expand its lineup of hybrids, enter into supply agreements with BMW and PSA for diesel engines and light commercial vehicles, and start to equip the RAV4 with BMW engines. The company actively tried to meet European demand; however, Eastern European economies, particularly Russia, continued to stagnate, mainly because of low oil prices. On the other hand, some regional markets grew rapidly. Annual sales in Turkey, Poland, and Israel reached record levels.

### Asia

Toyota considered that the long-term growth prospects in Asia were very good, and thus it was trying to create an efficient and self-reliant foundation for its business going forward. The competition, though tough, did not deter it from making strategic investments and developing relationships with local suppliers, and it strengthened its business in the region by improving the product lineup, expanding local procurement, and increasing its production capacities in Indonesia and Malaysia.

### China

Like other automakers, Toyota continued to depend on its joint venture partners. It worked with them to increase production capacity at a Sichuan plant and planned to replace an aging production line in Tianjin with a new one. It started a factory to produce hybrid batteries in China. Its market share in the country was about 6 percent, with its strengths being in engines smaller than 1.6-liters and increasingly SUVs. It tried to expand its Lexus sales in the country.

### Other Parts of the World

Toyota sales in other parts of the world (South and Central America, Oceania, Africa, and the Middle East) declined by 9.2 percent in 2016 compared to the previous year. The core models it sold in this region were the Corolla, Hilux, and Camry. Even with the decline, Toyota increased annual production capacity, as it expected the region to become progressively more important in the future. The company aimed to develop products to meet specific regional demands.

### (3) Adjusting the Brand and Model Mix

Toyota had hedged its bets well, but would the way it had hedged work as well in the future? In 2016, the Corolla was the bestselling car in the world, at more than 1.3 million vehicles. The Ford F-Series was second, at nearly 1 million vehicles; the VW Golf was a very close third, also at just under 1 million vehicles. The Toyota RAV4 was seventh, at about 0.72 million vehicles, and the Toyota Camry was tenth, at about 0.66 million vehicles. While Ford, VW, and Honda had two vehicles in the top ten, only Toyota had three vehicles in this category. However, Toyota had to be concerned, as Corolla sales were down 3.4 percent for the year, and Camry sales were down 11.5 percent for the year.

### Light Trucks

Given low gasoline prices, the bestselling vehicles in the United States were light trucks. The Ford F-Series, at 820,799 vehicles, saw sales grow by 5.2 percent in 2016 in comparison to 2015; and Chrysler RAM trucks, at 489,418 vehicles, saw sales increase by 8.7 percent. Toyota's RAV4 was the eighth most popular vehicle in the United States in 2016. At 352,139 vehicles sold, its sales were up 11.6 percent over the previous year. As a result of low gas prices, Toyota, like VW, had to put greater emphasis on recreational, sport utility vehicles, and pickup trucks. Other than the RAV4 that it sold in this category it sold the Sequoia, 4Runner, Highlander, FJ Cruiser, Land Cruiser, Tacoma, Tundra, Lexus SUVs, and the large minivans, the Alphard and Vellfire, in Japan and the Corolla Versa in Europe. Other minivans in its lineup were the Noah/Voxy, Esquire, Estima, Sienta in Japan, and the Sienna in North America. The buses and trucks it sold were under the Hino brand.

### Compacts and Subcompacts

The company was fighting the decline in compact and subcompact vehicles by introducing new models and remodeling old ones.

It introduced the Sienta and GS as new cars in Japan in 2016 and remodeled the Sienta, RX, Prius, and Passo. It bet heavily that the Scion iA, which Mazda designed, manufactured, and newly introduced to the market in 2015, would be a success. The mid-size models other than the Camry, which it sold, were the REIZ in China, the Avensis in Europe, and the Mark X in Japan. Its minivehicles bet was with Daihatsu, which sold about 5.6 million vehicles in Japan in 2016.

### Electrification

Toyota anticipated strong hybrid growth and hoped that a remodeled hybrid lineup could partially make up for the decline of the Corolla and Camry. Therefore, it enhanced hybrid engine power while improving fuel economy and put twenty-one new hybrid models on the market in 2015. At the same time, it announced that it was backing away from fully electric vehicles because of their range, costs, and how it long it took to charge them. Instead, the company was moving toward FCVs, where it offered the first mass-produced FCV MIRAI for sale in Japan in 2014 and in the United States and Europe in 2015.

### (4) Innovating

The company coordinated and integrated its R&D from basic to advanced research. It reviewed and evaluated projects to ensure that its investment in areas such as energy, the environment, information technology, telecommunications, and material would pay off. Its research expenditures remained substantial and continued to grow to ¥1,004 billion in 2015 and ¥1,055 billion in 2016. Its aims were to enhance vehicle functionality and increase the attractiveness of driving, make cars more comfortable and environmentally friendly, and help establish a low-carbon emission transportation system. It wanted to minimize the negative aspects of its vehicles, such as traffic accidents and environmental impact, and maximize driver gratification, comfort, and convenience. Strategic advantage would come if it could achieve early commercialization of next-generation environmentally friendly, energy-efficient, safe vehicles.

### Vehicle Functionality

Toyota was trying to enhance vehicle functionality in many ways. For instance, it connected vehicles to telecommunication systems and used communication sensor technologies for navigation. It gave drivers traffic, vehicle safety, and other real-time information, including parking maps. It operated emergency dial and threat protection systems. It collaborated with insurance companies and worked with a car-sharing company to advance big data research on changing mobility patterns.

### Driver Assistance

The driver assistance functions Toyota was developing had the aim of reducing the burden of driving and making it safer and more pleasurable. The company was commercializing ways to assist drivers in sensing external conditions, avoid danger, and make appropriate maneuvers. In a dynamic vehicle, the driver's operations were constantly monitored, the vehicle's situation assessed, and the engine, steering mechanisms, and brakes centrally managed. A pre-collision system perceived the possibilities of a crash with obstacles, other cars, or pedestrians through sensors. If a collision seemed likely, the system activated warnings and brake assistance, which could avoid the collision and reduce the damage. The dynamic vehicle approach was to address factors across a wide scope relevant to the vehicle's environment.

### Performance

With the collapse in gas and oil prices, although Toyota's revenue and net income increased, the overall number of vehicles it sold declined (Figure 15.7). It did not sell the right mix of vehicles to take maximum advantage of a low-fuel price environment. To the extent it sold more vehicles in the United States, the composition changed. Increasingly, it was selling larger crossovers and SUVs and not its mainstay Camrys and Corollas, which faced declining sales in the United States. At the end of 2016, VW again replaced Toyota and sold the most vehicles globally. Admittedly, VW's lead was small, and Toyota could reverse it, as VW and Toyota were not that far apart in the number of vehicles they sold.

## Restoring Quality and Focusing Less on EVs – The Correct Response?

Toyota stood out from other motor vehicle companies because of its focus on quality and its pioneering efforts in bringing hybrids to commercial success. These emphases helped it rise to the top among the world's automakers. However, the company suffered a setback when the unintended acceleration recall took place. It stumbled, and VW made inroads, but then VW had a bigger fall, Dieselgate, and Toyota again surpassed VW in global market share. However, it was running a very close race with VW, and its lead did not last long. VW soon came back and captured first place. This race was close and would continue to be so in a highly competitive sector which no firm dominated absolutely. In comparison to VW, Toyota was disadvantaged in China, the world's largest growing motor vehicle market, because of the historic antagonism between the two countries. Its disadvantageous position in China meant that it might never forge a large lead over VW.

Like other motor vehicle companies, if not more so, Toyota recognized the importance of safety, fuel economy, emissions control, and the vast array of regulations to which motor vehicle companies were quite justifiably subject. The changes, which took place in these regulations, were not ones that either Toyota or the other manufacturers could easily control and the ability of Toyota, like the other automakers, to comply with regulations, without costly and unprofitable adjustments, was difficult. Toyota was therefore in a race with the other automakers to make technological progress. They all sensed that new types of mobility, safer and less environmentally harmful, were available and that new forms of mobility might take the form of electrification, whether partial or complete, and that shared and autonomous driving, were also possible, if not in the present, then in the not-so-distant future. How this race would evolve involved great risk and uncertainty.

All the automakers including Toyota were in this race at the same time that the global economy still had not recovered entirely from the great financial meltdown of 2007–2008. It was in a better, albeit still uncertain, condition. The competition among automakers was intense, and none was completely dominant; the sector suffered from overcapacity. Every large automaker had done about all it could do to hedge its bets by expanding globally, proliferating brands into many niches, and trying, as best they could, to match models with regional and local needs. All of them had also hedged their bets against the risks and uncertainties they faced by taking out options in alternatives to the conventional internal combustion engine, the technology they knew so well. None of them could get around the fact that growth in demand for motor vehicles in most parts of the world, other than China, was not that strong, and without strong growth, or innovation, the best they could hope for was to take market share from each other.

Toyota's approach to hedging was similar to that of other motor vehicle firms. The theme to which they all adhered was foremost to ensure quality and safety. This was fundamental. Straying from this path had dreadful consequences, as they all learned. Next, they had to keep investing in global markets, fine-tuning their brand and model mix, and innovate. They all did this and they spent vast sums on innovation – their R&D budgets were substantial. They were in a race to find some edge, whether it was in safety, new mobility models, lighter materials, or new engine technology.

Toyota was distinct from the other automakers because of its history. It was the first among them to come close to perfecting the system, which became known as the Toyota Way, which allowed it to keep its costs down without sacrificing the quality of its vehicles. The system also allowed it to better adjust the mix of models and the lineup of vehicles it offered for sale to the needs of particular consumers in different parts of the world.

As Toyota was extremely well-diversified in terms of where it operated and in the kinds of vehicles it sold, like VW, it had a strong hedge against uncertain and risky conditions. The manner in which Toyota differed from VW was in how it acquired that hedge. To a much greater extent than Toyota, VW was a conglomerate of different brands amalgamated into its group one by one over time. Toyota, on the other hand, created most of its diversity organically. Although it adjusted its operations to local conditions in the countries in which it sold its vehicles and engaged in production locally nearly everywhere it operated, it functioned in a more uniform manner than VW.

Each of the major automakers carved out a particular niche in the market that helped them in their survival. Toyota's vehicles stood out for their functionality and for being good value for the money, unlike GM and Ford, which distinguished themselves on account of their strengths in trucks, and VW which was best known for its engineering prowess. The evolution of the major automakers was such that each enjoyed some advantage; without it, they would be much more exposed to adverse circumstance. The heterogeneous hedges they created for themselves led them in different directions. Toyota's strength was in Japan, North America, and passenger cars – in particular, its strong brands were the Camry, the Corolla, and the Prius. VW's strength was in Europe, China, and in diesel engines and its strongest brands were Audi, Porsche, and the Golf. Ford's strength was North America and

Europe, and at one end of the spectrum, its strongest brand was the F-150 series pickup truck, while at the other end, its strongest brands were the Focus and the Fiesta. GM's strength was in North America and China and it had a strong reputation in big trucks, in the Chevrolet brand, in Buick's strength in China, and in being the first major automaker to market an EV, the Chevy Bolt.

With gasoline prices plummeting, Toyota's comparative advantage slipped in value in North America where it competed against GM and Ford and also Fiat Chrysler. Its strength in passenger cars actually became something of a liability. In North America, Toyota's emphasis on fuel-efficient hybrids no longer delivered the growth in revenue and income that it had delivered in that market when fuel prices were higher. Toyota therefore had to change direction, as – like VW – it recognized the need to introduce additional light vehicle truck models into the United States. Compared to light trucks, the compact and subcompact cars and the hybrids that Toyota sold did not do as well in a period of low gasoline prices, but it did meet with some success with the Rav 4; this vehicle did very well in the North American market. An issue for Toyota was whether it would have to retreat and actually cut back on its commitment to passenger cars in North America.

In addition, Toyota pivoted from an all-electric vehicle and moved toward fuel cells. In this respect, as for its future vision, it was on a different path than other automakers, which saw less potential in FCVs than Toyota and more potential in EVs. Where the company should go next was unclear. If gasoline prices rose again, Toyota might be able to recapture lost ground in passenger cars, but if low prices remained, would Toyota have to revamp its strategy even more fundamentally?

Toyota had placed big bets on emerging economies in Asia, but these investments had not yet paid off in a significant way. It continued to be highly invested in hybrids. Could it build on its investments in emerging economies in Asia and in hybrids to gain on its competitors? Should Toyota reconsider the commitment it had made to fuel cells? Where should it go next with the Toyota Way? Could it take the lead in safety?

## Notes

1. Liker, Jeffrey K. *The Toyota Way: 14 Management Principles from the World's Greatest Manufacturer*. New York: McGraw-Hill, 2003;

Womak, James. *The Machine That Changed the World: The Story of Lean Production – Toyota's Secret Weapon in the Global Car Wars That Is Now Revolutionizing World Industry*. New York: Free Press, 2007.

2. Cusumano, Michael. *The Japanese Automobile Industry: Technology and Management at Nissan and Toyota*. Cambridge, MA: Harvard University Press, 1986.

3. *"Toyota Output Sets Industry Record."* www.wsj.com/articles/toyota-output-sets-industry-record-1390986041

4. Marcus, Alfred. *Innovations in Sustainability: Fuel and Food*. Cambridge, UK: Cambridge University Press, 2015.

5. *"Worldwide Sales of Toyota Hybrids Surpass 10 Million Units."* https://newsroom.toyota.co.jp/en/detail/14940871

6. *"Toyota Passes GM as World's Largest Automaker."* www.washingtonpost.com/wp-dyn/content/article/2009/01/21/AR2009012101216.html

7. *"How Toyota Lost Its Way."* http://archive.fortune.com/2010/07/12/news/international/toyota_recall_crisis_full_version.fortune/index.htm

8. *"Unintended Acceleration in Toyota Vehicles – National Highway Traffic Safety Commission."* https://one.nhtsa.gov/About-NHTSA/Press-Releases/2011/ci.U.S.-Department-of-Transportation-Releases-Results-from-NHTSA%E2%80%93NASA-Study-of-Unintended-Acceleration-in-Toyota-Vehicles.print; *"2009–11 Toyota Vehicle Recalls."* https://en.wikipedia.org/wiki/2009%E2%80%9311_Toyota_vehicle_recalls

9. *"An Inconvenient Truth about Toyota."* www.theglobeandmail.com/globe-drive/culture/commuting/an-inconvenient-truth-about-toyota/article588288/

10. *"Toyota Recall: More Sudden Acceleration Complaints Even After Fixes."* www.csmonitor.com/Business/2010/0305/Toyota-recall-More-sudden-acceleration-complaints-even-after-fixes

11. *"NHTSA Report on Toyota Unintended Acceleration Investigation."* file:///C:/Users/amarcus/Desktop/NHTSA-UA_report.pdf

12. *"Okla. Jury: Toyota Liable in Sudden Acceleration Crash."* www.cbsnews.com/news/okla-jury-toyota-liable-in-sudden-acceleration-crash/ *"Toyota Unintended Acceleration and the Big Bowl of 'Spaghetti' Code."* www.safetyresearch.net/blog/articles/toyota-unintended-acceleration-and-big-bowl-%E2%80%9Cspaghetti%E2%80%9D-code

13. *"Toyota Expects Recall to Cost $2 Billion."* www.forbes.com/2010/02/04/toyota-earnings-recall-markets-equities-prius.html#4d76ea4e5668

14. David Austen-Smith, Daniel Diermeier, and Eitan Zemel. "Unintended Acceleration: Toyota's Recall Crisis." Kellogg Business Case, 2016. http://sk.sagepub.com/cases/unintended-acceleration-toyotas-recall-crisis

15. "*Toyota Sustainability Report 2012*." www.toyota-global.com/sustain
ability/report/archive/sr12/pdf/sustainability_report12_fe.pdf; "*Toyota
Annual Report 2012*." www.toyota-global.com/pages/contents/inves
tors/ir_library/annual/pdf/2012/ar12_e.pdf
"*Toyota Sustainability Report 2013*." www.toyota-global.com/sustain
ability/report/sr/pdf/sustainability_report13_fe.pdf; "*Toyota Annual
Report 2013*." www.toyota-global.com/pages/contents/investors/ir_li
brary/annual/pdf/2013/ar13_e.pdf
"*Toyota Sustainability Report 2014*." www.toyota-global.com/sustain
ability/report/sr/pdf/sustainability_report14_fe.pdf
"*Toyota Annual Report 2014*." https://www.toyota-global.com/pages/
contents/investors/ir_library/annual/pdf/2014/ar14_e.pdf
"*VW Sustainability Report 2015*." http://annualreport2015.volkswagenag
.com/group-management-report/sustainable-value-enhancement/csr-and-
sustainability.html
"*Toyota Annual Report 2015*." www.toyota-global.com/pages/contents/
investors/ir_library/sec/pdf/20-FA_201503_final.pdf; "*Toyota Sustainability Report 2016*." www.toyota-global.com/pages/contents/investors/
ir_library/annual/pdf/2016/smr16_3_en.pdf
"*Toyota Annual Report 2016*." www.toyota-global.com/pages/contents/
investors/ir_library/sec/pdf/20-F_201603_final.pdf; "Toyota Sustainability Report 2017." www.toyota-global.com/sustainability/report/
archive/sr17/pdf/sdb17_full_en.pdf

# PART V

*Conclusion*

# 16 | Oil and Gas Companies' Strategic Moves 2017–2018

The purpose of this chapter is to update the moves of the major oil and natural gas companies – ExxonMobil, BP, Shell, and TOTAL in the eighteen months after 2016. What were the lingering effects of the drop in energy prices? As oil prices started to creep up again, what were these companies doing? In what ways did their strategies shift?

## ExxonMobil

ExxonMobil indicated that it was not preparing for peak oil. It was subject to continued criticism on climate change and renewables from activists.[1] The company tried to achieve a waiver from the sanctions that the US government had imposed on Russian investments, but failed. It emphasized shale and natural gas and tried to compete with the frackers. However, it had to control its investments, cut back, and write-down assets and it missed earnings estimates. Its problems lingered even under a new CEO Darren Woods, who imposed additional decision-making discipline. Under Woods, the company recommitted to its investments in oil exploration and development in Brazil, Papua New Guinea, and Mozambique, as well as Texas shale. It invested in high-tech computational power to enhance its ability to find and exploit fossil fuels and tried to find a way to bolster the future of the internal combustion engine (ICE).

### Peak Oil and Activists

Some of the world's other large oil companies were preparing for a decline in oil demand in the coming decades because of greater efficiency, electric vehicles, carbon legislation, and less economic growth in developing nations. ExxonMobil was not among them. The forecasts other companies made about peak oil demand varied. BP, in its main scenario, like the IEA and OPEC (see Chapter 4),

401

projected slower demand growth until about 2040 and a peak in that decade. Shell forecast a peak as early as 2025. It therefore changed its long-term investment plans to diversify away from oil and made big bets on the alternatives, like natural gas. In contrast, ExxonMobil did not change its position that an end to growth in demand for oil was likely. It expected that oil would be the dominant fuel source well beyond 2040, as demand for air and surface transportation and lightweight plastics would pick up because of growing incomes in Asia and lack of progress in fuel economy, electric and self-driving vehicles, and battery technology. It concluded that sizeable investments in oil projects, therefore, were imperative.

Activists also continued to target the company for concealing its prior knowledge of climate change. ExxonMobil persistently denied the charges and claimed they were a conspiracy by antagonists to smear its reputation. It pointed to its carbon tax and Paris climate accord endorsements, but the activists remained critical and considered these endorsements weak. They also held that the company stood out among its competitors for its failure to invest in renewable energy. However, with its strong abilities in fossil fuel, ExxonMobil did not want to invest in renewables like wind or solar where it lacked expertise. Instead of these investments, the company returned as much as half its earnings to shareholders in the form of dividends it made or share buybacks.

The company also continued to fight off the suits the New York and Massachusetts attorney generals brought against it for seeking to neutralize and obfuscate scientific research on climate change. The suits alleged that the company had misled investors about how it accounted for the impact of climate change. Since 2007, it had included in its assessment of new projects a proxy cost of how much governments could charge for carbon dioxide emissions. The suit claimed that from 2010 to 2014, the company publicly held that it applied a cost of $60 per ton, while internal documents showed it actually used a cost of $40 a ton. ExxonMobil asserted that these accusations of its downplaying climate change were inaccurate and stressed that it had turned a corner on this issue and along with other companies had opposed President Trump's intention to withdraw the United States from the Paris climate accord.

## Seeking a Russian Waiver

The company applied to the Treasury Department for a waiver from US sanctions on Russia in a bid to resume the joint venture it had created with Russian state oil company Rosneft. It was seeking US permission to drill with Rosneft in several areas in Russia. The company originally applied for a waiver to gain access to the Black Sea in 2015, but the government denied the waiver. Congress closely scrutinized the waiver since it was seeking to intensify sanctions on Russia for its interference with the US elections. Oil companies long had sought access to Russia's oil resources. As much as 100 billion barrels of oil might be untapped in the country, but sanctions held the companies back in their attempts to reach those reserves. The sanctions affecting Rosneft banned US companies from deals in the Arctic, Siberia, and the Black Sea that would require sharing cutting-edge drilling techniques. Congress instituted the sanctions after Russia annexed the Crimea region of Ukraine in 2014. It made dealings with Rosneft's chief executive, Igor Sechin, illegal and effectively blocked the exploration deal ExxonMobil signed with Rosneft in 2012 that would have given ExxonMobil access to Russia's Arctic waters, Siberia, and the Black Sea. ExxonMobil claimed losses of up to a billion dollars billion from the blocked ventures though it had not recognized them in its books because it hoped the government would lift the sanctions.

In 2014, when the world first imposed sanctions, ExxonMobil had obtained a temporary waiver and was able to begin drilling in the Russian Arctic. The company asked the government to allow it to complete this drilling, arguing it would not be safe to leave it behind before it finished. It received this extension and then withdrew from Russia when it finished. President Trump, under scrutiny for his Russian ties, rejected ExxonMobil's waiver bid. In any case, lower oil prices meant that the Russian projects were not worth pursuing. ExxonMobil made the deal to carry out the projects when oil prices topped $90 a barrel and prospects for prices remaining high seemed likely. With oil trading far below that number, it made sense for the company to withdraw and carry out other projects with better prospects for gain.

## Emphasizing Shale and Natural Gas

ExxonMobil announced plans to spend $50 billion to expand its US shale projects over five years. It invested $6.5 billion into doubling its acreage in Permian Basin's fields, increasing these holdings by buying Bass-family-owned companies for $5.6 billion in stock and up to $1 billion in additional payments. Once a dominant player in the region, ExxonMobil had to rebuild its portfolio. With oil prices rising above $50 a barrel, the value of land in the Permian basin had gone up. Although the purchase doubled the oil and gas ExxonMobil held in the area to the equivalent of 6 billion barrels, its holdings were smaller than rivals Chevron and Occidental Petroleum. The company planned to use the purchase to drill long horizontal wells that would reduce its costs by extending the drillings' reach. It planned to spend about $5.5 billion in 2017 in Texas, New Mexico and North Dakota, tapping wells that could turn a profit at a price of $40 a barrel. The company's ability to profit from shale was growing due to lower costs and better engineering, yet it still lagged behind the top independents, with their wells producing about twice as much oil and gas as ExxonMobil wells in some cases. Nevertheless, the company was trying to make improvements in its drilling mainly by using more sand to open the rock layers.

Since ExxonMobil could ramp up drilling for shale quicker than other types of production, it tempered oil price volatility. Although the hurdles were high and costs great, the company was trying to replicate the US fracking boom in a desolate part of Patagonia in western Argentina. The Argentinian fields potentially had as much oil and gas as the biggest in Texas and North Dakota. Nonetheless, the company recognized there was considerable peril in investing more money in shale, as small independent producers, which had lower breakeven points, did the same. Thus, it took a more modest approach to increasing drilling. It was apprehensive that the price advance in crude would lose its momentum and concerned that it and other companies might produce too much oil and the price would fall.

Some investors, moreover, preferred the independent frackers to ExxonMobil because of their superior record of stopping and starting production based on price changes. While investors in the independent fracking companies mainly sought production growth, investors in ExxonMobil wanted profits, less debt, and higher dividends. The frackers had a flare for finding more cost-effective ways to get oil and gas out of fields when oil prices dropped that ExxonMobil lacked. When the price of oil went down, almost half a million oil and gas jobs were lost and more than 200 US companies were in fracking filed for bankruptcy. Nonetheless, firms that fracked like EOG, Chesapeake Energy, and Pioneer Natural Resources survived and found many ways to lower costs.

EOG, for instance, claimed it produced about the same amount of oil in 2016 as it did in 2014 with a budget that was 67 percent lower. It could drill new horizontal wells in West Texas that were more than a mile long in twenty days, eighteen days less than in 2014. It estimated a 30 percent rate of return on the wells that it drilled at $40 a barrel. At $50 a barrel, it could boost production by 15 percent a year through 2020. EOG created its own device located behind the underground drill bit that transmitted information, including depth, direction, rocks, and presence of gas. The company analyzed the information using proprietary databases on rock location and the previous wells it had dug, and made course corrections within minutes. It also designed its own power drill motor, which allowed engineers to incorporate fixes to improve performance. It worked with smaller service providers, not big companies like Halliburton, because it could negotiate costs to keep them down and find expertise tailored to its needs. EOG expanded in the Permian region by 310,000 acres in 2017 when it acquired Yates Petroleum Corp. for $2.4 billion. Its trial-and-error improvement methods, common to smaller independent fracking, were not well suited to ExxonMobil's formal and bureaucratic way of doing business.

As ExxonMobil increased its investment in shale, its overall hydrocarbon production fell and the attention the company paid to natural gas picked up. From 2007 to 2016, ExxonMobil and its rivals had invested heavily in new natural-gas supplies and by 2017 ExxonMobil produced more natural gas than oil, much of it in LNG form, which it shipped throughout world. LNG demand was rising in China, where imports grew by 40 percent in 2017. Higher LNG imports were likely to follow in India, but the competition to supply these markets would be stiff as Qatar and Russia also planned to produce more LNG, which they would ship to the world. LNG prices in 2017 were relatively low as increased demand outside of China did not materialize and many countries had neither the infrastructure to import the fuel, nor the money to build this infrastructure.

ExxonMobil was in talks with Qatar for a partnership in which that country's state energy company, Qatar Petroleum, would invest in ExxonMobil's US natural gas resources. This joint venture would be with the company's subsidiary XTO, which developed the bulk of its shale resources. Qatar Petroleum would gain XTO experience in fracking. Natural gas extracted from shale was a bet on a relatively low-emissions bridge from coal to renewable energy. However, methane, a main component in natural gas, was a potent greenhouse gas and the issue of fugitive emissions from methane leaks drew more attention. To reduce these leaks, ExxonMobil joined seven other large energy companies and created an agreement to abide by a set of principles to drive down their methane emissions.

## Controlling Spending and Cutting Back Investments

Once known for its massive spending on ambitious exploration projects, ExxonMobil had to be more frugal. The emphasis it was giving to shale signified a retrenchment from the large, technically challenging international projects that had once been ExxonMobil's strength. A high percentage of the company's domestic production growth in 2017 was from shale. These investments produced quick cash flow and required less capital spending than the large capital-intensive projects the company previously preferred. This change reflected a fundamental shift in its strategy in which ExxonMobil had to live within its means and avoid the once common budget-busting projects in which it had been involved. The company concluded that it had to control its spending in the wake of the downturn in crude oil prices from what had been a high of $114 a barrel to a low of $27 a barrel. In 2017, prices had come back but at not much more than $50 a barrel, they had not yet stabilized at a comfortable level for ExxonMobil. With shale, there were lower exploration, political and financial risks. Fewer dry holes occurred and governments were not likely to nationalize oil fields. The flexibility was greater, for if prices fell, the company could cut back. The move from large, technically challenging projects to shale allowed ExxonMobil to cut its costs, become leaner, reduce its debt, and generate the cash it needed to rebuild its weakened balance sheet in the face of the rating agencies that had downgraded its debt. The company responded to investors, who demanded greater financial discipline and a more judicious approach to investing. The downside was the competition with the smaller, independent companies, who in 2017 grew their investments by over 25 percent in response to oil prices rising. Competing with them would mean lower profits for ExxonMobil in the long run.

ExxonMobil's 2016 capital spending was $12 billion lower than in 2016. In 2017, its capital spending grew but slightly; its plan was to spend about $22 billion in 2017, about 15 percent more than the prior year. Yet, ExxonMobil was the only large oil company that increased spending; all the rest were continuing to make cuts. As the company's focus was on low-cost shale that yielded fast returns, it remained cautious. The growth in total US shale rig count, even in the Permian Basis, where extraction was cheap, was quite slow. A lack of investment might lead to supply shortages in the future. If prices then increased, ExxonMobil might be able to back off from shale, as the higher prices would provide it with the incentive to return to the big and challenging projects in which it excelled.

ExxonMobil also got praise from President Trump for $20 billion in commitments to oil, gas, and chemical infrastructure projects on the Gulf Coast. However, the plans for these investments were old and under 7 percent of the company's total investments, and investments of this kind were becoming increasingly less attractive. In the first decade of the twenty-first century, ExxonMobil's upstream return on capital was over 33 percent. Downstream return was about 20 percent. From 2011 onward, this situation changed as downstream investments outearned upstream investments. Upstream returns fell to about 12 percent. They were less than the breakeven point for new projects, which was a 15 percent return on investment.

In 2010, ExxonMobil lobbied against federal regulation that mandated that energy companies disclose payments to foreign governments. It argued that the regulation put US companies at a disadvantage to foreign rivals. US lawmakers eliminated the requirement in 2016; however, ExxonMobil was no longer eager to do business in many of the countries in which it had operated and where these payments might have been necessary. It retreated from Angola, once a magnet for its investments when oil prices were about $100 a barrel. With oil prices under $60 a barrel, ExxonMobil considered Angola to be a challenging place in which to operate. For projects to break even, ExxonMobil calculated that oil prices had to climb above $73 a barrel. As a result, Angola's oil-drilling rig count fell from thirty-six in 2014 to three in 2017.

ExxonMobil planned to continue to invest in Guyana, where it made a major discovery in 2015, but at a substantially lower level. It pulled back from a 120,000 barrel-a-day Guyana coast project in 2017, which would have cost it more than $4.4 billion. Projects that it continued were subject to rigorous cost cutting and relied on simple, cheap methods that made use of standardized equipment. The company generally assumed that oil prices had to increase to more than $70 a barrel to open the way for it to approve the type of projects that it had previously carried out.

## Writing-Down Assets and Missing Earning Estimates

Because of an investigation by securities regulators, ExxonMobil had to write down the value of more than $2 billion of its US assets, The US Securities and Exchange Commission (SEC) contested the company's accounting practices. It questioned how the company valued future oil and gas wells and reserves. The probe also sought information about how ExxonMobil weighed the potential impact of future climate-change regulations. With fossil fuel prices declining, it had been the only major energy company not to recognize the lower value of its reserves. ExxonMobil cooperated with the investigation and tried to update its reporting to ensure that it met SEC standards. The SEC required companies to evaluate their future prospects based on the average price fossil fuel prices of the previous year. When expected future cash flow from reserves fell, the rules required that reserves be written down. In response to the SEC investigation, ExxonMobil wrote down the natural-gas assets in the Rocky Mountains it obtained when it acquired shale producer XTO Energy. The price of natural gas, which averaged $5.35 per million British thermal units when it announced the deal late in 2009, had slipped to $3.23 in 2017. ExxonMobil also had to acknowledge that as much as 4.6 billion barrels of its reserves, mostly in Canada's oil sands, were not profitable. Although not profitable, the company had stuck with them because the fixed costs of these operations were such that they would not allow ExxonMobil to shut them down easily.

Despite billions of dollars in spending cuts and a modest oil-price rebound, ExxonMobil did not make sufficient money in 2016 to cover all of its costs. It spent nearly $7 billion more in developing new projects and dividends than it generated in cash, though, according to its own metrics, which excluded dividends, it broke even. The company continued to distribute dividends at a high rate even when oil prices were down, adding to its debt. It sold off assets so shareholders would not suffer. According to analysts' estimates, the company needed the price of oil to be at more than $50 a barrel to balance the cash it generated against the capital expenditures it made and the dividends it generated.

ExxonMobil's first quarter 2018 profits missed Wall Street expectations. Seventy percent of its $8.4 billion net income in that quarter arose out of one-time tax change benefits. Earnings declined by 2.2 percent on an adjusted basis, which did not include the new tax law bonus. Production fell by about 3 percent compared to the prior year. The company's US drilling operations lost money for the twelfth consecutive quarter, an oddity given that US production as a whole rose to near record levels and was nearly equal to Saudi Arabia.

Hydrocarbons demand was not the issue, nor was the shift to renewable energy and electric vehicles. Global consumption of oil and natural gas was on the rise because of improved global growth. The problem was that giant oil companies, such as ExxonMobil, had been shut out of the lucrative state-firm controlled oil fields. They did not own and control a sufficient amount of the asset to share in the profits that came from a growth in demand.

ExxonMobil's focus had moved from complicated mega-projects, high cost and high risk and at the same time capable of yielding big profits, to smaller, less risky projects that smaller companies that were involved principally in shale could do better. ExxonMobil's shale investments were not as lucrative as the high risk high-yield projects in which it typically excelled; consequently, its returns tumbled. Nonetheless, the company remained committed to spending $50 billion over the next five years to triple Permian production. It also gave out its thirty-sixth annual dividend increase in a row. For 2017 overall, the firm's losses in its US upstream businesses were $459 million, which was an improvement on the nearly $2 billion in losses in 2016. Return on invested capital, once between 20 and 35 percent, did not rise above mid-single digits. The company had to report write-downs on additional oil and natural gas properties. The bright spot had been that a strong global economy had pushed up demand and increased refining profits, where margins surged by as much as 15 percent in the first quarter of 2018. In this sense, the hedging in which the company as an integrated firm engaged, did work.

## Lingering Problems and the New CEO's Discipline

In sum, ExxonMobil suffered from many problems. The company continued to face investigations of its accounting and tax practices as well as lawsuits by cities and states seeking funds to pay for the effects of climate change. Although it typically won these lawsuits, they continued to hurt its image. Moreover, the company was not seeing a payoff from its disciplined spending on projects that would make money even at low oil prices. Despite greater spending, its oil productions of about 4 million barrels a day and its proven oil and natural gas reserves of about 20 billion barrels were no higher than they had been in 1998. The result of these problems was that while the company once was the world's largest company by market value, it had fallen to tenth place in the middle of 2018 and by market value it was less than half the size of Apple.

These problems were compounded by the fact that ExxonMobil had chosen not to follow the path on which its competitors had started a move to depart from oil exploration and diversify into renewable energy in small ways. As oil prices rose to all-time highs of almost $150 a barrel, ExxonMobil had chased expensive prospects like Canada's oil sands and deep offshore drilling in Russia's Arctic, which required high oil prices for them to be profitable. By 2018, ExxonMobil had to acknowledge that 3.6 billion barrels of reserves in Canada from an oil sands project that cost more than $20 billion would not be profitable. It might have to reduce its exposure in a country where it had operated for 130 years. The company had also bet on finding oil in risky, expensive locations like the Russian Arctic, but as oil prices fell, those projects also would not pay off. ExxonMobil had made serious miscalculations about the political risks of doing business in Russia. Because of US and European sanctions, it had to back off from joint ventures with Rosneft to drill for oil in the Black Sea and Arctic waters. Another miscalculation was its 2010 purchase of fracking pioneer XTO for more than $40 billion. Although the fracking XTO did in the Permian basin in West Texas and New Mexico had been among the company's most profitable opportunities, ExxonMobil did not consistently make money from the activity. Moreover, it had to write down the value of its US natural gas assets, which included XTO, by $2.5 billion, because natural gas prices did not go up.

Under Rex Tillerson, ExxonMobil's production declined and it delivered lackluster financial results. New CEO, Darren Woods, rose through the refining division's ranks, where profits came from the company's ultra-efficient operations. This attention to detail spilled over to the company's risk and accountability methodology, known as the Operations Integrity Management System (OIMs). It was renowned for the results it produced and continued to produce in safety. Under Woods, the company introduced a process of painstakingly analyzing all its decisions, major and minor, and it judged projects on an assumed oil price that was as much 50 percent or more *below* current and forecast prices. Although it recognized the threats it faced from electric vehicles and climate change, it continued to assume that renewable energy would not be able to compete with fossil fuel. The centerpiece of the company's turnaround efforts under Woods, therefore, was to increase fossil fuel investment to the extent it was feasible. It continued its focus on drilling in Brazil, Papua New Guinea, and Mozambique as well as Texas in the hope that the company could produce the equivalent of an additional 1 million barrels of oil and natural gas a day. In 2018, the company planned to spend $28 billion on exploration, 45 percent more than in 2016, moving it in a direction different from its rivals, which were holding their exploration investment levels flat or reducing them below 2016 levels. Even though the price of crude rose about 60 percent in 2018, ExxonMobil share prices barely budged. Investors favored the smaller, nimbler shale companies with which ExxonMobil competed and ExxonMobil continued to underperform, producing returns lower than the S&P 500 and rivals like Shell.

## Improving Exploration and Bolstering the Internal Combustion Engine

To improve its ability to explore for and recover new oil and natural gas, ExxonMobil, like its rival BP, increased its investments in computational power. Working with the National Center for Supercomputing Applications, it ran simulations that used 716,800 processors, four times the number of processors anyone in the industry previously had used. With this order of magnitude increase in processing speed, the company hoped to be better able to optimize future oil and gas development. For years, like other companies, ExxonMobil had used supercomputers to analyze seismic data and assemble maps of geologic formations, which shaped where it would drill. The advantage of the new supercomputing initiative was it could do faster and more detailed modeling. In the capital-intensive industry in which ExxonMobil competed, prices fluctuated constantly. Thus, images that were crisper and more detailed, made better predictions, yielded less guesswork, and improved accuracy about all aspects of a project were of great importance. Moreover, they were useful in terms of potential environmental impacts. Better predictions, which relied on massive amounts of seismic data, historical production data, and other information would permit ExxonMobil to design more efficient and cost-effective strategies for oil and natural gas exploration and recovery.

In its past seismic imaging, the algorithms in each of ExxonMobil's computer worked independently on a small part of the problem. The computers functioned without regular communication among them. The new technique in which many computers worked in parallel on a problem was expensive but could save money because of its potential to avoid misplaced wells and poorly executed recovery projects. To harness this potential, ExxonMobil was outsourcing its demand for computing power and competing with Silicon Valley firms for talent.

The future of the internal combustion engine was important to maintaining demand for fossil fuels. Tough regulation and the advances that electric vehicles were making put the internal combustion engine in jeopardy. Thus, ExxonMobil and other oil companies had an interest in preserving the internal combustion engine and along with other oil companies and the automakers, it became involved in an effort to help sustain the technology. They spent millions of dollars a year to create a new super-slick oil that would make traditional engines more efficient. This oil might enable them to comply with stricter environmental rules and fight off the threat of zero-emission electric vehicles (EVs).

The threat to the internal combustion engine was real as many countries signalled they would ban it in coming years and implement tough new emission standards. The EU in 2017 came forward with a proposal to cut carbon-dioxide emissions from cars and vans 30 percent by 2030. China called for 20 percent of vehicle production and sales in that country to be electric and hybrid by 2025. The Trump administration, on the other hand, was relaxing US initiatives to tighten vehicle emissions standards. Regardless the auto companies promised to launch more EVs in the next decade. GM pledged to sell 1 million annually by 2026, Tesla 1 million by 2020, VW 3 million by 2025, and Toyota 5.5 million by 2030. Oil companies other than ExxonMobil invested in EV infrastructure. Still, it was in the interest of most oil and auto companies to extend the ICE's use. To extend its lifetime required that they make the ICE more efficient. Ultrathin oils would help reduce friction and allow for engines that could operate at high temperature and pressure. The auto companies then could build smaller, turbocharged engines that were powerful and up to 15–25 percent more efficient than current ICEs.

## BP

Unlike ExxonMobil, BP acknowledged that peak oil demand was likely.[2] While ExxonMobil felt the sting of the lost Russian opportunity, BP faced the ongoing challenge of making Deepwater Horizon payments. Consequently, it slowed its investments, tried to lower its breakeven point, and attempted to sell assets at a rate greater than ExxonMobil. Unfortunately, BP had to deal with another oil leak, albeit one far smaller and far less serious than Deepwater. Like ExxonMobil, it invested in supercomputing to advance exploration and production. However, unlike ExxonMobil, it also made investments in wind electricity. Finally, unlike ExxonMobil, its finances did start to improve.

### Acknowledging Peak Oil Demand

Moving in a direction different to ExxonMobil, BP acknowledged that oil demand was likely to peak in the next decades, as renewables surged and met a greater share of the world's energy needs. It projected that demand for oil would grow until around 2035, reaching 110.3 million barrels a day – 15.3 more million than in 2015 – before flattening and declining. Its new forecast suggested the arrival of peak-oil demand sooner than it had estimated in the past when it projected that oil demand would only stop growing in the 2040s. In comparison, Shell maintained that peak demand could come as early 2025, while ExxonMobil, as discussed previously, did not foresee a peak.

BP assumed that government policies, technology, and social preferences would evolve in ways similar to their past development.

Countries like the United Kingdom and France would continue to impose restrictions on the ICE. China would persist in pushing for expanded use of EVs. Under these circumstances, oil consumption, according to BP, would grow by an average of 0.14 percent annually. Its growth projection was lower than the US DOE, which had growth at 0.19 percent annually and lower than OPEC, which had growth at 0.17 percent annually, but higher than the IEA, which predicted that growth would be 0.12 percent annually. The majority of this growth, according to BP, would come from developing economies. Oil would constitute about 85 percent of total transport fuel demand in 2040, compared with 94 percent in 2017. The number of EVs would rise to about 320 million in 2040, accounting for about 30 percent of miles driven, an increase that would be augmented by autonomous vehicles, most of which would be electrically powered. BP also forecasted that US oil production would continue to grow and reach 18 percent of global output by 2040, well ahead of Saudi Arabia's output. According to BP, by 2040, global demand for oil, natural gas, coal, and various non-fossil fuels would be roughly equivalent. Each would account for about a quarter of the world's energy. Renewables, however, would supply more than 40 percent of the world's increase in demand.

## *Facing the Burden of Deepwater Horizon Payments and the Prospect of Less Investment*

In 2017, BP, unlike any other major oil and natural gas company, was still in the unenviable position of having to make more than $4 billion annual payments because of the 2010 Deepwater Horizon accident. These liabilities held it back even as the financial performance of other companies in the sector started to improve somewhat as oil prices rose. With nearly 400,000 claims from Gulf of Mexico residents and businesses still outstanding, the exact value of the company's future liability still was unknown. Since the accident, BP had not been able to sustain its position as the largest oil producer among publicly traded western companies. It slipped to third place after ExxonMobil and Shell and its growth prospects were the weakest among these companies.

BP still did not run its operations particularly tightly. The company continued to experience operational problems. In the

Prudhoe Bay region of Alaska, where it accounted for about 55 percent of Alaska's oil and gas production, it had a leak in 2017 because of a damaged pressure gauge. It had to notify the mostly Native American community within a fifty-mile radius, though it was not clear, however, how much was oil spilled and the degree to which it affected the snow-covered tundra. BP's crews could not immediately access the site because the danger of a natural gas release persisted after the leak terminated. Ultimately, the company's crews plugged the well and stopped its operation, containing the contamination without serious injury to humans or damage to wildlife. Fortunately, the company controlled the event before serious impacts occurred.

BP's investors were generally conservative and wanted it live within its means and focus on profits, debt reduction, and dividends. They did not reward it for growth in production, while investors in shale firms did. The company, therefore, had to be quite disciplined, selective, and judicious in the investments it made. Throughout the downturn, it continued to pay dividends. It had to meet its expenses and pay dividends with cash from operations. It had to use the excess cash it had to pay down its debt. Its debt had expanded to uncomfortable levels after oil prices dropped from more than $100 a barrel in 2014 to below $30 a barrel. BP's excessive borrowing was the reason the ratings agencies had downgraded its credit, as they had downgraded ExxonMobil. Under these circumstances, the company had to spend less than it grew its cash flow. This meant that it had to cancel projects that were not likely to generate relatively quick returns. As an example, the company chose to back away from a deep-water project in the Great Australian Bite that it otherwise might have pursued.

To the extent that BP continued to spend, it had to target less ambitious projects with shorter time horizons. Pursuing extravagant bets, like multibillion-dollar projects in Arctic waters or Kazakhstan's Caspian Sea (see Chapter 1), was no longer possible. It had to abandon the projects in favor of alternatives that were easy to carry out. With oil prices ranging from $50 to $55 a barrel, the surer bets were to return to old oil basins to determine if it could extract more fuel with the new technologies available.

BP needed to generate the cash so it could cover its capital spending and dividends. It was in a position where it had to focus on low-cost projects that could bring oil or gas to market within a few years, while avoiding projects that locked it into multibillion-dollar investments that lasted for long periods with uncertain results. Even if oil prices came back, it had to be wary of megaprojects. As oil prices moved to more than $50 a barrel, shale-oil companies raised their budgets by over 25 percent to revive drilling. BP continued to hold back spending and held to a cautious path. The oil price rebound might not continue or it might even go into reverse, which could happen if OPEC members did not keep to their promised cuts or if US shale firms produced oil and natural gas at a very high a rate.

### Driving Down the Breakeven Price and Selling Assets to Raise Cash

At the start of 2017, BP acknowledged that it needed oil to reach $60 a barrel price for it to break even. Its share price, therefore, slumped by 4 percent, even though $60 a barrel was far better than the previous price estimated of nearly $70 a barrel it needed to breakeven. To drive down its breakeven price to between $35 and $40 a barrel by 2021, the company initiated a plan that assumed oil prices would remain about the same as they were in 2017. This plan almost immediately showed results; in the middle of 2017, the company reported that due to the spending cuts it had made, it had reached a breakeven price of $47 a barrel for the first half of that year. Based on this news, its stock rose 2 percent. BP hoped it could lower its breakeven price even further and then increase production. It could achieve these goals only if it maintained strict cash discipline and the price of a barrel of oil stayed at about $50–$60 a barrel. It continued to drive down costs and focus on projects that generated strong returns. The aim was to stick to low-cost projects that provided quick paybacks. For instance, after giving up on its plans to explore in the Great Australian Bight, which was a potentially large new supply source, but one that was very risky to develop, it invested $2 billion in a 10 percent stake in oil fields in the UAE, which were easier to exploit and had low extraction costs.

BP announced it was still committed to the North Sea region, yet at the same time approached potential buyers for its assets in the region. While it discussed selling these assets, which produced about 150,000 barrels a day, because they were nearing the end of their production life, it also declared that it would try to increase North Sea production by more than a third in order to maximize extraction. It was in the company's interest to abandon fields like the nearly tapped-out North Sea, and to find cheaper options for producing oil, even though it had been a North Sea leader since the inception of exploration and production in the region in the mid-1960s and was reluctant to withdraw. Along with Shell and others, it had helped to create the basin, but by the 1990s, production peaked and started to go down. Extracting remaining barrels from aging fields like the North Sea was too expensive for BP to undertake given its financial circumstances. BP had sold part of its interest in the Magnus field in the North Sea to EnQues under pressure to raise cash to pay for Deepwater Horizon accident costs. Selling North Sea assets was not straightforward however as it cost billions of dollars to dismantle and dispose of fully tapped oil rigs. When Shell sold its North Sea fields, it had to pay the buyer about $1 billion in decommissioning costs. Therefore, BP put its plan to sell its North Sea holdings temporarily on hold. Figuring out that it needed to raise $5.5 billion via various other divestments, it developed plans to divest other assets, and moved forward with a proposal to sell a part of its US pipelines, a move that could earn it about $100 million

## Using Super-Computers to Enhance Production

Like ExxonMobil, BP increasingly relied on super-computers to help it answer vexing questions such as whether there were large amounts of oil under a 7,000-feet underwater salt dome in the Gulf of Mexico. With an algorithm, it could answer this question with a high level of confidence within two weeks. The supercomputer produced a clear seismic image of the 200 million barrels of oil. As opposed to ExxonMobil, which contracted out for super-computing technology, BP acquired its own devices, invested hundreds of millions in upgrades, and possessed some of the world's most powerful commercially owned supercomputers. It made a five-year $100 million investment in a supercomputer housed in a large room in a flood proof building in Houston. This technology, BP hoped, would allow it to produce fossil fuels more cheaply and efficiently. The computers were expensive but they could reduce oil-exploration time and save the company tens of millions of dollars. To harness the supercomputers' potential, BP, like ExxonMobil, was competing with Silicon Valley firms to recruit the world's best talent.

## Harvesting Wind

Unlike ExxonMobil, BP invested in wind energy. In a partnership with Dominion Energy and Sempra Energy, it operated more than half of Benton County Indiana's 560 wind turbines. Wind was a boon to this economically struggling region. Projects employed hundreds of construction workers, created over 100 permanent jobs, mostly technicians, who earned about $50,000 a year, and the projects brought in taxes that enabled the local government to finance schools and build roads. Moreover, they produced relatively cheap energy. Excluding subsidies, it cost about $47 per megawatt hour to generate electricity from wind over the lifetime of a facility, compared to $63 for natural gas and $102 for coal. In the neighboring state of Iowa, wind produced more than 36 percent of the state's electricity. The falling price of wind, along with its environmental benefits, helped to persuade companies such as Facebook, Microsoft, and Google to open data centers in Indiana.

## Achieving Better Returns

A nearly $1 billion loss related to US corporate-tax changes and a $1.7 billion charge from Deepwater Horizon accident settlements hurt BP's fourth quarter 2017 earnings, but otherwise the company performed well, assisted by oil prices coming close to $60 a barrel. The company's high debt levels and inability to push forward with new investment had alienated shareholders, but in 2017's fourth quarter, its cost cutting made inroads as it seemed the company was on track to achieve increased profits. As a sign of confidence, BP began a share buyback program. Excluding its nearly 20 percent stake in Russian state-oil company, Rosneft, its annual production rose by 12 percent. The company started many new projects around the world as part of a plan to add 900,000 barrels a day of new production by 2021. Achieving these results would bring it to a level roughly the same as it had been prior to the Deepwater Horizon accident. The company also announced a return to North Iraq for the first time since the Islamic State became a presence in 2014. The Iraqi Kurds had defended and held Kirkuk and its oil fields, but gave them back when Iraqi forces liberated the region. Iraq encouraged BP to help it boost production by 60 percent to its previous level of 750,000 barrels a day.

## Shell

Unlike ExxonMobil, but like BP, Shell conceded that peak oil demand was on the horizon.[3] Its investments in renewables, however, exceeded those of BP. Like BP and ExxonMobil, it sold assets in a serious way both when the price of oil was low and when it started to rise. Like both companies, it tried to introduce new technology to boost oil output. Similar to BP, Shell tried to lower its breakeven point. Like ExxonMobil, it looked for opportunities in fracking. Unfortunately, unlike either company, it had to fight off charges that it had been involved in bribery. It also had to fight off charges that its operations were causing earthquakes in the Netherlands. Shell worked with ExxonMobil and BP on ways to reduce pollution and increase the efficiency of the internal combustion engine. Like BP, and unlike ExxonMobil, Shell's finances improved. What distinguished Shell from ExxonMobil and BP was the degree to which it assumed that the future of the oil and natural gas sector would be quite different in the future than it had been in the past and therefore it put its hopes in natural gas more than any of these companies.

### Conceding to Peak Oil Demand and Investing in Renewables

Unlike ExxonMobil and like BP, Shell conceded that peak oil demand was on the horizon, but unlike BP, it put the date at an earlier point. Peak oil demand, according to Shell, might arrive as early as 2025. Shell anticipated that, as demand for oil peaked, driven by efforts to meet global climate goals, reliance on electricity would grow from about 20 to about 50 percent of energy consumed by 2050. Based on these projections, the company did not want to be stuck with long-term oil investments, whose values, were likely to decline. Thus, Shell reckoned that it was prudent not to undertake long-term investments in oil projects, whose returns might be negative. The company's CEO Ben van Beurden declared that because of tough new environmental rules, including the possibility of a cap on emissions or a carbon tax, and with electric cars and other technologies threatening to erode demand, the company had to start to move away from fossil fuels and become a world-class new energies player.

Thus, Shell started to move much more aggressively than BP toward early-stage investments in alternative energy. Its investments extended from electric-vehicle charging to offshore wind power. The company committed $1–$2 billion a year spending to these areas annually until

2020. To put this number in perspective, it was not large compared to the amounts Shell committed to fossil fuels, yet it was significant, inasmuch it elevated these projects to a new level of legitimacy within the firm. Shell bought a stake in US solar producer Silicon Ranch and purchased New Motion, one of Europe's largest EV charging firms. It acquired a midsize UK power supplier, First Utility, which gave it direct access to electricity consumers.

The company bet it could profit as renewables played a greater role. As an integrated player in renewable energy, the company considered itself to be hedged to be virtually failure proof, for regardless of how the world evolved, it would be in a position to profit. Shell's evolving business model was mainly to produce natural gas, use it in making electricity and then sell the power for EV charging as well as other purposes. It accepted that it would increasingly have to replace gasoline with electricity for the propulsion of automobiles. With natural gas, it could plug in the gaps, when intermittent solar and wind power did not function in making the electricity it needed.

Shell's 2017 "Energy Transition Report" envisioned a low fossil fuel future. Proof it was taking the needed steps to adapt to this vision was its $1–2 billion per year spending on alternative energies. By 2070, Shell anticipated a world where fossil fuels would be a small part of the global energy mix, and renewable energy would basically take over. According to Shell, even though right now the world was heavily dependent on fossil fuels, the company had to be prepared for that inevitability. North American and European energy needs would remain flat and these regions would be almost fossil fuel free by 2070. Asia would see its energy needs double, but its fossil fuel use nevertheless would be cut in half. Africa, despite its population doubling every thirty-five years, would manage to develop without resorting to a significant increase in fossil fuel use.

Shell was proud of the fact that in three out of the past five years, its reserve replacement of conventional oil and natural gas had been positive. Additions outpaced production and depletion. However, in the long-run, so long as production averaged almost 600 million barrels of oil per year, discoveries would not keep up. Dwindling conventional oil discoveries were industry-wide trends the company could not avoid. The world was moving toward low fossil fuel use and the company had to adapt. At some point, reserve additions through reclassification of existing resources, as well as the purchase of assets, such as BG would no longer be a viable solution. Among oil companies, Shell had a record of accomplishment in adjusting to trends. It was not afraid to make significant changes and divest from assets when they were not profitable, to cancel projects when they produced at a loss, and abandon them when the sum of long-term energy prices and capital costs did not equal the revenue.

## Selling Assets to Pay Off the Debts from the BG Acquisition

Because of Shell's purchase of the large British natural gas and oil firm, BG, it had a large debt, estimated to be $78 billion. The acquisition of BG, at $50 billion, gave Shell a very strong position in natural gas and in valuable offshore Brazilian oil fields, but Shell's debt-to-equity ratio of 29 percent was higher than that of competing oil and natural gas companies. Due to the BG acquisition, Shell's 2016 profits, $3.5 billion, were the lowest they had been in decade. Cash flow from operations, however, grew nearly 70 percent in the fourth quarter of 2016, compared to the previous year, because of the acquisition, and they rose to $9.2 billion, which was enough to cover the company's dividend. Shell sought to reposition itself as a natural gas leader, but now had to deal with the debt it had accumulated in making the transition. To deal with this debt, it promised investors that it would sell up to $30 billion in assets by 2018. These sales would allow it eliminate weak and less desirable parts of its holdings. Shell then would be in a better position to pay dividends in the future and it would have the cash in hand for making share buybacks.

The company wanted to dispose of assets but it found that it was not easy to accomplish this goal. In 2016, the company could sell only $5 billion in assets, almost $3 billion less than it had promised. It sold a stake in the Japanese refiner Showa Shell Sekiyu for $1.4 billion, a shale holding in Canada for $1 billion, and various pipeline interests for $1 billion. It made a variety of other smaller sales in Mexico, the Philippines, Africa, Australia, and New Zealand. Most of the assets it sold were in refining and marketing, where low oil prices depreciated the assets' value less than they depreciated the value of exploration and production assets. For most of 2016, with oil prices below $50 a barrel, the company could not fetch the prices it was seeking for the sale of upstream assets.

With oil prices increasing to more than $50 a barrel in 2017, Shell hoped to ramp up its asset sales and get better prices. Indeed, it was able to find buyers willing to pay it $3.8 billion for oil fields it owned in the North Sea and buyers willing to pay it $0.9 billion for natural gas fields it owned in Thailand. It sold nearly all of its Canadian oil-sands developments in deals worth $7.25 billion. These sales were a sharp reversal for its Canadian oil development, for in the decade prior to the 2014 oil-price collapse, Shell and other large oil companies had invested heavily in large projects in northern Alberta to tap the heavy oil reserves that were there. Shell also found buyers for properties in Gabon that were acquired for $0.74 billion. The company found a buyer for oil fields it had in Iraq. However, it wanted to maintain its natural gas holdings in that country as well as in Oman, Qatar, and Egypt. Cutting loose its Iraqi oil assets left Shell with Middle East oil assets only in Oman, which produced about 220,000 barrels a day. In 2003, Shell had generated 450,000 barrels of Middle East oil a day. The company retreated from the Middle East because of escalating security risks and the restrictive and unprofitable oil contracts Middle Eastern governments imposed on it. The company relinquished properties it had in New Zealand. It moved toward sixteen additional asset sales valued at more than $0.5 billion. However, as oil prices approached $60 a barrel, it was not certain it was obtaining a satisfactory return for the assets it sold. A second quarter sale of an Irish gas field netted only $0.48 billion because opponents of the construction of an associated pipeline caused years of delay and had halted production until 2015. In Nigeria, Shell had to close the Trans-Niger Bonny Light pipeline because of a fire and other attacks on the country's energy infrastructure. The asset sales and closures netted needed cash, but not enough to reduce Shell's debt in a significant way.

## Pursuing a Low Cost Breakeven Point

All of the major oil companies were in a race to get their production costs down so they would be better able to deal with price contingencies. Shell tilted toward frugal development projects in older oil basins, like the Mars oil field in the Gulf of Mexico, where it applied new technology to obtain additional output. In the Mars field, Shell could produce oil for $10–$15 a barrel by reopening old wells and using water and chemicals to flush out more oil from the ground, although, in carrying out these practices, it faced additional occupational health and safety risks. Like ExxonMobil and BP, Shell was spending less, de-emphasizing energy megaprojects with huge upfront costs and long-term payoffs over twenty to thirty years. It targeted less ambitious projects that had shorter payoff periods. Certainly out of the question were expensive engineering projects in regions like Kazakhstan's Caspian Sea, which had once seemed attractive (see Chapter 1). When 2017 oil prices rose, investment in US exploration returned to the levels they had been in 2015, but Shell reduced its US investments and canceled the ambitious plans it once had for Arctic development. At the start of 2017, these efforts paid off with Shell achieving a lower cost breakeven point than its competitors. At about $43 a barrel, its breakeven point was lower than ExxonMobil's, which was about $47 a barrel, TOTAL's which was about $51 barrel, and BP's, at about $60 a barrel.

Shell's advantage over its competitors provided it with the confidence to make some new investments. Now owner of BG's vast Brazilian holdings, it invested in deep-water projects offshore of Brazil, which it calculated had a breakeven point of less than $40 a barrel. Brazil's offshore geology was rich and experts considered it one of the lowest cost places left in the world to develop new oil. Shell planned to invest $10 billion in Brazil over five years, which would make it the largest foreign investor in Brazil's fields. New technology played a role. If it could implement a concept it called budget deepwater drilling, it could lower the breakeven point of its Brazilian projects to as little as $15 a barrel. This concept meant carrying out the projects faster using fewer supplies and less equipment and adopting techniques from onshore fracking, such as drilling horizontal water-injection into the wells, to maximize the recovery of oil that was possible. The problem with using these techniques was that in working in such a lean way Shell could have spills and endanger workers' lives – inherent risks in Brazilian deep-water drilling which Shell accepted.

Having fallen behind at an early stage in fracking in the United States to smaller companies, Shell, along with other large oil firms like ExxonMobil, considered Argentina a good opportunity to undertake new shale development. The Vaca Muerta region had a business-friendly government that encouraged drilling, but many hurdles existed; for instance, labor and infrastructure were significantly higher priced than in the United States. Nonetheless, Shell invested $200 million annually in this endeavor because the area in which it was able to drill was thought to have 27 billion barrels of recoverable oil and 802 trillion cubic feet of natural gas embedded in a shale layer up to 1,700 feet thick. Thus, the Vaca Muerta region was comparable to some of the best shale regions in the United States. Shell set up a facility there that had the capacity to process 10,000 barrels of shale oil and 6 million cubic feet of natural gas daily. However, Shell did not completely give up on the United States. Along with other large oil companies, it also invested in fracking in the US Permian basin despite the fact that like ExxonMobil it lagged behind the production of the smaller companies active in the basin. The justification for making the investments was that they were part of Shell's long-term commitment to the Permian, as opposed to smaller companies, whose goal was to maximize their short-term cash flows.

## Fighting Off Bribery and Earthquake Charges

Shell had to contend with both bribery and earthquake charges. With regard to bribery, Italian prosecutors pursued criminal charges against the company and the Italian oil company Eni, alleging that their employees knew that money they had dispensed for a Nigerian oil deal would be used for bribes. Shell admitted that it had given money to Nigerian government officials, but claimed that the purpose was not bribery. Italian prosecutors, on the other hand, maintained the money went illegally to business executives and government officials, including Goodluck Jonathan, the Nigerian president at the time. The amount of money involved, more than $1 billion, was among the most prosecutors in any country had ever accused oil companies of paying in a bribery case. The prosecutors accused Shell executives, including Malcolm Brinded, its then global exploration and production chief, of being involved. Although disappointed with this indictment, the company cooperated with authorities, as it recognized that such practices had been pervasive in many of the countries where it operated.

With regard to earthquakes, the Dutch government leveled charges against Shell's natural gas joint venture with ExxonMobil in Groningen, the Netherlands that they had caused earthquakes. The Dutch government, responding to a public outcry, attempted to impose production limits on Shell and ExxonMobil, which they resisted, as the Groningen facility produced about 10 percent of Exxon and Shell's combined global natural gas. The reserves found there were among the companies' largest undeveloped resources. Although the tremors were responsible for widespread damage, they caused no deaths. Nonetheless, the charges exposed Shell and ExxonMobil to a criminal probe and they had to pay millions of Euros in damages for reconstruction.

## Working with Competitors on Fuel Efficiency and Reducing Pollution

Shell became involved in the same project as ExxonMobil, other oil companies, and the major automakers to develop the next generation of thinner engine lubricants, which would reduce friction in small, powerful turbocharged ICE engines, increase their efficiency, and reduce pollution. The engines would be capable of getting 15–25 percent more miles per gallon than standard ICE engines and would help the automakers meet stricter standards in the United States and EU. Shell also worked with the other large oil companies to cut their methane emissions from natural gas facilities. The companies promised to lower emission, stimulate better performance on the part of all parties in the industry, improve transparency and data accuracy, and promote better, but not more, regulation.

## Increasing Earnings

In the second quarter of 2017, Shell's cost cutting and its reorienting of its business projects to those that could be completed quickly and produce rapid profits began to pay off. Ben van Beurden, the CEO, claimed that Shell had effectively transitioned to a world in which prices were likely to remain lower forever because of declining demand. In the third quarter of 2017, Shell succeeded in nearly tripling its profits compared to the previous year. It promised investors that it would restore cash dividends and resume its stock buybacks. Rising oil prices, which moved close to $60 a barrel, and strong performance in the company's refining and chemicals division reinforced the earnings growth. By the end of the year, the company reported profits of $12.1 billion, the highest it had achieved since oil prices plummeted in 2014. Shell also began to do better in paying down its debt.

It believed its sale of oil properties and its acquisition of the BG Group were worthwhile as they helped to transition the firm to a lower carbon, less greenhouse gas emission, natural gas-dominated world. Proof of the benefits was that Shell's natural gas profits doubled in 2017 to $5.1 billion.

## Total

TOTAL too sensed that peak oil demand was coming and took steps to diversify into solar power and batteries, but, unlike any of its competitors, having acquired two electric utilities, it was betting on electricity.[4] Like its competitors, it was becoming increasingly committed to natural gas, but in a step none of its competitors took, it invested in Iranian natural gas. Like them, it promoted LNG use and had to look for ways to reduce methane emissions. Like other companies, it also tried to find ways to replace the oil it produced. It chose to deemphasize diesel. The results of these moves proved to be beneficial, as TOTAL's stock market performance improved.

### Peak Oil Demand and Electricity

TOTAL, like BP and Shell, anticipated that demand for oil would peak though it did not give a specific date. In its view, electricity would replace petroleum and become the world's leading power source, however, like its peers, its capabilities rested on its ability to supply the world with oil and it had no doubt it would remain an oil and natural gas company, as it had large exploration, refining, and chemical businesses and fossil fuel operations in 130 countries. Its 2016 net income in 2016 was $6.2 billion, second among major oil companies only to ExxonMobil. However, so long as oil prices were low, TOTAL recognized that it was becoming increasingly unprofitable to explore for oil, to extract and refine it, and to make it into transportation fuels and chemicals. EVs would gain in popularity, and as the world tried to contain greenhouse gas emissions, demand for oil would go down.

More than 140 countries had ratified the 2015 Paris Accord to tackle climate change. Although the Trump administration had announced that it would pull out of the agreement, most US states were shifting from oil and coal to natural gas and renewables to generate electricity.

BP had invested in solar power in the early 2000s; Shell had invested in offshore wind in the late 2000s. They exited these businesses, and they were now reentering them. Producing cleaner energy had been more expensive when they had experimented earlier, but production costs for renewables like wind and solar panels had since dropped. Seeking to hedge its bets, TOTAL took out diversified positions in alternative energy companies. It paid $1.4 billion for a majority stake in California solar panel maker SunPower. It also paid about $1 billion for the French firm Saft, which made heavy-duty industrial batteries. It was trying to coordinate SunPower and Saft activities so they could compete with Tesla's solar power and battery businesses.

With the purchases of the Belgian utility Lampris and the French utility Direct Energy, TOTAL was increasing its wager on electricity. Among major oil companies, these moves were unique. Lampris relied mostly on natural gas and renewable energy to provide electricity to over 1 million European customers. Direct Energie had nearly 1.4 gigawatts gas-fired power and renewable installed electrical capacity. Only about 4 percent of the world's electricity was oil-based in 2017. This amount was likely to fall by half by the middle of the next decade. To defuse the risk of declining oil demand, TOTAL contemplated becoming more committed to electricity as a hedge against oil's decline. Achieving this goal would require a change in its business model. Most current electricity was natural gas or coal based, but renewables had made rapid advances. Coal's share was shrinking. With the acquisitions TOTAL had made, TOTAL not only had solar panel and battery businesses. It could generate electricity with natural gas and sell it to households and commercial users.

TOTAL reported that renewables, natural gas, and electric power yielded about 5 percent of its $9.42 billion operating income in 2016, a small percentage. However, its goal was to have 20 percent of the energy it produced come from renewables by 2035. While analysts expected demand for oil to increase at a 0.5 percent annual rate globally until 2040, they expected demand for electricity to grow at about a 2 percent annual rate. Oil came from different places in the world. Extracting it off the coast of Latin America and shipping it to China, TOTAL like other companies transported and sold oil nearly everywhere. Electricity could not be stored and transported long distances. To keep losses at a minimum, consumers had to consume the electricity as close as possible to where utilities generated it. Therefore,

TOTAL had in its plans the acquisition of other local electricity producers and distributors.

## Iranian Natural Gas and LNG

Betting on electricity also meant that TOTAL, like other large energy companies, had to increase its natural gas production. Consistent with these plans, TOTAL chose to invest $1 billion in a giant Iranian natural gas field in the Persian Gulf. Active in Iran before the Islamic revolution, it was first Western company to make a large commitment to Iran after the signing of the nuclear deal with that country. TOTAL had interest in such an agreement before the deal but did not go forward with it because of US sanctions. It also abstained because of low prices, and the uncertain financial terms that Iran had been willing to offer. The arrangement with Iran to which TOTAL agreed had flexible terms and a twenty-year period. TOTAL was the lead operator and its partners were the China National Petroleum and the Iranian company Petropar that put another $3.8 billion into the pact. Shell and the Italian oil company ENI were looking for their own agreements with Iran and Shell was working with the National Iranian Oil Company and the Chinese company Sinopec.

TOTAL had fewer reservations about working with Iran than other oil companies, which were more concerned about Iranian support for terrorism, its human rights violations, and its ballistic-missile technology. Companies like Shell, ExxonMobil, and BP viewed the options they had in other parts of the world to be more promising than the options they had in Iran. TOTAL was in a privileged position vis-à-vis Iran, because, as a French company, Iran was more interested in working with it than with US and UK companies. TOTAL's deal with Iran had large potential since Iran had the world's second largest natural gas reserves, but by investing in Iran, TOTAL risked alienating Saudi Arabia and Iran's Sunni rivals. Iran's oil output had plateaued after a brief rise following the end of sanctions. It grew from 2.7 million barrels a day to 3.9 million barrels a day, but the country still needed investment estimated to be in the range of $100 billion to reach its goals for oil and natural gas production by 2020.

With other companies, TOTAL had reason to be concerned about the methane emissions that accompanied natural gas production. These emissions amounted to around 76 million tons each year and they were potent greenhouse gases. TOTAL worked with other companies on efforts to reduce these emissions and signed the agreement to drive down the emissions, to encourage companies to improve their performance, and to achieve increased transparency, greater data accuracy, and better regulation.

As part of the emphasis on natural gas, TOTAL, like other large energy companies, promoted the use of LNG. All of them had made substantial investment in LNG, yet they had to do more to further ramp up global markets for the fuel. They supported its use in industrial trucking and shipping and encouraged the building of power plants reliant on LNG. The infrastructure to provide LNG to markets in Southeast Asia and Africa was deficient. Although the number of countries with the capacity to import LNG had increased from seventeen to forty in a decade, the cost of building terminals continued to be high and remained out of reach for many nations. TOTAL, therefore, partnered with Shell to construct an LNG terminal in the Ivory Coast and was contemplating providing Myanmar and South Africa with LNG infrastructure, as well as exporting LNG to these countries and building power plants that used LNG to produce electricity.

## *Low Breakeven Point*

TOTAL brought its breakeven point down to about $51 a barrel, an accomplishment that provided it with more freedom to invest. However, like the other large oil companies it was under pressure to make bets on projects that it could carry out quickly and bring returns within a few years. It could no longer invest regularly in large billion-dollar projects that could take more than a decade to complete and only then start to yield payoffs. Like other major oil companies, it had learned how to rein in spending during the downturn in which oil prices fell from more than $100 a barrel to under $30 a barrel. Like the other companies, it concluded that continued emphasis on potentially budget-busting projects was not acceptable. In the first quarter of 2017, the company's efforts to control spending paid off, and it improved its profitability after years of weak earnings. It surmounted this hurdle, and, like the other oil companies, it felt the imperative to continue to maintain capital discipline, as future oil price swings were a distinct possibility. Yet, it was difficult to maneuver in an environment of boom and bust oil prices, as TOTAL also had to try to find replacement for the oil it produced, which meant that it could not cease entirely from spending on exploration and development or on acquisitions. TOTAL chose to go the route of acquisition, buying the Danish oil conglomerate Maersk, which gave it an immediate 0.5 million barrel a day boost in production. This acquisition raised TOTAL's daily oil and natural gas production to the equivalent of 3 million barrels a day, which put it close ExxonMobil and Shell in daily production.

TOTAL's purchase of Maersk provided a boost to North Sea oil, once considered moribund because of high costs, aging infrastructure, and declining output. TOTAL became the second largest off shore operator in Europe. It paid for the deal with close to $5 billion in shares and took on $2.5 billion of Maersk's debt and $3 billion in the costs of decommissioning North Sea fields. Next to Shell's acquisition of BG, TOTAL's acquisition of Maersk was the largest acquisition by an oil and natural gas company in 2016–2017. While Shell and BP came close to abandoning the North Sea entirely, they were revisiting this assessment and had started to become interested in the region's revival. Shell had plans to spend between $0.6 and $1 billion a year on North Sea oil and BP was trying to double its North Sea production by 2020. All the companies that invested anticipated that they could slash North Sea production costs by more than 50 percent. They had the ambitious goal that they could get it down to the equivalent of $12 a barrel.

## Cutbacks in Diesel

The VW scandal was a blow to the expectation that diesel fuel demand for passenger cars might rise in Europe. It caused a backlash against diesel, which led TOTAL and other European refiners to cut back, soon after they had invested as much as $10 billion in upgrades and increases in production capacity. TOTAL and the other refiners decided to try to convert facilities meant for passenger car fuel to chemically similar fuels for airplanes and ships, a transformation that was not simple. Pollution regulation was in place to slash the amount of sulfur permitted in marine fuel ocean going vessels. Ships could no longer use bunker fuel composed of residual left over after refineries made diesel from crude. The producers were under intense competitive pressure from Asian and Middle Eastern refiners. The sector suffered from overcapacity. After Dieselgate, politicians in Germany and elsewhere in Europe no longer resisted the argument that nitrous oxide emission from diesel engines posed a problem. They were in the midst of tightening the control of the emissions, after TOTAL had invested $2.4 billion in diesel upgrades at its largest European facilities.

Since 2009, due to competitive pressures, companies had shut down twelve refineries in Europe, leaving only 105 in operation. The expectation was that by the mid-2030s, the European continent would need no more than fifty refineries. Bans the United Kingdom and France had imposed on ICEs would take effect after 2040 and EVs would be more popular. Under these circumstances, TOTAL was planning for the further streamlining and phasing out of its diesel refineries in Europe.

## Better Stock Market Performance

In the second quarter of 2017, TOTAL's ROI reached 10 percent and its earnings grew by about a third, but investors – aware that the oil industry's return to profits was largely due to spending cuts and a move to projects with quick paybacks – remained cautious about investing in TOTAL and in all the major oil companies. Among these companies, from 2015 to 2017, ExxonMobil did not advance very much, Shell did very well, BP made improvements, but TOTAL had the most stable growth in net income and revenue (Figure 16.1), and the stock market rewarded it for its stability. For the three-year period that started on May 4, 2015 and ended on May 4, 2018, it achieved higher gains for investors than ExxonMobil, BP, or Shell; the gains were 24 percent, while Shell and BP advanced by about 1 percent and ExxonMobil lost about 15 percent. Yet none of these firms came close to performing as well as the Dow Industrials as a whole, which rose around 60 percent.

## Conclusion – How Much Strategic Change Had Taken Place?

The strategic moves that the major integrated oil and natural gas companies made coming out of the 2012–2016 period, the period in which there had been a major boom and bust in petroleum prices that profoundly affected them, created large gaps among them. Already dissimilar before this time of volatility, their heterogeneity grew as they had different understandings of the risks and uncertainties they faced, had different assumptions about the future, and took different paths to hedge themselves against what they anticipated might come

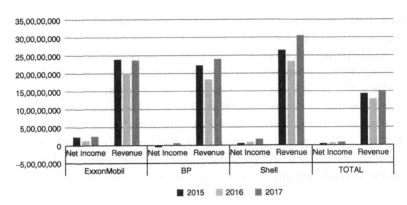

**Figure 16.1** The average quarterly income and revenue of major oil companies
2015–2017
Derived from Annual Reports

next. The gap between them widened, as they moved beyond positions
they had previously occupied.

ExxonMobil went from trying to stay the course, to clinging rather
aggressively to that course. It separated itself from the other major oil
and natural gas companies by refusing to acknowledge the possibility
of peak oil and by not opening up new avenues of investment in
alternative energy. Like all the integrated oil and natural gas companies, it had to cut back on its exploration and production expenses, but
the cutbacks it made were not as extreme. Like these companies, it put
a renewed emphasis on natural gas, but unlike them, it significantly
increased its investments in US shale oil and natural gas, an area where
it still had to prove that it had the expertise to compete effectively
against the independent operators.

With Deepwater Horizon payments continuing to burden BP, it had to
make greater cutbacks than ExxonMobil. The adjustments it could make
in the eighteen months after 2016 were small but it effectively lowered its
costs. All the major oil and natural gas companies were in a race to lower
their breakeven points so they could compete in an era of lower oil prices.
BP started at the worst point and made significant progress. It also
changed its assumptions about the future, envisioned peak demand coming in a few decades, and upped its commitment to wind power.

Shell broke with the past more than ExxonMobil or BP based on the
assumption that peak demand was imminent and could take place

within a decade and that in the long term it had to expect a low fossil fuel future. Shell invested in solar, EV charging, and electricity. It too pursued a lower breakeven point to position itself better to avoid gigantic losses should oil prices plunge again. It too shed assets and tried to acquire assets where the costs of production were lower. It had to sell these assets in a systematic and timely way in order to pay off the vast debt it had accumulated when it bought BG.

TOTAL made no explicit prognostications about peak demand but imagined a future in which electricity powered by natural gas and renewable energy would prevail. It maintained the investments it had in solar and batteries and started to acquire electric utilities, raised its investments in natural gas and LNG, and replenished its oil reserves via a North Sea acquisition.

All of the companies were constrained by financial weakness and had to make asset sales and reduce their capital spending and restrict it to projects with shorter and more certain payoffs. This change was substantial and was an important result of the ups and downs in energy prices they recently experienced. They tilted away from oil and toward natural gas, yet confronted a new obstacle, methane emissions, as they moved in this direction. For TOTAL, the tilt toward natural gas was fraught with danger since it depended on its ability to do business with Iran. When President Trump shut down US participation in the nuclear deal, TOTAL faced the dilemma of whether it could maintain its ties with that country.

All the companies made it an explicit priority to lower their breakeven point. Shell, which was very active in both selling and acquiring assets, got its breakeven point down to about $43 for a barrel of oil. ExxonMobil came in at about $47 for a barrel of oil. TOTAL was at about $51 for a barrel of oil, and BP was at about $61 but then lowered this number.

More than any company, ExxonMobil had to deal with its past miscalculations, which it had not corrected in its financial statements. It had to write down the investments it had made in Canadian tar sands and fracking. Yet it persisted, as indicated, unlike any of the other companies, in trying to exploit the opportunity for fracking in the United States via its XTO subsidiary. Shell also had some interest in fracking, but it confined that interest mainly to Argentina, and not the United States, where small independents – more nimble than the large integrated companies were and more experienced with fracking – had taken the lead.

ExxonMobil also had to give up on any immediate gain it could achieve through its partnership with Rosneft. Even after Trump's election, and Rex Tillerson's appointment as Secretary of State, the company could not achieve a waiver that would allow it to continue to operate in Russia. ExxonMobil was not the only company that had to deal with missteps and problems in its global operations. Shell faced bribery charges in Nigeria. In its home country, the Netherlands, it confronted accusations that its natural gas operations had caused earthquakes. BP continued to have leaks in the Prudhoe Bay in Alaska.

Although all the companies with the exception of ExxonMobil sensed that peak oil demand was coming, their assumption about their identities continued to be that they were primarily fossil-fuel companies. As such, even if this identity had been somewhat diluted, they still had to try to replenish their diminishing oil reserves for without replenishing these reserves, they could not keep their production going. Their time horizons, however, shrank because of the 2012–2016 boom and bust cycle in oil prices. They all withdrew from large-scale, expensive projects that had little likelihood of immediate payoff. The possible harm to their bottom lines was too great to sustain these types of investments. As oil companies, they were in retreat. This change was a big one in the oil and natural gas sector. Shell's solution to the problem of replenishing its oil reserves had been to acquire BG, not only for its vast natural gas holdings, but also for its position as Brazil's largest off-shore oil driller. Similarly, TOTAL solved this problem by acquiring the Danish firm Maersk, and in doing so choosing to try to revive North Sea fields that almost every firm had given up on as moribund just a few years earlier.

Would the bets these firms made pay off? The risks and uncertainties they faced continued to be high. For both BP and ExxonMobil, technology was an especially important part of their strategies. They bet on supercomputers and Silicon Valley to increase their ability to find oil and natural gas and remove it from the ground. The supercomputers and the Silicon Valley talent might be able to eliminate some of the uncertainty that plagued them when they explored for oil and extracted it from distant and dangerous locations. The move in this direction was promising, but uncertain.

In its development of Brazilian offshore oil, Shell was also relying on advanced technology. Its bet was that it could significantly lower extraction costs if it could apply horizontal drilling techniques that the frackers used to ocean drilling. The risk it was running was whether it could apply these techniques without accident in such a different environment. Like TOTAL, BP, and ExxonMobil, Shell, in trying to do away with the uncertainties and risks it confronted might be creating new ones.

The responses of these companies in 2017–2018 were disparate. The moves they made deepened the divisions among these firms and they created a more heterogeneous sector. The companies' perceptions of the risks and opportunities they confronted diverged more than they had in the past. Their assumptions about the future evolved in different ways. The specific hedges they took to protect themselves from future contingencies also diverged. Yet, the basic hedging mechanisms they had in place to deal with risks and uncertainties had not budged that much. They still put great emphasis on operational safety, for they had to, as one major mistake could be devastating. They still operated as upstream and downstream entities, in the hope that this type of organization could lower their costs and balance the flow of energy price fluctuations. Finally, they still innovated and experimented with different approaches and technologies, some of which were renewable and less climate altering and some of which were not.

## Notes

1. This review of ExxonMobil strategies comes from an analysis of the following *Wall Street Journal* articles about the company that appeared between January 1, 2017 and August 1, 2018. The articles are listed below in chronological order starting with the most recent articles first.

    Olson, Bradley. "Oil Profit Fails to Impress – Investors Expect to See More from Crude's Rally." *Wall Street Journal*, July 28, 2018.

    Olson, Bradley. "Exxon Is Running Low – The Once Mighty Oil Giant Is Struggling. Profits Are Down, and some Big Bets Failed to Pay Off. Now a New CEO Has a Plan to Spend the Company Back to Prosperity." *Wall Street Journal*, July 14, 2018.

    Faucon, Benoit, Summer Said, and Stephanie Yang. "Oil Soars as OPEC Agrees to Small Boost." *Wall Street Journal*, June 23, 2018.

Vyas, Kejal. "World News: Guyana Dreams of Oil Riches – An Exxon Mobil-Led Consortium Begins Offshore Drilling After Discovering Huge Find." *Wall Street Journal*, June 22, 2018.

Kent, Sarah. "Industry Aims to Spread Fracking Boom." *Wall Street Journal*, June 21, 2018.

Magalhaes, Luciana, and Paulo Trevisani. "Oil Drillers Buy Offshore Brazil Fields – Consortium Led by Exxon Snags Biggest Block in Auction that Drew Robust Interest." *Wall Street Journal*, June 8, 2018.

Jakab, Spencer. "Oil Prices Pinching Producers' Profits." *Wall Street Journal*, June 1, 2018.

Whelan, Robbie, Paulo Trevisani, and Bradley Olson. "Oil Drillers March to a Latin Beat." *Wall Street Journal*, May 22, 2018.

Wursthorn, Michael, and Akane Otani. "Energy Stocks Flip from Dud to Darling – The Sector Is Up More than 10% in the Past Month as Oil Prices, Company Earnings Rise." *Wall Street Journal*, May 9, 2018.

Olson, Bradley, and Sarah Kent. "Big Oil Gushes Cash but Reins in Spending." *Wall Street Journal*, April 28, 2018.

Jakab, Spencer. "Exxon's New, and Lower, Normal." *Wall Street Journal*, April 28, 2018.

McFarlane, Sarah, and Bradley Olson. "Exxon, Qatar Explore Gas Pact." *Wall Street Journal*, April 11, 2018.

Olson, Bradley. "In Oil Patch, Investors Push for New Frugality." *Wall Street Journal*, April 3, 2018.

Armental, Maria. "Exxon Fails to Stop Climate Inquiries." *Wall Street Journal*, March 30, 2018.

Patterson, Scott, Bradley Olson, and James V. Grimaldi. "Exxon Designed Deal to Skirt Scrutiny – Oil Giant Was Excited about Africa Prospect but Worried about US Laws." *Wall Street Journal*, March 30, 2018.

Matthews, Christopher M., and Bradley Olson. "Shale Deal Could Signal Consolidation in Permian." *Wall Street Journal*, March 29, 2018.

Gold, Russell. "Sanctions, Price of Oil Doom Exxon's Arctic Gambit." *Wall Street Journal*, March 2, 2018.

Eisen, Ben. "Energy Sector Tumbles by 4.1%." *Wall Street Journal*, February 5, 2018.

Jakab, Spencer. "No More Tigers in Exxon's Tank." *Wall Street Journal*, February 5, 2018.

Olson, Bradley. "Exxon, Chevron Come Up Short – Two Biggest US Oil Producers Disappoint Investors, Despite Big Gains Tied to Tax Law." *Wall Street Journal*, February 3, 2018.

Kent, Sarah. "Big Oil Drills again with Eye on Costs." *Wall Street Journal*, February 1, 2018.

"John Bogle and the Rockefeller Fund Respond." *Wall Street Journal*, January 30, 2018.

Kantchev, Georgi, and Benoit Faucon. "Oil Supplies Retreat, Bolstering Producers." *Wall Street Journal*, December 13, 2017.

Kent, Sarah, and Bradley Olson. "Energy Firms Commit to Cut Gas Pollution." *Wall Street Journal*, November 24, 2017.

Alessi, Christopher. "OPEC Expects Peak Demand by 2040." *Wall Street Journal*, November 8, 2017.

Cook, Lynn. "End to Gas Glut Predicted – Oil Companies Defend Big Bets, Citing the Rising Demand for LNG in China and India." *Wall Street Journal*, October 18, 2017.

Kiernan, Paul. "Brazil Holds Its Most Successful Oil Auction." *Wall Street Journal*, September 28, 2017.

Taplin, Nathaniel. "Producers Are Adjusting to Lower Oil Prices." *Wall Street Journal*, August 2, 2017.

Olson, Bradley. "Energy Firms Post Gusher of Earnings." *Wall Street Journal*, July 29, 2017.

Kent, Sarah. "Big Oil Urged to show Discipline – Investors Want Companies to Avoid Budget-Busting Projects of the Past." *Wall Street Journal*, July 27, 2017.

Rubenfeld, Samuel, Lynn Cook, and Ian Talley. "US and Exxon Spar Over Russia Sanctions." *Wall Street Journal*, July 21, 2017.

Faucon, Benoit. "Big Oil Remains Wary of Iran Dealings." *Wall Street Journal*, July 13, 2017.

Olson, Bradley, and Peter Nicholas. "Oil Giants Push Back on Russia Measure – Executives Warn Tougher Sanctions Could Shelve Energy Projects Around World." *Wall Street Journal*, July 5, 2017.

Kent, Sarah. "Panel Pushes for Climate Disclosure." *Wall Street Journal*, June 30, 2017.

Olson, Bradley. "Big Drillers Flock to Shale – Chevron and Others Expect More Success than Smaller Rivals in Permian Basin Region." *Wall Street Journal*, June 19, 2017.

Olson, Bradley. "Exxon's Accounting Draws Fire." *Wall Street Journal*, June 3, 2017.

Jakab, Spencer. "Paris Exit: Less than Meets the Eye." *Wall Street Journal*, June 2, 2017.

Olson, Bradley. "Investors to Exxon: Heed Climate – Shareholder Vote Backs 'Stress Test' of Oil Assets Amid Tough Environmental Rules." *Wall Street Journal*, June 1, 2017.

Olson, Bradley, Sarah Krouse, and Sarah Kent. "Big Investors Weigh Rebuking Exxon on Climate." *Wall Street Journal*, May 26, 2017.

Cook, Lynn, and Elena Cherney. "Innovations in Energy (A Special Report) – Get Ready for Peak Oil Demand: There's a Growing Consensus That the End of Ever-Rising Consumption Is in Sight; the Big Question that Many Oil Companies are Debating: When? A Lot Is Riding on the Answer." *Wall Street Journal*, May 22, 2017.

Olson, Bradley, and Jay Solomon. "Sanctions Fail to Curb Russian Oil." *Wall Street Journal*, May 9, 2017.

Kent, Sarah, and Taos Turner. "Big Oil Jumps on Argentina Shale – Shell, Exxon and Others That Were Late to US Boom Grab at New Opportunities." *Wall Street Journal*, May 5, 2017.

Olson, Bradley. "Exxon, Chevron Earnings Point to Industry Recovery." *Wall Street Journal*, April 29, 2017.

Jakab, Spencer. "'Big Oil' Is Getting Less Bold." *Wall Street Journal*, April 29, 2017.

Solomon, Jay, and Bradley Olson. "Trump Rebuffs Exxon on Russia." *Wall Street Journal*, April 22, 2017.

Solomon, Jay, and Bradley Olson. "Exxon Seeks Waiver for Russia Deal." *Wall Street Journal*, April 20, 2017.

Olson, Bradley, and Paul Kiernan. "Brazil's Deepwater Oil Lures Exxon." *Wall Street Journal*, April 5, 2017.

Kent, Sarah. "Oil Industry Struggles to Break Even – Despite Spending Cuts and a Modest Rebound, Top Companies Fight to Keep Up with Expenses." *Wall Street Journal*, April 3, 2017.

Ailworth, Erin. "Low Oil Price Ushers in Shale 2.0 – Texas Fracker EOG Pioneers Way to Turn Profit by Extracting Crude Faster and at Less Cost." *Wall Street Journal*, March 31, 2017.

Castellanos, Sara. "Exxon Harnesses Computing Power." *Wall Street Journal*, March 29, 2017.

Jakab, Spencer. "Exxon Mobil's New Reality: Fewer Risks, Lower Returns." *Wall Street Journal*, March 10, 2017.

Kent, Sarah, and Bradley Olson. "Oil Firms Now Favor Frugal Bets – Exxon, BP and Other Energy Companies Are Avoiding Expensive Engineering Projects." *Wall Street Journal*, March 9, 2017.

Olson, Bradley. "Exxon Places Big Wager on US Energy – Oil Giant's $20 Billion Spending Plan Shows How Sector Is Shifting Focus Toward America." *Wall Street Journal*, March 7, 2017.

Olson, Bradley. "Exxon Sharpens Focus on US Shale Oil." *Wall Street Journal*, March 2, 2017.

Kent, Sarah, Bradley Olson, and Georgi Kantchev. "Prices Leave Drillers in Crude Quandary – Stubborn Market, Climate Rules Cloud Equation on Bringing Oil Up Out of Ground." *Wall Street Journal*, February 18, 2017.

Jakab, Spencer. "Big Oil's Spending Gets Less Big." *Wall Street Journal,* February 8, 2017.

Olson, Bradley. "Exxon Takes a $2 Billion Charge – Oil Slump Results in Lowest Annual Profit in 20 Years; Company Dogged by SEC Probe." *Wall Street Journal,* February 1, 2017.

Olson, Bradley, and Sarah Kent. "Small Oil Firms Spend as Titans Hold Back." *Wall Street Journal,* January 30, 2017.

Olson, Bradley. "Exxon Joins Land Rush in Red-Hot Southwest – Oil Company Commits as Much as $6.6 Billion to Permian Basin in Texas and New Mexico." *Wall Street Journal,* January 18, 2017.

Jenkins, Holman W., Jr. "Exxon Vs. Russia Illusions." *Wall Street Journal,* January 11, 2017.

2. This review of BP strategies comes from an analysis of the following *Wall Street Journal* articles about the company that appeared between January 1, 2017 and August 1, 2018. The articles are listed below in chronological order starting with the most recent articles first. Some of the articles deal with the sector as a whole and are the same articles used in doing the ExxonMobil update.

Kent, Sarah. "Oil Prices Propel BP's Resurgence – Energy Producer's Quarterly Profit Soars; Deepwater Disaster Remains Financial Drag." *Wall Street Journal,* August 1, 2018.

Matthews, Christopher M. "Oil Mixes with Silicon Valley – But Warily." *Wall Street Journal,* July 25, 2018.

Kent, Sarah. "Big Oil Pulls Back, Threatens Supplies." *Wall Street Journal,* June 22, 2018.

Kent, Sarah. "BP's Grueling Recovery Gathers Momentum." *Wall Street Journal,* May 2, 2018.

Martuscelli, Carlo. "BP Names Industry Veteran as Its New Chairman." *Wall Street Journal,* April 27, 2018.

Kent, Sarah, and Christopher M. Matthews. "Oil Patch Catches Computer Bug – Technology Is Being Used to Speed Up Exploration Process, Avoid Misplaced Wells." *Wall Street Journal,* April 11, 2018.

Alessi, Christopher. "BP Sees Quicker March to Peak Oil Demand." *Wall Street Journal,* February 21, 2018.

Kent, Sarah. "BP Takes Tax Hit but Shows Strength." *Wall Street Journal,* February 7, 2018.

Kent, Sarah. "BP Takes on Its Doubters – Oil Company Pushes to Regain Prestige Lost After Deepwater Horizon Spill in 2010." *Wall Street Journal,* February 5, 2018.

Kent, Sarah. "Big Oil Drills again with Eye on Costs." *Wall Street Journal,* February 1, 2018.

Faucon, Benoit, and Sarah Kent. "BP Heads Back to Volatile Northern Iraq." *Wall Street Journal*, January 19, 2018.

Kent, Sarah. "BP Adds $1.7 Billion to Cover Costs of Deepwater Horizon." *Wall Street Journal*, January 17, 2018.

Kent, Sarah, and Nina Adam. "Norway, Others Rethink Oil Bets." *Wall Street Journal*, January 4, 2018.

Kent, Sarah. "BP to Take $1.5 Billion Tax Charge." *Wall Street Journal*, January 3, 2018.

Kantchev, Georgi, and Benoit Faucon. "Oil Supplies Retreat, Bolstering Producers." *Wall Street Journal*, December 13, 2017.

Salvaterra, Neanda. "Angola Loses Allure for Oil Firms." *Wall Street Journal*, December 9, 2017.

Yang, Stephanie, and Alison Sider. "Climb in Oil Prices Buoys Hopes of Energy Producers." *Wall Street Journal*, November 29, 2017.

Kent, Sarah, and Chester Dawson. "Combustion Engines Catch New Spark – Thinner Oils Improve Efficiency, Helping the Old Technology Stay Relevant as Electric Vehicles Gain Ground." *Wall Street Journal*, November 20, 2017.

Kent, Sarah. "BP Signals Optimism with New Buybacks." *Wall Street Journal*, November 1, 2017.

Olson, Bradley, and Sarah Kent. "Oil's Profits Fail to Draw Investors." *Wall Street Journal*, October 28, 2017.

Kent, Sarah. "Breaking Even Becomes Goal in Oil." *Wall Street Journal*, October 27, 2017.

Kantchev, Georgi, and Sarah Kent. "Energy Stocks Lag Behind Oil Prices." *Wall Street Journal*, October 26, 2017.

Kent, Sarah. "BP's Chairman Plans to Retire." *Wall Street Journal*, October 20, 2017.

Cook, Lynn. "End to Gas Glut Predicted – Oil Companies Defend Big Bets, Citing the Rising Demand for LNG in China and India." *Wall Street Journal*, October 18, 2017.

McFarlane, Sarah. "Energy Firms Hunt for LNG Buyers." *Wall Street Journal*, October 16, 2017.

Kiernan, Paul. "After Decade, Brazil Lets in Big Oil Firms – The Country Is Looking to Expand Its Crude-Production Potential and Revive Its Economy with an Auction This Week." *Wall Street Journal*, September 27, 2017.

Kent, Sarah. "North Sea, Surprisingly, Is Oil Hot Spot Again." *Wall Street Journal*, September 20, 2017.

Ailworth, Erin. "Wind Powers Rural US." *Wall Street Journal*, September 7, 2017.

Sider, Alison, and Rob Copeland. "Oil's $100 Million Man Pays Price for Bad Bets." *Wall Street Journal*, August 4, 2017.

Taplin, Nathaniel. "Producers Are Adjusting to Lower Oil Prices." *Wall Street Journal*, August 2, 2017.

Amon, Michael. "BP Says Its Break-Even Is $47 Oil." *Wall Street Journal*, August 2, 2017.

Kent, Sarah. "Big Oil Urged to Show Discipline – Investors Want Companies to Avoid Budget-Busting Projects of the Past." *Wall Street Journal*, July 27, 2017.

McFarlane, Sarah, Matt Jarzemsky, and Ben Dummett. "BP in Talks to Sell North Sea Assets – Discussions Are at an Early Stage, with Private-Equity Firms among Potential Buyers." *Wall Street Journal*, July 21, 2017.

Faucon, Benoit. "Big Oil Remains Wary of Iran Dealings." *Wall Street Journal*, July 13, 2017.

Kent, Sarah. "Panel Pushes for Climate Disclosure." *Wall Street Journal*, June 30, 2017.

Kantchev, Georgi, Sarah Kent, and Erin Ailworth. "Oil Companies Adapt to a Low-Price World." *Wall Street Journal*, June 20, 2017.

Kent, Sarah. "BP's India Natural-Gas Plans Advance." *Wall Street Journal*, June 16, 2017.

Cook, Lynn, and Elena Cherney. "Innovations in Energy (A Special Report) – Get Ready for Peak Oil Demand: There's a Growing Consensus That the End of Ever-Rising Consumption Is in Sight; the Big Question That Many Oil Companies Are Debating: When? A Lot Is Riding on the Answer." *Wall Street Journal*, May 22, 2017.

Molinski, Dan. "BP Says Well Leak Is Under Control." *Wall Street Journal*, April 18, 2017.

Molinski, Dan. "BP Well's Gas Leak Persists in Alaska." *Wall Street Journal*, April 17, 2017.

Kent, Sarah. "Oil Industry Struggles to Break Even – Despite Spending Cuts and a Modest Rebound, Top Companies Fight to Keep Up with Expenses." *Wall Street Journal*, April 3, 2017.

Jakab, Spencer. "Big Oil's Spending Gets Less Big." *Wall Street Journal*, February 8, 2017.

Olson, Bradley, and Sarah Kent. "Small Oil Firms Spend as Titans Hold Back." *Wall Street Journal*, January 30, 2017.

3. This review of Shell strategies comes from an analysis of the following *Wall Street Journal* articles about the company that appeared between January 1, 2017 and August 1, 2018. The articles are listed below in chronological order starting with the most recent articles first. These articles mainly concern Shell. The analysis also uses articles that cover the sector as a whole, found in the ExxonMobil and BP updates, for the Shell update.

Olson, Bradley. "Energy Firms Post Gusher of Earnings." *Wall Street Journal*, July 29, 2017.

Kent, Sarah. "Shell Girds for 'Lower Forever' Oil." *Wall Street Journal*, July 28, 2017.

Kent, Sarah. "Big Oil Urged to Show Discipline – Investors Want Companies to Avoid Budget-Busting Projects of the Past." *Wall Street Journal*, July 27, 2017.

Faucon, Benoit. "Big Oil Remains Wary of Iran Dealings." *Wall Street Journal*, July 13, 2017.

Amon, Michael. "Shell Faces Loss on Sale of Stake in Irish Gas Field." *Wall Street Journal*, July 13, 2017.

Kent, Sarah. "Dutch Quakes Rattle Exxon, Shell – Big Gas Field Is Causing Tremors, Exposing Energy Firms to Criminal Probe and Rising Bills." *Wall Street Journal*, June 26, 2017.

Kent, Sarah. "Groningen Field Disrupts Bucolic Farm Life." *Wall Street Journal*, June 26, 2017.

Matthews, Christopher M. "Shale Boom's Impact in One Word: Plastics – Petrochemicals Power US Manufacturing, Exports." *Wall Street Journal*, June 26, 2017.

Kantchev, Georgi, Sarah Kent, and Erin Ailworth. "Oil Companies Adapt to a Low-Price World." *Wall Street Journal*, June 20, 2017.

Kent, Sarah, and Eric Sylvers. "Nigerian Oil Deal Was Worry at Shell." *Wall Street Journal*, April 10, 2017.

Kent, Sarah. "Oil Industry Struggles to Break Even – Despite Spending Cuts and a Modest Rebound, Top Companies Fight to Keep Up with Expenses." *Wall Street Journal*, April 3, 2017.

Jakab, Spencer. "Big Oil's Spending Gets Less Big." *Wall Street Journal*, February 8, 2017.

Olson, Bradley, and Sarah Kent. "Small Oil Firms Spend as Titans Hold Back." *Wall Street Journal*, January 30, 2017.

4. This review of TOTAL strategies comes from an analysis of the following *Wall Street Journal* articles about the company that appeared between January 1, 2017 and August 1, 2018. The articles are listed below in chronological order starting with the most recent articles first. These articles mainly concern TOTAL. The analysis also uses articles that cover the sector as a whole, some found in the ExxonMobil, BP, and Shell updates, for the TOTAL update.

Molinski, Dan, and Christopher Alessi. "Oil Prices Extend Streak on Iran Fears." *Wall Street Journal*, August 22, 2018.

Faucon, Benoit. "Total Struggles Over Its Iran Stake." *Wall Street Journal*, August 21, 2018.

Matthews, Christopher M. "Oil Mixes with Silicon Valley – But Warily." *Wall Street Journal*, July 25, 2018.

Kent, Sarah, and Benoit Faucon. "Business News: Oil Giant Total Pursues Risky Bets – French Energy Firm, Undaunted by Setback in Iran, Doubles Down on Russia with Gas Deal." *Wall Street Journal*, June 06, 2018.

Olson, Bradley, and Sarah Kent. "Big Oil Gushes Cash but Reins in Spending." *Wall Street Journal*, April 28, 2018.

Kent, Sarah. "Oil Producer Pushes Strategic Shift." *Wall Street Journal*, April 19, 2018.

Meichtry, Stacy, and Margherita Stancati. "World News: Saudis Drum Up Business in France." *Wall Street Journal*, April 11, 2018.

Kent, Sarah. "Business News: Big Oil Drills again with Eye on Costs." *Wall Street Journal*, February 1, 2018.

Kent, Sarah, and Bradley Olson. "Business News: Energy Firms Commit to Cut Gas Pollution." *Wall Street Journal*, November 24, 2017.

Kent, Sarah. "Earnings: Shell's Profit nearly Triples – Recovering Oil Prices, Increased Production and Cost Cutting Help Lift Quarterly Results." *Wall Street Journal*, November 3, 2017.

Olson, Bradley, and Sarah Kent. "Oil's Profits Fail to Draw Investors." *Wall Street Journal*, October 28, 2017.

Kent, Sarah. "Breaking Even Becomes Goal in Oil." *Wall Street Journal*, October 27, 2017.

Matthews, Christopher M. "The Week Ahead: Big Oil Looks for Bumper Profits." *Wall Street Journal*, October 23, 2017.

McFarlane, Sarah. "The Week Ahead: Energy Firms Hunt for LNG Buyers." *Wall Street Journal*, October 16, 2017.

Kent, Sarah. "North Sea, Surprisingly, Is Oil Hot Spot again." *Wall Street Journal*, September 20, 2017.

Kent, Sarah, and Costas Paris. "Maersk Trims Sails by Selling Oil Assets – France's Total to Pay $4.95 Billion in Shares, as Danish Group Focuses on Shipping." *Wall Street Journal*, August 22, 2017.

Kent, Sarah. "Big Oil Urged to show Discipline – Investors Want Companies to Avoid Budget-Busting Projects of the Past." *Wall Street Journal*, July 27, 2017.

Trofimov, Yaroslav. "World News – Middle East Crossroads: Iran's Stature Grows as Its Adversaries Quarrel." *Wall Street Journal*, July 14, 2017.

Faucon, Benoit. "Big Oil Remains Wary of Iran Dealings." *Wall Street Journal*, July 13, 2017.

Faucon, Benoit, and Sarah Kent. "Business News: Total Gets Jump with Iran Pact." *Wall Street Journal*, July 5, 2017.

Kent, Sarah, and Benoit Faucon. "Business News: Total to Seal $1 Billion Iranian Gas Deal." *Wall Street Journal*, July 3, 2017.

Kent, Sarah. "Total to Invest $1 Billion in Iran Venture." *Wall Street Journal*, June 21, 2017.

Gold, Russell. "Oil Giant Sees a Future in Volts – France's Total, Sensing Peak Demand for Crude Oil, Bets it Can also Produce and Sell Electricity." *Wall Street Journal*, June 14, 2017.

Gold, Russell, and Alison Sider. "Long a Promise, Gas Goes Global – New Natural-Gas Infrastructure and Flexible Contracts Lead World's Prices to Converge." *Wall Street Journal*, June 7, 2017.

Cook, Lynn, and Elena Cherney. "Innovations in Energy (A Special Report) – Get Ready for Peak Oil Demand: There's a Growing Consensus That the End of Ever-Rising Consumption Is in Sight; the Big Question That Many Oil Companies Are Debating: When? A Lot Is Riding on the Answer." *Wall Street Journal*, May 22, 2017.

Faucon, Benoit. "OPEC Looks to Expand Production-Cut Pact." *Wall Street Journal*, May 13, 2017.

Fitch, Asa, and Benoit Faucon. "Iran Lures Foreign Investors – European Firms Jump in on Post-Sanction Deals, Though US Companies Largely Stay on Sidelines." *Wall Street Journal*, March 28, 2017.

Kent, Sarah, and Bradley Olson. "Business News: Oil Firms Now Favor Frugal Bets – Exxon, BP and Other Energy Companies Are Avoiding Expensive Engineering Projects." *Wall Street Journal*, March 9, 2017.

Kantchev, Georgi, and Benoit Faucon. "Traders Struggle to Gauge OPEC's Production Cuts." *Wall Street Journal*, February 15, 2017.

Jakab, Spencer. "Big Oil's Spending Gets Less Big." *Wall Street Journal*, February 8, 2017.

Sider, Alison, and Erin Ailworth. "Gusher of Speculation Drives Oil Rally – Wagers Pile Up That OPEC's Output Cut Will Push Up Crude Prices; 'Put Up Or Shut Up Time'." *Wall Street Journal*, January 6, 2017.

# 17 | Motor Vehicles Companies' Strategic Moves 2017–2018

The purpose of this chapter is to update the moves of the major motor vehicle companies – GM, Ford, VW, and Toyota – in the eighteen months after 2016. What were the lingering effects of the drop in energy prices? As oil prices started to creep up again, what were these companies doing? In what ways did their strategies shift?

## GM

GM faced many challenges in this period.[1] The upward momentum in gasoline prices jeopardized the choice it had made to focus on light trucks. The Trump administration's "America First" demands forced it to invest in US factories it might have preferred to locate elsewhere. To protect and grow its market share in China, it had to make a deal with its joint venture partner to manufacture and sell less expensive vehicles. It completed the European withdrawal, conceding it was unlikely ever again to regain the position of the world's leading automaker. It had to quit Venezuela because of political turmoil and India because it did not have a profitable line of vehicles to sell in that country, though it would continue to manufacture cars there. GM also made a series of new mobility investments in the anticipation that driverless vehicles and ridesharing could provide a new business model; as a transportation service company, relying on autonomous vehicles, GM calculated that it could quadruple its profit margins. It financed the new mobility transition with profits from its heavy truck division. Electric vehicle sales were disappointing and led to extended summer layoffs for the employees making these vehicles.

The company was in a bind over how to meet US fuel economy standards. Tentatively, it announced it planned to introduce carbon-fiber material in some vehicles, even if it meant higher prices and reduced sales. Light truck sales were already slipping, partly because of stiff Ford and Fiat-Chrysler competition and partly because of upward movement in gasoline prices. The company had to deal with US plant overcapacity, and the Trump administration's insistence on keeping jobs in the United States. Other issues it confronted were a strike in the Equinox SUV factory in Canada, new claims of ignition switch damages, and Cadillac's ongoing image impairment. In the face of these challenges, the company took the unprecedented step of ending monthly sales reporting, claiming that a thirty-day period was too short a time to understand its performance.

## Sticking to Light Trucks

GM's end of 2016 sales were at record levels, but 60 percent of the vehicles it sold in the United States consisted of pickup trucks, crossovers, and SUVs. Sales of these vehicles were 4 percent higher than they had been in 2015. The company benefitted from low gas prices and low interest rates. Sales of big, expensive vehicles like the Chevrolet Silverado pickup and the Cadillac Escalade boomed. These were the most profitable vehicles GM sold. With demand for small and midsize passenger cars slumping, dealers had a surplus of these vehicles, forcing GM to offer steep discounts and sell the excess cars to daily rental operators.

Like other automakers, GM had devoted too much capacity to passenger cars. In the five years leading up to 2015, it grew its capacity to make passenger cars to 1.2 million vehicles annually in North America, while it increased its capacity to make pickup truck, crossover, and SUV by 800,000 annually. The company had to cut back on its commitments to passenger cars. It planned to do away with the production of about 2 million of them annually and at the same time to add to its production of pickup trucks, crossovers, and SUVs. To do so, it would have to eliminate about 3,300 jobs at passenger-car factories in Ohio and Michigan, and it had to end the jobs of 250 employees at the Lordstown, Ohio plant, where it made Cruze sedans. The sales of the vehicles it made at the plants where it would eliminate jobs were off by 16.6 percent in 2016. On the other hand, due to growing demand, workers at GM factories that made pickup trucks, crossovers, and SUVs were enjoying bonuses in the form of profit-sharing checks that increased their standard hourly wage by about 10 percent.

In 2016, the United States gasoline prices had averaged $2.14 a gallon, their lowest since 2004, which created the perfect condition for the sale of pickup sales, but this situation did not last. The Saudis, OPEC, and the Russians stuck to a deal they made to curb output and in 2017 oil prices rose to more than $50 a barrel. The boom and bust cycle in gasoline prices that made decision making so difficult in the automotive sector set in. GM estimated that though gasoline prices started to move upward, the change would not affect demand for pickups, crossovers, and SUVs. A decade earlier, a similar rise in prices had hurt sales of these vehicles, but now they were lighter, had smaller engines, and had better fuel economy. GM assumed the company's customers were less likely to stop buying them simply because of the increase in gasoline prices. Based on this assumption, GM, therefore, continued with its layoffs in the passenger car factories and continued to take steps to bolster production of pickup trucks, crossovers, and SUVs. It planned to introduce even larger pickups and SUVs, since they generated a high percentage of the company's profits, even though they accounted for no more than 12 percent of total global sales. It raised average pickup prices by nearly $700, to well over $40,000, and customers did not seem to complain, although gasoline prices were increasing.

## Responding to "America First" Demands

The Trump administration threatened GM's economic performance by pressuring it, as well as other US automakers, to keep their assembly plants in the United States. The administration indicated that it intended to impose import tariffs on the vehicles US manufacturers imported from abroad. While Toyota and VW built new factories for auto production in the United States, US automakers closed many of their US factories as part of their post-financial crisis restructuring. After the signing of the North American Free Trade Agreement (NAFTA) in 1993, GM had expanded its ties with Mexico. It had the largest presence in that country among global automakers. It made about a fifth of the light trucks it sold in the United States in Mexico where the equivalent wages were about 85 percent lower than they were in the United States. In addition, the SUVs GM assembled in the United States had a high amount of Mexican content. The estimate of the National Highway Traffic Safety Administration (NHTSA) was that 38 percent of the parts in US-made SUVs came from Mexico.

A 20 percent Trump administration tariff on goods produced in Mexico, therefore, would cost GM $3 billion, which would eliminate about a quarter of its North American profits. Customers, facing higher prices, would buy fewer vehicles.

GM therefore had to respond to the threat of the Trump administration's "American First" policies. It announced plans to invest up to a $1 billion in US factories on top of the $1 billion it already had committed and create 2,000 new US jobs. It indicated it would open a supplier park near its Arlington, Texas sport-utility factory, resulting in the relocation of about 600 jobs from Mexico to the United States. Many of the supplier park employees would work for International Automotive Components Group, a Luxembourg-based interiors firm Commerce Secretary Wilbur Ross had started.

GM committed to increasing the amount of US parts in Chevrolet Suburbans and Cadillac Escalades. The company claimed it had added 25,000 US jobs from 2012 to 2016 and had removed 15,000 of the jobs from foreign production. It asserted that it made 83 percent of the vehicles it sold in the United States in the country. It concluded that it would build small cars in Mexico. Producing them in Mexico provided export opportunities not found in the United States as Mexico had trade deals with forty-five countries, consisting of half of the world's car market, while the US had such agreements with just twenty countries. The main reason GM sold the Cruze, which was not profitable in the United States, was to meet corporate average fleet fuel efficiency (CAFE) standards. GM would make the Cruze, mainly sold outside the United States, in Mexico.

### Aiming for Improved Chinese Performance

GM sold more cars overseas than it did in the United States. China was its number one foreign market. A 2016 Chinese tax cut on some vehicles it sold helped boost its Chinese sales to a record 3.9 million vehicles. Though the prices of the vehicles the company sold in China were increasing, its China sales – which accounted for 40 percent of the company's total sales – made up just 16 percent of its profits. Because of its relations with its joint venture partners, the risk of operating in China was that GM could face the loss of intellectual property. Its deal was a 50–50 partnership with SAIC to build Buicks, Chevrolets, and Cadillacs. The second most popular car in China, behind the VW brand, was the Buick, a car that GM had not sold in the United States in years.

Overall, GM sold more than a million vehicles in China in 2016; however, Chevy sales were down. They fell during the period 2014 2016, GM assumed because of a dearth of sport-utility models, whose popularity in China was growing. The Chinese consumer considered foreign branded vehicles, even the Chevy, upscale. GM's plan was to introduce twenty new or revamped Chevy models in China by 2020, replacing made-for China vehicles with US look-alikes that had better styling and technology.

GM's weakness in China was its inability to compete with local brands at the lower end of the market. It had particular trouble reaching first-time buyers in this segment. Thus, it was working with SAIC to produce smaller and cheaper cars that it would sell under the Chinese Baojun brand. GM would have a non-controlling 44 percent ownership in this venture. Baojun sales had grown from roughly 100,000 in 2013 to more than 760,000 in 2016. Its sedans and minivans sold at bargain prices in comparison to the other vehicles GM sold in China. A compact Baojun SUV, for instance, started at $8,250, far below the Chevrolet Equinox, which cost $26,300 and more. Largely because of its lower price, the Bajoun compact SUV outsold the Equinox eight to one. It had been the fastest growing brand in China since 2012 and in 2016 captured about 3.6 percent of the Chinese market, making it the third top seller in China behind VW and Buick. In 2017, SAIC and GM announced that they would invest an additional $2.4 billion in the Liuzhou factory where they would build 800,000 Bajoun vehicles per year.

## Retreating from Europe

Shortly after becoming GM's CEO, Mary Barra assured analysts that GM could turn around its loss-making European brand Opel and that its European operations would remain a vital part of the company. The longtime subsidiary had not returned an annual profit since 2000; in this period, it lost more than $15 billion. GM's vehicle portfolio in Europe had little resemblance to the rest of its product line, lessening the opportunities for synergies and economies of scale. European consumers were different from those in the rest of the world; they preferred diesels and passenger cars with styling different from that of vehicles

GM sold elsewhere. The European market was extremely competitive; too many companies were active, and consumers had too many brands from which to choose. The regulations the EU imposed after Dieselgate added to costs of doing business in Europe; they required that GM retool its factories. Following the United Kingdom's vote in 2016 to leave the EU, competing in Europe became even more challenging. The ensuing pressure on the pound generated more than $300 million in GM losses. The United Kingdom's decision shattered any remaining conviction GM had it could break even in Europe.

As far back as 2009, when GM was in the midst of its restructuring, it had considered selling the European division, but at that moment, it backed away and tried to fix it. It shut down a plant in Bochum, Germany, but that proved very difficult because of the country's strict labor laws. In 2016, it was using just 63 percent of its European capacity, while the industry average was 71 percent. Sales improved by about 5 percent in 2016, compared to the previous year, but most of the sales were low-margin passenger vehicles. Without sufficient higher-margin trucks, sports cars, and luxury brands in the mix, GM could not turn a profit in Europe. In contrast, its competitors in Europe, such as Ford and Fiat-Chrysler, were profitable. Yet, there was a downside to selling the European division, as it would mean a 10 percent decline in GM's overall sales volume and end any hope that GM could recapture the global market share lead it once had. GM would be the only major auto company in the world without a European presence. The European decision was not an easy one to make but GM followed through in order to increase its margins and release cash for more profitable investments. One of the bets on the future that GM could better fund because of its withdrawal from Europe was on future technologies, such as self-driving cars.

GM's buyer for the European division was Peugeot. By acquiring the Opel and Vauxhall brands, Peugeot became Europe's second biggest carmaker behind VW. In 2016, its combined European market share was 16.6 percent, second only to that of VW with a market share of 23.9 percent. The acquisition also gave Peugeot a more balanced geographic portfolio, as it would be strong in its home base of France and in Opel's home base of Germany. Peugeot's sales volume would go up by a million vehicles, or about a third. Moreover, Peugeot knew Opel well as it had collaborated with it since 2012 on common vehicle platforms and parts buying. Scrutiny of the acquisition came from the French government, a 14 percent owner of Peugeot, but the Peugeot family and the Chinese firm Dongfeng Motor Group each had a 14 percent stake in Peugeot, and they favored the acquisition. Peugeot agreed to pay GM €2.2 billion for the Opel and Vauxhall brands. However, GM had to return to Peugeot about €3 billion in pension obligations and it retained a pension deficit fund of about €6.5 billion. In the short term, GM decided to use most of the cash it obtained from the deal for share buybacks. In the long-run, with the burden of Europe behind it, it could hone in on areas where it intended to dominate – light trucks, China, and autonomous vehicles.

## Quitting Other Countries

GM chose not just to exit Europe. It also withdrew from Venezuela, which once had been South America's most lucrative market, following the government's seizure of its plant there. Venezuelan authorities had taken over its plant in the central Carabobo state, confiscating the facility and stock of cars; 2,700 workers lost their jobs. The Carabobo plant had the capacity to make 20,000 vehicles a month. A provincial court order in favor of a former local dealer, who sued GM for about $370 million over contract disagreements, triggered the takeover. GM's Venezuelan managers were unable to obtain hard currency to import parts because of currency controls. GM had to take a $100 million charge. Since taking power in 1999, the ruling party of Chavez and Maduro had nationalized more than 1,400 companies. Most of the seized companies were shutdown.

GM also planned to stop selling vehicles in India, but it would not leave the country entirely and would continue to make vehicles there to sell in other countries. It would continue to take advantage of low costs in India and make cars for export. Its Maharashtra plant tripled its production volumes in 2016 to about 53,000 vehicles. The car market in India was fragmented, and automakers mostly offered basic models. GM had entered the country in 1918, selling Chevrolets and opening a factory near Mumbai in 1928, but previously left the country in 1958 along with other foreign automakers because of nationalist pressures. It came back only in 1995, as a small player, selling just about 29,000 vehicles in India in 2016 for a market share of less than 1 percent. The market leader was Suzuki, which had a 40 percent market share.

Several other automakers had made gains in the Indian market with small crossover SUVs that were agile enough to drive in congested cities, but sufficiently durable for rugged country roads. While selling cars in India had the potential to increase the scale of GM's global operations, GM found it difficult to turn a profit in that country.

GM's concerns extended beyond India to South Africa, the Middle East, and several Asian countries, which produced a combined loss of $838 million for the company in 2016. It had plans to leave South Africa, where it was considering selling its manufacturing to Isuzu. The company chose to close a plant in the coastal South Korean city of Gunsan, a move that affected 2,000 workers, but remained committed to South Korea, where it would continue restructuring. The Gunsan plant accounted for about 7 percent of the 520,000 vehicles GM produced in the country in 2016. GM had three other factories there, which it acquired when it took over bankrupt Daewoo's in 2001. The South Korean plants produced cars mostly for export, including SUVs that GM sent to the United States. The closure of the Gunsan plant hurt relations with the union that represented South Korean autoworkers, which was seeking concessions and incentives before it would help GM restructure further.

## Making New Mobility Investments

GM invested about $600 million a year in self-driving, car sharing, and electric vehicles (EVs). To fend off potential future competition from Silicon Valley companies, its goal was to launch a safe driverless vehicle on a commercial scale. It claimed that autonomous vehicles would be better than humans in navigating in busy urban environments. It expected self-driving cars to be a $20 billion market by 2025. About 40 percent of the market would be in North America, 30 percent in Asia, and 30 percent in Europe. Before GM could build to scale, it needed capabilities in electrical architecture, sensors and a system of innovative software. To obtain these capabilities it took a number of steps.

**Acquiring Cruise and Strobe:** GM acquired San Francisco headquartered autonomous-car developer Cruise Automation in 2016. At the time of the purchase, Cruise Automation had about 150 employees and it had the goal to expand to 1,100 in five years. GM used Cruise to attract software talent. This startup collected the mapping data to lower dependence on human drivers in competition with Google spinoff Waymo; but Waymo was ahead of it in this activity. Cruise's advantage was that because of its association with GM, it could put demonstration cars on the road. It had a fleet of fifty electric cars, which GM was working to expand to 300, with the aim being to develop a commercial product. The app-based service to transport its employees around Silicon Valley in self-driving cars still had a safety driver at the wheel. Cruise tested such cars on roads in San Francisco, Scottsdale, Arizona, and in southeast Michigan near GM's headquarters. San Francisco was an especially complex environment because of the terrain and traffic. GM calculated that the challenges were at least sixty times as great as in Scottsdale. The demonstration rides that Cruise provided journalists in San Francisco were impressive, but the journalists observed that the vehicles were sometimes tentative and unsure about how to react to such obstacles as double-parked cars.

Seeking to bolster Cruises' capabilities in commercializing self-driving vehicles, GM also acquired Strobe. This startup, comprising eleven engineers, worked on lidar, the sensors that helped autonomous vehicles navigate complex environments. The technology relied on lasers to measure the distance of objects in a vehicle's field of vision. Autonomous-vehicle developers combined lasers with lidar and cameras to recognize street signs, pedestrians, vehicles, and other objects. By collapsing the lidar sensor down to a single chip, Strobe was hoping to make the system smaller and cheaper to use.

**Betting on Ride Sharing:** Ride sharing posed the risk of a declining need for cars; the decline in US vehicle sales might be as great as 40 percent over twenty-five years as car sharing and self-driving vehicles expanded, but GM anticipated that the system would lower cost, be safer, and result in more miles traveled. Its goal was to run a large-scale fleet of driverless cars in big cities as a taxi service as soon 2019. It planned to deploy fleets of cars in a number of cities, targeting what it suspected could be a $7 trillion industry in 2050. Offering rides for less than $1 a mile by 2025 was the goal, for at this price, the rides were less than half the cost of the current driver-based system. GM calculated that it could quadruple its margins by moving from manufacturing to offering this service. However, many barriers existed to widespread deployment, including regulatory and technical challenges. The companies and government involved had to figure out about how autonomous cars would interact with human drivers, pedestrians, and cyclists.

To reach its goal, GM invested in ride-hailing firm Lyft. GM wanted Lyft to test self-driving electric Bolts, but when GM fell behind in delivering the Bolts, Lyft engaged with other companies and made deals with Waymo and a Boston startup working with Renault. The future Lyft envisioned was one in which it managed a network of vehicles made by many manufacturers, not just GM. This future was not in alignment with what GM envisioned. As far as the competition went, Uber had ordered 24,000 Volvo sport-utility vehicles to convert to autonomous vehicles, but had not disclosed a timetable for commercial deployment. Waymo did not have as a goal an autonomous-taxi service, but it was planning to offer public demonstration rides of a vehicle without a safety operator. If more people found it easy to go without a car, the existence of too many mobility offerings was a potential threat to GM and other vehicle makers.

GM was carrying out tests to reveal which business model might work best. The car-sharing service Maven – which offered all kinds of vehicles – from cheap sedans to sports cars to big SUVs – for 27,000 members in seventeen US cities – was an example. GM also experimented with a subscription service for Cadillac drivers only. For $1,500 a month, members could drive ten Cadillac models for up to eighteen times a year. GM provided the service only in the New York City area but might expand it to Los Angeles and other metro areas. Nearly 5,000 people had registered on the plan's website, but it was unclear how many were paying and how many just using the free-trial offer. Atlanta-based Clutch Technologies, started in 2014, had a similar model, but gave customers access to multiple brands and models for $950–$1,400 a month.

## Dealing with the EV Slowdown and Funding New Mobility

Meanwhile, demand for the Bolt had not developed as fast as expected and workers assembling the car had to take a month off in the summer of 2017, because of the lukewarm demand. Output at GM's Orion Township, Michigan plant, where it built the Bolt, hit 15,000 before a summer pause, supposed to last two weeks, but extended because of the slow sales. The car cost $37,000 and qualified for a $7,500 tax credit; facing the possible expiration of the tax credit, Mary Barra had to lobby for its extension. GM had sold about 7,500 Bolts, though the car was not yet available in all fifty states. Sales were roughly equal to that of the Nissan Leaf, another electric car, but one whose range was less, compared to the Bolt that could get 238 on a single charge. The Leaf had been on the market in the United States for several years before GM introduced the Bolt. Altogether, EV sales in the United States made up about 0.6 percent of the total US auto market in 2017.

GM had plans for twenty new models powered solely by batteries or fuel cells within five years. It would have to spend a few billion dollars a year developing these vehicles. How would it fund the development of these new vehicles and the other new mobility initiatives when it was not a startup able to burn cash in the short term in the pursuit of a long-term dream? GM rejected the idea of spinning off Cruise Automation, Strobe, and Lyft along with the company's EV projects into a separate company, which would attract new technology seeking shareholders and talent. Instead, the main way the company funded its new mobility initiatives was by selling large pickup trucks in the United States. It sold more than 2.4 million large pickup trucks in the United States in 2016, 14 percent of all US sales and 3.6 greater than its sale of US pickup trucks in 2012. Low gasoline prices stimulated the pickup truck sales that GM used to finance its new mobility investments.

During GM's bankruptcy, it had considered selling off the GMC truck division, but that division had become a strong contributor to its income. GMC, which mostly sold very large pickup trucks and pre-mium SUVs, had about $24 billion in revenue in 2016, or about 16 percent of the company's total revenue. It also delivered more profit per sale than most GM brands. The average GMC vehicle sold for $44,000, 25 percent more than in 2012, 36 percent higher than the average Chevy, and $13,000 above the industry average. GM was sending a portion of the profits from these trucks into driverless and electric cars and other new mobility initiatives and was able to boost its spending on these long-range bets by two-thirds in 2017.

## Tougher Fuel-Economy Standards and Carbon Fiber

To maintain the profitable truck business, GM had to satisfy tightening fuel-economy standards. Its trucks were a serious challenge in meeting the fuel-efficiency standards. Regulators demanded greater efficiency, while customers still expected exceptional power. Ford's use of alumi-num in the market-leading F-Series was a response to this challenge; indeed, the EPA reported that the F-Series was close to meeting strict US 2025 standards. GM's trucks were further away from meeting this standard, so GM needed a solution. It was taking actions to meet the fuel-economy targets, including introducing new hybrid and diesel engines, but these actions were not sufficient.

Another approach to dealing with the problem was to build the pickups with lightweight carbon fiber. This change would increase pickup costs and it might reduce sales among some customers who would not buy at the higher price. However, Ford had started to use aluminum in its F-150 pickup trucks in 2014, which raised their price and gave GM the leeway to consider the move to carbon fiber. The reason GM did not follow Ford and use aluminum was that it considered the aluminum in Ford's pickup to be not as durable as carbon fiber and more prone to dents when involved in crashes. The carbon fiber was light – as much as 50–75 percent lighter than steel and 20 to 50 percent lighter than aluminum – but it was also strong and had the potential to increase dent resistance. The issue with carbon fiber was the motor vehicle industry's lack of experience in using it. If companies used it, it had been mostly in exotic sports cars. Another disadvantage was that carbon fiber was complicated to make. It required expensive equipment and took longer than making metal or aluminum. GM was working with Tokyo-based carbon-fiber producer Teijin to get it ready for wider adoption of carbon fiber. By waiting GM would not get a jump on Ford, for Ford also had a joint venture in Japan for this purpose with DowAksa. Between them, if GM and Ford introduced carbon fiber, they were likely to set a new weight standard, one that could spread throughout the industry.

A prior GM experiment with alternative materials had failed. In 2001, the company offered a pickup truck with composite plastics as an $850 Silverado option, but it ended the program in 2003 because it had quality and sales problems. In 2017, when GM introduced the redesigned Chevy Silverado and GMC trucks, it did not give customers a carbon filter option. This option would only be available in GM's highest-priced pickups in 2019, and the company reserved the right to change these plans if it encountered unexpected hurdles. In the meantime, GM used a collage of different materials to relieve the cost and regulatory pressure it experienced. Redesigned doors in Chevy Suburbans and large SUVs were made of aluminum, but GM continued to make the cabins of high-strength steel.

## Confronting Overcapacity Again

The lift in sales, helped along by low fuel 2015–2016 fuel prices, did not last forever. By the third quarter of 2017, GM had to deal with its sales falling short of its original forecast for the year. Fuel prices had crept up again, and after record growth, the entire industry faced a slowdown. GM's expectations for industry sales were in the low

17 million range, whereas it had previously hoped they could match the 17.55 million vehicle sales record set the previous year. Typically, when sales slowed auto companies increased their use of incentives and other tactics that benefitted customers to get them to buy. This time, since prices were already very competitive, they moderated their use of incentives. The sales slowdown meant that GM had to confront the issue of over-capacity again and eliminate excess capacity to lower costs. Its North American factory capacity in 2015–2017 averaged about 95 percent, while Ford and Toyota capacity exceeded 100 percent as these companies relied on third shift and weekend overtime work to make the cars they needed.

GM, therefore, had good reasons to eliminate US jobs and move production to Mexico where it made popular crossover SUVs. Its US factories tilted toward making unprofitable sedans and coupes, such as Cadillacs and the Chevy Malibu. The Malibu, which got great reviews from critics, did not elicit enthusiasm from buyers. Low gasoline prices in the United States had prompted buyers to abandon passenger cars like the Malibu for SUVs and pickup trucks and GM assumed that passenger cars were not coming back. Within a decade, they had declined from about half of US vehicle purchases to about a third. GM had seventeen assembly plants in North America. Most, except for five that made trucks and SUVs, made passenger cars, and had unused capacity GM could eliminate. The company's Detroit-Hamtramck assembly plant, the only factory GM had in the city, made 80,000 cars in 2016, while seventeen years earlier it had made 200,000. It was GM's least-productive assembly factory in North America. Demand for three of the four cars built there – the small Volt plug-in, the large Cadillac CT6, and the mid-size Buick LaCrosse – declined in the second quarter of 2017 in comparison to the previous year, the Volt by 32 percent, the Cadillac by 20 percent, and the LaCrosse by 43 percent. These cars, even though GM recently redesigned each, struggled to attract buyers. Only the Impala, also made at the Detroit-Hamtramck assembly plant, had grown its sales. However, complicating GM's ability to act was the Trump administration's demand that it assemble more vehicles in the United States and create US jobs. It would not be easy for it to lower its costs by shutting down US plants and relying on production in low-wage countries.

Under recent union contracts, GM had the right to employ temporary workers and lay off some permanent ones. This situation allowed it to let go nearly 4,000 workers at the plants that made passenger cars, to operate these plants on reduced schedules, and to convert some of them, like the one in the Kansas City area that had made the Malibu, to SUV assembly. While GM employees making passenger cars were underutilized, employees who made SUVs and pickups were working overtime. However, GM could not carry out the conversion of a plant like that in Kansas City to SUV assembly very quickly. It required several years of lead-time to install new assembly-line equipment and tooling. By the time it accomplished the switch, the market could be different. Gasoline prices might dictate a different set of choices. In response to booms and buses in gasoline prices, demand for light trucks could go down. Demand for passage cars could go up. For consumers, GM already had the sense of some movement in consumer sentiment. As it entered the third quarter of 2017, demand for its SUVs and big pickups started to slip. However, the Ford's F-Series pickups and Chrysler's Ram trucks continued to do well. As of May 2017, both Ford and Fiat Chrysler pickup sales had grown by more than 8 percent from a year earlier, while GM's sales fell by 5.6 percent. Ford, usually the number two seller in the United States, had a lead over GM in US market share for that quarter.

## Other Issues

Other issues GM dealt with were a strike in Canada, more ignition switch claims, and trying to revitalize the Cadillac brand.

**A Strike in Canada:** GM reached a tentative agreement with striking workers at its sport-utility plant in Canada. The strike interrupted production of the Equinox, GM's top-selling US SUV and its second most popular model. GM also made the Equinox at two plants in Mexico. The company had laid off several hundred Canadian workers after moving some production to Mexico. It warned it would increase Mexican production if the striking Canadian employees did not return to assembly line. The workers wanted GM to designate the Canadian facility as the primary place for Equinox production, lest the company move even more production to Mexico. For the Canadian workers, job security was the issue.

**Ignition Switching Claims:** GM faced more of these claims, a potential $1 billion payout depending on the outcome of an upcoming trial.

Plaintiffs had made prior deals with a trust that represented the old General Motors that had produced the cars. This trust was a leftover from the 2009 bankruptcy, but the plaintiffs wanted the current GM to hand over additional money to the trust to cover upcoming legal settlements.

**Revitalizing Cadillac:** The Cadillac brand trailed its luxury brand rivals and was in acute need of revitalization. The Cadillac's Escalade sport-utility had been a success, sales in China grew, but the brand's overall sales lagged behind BMW, Mercedes-Benz and other luxury makes, and it had lost US market share each year since 2014. Most consumers did not consider Cadillac to be in the same league as Audi or Tesla. GM stopped tactics that harmed the brand's image, such as sales to rental companies and steep end-of-the-month discounts and launched new models including a crossover SUV. It tried to improve service at its dealers, but it still had not found a formula to turn around the brand.

## Ending Monthly Sales Reports

In an unprecedented and widely discussed move, GM gave up on the practice of issuing monthly sales reports. It claimed that a short thirty-day period did not provide an adequate picture of its condition. This amount of time was not sufficient to separate real trends from short-term fluctuations. GM maintained it was not the first to make this change but that it was following other large companies such as Target and Walmart that had also stopped reporting their sales on a monthly basis.

## Ford

The eighteen months after 2016 when gasoline prices started to creep up again was a very turbulent period for Ford, as it was for GM.[2] The company faced many challenges. It had to deal with the Trump administration's threat of a border tax. The possibility of continued low gasoline prices resulted in a growing commitment to light trucks and SUVs. Yet, at the same time, like GM, Ford pursued the paradoxical path of investing in futuristic initiatives in smart mobility – it equipped its vehicles with virtual assistance capabilities, hired Silicon

Valley software engineers, and established a goal of having a functioning autonomous vehicle by 2021. Like GM, it backed up these initiatives by acquiring high-tech startups. To improve its lagging performance in China, it aggressively pursued electric vehicles with its joint venture partner. Nonetheless, with so much of its profitability dependent on the sale of light trucks, it was also very concerned about its ability to comply with strict US and European emission and fuel economy standards and it was looking for leniency or an extension of these rules. Like GM, it was between the rock of its dependence on light trucks and the hard place of a future when the dependence might ease.

With its performance failing to meet investor expectations, CEO Mark Fields reverted to cost cutting and downsizing. Unhappy with Fields, Ford sacked him and replaced him with the head of its Smart Mobility division, Jim Hackett, a former Steelcase CEO. Hackett was the favorite of board chair and family member Bill Ford, an ardent champion of the firm's new mobility endeavors. Hackett took steps to establish a new strategy for the firm, but did not convince shareholders he was necessarily on the right course. He moved the production of the Ford Focus from the United States to China, putting Ford in the position of importing more Chinese-produced vehicles into the United States than any firm previously had.

Like GM, Ford, because of the tightening in energy efficiency and emission standards, had to start to shift toward the use of carbon fiber and other lighter materials, and it also had to deal with safety and quality issues. As in the instance of GM, the upward momentum in gasoline prices jeopardized the choice it made to focus on light trucks. With gasoline prices increasing, the company's sales volume slipped. Unlike GM, Ford committed to India. Then, came its much-publicized move announcing that it would end entirely the sale of unprofitable sedans in the United States, with the exception of the Mustang and Focus, and redirect the $7 billion it would save to the development of trucks and sport-utility vehicles. The redirection of these funds to truck and sports-utility vehicles, Ford maintained, was just a short-term move that would enable the company in the long run to invest more in EVs and connected and driverless cars. Thus, Ford continued along a paradoxical path. Consistent with paradox was its solution to its energy efficiency dilemmas; that is, it would continue to try to rely on a light truck loophole in US law to avoid complying with more stringent vehicle requirements.

## The Trump Border Tax

Trump's border tax threat led Ford to abandon building a new $1.6 billion small car factory in Mexico. Instead, it decided that it would carry out future small-car production in an existing Mexican factory and invest $700 million to create 700 jobs in Michigan. Trump's threat came at a particularly in inopportune time for Ford. Fourth quarter results showed a net loss of $800 million, compared to the $1.9 billion in net income it earned in the prior year's last quarter. Revenues declined by 4 percent and the company had to make a special payment to its pension fund. Trump's threat, as seen by Ford, failed to acknowledge the full shift already underway in US auto production. Mexican auto exports to the US constituted about 80 percent of that country's total exports. Mexico's vehicle assembly capacity was scheduled to double in size from 2010 to 2020. US auto companies planned to build eleven new assembly plants in this period, nine of them in Mexico. Ford exclusively built low-margin passenger cars like the Fiesta and Fusion in Mexico in contrast to GM, which also made SUVs there. Nearly 90 percent of the cars US automakers manufactured in Mexico were sold in the United States.

The investments Ford promised to make in Michigan, unlike those in Mexico, were not exclusively in manufacturing. They included a $200 million data-storage center to help Ford design and manage the increasingly computerized and connected cars it sold. The company's US investments also included $150 million for converting a small-car plant to more profitable Ranger pickups and Bronco SUVs. Ford's moves were supposed to signify a commitment to US jobs, however, about half the components in vehicles like the Ranger and Bronco were not US made. Ford actually had made more than 80 percent of its $1.2 billion commitment to Michigan factories earlier as part of a 2015 agreement with the United Auto Workers (UAW). Included in the earlier announcement was a promise to spend $700 million to convert a Michigan plant to autonomous cars and electric vehicles and in so doing create 700 jobs. In return for its investments in the state of Michigan, Ford was seeking $30 million in tax incentives over fifteen years.

Conclusion

## Bigger Trucks and SUVs

Expectations were that gasoline prices would rise in 2017, but by how much was not certain. Betting that rising gasoline prices would not hurt demand for pickups and SUVs, as they previously had, Ford became even more committed to pickups and SUVs. Like GM, it assumed that demand would not slump as it had a decade earlier when gasoline prices rose, because the pickups and SUVs it made in 2017 were lighter and had smaller engines and therefore they had better fuel economy than the vehicles the company produced a decade earlier. From 2006 onward, the market had shifted to the point where nearly 60 percent of the 17.5 million vehicles automakers sold in the United States were light trucks. This trend toward large vehicles was in Ford's favor, as pickups and SUVs made up more than half of its North American pretax operating profit. If the trend toward large vehicles did not abate, the prudent course for Ford was to continue launching new trucks and SUVs despite persistent warnings that gasoline prices were volatile, that they were subject to booms and busts, and they could creep up and trigger a collapse in demand. Thus, Ford opted not only to revive the Bronco SUV and Ranger small pickup, but also launched larger versions of existing models like the F-150 and F-350 pickup trucks. The F-150 was already ample, but Ford stretched it out by another half-foot. At 7.2 feet between its front fenders, it was the widest light-duty vehicle sold, as wide as an original, military-style Hummer. It also was tall, with a roof height 6.5 feet, which provided 11.5 inches of ground clearance. Its base price was $53,140, but Ford was convinced that it would not deter consumers from buying the vehicle.

The width of the F-350 Super Duty Platinum Crew Cab 4x4 pickup also was large. The vehicle weighed more than 6,800 pounds, even with its aluminum-body construction that eliminated about 250 pounds. When GM criticized, the aluminum frame as being prone to dents Ford defended it by asserting that the frame was 95 percent high-strength steel and much stronger than its prior models. Equipped with a 6.7-liter turbo-diesel V8 option the F-350 averaged 14.2 miles per gallon, yet it qualified for a substantial federal tax credit to small-business owners, who were willing to declare they used it mostly for business. With a base price of $63,285, Ford was hoping the market would be large and lucrative grounded on its assumption that the

United States had experienced a structural shift toward bigger vehicles. With regard to SUVs, Ford gave the Expedition and Lincoln Navigator their first overhauls in nearly fifteen years. The company had been a major force in the market for such hulking SUVs, but from 2006 to 2014 CEO, Alan Mulally, had cut back in response to fuel efficiency and emission standards. His decision to cut back came at about the same time as GM, emerging from bankruptcy, bulked up the size of its SUVs, deeming that, given its weak position, profit margins were too attractive to relinquish even in the face of the stricter standards. Because of these decisions, GM had a very strong position in this segment. It advanced by regularly redesigning the Chevrolet Tahoe, Cadillac Escalade, and other models and outselling Ford by a four-to-one margin. Ford, searching for ways to bolster its profits, tried to catch up by retooling SUVs like the Expedition and Lincoln Navigator. With their aluminum body panels, they were on average 300 pounds lighter and more fuel-efficient than comparable GM vehicles, but they also cost more. Ford brought more to these SUVs than aluminum frames, as they introduced technologies like a wireless charging pad for smartphones and built-in Wi-Fi connectivity. The moves Ford was making toward launching bigger vehicles was good for employees, as the vehicles were popular and sold well and they were able to earn bonuses when working overtime on them. The average increase in pay that an employee in such a factory could earn in 2016 amounted to $9,000.

## Smart Mobility

Ford, like GM, was investing in smart mobility, whilst simultaneously making increasingly larger trucks. While trying to increase its profits by selling more pickups and SUVs, it launched a series of new technology investments, including a $4.5 billion electric-vehicle program and autonomous-car project. In addition, the company established the new division, Smart Mobility, to consolidate the efforts. To advance Smart Mobility's goals, Ford took steps to acquire a ride-sharing firm and to invest in companies that developed technology needed to program and pilot autonomous vehicles, such as a $1 billion bet it made in a startup that specialized in artificial intelligence. These moves, meant to contribute to the company's long-term profitability, had the short-term impact of eroding its profit margins. A reason the company took these moves was the need to convince investors that it could stand up to the threat from cutting-edge tech companies like Tesla, Apple, and Alphabet. Ford expanded its presence in Silicon Valley, where these tech giants were moving ahead with their own car-sharing ventures, driverless cars, and future mobility experiments. Ford, for example, worked with a bike-sharing firm in San Francisco and bought Chariot, an app-based shuttle service that plotted out routes based on user demand in order to try to better figure out how people in these places moved from place to place. Chariot had a growing presence in San Francisco and in New York, Seattle, and Austin. Like GM, Ford took a series of steps to advance the cause of smart mobility.

**Putting Virtual Assistants into Vehicles:** In response to automakers, like BMW and Hyundai, bringing virtual assistants into their cars, Ford announced that Amazon's Alexa voice-command software would be available in some vehicles. Drivers with Alexa devices at home could tap into car functions such as starting the engine and unlocking doors in their houses. Vehicles equipped with Ford's infotainment system Sync 3 with access to the Alexa app would allow drivers to do tasks like shopping and searching for addresses while driving.

**Allowing Buyers to Purchase Cars on the Internet:** Another of Ford's moves was to make it easier for its customers to buy and finance a car without going into a showroom. The company allowed car buyers to use software developed by AutoFi to shop and secure loans from dealers' websites. Ford dealers selected the banks, credit unions, and other lenders to pitch loans to car buyers on AutoFi and AutoFi collected a fee from the dealers and lenders if they used its service in their purchases. The hitch was that laws in many states required customers to visit a showroom to finish the paperwork.

**Hiring Software Engineers:** Another way Ford tried to increase its high-tech capabilities was by hiring 400 engineers from BlackBerry to help it develop internet-connected vehicles. This move doubled the size of the firm's mobile-connectivity team and boosted its software capabilities, as it tried to keep up with tech companies and rivals in the auto industry in these domains. Previously, the company had closely allied itself with Blackberry. In 2014, it had chosen the smartphone maker's QNX software for its SYNC infotainment systems.

**Acquiring Artificial Intelligence Startup Argo AI:** The company acquired Pittsburgh-based artificial-intelligence startup Argo AI and made plans to invest $1 billion over five years to expand the firm. Argo made the laser systems needed to operate cars without human intervention. Ford had exclusive access to the company's technology but Argo AI could license it to other automakers.

**Acquiring Lidar Sensor Technology Startup Princeton Lightwave:** Argo AI then bought Cranbury, NJ-based Princeton Lightwave for an undisclosed price – a move that gave it better access to lidar systems that used lasers to create a 3-D view of the world. The acquisitions of Argo AI and Princeton Lightwave paralleled GM's acquisitions of Cruise and Strobe and gave Ford capabilities in systems that were the key components in autonomous vehicles. Claiming that it had lowered production costs of these systems by 90 percent, Waymo was in the lead. Princeton Lightware's claim was that the lidar it made could identify objects nearly a quarter of a mile away traveling at sixty miles an hour. The founders, Bryan Salesky, formerly of Alphabet, and Peter Rander, formerly of Uber, continued to hold equity in the startup. Founded in 2000, it had about thirty employees and had sold sensors to clients in the telecom and defense industries.

**Setting 2021 as the Goal for an Autonomous Vehicle:** Ford anticipated that by 2030, autonomous cars would account for 20 percent of US sales. Its goal was to launch a self-driving vehicle by 2021, but whether it could achieve this goal was unclear. It was also seeking a patent for a drone system that could locate passengers who called for a self-driving robo-taxi. Another patent filing was for an air bag to protect occupants sitting in conference-room-style seating in self-driving cars.

## EV Commitments in China

As Ford's sales fell elsewhere, Ford, like other automakers, turned to China, the world's largest car market, for growth. It had a long way to go – while in the United States its sales in the first two months of 2017 fell by 7 percent, in China, they dropped by more than 30 percent. The expectation was that demand for its vehicles in China would continue to fall for the rest of the year and its margins would remain low, which gave Ford and Changan, its Chinese joint venture partner, the motivation to come up with plans to spur future sales. They would have no new launches in 2017. Instead, to attract favorable attention, they developed an aggressive and well-publicized electric-car strategy. Ford promised to meet China's ambitious electric-vehicle production targets, and in a departure from the past, to share whatever cutting-edge technology it developed with Changan. Most gasoline-powered cars made in China had foreign auto partners, but Chinese companies made almost all the EVs sold in the country. With its Changan partnership, Ford aimed to break with this pattern, but this move would not have much of an effect on the company's short-term performance in

China. Actual electric-vehicle sales in China were not high, compared to the sale of conventional vehicles. The hoped for payoff would be in the long term.

China's aim was to have as many as 32 million new-energy vehicles on the roads by 2025. This would be a substantial percentage of the world's total, as other countries proceeded more cautiously. The Chinese government had many supportive policies in place to spur the development of alternative vehicles. Local governments had targets for electrifying their bus and taxi fleets and were preparing the way by building EV charging infrastructure. The national government gave subsidies to companies that launched new electric vehicles. With its joint venture partner, Changan, Ford promised to offer Mondeo Energi plug-in hybrids in China in 2018. The two companies would make electric powertrains in China in 2020; by 2023, they would launch an all-electric sport-utility vehicle. By 2025, all models they sold in China would have electric versions.

## *Questioning Emission Rules*

Automakers had received criticism for years from environmentalists, government officials, and some customers for failing to produce sufficient numbers of electric cars and other alternative-fuel vehicles. However, by virtue of the purchasing decisions customers made, the automakers assumed there was not much real interest in these vehicles. Ford, therefore, questioned whether it could sell enough of them to meet US emission standards. Despite most of its profits coming from pickup trucks and SUVs, it had promised to spend $4.5 billion on electric cars and other alternative-fuel vehicles. Ford had invested heavily in these vehicles because of strict US and European emission rules, but its investments so far had not paid off.

Therefore, Ford, along with other automakers, was trying to obtain relief from EPA rules mandating that US-sold automobiles average 54.5 mpg by 2025. But, California, the largest car market in the United States, had its own rules that dictated that zero-emission vehicles constitute about 15 percent of auto company sales by 2025. This policy had been in place because the national government's mileage and emissions targets were not sufficient to yield the greenhouse gas reductions and air-quality improvements California wanted. Nine other US states followed California's lead and the California standards and those of the other states would stay in force even though the federal government under Trump had demonstrated its desire to ease national standards and it intended to challenge the right of California and the other states to have their separate rules. Demand for alternative vehicles had increased, but not as fast as had been hoped. More than 250,000 of them were on the road in California. In the rest of the United States, more than a half million were on the road. However, the Obama administration had once predicted that more than a million alternative vehicles would be on the road by 2015. To make up for the losses the automakers had accrued by selling alternative vehicles, they increased the average price of the cars they sold in the United States by an estimated of $350. So long as fuel prices were low, the automakers did not expect demand for alternative vehicles to grow. Even if higher fuel prices increased demand for these vehicles, the automakers anticipated that many customers would stick with less expensive, conventional vehicles that ran on gasoline.

The automakers had also invested billions of dollars in alternative vehicles to meet European standards. It was not just in the United States that they faced tough requirements. Yet, it was unlikely, even in the best of circumstances, that the efforts they had made would be adequate to meet either European or US benchmarks. Ford, for instance, could face fines as high as $6.6 billion in Europe for excess carbon emissions in 2021, an amount equivalent to more than 90 percent of its profits. Furthermore, Ford assumed that the trends in Europe were no different from those in the United States and most Europeans would continue to buy gasoline-powered vehicles. The conundrum for the company was how to challenge the demanding rules in place in Europe and US states like California without appearing insensitive to the need to reduce carbon emissions.

## Weak Performance and Ouster of CEO

Ford's financial performance fell in 2017; its first-quarter profits were off by 35 percent compared to the previous year. The company's overall volume was down by 7.1 percent, a reduction that was greater than any other automobile company. The company was also stung by an expensive $295 million recall of nearly half a million vehicles that had fire risks and faulty door latches, the second time in less than a year that a recall had reduced its profits. Revenue did rise 4 percent compared to the preceding year, but mostly because of high prices for pickup trucks and sport-utility vehicles. The average price buyers paid Ford for a vehicle in the first quarter hit a record of $31,380. However, the company was concerned that higher interest rates and the number of used cars on the market would lower vehicle affordability, and it anticipated that sales in 2017 and 2018 would stall and be lower than they had been in 2016. In response, it announced that it would have to cut costs by $3 billion in 2017.

However, the company decision to cut costs would not affect the scheduled introduction of two new full-size SUVs in the following year and the relaunch of the iconic Bronco in the following year. While Ford anticipated that the market for profitable SUVs and trucks would continue to be strong, it assumed that the market for sedans would be weak. This shift to larger vehicles was global and the company knew it played to its strengths. Yet, Ford was not doing well outside the United States. About 90 percent of its profits came from the United States, and its performance in Europe was weak. Profits in Europe were 60 percent lower than the previous year because of exchange rate and Brexit problems that offset higher sales volumes. In Asia Pacific, the company's profits had declined by about 45 percent because of reduced demand for its cars.

Under Alan Mulally, Ford shares had done well, but by 2017, under Mark Fields, weak performance led to Ford slipping behind GM and, worse yet, behind Tesla in its performance on the stock market. Tesla's success suggested that significant numbers of shareholders were anticipating that EVs were going to make substantial inroads on internal combustion engines someday. Indeed, Ford was behind GM, and not only Tesla, in developing an EV, as Tesla was still working on a medium priced EV, while GM had offered one for sale. Tesla, though, posed a special challenge. It was unprofitable, deeply indebted, and sold just 76,000 cars in 2016, but its valuation exceeded that of Ford, which had over twenty times the annual revenue, billions of dollars in profits, and sold millions of cars annually. Ford made moves to counter the threat of GM and Tesla in this area. As indicated, it promised to deliver a self-driving car by 2021 and it acquired and invested in tech startups. Nonetheless, Ford's market value had not increased by much since late 2010.

Shareholders, therefore, put pressure on CEO Mark Fields, seeking answers as to why the company's value had declined by more than a third of its value during his tenure. He had been pushing the company to move to new technologies such as electric and self-driving vehicles, but faced criticism for uneven progress in achieving these goals, while at the same time he had shifted the emphasis away from the conventional vehicles that accounted for virtually all of Ford's profits. The push into new areas aimed at reducing the company's vulnerability to boom and bust cycles was very expensive and would not pay off for years. Silicon Valley firms such as Alphabet, Apple, and Intel were buying startups at a more rapid pace than Ford and GM already had an EV on the road. Ford would not introduce a similar car until 2020. The future prospects of the company did not seem stellar and the present performance was lackluster. Ford's US market share fell to 15.1 percent in 2017, from 15.6 percent the previous year. Ford was also behind almost every one of its competitors in China. Field's failures came on the heels of his being awarded a $2.5 million stock incentive to broaden Ford's reach beyond the trucks and SUVs that provided for the bulk of its profits. His mandate was to develop a "lean mindset," and to pursue "moonshot ideas" like ride sharing. Shareholders apparently wanted Fields to sharpen the company's strategy.

Fields was uncertain how to respond. In his twenty-eight years with Ford, he had earned the reputation of being a cost cutter and had ample prior experience in downsizing. Thus, almost predictably, he announced a 10 percent cut in Ford's global workforce, largely aimed at salaried employees, so as not to cause a negative White House reaction. Instead of laying off hourly workers, Ford would stagger assembly-plant schedules and give workers weeks of downtime. With approximately 200,000 global employees, Ford had steadily grown its workforce in reaction to low gasoline prices and opportunities in China. It employed about half of its 200,000 employees in the United States, just under a quarter in Europe, and just under a quarter in Asia. Besides workforce reductions, Fields declared that he would bolster the underperforming areas of the core business and invest aggressively, but prudently, in emerging new mobility opportunities.

## Replacing Fields with Hackett

However, Ford looked elsewhere for leadership, ousting Fields and appointed Jim Hackett, head of the Smart Mobility unit, as his successor. The Ford family held a separate class of stock that gave it

40 percent of the voting shares in the company. Bill Ford, chair of the company's board, who owned 17.7 percent of these shares, expected more rapid decision making from Hackett and less concern about hierarchy. He wanted the new CEO to ease tension between groups, one of which he asserted made moonshot bets and invested in new technology, while the other tended to current operations, and felt left out. Since becoming chair of the board in 1999, Bill Ford had encouraged the company to make a shift to EVs and other new modes of transportation. He tirelessly spoke out about how traffic congestion and pollution were choking the world's major cities. He pointed out that in 2004, Ford was the first US auto company to introduce a hybrid, but admitted that the financial crisis intervened and it had to delay additional initiatives of this type. Meanwhile, other automakers moved ahead of Ford in deploying alternative technologies. Ford's sales of hybrids did increase, but its focus remained on profitable pickups and SUVs. With the prospect that a third of all cars produced could be electric or hybrids in 2025, Bill Ford was convinced that the company had to accelerate the pace of the shift to electrified vehicles; thus, he encouraged the company to adopt the plan to sell thirteen more electrified vehicles by 2022, including hybrid F-150s and Mustangs.

Hackett impressed Bill Ford and the other members of the board with his tech savviness and his turnaround experience at office furniture company Steelcase. He had also been temporary athletic director of the University of Michigan, which resulted in the hiring of Jim Harbaugh as the football coach. The board expected him to consider how to incorporate new technologies like data analytics and 3-D printing into Ford's operations. Though Hackett did not have extensive Silicon Valley experience, he had relied heavily on the design firm Ideo when he headed Steelcase. Another reason the Board chose Hackett was that he was not tainted by Ford's handling of its relations with Trump during the transition. The board was uneasy with Fields' communications with respect to this flap. Ford made the switch to Hackett despite Smart Mobility's struggles in comparison to GM, which had successfully launched the Bolt and invested in Lyft and Cruise Automation. Ford appointed Sherif Marakby, who had left Ford for Uber, as the new head of Smart Mobility and gave him the mandate to convert the technology that companies like Argo AI was developing into profitable revenue streams.

For the lingering decisions that Ford had to make, Hackett set up a "shot-clock" in imitation of a basketball rule. As part of his first 100-day agenda, he focused on costs and on weaknesses, such as slowing sedan sales. He also focused on futuristic ideas and on strengthening the core. Executives huddled in conference spaces at headquarters to come up with ideas. Analysts, however, remained unconvinced that Ford would be able to find the right balance between increasing its profitability and competitiveness and moving to the new emphasis on electrification and the other initiatives to which it had committed. They pressured Ford to take bolder steps to reduce costs. They pointed to GM, which had been willing to leave Europe. They also maintained that the company should not shift too much of its attention away from its current product portfolio in favor of such projects as car-sharing services that did not have the near-term potential to improve its profitability.

Ford's first step under Hackett was to move the production of Focus compacts intended for the US market to China (a decision that later had to be reversed because of Trump administration's import tariffs). The aim was to save costs, even if the initiative might run against Trump administration's efforts to keep auto-industry jobs in the United States. Ford would end production of the Focus in the United States in 2018 and begin importing cars from China in 2019. Chinese production would be from an existing plant that already made the Focus. According to calculations Ford made, moving production to the existing Chinese plant, rather than to Mexico, would save $0.5 billion. The company would convert the US Focus production facility to Bronco sport-utility vehicles and Ranger pickup production with no net loss in jobs. Importing as many as 170,000 Ford Focus cars from China would be by far the highest volume of vehicles shipments from a Chinese factory to the United States in the country's history.

## The Environment, Safety, Quality, and Miscellaneous Issues

Like GM, Ford started to consider whether it could rely on materials other than aluminum to make pickups and other vehicles. It was considering a patchwork of materials to replace heavier metals in trucks. Like other automakers, it had worked on nearly every vehicle component to lighten them and increase efficiency from body panels and engines to brackets and windshields. Almost every change it considered came at a price. For example, Ford reckoned that aluminum had lowered the weight of the F-150 by as much as 700 pounds but added $1,000 in costs. The mix of additional materials that the company might use included thinner and lighter steels, magnesium, and carbon fiber. Like GM, Ford was reluctantly taking a serious look at carbon fiber.

As Ford was trying to set a new materials strategy, it confronted safety and quality issues. NHTSA started an investigation after receiving complaints that steering-wheel fastening bolts were loosening in 2014–2016 Fusion midsize sedans. The investigation applied to over 800,000 cars. Drivers had not reported crashes or injuries, and Ford therefore had not initiated a recall, but the company had to take the reports seriously. In another realm, Ford offered fixes to owners of 1.4 million late-model Explorer SUVs to address exhaust fumes leaking into the vehicle cabins. The safety and quality problems had an effect on the company's financial performance, as its net income rose slightly in the second quarter, but the stock fell by nearly 2 percent in response. The company revised its full-year guidance for profits. It was likely that they would be 16–25 percent lower than the previous year.

The company's sales volume also continued to slide, although at a rate lower than analysts' had predicted. For the first half of 2017, Ford's vehicle sales were down by 7.4 percent, which was better than GM, whose sales were down by 15.4 percent, and Fiat Chrysler, whose sales were down by 10.5 percent. However, Toyota's sales grew by 3.6 percent in this period, reflecting its greater emphasis on passenger cars rather than pickup trucks and SUVs as gasoline prices started to increase. Toyota also benefitted from improvement in the company's performance in China. In an effort to raise sales, Ford's financing unit changed its approval process for new loans, choosing to look beyond credit scores, despite rising defaults. The new approval process would allow borrowers with low credit scores to obtain a loan to purchase a car even if they did not have the prior financing history.

Going in the opposite direction of GM, Ford announced a partnership with an Indian automaker in order to raise its presence in a market where the potential was great but profits hard to achieve. Ford linked up with Indian automaker Mahindra & Mahindra to collaborate on new technologies and increase sales. As well as leveraging the companies' dealer networks, Ford was considering working with Mahindra & Mahindra on EVs, new mobility services, and connected-car innovations. This initiative came on the heels of GM's exit from India, the world's fifth-largest car market by sales.

## *Abandoning the North America Sedan and Relying on a Loophole for Fuel Efficiency*

As buyers increasingly deserted sedans for larger vehicles, Ford tried to show it could make a bold decision, as analysts and shareholders seemed to demand. The decision was to abandon the sale of unprofitable sedans in the United States, with the exception of the Mustang and Focus, and redirect the $7 billion it would save to the development of trucks and sport-utility vehicles. This decision was in accord with the improved profits F-series truck sales had generated in the third quarter of 2017. The improvement mainly came from the redesign of super duty trucks that sold for more than $100,000. In a segment where GM and Fiat Chrysler had similar offerings, Ford was convinced that it had to protect its turf. It estimated that by 2020, large vehicles with relatively low fuel economy would make up 90 percent of the firm's North American sales. Abandoning the sedan in North America attacked the company's costs by deploying its capital in a product line that had superior growth prospects. Ford was copying what Fiat Chrysler had done in 2016, when it had also abandoned the small and midsize niche in North America. Fiat Chrysler had prospered by making this decision, as it had increased its sales of trucks and Jeeps. Now, Ford hoped to do the same. Yet, it promised that by 2020 most of its trucks and SUVs would be available in battery-powered as well as gasoline-powered models. The company was also committed to reducing its sales, marketing, engineering and other costs by $11.5 billion between 2019 and 2022, and, in addition, was considering exiting or selling loss-making operations in Europe and South America. These moves would better position it for a future in which it would have to invest more in EVs and connected and driverless cars. Thus, the company announced a shift of about a third of its investment in gasoline and diesel engines over five years, or about $500 million a year, into vehicles that ran fully or partly on batteries, a change that would add to the $4.5 billion the company had already promised to spend over five years to electrify its vehicles.

Ford reckoned that it would be able to switch almost entirely over to trucks and SUVs in North America because of a well-known loophole in fuel economy standards. Vehicles classified as light trucks were subject to lower standards than cars. The area within the perimeter of vehicles' four wheels determined the miles-per-gallon limit to which vehicles had to adhere. Vehicles with larger perimeters had to comply with progressively lower fuel economy standards. Therefore, they enjoyed lower compliance standards than smaller cars. Mainly for this reason, Ford had already increased the size of the Ford Explorer XL without negative fuel economy regulatory consequences. In 2008, the Ford Explorer XL was 193.4 inches long and 73.7 inches wide but by 2018, it had grown to 198.3 inches long and 78.9 inches wide. In any case, the EPA under Trump was intent on rolling back 2025 the CAFE standards established by the Obama administration. It also promised to try to rescind California's waiver under the Clean Air Act, which allowed California and other states to set their own rules. Ford CEO Hackett and board chair Bill Ford, however, distanced themselves from this initiative and called for compromises on clean air and fuel economy rules.

## VW

Unlike GM and Ford, which were free of this problem, the cheating scandal dominated VW attention in the post-2016 period.[3] Projections of the ultimate cost of the scandal rose to more than $30 billion, European governments were still in the midst of investigations, and many court cases were pending. The US government brought criminal charges against VW executives and German authorities seemed close to proving that ex-CEO Martin Winterkorn had been personally involved. Despite the scandal, company revenues continued to grow. Its global rivals apparently had not been able to use the scandal for their benefit. The company was so large and diversified that it was very well-hedged to prevent long-term damage. While sales fell in the United States and Western Europe, they rose in the rest of the world. The VW brand suffered, but the other brands in the firm's diversified portfolio did well, and sales of nearly all of them increased.

Nonetheless, the scandal had serious implications for the company's strategy, in that it had to start to plan for a post-diesel world. Though many of its top executives were not pleased with this outcome, VW had little choice as European laws had turned against diesel and diesel had lost its image as a cleaner alternative to gasoline-powered automobiles.

CEO Mathias Mueller engaged the company in a series of initiatives very similar in nature to those in which GM and Ford had engaged. Like GM and Ford, VW invested in EVs, self-driving vehicles, and shared mobility. In comparison to GM and Ford, VW had extremely aggressive EV and hybrid goals, which were to launch fifty electric models and thirty hybrids by 2025 and electric versions of all its models by 2030. VW established a partnership with Didi Chuxing of China, the world's largest ride-hailing company.

In the United States, VW, like GM and Ford, initially benefitted from the investments it had made in crossovers and SUVs. In a low-price gasoline environment, the money VW sunk into the mid-size Tiguan crossover and the large Atlas SUV had paid off. However, as gasoline prices started to rise, the company's earnings, like those of GM and Ford, started to fall. The decline in earnings did not deter VW from trying to expand the reach of its light truck business in the United States. As a foreign motor company operating in the United States, it had to take action to protect its position against disadvantageous import tariffs. Thus, VW committed to expanding its production of its SUVs in its US facility in Tennessee.

Mueller fought off rumors that VW might acquire Fiat Chrysler and make other acquisitions or divestments. He was open and vocal and made changes that antagonized some of the firm's board members; thus, the board chose to remove him and replace him with Herbert Diess, an ex-BMW executive, who then reorganized the company to gain more control over its diverse brands and divisions. Dies, though, promised not to go back on the commitments that VW had made to electrification and alternative business models and technologies.

VW, in its own way, dealt with the same contradictions as those faced by GM and Ford. It pursued the lure of immediate profits by ramping up SUV and crossover production in the United States, while at the same time investing in a future that it anticipated might be far different. In the case of VW, however, the management paradoxes were somewhat different in that, following the cheating scandal, VW had to abandon its commitment to diesel, which had been its distinctive differentiating factor and area of excellence. Neither GM nor Ford had to take such a drastic step. Moreover, VW gave up on diesel in humiliating circumstances, and for this proud German company, to phase out of diesel was no easy task.

## The Emissions Cheating Scandal

VW CEO Matthias Müller estimated that since becoming CEO in 2015, he spent half his time managing the crisis. In the United States, the cost of the affair had ballooned to nearly $25 billion in fines, penalties and compensation, and in other countries, there were costs still to be determined and repercussions that could last for another decade. The company as well as two of its employees had pleaded guilty to criminal charges in the United States of defrauding the government and violating environmental law. US courts had sentenced VW employees to prison time. The company had agreed to pay about $20 billion to nearly 535,000 consumers and car dealers in the United States. Alleging that the software it used as a defeat device was not illegal in Europe, it had refused to make similar payments to the nearly 9 million European customer affected by the scandal. Suits cropped up in Germany, however. An owner of a defective VW sought consumer compensation for damages in a test case, which could lead to payments for millions of European customers. The German courts did not have US class-action rules, but they responded to the case of a single plaintiff that became a model for other suits affected parties brought. At least 100,000 German customers were ready to press the company for payment depending on the outcome of the first German trial.

The US settlement was unprecedented. VW pleaded guilty to criminal wrongdoing and paid a $4.3 billion penalty in response to a Justice Department probe of cheating. It pleaded guilty to fraud, obstruction of justice, and violating both the Clean Air Act and import rules. It admitted that it had equipped nearly 11 million diesel vehicles worldwide, including more than a half million in the United States, with software that enabled it to deceive the government on emissions tests. The cars it sold emitted toxic fumes from their tailpipes that were much higher than legal limits. The Justice Department reproached the company for a clean diesel campaign meant to deceive the public and an attempted cover up, in which employees had deleted documents, and it subjected the company to an independent monitor to audit its compliance practices.

The Justice Department asserted that it could have fined the company up to $34 billion, but accepted a lower figure because the company cooperated and had agreed to make payments in prior civil claims. The fine from the Justice Department was on top of the more than $20 billion in civil claims VW had to pay to consumers, regulators, dealers, and state attorney generals. Because of tough US emission and fuel-economy rules, the costs of fixing the cars ended up being higher than VW anticipated. The company had to buy back or fix Jettas, Golfs, Passats, and Beetles going back to 2009. Car owners also had the right to cash payments. Dealers had to fix many cars more than once, because the first fix did not take.

The Justice Department fine exceeded the $19.2 billion VW had set aside for the penalties. The total amount the company set aside grew to almost $30 billion. Matthias Mueller apologized for the company's egregious behavior and VW agreed to contribute billions of dollars toward promoting zero-emissions vehicles. A VW engineer, James Liang, pleaded guilty to helping with the cheating and agreed to cooperate with the government in the prosecution of others in exchange for a delay in his sentencing. Liang knew about the defeat device from a colleague who wrote in an email that the scheme was "watertight." He was part of group that responded to the government that tried to prevent it from finding out what was happening. Based partly on what Liang revealed, a federal grand jury indicted seven other VW employees for fraud. Many lived in Germany and refused to come to the United States to face charges, but the FBI was able to seize Oliver Schmidt, as he was getting ready to return to Germany. Schmidt had been in charge of US emissions compliance. Upon learning of the West Virginia University study that showed higher levels of emissions on the road than in the lab, he wrote in an email that the company had to choose between lying and telling the truth. He then helped prepare slides for a key meeting held in Germany, which pointed out that that without an adequate explanation the US government was likely to indict the company. Schmidt pleaded guilty and faced up to seven years in prison. He would have to pay a fine between $40,000 and $400,000. Upon completing his prison sentence, the United States had the right to deport him. Liang also faced jail time and would have to pay a fine for his involvement. The other VW executives the Justice Department indicted were: Jens Hadler, who ran engine development and powertrain development groups; Heinz-Jakob Neusser, who was a member of the brand-management board; Richard Dorenkamp, an engineer who worked on exhaust systems; Bernd Gottweis, a quality-control chief; and another engineer Jurgen Peter. The government later charged former

Audi engine-development manager Giovanni Pamio for his role in installing the software.

In Europe, governments were carrying out a number of separate investigations and arrests. The EU's antifraud office was investigating whether Volkswagen knowingly misused loans the European Investment Bank gave it to fraudulently boost its environmental performance. EU's antitrust regulators claimed that VW together with Daimler and BMW had engaged in collusive behavior by coordinating their answers to questions. German authorities arrested former engine chief Wolfgang Hatz, a senior executive and confidant of Martin Winterkorn, who had resigned as chief executive days after the scandal became public (see Chapter 15). The German authorities named Winterkorn a suspect, alleging that he probably knew about the fraud earlier than he acknowledged and may have been knowingly involved. The authorities also ordered the arrest of Jorg Kerner, Porsche's head of engine development and accused Michael Steiner, a Porsche board member, of not taking action when he knew what was taking place. Ongoing investigations were looking into whether current chief executive Mueller and other board members and executives including Porsche chair Hans Dieter Potsch had adequately disclosed the financial liabilities related to the scandal and whether VW had falsified carbon dioxide levels listed on its vehicle certifications.

## Sales Growth Despite the Scandal

Despite the ongoing emissions scandal, VW sales grew in 2016. The company sold 10.3 million vehicles, 3.8 percent more than in 2015, and its sales were higher than any carmaker. It was well positioned to weather the storm because it was well hedged by its global reach and diverse brands that protected it from the cheating scandal's full impact. While sales in the United States and Western Europe dropped by more than 7 percent in 2016, compared to the previous year, sales in China and Central and Eastern Europe grew by about 7 percent in the same period. China, where sales in 2016 surged to 2.9 million vehicles, was the firm's biggest source of growth. In Western Europe, VW's second biggest market, however, its market share fell after it admitted that it had cheated, and various countries took actions against the company. South Korea banned VW sales entirely. In Australia, sales fell by 9 percent, but VW did very well in

Mexico, its sales growing by nearly 15 percent in 2016, compared to the previous year.

Growth in sales in China and Central and Eastern Europe insulated VW from the full effects of the emission scandal. The diversity of the company's brands, which ranged from Skoda to Audi to Porsche, also protected it. Sales of cars with the VW brand were down by 1.3 percent and sales of cars with the Audi brand were down by 7.3 percent in comparison to the preceding year. However, sales of other brands grew in this period. Sales of Skoda grew by 2.5 percent; sales of VW trucks grew by 8 percent; Seat sales grew by 14 percent; Porsche sales grew by 6.6 percent; those of MAN grew by 7.5 percent; and sales of Scania grew by 12 percent.

Ironically, the buyback program VW had to start in the United States after the scandal helped US sales. The company spent more than $10 billion to buy back or terminate the leases of 125,000 diesel vehicles in the United States because of the emissions-cheating scheme, but VW dealers estimated that as many as 40 percent of customers ended up repurchasing a VW vehicle. The SUVs VW introduced into the US market, because of lower gasoline prices, also boosted US sales. Therefore, like Ford, VW announced plans to introduce an even larger SUV in the United States. It would manufacture this SUV in its Tennessee factory. Another factor spurring an upturn in US sales was a boom in luxury car sales such as Porsche. After Trump's election, Porsche sales climbed. The company's stock price picked up slowly because of continued growth despite the scandal. The concern of investors, apparently, was not with the scandal itself but with VW's weak earnings. Its operating margins were just 2 percent. VW promised to double these margins by 2020, but an agreement with its powerful union, which had ten seats on the board, prohibited the company from carrying out any forced layoffs for a decade. In not being able to make these forced layoffs, VW was in a different position than Ford or GM. Investors were also concerned that VW had invested in a wide range of electric-powertrain technologies that would not yield significant near-term results.

## Planning for a Post-Diesel World

The lesson that VW carried with it from the crisis was that it had to plan for a post-diesel world. Large European cities from Munich to Madrid had plans to ban or restrict diesels due to toxic emissions. Court orders had forced the European cities to act. Paris outlawed all diesels made before 2001 and promised a total ban by 2025. Madrid aimed to prohibit diesels from the city center by 2025. London pledged to replace them in municipal fleets and public transportation. Athens would exclude them from its city center starting in 2025. Oslo imposed high tolls on them. German cities like Munich, Stuttgart, and Hamburg were also in the process of outlawing or restricting older diesels from city centers. Hamburg's pledge was to replace diesels in its city fleets and public transportation by 2030. Though some drivers had deep attachments to diesel, VW could not count on diesel's reputation as a clean fuel. It could not continue to be as committed to diesel it had been. European cities, prodded by strong environmental pressure, were spearheading the changes that compelled VW to rethink its plans.

For VW, the issue was not just the cities' bans. To prevent future abuses like Dieselgate, European governments backed up their regulations with tight enforcement, which included spot checks, and high fines – as much as $35,000 for a single non-compliant vehicle. The cost of failing to comply with European emission and fuel economy regulations was likely to be prohibitive. VW and other European carmakers responded by initiating a campaign to remove the worst polluting diesel vehicles from roads by offering their owners up to a €10,000 discount on a new car if they retired their old one. VW admitted that the plan would cost it as much as €1.2 billion to implement.

Only about 5 percent of cars sold in the United States were diesel, but in Europe diesels made up more than half of sales. Companies, like VW, had reckoned they could meet EU targets to reduce carbon dioxide emissions with diesels, since the cars powered by them were more efficient and they emitted less carbon dioxide than gasoline-powered cars. European governments had previously subsidized diesel's use with low taxes because of these apparent clean properties. However, VW could no longer refrain from action based on the assumption that European governments would be supportive. Without diesel as an option, VW and other carmakers would find it very hard to meet European greenhouse-gas targets. The alternative, to go electric, was, in the view of many of VW's top managers, in its very early stages. Yet, tighter diesel emission regulation on top of the EU's mandated 30 percent cut in carbon-dioxide emissions gave the company little choice but to move in this direction. Globally, EVs made up less than 2 percent of auto sales in 2016, and in Europe, EVs and hybrids amounted to no more than 1 percent of the vehicles sold. The auto unions, a powerful influence on VW, because of their seats on the board, were anxious about the job implications of increased reliance on electric and hybrid vehicles. The price of these vehicles was significantly higher than that of diesels; they could hurt demand, and they could reduce the number of cars made and result in layoffs.

Matthias Mueller, appointed chief executive of VW after the emissions scandal, tried to move the company in the direction of electric and self-driving cars and ride sharing. Not only did he encounter union opposition to these initiatives, but many of VW's top managers resisted and did not want to abandon diesel. Mueller's challenge to win over the employees was not easy. To appease labor, he revoked job cuts that Herbert Diess, CEO of the VW brand, had planned. Despite the opposition, VW planned to invest around $40 billion over five years to develop electric vehicles, self-driving cars, and Uber-like mobility app services.

**Investing in EVs:** VW's dedication to diesels left it behind in electric vehicle (EV) technology. Its share of the global plug-in passenger-car market was just 8.2 percent in 2016. To catch up, the company opted to develop a new family of electric cars, named the ID. The prototype would resemble the Golf. VW tripled its investment in electric vehicles to $10 billion through 2025. It aimed to launch fifty new electric models and thirty new hybrids by that year and to create electric versions of all its more than 300 models by 2030. Starting in 2019 it would launch a new electric vehicle almost every month. It would build the cars in Germany, China, and the United States and aimed to create at least sixteen new electric-vehicle plants in these countries by 2025, with nine of the plants expected to be in operation by 2020.

With regard to the infrastructure for EVs, the company was teaming with BMW, Daimler, and Ford. In Europe, they would help build an electric car-charging network. In the United States, VW launched a subsidiary called Electrify America to administer $2 billion in investments in order to promote zero-emission vehicles as it promised after the cheating scandal. Electrify America planned to build a network of charging stations that could supply 10 percent of US needs. It would create these charging stations in thirty-nine states at workplaces, retail centers, and other locations. It would also construct ultrafast charging stations in highway corridors. While VW maintained that the

US charging stations would be compatible with other companies' plans to build such stations, Ford complained that VW was not designing them this way. VW's exclusiveness would have a negative effect on the electrification of the US driving fleet. This accusation did not deter VW. With its extensive rollout of charging stations, battery, production facilities, and hybrid models over five years, its goal was to overtake Tesla. The company wanted to sell three million electric vehicles a year by 2025. In comparison, Tesla sold 102,807 cars in 2016 and had about 500,000 orders for the Model 3.

The Chinese market was particularly attractive for EVs. EV sales in China amounted to an estimated 350,000 vehicles in 2016, which was roughly half the global total. This market was supposed to grow very quickly as China moved to reduce air pollution and it offered incentives for EVs. VW estimated that as many as two million electric and plug-in hybrid vehicles would be sold in China in 2020. The company solved the problem of the Chinese requiring that EVs built in China use Chinese made batteries. It invested nearly half the €50 billion it set aside for batteries, acquiring them from Chinese company Contemporary Amperex Technology.

**Investing in Self-Driving Vehicles:** VW imagined that the EVs would ultimately drive autonomously. To achieve its autonomous vehicle goals, VW collaborated with Nvidia to develop artificial-intelligence applications. Together with Intel, BMW, and Daimler it had a stake in Here International, a digital mapmaker that created navigation technology to ensure self-driving car safety. VW also collaborated with Hyundai, with whom it invested in Silicon Valley startup Aurora Innovation. Aurora Innovation had been started in 2016 by former autonomous vehicle leaders from Google and Tesla. Their goal, like startups in which GM and Ford had invested, was to create a rival to Waymo. Using a mixture of robotics lasers, radar cameras and machine learning, they aimed to put their self-driving software in production vehicles by 2021. The company's offices were in Pittsburgh. Its chief executive, Chris Urmson, had ties to Carnegie Mellon University and he had helped start Google's program. Sterling Anderson, a co-founder, had been a participant in the development of Tesla's program.

**Investing in Ride Hailing:** VW had been behind other firms in new mobility services such as car sharing and ride-hailing. For instance, it trailed Daimler, whose Car2Go was Europe's biggest car-sharing company, with 2.3 million world-wide members. VW had to move into such services, to replace revenue it would lose if customers bought fewer vehicles. However, many VW executives were disdainful of businesses like car sharing and ride-hailing. Nonetheless, VW took a stake in Gett, an app-based business that was like Uber's ride-hailing service. Gett, an Israeli-based company, became the nucleus for a brand VW called Moia, which was the world's tenth largest car-hailing service. Drivers were using their own vehicles, but VW eventually wanted to provide them with vehicles. Car-sharing applications had the potential to create additional revenue streams, for example, location-based services, that steered drivers to hotels or restaurants. VW could also sell the data, which the car-sharing services generated. A 2016 McKinsey study projected shared-mobility and data services could create up to $1.5 trillion in additional revenue for auto companies by 2030 if the automakers could develop digital technology and business models to capture this revenue.

Didi Chuxing of China had the largest ride-hailing market share of any company in the world at about 33 percent in comparison to Uber's 30 percent. VW formed a joint venture with Didi to share technology and develop mobility services in China. The deal was more than about ride-hailing, as the two companies intended to explore autonomous driving and robo-taxis as well as other mobility projects. As a first step, VW agreed to provide Didi Chuxing with around 100,000 vehicles, plus electric and autonomous-vehicle technology, and to help manage the company's vehicle fleet. VW held a 40 percent in the venture and would acquire another 10 percent later.

## Performance, SUVs, and Acquisitions

Based on strong sales of new models and cost-cutting, VW's 2017 first-quarter earnings beat expectations. Refurbishing models to take advantage of robust global demand for SUVs had positive results in a low gasoline price environment. The new Tiguan, a midsize crossover, as well as the larger and the higher priced seven-seat Atlas SUV, which VW specially designed for the US market, sold very well. Cost cutting and better pricing in Western Europe also helped improve the company's performance. VW's first quarter earnings were 29 percent higher than the previous year and ahead of analysts' forecasts. However, in the third quarter of 2017, VW's earnings dropped, as gasoline prices started to move upwards and diesel-emissions scandal costs again assumed significance. The company took a one-time diesel-related charge of $3 billion against quarterly earnings, which caused its net income in the quarter to fall by more than 50 percent compared to the previous year. Ignoring the onetime charge, the company's profits grew by 15 percent as revenue from VW brands like Audi, Porsche, VW, Lamborghini, MAN, Scania, and Ducati were higher than expected. However, sales growth in the saturated Western Europe market was weak.

As part of its plan to boost its US performance, VW like other automakers had made investments in SUVs. To offset a trade dispute, it pledged to invest $340 million in manufacturing a new sport-utility vehicle in Tennessee. Previously it had spent $900 million on the plant and built the Atlas in Tennessee. Under existing import rules, the United States could establish a 2.5 percent tariff on passenger cars imported from Europe, but on pickup trucks and vans imported from Europe it could impose a 25 percent tariff. In contrast, the EU did not distinguish between passenger cars, pickup trucks, and vans. It could set 10 percent across-the-board tariff on both cars and trucks imported from the United States.

To achieve VW's goal of growing its US market share, it had to maneuver around these rules. In 2017, its US market share was just 3 percent. Its aim was to grow its US market share to 5 percent. Therefore, it made the Jetta passenger car as well as the Atlas SUV in Tennessee. Because of high labor costs and other factors, the United States was not the ideal place for auto manufacturing. NAFTA, though, presented an opening. In Puebla, Mexico, VW built the Golf and a number of other models that it exported to the United States from one of its largest worldwide factories. VW had to be prepared to shift more of its production to the United States if the Trump administration terminated NAFTA or imposed onerous tariffs on Mexico.

Being in possession of so many assets, VW was in a position where it could sell some to raise cash to make investments in electric vehicles, self-driving cars, and mobility. The MAN and Scania brands, for instance, were assets the company could sell. On the other hand, VW could choose to get bigger rather than to sell assets. VW at first denied persistent rumors that it might buy Fiat Chrysler. Mueller claimed the company had enough to deal with after the scandal. It was not in a position to consider a large-scale takeover like Fiat Chrysler. Then, VW declared that it *might* be open to such talks. However, it qualified what it said and maintained that it was regularly engaged in exploratory talks with many companies and was unlikely to conclude any deal soon. Rumors also persisted that VW might sell its premium Italian motorcycle maker Ducati to Harley-Davidson. An issue was that the board would have to accept any restructuring the company did, and the board, which included labor representatives, was not likely to be open to changes that could involve job losses.

## Replacing the CEO

Mueller aroused much opposition because of the moves he made. Thus, VW decided to replace him and install instead the head of the VW brand and former BMW executive Herbert Diess, a longtime Mueller antagonist, as CEO. Diess rose to the top of Porsche and became its CEO in 2015 after the emissions test cheating scandal. Mueller had been an ultimate VW insider. His ouster was a surprise after what he had done to help the company get through the emissions crisis, including restoring profits and initiating new efforts to develop electric and self-driving vehicles. Diess had previously been passed over as chief executive at BMW. Ferdinand Piech, a former VW CEO and a grandson of Ferdinand Porsche, recruited Diess to VW. It was Piech who apparently orchestrated a boardroom coup, urging shareholders to oust Mueller. Diess promised to accelerate changes Mueller had started. Change at VW was very hard to accomplish because of the ownership structure and the board's influence. The heirs to Porsche family and the German state of Lower Saxony together held more than 70 percent of the company's voting stock. The IG Metall trade union, which represented employees, had ten seats on the board. Under these circumstances, protecting jobs usually took precedence over increasing profits. Organized labor viewed Diess with suspicion because of his reputation as a cost cutter, but it seemed that prior to his appointment he was able to patch up his relations with labor.

A theory about Mueller's ouster was that it was a result of his push into electric and self-driving cars, which many VW executives and engineers opposed, but Mueller appeared to have the board's backing for this change. Another theory was that his candidness and strong opinions were related to his ouster. As CEO of VW, he should have been more circumspect. He was too open in stating that VW might be willing to accept an end to tax subsidies for diesels, a shift to government funding to electric vehicles, and the sale of Ducati and other VW assets. These opinions might have alienated the Porsche family, Lower Saxony, and the IG Metall trade union that dominated the company's board. Mueller also bluntly expressed his disgust when the media revealed that VW employees had participated in experiments that forced monkeys to inhale diesel exhaust.

The first move Diess made as CEO was to initiate a restructuring. He brought together the firm's mass volume car brands VW, Seat, and Skoda. He split out Porsche, Lamborghini, Bugatti and Bentley as a super-premium division, kept Audi separate as the premium division, and prepared the VW Truck & Bus group for a potential divestment. This move gave Diess greater control over the direction of the company, in contrast to Mueller who had granted more autonomy to the separate brands. But Diess promised not to reverse Mueller's overall strategy on electric cars and new auto technology. At the same time, he considered a full-scale takeover of Navistar International, one of the largest truck makers in the United States. VW already owned 16.6 percent of Navistar, which was one of the successor companies to International Harvester.

## Toyota

Toyota was caught in some of the same binds as GM, Ford, and VW.[4] It too drew Trump's ire and had to make non-optimal plant location decisions. It had to bolster its US presence to ensure that it would not be subject to punitive tariffs. In locating in the United States, it took advantage of the high level of incentives states and localities offered to have it locate to their jurisdictions. Unlike GM and Ford, Toyota struggled with low gasoline prices. Its distinct competence and market lead was in passenger cars. The most important markets for Toyota were Japan and the United States. As US demand shifted to SUVs and small trucks, Toyota lost US market share to its competitors. It had to increase the incentives it gave to consumers to get them to buy passenger cars. It increased its SUV, truck, and crossover offerings and production, because the US market demanded that it pivot in that direction. The C-HR crossover ultimately proved to be a success in the United States as it had been in other parts of the world, but Toyota had trouble producing enough of these vehicles for the US market. Its plans were to stick with the Camry and Corolla in the United States, produce other new models in the country, and not go all out with SUVs, trucks, and crossovers like the C-HR.

Toyota like other automakers set electrification goals. Its aim – to sell 5.5 million hybrids, fully electric, and FCVs by 2030 – exceeded that of any automaker. Like other automakers, it viewed China as being the first large market for fully electric vehicles. Collaborating with Panasonic, Tesla's supplier of batteries, it aimed to produce and sell EV batteries to other automakers. Along with Panasonic, it innovated in the lithium ion battery used in electric vehicles. It patented a battery that was lighter, quicker to charge, and lasted longer, but it still had to figure out how to manufacture it cheaply and to scale.

In pursuit of the goal of 5.5 million electrified vehicles by 2030, it aimed to solidify and extend its 2017 lead in hybrids. It introduced a new model of the regular Prius and a plug-in Prius. However, the new plug-in hybrid did not have the features that would make it competitive with Chevy's Volt, suggesting that Toyota's commitment to the plug-in Prius was weak and that it preferred that customers stick with the non-plug-in version. Like other automakers, Toyota had autonomous vehicle goals but it was more circumspect than the other automakers in publicizing its plans. In comparison to other automakers, Toyota was mostly inactive in the ride-sharing realm. Finally, Toyota continued to face claims for liability in the Takata airbag recall and unlike GM, but like Ford, it took steps to expand the scope of its activities in India.

## Drawing Trump's Ire

Trump attacked Toyota for the new $1 billion Corolla plant it was building in Mexico and threatened to levy a tariff on imported cars. Toyota's response was to try to cooperate with the new administration. Maintaining that the new plant would not replace US employment, the company stated that the relocation of Corolla production was from Canada, not the United States and that it still would assemble Corolla, the second-best-selling US compact car after the Honda Civic, in Mississippi. For Toyota, it was important to be able to produce vehicles it sold in North America and in other countries outside Japan because of the Yen's fluctuations. If the Trump administration exited NAFTA, the light trucks Toyota made in Mexico could face a 25 percent duty. Previously, Toyota had announced plans to increase production of pickup trucks in Mexico, as NAFTA allowed the company and other automakers to import light trucks from Mexico to the United States duty free. In 2016, automakers imported more than $18.5 billion worth of light trucks from Mexico to the United States. Mexico's share of North American auto production had grown to about 20 percent. Its auto-parts suppliers employed more than 700,000 workers. If Toyota canceled the new plant in Mexico, parts supplier Aisin Seiki might also have to cancel plans to build a $60 million Mexican plant.

To deal with the threat, Toyota pledged to invest $1.6 billion in a Camry plant in Kentucky. It promised to build another $1.6 billion assembly plant in the United States with Mazda that would produce 300,000 vehicles a year and create 4,000 jobs. The new US assembly plant would make Corollas and crossovers that relied on the Corolla's architecture. Mazda too would make crossovers in the new plant as well as SUVs and some passenger cars. Toyota hoped that by building this new plant, it would be able to increase production of high-margin sport-utility vehicles in Canada and pickup trucks in Mexico. These initiatives signaled a change in Toyota's strategy. In 2015, concerned about overproduction, it stopped creating new production capacity; and Mazda had not built cars in the United States since it stopped co-production with Ford in 2012.

Toyota's shortlist of locations bidding for the new factory included a host of states mostly in the Southeastern and Southwestern parts of the United States, but also including Illinois, Indiana, Iowa, and Michigan. The Southeast was Toyota's favorite because of weak union laws, the availability of suppliers, and inducements that Toyota and Mazda expected from local governments – tax breaks, free land, infrastructure, and training. These inducements were worth hundreds of millions of dollars. Alabama ultimately won the bid for the Toyota-Mazda plant with a package of incentives worth about $700 million. More than half came from the state and the rest came from the city of Huntsville, where Toyota and Mazda would locate the plant. Toyota promised to invest another $6.8 billion in the United States by 2020.

Toyota and other foreign carmakers added capacity and increased their workforces in the United States to the point that they produced more vehicles and had more workers in the United States than the domestic automakers. Foreign automakers dominated US sales, controlling 56 percent of the market. In the first quarter of 2018, they made

1.4 million vehicles in the United States. They were unencumbered by pensions and lured by the strong US incentive packages. In contrast, US carmakers, burdened by costly overhead and too much US capacity, preferred to locate their new factories outside the country. They were increasing the number of vehicles they imported. Because of low gasoline prices, they had scaled back production of low-margin sedans in favor of more profitable trucks and SUVs.

## SUVs, Crossovers, and Trucks

In contrast to GM, Ford, and Fiat Chrysler, Toyota was not well-positioned to meet growing demand for light trucks and SUVS, whose sales surged because of the low gasoline prices. In 2016, Toyota had to surrender the title of being the world's largest carmaker by sales volume, a status it had since 2012. VW slipped ahead of Toyota in 2016. VW sold 10.3 million vehicles in 2016 compared to Toyota that sold 10.2 million vehicles. VW advanced mainly because of its strong showing in China. In contrast, Toyota's overall sales declined because it depended heavily on Japan and the United States. Economic growth in Japan was slow, while US auto sales were driven by low gasoline prices and Toyota did not excel in the SUVs and light trucks that were popular in the United States. Toyota's strength was in sedans like the Camry, a part of the US market, which was not advancing. Toyota struggled in an era of low gasoline prices. It was not on the right side of the shift in US demand to SUVs and light trucks. In the first quarter of 2017 Toyota had its first operating loss in North America in five years. It had to spend more to attract US buyers, increasing incentives by an average of $250 a vehicle to $4,000. For the first time it sold more light trucks than cars in the United States. US sales of midsize sedans like the Camry fell by 15 percent in the first quarter of 2017 compared to a year earlier, while US crossover and SUV sales rose by more than 8 percent. In that quarter, Toyota's US market share dropped from 16.2 percent to 14 percent.

To stem this tide, Toyota boosted production of SUVs, trucks, and crossovers. The company chose to stop making Corollas in Canada in favor the RAV4 SUV, which was its top-selling US vehicle. The company increased the assembly not only of the RAV4 but also of Highlander SUVs, and Tacoma pickups. It redid its factory in Guanajuato, Mexico to nearly double production of North American

Tacoma pickups to 400,000 vehicles a year. Uncharacteristically, Toyota tried to compete in the full-size luxury SUV model with the Land Cruiser, a low MPG vehicle. The Land Cruiser, loaded with extras, sold for about $85,000. It attracted sales of just around 4,000 US buyers per year. Most buyers viewed the Ford Range Rover as a much better bargain. It weighed about 1,000 pounds less than the Land Cruiser and at 19 mpg it got about 20 percent better fuel economy.

Toyota also had plans to retool production lines to make more crossovers, like its new C-HR compact, instead of sedans. The new US factory with Mazda, which would be completed by 2021, would have the flexibility to produce other vehicles on the Corolla platform including the CH-R. Toyota built the C-HR crossover on a sedan or hatchback platform. It was more fuel-efficient than a full-size SUV constructed on a truck frame, but resembled an SUV in that it had more passenger space than a sedan. To perk consumer interest, the C-HR had an unusual design. In Europe and Japan it sold very well, about 150,000 C-HRs in the first half of 2017, which was over 10 percent of Toyota's total European and Japanese sales. The C-HR also sold very well in Japan. Furthermore, its US price started at $22,500, which put it in reach of first-time car buyers. Yet Toyota only sold a few thousand C-HRs in the United States per month in 2016, which was a small fraction of its sales of larger and more expensive RAV4 and Highlanders. So long as gasoline prices were low, customer demand for large vehicles held back C-HR US sales. Another reason for weak sales was supply constraints. Almost all C-HRs Toyota sold in the United States and in Europe came from Turkey, where Toyota's assembly lines had to work overtime to meet global demand. In the second quarter of 2017, as gasoline prices began to rise, motor vehicle sales in the United States slumped, yet Toyota did better on improved crossover sales. Buyers continued to move away from sedans, but they lost some of their interest in SUVs and trucks. The booms and busts in energy prices now favored Toyota. Toyota raised profit projections based on the expectation that its sales would continue to grow, but in the third quarter of 2017, operating margins in North America fell about 2 percent compared to the previous year. The RAV4 did become the best-selling US vehicle not made on a truck platform. However, growing RAV4 sales, did not compensate for the increased incentives Toyota had to pay to sell passenger cars. The company had to offer customers an average $3,291 incentive to purchase passenger cars, compared to just $2,063 for trucks, SUVs, and crossover.

Toyota faced a shortage of RAV4s, Highlanders, and Tacoma pickups because of its 2015 moratorium on new plant construction. Its dealers estimated that the company could sell an additional 100,000 Tacomas, but its two truck plants in San Antonio, Texas and Baja California, Mexico, did not have additional capacity. The company did not expect to ease the Tacoma shortage until the opening of a Mexican factory in 2019. Toyota was pushing for the start of production a year early to meet growing demand. It had anticipated incorrectly that passenger-car sales would be the main driver of US sales.

## Electrification Goals

Meanwhile, like other automakers, Toyota set ambitious targets for the electrification of its fleet, promising that hybrid and electric vehicles would constitute up to half of global sales by 2030. The company formed a partnership on battery technology with Panasonic. Hybrids already constituted about 14 percent of Toyota sales in 2016. Its global market share was about 40 percent. Outside hybrids, the remaining vehicles Toyota needed to meet its 2030 goals were plug-in hybrids, completely electric vehicles, and FCVs. The aim was to sell 5.5 million of this type of vehicle, 4.5 million hybrids and plug-in hybrids and the remainder completely electric and fuel cells.

**Maintaining the Lead in Hybrids:** Toyota maintained the global lead in hybrids. In the United States as of November 2017, Toyota/Lexus sold 184,124 hybrids. Ford/Lincoln sold 68,011. Kia/Hyundai sold 31,539, and other automakers sold 31,539. Toyota promised ten new electrified models by the early 2020s. By about 2025, it pledged that every Toyota and Lexus model would have an electrified option. Many of the models it would sell would be hybrids. It lagged behind GM and Nissan, which already had fully electric vehicles. Other rivals indicated they would reach their electric goal earlier than Toyota.

GM promised to introduce twenty electric models globally within six years, about twice the number that Toyota promised. Toyota set electrification goals because regulators in China, Europe, and elsewhere had tough emission and fuel-efficiency targets. Like its competitors, it indicated that it would start to build fully electric vehicles in China and sell them first in that country before gradually introducing them into Japan, India, the United States, and Europe. However, Toyota's goal of having half of its vehicle sales come from electrified vehicles fell short of Honda's goal of two-thirds. It projected sales of 10.2 million vehicles in 2030, of which 5.5 million would be electrified, while Honda projected sales of 4.7 million vehicles, of which 3.1 million would be electrified. VW projected sales of 10.3 million vehicles in 2025, of which 2.6 million would be electrified.

**Making Batteries for other Manufacturers' EVs:** Toyota and Panasonic planned to make batteries for other automakers. Toyota's spending on electric vehicle R&D would be $13 billion by 2030, with more than half this investment reserved for battery development carried out with Panasonic. Toyota sold the final part of the $50 million stake it had in Tesla in 2016, formally ending a partnership between the carmakers that had started in 2010. Tesla had agreed to make components for the all-electric RAV4 SUV in return for Toyota's investment, but in 2014, Toyota stopped selling this vehicle. Besides Panasonic, Toyota's other partners in developing electric vehicle technology were Mazda and the parts supplier, Denso. Together they set up a new company called EV Common Architecture Spirit, with Toyota having a 90 percent stake in the venture, and Mazda and Denso and Mazda each having 5 percent shares. The aim of the venture was to create a common architecture for electric powertrains. The conundrum Toyota faced, similar to that of GM, Ford, and VW, was that its ability to meet its electrification goals was limited because of pressing immediate demand for trucks and SUVs. Toyota heavily invested in expanding truck and SUV production, which conflicted with its need to electrify. Another challenge Toyota faced was Ford's plans to surpass it in annual US hybrid sales by 2021. To build a lead in a segment where other US automakers had fallen behind, Ford was attempting to increase hybrid demand by adding the option to its popular F-150, Mustang, and Explorer models. Ford's wanted to be as well-known for hybrids as Toyota.

While it struggled with other automakers for electric dominance, Toyota neared a technological breakthrough in batteries. The technology was a solid electrolyte that made smaller, lighter lithium-ion batteries possible. It could lower charging time since it could safely handle higher currents. It held twice the charge, thereby expanding electric vehicle range. The problem the materials in the glasslike electrolyte in the battery overcame was fire risk that prevented packing the current lithium-ion battery more tightly together. Though Toyota only had shown how the new battery was effective on a small scale in a laboratory, it expected that it could sell vehicles with it by the early 2020s. The company described how it produced the battery and made the safety features known in patent filings. It was in the process of determining how to produce large quantities at reasonable cost.

**Introducing a new Prius Plug-In:** Toyota called the plug-in version the Prius Prime and it sold this car for about $35,000, which was similar to the Chevy Volt, but it had less advanced features. Its maximum range was twenty-five miles, while the Volt could travel up to forty miles on a single charge under good conditions. The Prime also had fewer seats than the Volt and its drive was more sluggish. The twenty-five-mile range was better than the prior Prius plug-in, which had a range of just eleven miles. Toyota treated it as a transition to a fully electric vehicle. Toyota built the Prime on its New Generation Vehicle Architecture rather than a dedicated platform, a cost-saving decision that limited battery space and configuration. The battery pack took up about five more cubic feet of cargo space than a standard Prius and it was located in a rear-center seat position. The weight – 300 pounds more than standard Prius -led to slow acceleration. Toyota continued to hold back on plug-in technology, reasoning that the return on investment was not sufficient, given the added cost, complication and weight, while the standard Prius was remarkably efficient. Its preference was that consumers buy a standard Prius.

**Planning For Autonomous Vehicles:** Unlike GM, Ford, and VW, Toyota was relatively silent about its autonomous vehicle plans. It offered information that its artificial-intelligence project, called Yu, aimed to install an onboard virtual assistant that evaluated a driver's mood, engaged in chitchat, and offered to drive autonomously if it sensed sleepiness or distractions. Rivals, Honda, as well as Amazon and Apple had similar plans, but Toyota planned to start testing cars equipped with the system in Japan in 2020. The seats in its car that were driven in an autonomous mode, reclined and massaged the driver's back. After an Uber self-driving car killed an Arizonan pedestrian, Toyota suspended autonomous-vehicle testing tests on public roads in California and Michigan, but not Japan.

## *Airbags and India*

Toyota still had to deal with suits arising out of the defective airbags that Takata had made. A bankruptcy judge issued a temporary stay on these suits. The stay did not affect the recall itself, the largest in US history, which had to continue. The judge's order also did not affect Takata, because it had filed for US Chapter 11 bankruptcy protection. The exception to the judge's order was Florida. In Florida, he allowed consumers to collect for losses, such as the need to rent cars while companies fixed their air bags. The judge gave permission to state actions brought by authorities in New Mexico, Hawaii, and the US Virgin Islands against Toyota, Honda, Subaru, and other manufacturers to move forward in ninety days. He allowed these actions to move forward, since weather in these states made the Takata-airbags more dangerous than elsewhere. Because of the heat, they were more likely to set off explosions, sometimes with lethal effect. The trial against carmakers in other jurisdictions would have to wait to the spring of 2018.

With regard to India, Suzuki's local unit, Maruti Suzuki, held 47 percent of India's passenger-car market, while Toyota's share of overall sales was about 5 percent. Toyota and Suzuki decided to collaborate, sharing models to capture more of this rapidly expanding market. Toyota provided its locally made Corolla sedan to Suzuki to sell. In return, Toyota sold two of Suzuki's popular models, the Baleno hatchback and the Vitara Brezza SUV. The deal helped fill gaps in the companies' Indian lineups. The Baleno hatchback and Vitara Brezza SUV were small, fuel-efficient models, while Indian consumers viewed the Corolla as a high-end vehicle.

## Conclusion – How Much Strategic Change Had Taken Place?

Toyota confronted some of the same contradictions as the other automakers but the company and the circumstances were different. A few main differences stand out. Toyota was behind GM and Ford when it came to SUVs and trucks. It was catching up and even surpassing these companies in crossovers, which were emerging as a new battleground for automakers. The company was way ahead of competitors in hybrids and its lead motivated it to set more far-reaching electrification goals than them. Whether any of the auto companies could achieve their electrification goals was unknown. All of them experienced pressures to meet consumer demand for large, less efficient vehicles, especially in the United States, on the one hand; and to innovate and offer electrified vehicles, autonomous driving choices, and ride-sharing possibilities, on the other hand. Their transformation was taking place within a dynamic setting of gasoline price changes that influenced consumer preferences that in turn affected their ability to innovate.

Boom and bust gasoline prices and auto efficiency regulations led GM and Ford to overcommit to passenger cars in the United States and to have too much capacity for their production. They had to cut back, close factories, and lay off workers. US auto production made a significant move to Mexico. The migration to Mexico would have been more significant were it not for the Trump backlash, which did not stop it, but which made the auto companies more cautious. The Trump administration played a role in the decision making of each of the companies. All of the companies faced pressure to produce ever larger and potentially more profitable SUVs and trucks for the US market; however, this pressure abated somewhat as oil prices again started to creep up. All of them anticipated that they could make the most headway selling electric vehicles in China. Maintaining and expanding their market presence in China was an important imperative. GM finalized its retreat from Europe and other countries. Both GM and Ford searched for lighter materials to use so they could comply with upcoming energy efficiency standards. Ford gave up on the sedan in the North American market and continued to use a legal loophole to get around the need to comply with fuel-efficiency standards.

Within this dynamic setting of volatile prices, the auto companies had to manage a paradox of being firmly rooted in the present and striving for an uncertain future. Each managed this paradox somewhat differently, based on the specific challenges they confronted. Ford and VW saw their CEOs sacked and new ones appointed. VW had to plan for a world without diesels, a choice it really did not want to make, but one it brought on itself because of its egregious behavior in the Dieselgate scandal. Of all the firms, VW was best-hedged against risks and uncertainties because of its global reach and brand diversity. The historic hedges of these automakers – the needs to emphasize safety and quality, to have a global reach, to offer a broad set of vehicles, and to innovate – however only went so far in protecting them against change and providing stability in an environment that was anything but stable.

## Notes

1. This review of GM strategies comes from an analysis of the following *Wall Street Journal* articles about the company that appeared between January 1, 2017 and August 1, 2018. The articles are listed below in chronological order starting with the most recent articles.

   Wilmot, Stephen. "The Fool's Game of Picking the Electric Car Champ." *Wall Street Journal*, July 28, 2018.

   Colias, Mike, and Chester Dawson. "Big Auto Makers Trim Forecasts – Tariffs on Aluminum and Steel Exact a Toll; Currency Devaluations, China also Hit Results." *Wall Street Journal*, July 26, 2018.

   Schlesinger, Jacob M. "Trump Sees Car Tariffs as Big Trade Weapon." *Wall Street Journal*, July 2, 2018.

   Colias, Mike, and Chester Dawson. "Car Makers Bring Fuel Efficiency to Trucks." *Wall Street Journal*, June 18, 2018.

   Higgins, Tim. "Driverless Autos Get Help from Humans Watching Remotely." *Wall Street Journal*, June 7, 2018.

   Colias, Mike. "Heavy-Pickup Contest Heats Up – with a New Entry, GM Hopes to Cut into Ford's Traditional Lead in a Growing Market." *Wall Street Journal*, May 17, 2018.

   Colias, Mike. "Trump Presses Car Makers to Hire – Auto Executives Urged to Boost Factory Jobs; 20% Tariff Proposed for Imported Vehicles." *Wall Street Journal*, May 14, 2018.

   Roberts, Adrienne. "Sedan Weakness Dents Auto Sales." *Wall Street Journal*, May 2, 2018.

   Wilmot, Stephen. "Auto Investors Focus on Change Ahead of a Murky Future." *Wall Street Journal*, April 30, 2018.

   Colias, Mike. "GM Takes Hit from South Korean Unit." *Wall Street Journal*, April 27, 2018.

   Colias, Mike. "Electric-Car Startups Lure Big Talent." *Wall Street Journal*, April 23, 2018.

   Colias, Mike. "GM Gives Cadillac Push with New Chief." *Wall Street Journal*, April 19, 2018.

   Colias, Mike, and Christina Rogers. "Car Makers Step Back from Cars." *Wall Street Journal*, April 5, 2018.

   Colias, Mike, and Adrienne Roberts. "GM Scraps a Standard in Sales Reporting – Decision to Drop Monthly Auto Sales Disclosure could Obscure Broad Trends." *Wall Street Journal*, April 3, 2018.

   Higgins, Tim, Mike Spector, and Mike Colias. "Self-Drive Focus Shifts to Humans." *Wall Street Journal*, April 3, 2018.

   Colias, Mike, and Mike Spector. "Business & Technology: Electric Cars Get Makeover." *Wall Street Journal*, March 10, 2018.

Colias, Mike, and Russell Gold. "GM's Barra Urges further Tax Credits." *Wall Street Journal*, March 8, 2018.

Colias, Mike. "GM's Cadillac Gets New Marketing Chief." *Wall Street Journal*, March 7, 2018.

Colias, Mike "GM Truck Unit Carries Big Load – Pickups and SUVs Will Help Auto Maker Fund Development of Driverless, Electric Cars." *Wall Street Journal*, February 27, 2018.

Colias, Mike "GM to Close South Korean Plant – Auto Maker to Seek Cuts at Other Factories in the Country as it Downsizes Globally." *Wall Street Journal*, February 13, 2018.

Colias, Mike, and Chester Dawson. "GM Picks Up Speed in North America, Outmuscling Toyota." *Wall Street Journal*, February 7, 2018.

Colias, Mike. "GM to Book Write-Down, but Outlook is Brighter." *Wall Street Journal*, January 17, 2018.

Colias, Mike. "Chevrolet Aims to make Trucks Handsomer." *Wall Street Journal*, January 16, 2018.

Dawson, Chester, and Mike Spector. "Auto Makers Miss Emissions Goal." *Wall Street Journal*, January 12, 2018.

Roberts, Adrienne, and John D. Stoll. "Foreign Car Makers to Take US Lead." *Wall Street Journal*, January 11, 2018.

Colias, Mike, and Adrienne Roberts. "Auto Sales Growth Stalls – Annual Drop of 1.8% is First in Eight Years, but Pickups and SUVs Bolster US Results." *Wall Street Journal*, January 4, 2018.

Spector, Mike. "GM Tries to Stop $1 Billion Payout." *Wall Street Journal*, December 18, 2017.

Moss, Trefor. "GM's China Brand Surges." *Wall Street Journal*, December 4, 2017.

Roberts, Adrienne, and John D. Stoll. "For US Car Makers, Smaller Share Drives Bigger Profit." *Wall Street Journal*, December 2, 2017.

Colias, Mike. "GM is Counting on Self-Driving Taxis." *Wall Street Journal*, December 1, 2017.

Moss, Trefor. "Electric Vehicles Struggle in China." *Wall Street Journal*, November 18, 2017.

Colias, Mike. "The Quest to make Cadillac Hum again – President Johan De Nysschen Looks Toward Growth in China as He Confronts the Auto Brand's Falling US Market Share." *Wall Street Journal*, October 26, 2017.

Heller, Jamie. "GM's Strategy for the Autonomous Car: President Dan Ammann on what the Company is Doing – and what the Timetable is." *Wall Street Journal*, October 24, 2017.

Stoll, John D. "GM's Recent Moves Give Shares a Lift – Bets on Driverless-Car Efforts, New Industry Technologies Help to Dispel 'Dinosaur' Image." *Wall Street Journal*, October 23, 2017.

Colias, Mike. "GM, Union Reach Tentative Accord." *Wall Street Journal*, October 14, 2017.

Colias, Mike "GM Plans to Idle Plant, Eliminate Jobs – Move is Prompted by Cooling Auto Sales in the US, especially of Passenger Cars." *Wall Street Journal*, October 13, 2017.

Colias, Mike. "GM Wrestles with Excess Capacity – Auto Maker is Operating Too Many US Plants, which Saddles it with Higher Fixed Costs." *Wall Street Journal*, October 10, 2017.

Roberts, Adrienne. "Car is 'made in America'? Well, Maybe – Data on National Origin of Auto Parts Isn't always Helpful; Canada is 'Domestic'." *Wall Street Journal*, October 7, 2017.

Moss, Trefor. "China's Leap in Electric Cars – Beijing's Subsidies Conjure Vast Market, Pulling Western Auto Makers Along in its Wake." *Wall Street Journal*, October 3, 2017.

Higgins, Tim, and Mike Colias. "How to Control a Self-Driving Car – Manufacturers Wrestle with the Challenge of Safely Meshing Autopilot with Driver." *Wall Street Journal*, October 2, 2017.

Colias, Mike, and Christina Rogers. "Car Sales Wheeze After Long Climb." *Wall Street Journal*, September 2, 2017.

Colias, Mike. "Cadillac Surges – in China." *Wall Street Journal*, August 31, 2017.

Colias, Mike, and Christina Rogers. "The Week Ahead: Slowing US SUV Sales Signal Turn." *Wall Street Journal*, August 28, 2017.

Stoll, John D. "Business & Technology: GM Detects Problem with Bolt Remotely." *Wall Street Journal*, August 26, 2017.

Colias, Mike. "GM Unit Launches Ride-Hailing App." *Wall Street Journal*, August 9, 2017.

Colias, Mike, and Nick Kostov. "After Europe Exit, GM Retools." *Wall Street Journal*, August 2, 2017.

Rogers, Christina, and Mike Colias. "Slump in Auto Sales Extends to 7th Month." *Wall Street Journal*, August 2, 2017.

Stoll, John D., and Adrienne Roberts. "Family Cars Yearn to be Sexy again – Sedan Designers Strive to Lure Buyers with Vehicles Inspired by Sprinters and Ballerinas." *Wall Street Journal*, August 1, 2017.

Colias, Mike. "GM's European Exit Takes Toll on Profit – Earnings Drop 42%, Overshadowing Strength of Core North American Business." *Wall Street Journal*, July 26, 2017.

Roberts, Adrienne. "GM Small-Car Plant Takes a Rest." *Wall Street Journal*, July 21, 2017.

Colias, Mike, and Adrienne Roberts. "Auto Makers Try to Navigate Sales Slowdown." *Wall Street Journal*, July 5, 2017.

Colias, Mike. "GM Lowers Outlook for Industrywide Sales." *Wall Street Journal*, June 27, 2017.

Higgins, Tim, and Mike Colias. "GM Puts Mapping Effort into High Gear – Cruise Unit Joins Race to Overtake Google in Development of Self-Driving Cars." *Wall Street Journal*, June 19, 2017.

Colias, Mike, and William Mauldin. "GM to Move 600 Jobs from Mexico." *Wall Street Journal*, June 17, 2017.

Colias, Mike. "GM Throttles Down on Passenger-Car Production." *Wall Street Journal*, June 15, 2017.

Colias, Mike. "GM Meets Activist in Face-Off Over Stock." *Wall Street Journal*, June 5, 2017.

Stoll, John D., and Adrienne Roberts. "GM Falls Behind in Flat Market – Auto Maker Struggles with Softer Demand for its Cars and Trucks; More Job Cuts Coming." *Wall Street Journal*, June 2, 2017.

Colias, Mike. "Head of GM Enjoys Her Board's Support." *Wall Street Journal*, May 23, 2017.

Colias, Mike. "GM to End Sales in India." *Wall Street Journal*, May 19, 2017.

Stoll, John D., and Mike Colias. "Car Makers Pull Back on Jobs Pledge." *Wall Street Journal*, May 17, 2017.

Wilmot, Stephen. "How General Motors might Unlock a Tesla-Like Valuation." *Wall Street Journal*, May 6, 2017.

Roberts, Adrienne, and Mike Colias. "Auto Sales Shrink, Inventories Grow." *Wall Street Journal*, May 3, 2017.

Vyas, Kejal. "General Motors Books $100 Million Charge for Venezuela Woes." *Wall Street Journal*, May 3, 2017.

Wilmot, Stephen. "What is Keeping GM Strong Likely Won't Last." *Wall Street Journal*, May 1, 2017.

Colias, Mike. "General Motors Keeps Riding its Trucks – GM Posts another Strong Quarter, Even as US Auto Market Begins to Soften." *Wall Street Journal*, April 29, 2017.

Barone, Michael. "When the Plant Shuts Down." *Wall Street Journal*, April 26, 2017.

Stech, Katy, and Mike Spector. "GM Loses Bid to Curb Ignition Suits." *Wall Street Journal*, April 25, 2017.

Kurmanaev, Anatoly, and Kejal Vyas. "GM Quits Venezuela After Seizure – Authorities Take Over Car Maker's Plant, Forcing Company to Lay Off 2,700 Workers." *Wall Street Journal*, April 21, 2017.

Colias, Mike. "Chevrolet Bolt Drops GPS – Built-in Systems Fall by the Side of the Road as More Drivers Find their Way with Phones." *Wall Street Journal*, April 17, 2017.

Benoit, David, and Mike Colias. "GM Under Pressure to Divide Stock – Auto Maker Rejects Investor Proposal for Dividend-Paying Shares and a Growth Class." *Wall Street Journal*, March 29, 2017.

Michaels, Daniel. "Driving US Factories: Foreign Robotics – Manufacturing Rebound Means Buying Modern Machinery from Overseas." *Wall Street Journal*, March 27, 2017.

Colias, Mike. "GM's Cadillac Tries a Netflix for Cars – for Fee, Members can Trade into and Out of Top 10 Models Up to 18 Times a Year." *Wall Street Journal*, March 20, 2017.

Colias, Mike, and John D. Stoll. "GM Takes Exit from Global Rush – Auto Maker Diverges from Rivals with Sale of Opel to Peugeot; Cutting its Losses." *Wall Street Journal*, March 7, 2017.

Wilmot, Stephen. "GM Pays Price to Exit from Europe." *Wall Street Journal*, March 7, 2017.

Colias, Mike, and John D. Stoll. "For GM, Opel Deal Ends Fund Source." *Wall Street Journal*, March 6, 2017.

Colias, Mike, and Nick Kostov. "GM's Deal to Sell Opel Unit Firms Up." *Wall Street Journal*, March 4, 2017.

Higgins, Tim. "Tension Grows as Auto, Tech Industries Converge." *Wall Street Journal*, February 27, 2017.

Colias, Mike, and Nick Kostov. "GM Signals Retreat from Europe – Auto Maker Explores Sale of Opel Business to France's Peugeot as it Focuses on Profit." *Wall Street Journal*, February 15, 2017.

Wilmot, Stephen. "General Motors' Adieu to Europe – and to Global Scale." *Wall Street Journal*, February 15, 2017.

Roberts, Adrienne, and John D. Stoll. "Big Auto-Maker Ranks Growing." *Wall Street Journal*, February 9, 2017.

Colias, Mike, and John D. Stoll. "GM Profit: Strong but Vulnerable – Mexican-made Trucks Help Drive Performance at a Time when Trump has Threatened Tariffs." *Wall Street Journal*, February 8, 2017.

Colias, Mike. "GM Hits Hurdles in Europe." *Wall Street Journal*, February 6, 2017.

Colias, Mike, Christina Rogers, and Joann S. Lublin. "Auto Makers in the Crosshairs – President Puts Detroit's Big Three on the Defensive about their Commitment to US Jobs; 'New Territory for most of Us'." *Wall Street Journal*, January 24, 2017.

Colias, Mike. "GM to Invest $1 Billion in US Factories." *Wall Street Journal*, January 17, 2017.

Dawson, Chester. "Autos: Gas Prices Take Backseat for Auto Makers – Car Companies Launch More Profit-Driving SUVs, Pickups Even as Pump Costs Rise." *Wall Street Journal*, January 11, 2017.

Colias, Mike, John D. Stoll, and Chester Dawson. "Auto Makers in Hot Seat as Political Pressure Rises." *Wall Street Journal*, January 9, 2017.

Roberts, Adrienne, and John D. Stoll. "Auto Sales Zip to Annual Record." *Wall Street Journal*, January 5, 2017.

Rogers, Christina, William Mauldin, and Mike Colias. "Trump Puts Auto Makers, Trade Policy in Spotlight." *Wall Street Journal*, January 4, 2017.

2. This review of Ford strategies comes from an analysis of the following *Wall Street Journal* articles about the company that appeared between January 1, 2017 and August 1, 2018. The articles are listed below in chronological order starting with the most recent articles.

Wilmot, Stephen. "The Fool's Game of Picking the Electric Car Champ." *Wall Street Journal*, July 28, 2018.

Colias, Mike, and Chester Dawson. "Big Auto Makers Trim Forecasts – Tariffs on Aluminum and Steel Exact a Toll; Currency Devaluations, China also Hit Results." *Wall Street Journal*, July 26, 2018.

Colias, Mike, and Aisha Al-Muslim. "Ford Takes Step to Help Finance Self-Driving Push." *Wall Street Journal*, July 25, 2018.

Dawson, Chester, and Josh Zumbrun. "Trump Pushes Auto Tariffs Despite Opposition." *Wall Street Journal*, July 19, 2018.

Moss, Trefor. "Ford's Sales Slide 26% in China – Trade Tensions Rise as Company Seeks a Revival in World's Largest Car Market." *Wall Street Journal*, July 12, 2018.

Schlesinger, Jacob M. "Trump Sees Car Tariffs as Big Trade Weapon." *Wall Street Journal*, July 2, 2018.

Al-Muslim, Aisha. "Ford Finds some Help in China – Search Giant Baidu Will Work with Auto Maker to Develop in-Car Digital Services." *Wall Street Journal*, June 28, 2018.

Colias, Mike, and Chester Dawson. "Car Makers Bring Fuel Efficiency to Trucks." *Wall Street Journal*, June 18, 2018.

Rogers, Christina. "Ford's Driverless Hopes are Riding on Startup." *Wall Street Journal*, June 13, 2018.

Higgins, Tim. "Driverless Autos Get Help from Humans Watching Remotely." *Wall Street Journal*, June 7, 2018.

Roberts, Adrienne. "SUVs, Pickups Continue to Drive US Auto Sales." *Wall Street Journal*, June 2, 2018.

Rogers, Christina, and Trefor Moss. "Ford's China Push Stalls Out as New Models Warm Up." *Wall Street Journal*, May 11, 2018.

Puko, Timothy, and Chester Dawson. "Auto Summit to Take Up Emissions." *Wall Street Journal*, May 11, 2018.

Rogers, Christina. "Ford's Pickup Assembly Takes Hit." *Wall Street Journal*, May 9, 2018.

Ramkumar, Amrith, Scott Patterson, and Sarah McFarlane. "Volatile Aluminum Price Stirs Concerns – Investors, Companies Worry about Inflation Rising, Profit Margins Getting Squeezed." *Wall Street Journal*, May 8, 2018.

Neil, Dan. "OFF DUTY – Gear & Gadgets – Rumble Seat: Mass Appeal: So Long, Normal-Size Sedans." *Wall Street Journal*, May 5, 2018.

Roberts, Adrienne. "Sedan Weakness Dents Auto Sales." *Wall Street Journal*, May 2, 2018.

Wilmot, Stephen. "Auto Investors Focus on Change Ahead of a Murky Future." *Wall Street Journal*, April 30, 2018.

Rogers, Christina. "The Week Ahead: Ford Takes Steps to Rein in Costs." *Wall Street Journal*, April 23, 2018.

Colias, Mike. "Electric-Car Startups Lure Big Talent." *Wall Street Journal*, April 23, 2018.

Colias, Mike, and Christina Rogers. "Car Makers Step Back from Cars." *Wall Street Journal*, April 5, 2018.

Dawson, Chester. "'Footprint' Rule Undercuts Push for Fuel Efficiency." *Wall Street Journal*, April 4, 2018.

"The Fuel Economy Fraud." *Wall Street Journal*, April 4, 2018.

Roberts, Adrienne, and John D. Stoll. "Bigger Vehicles Hog Road to Sales Gains – Strong Tally for March Reflected Extra Selling Day, Better Weather, Increased Incentives." *Wall Street Journal*, April 4, 2018.

Higgins, Tim, Mike Spector, and Mike Colias. "Self-Drive Focus Shifts to Humans." *Wall Street Journal*, April 3, 2018.

Stoll, John D. "Ford Looks to Beat Toyota Hybrids." *Wall Street Journal*, March 16, 2018.

Colias, Mike, and Mike Spector. "Electric Cars Get Makeover." *Wall Street Journal*, March 10, 2018.

Roberts, Adrienne, and Mike Colias. "Car Sales Start Year at Uneven Pace." *Wall Street Journal*, February 2, 2018.

Colias, Mike. "Two Ford Acquisitions Put Focus on Software." *Wall Street Journal*, January 26, 2018.

Colias, Mike "Ford Struggles to Improve Profit Margins." *Wall Street Journal*, January 25, 2018.

Stoll, John D. "Ford Projects Lower Operating Profit." *Wall Street Journal*, January 17, 2018.

Colias, Mike."Ford Motor Doubles Down on Electric-Vehicle Push." *Wall Street Journal*, January 16, 2018.

Dawson, Chester, and Mike Spector. "Auto Makers Miss Emissions Goal." *Wall Street Journal*, January 12, 2018.

Roberts, Adrienne, and John D. Stoll. "Foreign Car Makers to Take US Lead." *Wall Street Journal*, January 11, 2018.

Higgins, Tim. "Driverless Cars Pick Up Speed – Industry shows how Vehicles can be used in Ways to Pursue Commercial Success." *Wall Street Journal*, January 9, 2018.

Colias, Mike, and Adrienne Roberts. "Auto Sales Growth Stalls – Annual Drop of 1.8% is First in Eight Years, but Pickups and SUVs Bolster US Results." *Wall Street Journal*, January 4, 2018.

George-Cosh, David, and Jacquie McNish. "BlackBerry Goes Driving – Former Phone Giant Pins Growth Prospects on Software for Autonomous Vehicles." *Wall Street Journal*, December 20, 2017.

Roberts, Adrienne, and John D. Stoll. "For US Car Makers, Smaller Share Drives Bigger Profit." *Wall Street Journal*, December 2, 2017.

Spector, Mike, and Mike Colias. "Recalls Mar Ford's Drive for New Vigor – Safety-Related Costs Climb at Same Time CEO Steers a Move to Electric, Driverless Cars." *Wall Street Journal*, November 27, 2017.

Moss, Trefor. "Electric Vehicles Struggle in China." *Wall Street Journal*, November 18, 2017.

Totty, Michael. "Big Issues: Energy (A Special Report) – Will Electric Vehicles Replace Gas-Powered Ones?" *Wall Street Journal*, November 14, 2017.

Higgins, Tim. "Ford Adds Laser Maker to Driverless-Car Effort." *Wall Street Journal*, October 28, 2017.

Colias, Mike, and John D. Stoll. "Ford's Workhorse Trucks Haul in Solid Profit." *Wall Street Journal*, October 27, 2017.

Roberts, Adrienne. "Car is 'made in America'? Well, Maybe – Data on National Origin of Auto Parts Isn't always Helpful; Canada is 'Domestic'." *Wall Street Journal*, October 7, 2017.

Moss, Trefor. "China's Leap in Electric Cars – Beijing's Subsidies Conjure Vast Market, Pulling Western Auto Makers Along in its Wake." *Wall Street Journal*, October 3, 2017.

Rogers, Christina. "Ford's Boss Gets Ready to Tinker." *Wall Street Journal*, October 2, 2017.

Higgins, Tim, and Mike Colias. "How to Control a Self-Driving Car – Manufacturers Wrestle with the Challenge of Safely Meshing Autopilot with Driver." *Wall Street Journal*, October 2, 2017.

Kubota, Yoko, and Trefor Moss. "China Speeds Push for Electric Vehicles." *Wall Street Journal*, September 29, 2017.

Rogers, Christina. "Ford Idles 5 Plants Amid Slowing Sales." *Wall Street Journal*, September 20, 2017.

Rogers, Christina. "Ford Links Up with Indian Firm." *Wall Street Journal*, September 19, 2017.

Colias, Mike, and Christina Rogers. "Car Sales Wheeze After Long Climb." *Wall Street Journal*, September 2, 2017.

Colias, Mike, and Christina Rogers. "The Week Ahead: Slowing US SUV Sales Signal Turn." *Wall Street Journal*, August 28, 2017.

Andriotis, AnnaMaria. "Ford Begins Car-Loan Push." *Wall Street Journal*, August 26, 2017.

"Ford Starts China Electrics Project." *Wall Street Journal*, August 23, 2017.

Rogers, Christina, and Joann S. Lublin. "Bill Ford Thinks Ford Needs a Vision – His – Chairman Wants Company to Shift Faster into Electric, Self-Driving Cars." *Wall Street Journal*, August 9, 2017.

Stoll, John D., and Adrienne Roberts. "Family Cars Yearn to be Sexy again – Sedan Designers Strive to Lure Buyers with Vehicles Inspired by Sprinters and Ballerinas." *Wall Street Journal*, August 1, 2017.

Rogers, Christina. "Ford's Net Rises, but its Shares Take a Hit." *Wall Street Journal*, July 27, 2017.

Colias, Mike, and Adrienne Roberts. "Auto Makers Try to Navigate Sales Slowdown." *Wall Street Journal*, July 5, 2017.

Rogers, Christina. "Ford CEO Presses Decision Making." *Wall Street Journal*, July 1, 2017.

Roberts, Adrienne. "Driverless Isn't Complaint-Less." *Wall Street Journal*, June 22, 2017.

Rogers, Christina, and Mike Colias. "Ford's Plan to Import Cars Veers from Mexico to China." *Wall Street Journal*, June 21, 2017.

Gold, Russell, and Lynn Cook. "Trump's Climate Shift: Move Unlikely to Alter Companies' Course – Shareholder Demands and State Rules have Already Pushed Firms on Climate Change." *Wall Street Journal*, June 2, 2017.

Roberts, Adrienne. "Ford's New CEO Tackles Challenges Posed by Tech." *Wall Street Journal*, May 24, 2017.

Rogers, Christina, and Joann S. Lublin. "US News: Ford Picks Leader to make New Inroads." *Wall Street Journal*, May 23, 2017.

Rogers, Christina, and John D. Stoll. "Ford Taps New Boss to Close Tech Gap." *Wall Street Journal*, May 23, 2017.

Stoll, John D. "US News: Fields Got Caught in Crosshairs of Trump." *Wall Street Journal*, May 23, 2017.

Wilmot, Stephen. "New Boss Won't Fix Ford Quickly." *Wall Street Journal*, May 23, 2017.

Rogers, Christina, Joann S. Lublin, and John D. Stoll. "Ford Weighs Executive Shake-Up." *Wall Street Journal*, May 22, 2017.

Stoll, John D., and Mike Colias. "Car Makers Pull Back on Jobs Pledge." *Wall Street Journal*, May 17, 2017.

Rogers, Christina. "Ford Looks to Cut Jobs 10% Globally." *Wall Street Journal*, May 16, 2017.

Rogers, Christina. "Ford CEO, Chairman Feel Heat." *Wall Street Journal*, May 12, 2017.

Rogers, Christina, and Joann S. Lublin. "Pressure Mounts on Ford's Chief." *Wall Street Journal*, May 10, 2017.

Roberts, Adrienne, and Mike Colias. "Auto Sales Shrink, Inventories Grow." *Wall Street Journal*, May 3, 2017.

Roberts, Adrienne, and Christina Rogers. "Ford's Pace Eases After Long, Hot Run – Demand for Trucks Remains Solid, but US Auto Market as a Whole is Downshifting." *Wall Street Journal*, April 28, 2017.

Barone, Michael. "When the Plant Shuts Down." *Wall Street Journal*, April 26, 2017.

Moss, Trefor, and Mike Colias. "Car Makers Plug into China." *Wall Street Journal*, April 22, 2017.

Moss, Trefor. "Ford Plans Electric Vehicles in China." *Wall Street Journal*, April 7, 2017.

Trivedi, Anjani. "Ford Takes a Chance on China Plan." *Wall Street Journal*, April 7, 2017.

Stoll, John D. "Ford Aims to Pivot in Raising CEO's Pay." *Wall Street Journal*, April 1, 2017.

Rogers, Christina, and John D. Stoll. "Ford Raises Spending in Michigan." *Wall Street Journal*, March 29, 2017.

Michaels, Daniel. "Driving US Factories: Foreign Robotics – Manufacturing Rebound Means Buying Modern Machinery from Overseas." *Wall Street Journal*, March 27, 2017.

Dawson, Chester. "Big Tech Reshapes Automotive Sector." *Wall Street Journal*, March 15, 2017.

Spector, Mike, and Amy Harder. "US News: EPA to Undo Fuel-Economy Goals." *Wall Street Journal*, March 6, 2017.

Higgins, Tim. "Tension Grows as Auto, Tech Industries Converge." *Wall Street Journal*, February 27, 2017.

Spector, Mike. "Car Makers Lobby to Undo Fuel Rules." *Wall Street Journal*, February 22, 2017.

Neil, Dan. "OFF DUTY – Gear & Gadgets – Rumble Seat: Ford F-350: The Country Boy's Rolls-Royce." *Wall Street Journal*, February 18, 2017.

Whelan, Robbie. "'Chicken Tax' Looms Over Imported Trucks – if Nafta is Gutted, LBJ-Era Tariff could Raise Price of Pickups made in Mexico." *Wall Street Journal*, February 16, 2017.

Spector, Mike. "California Steers Agenda on Cleaner Cars – State has Power to Set its Own Mandate for Zero-Emission Vehicles, Separate from Washington's Rules." *Wall Street Journal*, February 13, 2017.

Higgins, Tim. "Ford Takes the Wheel at Startup – Move for Argo AI is Latest to Extend its Reach into Developing Self-Driving Technology." *Wall Street Journal*, February 11, 2017.

Rogers, Christina, and Mike Colias. "Ford Bulks Up in SUVs." *Wall Street Journal*, February 8, 2017.

Colias, Mike, Christina Rogers, and Joann S. Lublin. "Auto Makers in the Crosshairs – President Puts Detroit's Big Three on the Defensive about their Commitment to US Jobs; 'New Territory for most of Us'." *Wall Street Journal*, January 24, 2017.

Rudegeair, Peter. "Ford Invests to Promote Online Auto Loans." *Wall Street Journal*, January 24, 2017.

Dawson, Chester. "Autos: Gas Prices Take Backseat for Auto Makers – Car Companies Launch More Profit-Driving SUVs, Pickups Even as Pump Costs Rise." *Wall Street Journal*, January 11, 2017.

Stoll, John D., and Adrienne Roberts. "Autos: 'Chicken Tax' Surfaces in Talk of Auto Tariffs." *Wall Street Journal*, January 11, 2017.

Colias, Mike, John D. Stoll, and Chester Dawson. "Auto Makers in Hot Seat as Political Pressure Rises." *Wall Street Journal*, January 9, 2017.

Roberts, Adrienne, and John D. Stoll. "Auto Sales Zip to Annual Record." *Wall Street Journal*, January 5, 2017.

Rogers, Christina, William Mauldin, and Mike Colias. "Trump Puts Auto Makers, Trade Policy in Spotlight." *Wall Street Journal*, January 4, 2017.

3. This review of VW strategies comes from an analysis of the following *Wall Street Journal* articles about the company that appeared between January 1, 2017 and August 1, 2018. The articles are listed below in chronological order starting with the most recent articles.

Bernhard, Max. "Volkswagen is Dogged by Emissions Scandal." *Wall Street Journal*, August 2, 2018.

Wilmot, Stephen. "The Fool's Game of Picking the Electric Car Champ." *Wall Street Journal*, July 28, 2018.

Colias, Mike, and Chester Dawson. "Big Auto Makers Trim Forecasts – Tariffs on Aluminum and Steel Exact a Toll; Currency Devaluations, China also Hit Results." *Wall Street Journal*, July 26, 2018.

Dawson, Chester, and Josh Zumbrun. "Trump Pushes Auto Tariffs Despite Opposition." *Wall Street Journal*, July 19, 2018.

Neil, Dan. "Volkswagen's Race to Climb Out of its PR Hole." *Wall Street Journal*, July 7, 2018.

Schlesinger, Jacob M. "Trump Sees Car Tariffs as Big Trade Weapon." *Wall Street Journal*, July 2, 2018.

Boston, William. "Audi CEO is Arrested in Emissions Scandal." *Wall Street Journal*, June 19, 2018.

Boston, William. "Volkswagen Fined $1 Billion in Germany – Auto Maker Says it Won't Appeal Penalty for Oversight Lapses in Emissions Scandal." *Wall Street Journal*, June 14, 2018.

Boston, William. "Germans Probe Audi Chief." *Wall Street Journal*, June 12, 2018.

Boston, William. "Extradition Unlikely in VW Case." *Wall Street Journal*, May 5, 2018.

Roberts, Adrienne, and Christina Rogers. "US Indicts VW's Former Chief." *Wall Street Journal*, May 4, 2018.

Roberts, Adrienne. "Sedan Weakness Dents Auto Sales." *Wall Street Journal*, May 2, 2018.

Wilmot, Stephen. "Auto Investors Focus on Change Ahead of a Murky Future." *Wall Street Journal*, April 30, 2018.

Wilmot, Stephen. "VW's Rebound Faces Old Reality." *Wall Street Journal*, April 19, 2018.

Boston, William. "VW Finds Navistar Tempting." *Wall Street Journal*, April 17, 2018.

Boston, William. "Business & Technology: Volkswagen CEO Sets His Course – New Leader Commits to 'Evolution' – but at a Faster Pace to Cut Costs, Boost Brands." *Wall Street Journal*, April 14, 2018.

Boston, William. "VW Picks Chief After Boardroom Coup – Herbert Diess Gets Top Role; Move Comes nearly Three Years After Diesel Scandal Hit Car Maker." *Wall Street Journal*, April 13, 2018.

Boston, William. "Volkswagen Prepares to Replace CEO." *Wall Street Journal*, April 11, 2018.

Colias, Mike, and Christina Rogers. "Car Makers Step Back from Cars." *Wall Street Journal*, April 5, 2018.

Roberts, Adrienne, and John D. Stoll. "Bigger Vehicles Hog Road to Sales Gains – Strong Tally for March Reflected Extra Selling Day, Better Weather, Increased Incentives." *Wall Street Journal*, April 4, 2018.

Roberts, Adrienne. "Volkswagen to Expand US Plant." *Wall Street Journal*, March 20, 2018.

Boston, William, and Max Bernhard. "VW Amps Up Electric-Car Plans – Auto Maker Wants to Charge Past Tesla with Growing Lineup of Battery, Hybrid Models." *Wall Street Journal*, March 14, 2018.

Roberts, Adrienne, and Mike Colias. "Car Sales Start Year at Uneven Pace." *Wall Street Journal*, February 2, 2018.

Viswanatha, Aruna, and Mike Spector. "US Probes Supplier to VW." *Wall Street Journal*, February 1, 2018.

Dawson, Chester, and Mike Spector. "Auto Makers Miss Emissions Goal." *Wall Street Journal*, January 12, 2018.

Roberts, Adrienne, and John D. Stoll. "Foreign Car Makers to Take US Lead." *Wall Street Journal*, January 11, 2018.

Higgins, Tim. "CES2018: Driverless Cars Pick Up Speed – Industry Shows how Vehicles can be used in Ways to Pursue Commercial Success." *Wall Street Journal*, January 9, 2018.

Colias, Mike, and Adrienne Roberts. "Auto Sales Growth Stalls – Annual Drop of 1.8% is First in Eight Years, but Pickups and SUVs Bolster US Results." *Wall Street Journal*, January 4, 2018.

Spector, Mike, and Mike Colias. "VW Manager Sentenced in Fraud." *Wall Street Journal*, December 7, 2017.

Boston, William. "VW Bets Big on Electric Cars." *Wall Street Journal*, November 18, 2017.

Moss, Trefor. "Electric Vehicles Struggle in China." *Wall Street Journal*, November 18, 2017.

Totty, Michael. "Big Issues: Energy (A Special Report) – Will Electric Vehicles Replace Gas-Powered Ones?" *Wall Street Journal*, November 14, 2017.

Boston, William. "VW Profit Drops on Diesel Charge." *Wall Street Journal*, October 28, 2017.

Roberts, Adrienne. "Car is 'made in America'? Well, Maybe – Data on National Origin of Auto Parts Isn't always Helpful; Canada is 'Domestic'." *Wall Street Journal*, October 7, 2017.

Moss, Trefor. "China's Leap in Electric Cars – Beijing's Subsidies Conjure Vast Market, Pulling Western Auto Makers Along in its Wake." *Wall Street Journal*, October 3, 2017.

Kubota, Yoko, and Trefor Moss. "China Speeds Push for Electric Vehicles." *Wall Street Journal*, September 29, 2017.

Boston, William. "Arrest made in German VW Probe – Former Engine Chief Charged in Connection with Plot to Rig Emission Tests." *Wall Street Journal*, September 29, 2017.

Boston, William. "VW Chief Contends with Scandal – Matthias Mueller Says He is Trying to Accelerate Change at the Auto Maker." *Wall Street Journal*, September 13, 2017.

Boston, William. "VW Stays on Restructuring Path – Auto Maker's CEO Dismisses Talk of Possible Fiat Chrysler Merger as 'Speculation'." *Wall Street Journal*, September 8, 2017.

Colias, Mike, and Christina Rogers. "Car Sales Wheeze After Long Climb." *Wall Street Journal*, September 2, 2017.

Roberts, Adrienne, and Mike Spector. "VW Engineer is Sentenced." *Wall Street Journal*, August 26, 2017.

Spector, Mike, and Mike Colias. "Ex-VW Official Admits Role in Emissions Cheating." *Wall Street Journal*, August 5, 2017.

Boston, William. "VW CEO has Skeptics – His Own Managers – Matthias Mueller Wants the World's Top Auto Maker to Embrace World of Uber and Tesla." *Wall Street Journal,* August 2, 2017.

Rogers, Christina, and Mike Colias. "Slump in Auto Sales Extends to 7th Month." *Wall Street Journal,* August 2, 2017.

Neil, Dan. "VW Atlas: What Germany Knows America Wants." *Wall Street Journal,* July 29, 2017.

Spector, Mike. "Ex-VW Executive Pleads Guilty." *Wall Street Journal,* July 26, 2017.

Wilmot, Stephen. "Car Makers' Diesel Woes Persist." *Wall Street Journal,* July 25, 2017.

Boston, William. "Harley Circles Around VW's Ducati." *Wall Street Journal,* June 24, 2017.

Spector, Mike. "VW Under Fire Over Plans for Charger Stations." *Wall Street Journal,* June 7, 2017.

Gold, Russell, and Lynn Cook. "Trump's Climate Shift: Move Unlikely to Alter Companies' Course – Shareholder Demands and State Rules Have Already Pushed Firms on Climate Change." *Wall Street Journal,* June 2, 2017.

Spector, Mike. "Ex-VW Official to Stay in Jail." *Wall Street Journal,* May 26, 2017.

Boston, William. "VW again Says it is on Cusp of US Turnaround." *Wall Street Journal,* May 8, 2017.

Colias, Mike. "Unleashed, VW Diesels Race Off." *Wall Street Journal,* May 6, 2017.

Boston, William. "Volkswagen Looks Down the Road." *Wall Street Journal,* May 5, 2017.

Boston, William. "Volkswagen Recovers from Scandal as Profit Soars." *Wall Street Journal,* May 4, 2017.

Roberts, Adrienne, and Mike Colias. "Auto Sales Shrink, Inventories Grow." *Wall Street Journal,* May 3, 2017.

Moss, Trefor, and Mike Colias. "Car Makers Plug into China." *Wall Street Journal,* April 22, 2017.

Boston, William. "VW Truck and Bus Unit Expects Boost in Profit." *Wall Street Journal,* March 21, 2017.

Wilmot, Stephen. "VW's Trouble Spells Opportunity." *Wall Street Journal,* March 20, 2017.

Boston, William. "VW Boss is Open to Talks with Fiat." *Wall Street Journal,* March 15, 2017.

Spector, Mike, and Amy Harder. "EPA to Undo Fuel-Economy Goals." *Wall Street Journal,* March 6, 2017.

Boston, William. "VW Revamps Pay, Imposes Caps." *Wall Street Journal*, February 25, 2017.

Roberts, Adrienne. "Diesel Buybacks Aid VW's Sales." *Wall Street Journal*, February 23, 2017.

Spector, Mike. "California Steers Agenda on Cleaner Cars – State has Power to Set its Own Mandate for Zero-Emission Vehicles, Separate from Washington's Rules." *Wall Street Journal*, February 13, 2017.

Roberts, Adrienne. "VW Forms Clean-Energy Unit in US." *Wall Street Journal*, February 8, 2017.

Viswanatha, Aruna, William Boston, and Mike Spector. "US Indicts Six in VW Diesel Case." *Wall Street Journal*, January 12, 2017.

Boston, William, Mike Spector, and Aruna Viswanatha. "VW Set to Pay $4.3 Billion to US in Emissions Cheat." *Wall Street Journal*, January 11, 2017.

Dawson, Chester. "Autos: Gas Prices Take Backseat for Auto Makers – Car Companies Launch More Profit-Driving SUVs, Pickups Even as Pump Costs Rise." *Wall Street Journal*, January 11, 2017.

Boston, William, Arian Campo-Flores, and Aruna Viswanatha. "VW Executive is Arrested in US." *Wall Street Journal*, January 10, 2017.

Boston, William. "Autos: VW shows Strong Growth Despite Scandal." *Wall Street Journal*, January 10, 2017.

Viswanatha, Aruna, and Mike Spector. "VW Nears Emissions Settlement – Deal would Resolve US Criminal Case with Financial Penalty of several Billion Dollars." *Wall Street Journal*, January 7, 2017.

Roberts, Adrienne, and John D. Stoll. "Auto Sales Zip to Annual Record." *Wall Street Journal*, January 5, 2017

Grimm, Christian, and Friedrich Geiger. "VW Faces Suit in Germany." *Wall Street Journal*, January 4, 2017.

Rogers, Christina, William Mauldin, and Mike Colias. "Trump Puts Auto Makers, Trade Policy in Spotlight." *Wall Street Journal*, January 4, 2017.

4. This review of Toyota strategies comes from an analysis of the following *Wall Street Journal* articles about the company that appeared between January 1, 2017 and August 1, 2018. The articles are listed below in chronological order starting with the most recent articles.

McLain, Sean. "RAV4 Drives Up Profit at Toyota." *Wall Street Journal*, August 4, 2018.

Steinberg, Julie, and Liza Lin. "Asian Ride Service Hails $2 Billion." *Wall Street Journal*, August 2, 2018.

Colias, Mike, and Chester Dawson. "Big Auto Makers Trim Forecasts – Tariffs on Aluminum and Steel Exact a Toll; Currency Devaluations, China also Hit Results." *Wall Street Journal*, July 26, 2018.

McLain, Sean, and Newley Purnell. "Toyota Piles into Ride-Hailing Service." *Wall Street Journal*, June 14, 2018.

Roberts, Adrienne. "SUVs, Pickups Continue to Drive US Auto Sales." *Wall Street Journal*, June 2, 2018.

McLain, Sean. "Tariffs Threaten Toyota's Run – Car Maker's Imports to US from Japan Up 22%; Duties would Weigh on the Popular RAV4." *Wall Street Journal*, May 31, 2018.

McLain, Sean. "Toyota Races to Improve Sales in US." *Wall Street Journal*, May 10, 2018.

Roberts, Adrienne. "Toyota to Invest in Two Canadian Plants." *Wall Street Journal*, May 5, 2018.

McLain, Sean. "Japanese Bet on Sedans Goes Bad – Toyota, Nissan, Honda Feel Sting as Drivers in the US Shift to SUVs; Discounting Takes Hold." *Wall Street Journal*, May 3, 2018.

Roberts, Adrienne. "Sedan Weakness Dents Auto Sales." *Wall Street Journal*, May 2, 2018.

Moss, Trefor, and Yoko Kubota. "Electric Car Makers Lean on China." *Wall Street Journal*, April 26, 2018.

Colias, Mike, and Christina Rogers. "Car Makers Step Back from Cars." *Wall Street Journal*, April 5, 2018.

Roberts, Adrienne, and John D. Stoll. "Bigger Vehicles Hog Road to Sales Gains – Strong Tally for March Reflected Extra Selling Day, Better Weather, Increased Incentives." *Wall Street Journal*, April 4, 2018.

McLain, Sean. "Japanese Car Makers Join Hands in India." *Wall Street Journal*, March 30, 2018.

Stoll, John D. "Ford Looks to Beat Toyota Hybrids." *Wall Street Journal*, March 16, 2018.

Bellman, Eric. "Car Makers Race to Go Electric Cheaply – Industry Aims to Build Affordable Cars for Drivers in Emerging Economies." *Wall Street Journal*, February 24, 2018.

Roberts, Adrienne, and Mike Colias. "Car Sales Start Year at Uneven Pace." *Wall Street Journal*, February 2, 2018.

Neil, Dan. "Toyota Camry: Upgrading Old Faithful." *Wall Street Journal*, January 27, 2018.

Bauerlein, Valerie. "US News: Rural North Carolina is One Tough Sell – as Companies Pit States Against each Other, Cities Thrive but Countrysides Lag." *Wall Street Journal*, January 23, 2018.

Roberts, Adrienne. "State Gave Toyota, Mazda Incentives." *Wall Street Journal*, January 12, 2018.

Roberts, Adrienne, and John D. Stoll. "Foreign Car Makers to Take US Lead." *Wall Street Journal*, January 11, 2018.

Colias, Mike, and Adrienne Roberts. "Auto Sales Growth Stalls – Annual Drop of 1.8% is First in Eight Years, but Pickups and SUVs Bolster US Results." *Wall Street Journal*, January 4, 2018.

Landers, Peter. "Toyota Details Electric-Vehicle Plan." *Wall Street Journal*, December 19, 2017.

Tsuneoka, Chieko. "Toyota Sets Big Target for Hybrids." *Wall Street Journal*, December 14, 2017.

Wilmot, Stephen. "Battery Makers Power Up Hunt for Winners." *Wall Street Journal*, November 29, 2017.

Moss, Trefor. "Electric Vehicles Struggle in China." *Wall Street Journal*, November 18, 2017.

Totty, Michael. "Big Issues: Energy (A Special Report) – Will Electric Vehicles Replace Gas-Powered Ones?" *Wall Street Journal*, November 14, 2017.

McLain, Sean. "Toyota Improves Profit Forecast – Auto Maker Still Faces Obstacles in US from Rising Sales Incentives and Vehicle Shortages." *Wall Street Journal*, November 8, 2017.

McLain, Sean "Toyota Wants a Talking Car to be Your Pal." *Wall Street Journal*, October 31, 2017.

McLain, Sean, and Chester Dawson. "Toyota Cuts Target for Mexican Factory." *Wall Street Journal*, October 26, 2017.

Roberts, Adrienne. "Car is 'made in America'? Well, Maybe – Data on National Origin of Auto Parts Isn't always Helpful; Canada is 'Domestic'." *Wall Street Journal*, October 7, 2017.

Moss, Trefor. "China's Leap in Electric Cars – Beijing's Subsidies Conjure Vast Market, Pulling Western Auto Makers Along in its Wake." *Wall Street Journal*, October 3, 2017.

Neil, Dan. "Toyota C-HR: Time to Think Little Picture." *Wall Street Journal*, September 30, 2017.

Kubota, Yoko, and Trefor Moss. "China Speeds Push for Electric Vehicles." *Wall Street Journal*, September 29, 2017.

Colias, Mike, and Christina Rogers. "Car Sales Wheeze After Long Climb." *Wall Street Journal*, September 2, 2017.

Colias, Mike, and Christina Rogers. "Slowing US SUV Sales Signal Turn." *Wall Street Journal*, August 28, 2017.

McLain, Sean. "Toyota Rides Crossover's Sales Gains – C-HR Compact Leads Car Maker's Growth in Europe and Japan; a Departure in Design." *Wall Street Journal*, August 25, 2017.

Trivedi, Anjani. "Japanese Car Makers Pay Up to Grab US Market Share." *Wall Street Journal*, August 5, 2017.

Dawson, Chester, and Sean McLain. "Toyota's Bet on US has Wider Aims – Venture with Mazda is a Chance to Boost Output of Trucks, SUVs in Mexico and Canada." *Wall Street Journal*, August 5, 2017.

Roberts, Adrienne. "Toyota and Mazda to Build US Plant." *Wall Street Journal*, August 4, 2017.

Rogers, Christina, and Mike Colias. "Slump in Auto Sales Extends to 7th Month." *Wall Street Journal*, August 2, 2017.

McLain, Sean. "Toyota: Battery can make Electric Cars Go Farther." *Wall Street Journal*, July 28, 2017.

Colias, Mike, and Adrienne Roberts. "Auto Makers Try to Navigate Sales Slowdown." *Wall Street Journal*, July 5, 2017.

Gold, Russell, and Lynn Cook. "Trump's Climate Shift: Move Unlikely to Alter Companies' Course – Shareholder Demands and State Rules have Already Pushed Firms on Climate Change." *Wall Street Journal*, June 2, 2017.

Neil, Dan. "Toyota Land Cruiser: An SUV from Days of Yore." *Wall Street Journal*, May 6, 2017.

Roberts, Adrienne, and Mike Colias. "Auto Sales Shrink, Inventories Grow." *Wall Street Journal*, May 3, 2017.

McLain, Sean. "Japan Pushes Automatic Braking." *Wall Street Journal*, April 21, 2017.

Spector, Mike, and Amy Harder. "US News: EPA to Undo Fuel-Economy Goals." *Wall Street Journal*, March 6, 2017.

Spector, Mike. "California Steers Agenda on Cleaner Cars – State has Power to Set its Own Mandate for Zero-Emission Vehicles, Separate from Washington's Rules." *Wall Street Journal*, February 13, 2017.

McLain, Sean. "Strong Yen Slices into Toyota's Latest Earnings." *Wall Street Journal*, February 7, 2017.

Dawson, Chester. "Autos: Toyota Supplier Muses on Mexico." *Wall Street Journal*, January 11, 2017.

Dawson, Chester. "Autos: Gas Prices Take Backseat for Auto Makers – Car Companies Launch More Profit-Driving SUVs, Pickups Even as Pump Costs Rise." *Wall Street Journal*, January 11, 2017.

Roberts, Adrienne, and Chester Dawson. "Toyota Draws Trump's Outrage." *Wall Street Journal*, January 6, 2017.

# 18 | *Ambivalence, Paradox, and Hedging*

The future is uncertain, especially in the energy industry, defined in this book as the oil and natural gas and motor vehicles sectors. Companies in these sectors have made expensive miscalculations in the past. They have bet incorrectly on what is to come next. The experience of price volatility, the boom and bust cycle in petroleum prices that took place from 2012 to 2016, along with climate change, meant that the strategic decisions faced by companies in the energy industry were difficult and complex. Keynes argued that under conditions of uncertainty decision makers act from emotions according to what he referred to as "animal spirits," which do not exclude calculation, but also do not eliminate the biases that affect their choices. Under these circumstances, different companies in the energy industry made different choices.

These variations are a key theme in the case studies discussed in this book. The strategic investments companies made in the period covered in the book were made with imperfect knowledge about the economy, society, technology, and politics, how these forces impact their industry, and what they should do next. The energy industry companies made dissimilar bets. The non-homogenous responses of the energy industry companies have and will have significant implications for the companies and for society.

## How Far to Go

The extent to which technologies on the horizon were disruptive or sustaining in relation to past practice was unclear. How far should decision makers take their companies? They have had to project the image of having answers to the questions that beset their companies. Buffeted by complex and dynamic environments and having to cope with multifaceted goals and issues they have had to project confidence, even if they could not realistically act with complete assurance. They knew of various responses their companies could make, but could not

514

compare them systematically and rigorously and be entirely certain of their relative effectiveness. They understood that unintended consequences regularly took place; they were inevitable and unavoidable. These understandings led to ambivalence.[1] They resulted in the paradox that energy decision makers developed conflicting strategies.[2] The strategic investments to which they committed their companies assumed on the one hand that the world would remain essentially the same. It would continue to be a world controlled by fossil fuels, while concurrently the investments they made rested on the assumption that the world was veering off in an entirely new direction far from the fossil-fuel domination of the past.

These contrasting perspectives drove the choices of decision makers. On the one hand, they saw the world remaining heavily dependent on fossil fuels; the internal combustion engine would continue to be dominant, and electric engines and other alternatives modes of transportation would never overturn this dominance. On the other hand, they also perceived that the world was on the verge of abandoning fossil fuels for innovative technologies such as electric vehicles, ride-sharing, and autonomous driving, and the internal combustion engine was close to being obsolete. These developments, they sensed, while they posed a threat, were also a potential opportunity.

Ambivalence and paradox led these decision makers to hedging. They needed to take strategic actions to protect their organizations from failure, at the same time that they had to take actions to enable their organizations to seize the opportunities that might exist. Their hedges began with basics. The first element was to allocate sufficient resources to maintain and improve quality and safety. Energy industry decision makers had to produce quality and safe products to satisfy current customers. They could not endanger communities or their employees. However, their hedges went well beyond assuring safety and quality. In the oil and natural gas sector, companies searched for resources throughout the world, anticipating that if petroleum fell out of favor, then natural gas or an unconventional or alternative type of energy would replace it. They also operated at different points in the value chain, hoping that doing so would have a countercyclical effect on price volatility. If prices declined and the rewards of finding new oil, natural gas, and other forms of energy fell, then the input costs to the refineries that the integrated oil and natural gas operated would go down.

To protect and buffer their organizations, companies in the motor vehicle sector had their own approach to hedging. They too had a strong emphasis on quality and safety. They too had a diverse set of global investments, based on the reasoning that not all countries or regions in the world were advancing at the same pace and they had to be invested in the world's most rapidly expanding and profitable markets. They also hedged by having a diverse product portfolio, because if consumers rejected one vehicle, brand or model, they might flock to other vehicles, brands, or models. Finally, they hedged in their research, where they attempted to innovate both in the domain of conventional internal combustion technology and in the domain of alternatives to the conventional internal combustion engine.

These types of hedges were attempts to protect energy industry companies from the risks and uncertainties they confronted and to allow them at the same time to take advantage of opportunities that might be emerging. Regardless of what happened, they would survive, and, perhaps if they hedged correctly, they would thrive. They were not making optimal decisions, because it was not possible to make optimal choices given the information they had about the future. Nor were they being boundedly rational; that is, going as far in the direction of making optimal choices as they could given the information they had. They were not aiming for the best decisions under these circumstances. Rather they were hedging their bets by layering their organizations with a series of safeguards in the hope that the set of defensive positions they had chosen could prevent the worst, and perhaps benefit them in an exceptional way if one of the options they had chosen – or, better put, the bets they had made – paid off in an exceptional way.

The hedges meant they did not just exploit their existing strengths, but explored for new ones. Risks and uncertainties abounded therefore, in charting innovative paths they could not stake out one future direction to the exclusion of all others, but had to make paradoxical moves. Motor vehicle companies strategically invested in opposing visions: a world of fossils and a world of renewable; a non-electric world and an electric world; and a world of private vehicle ownership and driving and a world of autonomous vehicles and ride-sharing. Different companies expressed these ambivalences differently and took different sets of paradoxical actions and hedged in different ways. The importance of their heterogeneous responses cannot be overemphasized, yet the basic pattern was similar: emphasize safety and quality; diversify in the value chain, globally, and in brands and products; and innovate along divergent paths in the hope of finding a match with future developments.

Ambivalence led to paradoxical moves that resulted in different sets of hedges. On the one hand, companies in the energy industry hedged by tightening discipline, trying to maximize efficiency, defending their organizations' niches, and exploiting their current strengths. On the other hand, they aimed to be agile, flexible, and to innovate, explore, and find new avenues of growth. In tackling exploitation and exploration simultaneously, they faced up to the tension between the near and long term, between the requirements of the moment and what might be needed in a more distant horizon.[3] They aimed to balance change and stability by launching exploratory businesses alongside an exploitative core, each company handling the conflict between these opposing ends differently and in its own way.

## Accommodating the Tensions

O'Reilly and Tushman frame the problem as one of ambidexterity.[4] Yet the energy industry companies were more than ambidextrous. They engaged in very layered and complex hedging. The complex environments in which they operated imposed goal conflicts and competing demands and the tensions did not result in simple trade-offs. The opposing elements in their responses also had underlying interdependencies. The paradoxical elements supported as well as opposed one another.[5] Lighter automotive body parts could be placed in older models with conventional internal combustion engines and in newer models with all electric engines. Accepting, confronting, and transcending the tensions triggered loose coupling, which increased agility whilst concurrently stimulating redundancy and reliability.

The managerial issue that each company faced was how to accommodate the tensions and cope with contradictory tendencies. There was no single best way to do so. Poole and Van de Ven have depicted a number of methods companies use to cope with contradictions: accepting tensions and simply living with them; dividing them in space and time by placing them in different organizational units; and emphasizing alternative tendencies at different moments.[6] In the end, Poole and Van de Ven are optimistic that organizations can synthesize opposing forces and become stronger. They imagine learning spirals in which organizations move through stages of exploitation and exploration and achieve convergence.[7] According to Poole and Van de Ven, organizations exploit their existing competencies and capabilities, but without exploration, exploitation eventually leads to too much stability and the likelihood of failure. Thus, they move to divergence in which they pursue dual and contradictory processes of exploration and experimentation as well as exploitation. Through this dialectical process, Poole and Van de Ven affirm that organizations make progress. One would hope so, but perhaps organizations never transcend the tensions entirely – the tensions are innate factors that stay with them. The contradiction between change and stability is never fully eliminated, and instead of upward learning spirals, organizations also can and do get caught in downward spirals of folly. Indeed, learning demands rounds of sense making and each round may be less than perfect. Each can have unintended consequences that trigger more ambiguity and further sense making and additional paradox, which can result in endless cycles rather than progress. The successive rounds of imperfect sense making and paradoxical moves end in troubled transformational journeys.

Companies may learn and develop capacities to understand and cope with tensions they confront, but the lessons learned do not necessarily have to be good ones. They still have to act without knowing what comes next and because they do not know what comes next they can err, and their errors can be small and relatively easily remedied or large and damaging both to themselves and society. Of course, there are no perfectly right answers but over time the decision-making powers of companies can erode, rather than advance. To their detriment and everyone's, organizations can be involved in negative as well as positive learning spirals. There is no inevitability that the process necessarily will be positive. Organizations experience incomplete as well as complete learning. They can take major steps backward as well as forward. Their learning can be spurious and does not have to generate advances; rather it can lead to unfortunate outcomes, that set the stage for their harm and harm to all of us.

The companies studied in this book were certainly on journeys, but where they will lead is unknown and still to be determined. The future will reveal the degree to which the learning they have accumulated will be positive or negative for them and for society.

All the integrated oil and natural gas companies and the motor vehicle firms faced risks and uncertainties. All of them experienced ambivalence, when confronted by these risks and uncertainties, and engaged in hedging that arose out of the ambivalence they experienced. This book has revealed differences among these firms in how they managed the ambiguity and how they engaged in paradoxical behaviors and hedging. It has shown the degree to which some firms escalated commitment to their current course of action, others adapted, and others staked out leadership positions in new directions. Among the oil and natural gas companies, ExxonMobil was the most resistant to change, while Shell and TOTAL resisted it least. Among the motor vehicle firms, Ford was seriously ambivalent about where to go next, while Toyota seemed to be more seamlessly adapting. Though it is possible to make such distinctions, they may be premature, since only time will tell how well the decision making of these companies will fare. All the companies examined in the book have struggled with what to do next. They exploited their current business models, but also looked for new approaches. They flip-flopped because of the inherent tensions they met in a boom and bust period of plummeting gasoline prices and growing climate change pressures. They developed their hedges to shield them from the worst that could take place and perhaps allow them to benefit sometime in the future.

## Hedging

This book has raised the question of how these companies managed the organizational contradictions they confronted. How did they aim for some type of balance, however imperfect, between exploiting their current assets and exploring for new business opportunities? The book has argued their ambivalence in the face of the risks and uncertainties they encountered led to paradoxical behaviors (Figure 18.1). Hedging their bets played an important role in how they responded, how they tried to insulate and protect themselves from conditions that were hard to manage and control, and perhaps

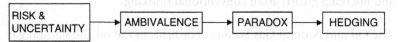

**Figure 18.1** Risk, uncertainty, ambivalence, paradox, and hedging

how they could benefit at some point in the future. Their hedging consisted of recognizing the risks and uncertainties, making assumptions, and then taking strategic actions in areas such as safety and quality, diversified investments, and innovation.

**Recognizing the Risks and Uncertainties and Making Assumptions:** The companies were required to establish a justification for the strategic choices they made in public documents like annual reports. They had to provide reasons for how they were investing shareholder money to increase their growth and profitability and prevent losses. In these public documents addressed to shareholders and the public, the laws of disclosure, under which publicly traded companies operated, meant they had to give a reckoning of the risks and uncertainties and they had to establish a set of assumptions, which formed the basis for the actions they took.

**Making Strategic Investments:** Then, based on these assumptions, they indicated the set of strategic investments they would make. By law, they had to reveal the decisions they were making so that investors could evaluate whether or not they had chosen correctly and were on the right path. Given that substantial residual risk and uncertainty remained, the companies in the energy industry examined in this book, in indicating their set of strategic investments, took steps to insulate and protect their firms from future unknowns. However, they could not foreseeably insulate their companies from all the known and unknown unknowns the companies might confront.

Regardless, they tried to cover certain bases so that their companies would remain standing and avoid serious jeopardy. Their disclosure to investors had to show that they were capable of taking bold actions, but they also had to take these actions prudently and cautiously and within limits, lest they err greatly and shareholders hold them accountable for irresponsibility. Decision makers had to persuade shareholders that they had some control over the fate of their companies, whether or not they really did, and in making these arguments to shareholders, they were restricted in their scope of action. Hedging prevented them from straying too far from accepted norms, from shifting too much, and breaking greatly from conventional thinking.

**The Oil and Natural Gas Sector:** For firms in the oil and natural gas sector, the bases that they had to cover were taking actions to ensure safety, balancing their exploration for new oil and natural gas resources with their downstream chemical and refining investments, and innovating. They innovated both within their existing business models for new ways to better extract oil and natural gas and convert it into useful products and, to a much smaller extent, with alternative forms of energy.

Each firm within the oil and natural gas sector examined in this book struck this balance somewhat differently. They did not make exactly the same trade-offs, because they had slightly different perceptions of the risks and uncertainties and different assumptions about the future. Their assumptions about peak demand for oil diverged in a particularly distinct way in the 2017–2018 period. ExxonMobil denied that peak demand would take place. BP envisioned it taking hold some time in the 2040s. Shell viewed it as imminent, possible occurring as early as 2025, and TOTAL simply accepted that someday it would happen. Because of these assumptions, how they hedged the future, their actual strategic initiatives, diverged more and more. They increasingly diverged in how they resorted and reassembled their asset base via divestiture and liquidation and the types of investments they made in different types of energy from oil and natural gas to wind, solar power, and electricity.

**The Motor Vehicle Sector:** For firms in the motor sector, the bases that they had to cover to hedge their bets started with taking action to ensure the safety and quality of vehicles. These actions were fundamental and were a priority as each of them had to avoid recalls and customer dissatisfaction. In addition, they had to balance the extent of their global reach with the types of brands and the car models they offered. They confronted and made different decisions about whether they should abandon investments in certain countries, or up their commitment. Almost all of them chose to increase their commitment to China, the world's fastest growing market for motor vehicles. However, there were differences in how they chose to increase this commitment and the extent to which they emphasized electric vehicles, given the Chinese government's interest in fighting pollution and developing an electric vehicle industry. With regard to the US market, still an important one, Toyota, the leader in this market, the laggard VW, and the traditional US players GM and Ford, had to contend with an ongoing movement to SUVs, light trucks, and crossovers. They also had to judge the degree to which they could continue to sell passenger cars profitably in this market. All of the companies backed away from passenger cars, but especially Ford in its surprising decision to stop selling passenger cars in the United States other than the Focus and the Mustang. All of the companies in the sector scrambled to accumulate capacity to build SUVs, light trucks, and crossovers for the US market under warnings from the Trump administration not to locate that new capacity outside the United States.

Each firm in the motor vehicle sector innovated to an extent probably greater than firms in the oil and natural gas sector. The investments they made in new forms of mobility, partially carried out to protect themselves from the inroads of Silicon Valley companies and partially due to estimates that the profit margins would be far greater than manufacturing and selling auto-mobiles, had the potential to radically change the face of transpor-tation in the United States and the rest of the world. Each company set far-reaching goals for electrification, which, if achieved and if accompanied by consumer acceptance, could lower the demand for gasoline. In moving toward electrification, the automakers were hedging to protect themselves against increasingly stringent regula-tions in Europe, China, and the United States. In moving toward electrification, they were also knowingly or perhaps unknowingly altering the estimates of the firms in the oil and natural gas sectors about future oil demand.

**Different Choices:** As with the oil and natural gas firms, each motor vehicle firm made these investments slightly differently. Their percep-tions of the risks and uncertainties and assumptions about the future were not exactly alike. As a result, they hedged their bets about the future in slightly different ways. Some of the factors mentioned earlier in the book proved to very important in the different ways they hedged:

- the degree to which they perceived external change as competence enhancing or detracting;
- the extent to which they had stranded assets;
- the ways in which their organizations were performing in compar-ison with peers and other reference points;
- the extent to which their organizations had slack resources to experi-ment and make changes.

Regardless of the reasons, these companies tried to have sufficient backups in place to deal with diverse contingencies. In the face of multiple possibilities, they experienced ambivalence and made paradoxical choices to increase the chances that their companies would survive and thrive no matter what ensued. By hedging their bets, they attempted to increase their gains, limit the downside losses, and reduce the volatility.

## Contribution to the Literature

Conceptualizations of ambivalence and especially paradox and the dilemmas they both pose for managers are well conceived and developed in the management literature. This book's contribution to the literature is that it has introduced hedging as a coping mechanism for dealing with risk and uncertainty, ambivalence, and the paradoxical choices that risk, uncertainty, and ambivalence impose on companies. It has illustrated how hedging played itself out in the energy sector in a period of great volatility brought on by plummeting oil prices and increased pressure on climate change. In the two sectors this book has examined, risk and uncertainty prevailed regarding the future, which led to ambivalence and paradoxical actions, which in turn manifested themselves as elaborate hedges incorporated into company strategies. Each company, as the institutional literature increasingly highlights, hedged in a slightly different way.[8]

In sum, the decision makers in these companies resorted to hedging to manage the risks and uncertainties, the ambivalences they sparked, and the paradoxical behaviors they prompted. Hedging constituted their strategy for managing the uncertainty that booms and busts in prices and changes in the climate brought about. Whether their hedges will lead to a better future for them and for all of us remains to be seen.

## Notes

1. Ashforth, Blake E., et al. "Ambivalence in Organizations: A Multilevel Approach." *Organization Science* 25.5 (2014): 1453–1478.
2. Andriopoulos, Constantine, and Marianne W. Lewis. "Exploitation-exploration Tensions and Organizational Ambidexterity: Managing Paradoxes of Innovation." *Organization Science* 20.4 (2009): 696–717;

Miron-Spektor, Ella, et al. "Microfoundations of Organizational Paradox: The Problem is How We Think About the Problem." *Academy of Management Journal* 61.1 (2018): 26–45; Miron-Spektor, Ella, Miriam Erez, and Eitan Naveh. "The Effect of Conformist and Attentive-to-detail Members on Team Innovation: Reconciling the Innovation Paradox." *Academy of Management Journal* 54.4 (2011): 740–760; Lavie, Dovev, Uriel Stettner, and Michael L. Tushman. "Exploration and Exploitation within and Across Organizations." *The Academy of Management Annals* 4.1 (2010): 109–155.

3. James G. March, "Exploration and Exploitation in Organizational Learning." *Organization Science* 2.1 (1991): 71-87 also see Mary J. Benner, "Securities Analysts and Incumbent Response to Radical Technological Change: Evidence from Digital Photography and Internet Telephony." *Organization Science* 21.1 (2010): 42–62.

4. Tushman, Michael L., and Charles A. O'Reilly III. "Ambidextrous Organizations: Managing Evolutionary and Revolutionary Change." *California Management Review* 38.4 (1996): 8–29.

5. Farjoun, Moshe. "Beyond Dualism: Stability and Change as a Duality." *Academy of Management Review* 35.2 (2010): 202–225.

6. Poole, Marshall Scott, and Andrew H. Van de Ven. "Using Paradox to Build Management and Organization Theories." *Academy of Management Review* 14.4 (1989): 562–578.

7. Raisch, Sebastian, Timothy J. Hargrave, and Andrew H. Van De Ven. "The Learning Spiral: A Process Perspective on Paradox." *Journal of Management Studies.*

8. See Greenwood, Royston, Oliver, C., Lawrence, T. B., and Meyer, R. E. eds. *The Sage Handbook of Organizational Institutionalism.* Thousand Oaks, California: Sage, 2017; and Greenwood, R., Raynard, M., Kodeih, F., Micelotta, E. R., and Lounsbury, M. "Institutional complexity and organizational responses." *Academy of Management Annals*, (2011). 5(1),317–371.

# Bibliography

Aleklett, Kjell. *Peeking at Peak Oil*. New York: Springer, 2012.

Austen-Smith, David, Daniel Diermeier, and Eitan Zemel. "Unintended Acceleration: Toyota's Recall Crisis." Kellogg Business Case, 2016.

Blair, John M. *The Control of Oil*. New York: Pantheon, 1976.

Braziel, E. Russell. *The Domino Effect: How the Shale Revolution Is Transforming Energy Markets, Industries, and Economies*. Madison, WI: NTA Press, 2016.

Brinkley, Douglas. *Wheels for the World: Henry Ford, His Company, and a Century of Progress*. New York: Penguin, 2003.

Brown, Lester. *The Great Transition*. New York: W.W. Norton, 2015.

Busch, Timo and Paul Shrivastava. *The Global Carbon Crisis*. Sheffield, UK: Greenleaf, 2011.

Chabris, Christopher and Daniel Simons. *The Invisible Gorilla*. New York: MJF Books, 2010.

Coll, Steven. *ExxonMobil and Private Power*. New York: Penguin, 2012.

Cusumano, Michael. *The Japanese Automobile Industry: Technology and Management at Nissan and Toyota*. Cambridge, MA: Harvard University Press, 1986.

Danielsen, Albert L. *Evolution of OPEC*. New York: Harcourt Brace Jovanovich, 1982.

Dicker, Dan. *Shale Boom Shale Bust: The Myth of Saudi Arabia*. Digital Edition, 2015.

Dobbs, Richard, James Manyika, and Jonathan Woetzel. *No Ordinary Disruption*. New York: Public Affairs, 2015.

Douglas, Mary. and Wildavsky, Aaron. *Risk and Culture*. Berkeley: University of California Press, 1983.

EIA. *World Energy Outlook to 2040*. Washington, DC: US Department of Energy, 2016.

Engler, Robert and Arthur Beeby-Thompson. *The Politics of Oil*. Chicago: University of Chicago Press, 1961.

Euromonitor. *Global Economies and Consumers in 2017*. Paris: Euromonitor, 2017.

Ferguson, Charles. *Nuclear Energy*. New York: Oxford University Press, 2011.

Fialka, John. *Car Wars*. New York: St. Martins, 2015.

Freeman, S. David and Leah Parks. *All-Electric America*. San Francisco: Solar Flare Press, 2016.

Fremeth, Adam and Alfred A. Marcus. "The Role of Governance Systems and Rules in Wind Energy Development: Evidence from Minnesota and Texas." *Business and Politics* 18, 3 (2016): 337–365.

Funston, Frederick and Stephen Wagner. *Surviving and Thriving in Uncertainty*. Hoboken, NJ: Wiley, 2010.

Ginsburg, Douglas H. and William J. Abernathy, eds. *Government, Technology, and the Future of the Automobile*. New York: McGraw-Hill Companies, 1980.

Goldember, Jose. *Energy What Everyone Needs to Know*. Oxford, UK: Oxford University Press, 2012.

Gordon, Robert. *The Rise and Fall of American Growth: The US Standard of Living Since the Civil War*. Princeton, NJ: Princeton University Press, 2017.

Graetz, Michael. *The End of Energy: The Unmaking of America's Environment, Security, and Independence*. Cambridge, MA: MIT Press, 2011.

Guillen, Maurro and Emilio Ontiveros. *Global Turning Points*. Cambridge, UK: Cambridge University Press, 2016 (2nd edition).

Hardy, Cynthia and Steve Maguire. "Organizing Risk: Discourse, Power, and 'Riskification'." *Academy of Management Review* 41, 1 (2016): 80–108.

Hilgartner, Stephen. "The Social Construction of Risk Objects: Or, How to Pry Open Networks of Risk." *Organizations, Uncertainties, and Risk* (1992): 39–53.

Hiott, Andrea. *Thinking Small: The Long, Strange Trip of the Volkswagen Beetle*. New York: Random House, 2012.

Hodge, Nick. *Energy Investing for Dummies*. Hoboken, NJ: Wiley, 2013.

Hoffman, Andrew J. and Marc J. Ventresca. *Organizations, Policy and The Natural Environment: Institutional and Strategic Perspectives*. Palo Alto: Stanford University Press, 2002.

Huff, Anne Sigismund and James Oran Huff. *When Firms Change Direction*. Oxford, UK: Oxford University Press, 2001.

IBIS World Industry Report. "SUV and Light Truck Manufacturing in the US." 2016.

"Automobile Brakes in US." 2016.

"Automobile Interior Manufacturing in the US." 2016.

"Automobile Steering and Suspension in the US." 2016.

"Automobile Transmission Manufacturing in the US." 2016.

"Average Age of Vehicle Fleet." 2016.

"Battery Manufacturing in the US." 2016.

"Car and Automobile Manufacturing in the US." 2016.

"Coal & Natural Gas Power in the US." 2016.

"Electric Power Transmission in the US." 2016.

"Global Automobile Engine and Parts Manufacturing." 2016.

"Global Automobile Engine and Parts Manufacturing." 2016.

"Iron and Steel Manufacturing in the US." 2016.

"Metal Stamping and Forging in the US." 2016.

"New Car Sales." 2016.

"Nuclear Power in the US." 2016.

"Petroleum Refining in the US." 2016.

"SUV and Light Truck Manufacturing in the US." 2016

"Tire Manufacturing in the US." 2016.

IEA. *World Energy Outlook 2016*. Paris: International Energy Association, 2016.

IMF. *World Economic Outlook*. Washington, DC: International Monetary Fund, 2016.

Incropera, Frank. *Climate Change: A Wicked Problem*. New York: Cambridge University Press, 2016.

Ip, Greg. "The Innovation Paradox: The Global Economy's Hidden Problem – Innovation Is Slowing, Hampering Improvements in Living Standards." *Wall Street Journal* 7 December 2016: A1.

Kahneman, Daniel. *Thinking, Fast and Slow*. New York: Farrar, Straus, and Giroux, 2013.

Kalicki, Jan H. *2015 Global Energy Forum: Revolutionary Changes and Security Pathways*. Washington, DC: Wilson Center, 2015.

Keynes, John Maynard. *The General Theory of Employment, Interest, and Money*. New York: Springer, 2018.

Knight, Frank. *Risk, Uncertainty and Profit*. Mineola, New York: Dover Publications, 2012.

Lacalle, Daniel and Diego Parrilla. *The Energy World Is Flat: Opportunities from the End of Peak Oil*. Chichester, West Sussex: Wiley, 2015.

Lasky, Mark. *The Outlook for US Production of Shale*. Washington, DC: Congressional Budget Office, 2016.

Levi, Michael. *The Power Surge*. Oxford, UK: Oxford University Press. 2013.

Lewis, M. W. "Exploring Paradox: Toward a More Comprehensive Guide." *Academy of Management Review* 25 (2000): 760–776.

Liker, Jeffrey K. *The Toyota Way: 14 Management Principles from the World's Greatest Manufacturer*. New York: McGraw-Hill, 2003.

Lovins, Amory. *Reinventing Fire: Bold Solutions for the New Energy Era*. White River Junction, VT., 2011.

Maguire, Steve and Cynthia Hardy. "Organizing Processes and the Construction of Risk: A Discursive Approach." *Academy of Management Journal* 56,1 (2013): 231–255.

Maital, Shlomo. *Executive Economics: Ten Essential Tools for Managers.* New York: Free Press, 2011.

Makridakis, Spyros. *Forecasting, Planning, and Strategy for the 21st Century.* New York: Free Press, 1990.

Malen, Joel, and Alfred A. Marcus. "Promoting Clean Energy Technology Entrepreneurship: The Role of External Context." *Energy Policy* 102 (2017): 7–15.

March, James G., Lee S. Sproull, and Michal Tamuz. "Learning from Samples of One or Fewer." *Organization Science* (1991): 1–13.

Marcus, Alfred. *Controversial Issues in Energy Policy.* Newbury Park, CA: Sage, 1992.

*Innovations in Sustainability: Fuel and Food.* Cambridge, UK: Cambridge University Press, 2015.

*Promise and Performance: Choosing and Implementing An Environmental Policy.* Santa Barbara, CA: Praeger, 1980.

"Risk, Uncertainty, and Scientific Judgement." *Minerva* (1988): 138–152.

*Strategic Foresight: A New Look At Scenarios.* New York: Palgrave MacMillan, 2009.

*The Adversary Economy.* Westport, CT: Quorum Books, 1984.

Marcus, Alfred and Andrew Van de Ven. "Managing Shifting Goal Consensus and Task Ambiguity in Making the Transition to Sustainability," in Henderson, R., Gulati, R., and Tushman, M. (Eds.) *Leading Sustainable Change: An Organizational Perspective.* Oxford, UK: Oxford University Press, 2015: 298–323.

Marcus, Alfred, and Donald Geffen. "The Dialectics of Competency Acquisition: Pollution Prevention in Electric Generation." *Strategic Management Journal* 19.12 (1998): 1145–1168.

Marcus, Alfred A. and Susan K. Cohen. "Public Policies in a Regulated Entrepreneurial Setting." *Business and Politics* 17,2 (2015): 221–251.

Marcus, Alfred, J. Alberto Aragon-Correa, and Jonatan Pinkse. "Firms, Regulatory Uncertainty, and the Natural Environment." *California Management Review* (2011): 5–16.

Mathews, J. A. "Ricardian Rents or Knightian Profits? More on Austrian Insights on Strategic." *Strategic Organization* (2006): 97–108.

Mattione, Richard. *OPEC's Investments and the International Financial System.* Washington, DC: Brookings, 1985.

McNally, Robert. *Crude Volatility.* New York: Columbia University Press, 2017.

Milliken, Frances J. "Three Types of Perceived Uncertainty about the Environment: State, Effect, and Response Uncertainty." *Academy of Management Review* (1987): 133–144.

Mills, Robin. *Risky Routes: Energy Transit in the Middle East.* Doha: Brookings, 2016.

Minsky, Hyman. *Stabilizing an Unstable Economy.* New York: McGraw Hill Education, 2008.

Moore, Peter. *The Business of Risk.* Cambridge, UK: Cambridge University Press, 1983.

Nisbett, Richard. *Mindware: Tools for Smart Thinking.* New York: Farrar, Strauss, and Giroux, 2015.

OPEC. *2016 World Oil Outlook.* Vienna: Organization of Petroleum Exporting Countries, 2016.

Owen, David. *The Conundrum: How Scientific Innovation, Increased Efficiency, and Good Intentions Can Make Our Energy and Climate Problems Worse.* New York: Riverhead Books, 2011.

Pearl, Judea. *Causality: Models, Reasoning, and Inference.* New York: Cambridge University Press, 2009.

Peterson, John E. *Politics of Middle Eastern Oil.* Washington, DC: Middle East Institute, 1983.

Pooley, Eric. *The Climate War: True Believers, Power Brokers, and the Fight to Save the Earth.* New York: Hyperion, 2010.

Power, Michael. *Organized Uncertainty: Designing a World of Risk Management.* Oxford, UK: Oxford University Press, 2007.

PWC. *The World in 2050: Will the Shift in Global Economic Power Continue.* PWC: London, 2015.

Quinn, Dennis Patrick. *Restructuring the Automobile Industry.* New York: Columbia University Press, 1988.

Ramaswamy, A. K. *Gazprom: The Evolution of a Giant in the Oil and Gas Industry.* Phoenix: Thunderbird, 2009.

Rattner, Steven. *Overhaul: An Insider's Account of the Obama Administration's Emergency Rescue of the Auto Industry.* Boston: Houghton Mifflin Harcourt, 2010.

Rieger, Bernhard. *The People's Car: A Global History of the Volkswagen Beetle.* Cambridge, MA: Harvard University Press, 2013.

Rumsfeld, Donald. *Known and Unknown: A Memoir.* New York: Penguin, 2011.

Sampson, Anthony. *The Seven Sisters: The Great Oil Companies and the World They Shaped.* New York: Viking Press, 1975.

Schnaars, Steven. *Megamistakes: Forecasting and the Myth of Rapid Technological Change.* New York: Free Press, 1989.

Schoemaker, Paul. *Profiting from Uncertainty: Strategies for Succeeding No Matter What the Future Brings*. New York: Simon and Schuster, 2012.

Schwartz, Peter. *The Art of the Long View: Planning for the Future in an Uncertain World*. New York: Doubleday, 1996.

Seba, Tony. *Clean Disruption*. Silicon Valley, CA: Clean Planet Ventures, 2014.

Sieminski, Adam. *International Energy Outlook 2016*. Washington, DC: Center for Strategic and International Studies, 2016.

Smil, Vaclav, *Natural Gas*. Chichester, West Sussex: Wiley, 2015.

*Energy: Myths and Realities*. Washington, DC: AEI Press, 2010.

Smithson, Charles W., Clifford W. Smith, and D. Sykes Wilford. *Managing Financial Risk: A Guide to Derivative Products, Financial Engineering, and Value Maximization*. New York: McGraw-Hill, 1998.

Sperling, Daniel. *New Transportation Fuels: A Strategic Approach to Technological Change*. Berkeley: University of California Press, 1990.

*Three Revolutions: Steering Automated, Shared, and Electric Vehicles to a Better Future*. Washington, DC: Island Press, 2018 (2nd edition).

Spiegel, Eric and Neil McArthur. *Energy Shift*. New York: McGraw Hill, 2009.

Sund, Kristan J., Robert Galavan, and Anne Huff (eds.). *Uncertainty and Strategic Decision Making*. Bingley, UK: Emerald, 2016.

Syrett, Michael and Marion DeVine. *Managing Uncertainty*. Hoboken, NJ: Wiley, 2012.

Taleb, Nassim Nicholas. *The Black Swan: The Impact of the Highly Improbable*. New York: Random House, 2007.

Tetlock, Philip E. and Dan Gardner. *Superforecasting: The Art and Science of Prediction*. New York: Random House, 2016.

Tilleman, Levi. *The Great Race: The Global Quest for the Car of the Future*. New York: Simon and Schuster, 2015.

Tong, Tony W. and Jeffrey J. Reuer. "Real Options in Strategic Management." *Real Options Theory*. Bingley, West Yorkshire, England: Emerald Group Publishing Limited, 2007. 3–28.

Tuckey, Bill. *Sunraycer*. St. Leonards, Australia: Chevron Publishing Group, 1989.

Tversky, Amos and Daniel Kahneman. "Loss Aversion in Riskless Choice: A Reference-Dependent Model." *The Quarterly Journal of Economics* (1991): 1039–1061.

Vogel, David. *The Market for Virtue: The Potential and Limits of Corporate Social Responsibility*. Washington, DC: Brookings Institution Press, 2007.

The Politics of Precaution: Regulating Health, Safety, and Environmental Risks in Europe and the United States. Princeton: Princeton University Press, 2012.

*California Greenin'.* Princeton: Princeton University Press, 2018.

Womak, James. *The Machine That Changed the World: The Story of Lean Production – Toyota's Secret Weapon in the Global Car Wars That Is Now Revolutionizing World Industry.* New York: Free Press, 2007.

Yergin, Daniel. *The Prize: The Epic Quest for Oil, Money, and Power.* New York: Free Press, 2008.

*The Quest: Energy, Security, and the Remaking of the Modern World.* New York: Penguin, 2012.

Yetiv, Steve. *Myths of the Oil Boom.* Oxford, UK: Oxford University Press, 2015.

Zuckerman, Gregory. *The Frackers: The Outrageous Inside Story of the New Billionaire Wildcatters.* New York: Portfolio, 2013.

# Index